Verdi's *Falstaff* in Letters and Contemporary Reviews

VERDI'S

Falstaff

IN
LETTERS
AND
CONTEMPORARY
REVIEWS

Edited and Translated by Hans Busch

INDIANA UNIVERSITY PRESS   BLOOMINGTON & INDIANAPOLIS

The small musical examples in the letters in Verdi's hand are reproduced
with the permission of G. Ricordi & C.

The paper used in this publication meets the minimum requirements of American National
Standard for Information Sciences—Permanence of Paper for Printed Library Materials, ANSI
Z39.48–1984.

Manufactured in the United States of America

Library of Congress Cataloging-in-Publication Data

Verdi's Falstaff in letters and contemporary reviews / edited and translated by Hans Busch.
    p.   cm.
    Includes bibliographical references (p.) and index.
    ISBN 0-253-32980-9 (cloth : alk. paper)
    1. Verdi, Giuseppe, 1813–1901. Falstaff. 2. Verdi, Giuseppe, 1813–1901—
Correspondence. I. Verdi, Giuseppe, 1813–1901. II. Busch, Hans, date.
ML410.V34 1998   96-32273
782.1—dc20

1 2 3 4 5   03 02 01 00 99 98

To

CAROLYN

my wife and collaborator

CONTENTS

CONTENTS

Preface

Letters are worth so much, because they
preserve the immediacy of our existence.[1]

The pages that follow reflect a drama in letters by most of those directly and indirectly involved with the creation and first productions of Verdi's last opera, *Falstaff*. The vast panorama of written communications exchanged during the almost six years (1889–1894) leading to the first three productions is presented in chronological order. This correspondence delves into the hearts and minds of the writers, with frequent abrupt changes of scene, plays of light and shadow, shifting colors and counterpoints, actions and reactions.

The 678 letters and telegrams appearing in this contribution to the present wealth of Verdi literature offer new perspectives on *Falstaff* and the atmosphere of the *fin de siècle* in which this unique comedy was created. Facts, not opinions, are found in these pages, and readers must reach their own conclusions. This book differs from my earlier ones[2] in that Verdi shares the limelight, even more than before, with his librettist Arrigo Boito and their publisher, Giulio Ricordi. The growing friendship of this triumvirate and their multifaceted relationship warrant a deeper acquaintance with the composer's collaborators than most previous publications have presented. In fact, Alessandro Luzio, the distinguished editor of Verdi's letters, considered a complete edition of the Verdi-Ricordi correspondence indispensable. He refers to those letters as *torrenti di luce*, torrents of light.[3] While a number of them appear translated in this volume as well as in my earlier books, many others still await publication.

Much of the correspondence in this book—never intended for any third person's eyes—mirrors the writers' innermost feelings and thoughts, far beyond their immediate involvement with *Falstaff*. Hence I have included a few of the many intimate letters Arrigo Boito and the legendary actress Eleonora Duse[4] exchanged during the *Falstaff* years.[5] They give much insight into the emotional and geographical whereabouts of this aristocratic, extremely discreet, and complex man, Verdi's last and most congenial librettist.

To comprehend fully the genesis and creation of *Falstaff* and its three initial productions,[6] we should consider the correspondence contained in this volume as an interrelated entity. For example, Verdi and Boito discuss their mutual admiration of Palestrina and Shakespeare. Verdi's letters to Giuseppe De Amicis,[7] on the other hand, concern mainly domestic issues and prosaic affairs, but also illuminate some of the Maestro's noblest traits. Giulio Ricordi's sometimes tedious communications about legal and copyright matters demonstrate Verdi's minute attention to business, while other letters reveal the more human aspects of their relationship.

The variety of the letters and telegrams collected here is quite extensive, but in view of the extraordinary amount of existing published as well as unpublished material, it is only a selection, illustrating the creative process in the midst of everyday life. From dreams to realities, despite—and because of—many disturbing and depressing events, Verdi and his collaborators reached their delightful goal.

No original production books for *Falstaff* exist, as there are for *Aida, Simon Boccanegra,* and *Otello.*[8] However, the reader is compensated by the vast number of musical corrections contained in Verdi's letters to Ricordi before and even after the *Falstaff* première at La Scala on 9 February 1893. The facsimile of the autograph orchestra score, 510 copies of which were published in 1951 to commemorate the fiftieth anniversary of Verdi's death, shows numerous erasures and changes reflecting the composer's constant quest for perfection. Moreover,

> that mysterious moment of transition in which a verse, a melody, emerges out of the invisible, out of the vision and intuition of a genius, and is graphically fixed in a material form—where else can it be so well examined and observed as in the tortured or trance-born manuscript of the master? I do not know enough about an artist if I am familiar only with his finished work, and I agree perfectly with Goethe when he says that to understand completely great creations one must have seen them not only in their perfection but also have pursued the process of their creation.[9]

Verdi's gift to the victims of an earthquake in Calabria and Sicily in November 1894 caps the chronological sequence of the letters.[10] His little-known prayer, which he wrote with Boito's help, appears at the end.

The appendixes contain articles and reviews by writers who attended some of the first productions of the new opera.

PREFACE

The privilege of spending decades immersed in Giuseppe Verdi's letters has vastly increased my appreciation of his greatness, both as an artist and as a human being. Occasionally, when deciphering the scratches and scrawls in his autographs, we might almost hear him talk, laugh, and swear. His shifting moods and opinions, even his contradictions and all-too-human frailties, have the power to invigorate, amuse, and comfort us in our own vicissitudes. Despite today's tendency to emphasize the shortcomings of great personalities—in contrast to one-sided Victorian glorifications—Franz Werfel's view of Verdi still seems every bit as valid as it did seventy years ago: "At such a moment as this, in which vulgar disbelief in all higher levels of existence is rising in a torrent, a life full of truth and without illusions, like that of the poet and farmer Giuseppe Verdi, appears a very star in the murk."[11]

Indiana University, 1995   Hans Busch

NOTES

1. Johann Wolfgang von Goethe in praise of his mother (*Gedenkausgabe,* ed. Ernst Beutler, vol. 10, p. 855 [Zurich: Artemis, 1948]).

2. Documentary studies of *Aida, Otello,* and the revision of *Simon Boccanegra.*

3. Alessandro Luzio, ed., *Carteggi Verdiani,* vol. iv, p. 216.

4. See below, Biographical Sketch.

5. Excerpts from Raul Radice, *Eleonora Duse–Arrigo Boito: Lettere d'amore.*

6. James Hepokoski clearly describes the changes Verdi made, after the première at La Scala, for Rome in 1893, and in the French version for Paris in 1894 (*Giuseppe Verdi: Falstaff,* pp. 54–84).

7. Giuseppe De Amicis (1823–1910) was an engineer, a bachelor, and cousin of the writer Edmondo De Amicis (1846–1908). When he first met the Verdis at a Genoese construction site, presumably in the mid-1850s, the composer introduced himself as a farmer, but his wife revealed his true identity (Mary Jane Phillips-Matz, *Verdi: A Biography,* p. 407; George Martin, *Verdi: His Music, Life and Times,* p. 412; Leonello Sartoris, *Nuovi inediti verdiani,* pp. 31, 266). Giuseppe De Amicis became the Verdis' most devoted and helpful friend.

8. See Document XII in Hans Busch, *Verdi's Aida,* and Documents I and II in Hans Busch, *Verdi's Otello and Simon Boccanegra (revised version) in Letters and Documents,* vol. ii.

9. Stefan Zweig, *The World of Yesteryear,* p. 162.

10. Verdi to Boito, 3 December 1894, n. 1.

11. Franz Werfel (1890–1945) in *Verdi: The Man in His Letters,* trans. Edward Downes.

Acknowledgments

This book owes its existence, more so than any of my previous ones, to a unique team of collaborators. Among the many helpful individuals in the Old World and the New who contributed materials, advice, and information, I was blessed with a quartet of most talented and generous collaborators, who became actual co-authors.

Had it not been for Lia Frey-Rabine, a former student at Indiana University, I would not have undertaken another book on Verdi in English. In the midst of a remarkable career as a dramatic soprano, and with all her dedication to her family, she has been unstinting in her encouragement and active assistance during all the years of my Verdi research. Sparing no effort, she not only meticulously criticized and significantly improved my translations, but also offered much persuasive advice.

Donald Wilson is a connoisseur of music and an enthusiastic admirer of Arturo Toscanini. Not originally drawn to Verdi, he discovered the Italian master through recordings of Toscanini's *Falstaff* broadcasts on 1 and 8 April 1950, which motivated him to further study. His judicious editorial comments have infinitely enriched this work.

Carolyn Lockwood, my wife, who has suffered my Verdi addiction for decades, was instrumental in identifying the numerous musical examples throughout the composer's correspondence with Giulio Ricordi. Her work in deciphering and comparing these examples in Verdi's scratchy hand with the facsimile autograph of the *Falstaff* orchestra score and with several piano-vocal scores has been invaluable.

Ali Shashaani guided me into the magical world of the computer. With indefatigable patience, he not only set up the entire program but also taught me how to apply it to writing these pages.

Special thanks go to Prof. Corrado Mingardi, head of the Biblioteca della Cassa di Risparmio e Monte di Credito su Pegno in Busseto, a gentleman and author of vast knowledge, which he is always ready to share with young and old. He has given me inestimable help with material and information during the twenty-five years of my investigations in and around Busseto's impressive eighteenth-century library.

All this work would have been inconceivable, however, without the continued cooperation of the House of Ricordi. Beginning in 1970 Signora Luciana Pestalozza made available photocopies of Verdi's letters to his publishers; her successor, Maestro Gabriele Dotto, again with Signora Mimma Guastoni's permission, augmented them. I also wish to thank Maestro Fausto Broussard and Signor Carlo Clausetti for all the generous advice they have given me over the years.

Signora Gabriella Carrara Verdi allowed me to make photocopies of Giulio Ricordi's and Arrigo Boito's many letters to Verdi, which are preserved at St. Agata. They form an integral part of this collection, and I gratefully acknowledge her permission to publish them.

The lucky star that in 1972 had led me to Arrigo Boito's heiress, the late Countess Elena Carandini Albertini in Rome, who invited me to study all of Verdi's 141 letters to Boito, shone brightly again when her daughter, Signora Maria Antonelli, drove me to their medieval castle at Torre in Pietra near the capital, to study a large, unknown trove of Boito's annotations and correspondence. Her kind permission for publication enabled me to include a number of these discoveries in this book.

In all my literary endeavors, my permanent gratitude goes to J. Hellmut Freund, senior editor at S. Fischer Verlag in Frankfurt-am-Main. His constant inspiration and advice led to the first German edition of Verdi's entire correspondence with Boito.

Prof. Leonhard M. Fiedler, of the Johann Wolfgang Goethe-University in Frankfurt-am-Main, offered many convincing suggestions.

Bruce Phillips and Oxford University Press gave permission for numerous quotations, and even a few reprints, from my two volumes on Verdi's *Otello* and *Simon Boccanegra* (revised version), which were published in 1988.

Had James Hepokoski's excellent book on *Falstaff*, published by Cambridge University Press, not taken a decidedly different approach to the subject, this book would have been superfluous. In many instances, I refer my readers to Mr. Hepokoski's publication; I gratefully acknowledge his permission to quote from this text. The same applies to Guglielmo Barblan's and Julian Budden's writings on *Falstaff*, which, like Prof. Hepokoski's, provide valuable stores of information.

I am also obliged to Raul Radice for his transcriptions of the Arrigo Boito—Eleonora Duse letters, a few of which appear here in English translation. And I thank Leonello Sartoris for his publication of Verdi's correspondence with Edoardo De Amicis, which has also been excerpted in English translation.

William Weaver and his publisher, W. W. Norton & Co., deserve my particular gratitude for their permission to quote from his translation of the *Falstaff* libretto, and I am indebted to Harcourt Brace Jovanovich for quotations from Weaver's superb biography of Eleonora Duse.

To Mary Jane Phillips-Matz I owe thanks for providing interesting information over many years. I also appreciate the permission by Oxford University Press to quote from her writings.

George Martin and his publisher, Dodd, Mead, once again allowed me to quote from his biography of Verdi. His esteem and moral support over the years greatly oblige me, as does William Ashbrook's, Malcolm Brown's, and Julian Budden's faith in my efforts.

Continued grants from Indiana University have done much to bring about the realization of this book. In addition, the American Philosophical Society, which first supported my Verdi research in 1972, came to my aid once more in 1993.

I reiterate my gratitude to the American Council of Learned Societies and the National Endowment for the Humanities, which, together with my former collaborators—John Cullars, Mimi Rudulph, and Hilary Walford —helped lay the foundation for the present book.

Countless major and minor contributions were provided by more people, living and dead, than I will ever be able to acknowledge. To name but a few of those directly involved, I am especially obliged to: Dr. Peter Boerner, Dr. Otto Biba, Giuliana Busch, Dr. Andrea Ciccarelli, Adriana Corbella, Dr. Eugene Eoyang, Dr. Rudolf Friedl, Dr. Margarete Fries, Thomas Glastras, Dr. Philip Gossett, Clayton L. Householder, Susanne Kutschera, David Lasocki, Dr. Marcel Prawy, Prof. Walter Robert, Eta Singher, Christa Stracke, Dr. Giampiero Tintori, Dr. Stefano Zamboni, and Dr. Heinrich Zimmermann. Theodore Front, Thomas Holliday, and Michael Ingham contributed particular editorial advice.

To three distinguished lawyers, my late friend Alfredo Amman, Giorgio Jarach, and Dr. Ferdinand Sieger, I am grateful for clear and precise answers to complex international copyright questions.

Natalie Wrubel, at Indiana University Press, deserves my special thanks for her work in the complicated editing of this book.

I should also like to express appreciation for numerous published works of Verdi and Boito scholarship which have aided and reinforced my research over the years. In particular I wish to recognize Gaetano Cesari, Marcello Conati, Carlo Gatti, Alessandro Luzio, Mario Medici, Piero Nardi, Andrew Porter, Giovanna Scarsi, and Frank Walker, as well as Franz Werfel, whose pioneering edition of Verdi letters, in German translation, first ignited my interest in Verdi research six decades ago.

Abbreviations

Abbreviations Used in the List of
Letters and Telegrams

AUTOGRAPH LOCATIONS

AC   Accademia Nazionale dei Lincei, Rome

Br.   Biblioteca Nazionale Braidense, Milan

Bo.   Conservatorio di Musica "G. B. Martini," Bologna

Ca.   Archivio Carandini, Rome

Ci.   Fondazione Giorgio Cini, Venice

EP   Eredi Persico

GE   Archivio di Stato, Genoa

HA   Houghton Library, Harvard University, Cambridge, Mass.

IP   Istituto di Studi Verdiani, Parma

Pa.   Biblioteca Palatina, Parma

Ri.   Archivio Ricordi, Milan

SA   Collezione Carrara Verdi, St. Agata

Sc.   Museo Teatrale alla Scala, Milan

VI   Gesellschaft der Musikfreunde, Vienna

PUBLISHED SOURCES

Abb.   Franco Abbiati. *Giuseppe Verdi,* 4 vols. (Milan: G. Ricordi, 1959).

Cart.   *Carteggi Verdiani*, ed. Alessandro Luzio, vols. i and ii (Rome: Reale Accademia d'Italia, 1935); vols. iii and iv (Rome: Accademia Nazionale dei Lincei, 1947).

Cart.V-B   *Carteggio Verdi-Boito*, ed. Mario Medici e Marcello Conati con la collaborazione di Marisa Casati, 2 vols. (Parma: Istituto di Studi Verdiani, 1978).

Cop.   *I copialettere di Giuseppe Verdi*, ed. Gaetano Cesari e Alessandro Luzio (Milan: Comune di Milano, 1913).

CP   *Giuseppe Verdi. Giulio Ricordi: Corrispondenze e immagini 1881–1890,* ed. Franca Cella e Pierluigi Petrobelli (Milan: Teatro alla Scala, 1982).

De R.   *Lettere di Arrigo Boito,* ed. Raffaello De Rensis (Rome: Società Editrice di "Novissima," 1932).

LS.   *Nuovi inediti verdiani*, ed. Leonello Sartoris (Genoa: Editrice Lo Sprint, n.d.).

Mi.   Corrado Mingardi. *Verdi e il suo Ospedale 1888–1988* (Comune di Villanova sull'Arda: Cassa di Risparmio di Piacenza e Vigevano, 1988).

Mo.   Gino Monaldi. *Verdi, 1839–1898* (Turin: Fratelli Bocca, 1899, 1926).

Ob.   Aldo Oberdorfer. *Giuseppe Verdi: Autobiografia dalle lettere*, ed. Aldo Oberdorfer (Milan: Rizzoli, 1951).

RR.   Raul Radice, ed. *Lettere d'Amore* (Milan: Il Saggiatore, 1979).

Abbreviations Used in the Footnotes

PUBLISHED WORKS FREQUENTLY MENTIONED

Abbiati
: Franco Abbiati. *Giuseppe Verdi,* 4 vols. (Milan: G. Ricordi, 1959).

Aida
: Hans Busch, ed. and trans. *Verdi's 'Aida': The History of an Opera in Letters and Documents* (Minneapolis: University of Minnesota Press, 1978).

Carteggi
: Alessandro Luzio, ed. *Carteggi Verdiani,* vols. i and ii (Rome: Reale Accademia d'Italia, 1935); vols. iii and iv (Rome: Accademia dei Lincei, 1947).

Carteggio
: Mario Medici e Marcello Conati con la collaborazione di Marisa Casati, eds. *Carteggio Verdi-Boito,* 2 vols. (Parma: Istituto di Studi Verdiani, 1978).

Conati
: Marcello Conati, ed., trans. Richard Stokes. *Encounters with Verdi* (Ithaca, NY: Cornell University, 1984).

Copialettere
: Gaetano Cesari e Alessandro Luzio, eds. *I copialettere di Giuseppe Verdi* (Milan: Comune di Milani, 1913).

De Rensis
: Raffaello De Rensis, ed. *Lettere di Arrigo Boito* (Rome: Società Editrice di "Novissima," 1932).

Hepokoski
: James A. Hepokoski. *Giuseppe Verdi: 'Falstaff'* (Cambridge: Cambridge University Press, 1983).

Marek
: George R. Marek. *Puccini: A Biography* (New York: Simon and Schuster, 1951).

Nardi
: Piero Nardi. *Vita di Arrigo Boito* (Verona: A. Mondadori, 1942).

Otello	Hans Busch, ed. and trans. *Verdi's 'Otello' and 'Simon Boccanegra' (revised version) in Letters and Documents* (2 vols.; Oxford: Clarendon Press, 1988).
Phillips-Matz	Mary Jane Phillips-Matz. *Verdi: A Biography* (Oxford and New York: Oxford University Press, 1993).
Weaver	William Weaver. *Duse: A Biography* (London: Thames & Hudson, 1984).

Editorial Notes

The "List of Letters and Telegrams," pp. xli–lix, gives basic details of the correspondence in this volume. The destination of the letters and telegrams is listed whenever possible, taken from extant envelopes or from corroborative evidence in the correspondence or chronologies; a question mark appears when there is any doubt. Brackets indicate that I have supplied details in the dates; a question mark means that there is still some doubt. The location of the original autographs is given when known. A major publication is listed even when only a small section of the original text is excerpted.

The correspondence appears in chronological order, with places and dates given at the head of each letter or telegram. For the sake of consistency, all dates are given in European style. Details that I have supplied are in brackets, and a question mark indicates any doubt. Several incorrect dates appearing in other publications have been silently corrected; any special explanations are given in the notes.

Translations are from autographs wherever possible. This is the case with the Verdi-Boito and Verdi-Ricordi correspondence. Verdi's letters to the House of Ricordi are in the publisher's archives in Milan; Ricordi's letters to Verdi are at St. Agata.

Where autographs are unavailable, translations originate mainly from Cesari and Luzio's *I copialettere di Giuseppe Verdi* and Luzio's four-volume *Carteggi verdiani*. *I copialettere*, originally published, with Boito's help, for the centenary of Verdi's birth, is based on letters Verdi drafted and copied in five simple copybooks, approximately 9½" × 7", along with all kinds of financial annotations and calculations scribbled in between the letters. These books, along with five others in his wife's hand, are held at St. Agata. Luzio's *Carteggi*, a major source of information, is unfortunately out of print.

Translations of Verdi's telegrams to Boito are from the Albertini-Carandini archive, as well as from Medici, Conati, and Casati's *Carteggio Verdi-Boito*. The telegrams from the latter were transcribed by Piero Nardi. The late Frank Walker bequeathed these transcriptions to the Istituto di Studi Verdiani in Parma.

In translating the letters and telegrams, my aim was to adhere to the original style of the writers. Unfortunately, subtle yet important nuances in the Italian forms of address—the formal "Lei," the more personal "Voi," the intimate "Tu"—cannot be rendered in English. In Verdi's letters, his old friend Giuseppe Piroli is addressed as "Tu," but Boito and Ricordi as "Voi." Both Boito and Ricordi always address Verdi as "Lei"; Ricordi sometimes also applies the old-fashioned term "Ella."

Verdi's scratchy handwriting is sometimes difficult, in rare instances impossible, to decipher. Dates and salutations are often abbreviated; for example, "C. Giulio," for "Caro Giulio," is spelled out in these translations as "Dear Giulio." Greetings at the end of letters, including the usual "addio" [farewell], are frequently illegible and have had to be surmised. But his signature, even to friends, is invariably "G. Verdi"; and several letters, especially to strangers, are headed "Busseto" rather than nearby St. Agata.

In contrast, Boito's and Ricordi's letters are, with few exceptions, quite legible. While Boito seldom dates his letters completely, he always signs his full name—except in his letters to Eleonora Duse, of course, and on extremely rare occasions, to Verdi.

Many of Ricordi's letters are too long to be quoted in full in this volume, and his flowery nineteenth-century style needed simplifying in translation. Even some of Verdi's and Boito's letters are abbreviated, particularly where they overlap with correspondence regarding the French *Othello*, which is published in my *Otello* book. Almost the entire Boito-Duse correspondence in this book is excerpted, and so are a number of letters not directly concerning *Falstaff*.

In presenting the letters, every effort has been made to follow the original text. Therefore, such matters as paragraph breaks, misspellings of names, idiosyncratic punctuation, groups of dots and dashes, or the word *hotel* with or without circumflex, etc., are all reproduced as they appear in the autographs.

Any emphasis in the original letter is indicated by italics. Italics are also used for foreign words and phrases, which are translated in roman type within brackets. However, changes have been made to avoid ambiguity between titles of operas and plays and names of characters; titles are always in italics, names of characters in roman type.

Some draft letters have no signatures; other published letters lack greetings and/or signatures. Any enclosures are set in small type immediately after the letters.

Extracts of the *Falstaff* libretto are quoted in the original Italian, followed by William Weaver's translations, as they appear in his *Seven Verdi Librettos* (New York: W. W. Norton, 1977).

With few exceptions, all musical examples are reproduced from the autographs. Footnotes refer to their printed equivalents in Ricordi's *Falstaff* piano-vocal score (abbreviated as "PV"), plate number 96342.

Translating certain technical terms proved a difficult task. For example, Verdi uses the term *stampato* [printed] to refer also to something which may be proofed, engraved, or typeset, but not actually printed. Such uses are translated according to the sense.

The Italian *impresario* and *impresa* usually appear, respectively, as "manager" and "management."

Letters or telegrams which have not been located are referred to as "Missing" in the footnotes.

Wherever feasible, duplication of information contained in other publications has been avoided. In particular, James A. Hepokoski's exhaustive Cambridge Opera Handbook on *Falstaff* cannot be improved upon, and is frequently referred to, as is his article on Giuseppina Pasqua in *19th Century Music,* March 1980. The same applies to William Weaver's translation of the *Falstaff* libretto and his biography of Eleonora Duse. Frequent references to and quotations from these and other publications are mentioned in the footnotes.

As in the case of Verdi's correspondence with Ricordi and Boito concerning the French *Othello,* the reader is occasionally referred to my earlier *Otello* book. Some references to my book on *Aida* also seemed unavoidable in order to avoid repetition.

As noted above, the abbreviation "PV" refers to piano-vocal score. The three numbers that follow indicate the page, staff, and measure: e.g., p. 23, 2/4.

A biographical note about every person mentioned in the letters is given in a footnote at his or her first appearance.

Introduction

Une oeuvre de vie, de santé,
de lumière et de joie.[1]

"*The Merry Wives,*" Richard Strauss observed, "is a pretty opera; *Falstaff,* however, is one of the greatest masterworks of all time."[2] Verdi's final opera abundantly justifies such high praise. From its scintillating *parlando* style, ideal for a text that is at once lyrical and supremely literate, to an orchestration whose wit and sophistication create incomparable fun, with ardent sighs easily alternating with belly laughs, *Falstaff* is a comedy without parallel in all of opera. For Arturo Toscanini, the lightness and effervescence of *Falstaff* made it "quicksilver."[3]

Strauss may not have been aware that Verdi had been hoping all his life to write such a comedy. As early as 1847 Verdi is said to have thought about writing an opera based on Falstaff's adventures.[4] In 1868 a Milan newspaper reported that he was composing a *Falstaff* to a libretto by Antonio Ghislanzoni.[5] The latter denied the assertion in *La Gazzetta musicale di Milano* of 19 July 1868; yet Verdi's close friend Count Opprandino Arrivabene[6] wanted to learn the whole truth, and Verdi replied to him, in a letter of 28 July 1868, that he was composing "neither *Falstaff* nor any other opera." *Falstaff* was nevertheless remotely on Verdi's mind, as evidenced by this letter to Clara Maffei[7] of 20 October 1876: "To copy the truth may be good, but it is better *to invent the truth.* But ask Papa [Shakespeare]. It's possible that he, the Papa, has met some Falstaff, but he will hardly have met a villain like Iago, and never such angels as *Cordelia, Imogene, Desdemona,* etc., etc., who are all so real!"

Three years later Verdi vented his anger over what he deemed a stupid prejudice which attempted to categorize him as a composer of tragedy. In Ricordi's *Gazzetta musicale* he had read the following comment by Rossini:

> Verdi is a composer of serious, melancholy character; his sense of color is dark and gloomy; it gushes forth richly and spontaneously from his

being, and just for this reason it is extremely commendable; I hold him in the highest esteem, but at the same time he will without a doubt never write an *opera semi-seria* such as *Linda* [*di Chamounix*], much less a buffa like *Elisir d'amore*.[8]

To this Verdi reacted in a letter to Giulio Ricordi from St. Agata on 26 August 1879:

> In your *Gazzetta* I have read [. . .] the judgment of Zeus Rossini (as Meyerbeer called him).

> But what do you know about that!! For twenty years I have been looking for a libretto for an opera buffa, and now, when I have found it, so to speak,[9] you encourage the public with this article to boo the opera before it has even been written; and thus you ruin my interests as well as your own.

> But never fear.— In case my weak spirit should through chance, bad luck or calamity, in spite of the judgment of the Great One, move me to write this opera buffa, I repeat, just never fear . . . . I will ruin another publisher!

Giulio Ricordi apologized two days later in a lengthy letter in which he asked, "Is it true what you tell me about that libretto? . . . Don't you realize that you have just managed to give me some great news?" In a postscript he went on to say that, had he read the article in his *Gazzetta musicale* before it was printed, he would have added the following words:

> Verdi has proved how wrong this judgment was in *La forza del destino*, where in Fra Melitone he created an utterly new kind of character, one that is at once comic and serious. And he gave this character the most novel music, which has no equivalent in any other opera, and which reveals to us the author of so many masterpieces in an entirely new light. This cranky, wily, inquisitive, grouchy bear of a friar could not have been better portrayed than Verdi has done.

Eleven years later, Giulio learned of the forthcoming birth of *Falstaff* when Boito broke the news at a dinner in Milan on 26 November 1890, and Giulio was far from ruined.

Sir John Falstaff has his origin in a historical figure, Sir John Oldcastle, who actually bore little resemblance to the literary character into which he evolved. Oldcastle was a soldier and prominent leader of the Lollards, a late Medieval English sect which propagated the religious teachings of John Wycliffe. In 1413 Oldcastle was convicted of heresy; after his escape from the Tower and subsequent recapture he was hanged, in 1417, over a fire that consumed the gallows. There is much confusion over the date of his birth, to which Elizabethan dramatists added by portraying him as the aged counselor and companion of Henry V's wild youth. This, however, is highly unlikely, since historical sources agree that Oldcastle was at this time already a prominent Lollard. In the anonymous play *The Famous Victories of Henry V*, written before 1588, he appears as a cynical accomplice of the prince in his robberies. Shakespeare adopted him, elaborating the character into the fat knight of *Henry V*. When the play appeared in print in 1598, Oldcastle was named Falstaff, and came to personify the irrepressible good-for-nothing, the besotted, self-indulgent reveler, the lascivious pleasure-seeker, who even in his old age is unsurpassed in wit and jest. Queen Elizabeth I herself is reputed to have asked the poet to write another part for Falstaff in which he is presented as a lover. Apparently Shakespeare had a scant three weeks in which to complete the new work, and in his haste and lack of interest, he ostensibly borrowed models for his characters from familiar Italian comedies. *The Merry Wives of Windsor* turned out to be a second-rate comedy, in which the jolly knight, scarcely recognizable, is hoaxed and humbled by a few spirited provincial women and reduced to a silly old fool.

Even before Nicolai's *Merry Wives*, Falstaff had been the leading character of several forgotten operas by composers including those by Dittersdorf (1796), Antonio Salieri (1798), Michael William Balfe (1838), and Adolphe Adam (1856). In *Songe d'une nuit d'été* by Ambroise Thomas, Falstaff appears as a contemporary of Shakespeare and Queen Elizabeth. But only Boito's libretto—a masterful version of *The Merry Wives*, combined with episodes from both parts of *Henry IV*—enabled Verdi to make Falstaff the harassed hero of an unparalleled opera.

In contrast to *Otello*, Boito this time had to create an entirely new work, one that Shakespeare himself might have admired and approved. Even without Verdi's music it could stand alone as a play. Of the twenty-two speaking roles in Shakespeare's rather weak comedy, Boito kept only ten plus three non-speaking ones. Anne Page became Nannetta Ford, while the parts of Dr. Cajus and Bardolph were combined with deleted characters. Mistress Quickly, Dr. Cajus' servant in *The Merry Wives*, the innkeeper's wife in *Henry IV*, and Pistol's wife in *Henry V*, was given the central role of the feigned procuress. Boito rejected out of hand the pale reflection of Falstaff that appears in *The Merry Wives*, taking from that play only the most colorful and comical passages. These he joined with sections of both parts of *Henry IV* to make a unified whole, to which he added his own entirely original finale.

When Boito lets his Falstaff strike up the reconciling fugue that closes the opera, allowing him and his adversaries to become brothers, he raises Sir John to a level of human greatness that Shakespeare had never accorded him. For the words to this glorious fugue, "Tutto nel mondo è burla" [Everything in the world is jest], Boito may have been inspired by Jacques' remark "All the world's a stage" in *As You Like It*. On Verdi's stage, however, the masks have fallen, and, for a brief, startling moment, joyful exuberance yields suddenly to profound seriousness before the happy conclusion.

Since his early youth Verdi, himself an avid reader, had been attracted to Shakespeare, although his interest was on a more intuitive level than that of Boito, the intellectual. Just how close Verdi was to Shakespeare—even though he consistently misspelled his name—is proved by his protest against a Paris review of his *Macbeth* in 1865: "That I do not know Shacpearce, that I do not understand and feel him—no, by God, no. He is one of my favorite poets, [. . .] whom I read again and again."[10]

Beyond Verdi's letters to many different contemporaries during the last two decades of his life, his correspondence with Arrigo Boito and Giulio Ricordi is of unique interest. Boito and Ricordi, both in their fifties at that time, were friends and, as Verdi's closest collaborators, developed an almost filial relationship with him. This triumvirate first was responsible for the revision of *Simon Boccanegra* and then for the creation of *Otello* and *Falstaff*.

Boito, the urbane, sophisticated intellectual, poet, musician, and genuine scholar, yet "a dandy"[11] and a discreet ladies' man, found his greatest fulfillment in his *servitude volontaire* to Verdi, "this real, most noble and truly great man."[12] Generously giving of himself to his Maestro and to others of lesser importance, he never saw the curtain rise on his own opera *Nerone*, his frustrating, elusive dream. When Boito died—in Milan, on 10 June 1918, at the age of seventy-five—his friend Ferruccio Busoni,[13] the composer of *Dr. Faust*, who had much in common with his one-time mentor, expressed these sad and honest thoughts in the *Neue Zürcher Zeitung* of 18 June 1918:

> Now he is gone, without ever seeing his *Nero* come to life on the stage. Even on his deathbed, it is said, he was still announcing his intention of seeing to certain changes in the score. [. . .] His sense of responsibility for his promised *Nero* grew and grew until it had become an enormous burden upon his shoulders, like old debts that are accumulating interest. After twenty years of shouldering this burden he found that tastes and tendencies in art had changed. [. . .] In the interim renowned composers had grown to maturity and were producing success after success.
>
> Boito, who once had a strong thirst for the new, had slowly turned his back on the present and looked toward the past. Always in a state of inner torment, always trying to come to terms with himself, he made change

after change in the work. The craftsmanship of the first act that he once wrote could no longer satisfy him; the younger generation of composers had outstripped him. He studied Johann Sebastian Bach, the last quartets of Beethoven. But he would sooner remain an Italian, so it was with good reason that he placed himself in the service of the patriarch Verdi. [. . .] But to return to the here and now, how is one ever to find a rational explanation for what is highly irrational in this artist's life? What, in the end, was the cause of Boito's colossal problem?

"Ô rare mélange de Latin et de Slave, de précision méridionale et de poésie du Nord," Camille Bellaigue once exclaimed regarding Boito's Italian-Polish origin.[14] With such duality and such talents for both music and literature, Dante, Bach, and Shakespeare were Boito's idols. Born in Padua, he felt Italian; but as a true European, the son of a Polish countess, he also felt at home in the north—in France, in Poland, and in Germany. Moved by thoughts and sentiments of German romanticism, he wrote stories remotely inspired by E. T. A. Hoffmann. Boito translated into Italian Weber's *Der Freischütz* and several works by Richard Wagner, including *Rienzi*, *Tristan und Isolde*, and the *Wesendonck-Lieder*. How could the young poet and musician escape the magic attraction of such a genius?[15] A member of the *scapigliatura*—a Milanese anti-establishment group of writers, painters, and musicians during the 1860s, who advocated sexual freedom and drugs—Boito wrote his first poems under the influence of Baudelaire. In *Dualismo* he speaks of his own light and shadow. His grotesque fable *Re Orso* [King Bear] is rich in wit and irony, bizarre puns, and fanciful, capricious rhymes that foreshadow his texts for *Otello* and *Falstaff*. The phenomenon of evil fascinated him in the characters of Mephistopheles, Nero, Iago, and also Barnaba, in his libretto for Ponchielli's *La Gioconda*. The dominant motive of Boito's works, the eternal struggle between divine and satanic powers, is the theme of his bold opera *Mefistofele*, based on both parts of Goethe's *Faust;* of the morbid, decadent *Nerone;* and of *Otello*, which initially had the title *Jago*.

Mefistofele was a resounding fiasco when it was first performed at La Scala in 1868. Boito destroyed most of the score, then revised and shortened it by an entire act. He rewrote the baritone part of Faust for a tenor and inserted a duet from his sketch for *Ero e Leandro*, another opera that he never finished. In 1875, the new *Mefistofele* was enthusiastically applauded by the avant-garde in Bologna. A year later Boito enriched the score for Venice with Margherita's final scene, and it is in this version that the opera continues to be performed with growing success throughout the world.

No one was able to appreciate the poet Boito more deeply than Benedetto Croce,[16] who strongly defended him against his critics:

His voice is that of a latecomer outside of time, of a survivor. And frequently every effort is made to dismiss him as being unimportant; some people consider Boito's music to be his strength and his poetry insignificant.

[. . .] Romanticism as a warped, tormenting, and antithetical aspect of life in Italy had no poet prior to 1860. Then came Arrigo Boito. [. . .] The play of life appears to him as a tragedy in which the predominance of destructive powers, passion, sin, crime and death strike weak, broken, wind-swept flowers, compliant Desdemonas, love, kindness, tenderness. [. . .] Every once in a while he overpowers tragedy and horror, death and evil, the submission of all that is good, through laughter; not through cynicism, which is dryness of the heart, but with humor. [. . .] His fault is that of a man who fights to express his feelings, not of one who has none and lightly glides with traditional literary form over the ice of his soul.

The underlining and annotations that appear in Boito's volumes of François-Victor Hugo's French translations of Shakespeare[17] indicate intensive studies. For Eleonora Duse, Boito translated *Antony and Cleopatra;* his first libretto had been a *Hamlet* for Franco Faccio,[18] and even after *Falstaff* he began a *King Lear* libretto for Verdi.[19]

Aware of his own weaknesses, Boito once wrote to Eugenio Tornaghi, the secretary of the Ricordi firm:[20]

Sirmione [Lake Garda], 11 May 1902

We need not regret the slowness of my work, and even less deplore it, for even if it is slow, it is incessant and entirely directed toward the goal shown me by my artistic and personal conscience. If I had a great deal more talent than I have, I would study less and work faster; if I were a bit more of an animal, I would study less and work faster; but I can only work with the brain that God has given me and in the manner that my brain allows.

A treasure of unpublished Boito papers still resides in the Albertini-Carandini Archive at Torre in Pietra near Rome. Innumerable annotations on the widest scope of universal philosophical, literary, musical, mathematical, and scientific studies bear witness to the obsessive working habits of this highly erudite artist. However, Boito was by no means devoid of temperament. In Naples, when his challenge to a duel was refused, he flew into a rage, smashing the furniture in his hotel room.[21] For the most part, however, Boito was uncommonly gracious in his behavior, and his air of aristocratic elegance, enhanced by his impressive height, was quite in keeping with his amiable nature.

The restless Eleonora Duse found peace with Boito, while he himself was torn by inner strife. Having been forced into acting in early childhood, she hated her profession and was as obsessed with the truth in life as she was on the stage. Their existing correspondence[22] lacks any mention of Boito's artistic endeavors, except for his unsuccessful version of *Antony and Cleopatra* for her; the only reference to *Falstaff* appears in her letter of 8 June 1894 from London, where it impressed her as being "such a melancholic thing." For fear, perhaps, that their letters could fall into the hands of strangers, the two famous artists never refer to Verdi by name, but as "the man of the Latin inscription" on the Palazzo Doria in Genoa,[23] where he resided in the winter. Even of themselves and each other they sometimes speak only in the third person. Other oddities abound, among them an utter lack of humor in their most intimate letters. Time and time again, Boito saves Duse from chaos and despair, truly deserving to have been her *Santo*, with whom she felt united beyond his death.

The depth of Boito's lifelong friendship with Franco Faccio is reflected in his letters to Verdi and Duse in March and April 1890. After his separation from Duse in 1898, Boito was increasingly drawn to his friends and acquaintances, among them several French and Italian writers whose prominence endured beyond their own era. He shared a large and elegant house in Milan's Principe Amedeo No. 1 with his elder brother Camillo,[24] the architect, who had protected and supported him in his early days. A lifelong bachelor, the aging Arrigo Boito found warmth and harmony, along with stimulating discourse, amid the families of Camille Bellaigue and the Swiss neuropathologist Paul Dubois.[25]

As a critical and influential consultant to the conservatories of united Italy, Boito introduced important reforms; as an official delegate to international conferences he was held in high regard. Cambridge University awarded him an honorary doctor's degree in 1893, and at the age of seventy he became a senator in Rome.

After *Otello*, the pinnacle he and Verdi had achieved together, Boito's letters to the composer reflect growing confidence in his own talent and in their collaboration. Having been abandoned as a little boy by his runaway father, Boito in all probability was subconsciously drawn to the aging Verdi, who for his part increasingly leaned on him like a son. Their shared concern for Franco Faccio during his devastating illness united the composer and his librettist in friendship. The 301 surviving letters and notes they exchanged bear witness to their mutual faith and affection. With Verdi's death, the sun set for Boito. The seventeen years he outlived Verdi were filled with nostalgic memories. Boito's letters to Camille Bellaigue tell us much of that story. In one he writes: "Savoir comprendre, savoir aimer,

savoir exprimer, voiçi les grandes joies de l'esprit humain."²⁶ These words
read like an epitaph for the friendship that gave us *Otello* and *Falstaff*.

In sharp contrast stand the relationship of Giulio Ricordi with his
exalted Maestro, and Verdi's reactions to him. Born into a prominent and
wealthy Milanese music-publishing family of Spanish descent,²⁷ Giulio
Ricordi was an urbane, ambitious champion of the Industrial Revolution,
a powerful and influential citizen, and a gifted musician and writer. He
became not only Verdi's publisher but also his personal representative and
producer.

The approximately 2,500 letters—many still unpublished—which
Giulio Ricordi, Verdi, and Verdi's wife exchanged over the course of three
decades contribute essential details to our knowledge of Verdi and his time.
Giulio's reverence for the Maestro, who was a second father to him, knew no
bounds. It appeared to be motivated not only by business interests but by
honest sentiment as well—although his life was often made difficult by
relations with this most prominent, as well as most demanding, of his
composers. Nevertheless, Verdi's trust in Giulio Ricordi underwent a severe
test in 1875 because of an incorrect rendering of his account.²⁸ And yet,
after he had received a large sum that Ricordi owed him, Verdi still made
a loan to the firm when it was in financial trouble. According to the terms
of his will, the loan was to be repaid after his death to the Casa di Riposo.

While concerned above all with the prestige and economic interests of
the House of Ricordi, and sincerely admiring Verdi the man and his works,
Signor Giulio ministered untiringly to his most famous composer. The
reader should be forewarned of the style of his letters, which is unique even
for the Victorian era. Ricordi's long-winded epistles, sprinkled with Latin
quotations as well as colloquialisms, betray extraordinary degrees of servil-
ity, flattery, and redundancy, not to mention naive exaggerations and rather
obvious ulterior motives. As if stuttering in awe or in fear of the Maestro's
displeasure, Giulio embellishes his impeccable calligraphy with an infinite
number of dots. His letter of 31 May 1891 seems like a cat-and-mouse
game; that of 3 April 1892 reads like sheer blackmail. How could the aged
Verdi, wise and humble as he was, tolerate year after year such displays of
primitive diplomacy and effusive adulation? Brief and to the point in his
own writing, why did he never seem to lose patience with Giulio's flowery
prose? The history of Verdi's nearly lifelong association with three generations of the House of Ricordi might to some extent explain his endurance
of Giulio's cloying style. As late as 1851, when Verdi was short of funds,
Giulio's father, Tito, had lent the Maestro a substantial sum;²⁹ Verdi recip-

rocated in later years, disregarding his discovery of Giulio's incorrect accounting in 1875. After Tito's death, in 1888, Verdi even became a shareholder in the Ricordi firm. Intricate financial ties and common interests were no doubt part of Verdi's friendship with the Ricordi family. Special bonds of mutual trust appear between Giulio and Giuseppina Verdi, whose feminine sensitivity occasionally comes to his aid when harmony must reign for her husband and all concerned.

With all his shortcomings, Giulio Ricordi achieved a lasting triumph with the union of Arrigo Boito and Giuseppe Verdi, which evolved into a unique artistic partnership after passing through a curious sequence of preliminary stages: initial contact, followed by cautious distance, and finally genuine accord. On Giuseppina Verdi's advice, Ricordi pursued his goal for many years, with perseverance and diplomacy, against perilous odds, until the two men's collaboration on *Simon Boccanegra* led to their *Otello*, the then apparent climax of Verdi's career.

The same Giulio, this person of frail constitution, so frequently disgusted and depressed by the greed and dishonesty which surrounded him, turned out, with firm determination, to be a genuine midwife to *Falstaff*, once he learned of the unexpected latecomer's birth. When the Maestro's admirable health and energy began to decline, Giulio Ricordi, forty years younger, emerged as the driving force. For example, caught between the hypersensitive Verdi's stubborn resolve not to set foot in La Scala under Piontelli's management[30] and his own keen desire that the *Falstaff* première be held in that theatre, Ricordi prevailed; his local pride would not allow the *pancione* [potbelly] to make his first appearance on any other stage.

The publisher's correspondence with Verdi does not concern *Falstaff* until 15 December 1890, after the authors had finally let him in on their secret. Sickness and death within the Ricordi family, including Giulio's own malaises bordering on hypochondria, are—next to the lawsuit in Paris—the most frequent topics of his letters until that time. Subsequently, however, Giulio, as practical a man of the theatre as the Maestro himself, spared no pain in the casting, organization, and technical preparation for the *Falstaff* première at La Scala. His meticulous attention to every detail tolerated no shortcuts to the goal of producing a total work of art and maintaining its integrity.

One of the most impressive achievements of Giulio Ricordi and his engravers were their editions of the *Falstaff* orchestral and piano-vocal scores. Countless musical examples in the composer's letters between 13 September 1892 and 4 April 1893 caused unusual problems, which were conscientiously and patiently solved in the first editions. Regardless of what corrections may still present themselves, these publications remain a monument to the House of Ricordi.

Bypassed in war and peace by the Roman Via Emilia, by the fast railroad linking Italy's north and south, and by today's busy autostrada, Verdi's St. Agata lies quietly in the plains between the Apennine Mountains and the Adriatic Sea. His lands extend to the southern bank of the River Po and are bordered on the north by Cremona, home of Monteverdi and Stradivari. In 1851, the Maestro and his wife had moved to the villa at St. Agata outside Busseto, the little town in the province of Parma where Verdi had spent his early days. During the *Falstaff* years, we find them in that rural solitude from spring to autumn, taking the waters at the spa of Montecatini in Tuscany each July, and wintering in the milder climate of Genoa in an apartment at the Palazzo Doria.

About two months before the opening of *Otello* at La Scala in 1887, Boito had answered a journalist's question in regard to Verdi's private life:

> For many years, the life of our Maestro has been so calm and so completely focused on study and home that no events worth mentioning, no curious anecdotes occur. The most exciting thing about it is (compared with the lives of other excellent contemporaries) that there is nothing exciting to report. This uniqueness is of no help to the biographer, but deserves to be noted, because it reveals the great simplicity of the artist and the man.[31]

Verdi the Antistar! A genuine sense of values, coupled with inborn dignity and a certain patrician reticence, had from the outset kept him free of ostentation. Apart from Boito's intimate bit of information about the then 73-year-old man, many letters in this and other volumes testify to the Maestro's abhorrence and outright fear of publicity and invasions of his personal life. His unwillingness to appear in public required infinite patience on the part of his collaborators; his reluctance to attend the first performances of *Falstaff* in Rome and Paris, for example, was part of a pattern his friends had learned to anticipate. We can imagine their frustration, their shoulder-shrugging, their sighs. How could their Maestro have been so inconsiderate? Such behavior might appear as puzzling a phenomenon as Verdi's endurance of Ricordi's endless flatteries and long-winded arguments. They are all, however, but various aspects of this utterly human, multifaceted genius in the fullness of his years, arriving at a higher degree of wisdom than most men find at that or any age.

"The most noble science" of agriculture, as Verdi called it in his letter to

Ferdinando Resasco of 21 October 1891, was for him a serious occupation, not a hobby; his closeness to nature unquestionably helped account for his long-lasting health of body and mind. To his friend Arrivabene he had written from St. Agata on 14 September 1880:

> Here I am breathing all the air I want, but I have nothing else to admire besides my cows, my oxen, horses, etc., etc., being farmer, mason, carpenter and laborer when necessary. Let me explain. I have many farmhouses in ruin, as they all are around here. I have made up my mind to repair them, as long as there is time, and to build some so that sooner or later somebody or other isn't killed. So I am architect, master mason, blacksmith, a bit of everything. Therefore, goodbye books, goodbye music. I feel that I have forgotten and don't know music any more.[32]

Verdi is said to have planted every tree in his park at St. Agata. On 16 June 1881 he took pride in informing Arrivabene once again about his practical talents:

> The Maestro Verdi [. . .] has hit upon the idea of having constructed a steam engine to pump water out of a little brook that runs past the house. In order to carry out this intention, a 25-meter-long pipe is needed 6 meters below the ground, as well as an approximately 7-meter-deep well. [. . .] The Maestro, laudably mentioned above, is staying down there all day long to encourage or admonish the workmen, but first of all to direct them.[33]

Another letter to Arrivabene from Genoa on 23 December 1881 provides further proof of Verdi's unselfish concern for his peasants:

> Last year I built a dairy, this year two that are even larger. There are about two hundred laborers who have been working up till now, and to whom I have to give instructions for future works, as soon as the frost permits. These are useless works for me, since these buildings won't give me another cent of income from the land, but in the meantime the people are earning money and aren't emigrating from my village.[34]

Such philanthropy and altruism are well documented, as is Verdi's extraordinary consideration for the feelings of his fellow man, expressed in a letter to De Amicis on 12 May 1893. Verdi's ever-increasing preference to give rather than receive gifts causes a dilemma involving the repair of his two pianos[35] and is also evidenced in his quirky manner of thanking the Ricordis, on 26 December 1892 and 1893, for their annual Christmas panettone. Two brief letters to Giulio Ricordi of 10 and 11 January 1894 bear witness to the Maestro's almost obsessive correctness in financial matters, as in all human relations. Verdi avoided funerals but observed the anniversaries or deaths of his colleagues.[36] The hospital he built for his peasants—like the Casa di Riposo, the home he established for aged musicians—seems reminiscent of Goethe's Faust, whose good deeds redeem the sins of his past.[37]

Friendship was sacred to Verdi; his exchange of letters with Boito about Franco Faccio's terminal illness, his energetic but futile efforts to help Emanuele Muzio in his final days, and his helpless encouragement to his dying friend Giuseppe Piroli, all bear witness to this. Much of his correspondence reflects his concern for the fragile health of his wife, Giuseppina, which must have been a constant drain on his energies.

These sad and depressing circumstances served to delay the birth of *Falstaff*. The ugly lawsuit against Bénoit in Paris, however, seems to be most responsible for Verdi's inability to finish the score any sooner.[38] He briefly sums up the cause of the suit and its consequences in a letter to Giuseppina Negroni Prati[39] of 15 March 1891; and he often complains bitterly to Ricordi about the exasperating duration of this frustrating affair, which keeps him from composing. Trivialities take their toll, too, as in the case of noisy workmen in his apartment in Genoa, where an inconsiderate landlord prompts the great man to consider finding other accommodations.[40]

Other correspondents and journalists refer to the admirable mental and physical health of the old Verdi. He, himself, however, is quite aware of his age, becoming more careful and distrustful, forgetful and repetitious, to the point of pedantry.[41] His handwriting is often shaky and harder to decipher than ever.

A sore throat and an injured finger disturb the Maestro during the weeks in autumn 1892, when he is coaching the members of the *Falstaff* cast at Palazzo Doria in Genoa, as he mentions to Ricordi on 25 November 1892 and on other days. At the same time, his critical evaluations of the singers, his precise observations on vocal production, enunciation, musicianship, and acting are as valid today as when they were written. Another letter to Ricordi, of 10 December 1893, concerning a young lady from Chicago, bears witness to his deep concern for the highest artistic standards as well as for the future of aspiring artists.

The Maestro's lines of 15 June 1893 to his exuberant young friend Edoardo Mascheroni[42] are a rare example of generous advice, wisdom, and common sense. In other letters to this young conductor, Verdi shares his delightful sense of humor after the tension he endured before *Falstaff* in Rome. On other occasions, he tries to console and encourage Mascheroni, who was caught in the web of backstage intrigue and vanity, caused largely by Victor Maurel,[43] whose arrogance, alas, paralleled his talent. The French baritone's outrageous demands for the title role in the summer of 1892 had been so upsetting to Verdi that, in his letter to Ricordi of 1 September, he threatens to burn the almost completed score.

Doubts regarding the dramatic flow of the second-act finale plague Verdi and, consequently, Ricordi, for weeks after the première of *Falstaff*, until he decides to cut sixteen bars of enchanting music. Thus Verdi answers the age-old question "Prima la musica, poi le parole?" [First the music, then the words?] in favor of the action. Boito and Ricordi disagree, as do others, but respectfully bow to the Maestro's somewhat hesitant judgment, as manifested in his letters to Ricordi in March 1893.

As always before first productions, Verdi is skeptical and even pessimistic about the first performance of the French *Falstaff* at the Paris Opéra-Comique on 18 April 1894. If he ever reread his letter to Teresa Stolz[44] of the following day, he must have realized how wrong his prognosis had been.

When he learns from Camille Bellaigue's letter of 27 May 1894 that, in subsequent performances at the Comique, Maurel has had the audacity to impose shocking cuts, the Maestro is furious. Nevertheless he lets Maurel go on as Iago in the first French *Othello* at the Opéra in the autumn. The success of that *Othello* performance means more to him than personal revenge. And, ironically, this success represents the climax of his career. Verdi's understandable patriotism, coupled with his resentment and prejudice against the French[45] and their Opéra, that "grande boutique" [big shop], had not allowed him to foresee such a glorious end.

Artistic reservations, rather than national prejudice, had, at the time of *Aida*, delayed his appreciation of the Bohemian soprano Teresa Stolz and the Viennese mezzo-soprano Maria Waldmann.[46] In different ways they had become his intimate friends. Even when she became the Duchess of Ferrara, Maria Waldmann remained like a daughter to him. The letters from the octogenarian to her feel as though they were written in sunshine, echoing the music he gave to his young lovers in *Falstaff*.

Although, with Boito's and Ricordi's help, *Falstaff* took less time to complete than any of Verdi's operas after *La Traviata*, its gestation was slowed by many factors. Not the least was Verdi's inherent pessimism, as he saw Europe inching toward the abyss of World War I, which he had in fact predicted many years earlier.[47] Yet, amidst personal sadness, the loss of friends, and forebodings of global suffering, Giuseppe Verdi, the farmer of St. Agata, found relief and escape as he gave himself and all of us the miracle that is *Falstaff*.

INTRODUCTION

He left a sheet within the pages of his autograph score, a farewell discovered by Arturo Toscanini in the archive of the House of Ricordi:

The final notes of Falstaff

All is finished!
Go, go, old John . . .
Be on your way,
as long as you can . . . .
Enchanting, eternal rogue;
Ever true, behind different
masks, at every time, in
every place!!
Go . . . . Go . . . .
On your way On your way.
Farewell !!!

NOTES

1. Camille Bellaigue in *Revue des deux mondes*, 1 May 1894: "A work of life, health, light and joy." (See Biographical Sketch and Appendix III.)

2. Edgar Istel, *Verdi und Shakespeare*, p. 119. The composer of *Die lustigen Weiber von Windsor* was the German Otto Nicolai (1810–49), who turned down the libretto to *Nabucco*, the young Verdi's first success, in 1842.

3. The celebrated conductor (1867–1957) and friend of Boito made this remark to Samuel Chotzinoff. (*Toscanini: An Intimate Portrait*, pp. 20–1.) See Appendix III, in particular.

4. A questionable statement by Raffaello Barbiera (see Bibliography) in a special issue of *Ilustrazione italiana*, p. 2, on the occasion of the *Falstaff* première in Milan, on 9 February 1893.

5. Ghislanzoni (1824–93) was a baritone, impresario, writer, and one of the most prominent Italian librettists of the nineteenth century. In 1867 he helped with the Italian translation of the French text of *Don Carlos;* in 1869 he assisted Verdi with the revision of *La forza del destino,* and in 1870 he wrote the Italian libretto of *Aida,* based on the French scenario by Camille Du Locle (see *Aida* and Verdi to Ricordi, 21 May 1893, n. 1).

6. Arrivabene (1807–87), a prominent journalist, was a descendant of the ducal family Gonzaga of Mantua and the Byzantine imperial house. As a partisan of Mazzini and Cavour, he played a major role in the Rinascimento and in Verdi's life (*Otello* ii, pp. 806–7).

7. Countess Clara Maffei (1814–86), one of the most attractive personalities in nineteenth-century Italy and Verdi's closest friend. Her salon was the heart of the intellectual and political Risorgimento in Milan (*Otello* ii, pp. 838–9).

8. On the other hand, Beethoven supposedly maintained that Rossini would never write a serious opera.

9. An unknown libretto, possibly related to *Falstaff*. Giulio Ricordi, however, seems either not to have known or to have forgotten that, after the failure of *Un giorno di regno*, Verdi considered another comic opera in the spring of 1870, before embarking on *Aida* (*Aida*, p. 17).

10. In a letter to his publisher and producer, Léon Escudier (1828–81) in Paris (*Carteggi* iv, p. 159).

11. Countess Elena Albertini Carandini (1902–90) thus described Arrigo Boito's appearance to me. Her father, Luigi Albertini (1871–1941), anti-fascist editor-in-chief of *Il Corriere della Sera,* was a close friend of Boito's and executor of his will.

12. Boito to Camille Bellaigue on 3 July 1908 (De Rensis, p. 342).

13. One of the greatest pianists of his time (1866–1924), composer, and writer. Boito noticed his talents at once when he met the sixteen-year-old Busoni in 1882 (*Otello* ii, pp. 797, 814).

14. In a letter to Boito of 15 November 1904 (Nardi, p. 661).

15. The reaction of Richard Wagner (1813–83) to Boito's admiration is reflected in his "Letter to an Italian friend about the performance of *Lohengrin* in Bologna." (*Richard Wagner: Sämtliche Schriften und Dichtungen*, vol. 9, pp. 287–91.) This publication does not entirely agree with the autograph preserved in the library of La Scala.

16. Philosopher, historian, literary critic, steadfast anti-fascist, and statesman (1866–1952). Essay in *La Letteratura della Nuova Italia, Saggi Critici,* vol. I, pp. 257–74 (see also *Otello* ii, pp. 768–9).

17. François-Victor Hugo (1828–73), the son of Victor Hugo (1802–85), translated Shakespeare into French. Five of Boito's volumes (III, V, VI, VIII, XIV), showing his penciled underlinings and notations, are preserved in the library of La Scala (see Nardi, p. 594). Similar volumes are among Boito's books in his studio at the Conservatory named in his honor in Parma.

18. See Biographical Sketch.

19. Nardi, pp. 593–4, 625. Three other complete librettos of *King Lear*, including one in Verdi's own hand, are preserved at St. Agata.

20. See Verdi to Eugenio Tornaghi, 24 August 1889, n. 1.

21. Naples twice happened to be the city of Boito's nemesis. In 1884, the indiscretion of a Neapolitan journalist—at one time, unbeknownst to Boito, the young Eleonora Duse's seducer—almost wrecked his collaboration with Verdi on *Otello* (*Otello* i, pp. 156–64). In 1893, a challenge to fight a duel with the publisher Edoardo Sonzogno in that city might have cost him his life, had it not been averted (Ricordi to Verdi and Frederick Cowen to Boito, 14 December 1893; Verdi to Ricordi, 15 December 1893; Frederick Cowen to Boito, 18 December 1893; Verdi to Ricordi, 20 and 21 December 1893; Boito to Verdi, 21 December 1893; Verdi to Ricordi, 22 December 1893).

22. See Preface, n. 5. There are no known surviving letters from 1892 and 1893 except for Duse's of 31 December 1893.

23. See Duse to Boito, 26 October 1889, n. 1; Boito to Duse, 14 November 1889, n. 1; Boito to Duse, 1 January 1890, n. 2; Boito to Duse, 1 May 1890, n. 2.

24. See Biographical Sketch.

25. Professor at the University of Bern (1848–1918) and author of several books, *inter alia* on the influence of the mind on the body.

26. "To understand, to love, to express oneself, these are the great joys of the human spirit" (Boito to Camille Bellaigue, 25 April 1894).

27. *Otello* ii, pp. 851–3.

28. *Aida*, pp. 383–4.

29. Phillips-Matz, pp. 299–300.

30. See Verdi to Boito, 18 August 1889, n. 3.

31. Eugenio Checchi, *Giuseppe Verdi: Il genio e le sue opere*, pp. 106–7.

32. *Otello* i, pp. 23–4.

33. Arrivabene, *Verdi intimo*, ed. Alberti, p. 78.

34. *Otello* i, p. 126.

35. Verdi to De Amicis, 8 May, 2 and 7 November 1890.

36. E.g., Verdi to Ambroise Thomas, 23 January 1891; to Edoardo Mascheroni, 10 August 1893; to Johann Strauss, 29 September 1894.

37. In pursuit of the truth, Phillips-Matz reveals in her biography of Verdi, as well as in her article "A Time of Stress" (see Bibliography), a number of character flaws in his earlier life. These make all the more remarkable his growth to greatness as a human being and his increasingly noble actions in later years.

38. See Hepokoski, pp. 35–6.

39. Countess Giuseppina Negroni Prati (1824–1909), a Swiss-born Milanese aristocrat and daughter of Verdi's close friend Countess Emilia Morosini (1804–75), was also a friend to Verdi and his wife.

40. Verdi to De Amicis, 29 November 1893, and 26 August 1894.

41. See Hepokoski, p. 42.

42. See Biographical Sketch.

43. See Biographical Sketch.

44. See Biographical Sketch.

45. Cf., e.g., Verdi to Negroni Prati, 10 September 1893, and to Ricordi, 11 January 1894.

46. See Biographical Sketch.

47. Verdi to Clara Maffei, 30 September 1870 (see *Aida*, pp. 72–4).

List of Letters and Telegrams

PH = photocopy of an autograph
FAC = facsimile of a letter
* = letter written in French
† = telegram
For other abbreviations, see pp. xvii–xviii.

FROM	TO	DESTINATION	DATE	AUTOGRAPH LOCATION	PUBLISHED SOURCE
Verdi	Boito	Milan	6 July 89	IP	*Cart. V-B* i, 142
Boito	Verdi	Montecatini	7 July 89	SA	*Cart. V-B* i, 144-5
Verdi	Boito	Milan	7 July 89	IP	*Cart. V-B* i, 143
Boito	Verdi	Montecatini	9 July 89	SA	*Cart. V-B* i, 145-7
Verdi	Boito	Milan	10 July 89	IP	*Cart. V-B* i, 147
Boito	Verdi	Montecatini	11 July 89	SA	*Cart. V-B* i, 148
Verdi	Boito	Milan	11 July 89	IP	*Cart. V-B* i, 148-50
Boito	Verdi	Montecatini	12 July 89	SA	*Cart. V-B* i, 150
Verdi	Faccio	Milan?	14 July 89	IP (PH)	*Cop.* 702
Verdi	Piroli	Rome	16 July 89	AC	*Cart.* iii, 194
Piroli	Verdi	Montecatini?	19 July 89	SA	*Cart.* iii, 194
Boito	Verdi	St. Agata	1 Aug. 89	SA	*Cart. V-B* i, 151
Verdi	Boito	Ivrea	2 Aug. 89	IP	*Cart. V-B* i, 151
Verdi	Boito	Ivrea	18 Aug. 89	IP	*Cart. V-B* i, 152-3
Boito	Verdi	St. Agata	20 Aug. 89	SA	*Cart. V-B* i, 153–5
Verdi	Tornaghi	Milan	24 Aug. 89	Ri.	
Verdi	Ricordi	Milan	24 Aug. 89	Ri.	
Verdi	Ricordi	Milan	27 Aug. 89	Ri.	
Verdi	Piroli	Rome	28 Aug. 89	AC	*Cart.* iii, 195
Ricordi	Verdi	St. Agata	31 Aug. 89	SA	
Verdi	Piroli	Rome	24 Sept. 89	AC	*Cart.* iii, 196
Ricordi	Verdi	St. Agata	3 Oct. 89	SA	
Verdi	Negroni	Milan	14 Oct. 89	Sc	
Verdi	C. Boito	Milan	? Oct. 89		Abb. IV, 392

LIST OF LETTERS AND TELEGRAMS

FROM	TO	DESTINATION	DATE	AUTOGRAPH LOCATION	PUBLISHED SOURCE
Verdi	De Amicis	Genoa	22 Oct. 89	GE	LS. 154
Boito	Duse	Palermo	22 Oct. 89	Ci.	RR. 573–4
Duse	Boito	Milan	26 Oct. 89	Ci	RR. 576–7
Boito	Verdi	St. Agata	30 Oct. 89	SA	*Cart. V-B* i, 155–6
Duse	Boito	Milan	31 Oct. 89	Ci.	RR. 580–1
Boito	Duse	Palermo	2 Nov. 89	Ci.	RR. 584
Verdi †	Boito	Milan	3 Nov. 89	IP	*Cart. V-B* i, 134
Ricordi	Verdi	St. Agata	3 Nov. 89	SA	
Verdi	Ricordi	Milan	4 Nov. 89	Ri.	Abb. iv, 390
Boito	Duse	Palermo	4 Nov. 89	Ci.	RR. 587–8
Ricordi	Verdi	St. Agata	7 Nov. 89	SA	
Verdi	De Amicis	Genoa	10 Nov. 89	GE	LS. 155
Boito	Duse	Messina	10 Nov. 89	Ci.	RR. 589–90
Verdi	Boito	Milan	11 Nov. 89	IP	*Cart. V-B* i, 156
Boito	Verdi	St. Agata	12 Nov. 89	SA	*Cart. V-B* i, 156–7
Boito	Duse	Messina	12 Nov. 89	Ci.	RR. 594
Boito	Duse	Syracuse	14 Nov. 89	Ci.	RR. 595–6
Verdi	Ricordi	Milan	17 Nov. 89	Ri.	Abb. iv, 391
Verdi †	Umberto I	Rome	17 Nov. 89		
Verdi	De Amicis	Genoa	24 Nov. 89	GE	LS. 156
Verdi	Carducci	Bologna	3 Dec. 89		*Cop.* 354–5
Verdi	De Amicis	Genoa	3 Dec. 89	GE	LS. 157
Boito	Duse	Catania	3–4 Dec. 89	Ci.	RR. 608–9
Ricordi	Verdi	Genoa	12 Dec. 89	SA	
Boito	Duse	Alexandria	22 Dec. 89	Ci.	RR. 616
Duse	Boito	Nervi	23 Dec. 89	Ci.	RR. 617
Ricordi	Verdi	Genoa	29 Dec. 89	SA	
Boito	Duse	Cairo	31 Dec. 89	Ci.	RR. 621
Verdi	Waldmann	Ferrara	1 Jan. 90	Bo.	*Cart.* ii, 263
Boito	Duse	Cairo	1 Jan. 90	Ci.	RR. 622–3
Giuseppina V.	G. De Sanctis	Naples	2 Jan. 90	IP (PH)	*Cart.* i, 210
Verdi	Boito	Nervi	6 Jan. 90	IP	*Cart. V-B* i, 157
Ricordi	Verdi	Genoa	7 Jan. 90	SA	
Boito	Duse	Cairo	10 Jan. 90	Ci.	RR. 628–9
Ricordi	Verdi	Genoa	11 Feb. 90	SA	CP 72–3
Verdi	Boito	Nervi	15 Feb. 90	IP	*Cart. V-B* i, 157–8
Boito	Duse	Barcelona	17 Feb. 90	Ci.	RR. 645–6
Duse	Boito	Nervi	21 Feb. 90	Ci.	RR. 646–7

LIST OF LETTERS AND TELEGRAMS

FROM	TO	DESTINATION	DATE	AUTOGRAPH LOCATION	PUBLISHED SOURCE
Ricordi	Verdi	Genoa	23 Feb. 90	SA	CP 73
Boito	Duse	Barcelona	25 Feb. 90	Ci.	RR. 648–9
Boito	Verdi	Genoa	1 Mar. 90	SA	*Cart. V-B* i, 158
Verdi	Boito	Nervi	2 Mar. 90	IP	*Cart. V-B* i, 159
Verdi	Boito	Nervi	8 Mar. 90	IP	*Cart. V-B* i, 160
Verdi †	Boito	Nervi	9 Mar. 90	IP	*Cart. V-B* i, 159
Boito	Verdi	Genoa	9 Mar. 90	SA	*Cart. V-B* i, 160
Boito	Duse	Barcelona	10 Mar. 90	Ci.	RR. 649–50
Duse	Boito	Nervi	11 Mar. 90	Ci.	RR. 650–1
Boito	Verdi	Genoa	13 Mar. 90	SA	*Cart. V-B* i, 161
Boito	Duse	Barcelona	14 Mar. 90	Ci.	RR. 651–2
Boito	Duse	Barcelona	15 Mar. 90	Ci.	RR. 652–3
Boito	Verdi	Genoa	16 Mar. 90	SA	*Cart. V-B* i, 161–2
Verdi	Boito	Milan	17 Mar. 90	IP	*Cart. V-B* i, 163
Boito	Verdi	Genoa	20 Mar. 90	SA	*Cart. V-B* i, 163–4
Verdi	Waldmann	Ferrara	21 Mar. 90	Bo.	*Cart.* ii, 263–4
Boito	Verdi	Genoa	25 Mar. 90	SA	*Cart. V-B* i, 164–6
Boito	Duse	Barcelona	29 Mar. 90	Ci.	RR. 664
Verdi	Boito	Milan	31 Mar. 90	IP	*Cart. V-B* i, 166–7
Verdi	Noseda	Milan	1 Apr. 90	?	*Cop.* 355–6
Ricordi	Verdi	Genoa	3 Apr. 90	SA	
Boito	Verdi	Genoa	7 Apr. 90	SA	*Cart. V-B* i, 167–8
Verdi	Boito	Milan	8 Apr. 90	IP	*Cart. V-B* i, 168
Verdi †	Boito	Milan	10 Apr. 90	IP	*Cart. V-B* i, 169
Boito	Duse	Madrid	10 Apr. 90	Ci.	RR. 666
Duse	Boito	Milan	14 Apr. 90	Ci.	RR. 667–8
Boito	Verdi	Genoa	15 Apr. 90	SA	*Cart. V-B* i, 169–70
Verdi	Boito	Milan	17 Apr. 90	IP	*Cart. V-B* i, 170
Boito	Verdi	Genoa	18 Apr. 90	SA	*Cart. V-B* i, 171
Verdi	Boito	Milan	20 Apr. 90	IP	*Cart. V-B* i, 172–3
Verdi	Maurel	Paris?	21 Apr. 90	?	Mo. 188
Boito	Duse	Madrid	1 May 90	Ci.	RR. 673
Verdi	De Amicis	Genoa	8 May 90	GE	LS. 159
Ricordi	Verdi	St. Agata	9 May 90	SA	
Boito	Duse	Madrid	10 May 90	Ci.	RR. 679
Boito	Verdi	St. Agata	21 May 90	SA	*Cart. V-B* i, 173–4
Boito	Duse	Madrid	22 May 90	Ci,	RR. 688–9
Verdi	Boito	Milan	23 May 90	IP	*Cart. V-B* i, 175

LIST OF LETTERS AND TELEGRAMS

From	To	Destination	Date	Autograph Location	Published Source
Boito	Duse	Madrid	24 May 90	Ci.	RR. 694–5
Ricordi	Verdi	St. Agata	25 May 90	SA	CP 26
Boito	Duse	Madrid	26 May 90	Ci.	RR. 696
Boito	Duse	Madrid	3 June 90	Ci.	RR. 705–6
Ricordi	Verdi	St. Agata	3 June 90	SA	
De Amicis	Verdi	St. Agata	7 June 90	SA ?	LS. 160
De Amicis	Giuseppina V.	St. Agata	7 June 90	SA ?	LS. 161
Boito	Duse	Madrid?	9 June 90	Ci.	RR. 714–5
Ricordi	Verdi	St. Agata	10 June 90	SA	CP 26–8
Boito	Duse	Madrid	11 June 90	Ci.	RR. 715
Boito	Duse	Madrid	15 June 90	Ci.	RR. 720–1
Boito	Duse	Madrid	25 June 90	Ci.	RR. 732–3
Verdi	Muzio	Paris	30 June 90	?	*Cop.* 704–5
Ricordi	Verdi	St. Agata	5 July 90	SA	
Verdi	Stolz	Milan	12 Aug. 90	?	Abb. iv. 402
Ricordi	Verdi	St. Agata	22 Aug. 90	SA	
Verdi	Piroli	Rome	31 Aug. 90	AC	*Cart.* iii, 198
Verdi	Piroli	Rome	6 Sept. 90	AC	*Cart.* iii, 198–9
Boito	Duse	Barcelona	11 Sept. 90	Ci.	RR. 755–6
Verdi	Persico	Villanova	11 Sept. 90	EP	MI. 33
Verdi	De Amicis	Genoa	27 Sept. 90	GE	LS. 165
Ricordi	Verdi	St. Agata	28 Sept. 90	Pa.	CP 74
Ricordi	Verdi	St. Agata	28 Sept. 90	SA	
De Amicis	Verdi	St. Agata	2 Oct. 90	SA ?	LS. 166
Boito	Duse	Turin	2 Oct. 90	Ci.	RR. 765–6
Boito	Verdi	St. Agata	3 Oct. 90	SA	*Cart.* V-B i, 175–6
Verdi	Boito	Milan	6 Oct. 90	IP	*Cart.* V-B i, 176–7
Muzio	Verdi	St. Agata	[22 Oct. 90]		*Cart.* iv, 239
Verdi	Piroli	Rome	24 Oct. 90	AC	*Cart.* iii, 199
Ricordi	Verdi	St. Agata	24 Oct. 90	SA	
De Amicis	Verdi	St. Agata	25 Oct. 90	SA ?	LS. 167
Verdi	Ricordi	Milan	27 Oct. 90	Pa.	CP 74
Ricordi	Verdi	St. Agata	29 Oct. 90	SA	
Verdi	Piroli	Rome	30 Oct. 90	AC	*Cart.* iii, 200
Ricordi	Verdi	St. Agata	1 Nov. 90	SA	CP 75
Ricordi	Verdi	St. Agata	2 Nov. 90	SA	CP 75
Verdi	De Amicis	Genoa	2 Nov. 90	GE	LS. 168
Verdi	Ricordi	Milan	4 Nov. 90	RI	*Cop.* 358–9

LIST OF LETTERS AND TELEGRAMS

FROM	To	DESTINATION	DATE	AUTOGRAPH LOCATION	PUBLISHED SOURCE
Boito	Duse	Turin	6 Nov. 90	Ci.	RR. 774
Ricordi	Verdi	St. Agata	7 Nov. 90	SA	
Verdi *	Erard	Paris	7 Nov. 90	?	*Cop.* 359–60
Ricordi	Verdi	St. Agata	12 Nov. 90	SA	
Verdi	Persico	Villanova	16 Nov. 90	EP	MI. 33–4
Verdi	De Amicis	Genoa	22 Nov. 90	GE	LS. 169
Verdi	Persico	Villanova	23 Nov. 90	EP	MI. 34
Verdi	De Amicis	Genoa	25 Nov. 90	GE	LS. 170
Verdi	De Amicis	Genoa	26 Nov. 90	GE	LS. 171
Verdi	De Amicis	Genoa	28 Nov. 90	GE	LS. 172
Verdi	De Amicis	Genoa	28 Nov. 90	GE	LS. 172
Ricordi	Verdi	Genoa	3 Dec. 90	SA	
Verdi	Monaldi	Rome?	3 Dec. 90	?	*Cop.* 712
Verdi	Waldmann	Ferrara	6 Dec. 90	Bo.	*Cart.* ii, 264
Boito	Verdi	Genoa	9 Dec. 90	SA	*Cart. V-B* i, 177–8
Ricordi	Verdi	Genoa	19 Dec. 90	SA	
Giuseppina V.	G. De Sanctis	Naples	28 Dec. 90	IP (PH)	*Cart.* i, 211
Verdi	Ricordi	Milan	28 Dec. 90	Ri.	
Verdi	Waldmann	Ferrara	29 Dec. 90	Bo.	*Cart.* ii, 264
Verdi	Negroni	Milan	30 Dec. 90	Sc.	
Verdi	Checchi	Milan?	30 Dec. 90	?	*Cop.* 712
Ricordi	Verdi	Genoa	30 Dec. 90	SA	
Boito	Verdi	Genoa	31 Dec. 90	SA	*Cart. V-B* i, 178
Verdi	Boito	Milan	1 Jan. 91	IP	*Cart. V-B* i, 179
Verdi	Ricordi	Milan	1 Jan. 91	Ri.	*Cop.* 712–13
Verdi	Monaldi	Rome?	11 Jan. 91	?	*Cop.* 362
Ricordi	Verdi	Genoa	18 Jan. 91	SA	
Verdi	Ricordi	Milan	19 Jan. 91	Ri.	*Cop* . 362–3
Verdi	Ricordi	Milan	20 Jan. 91	Ri.	
Verdi	C. Boito	Milan	Jan. 91	SA	
Verdi*	Thomas	Paris	23 Jan. 91	?	*Cop.* 364
Verdi	Fortis	Milan	26 Jan. 91	?	*Cop.* 364–5
Verdi	Ricordi	Milan	27 Jan. 91	Ri.	*Cop.* 706–8
Verdi	Ricordi	Milan	28 Jan. 91	Ri.	
Verdi	Ricordi	Milan	30 Jan. 91	Ri.	*Cop.* 708–9
Verdi	Ricordi	Milan	3 Feb. 91	Ri.	
Verdi	Ricordi	Milan	5 Feb. 91	Ri.	
Verdi	Ricordi	Milan	7 Feb. 91	Ri.	*Cart. V-B* ii, 404

LIST OF LETTERS AND TELEGRAMS

From	To	Destination	Date	Autograph Location	Published Source
Verdi	De Amicis	Genoa	3 Mar. 91	GE	LS. 173
Verdi	Negroni	Milan	8 Mar. 91	Sc.	*Cop.* 505
Giuseppina V.	Calvi Carrara	Busseto?	14 Mar. 91	?	Abb. iv, 417
Verdi	Negroni	Milan	15 Mar. 91	Sc.	
Boito	Giuseppina V.	Genoa	19 Mar. 91	SA	*Cart. V-B* i, 179–80
Ricordi	Verdi	Genoa	19 Mar. 91	SA	
Verdi	Ricordi	Milan	19 Mar. 91	Ri.	Abb. iv, 418
Verdi	Boito	Milan	21 Mar. 91	IP	*Cart. V-B* i, 180–1
Verdi	Ricordi	Milan	21 Mar. 91	Ri.	
Boito	Verdi	Genoa	22 Mar. 91	SA	*Cart. V-B* i, 181–2
Ricordi	Verdi	Genoa	31 Mar. 91	SA	*Cart. V-B* ii, 403
Ricordi	Verdi	Genoa	5 Apr. 91	SA	
Ricordi	Verdi	Genoa	12 Apr. 91	SA	
Ricordi	Verdi	Genoa	24 Apr. 91	SA	
Boito	Verdi	Genoa	25 Apr. 91	SA	*Cart. V-B* i, 182–3
Verdi	Boito	Milan	26 Apr. 91	IP	*Cart. V-B* i, 183
Verdi	Boito	Milan	27 Apr. 91	IP	*Cart. V-B* i, 184
Boito	Verdi	St. Agata	29 Apr. 91	SA	*Cart. V-B* i, 185–6
Verdi	Boito	Milan	1 May 91	SA	*Cart. V-B* i, 186
Boito	Verdi	St. Agata	2 May 91	SA	*Cart. V-B* i, 187
Verdi	Boito	Milan	5 May 91	IP	*Cart. V-B* i, 187
Ricordi	Verdi	St. Agata	9 May 91	SA	
Ricordi	Verdi	St. Agata	22 May 91	SA	
Verdi	Ricordi	Milan	25 May 91	Ri.	*Cart. V-B* i, 409
Boito	Verdi	St. Agata	28 May 91	SA	*Cart. V-B* i, 188
Boito	Verdi	St. Agata	29 May 91	SA	*Cart. V-B* i, 188–9
Ricordi	Verdi	St. Agata	31 May 91	SA	
Verdi	Boito	Milan	May–June 91	IP	*Cart. V-B* i, 282
Verdi	Ricordi	Milan	2 June 91	Ri.	Abb. iv, 421
Ricordi	Verdi	St. Agata	6 June 91	SA	
Boito	Verdi	St. Agata	9 June 91	SA	*Cart. V-B* i, 189–90
Verdi	Ricordi	Milan	9 June 91	Ri.	*Cop.* 713
Ricordi	Verdi	St. Agata	12 June 91	SA	
Verdi	Boito	Milan	12 June 91	IP	*Cart. V-B* i, 190
Boito	Verdi	St. Agata	14 June 91	SA	*Cart. V-B* i, 191
Ricordi	Verdi	St. Agata	16 June 91	SA	
Verdi	Boito	Milan	5 July 91	IP	*Cart. V-B* i, 191–2
Verdi	Ricordi	Milan	23 July 91	Ri.	

LIST OF LETTERS AND TELEGRAMS

From	To	Destination	Date	Autograph Location	Published Source
Verdi	Boito	Milan	23 July 91	IP	*Cart. V-B* i, 192–3
Boito	Verdi	St. Agata	24 July 91	SA	*Cart. V-B* i, 193
Ricordi	Verdi	St. Agata	26 July 91	SA	
Ricordi	Verdi	St. Agata	21 Aug. 91	SA	
Verdi	Ricordi	Milan	23 Aug. 91	Ri.	Abb. iv, 424
Verdi	Ricordi	Milan	30 Aug. 91	Ri.	
Ricordi	Verdi	St. Agata	1 Sept. 91	SA	
Verdi	Ricordi	Milan	3 Sept. 91	Ri.	
Boito	Verdi	St. Agata	3 Sept. 91	SA	*Cart. V-B* i, 194
Verdi	Mariotti	Parma	4 Sept. 91	?	*Cop.* 370–1
Boito	Mariotti	Parma	4 Sept. 91	?	*Cart. V-B* ii, 415
Verdi	Boito	Milan	5 Sept. 91	IP	*Cart. V-B* i, 194–5
Boito	Verdi	St. Agata	8 Sept. 91	SA	*Cart. V-B* i, 195
Mariotti	Verdi	St. Agata	9 Sept. 91	?	
Ricordi	Verdi	St. Agata	9 Sept. 91	SA	
Verdi	Boito	Milan	10 Sept. 91	IP	*Cart. V-B* i, 196
Verdi	Boito	Milan	15 Sept. 91	IP	*Cart. V-B* i, 196–7
Boito	Verdi	St. Agata	16 Sept. 91	SA	*Cart. V-B* i, 197–8
Ricordi	Verdi	St. Agata	19 Sept. 91	SA	
Ricordi	Verdi	St. Agata	2 Oct. 91	SA	
Boito	Verdi	St. Agata	3 Oct. 91	SA	*Cart. V-B* i, 198–9
Verdi	Resasco	Genoa	21 Oct. 91	?	*Cop.* 515–6
Verdi	Negroni	Milan	26 Oct. 91	Sc.	Ob. 106
Verdi	Ricordi	Milan	6 Nov. 91	SA	Abb. iv, 426–7
Verdi	Bramanti	Ravenna	14 Nov. 91	?	*Cop.* 372
Verdi	Gallignani	Parma?	15 Nov. 91	?	*Cop.* 373
Ricordi	Verdi	Genoa	15 Dec. 91	SA	
Ricordi	Verdi	Genoa	29 Dec. 91	SA	
Boito	Verdi	Genoa	1 Jan. 92	SA	*Cart. V-B* i, 200
Verdi	Boito	Milan	2 Jan. 92	IP	*Cart. V-B* i, 200
Verdi	Waldmann	Ferrara	3 Jan. 92	Bo.	*Cart.* ii, 264–5
Ricordi	Verdi	Genoa	4 Jan. 92	SA	
Verdi	Ricordi	Milan	7 Jan. 92	Ri.	
Ricordi	Verdi	Genoa	8 Jan. 92	SA	
Verdi	Ricordi	Milan	9 Jan. 92	Ri.	
Ricordi	Verdi	Genoa	11 Jan. 92	SA	
Verdi	Monaldi	Rome?	18 Jan. 92	?	Mo. 265
Ricordi	Verdi	Genoa	19 Jan. 92	SA	

LIST OF LETTERS AND TELEGRAMS

FROM	TO	DESTINATION	DATE	AUTOGRAPH LOCATION	PUBLISHED SOURCE
Verdi	Boito	Milan	23 Jan. 92	IP	*Cart. V-B* i, 201
Boito	Verdi	Genoa	23 Jan. 92	SA	*Cart. V-B* i, 201–2
Verdi	Persico	Villanova	23 Jan. 92	EP	*Cart. iv,* 299–300
Ricordi	Verdi	Genoa	25 Jan. 92	SA	
Verdi	Ricordi	Milan	31 Jan. 92	Ri.	
Ricordi	Verdi	Genoa	1 Feb. 92	SA	
Verdi	Ricordi	Milan	2 Feb. 92	Ri.	
Ricordi	Verdi	Genoa	5 Feb. 92	SA	
Verdi	Ricordi	Milan	9 Feb. 92	Ri.	
Boito	Verdi	Genoa	10 Feb. 92	SA	*Cart. V-B* i, 202–3
Verdi	Ricordi	Milan	10 Feb. 92	Ri.	
Verdi	Ricordi	Milan	12 Feb. 92	Ri.	
Verdi	Boito	Milan	12 Feb. 92	IP	*Cart. V-B* i, 203–4
Ricordi	Verdi	Genoa	16 Feb. 92	SA	
Verdi	De Amicis	Genoa	16 Mar. 92	GE	LS. 181
Verdi	Waldmann	Ferrara	22 Mar. 92	Bo.	*Cart.* ii, 265
Ricordi	Verdi	Genoa	25 Mar. 92	SA	
Verdi	Ricordi	Milan	26 Mar. 92	Ri.	
Ricordi	Verdi	Genoa	30 Mar. 92	SA	
Verdi	Ricordi	Milan	31 Mar. 92	Ri.	
Verdi	Ricordi	Milan	2 Apr. 92	Ri.	Abb. iv, 436–7
Ricordi	Verdi	Genoa	3 Apr. 92	SA	
Verdi	Ricordi	Milan	4 Apr. 92	Ri.	Abb. iv, 437
Verdi	Ricordi	Milan	5 Apr. 92	Ri.	
Bülow	Verdi	Genoa	7 Apr. 92	SA	*Cop.* 375
Verdi	Ricordi	Milan	8 Apr. 92	Ri.	Abb. iv, 437
Verdi	Ricordi	Milan	11 Apr. 92	Ri.	Abb. iv, 439
Giuseppina V.	Ricordi	Milan	14 Apr. 92	Ri.	Abb. iv, 438
Verdi	Ricordi	Milan	14 Apr. 92	Ri.	Abb. iv, 438
Verdi	Bülow	Hamburg	14 Apr. 92	?	*Cop.* 375–6
Verdi	Boito	Milan	15 Apr. 92	IP	*Cart. V-B* i, 204–5
Boito	Verdi	Genoa	17 Apr. 92	SA	*Cart. V-B* i, 205
Ricordi	Verdi	Genoa	26 Apr. 92	SA	
Verdi	Ricordi	Milan	27 Apr. 92	Ri.	
Verdi	Ricordi	Milan	? Apr. 92	Ri.	
Ricordi	Verdi	Genoa	1 May 92	SA	
Boito	Verdi	St. Agata?	9 May 92	SA	*Cart. V-B* i, 206
Verdi	Boito	Milan	11 May 92	IP	*Cart. V-B* i, 207

LIST OF LETTERS AND TELEGRAMS

From	To	Destination	Date	Autograph Location	Published Source
Tornaghi	Verdi	St. Agata	14 May 92	SA	
Verdi	Panattoni	Paris	24 May 92	Ri.	
Verdi	Tornaghi	Milan	24 May 92	Ri.	
Ricordi	Verdi	St. Agata	30 May 92	SA	
Verdi	Ricordi	Milan	1 June 92	Ri.	Abb. iv, 441
Ricordi	Verdi	St. Agata	5 June 92	SA	*Cart. V-B* ii, 424
Verdi	Ricordi	Milan	7 June 92	Ri.	*Cart. V-B* ii, 441–2
Ricordi	Verdi	St. Agata	9 June 92	SA	
Verdi	Ricordi	Milan	10 June 92	Ri.	
Ricordi	Verdi	St. Agata	11 June 92	SA	
Verdi	Ricordi	Milan	13 June 93	Ri.	
Verdi	Ricordi	Milan	14 June 92	Ri.	
Verdi	Ricordi	Milan	15 June 92	Ri.	
Ricordi	Verdi	St. Agata	15 June 92	SA	*Cart. V-B* ii, 424–5
Ricordi	Verdi	St. Agata	16 June 92	SA	
Ricordi	Verdi	St. Agata	16 June 92	SA	
Verdi	Ricordi	Milan	17 June 92	Ri.	Abb. iv, 444–5
Ricordi	Verdi	St. Agata	17 June 92	SA	
Ricordi	Verdi	St. Agata	21 June 92	SA	
Verdi	Ricordi	Milan	12 July 92	Ri.	
Verdi	Ricordi	Milan	12 July 92	Ri.	
Ricordi	Verdi	St. Agata	14 July 92	SA	
Verdi	Ricordi	Milan	14 July 92	Ri.	Abb. iv, 447
Verdi	Ricordi	Milan	17 July 92	Ri.	
Ricordi	Verdi	St. Agata	18 July 92	SA	
Verdi	Ricordi	Milan	19 July 92	Ri.	
Ricordi	Verdi	St. Agata	19 July 92	SA	
Ricordi	Verdi	St. Agata	20 July 92	SA	
Verdi	Ricordi	Milan	21 July 92	Ri.	
Verdi	Ricordi	Milan	22 July 92	Ri.	
Verdi	Ricordi	Milan	23 July 92	Ri.	
Giuseppina V.	Ricordi	Milan	4 Aug. 92	Ri.	Abb. iv, 449
Ricordi	Verdi	St. Agata	5 Aug. 92	SA	
Verdi	Ricordi	Milan	5 Aug. 92	Ri.	
Verdi	Boito	Milan	6 Aug. 92	IP	*Cart. V-B* i, 207–8
Verdi	Ricordi	Milan	8 Aug. 92	Ri.	Abb. iv, 451
Boito	Verdi	St. Agata	9 Aug. 92	SA	*Cart. V-B* i, 209–10
Ricordi	Verdi	St. Agata	12 Aug. 92	SA	

LIST OF LETTERS AND TELEGRAMS

FROM	TO	DESTINATION	DATE	AUTOGRAPH LOCATION	PUBLISHED SOURCE
Verdi	Ricordi	Milan	14 Aug. 92	Ri.	Abb. iv, 451
Tornaghi	Verdi	St. Agata	16 Aug. 92	SA	
Ricordi	Verdi	St. Agata	17 Aug. 92	SA	
Verdi	Tornaghi	Milan	17 Aug. 92	Ri.	
Verdi	Ricordi	Milan	19 Aug. 92	Ri.	
Tornaghi	Verdi	St. Agata	20 Aug. 92	SA	
Ricordi	Verdi	St. Agata	21 Aug. 92	SA	
Ricordi	Verdi	St. Agata	22 Aug. 92	SA	
Verdi	Boito	Milan	22 Aug. 92	IP	*Cart. V-B* i, 210
Verdi	Tornaghi	Milan	22 Aug. 92	Ri.	
Tornaghi	Verdi	St. Agata	23 Aug. 92	SA	
Verdi	Ricordi	Milan	23 Aug. 92	Ri.	
Boito	Verdi	St. Agata	23 Aug. 92	SA	*Cart. V-B* i, 211
Verdi	Ricordi	Milan	30 Aug. 92	Ri.	Abb. iv, 454
Ricordi	Verdi	St. Agata	30 Aug. 92	SA	
Verdi	Ricordi	Milan	31 Aug. 92	Ri.	
Ricordi †	Verdi	Busseto	31 Aug. 92	SA	
Ricordi †	Verdi	Busseto	1 Sept. 92	SA	
Ricordi	Verdi	St. Agata	1 Sept. 92	SA	
Verdi	Ricordi	Milan	1 Sept. 92	Ri.	*Cop.* 377–8
Verdi	Ricordi	Milan	2 Sept. 92	Ri.	
Ricordi	Verdi	St. Agata	2 Sept. 92	SA	
Ricordi †	Verdi	Busseto	2 Sept. 92	SA	
Ricordi	Verdi	St. Agata	2 Sept. 92	SA	
Ricordi	Verdi	St. Agata	3 Sept. 92	SA	
Maurel †	Verdi	Busseto	5 Sept. 92	SA	
Verdi	Ricordi	Milan	5 Sept. 92	Ri.	
Verdi	Ricordi	Milan	7 Sept. 92	Ri.	
Verdi	Stolz	Milan	9 Sept. 92	?	Abb. iv, 457
Ricordi	Verdi	St. Agata	10 Sept. 92	SA	
Boito	Verdi	St. Agata	11 Sept. 92	SA	*Cart. V-B* i, 212
Verdi	Ricordi	Milan	13 Sept. 92	Ri.	
Ricordi	Verdi	St. Agata	17 Sept. 92	SA	
Verdi	Ricordi	Milan	18 Sept. 92	Ri.	*Cop.* 379–82
Verdi	Boito	Milan	20 Sept. 92	IP	*Cart. V-B* i, 212–3
Ricordi	Verdi	St. Agata	24 Sept. 92	SA	
Boito	Verdi	St. Agata	25 Sept. 92	SA	*Cart. V-B* i, 213
Boito	Verdi	St. Agata	27 Sept. 92	SA	*Cart. V-B* i, 214–5

LIST OF LETTERS AND TELEGRAMS

From	To	Destination	Date	Autograph Location	Published Source
Verdi	Ricordi	Milan	27 Sept. 92	Ri.	
Ricordi	Verdi	St. Agata	30 Sept. 92	SA	*Cart. V-B* ii, 427
Tito Ricordi	Verdi	St. Agata	30 Sept. 92	SA	
Verdi	Ricordi	Milan	9 Oct. 92	Ri.	Abb. iv, 463–4
Verdi	Ricordi	Milan	10 Oct. 92	Ri.	Abb. iv, 464
Verdi	Ricordi	Milan	21 Oct. 92	Ri.	
Verdi	Ricordi	Milan	4 Nov. 92	Ri.	
Boito	Ricordi	Milan	5 Nov. 92	Ri.	*Cart. V-B* ii, 429
Ricordi	Verdi	Genoa	6 Nov. 92	SA	
Ricordi	Verdi	Genoa	7 Nov. 92	SA	
Verdi	Pasqua	?	7 Nov. 92	?	*Cop.* 714
Verdi	Maurel	?	8 Nov. 92	?	
Verdi	Ricordi	Milan	8 Nov. 92	Ri.	
Ricordi	Verdi	Genoa	8 Nov. 92	SA	
Ricordi	Verdi	Genoa	8 Nov. 92	SA	
Verdi	Ricordi	Milan	9 Nov. 92	Ri.	Abb. iv, 465–6
Ricordi	Verdi	Genoa	10 Nov. 92	SA	
Ricordi	Verdi	Genoa	10 Nov. 92	SA	
Tito Ricordi	Verdi	Genoa	10 Nov. 92	SA	
Verdi	Ricordi	Milan	10 Nov. 92	Ri.	
Ricordi	Verdi	Genoa	14 Nov. 92	SA	
Verdi	Ricordi	Milan	14 Nov. 92	Ri.	
Verdi	Ricordi	Milan	16 Nov. 92	Ri.	Abb. iv, 466
Ricordi	Verdi	Genoa	17 Nov. 92	SA	
Verdi	Ricordi	Milan	17 Nov. 92	Ri.	
Verdi	Ricordi	Milan	18 Nov. 92	Ri.	Abb. iv, 467
Ricordi	Verdi	Genoa	19 Nov. 92	SA	*Cart. V-B* ii, 430
Verdi	Ricordi	Milan	20 Nov. 92	Ri.	*Cart. V-B* ii, 430
Ricordi	Verdi	Genoa	21 Nov. 92	SA	
Verdi	Ricordi	Milan	21 Nov. 92	Ri.	
Verdi	Ricordi	Milan	21 Nov. 92	Ri.	
Verdi	Ricordi	Milan	23 Nov. 92	Ri.	
Ricordi	Verdi	Genoa	24 Nov. 92	SA	
Ricordi	Verdi	Genoa	25 Nov. 92	SA	
Verdi	Ricordi	Milan	25 Nov. 92	Ri.	*Cart. V-B* ii, 430
Verdi	Ricordi	Milan	25 Nov. 92	Ri.	
Verdi	Ricordi	Milan	27 Nov. 92	Ri.	Abb. iv, 467
Ricordi	Verdi	Genoa	28 Nov. 92	SA	

LIST OF LETTERS AND TELEGRAMS

FROM	TO	DESTINATION	DATE	AUTOGRAPH LOCATION	PUBLISHED SOURCE
Verdi	Ricordi	Milan	28 Nov. 92	Ri.	
Verdi	Ricordi	Milan	29 Nov. 92	Ri.	
Ricordi	Verdi	Genoa	29 Nov. 92	SA	
Ricordi	Verdi	Genoa	30 Nov. 92	SA	
Verdi *	Heugel	Paris	Nov. 92		*Cop.* 382–3
Verdi	Ricordi	Milan	1 Dec. 92	Ri.	Abb. iv, 467–8
Ricordi	Verdi	Genoa	2 Dec. 92	SA	
Verdi	Ricordi	Milan	2 Dec. 92	Ri.	
Verdi	Ricordi	Milan	5 Dec. 92	Ri.	
Verdi	Ricordi	Milan	7 Dec. 92	Ri.	Abb. iv, 468
Verdi	Ricordi	Milan	8 Dec. 92	Ri.	
Verdi	Ricordi	Milan	9 Dec. 92	Ri.	
Verdi	Persico	Villanova	9 Dec. 92	EP	*Cart.* iv, 300–1
Ricordi	Verdi	Genoa	10 Dec. 92	SA	
Verdi	Ricordi	Milan	11 Dec. 92	Ri.	
Verdi	Ricordi	Milan	12 Dec. 92	Ri.	
Verdi	Ricordi	Milan	13 Dec. 92	Ri.	
Ricordi †	Verdi	Genoa	13 Dec. 92	SA	
Verdi	Ricordi	Milan	14 Dec. 92	Ri.	
Verdi	Ricordi	Milan	16 Dec. 92	Ri.	
Ricordi	Verdi	Genoa	19 Dec. 92	SA	
Verdi	Ricordi	Milan	21 Dec. 92	Ri.	Abb. iv, 468–9
Verdi	Ricordi	Milan	22 Dec. 92	Ri.	
Verdi	Ricordi	Milan	23 Dec. 92	Ri.	
Ricordi	Verdi	Genoa	24 Dec. 92	SA	
Verdi	Ricordi	Milan	25 Dec. 92	Ri.	
Verdi	Waldmann	Ferrara	25 Dec. 92	Bo.	*Cart.* ii, 265
Verdi	Ricordi	Milan	26 Dec. 92	Ri.	Abb. iv, 470
Ricordi †	Verdi	Genoa	27 Dec. 92	SA	
Verdi	Ricordi	Milan	27 Dec. 92	Ri.	Abb. iv, 470–1
Verdi	Ricordi	Milan	31 Dec. 92	Ri.	
Giuseppina V.	De Sanctis	Naples	31 Dec. 92	IP (PH)	*Cart.* i, 213
Verdi	Ricordi	Milan	? Jan. 93	Ri.	
Ricordi	Verdi	Milan	? Jan. 93	SA	
Ricordi	Verdi	Milan	28 Jan. 93	SA	
Verdi	Ricordi	Milan	28 Jan. 93	Ri.	
Verdi	Ricordi	Milan	Jan.–Feb. 93	Ri.	
Verdi	Boito	Milan	Jan.–Feb. 93	IP	*Cart. V-B* i, 283

LIST OF LETTERS AND TELEGRAMS

From	To	Destination	Date	Autograph Location	Published Source
Verdi	Boito	Milan	Jan.–Feb. 93	IP	*Cart. V-B* i, 283
Giuseppina V.	B. Strepponi	Cremona	Feb. 93		Abb. iv, 472
Bellaigue *	Verdi	Milan	3 Feb. 93	Sc.	*Cart.* ii, 301–2
Journalists *	Verdi	Milan	4 Feb. 93	SA?	*Cop.* 383–4
Verdi *	Journalists	Milan	5 Feb. 93	?	*Cop.* 383–4
Verdi *	Bellaigue	Paris	9 Feb. 93	Sc.	*Cart.* ii, 302
Umberto I †	Verdi	Milan	9 Feb. 93	?	*Cop.* 715
Verdi	Martini	Rome	11 Feb. 93	?	*Cop.* 715
Martini	Verdi	Milan	12 Feb. 93		Abb. iv, 475–6
Verdi *	Bellaigue	Paris	12 Feb. 93	Sc.	*Cart.* ii, 302
Bellaigue *	Verdi	Milan	12 Feb. 93	Sc.	Abb. iv, 477
Giuseppina V.	De Sanctis	Naples	15 Feb. 93		*Cart.* i, 213
Boito *	Bellaigue	Paris	16 Feb. 93	Sc.	De R. 317–8
Verdi	De Amicis	Genoa	23 Feb. 93	GE	LS. 187
Verdi	Maurel	?	Feb. 93	?	
Verdi	Ricordi	Milan	3 Mar. 93	Ri.	Abb. iv, 478
Ricordi	Verdi	Genoa	4 Mar. 93	SA	
Verdi	Ricordi	Milan	5 Mar. 93	Ri.	
Monaldi †	Verdi	Genoa	7 Mar. 93	Ri.	
Verdi	Ricordi	Milan	7 Mar. 93	Ri.	Abb. iv, 499
Verdi	Ricordi	Milan	8 Mar. 93	Ri.	Abb. iv, 500
Ricordi	Verdi	Genoa	9 Mar. 93	SA	*Cart. V-B* ii, 433
Verdi	Ricordi	Milan	10 Mar. 93	Ri.	*Cart. V-B* ii, 433–4
Ricordi †	Verdi	Genoa	11 Mar. 93	SA	
Verdi	Ricordi	Milan	11 Mar. 93	Ri.	
Ricordi	Verdi	Genoa	13 Mar. 93	SA	*Cart. V-B* ii, 434
Verdi	Ricordi	Milan	14 Mar. 93	Ri.	
Ricordi	Verdi	Genoa	15 Mar. 93	SA	
Verdi	Ricordi	Milan	15 Mar. 93	Ri.	*Cart. V-B* ii, 434
Giuseppina V.	Ricordi	Milan	16 Mar. 93	Ri.	
Verdi	Ricordi	Milan	17 Mar. 93	Ri.	Abb. iv, 501
Verdi	Waldmann	Ferrara	18 Mar. 93	Bo.	*Cart.* ii, 265
Verdi	Spatz	Milan	19 Mar. 93		*Cop.* 516
Boito	Verdi	Genoa	19 Mar. 93	SA	*Cart. V-B* i, 215–6
Verdi	Ricordi	Milan	29 Mar. 93	Ri.	Abb. iv, 501–2
Verdi	Ricordi	Milan	29 Mar. 93	Ri.	Abb. iv, 502–3
Ricordi	Verdi	Genoa	31 Mar. 93	SA	
Verdi	Ricordi	Milan	31 Mar. 93	Ri.	

LIST OF LETTERS AND TELEGRAMS

From	To	Destination	Date	Autograph Location	Published Source
Verdi	Ricordi	Milan	1 Apr. 93	Ri.	Abb. iv, 503
Verdi	Ricordi	Milan	2 Apr. 93	Ri.	
Ricordi	Verdi	Genoa	4 Apr. 93	SA	*Cart. V-B* ii, 431–2
Verdi	Ricordi	Milan	4 Apr. 93	Ri.	
Verdi	Ricordi	Milan	5 Apr. 93	Ri.	
Verdi	Ricordi	Genoa?	8 Apr. 93	Ri	
Verdi	Ricordi	Genoa?	11 Apr. 93	Ri.	Abb. iv, 503
Verdi	Ricordi	Genoa?	11 Apr. 93	Ri.	
Verdi	Mascheroni	Rome	23 Apr. 93	?	*Cop.* 716
Ricordi	Verdi	Genoa	26 Apr. 93	SA	
Verdi	Ricordi	Milan	27 Apr. 93	Ri.	
Verdi	Mascheroni	Rome	27 Apr. 93	?	*Cop.* 716–7
Verdi	Ricordi	Milan	30 Apr. 93	Ri.	Abb. iv, 505
Verdi	Mascheroni	Venice?	3 May 93	?	*Cop.* 717
Verdi	Ricordi	Milan	5 May 93	Ri.	
Verdi	Mascheroni	Trieste?	7 May 93	HA	*Cop.* 717–8
Verdi	De Amicis	Genoa	12 May 93	GE	LS. 190
Ricordi †	Verdi	Busseto	12 May 93	SA	
Mascheroni	Verdi	St. Agata	12 May 93	SA	Abb. iv, 507
Verdi	Mascheroni	Vienna?	15 May 93	HA	*Cop.* 633
Verdi	Ricordi	Milan	16 May 93	Ri.	
Ricordi †	Verdi	Busseto	17 May 93	SA	
Verdi	Ricordi	Milan	21 May 93	Ri.	Abb. iv, 509
Verdi	Ricordi	Milan	23 May 93	Ri.	Abb. iv, 509
Verdi	Ricordi	Milan	24 May 93	Ri.	
Verdi	Ricordi	Milan	24 May 93	Ri.	
Ricordi	Verdi	St. Agata	27 May 93	SA	
Verdi	Ricordi	Milan	29 May 93	Ri.	
Ricordi	Verdi	St. Agata	30 May 93	SA	*Cart. V-B* ii, 436
Ricordi	Verdi	St. Agata	31 May 93	SA	
Ricordi	Verdi	St. Agata	1 June 93	SA	
Mascheroni †	Verdi	Busseto	2 June 93	SA	
Verdi	Ricordi	Milan	2 June 93	Ri.	
Verdi	Ricordi	Milan	5 June 93	Ri.	
Verdi	Negroni	Milan	5 June 93	Sc.	
Verdi	Mascheroni	?	8 June 93	HA	*Cop.* 718–9
Verdi	Ricordi	Milan	8 June 93	Ri.	
Verdi	Ricordi	Milan	9 June 93	Ri.	

LIST OF LETTERS AND TELEGRAMS

From	To	Destination	Date	Autograph Location	Published Source
Verdi	Ricordi	Milan	14 June 93	Ri.	
Verdi	Mascheroni	Varese	15 June 93	HA	?
Verdi	Ricordi	Milan	16 June 93	Ri.	
Verdi	Ricordi	Milan	18 June 93	Ri.	
Ricordi	Verdi	St. Agata	20 June 93	SA	*Cart. V-B* ii, 436
Ricordi	Verdi	Montecatini	6 July 93	SA	
Verdi	Ricordi	Milan	10 July 93	Ri.	
Ricordi	Verdi	Montecatini	14 July 93	SA	
Verdi	De Amicis	Genoa	18 July 93	GE	LS. 192?
Verdi	Ricordi	Milan	18 July 93	Ri.	
Verdi	Tornaghi	Milan	24 July 93	Ri.	
Verdi	Tornaghi	Milan	29 July 93	Ri.	
Ricordi	Verdi	St. Agata	31 July 93	SA	
Verdi	Tornaghi	Milan	1 Aug. 93	Ri.	
Verdi	Ricordi	Milan	4 Aug. 93	Ri.	Abb. iv, 516–7
Verdi	Ricordi	Milan	8 Aug. 93	Ri.	
Ricordi	Verdi	St. Agata	10 Aug. 93	SA	
Verdi	Mascheroni	Brescia?	10 Aug. 93	HA	*Cop.* 719–20
Verdi	Mascheroni	Brescia	16 Aug. 93	?	*Cop.* 720
Verdi	Mascheroni	Brescia	18 Aug. 93	HA	
Ricordi	Verdi	St. Agata	18 Aug. 93	SA	
Verdi †	Mascheroni	Brescia	31 Aug. 93	HA	
Verdi	Ricordi	Milan	2 Sept. 93	Ri.	Abb. iv, 517
Boito	Verdi	St. Agata	4 Sept. 93	SA	*Cart. V-B* i, 216–7
Verdi †	Boito	Milan	6 Sept. 93	IP	*Cart. V-B* i, 217
Verdi	Negroni	Milan	10 Sept. 93	Sc.	*Cop.* 721
Ricordi	Verdi	St. Agata	10 Sept. 93	SA	
Verdi	Ricordi	Milan	14 Sept. 93	Ri.	
Verdi	Boito	Milan	15 Sept. 93	IP	*Cart. V-B* i, 218
Boito	Verdi	St. Agata	17 Sept. 93	SA	*Cart. V-B* i, 218–9
Ricordi	Verdi	St. Agata	20 Sept. 93	SA	
Verdi	Ricordi	Milan	21 Sept. 93	Ri.	Abb. iv, 518
Ricordi	Verdi	St. Agata	29 Sept. 93	SA	
Verdi	Ricordi	Milan	2 Oct. 93	Ri.	Abb. iv, 518–9
Ricordi	Verdi	St. Agata	10 Oct. 93	SA	
Verdi	Ricordi	Milan	16 Oct. 93	Ri.	
Boito	Verdi	St. Agata	1 Nov. 93	SA	*Cart. V-B* i, 219
Verdi	Boito	Milan	3 Nov. 93	IP	*Cart. V-B* i. 220

LIST OF LETTERS AND TELEGRAMS

From	To	Destination	Date	Autograph Location	Published Source
Verdi *	Bellaigue	Paris	18 Nov. 93	Sc.	*Cart.* ii, 303–4
Verdi	De Amicis	Genoa	29 Nov. 93	GE	LS. 195
Verdi	Ricordi	Milan	4 Dec. 93	Ri.	
Ricordi	Verdi	Genoa	7 Dec. 93	SA	
Verdi	Mascheroni	Milan?	8 Dec. 93	?	Abb. iv, 521–2
Mascheroni	Verdi	Genoa	c. 10 Dec. 93	SA	Abb. iv, 522–3
Verdi	Ricordi	Milan	10 Dec. 93	Ri.	
Ricordi	Verdi	Genoa	14 Dec. 93	SA	
Cowen	Boito	Milan	14 Dec. 93	Ca.	
Verdi	Ricordi	Milan	15 Dec. 93	Ri.	Abb. iv, 526
Verdi	Zilli		15 Dec. 93		Ob. 104
Cowen	Boito	Milan	18 Dec. 93	Ca.	
Verdi	Ricordi	Milan	20 Dec. 93	Ri.	
Verdi	Ricordi	Milan	21 Dec. 93	Ri.	Abb. iv, 527
Boito	Verdi	Genoa	21 Dec. 93	SA	*Cart. V-B* i, 220–1
Verdi †	Ricordi	Milan	22 Dec. 93	Ri.	
Verdi †	Boito	Milan	22 Dec. 93	IP	*Cart. V-B* ii, 438
Boito *	Bellaigue	Paris	26 Dec. 93	Sc.	De R. 311–3
Verdi	Ricordi	Milan	26 Dec. 93	Ri.	
Verdi	Gallignani		27 Dec. 93		*Cop.* 633–4
Ricordi	Verdi	Genoa	28 Dec. 93	Ri.	
Verdi	Waldmann	Ferrara	30 Dec. 93	?	*Cart.* ii, 266
Boito	Verdi	Genoa	31 Dec. 93	SA	*Cart. V-B* i, 221
Verdi	Mascheroni	Milan	31 Dec. 93	HA	
Duse	Boito	Milan	31 Dec. 93	Ci.	RR. 805
Verdi	Ricordi	Milan	10 Jan. 94	Ri.	
Ricordi	Verdi	Genoa	11 Jan. 94	SA	
Verdi	Ricordi	Milan	11 Jan. 94	Ri.	Abb. iv, 528
Duse	Boito	Milan	12 Jan. 94	Ci.	RR. 806
Ricordi	Verdi	Genoa	13 Jan. 94	SA	
Boito	Verdi	Genoa	18 Jan. 94	SA	*Cart. V-B* i, 222–3
Verdi	Boito	Milan	19 Jan. 94	IP	*Cart. V-B* i, 223
Ricordi	Verdi	Genoa	19 Jan. 94	SA	
Verdi	Ricordi	Milan	19 Jan. 94	Ri.	
Verdi	Ricordi	Milan	20 Jan. 94	Ri.	
Verdi	Ricordi	Milan	21 Jan. 94	Ri.	*Cart. V-B* ii, 445
Boito *	Bellaigue	Paris	22 Jan. 94	Sc.	De R. 315–6

LIST OF LETTERS AND TELEGRAMS

FROM	TO	DESTINATION	DATE	AUTOGRAPH LOCATION	PUBLISHED SOURCE
Tornaghi	Verdi	Genoa	24 Jan. 94	SA	
Tornaghi	Verdi	Genoa	29 Jan. 94	SA	
Verdi	Carvalho	Paris	11 Feb. 94	?	Abb. iv, 533
Duse	Boito	Milan	15 Feb. 94	Ci.	RR. 807
Maurel *	Verdi	Genoa	16 Feb. 94	SA	
Verdi *	Bellaigue	Paris	3 Mar. 94	Sc.	*Cart.* ii, 304
Ricordi	Verdi	Genoa	9 Mar. 94	SA	*Cart. V-B* ii, 447
Verdi	Ricordi	Milan	12 Mar. 94	Ri.	Abb. iv, 534–5
Verdi	Ricordi	Milan	12 Mar. 94	Ri.	
Giuseppina V.	De Sanctis	Naples	13 Mar. 94	IP (PH)	Abb. iv, 534
Verdi	Boito	Milan	14 Mar. 94	IP	Abb. iv, 533
Ricordi	Verdi	Genoa	15 Mar. 94	SA	
Boito	Verdi	Genoa	16 Mar. 94	SA	Abb. iv, 536–7
Verdi	Ricordi	Milan	17 Mar. 94	Ri.	Abb. iv, 535–6
Verdi	Waldmann	Ferrara	18 Mar. 94	Bo.	*Cart.* ii, 266
Verdi	Ricordi	Milan	18 Mar. 94	Ri.	
Verdi	Ricordi	Milan	23 Mar. 94	Ri.	Abb. iv, 538–9
Ricordi	Verdi	Genoa	23 Mar. 94	SA	
Verdi	Ricordi	Milan	24 Mar. 94	Ri.	
Verdi	Ricordi	Milan?	25 Mar. 94	Ri.	Abb. iv, 539–40
Verdi	Ricordi	Paris	28 Mar. 94	Ri.	
Verdi	Ricordi	Paris	31 Mar. 94	Ri.	Abb. iv, 540
Verdi	Ricordi	Paris	1 Apr. 94	Ri.	
Verdi	Stolz	Milan	19 Apr. 94	?	
Duse	Boito	Paris	23 Apr. 94	Ci.	RR. 810
Verdi	Waldmann	Ferrara	24 Apr. 94	?	*Cart.* ii, 266
Boito *	Bellaigue	Paris	[25] Apr. 94	Sc.	De R. 316–7
Verdi	Ricordi	Milan	27 Apr. 94	Ri.	*Cart. V-B* ii, 448
Ricordi	Verdi	Genoa	28 Apr. 94	SA	
Duse	Boito	Paris?	30 Apr. 94	Ci.	RR. 812
Ricordi	Verdi	Genoa	1 May 94	SA	
Verdi	Ricordi	Milan	3 May 94	Ri.	
Verdi	Ricordi	Milan	6 May 94	Ri.	
Duse	Boito	Milan	8 May 94	Ci.	RR. 815
Verdi †	Boito	Milan	8 May 94	IP	*Cart. V-B* i, 227
Ricordi	Verdi	St. Agata	9 May 94	SA	
Duse	Boito	Milan	10 May 94	Ci.	RR. 816–7

LIST OF LETTERS AND TELEGRAMS

FROM	TO	DESTINATION	DATE	AUTOGRAPH LOCATION	PUBLISHED SOURCE
Verdi	Ricordi	Milan	10 May 94	Ri.	Abb. iv, 541
Verdi	Boito	Milan	12 May 94	IP	*Cart. V-B* i, 228
Verdi	Ricordi	Milan	14 May 94	Ri.	
Boito	Verdi	St. Agata	14 May 94	SA	*Cart. V-B* i, 229
Ricordi	Verdi	St. Agata	17 May 94	SA	*Cart. V-B* ii, 450
Tito Ricordi †	Verdi	St. Agata	19 May 94	SA	
Bellaigue *	Verdi	St. Agata	27 May 94	Sc.	*Cart.* ii, 304–5
Verdi	Ricordi	Milan	1 June 94	Ri.	Abb. iv, 544
Verdi	Ricordi	Milan	1 June 94	Ri.	
Duse	Boito	Milan	7 June 94	Ci.	RR. 828–9
Duse	Boito	Milan	8 June 94	Ci.	RR. 829–31
Verdi *	Bellaigue	Paris	8 June 94	Sc.	Abb. iv, 545
Verdi	Ricordi	Milan	8 June 94	Ri.	
Ricordi	Verdi	St. Agata	9 June 94	SA	*Cart. V-B* ii, 452
Verdi	Ricordi	Milan	9 June 94	Ri.	*Cop.* 395–6
Duse	Boito	Milan	11 June 94	Ci.	RR. 832
Ricordi	Verdi	St. Agata	12 June 94	SA	*Cart. V-B* ii, 453
Verdi	Ricordi	Milan	13 June 94	Ri.	Abb. iv, 546
Verdi	Ricordi	Milan	14 June 94	Ri.	Abb. iv, 546
Ricordi	Verdi	St. Agata	15 June 94	SA	
Verdi	Ricordi	Milan	16 June 94	Ri.	Abb. iv, 546
Verdi	De Amicis	Genoa	18 June 94	GE	LS. 197
Verdi	Gallignani	?	20 June 94	?	?
Verdi	De Amicis	Genoa	29 June 94	GE	LS. 198
Verdi	Negroni	Milan	12 Aug. 94	Sc.	
Verdi	De Amicis	Genoa	26 Aug. 94	GE	LS. 199
Verdi	J. Strauss	Vienna	29 Sept. 94	VI	
Duse	Boito	Milan	? Oct. 94	Ci.	RR. 833
Verdi	Ricordi	Milan	17 Oct. 94	Ri.	Abb. iv, 556
Duse	Boito	Milan	22–23 Oct. 94	Ci.	RR. 833
Ricordi	Verdi	Genoa	24 Oct. 94	SA	
Verdi	Gallignani	Parma?	29 Oct. 94	?	Abb. iv, 560
Verdi	Gallignani	Parma?	4 Nov. 94	?	Abb. iv, 560
Verdi	Ricordi	Milan	7 Nov. 94	Ri.	
Verdi	Ricordi	Milan	11 Nov. 94	Ri.	
Verdi	Frenchman	Paris?	20 Nov. 94	?	
Verdi	Ricordi	Milan	29 Nov. 94	Ri.	

LIST OF LETTERS AND TELEGRAMS

FROM	TO	DESTINATION	DATE	AUTOGRAPH LOCATION	PUBLISHED SOURCE
Boito	Verdi	Genoa	2 Dec. 94	SA	*Cart. V-B* i, 233–4
Verdi	Boito	Milan	3 Dec. 94	IP	*Cart. V-B* i, 235
Boito	Verdi	Genoa	4 Dec. 94	SA	*Cart. V-B* i, 236
Verdi	Boito	Milan	5 Dec. 94	IP	*Cart. V-B* i, 237
Boito	Verdi	Genoa	6 Dec. 94	SA	*Cart. V-B* i, 238

Verdi's *Falstaff* in Letters and Contemporary Reviews

1889

In the world of dreams[1]

I n late June, on the way from St. Agata to their annual cure at the spa of Montecatini, Verdi and his wife, Giuseppina, spend a few days in Milan. At that time Boito most likely gives Verdi the sketch of a *Falstaff* libretto, which he had apparently mentioned to him in April. Verdi reads it in Montecatini, if not en route on the train on 4 July.[2] His response of 6 July is enthusiastic. "Let's do *Falstaff*, then!" he writes to Boito on 10 July and looks forward to receiving "at least the first two acts" of the actual libretto in October, as Boito suggests in his letter of 11 July.[3] The Verdis leave Montecatini on 21 July for Tabiano, a spa not far from Busseto, where Giuseppina continues the cure alone. On the 23rd the Maestro is home at St. Agata. In August he unsuccessfully attempts to persuade Franco Faccio[4] to accept the directorship of the Conservatory of Parma.[5] A small hospital Verdi had built for his peasants and had inaugurated the previous November, at nearby Villanova, becomes a persistent source of troubles.[6] In October he purchases a piece of land in Milan as the site of the Casa di Riposo, a home for aged musicians, which, like the hospital at Villanova, is still in existence today. Arrigo Boito's brother Camillo[7] is commissioned as the architect for the Casa di Riposo. Verdi signs the contract with him and on 18 October makes a down payment in Milan, where he also sees Arrigo. On 3 November Ricordi informs Verdi, by letter, about a lengthy frustrating suit against the publisher Bénoit in Paris.[8] Boito arrives with the first two acts of *Falstaff* the following day. En route from St. Agata to their winter home in Genoa, the Verdis are again in Milan from 23 November to 6 December. There the Maestro discusses the construction of the Casa di Riposo with Camillo Boito and, quite likely, *Falstaff* with Arrigo. Unable to prevent, and escaping from, celebrations on the occasion of the fiftieth anniversary of his first opera, *Oberto, Conte di San Bonifacio,* Verdi thanks the King[9] and Giosuè Carducci[10] for their congratulations. Boito and Emanuele Muzio join the Verdis at Palazzo Doria in Genoa for the holidays.

Ricordi, who is unaware of Verdi and Boito's secret *Falstaff* project, is largely concerned this year with a revival of *Otello* at La Scala and with productions of that opera on other stages. He is also preoccupied with Puccini's early career and involved in preparations at La Scala for the first Italian *Meistersinger.* Meanwhile the ongoing litigation in Paris with the music publisher Bénoit continues to disturb him. In August Ricordi and Faccio attend a performance of *Die Meistersinger* in Bayreuth,[11] conducted by Hans Richter.[12] At the end of September, Ricordi and his wife, Giuditta, are the Verdis' guests at St. Agata.

All the time that Boito is writing the *Falstaff* libretto, his secret love, the actress Eleonora Duse,[13] appears to be constantly in his thoughts. Since February, a gynecological ailment has kept her in Naples, forcing her to cancel most of her engagements.[14] On 13 July he visits her in Naples, is back in Milan on the 17th, and on the 22nd stays at a former monastery at San Giuseppe, their refuge in the mountains of Piedmont. Duse joins him there from 25 July until 14 August. Boito then remains alone at San Giuseppe, concentrating on the *Falstaff* text,[15] but he meets Duse briefly in Milan on 3 September. In between his work on *Falstaff* at San Giuseppe and Duse's performances in Turin, he visits her in that city. By 25 September Boito is the guest of Donna Vittoria Cima,[16] at the Villa d'Este in Cernobbio, near Como. Tormented by fits of jealousy, Duse is working with her company in Milan, where Boito sees her, attending a performance on 5 October of his translation of Shakespeare's *Antony and Cleopatra.*[17] She embarks in Naples for Palermo on 18 October; he visits St. Agata from 4 until 10 November, with the first two acts of *Falstaff.* Later in the month and in early December he also meets Verdi in Milan. On 9 December he travels secretly to Naples for a few unhappy hours with Duse, between her arrival from Sicily on the 10th and her departure for Egypt the following day. The end of the year finds Boito at the Hotel Eden in Nervi, and with the Verdis at the Palazzo Doria in Genoa.

NOTES

1. Verdi to Boito, 6 July.

2. It seems more likely that Boito handed rather than sent Verdi this sketch, as is generally assumed. (*Carteggio* ii, pp. 383–4.)

3. See Hepokoski, pp. 21–4.

4. See Biographical Sketch.

5. Verdi to Boito, 18 August.

6. Verdi to Piroli, 28 August.

7. See Biographical Sketch.

8. See Ricordi to Verdi, 3 November, n. 5.

9. Verdi to King Umberto I, 17 November, n. 1.

10. Verdi to Carducci, 3 December, n. 1.

11. See Abbiati IV, pp. 378–9.

12. Ricordi to Verdi, 5 June 1892, n. 3.

13. See Biographical Sketch.

14. Weaver, pp. 78–9.

15. Boito to Verdi, 1 August, and Verdi to Boito, 2 August.

16. Italian aristocrat (1834–?), gifted pianist and friend of Boito.

17. Its Milan première the previous year had been a failure. (Weaver, pp. 75–8.)

 Verdi to Boito

Montecatini, 6 July 1889

Dear Boito,

Excellent! Excellent!

Before reading your sketch, I wanted to reread the *Merry Wives*, the two parts of *Henry IV,* and *Henry V*; and I can only repeat *excellent,* for one could not do better than you have done.

A pity that the interest (it's not your fault) does not increase until the end. The culmination is the finale of the second act; and the appearance of Falstaff's face amid the laundry, etc., is a true comic idea.

I also fear that the last act, in spite of its bit of fantasy, will end up weak with all those little pieces, songs, ariettas, etc., etc. You let *Bardolfo* reappear! And why wouldn't you also let *Pistol* reappear, so that both of them could come up with some small or large prank?——

You have only two weddings! So much the better, for they have little to do with the main plot.[1]

The two trials by water and fire suffice to punish Falstaff well; nevertheless, I would have also liked to see him get a good thrashing.[2]

I'm just saying so . . . and don't mind what I say. Now we have quite different matters to discuss, so that this *Falstaff* or the *Wives,* who two days ago were still in the world of dreams, may now take shape and become reality! When? How? . . . Who knows!! I'll write you about it tomorrow or later.

Greetings from Peppina. Addio.

Affectionately
G. Verdi

NOTES

1. See Shakespeare, *The Merry Wives of Windsor*, V. iii.

2. Verdi refers to the scene in Shakespeare's *Merry Wives* where Falstaff is thrown into the Thames (water) in III.iii, and then to "they burn him with their tapers" (fire) in V.v.88–106. Boito, however, replaced Shakespeare's symbolic but—in this setting—too brutal trial by fire and water with Verdi's "good thrashing."

 *Boito to Verdi*

1st Letter   [Milan] 7 July [1889][1]

Dear Maestro,

No doubt, the third act is the weakest. And in the theatre this is a serious mistake.— Unfortunately, this is a general law of comedy. Tragedy has the opposite law. The approach of the catastrophe in a tragedy (whether it be foreseen as in *Othello,* or unforeseen as in *Hamlet*) tremendously increases our interest, because the end is terrible.—Thus the last acts of tragedies are always the most beautiful ones.—

In comedy, our interest always diminishes when the knot is about to be untied, because there is a happy ending.

You have recently reread Goldoni, and you will remember how in the last scenes—although the whole marvelous context of the dialogue is admirable—the action almost always declines, and with it our interest.—In the *Merry Wives,* even Shakespeare, with all the power that he had, could not escape this general law.—And so Molière, and so Beaumarchais, and so Rossini. The last scene of the *Barbiere* has always seemed less admirable to me than the rest.— Correct me if I am wrong.

In comedy there comes a point where the audience says: it's *finished*, whereas on the stage it [the plot] is not yet finished yet.

A knot cannot be untied without first being loosened, and when it is loosened we foresee how it will be untied, so that our interest is untied before the knot.

Comedy unties the knot, tragedy breaks or cuts it.—Therefore, the third act of *Falstaff* is certainly the weakest. But no matter how general that law may be, the trouble is less serious than one may think. We will bring warmth to this act, and make it brisker and less fragmented. Above all, as much as possible that is advantageous must be extracted from the last scene. The atmosphere of fantasy, never touched upon in the rest of the opera, can be helpful; it lends a fresh tone, light and new. Then we have three rather good comic moments: 1st. Falstaff's monologue with the horns. 2nd. The interrogation (we'll have it performed by Bardolfo and Pistola to the sound of blows on the outstretched Falstaff's belly as he confesses a sin at each blow). 3rd. The blessing of the two masked weddings.—

We'll put Fenton and Nannetta's little duet into the first part of the same act, as evening descends.[2]

This amorous play between Nannetta and Fenton must appear in very frequent spurts; in all the scenes where they are present they will steal kisses hidden in corners, slyly, boldly, without letting themselves be discovered, with fresh little phrases and short little dialogues, very rapid and cunning from the beginning to the end of the comedy. It will be a most cheerful love, always disturbed and interrupted, and always ready to begin again.—This color, which I think is good, must not be forgotten. Fenton's song is added certainly to give the tenor a solo, and that is bad. Shall we omit it?[3]

The correspondence resumes.— I am awaiting the letter you announce.

Many cordial greetings to Signora Peppina and to you, dear Maestro— And a good cure.

Your
Arrigo Boito

NOTES

1. Apparently, Boito wrote from his home in Milan, where Verdi addressed his letters from Montecatini during July.

2. This idea was later discarded.

3. Fenton's Sonnet at the beginning of III.ii became one of the jewels of the score.

 Verdi to Boito

Montecatini, 7 July 1889

I told you yesterday that I would write today, and I keep my word, even at the risk of annoying you.

As long as we roam in the world of ideas, everything smiles upon us, but when we come down to earth, to practical matters, doubts and distresses arise.

When drafting *Falstaff*, did you ever think of the enormous number of my years? I know well that you will answer me, exaggerating the good, excellent, robust state of my health. . . And so may it be; but in spite of this you will agree with me that I could be accused of great temerity for taking on such a task!—And if I shouldn't withstand the labor?!—And if I shouldn't get to finish the music?—

Then you would have wasted time and labor in vain! I would not want this for all the gold in the world. This idea is intolerable to me; and all the more intolerable if you, while writing *Falstaff* had, if not to abandon, at least to distract your mind from *Nerone* or delay the date of its production. I would be blamed for this delay, and the thunderbolts of the public's ill will would fall upon my shoulders.

Now, how to overcome these obstacles? . . Do you have a good reason to oppose my own? I hope so, but do not believe it. Still, let's think it over (and watch out not to do anything that might harm your career), and if you could find a *single* reason, and if I knew how to shrug ten years off my shoulders, then . . . . What joy! Being able to tell the public:

> *"We are still here!!*
> *Make way for us!!"*

Addio, addio.

Affectionately,
G. Verdi

 *Boito to Verdi*

2nd Letter   [Milan] 9 July [1889]
Dear Maestro,

Here you see two letters; I did not mail the first one, because I thought that I should await the one that you announced to me. At that time I still wanted to wait before responding to your doubts. After 24 hours I respond; my thought is ripe. The fact is that I never think of your age when I talk to you or when I write to you or when I work for you.

The fault is yours.

I know that *Otello* is only a little over two years old, and that, as I write you, it is understood as it should be by Shakespeare's countrymen.[1] But there is an even stronger argument which has nothing to do with age, and this is: It was said of you after *Otello*: *"A better end is impossible!"*

This is a great truth which contains great and very rare praise. This is the only serious argument. It is serious for one's contemporaries, but not for history, which wants to appraise above all the essential value of men.—Yet it is extremely rare to see an artist's life concluded with a worldwide victory. *Otello* is this victory. All the other arguments: *age, strength, your labor, my labor,* etc., etc., do not count and do not stand in the way of a new work. Since you compel me to speak to you about myself, I will tell you that despite the commitment I would assume for *Falstaff,* I can complete my work within the promised time.[2] I am sure of that.—Let us go on to the other doubts.

Writing a comic opera, I believe, would not tire you.

Tragedy *makes* the one who writes it *really suffer;* the spirit suffers a painful suggestion that morbidly plays on the nerves.

But the fun and laughter of comedy exhilarate body and soul.—

"Un sorriso aggiunge un filo alla trama della vita." [A smile adds a thread to the fabric of life.]

I don't know whether this is Foscolo's exact phrase,[3] but it is certainly true.

You have a great will to work; this is an indubitable proof of health and power. The *Ave Marias*[4] are not enough for you, you need something else.

Throughout your life you have wanted a nice theme for a comic opera; this is a sign that the noble vein of merry art exists essentially in your brain; instinct is a good counselor. There is only one way to end better than with *Otello,* and that is to end victoriously with *Falstaff.* Having made all the cries and lamentations of the human heart resound, to end with an immense outburst of cheer! That will astonish!

Try then, dear Maestro, to think again about the theme I have sketched out for you; find out if you feel the germ of the new masterwork in it. If that germ is there, the miracle has happened. And meanwhile we promise each other the most scrupulous secrecy.

I have not mentioned it to *anyone.* If we work in secret, we shall work in peace. I await your decision, which will be free and resolute as usual. I must not influence you; your decision will be wise and firm in any case, whether you say *enough* or *once again.*

Your most affectionate
Arrigo Boito

NOTES

1. Franco Faccio had conducted the very successful first performance of *Otello* in England at London's Lyceum Theatre on 5 July.

2. The opera *Nerone,* which Boito never completed.

3. The Italian poet and literary historian Ugo Foscolo (1778–1827) wrote, translating Laurence Sterne's *A Sentimental Journey* (London, 1768): "Lettori miei: Era opinione del reverendo Lorenzo Sterne parocco in Inghilterra: Che un sorriso possa aggiungere un filo alla trama brevissima della vita." [Dear Reader: The reverend Parish priest Laurence Sterne in England was of the opinion: That a smile could add a thread to the very brief fabric of life.] The Italian title of Sterne's book—translated by Foscolo under the pseudonym Didimo Chierico—is *Viaggio sentimentale di York lungo la Francia e l'Italia* (Pisa, 1813). Cf. Budden iii, p. 423, n. †.

4. Boito refers to Verdi's *Ave Maria* (after words by Dante) for soprano and strings, premiered by Faccio at La Scala on 18 Aprll 1880, and to another one they discussed in their letters of 6 and 7 March (*Otello* i, pp. 366–7). The latter, for four-part chorus, was premiered as one of the *Quattro Pezzi Sacri* in Vienna on 13 November 1898.

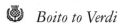 *Verdi to Boito*

Montecati[ni], 10 July 1889

Dear Boito,

Amen; and so be it!

Let us do *Falstaff*, then! For the moment we won't think of obstacles, of age, of illness!

I too wish to maintain the most profound *secrecy;* a word I too underline three times to tell you that no one must know anything about it! . . . But wait . . . Peppina knew it, I believe, before I did! . . . Do not doubt: She will keep the secret.—When women have this quality, they have it to a greater degree than we do.

I bear in mind your phrase, *"Despite the commitment I would assume for* Falstaff*, I can complete my work within the promised time."*

And now a final word. A rather prosaic word, yet, especially for me, necessary and proper. But no, no . . . Today I have *Falstaff* too much in mind to talk with you about another matter. I'll talk to you about the *other matter* tomorrow.

Meanwhile, if you feel like it, just start to write. In the first two acts there is nothing to change except, perhaps, the monologue of the jealous husband, which might work out better at the end of the first part than at the start of the second. It would have more fire and force.

'Til tomorrow. With Peppina's greetings I tell you

Addio, addio.
Cordially,
G. Verdi

Boito to Verdi

[Milan] 11 July [1889]

Dear Maestro,

Evviva!!!

Swiftly it will be done. Without doubt I'll bring at least the first two acts to you in St. Agata in October.

I need the rest of July to settle a few details of my work.[1]

In the very first days of August I shall start with ours. Signora Giuseppina knew it before we did! This is the miracle of feminine intuition.

Now, dear Maestro, the other miracle is up to you!—

1889

Many greetings to Signora Giuseppina, the prophetess.
An embrace

from your
affectionate
Arrigo Boito

NOTE

1. Presumably on *Nerone*.

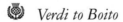 *Verdi to Boito*

Montecatini, 11 July 1889

Dear Boito,

 . . . . I continue yesterday's letter.— Upon completion of your work you would cede the property to me for the compensation of . . . (to be agreed upon). And if ever, through age or disability, or for any other reason, I should not be able to finish the music, you would recover your *Falstaff*: a property I myself offer you in remembrance of me, and which you will put to use as you please.

 I am in perfect agreement with you as to the requirements and the nature of tragedy and comedy; the examples you quote confirm what you say. But if in comedy (as you say) there is a point where the audience says: it is *finished!*, and on the stage it is still not *finished,* then something must be found that can strongly rivet attention in a comical or musical way.

 You have already improved this third act.

 The little duet *Fenton-Nannetta* fits better in the first part.

 The fantasy part with the Song of the Fairies is good.

 Falstaff's Monologue is good. Also good is the interrogation to the sound of the blows, etc. . . . But then the weddings interrupt the attention, which ought to be turned altogether to Falstaff, and the action grows cold. At this point there would be a ready-made musical piece in Shaespeare[1]—

Mis P.	Non spingiamo più oltre la burla.
Fals	E queste son le Fate?
Mis Ford	E credete Voi che volendo peccare avressimo scelto un'uomo come Voi?!
Ford	Una balena!

Fals	Bene! . . .
Altro	Un'uomo di crema!
Fals	Bene!
Altro	Un vecchio appassito
Fals	Molto bene
Altro	Maledico come Satana
Fals	Sempre bene
Altri	Povero come Giobbe
[*Fals*]	Benissimo
Tutti	E dedito alle fornicazioni alle taverne, al vino, alle crapule, giurando, spergiurando e bestemmiando Dio . . .
Fals	Amen . . . e così sia
Mis	Ed ora Sir Giovanni, come amate le donne di Vindsor?
Fals	Or incomincio a credere che sono un'asino.
Tutti	Bravo! Ben detto! ben detto! Viva Viva Viva! . . . *Battono le mani e cala il sipario.*

[*Mrs. Page*	Let's not push the jest any further.
Fal.	And these are the Fairies?
Mrs. Ford	And you think that, wishing to sin, we would have chosen a man like you?!
Ford	A whale!
Fal.	Well! . . .
Another	The cream of the aristocracy!
Fal.	Good!
Another	An old withered man
Fal.	Very good
Another	I curse you like Satan
Fal.	Always good
Others	Poor as Job
Fal.	Excellent
All	And given to fornications, to taverns, to wine, to gluttonies, swearing, perjuring and blaspheming God . . .
Fal.	Amen . . . and so be it.
Mrs. Page	And now, Sir John, how do you like the wives of Windsor?
Fal.	Now I begin to believe that I'm an ass.
All	Bravo! Well said! Well said! Hurrah, hurrah, hurrah! . . . *They clap their hands and the curtain falls.*]

And what shall we do with the weddings, you will say? I don't know!
But you, who have been so lucky with the *idea* of Falstaff's face appearing

II

1889

among the laundry in the second act, will easily come up with some other deviltry.

Addio for now.

Cordially,
G. Verdi

NOTE

1. Considerably altered and abbreviated by Verdi. (Cf. Shakespeare, *The Merry Wives of Windsor*, V.v.110–69.)

 *Boito to Verdi*

[Milan] 12 July [1889]

Dear Maestro,

All your thoughts are good. I thank you with all my heart, and the pact is made. In about two weeks I'll get to work on our comedy. The fragment of the dialogue you quoted was already marked to be inserted. But there have to be nuptials; without the weddings there is no contentment (don't mention this to Signora Giuseppina; she would start again to talk to me about matrimony!) and Fenton and Nannetta must marry.

I like their love; it serves to refresh and solidify the entire comedy. That love must enliven each and everything, and always in such a way that I would almost skip the duet of the two sweethearts.[1]

In every ensemble scene, that love is present in its own way.

It is present in the 2nd part of the 1st act.

In the 2nd part of the 2nd act.

In the 1st and 2nd parts of the third.[2]

Therefore it is useless just to let the two of them sing together in a real duet. Even without the duet their part will be very effective; it will be even more effective without it. I cannot explain myself; I would like, as sugar is sprinkled on a cake, to sprinkle the whole comedy with that merry love without accumulating it at any point.

Cordial greetings to you and Signora Giuseppina.

Your
Arrigo Boito

NOTES

1. This duet was ultimately omitted. (See Boito to Verdi, 7 July, n. 5.)
2. Ultimately only in the 2nd part of the 2nd act and in the 2nd part of the 3rd.

🌼 *Verdi to Franco Faccio*

Montecatini, 14 July 1889[1]

From the telegrams and from Muzio I had news of *Otello* in London.[2] Now you confirm this news, and it pleases me, even though at my age, and with the present conditions of our music, a success is useless. You speak of the "triumph of Italian art"!! You deceive yourself! Our young Italian composers aren't good patriots. If the Germans, starting with Bach, have arrived at Wagner, they make opera like good Germans, and that's all right. But we descendants of Palestrina commit a musical crime by imitating Wagner, and we do useless, even harmful, work.

I know that they spoke very well of Boito, and that gives me the greatest pleasure, since praise attributed to *Otello* in Shakespeare's homeland is worth much. [. . .]

NOTES

    1. See *Otello* i, p. 373.
    2. Under Faccio's baton at the Lyceum Theatre on 5 July. (See Boito to Verdi, 9 July.)

🌼 *Verdi to Giuseppe Piroli*[1]

Montecatini, 16 July 1889

You scoundrel! . . . Is this the way to behave? To make a promise, and not to keep it! You scoundrel! You scoundrel!

However, if you couldn't come for more than three days, you did well to spare yourself the fatigue of a rather long journey here . . . and in this heat!

'Til we see each other, then, in September . . . but without fail.

I am glad to hear from you that your health is so much better . . . We will depart from Montecatini Sunday evening and get off at Borgo [San Donnino][2] at 3:37 on Monday morning, because Peppina will go to Tabiano[3] for two weeks. I will accompany her and then return right away to St. Agata. [. . .]

NOTES

    1. See Biographical Sketch.
    2. Borgo San Donnino lies on the main railway line Milan-Piacenza-Parma-Bologna, which was opened in 1865. It is approximately 13 km southwest of Busseto. Because of its Roman origins (*Fidentia Julia*) the name of this town was changed by royal decree to Fidenza on 9 June 1927. The railway from Borgo San Donnino to Busseto and Cremona

1889

was not inaugurated until 1908. The Verdis and their visitors proceeded by rail to Borgo San Donnino, Alseno, Fiorenzuola, or Piacenza, and then by coach to St. Agata, 15 to 25 km away.

3. Spa near Salsomaggiore Terme, 10 km southwest of Fidenza.

 *Giuseppe Piroli to Verdi*

Rome, 19 July 1889

[. . .] I wonder how true it might be that you are busy with a *Giulio Cesare,*[1] but I think that you should really rest at this time; yet, I also think and hope that, as in Mt. Aetna, a sacred fire will work in you that must burst out again with the terrible power and might of the inexhaustible genius revealed in all your new works. [. . .]

NOTE

1. An idle rumor.

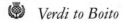 *Boito to Verdi*

Ivrea[1] per S. Giuseppe, 1 August [1889]

Dear Maestro,

I am ready. Please return the outline of *Falstaff*[2] to me; rereading it and thinking it over again, I shall work more easily.

Cordial greetings

from your
Arrigo Boito

NOTES

1. Industrial city near the former monastery of San Giuseppe in the province of Aosta, Piedmont.

2. This "schema del *Falstaff,*" called a "schizzo" [sketch] by Verdi in the following letter, has not been located. Boito might have thrown it away after it had served its purpose.

 *Verdi to Boito*

St. Agata, 2 August 1889

Dear Boito,

Bravo, bravo, three times bravo! How punctual you have been!!![1]

Here is the sketch of . . . . . and on to work . . . Evviva, it seems like a dream to me!—

Addio

Your
G. Verdi

NOTE

1. See Boito to Verdi, 11 July and 1 August.

 *Verdi to Boito*

St. Agata, 18 August [1889]

Dear Boito,

Help me to do a good deed.—You know that the position of Director of the Conservatory of Parma is vacant.[1] I thought of Faccio. He would have a stipend of 6000 Lire plus 1000 Lire for lodging; (in Parma he would spend half of that for suitable lodging). Furthermore, the City would be disposed to assign 4000 Lire to the conductor of the performances at the theatre. And even if the City should not wish to give performances for some seasons, payment would go on. Because the Conservatory is now a government institution, he would be entitled to a pension, and the years of service to the Conservatory in Milan would also be counted.—I wrote to Faccio[2] that in his place I would have accepted before *getting to the end of my letter;* that the offers which can be made to him elsewhere are precarious; that his very position at La Scala is precarious, etc., etc. . . .

Supposing that in the present musical upheaval some *Piontelli* [3] became the manager of La Scala, the conductor would be a Cimino.[4] Furthermore, Faccio should understand that the air which he now breathes in Milan is no longer as pure for him as it was ten years ago! Also a misfortune for him is the *Meistersinger.* If it goes well, he will be given very little credit; if it goes badly, the fault will be his.[5] Faccio will trust Giulio, and that's all right; but Giulio has his own interests and must account for his actions to his shareholders, whose interests might be contrary to Faccio's.—He wants to talk with me! But I have nothing more to tell him. He hesitates as usual, and as usual he will do something foolish!—

You, the oldest and dearest of his friends, write him, if you are of my opinion, to accept; and if you don't write to him, write to me a bit forcefully, and I will show him your letter, and who knows!! . . Amen, amen.—

1889

You are working, I hope? The strangest thing is that I am working too!
... I am amusing myself by writing fugues! .. Yes, sir: a fugue ... and a *comic fugue* .. that may go well in *Falstaff*! ... But how come a comic fugue? Why comic? you will say? ... I don't know *how*, or *why*, but it is a comic fugue!

I shall tell you in another letter how this idea came about![6]

Meanwhile, greetings and addio from the heart.

Cordially,
G. Verdi

NOTES

1. After the death of the world-famous double-bassist and conductor Giovanni Bottesini (1821–89). Upon Verdi's recommendation, Bottesini had been appointed director of the Conservatory of Parma in 1889, where he died six months later.

2. Published without date by De Rensis, *Franco Faccio e Verdi*, pp. 264–5. (*Carteggio* ii, p. 387.)

3. Luigi Piontelli (?–1908), double-bass player, noted impresario, friend, and early promoter of Toscanini. Piontelli was in charge of various Italian opera houses, including the Teatro Carlo Felice in Genoa, and of La Scala from 1892 to 1893. He also managed the *Falstaff* tour in 1893. (See Verdi to Ricordi, 2 June 1891, n. 4; 31 January 1892, n. 1; *Otello* i, pp. 380–2.)

4. Gaetano Cimini (1852–1907), composer and distinguished conductor.

5. Under Faccio's baton, the first performance at La Scala, on 26 December, signaled Wagner's breakthrough in Italy.

6. Such a letter apparently does not exist. Verdi probably discussed the Fugue with Boito at St. Agata in early November.

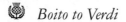 *Boito to Verdi*

San Giuseppe (Ivrea)
20 August [1889]

Dear Maestro,

I am reading your letter and answer immediately.

If I were in Faccio's shoes, I too would not hesitate to accept the position that is offered to him in Parma.

But Faccio will hesitate. The peculiar sentimentality of his character induces him to hesitate whenever he is forced to leave Milan in order to improve his living conditions. And having hesitated, he refuses.

If today this most fatal sentimentality should reawaken in him, I would no longer see either security or peace for my friend. After thirty years of work (or slightly less), he finds himself today, with much praise and little savings, in a rather unenviable, yet illustrious, but also precarious position.

In that city which he loves, there is continuous war, animated by deceit and envy. The position he holds today, uncertain if he will hold it for any length of time, has always been fought over hatefully. No one has lasted there any longer and more securely than he, but this security already shows signs of being shaken. And these signs would be a tremendous good fortune for him if they could make him decide to give up that position in time for the other one offered to him, which is honorable, secure, peaceful and profitable.

You write me that the salary for the directorship of the Parma Conservatory is 6000 Lire, plus 1000 for lodging; 7000 Lire in Parma is equivalent to 12,000 in Milan—not counting the theatre, which would raise the salary by 4000 Lire, and without considering the fact that during the vacation months, Faccio could perhaps take on other important engagements. I am convinced that Faccio would be an outstanding conservatory director.

In theory and practice he knows everything that the director of a conservatory must know. And he keeps his indecision to himself, as his own business, like a fine pearl, not sharing it with others. It follows that he can command even rough and unruly masses, and that he can make them pay him strict obedience, for intuitively he clearly understands order and equity. Therefore, he will be quite readily obeyed by the students of a newly reformed conservatory that has no rotten traditions and ingrained flaws, like those in Naples, Florence or Palermo. Parma will be his peace and his fortune, as long as he goes there alone without his family and domestic worries.

Dear Maestro, you should insist on encouraging our friend; and if you think that my words can influence him, I beg you to let him read this letter, which is the frank expression of my thoughts.

My affectionate wishes for you and Signora Giuseppina.

Your
Arrigo Boito

And this page, dear Maestro, is for you.

A comic fugue is just what we need; the place to insert it will not be lacking.

The plays of art are made for the playful art.

I live with the immense Sir John, with the potbelly, with the breaker of beds, with the smasher of chairs, with the mule-driver, with the bottle of sweet wine, with the lively glutton, between the barrels of Xeres [sherry] and the merriment of that warm kitchen at the Garter Inn.

In the month of October you will live there, too.

During the first few days I was in despair. To sketch the characters in a few strokes, to weave the plot, to extract all the juice from that enormous Shakespearian pomegranate, without letting useless pits ripple into the

1889

little glass; to write colorfully, clearly and briefly, to outline the musical plan of the scene, so that an organic unity may result that should and yet should not be a *piece of music*; to make the merry comedy live from beginning to end, to make it live with natural and communicative cheer is difficult, difficult, difficult; but it must seem easy, easy, easy.—

Courage and forward.

I am still in the first act. In September, the second. In October, the third. This is the program. Forward.

Once again a good and strong handshake to regain courage.

Your
Arrigo Boito

 *Verdi to Ricordi*

Busseto St. Agata, 24 August 1889 [1]

Dear Giulio,

I believe you will receive this letter of mine in Milan, and I hope that the cure in Levico[2] was beneficial to you and all of you; this is our, the savages of St. Agata, warmest wish.

I am sending you your copy of our usual statement, which is all right.

I expect to be in Milan Wednesday evening, and if we could formally sign this statement on Thursday, or Friday morning at the latest, I could leave the same Friday at 2:25 for Genoa.

I have already written to Tornaghi in order to collect the sum of 20 thousand Lire on Thursday or Friday morning.

Stay well always, and addio ad.

G. Verdi

P.S. Wire me if there is any obstacle.

NOTES

1. Postmark: BUSSETO 25/8/89. (The letter was registered on this Sunday.)
2. A spa in the Valsugana region near Trento.

 *Verdi to Eugenio Tornaghi*[1]

St. Agata, 24 August 1889

Esteemed Signor Tornaghi,

Certain of Giulio's arrival in Milan on Monday, I shall also come to your capital Wednesday evening. I am notifying you in advance so that I may collect the sum of L. 20,000 on Thursday morning. I will collect the rest a few days later.

Tomorrow I shall send Giulio the papers concerning the known affair.[2] Thank you, [Signor?] Tornaghi.

Sincerely,

G. Verdi

NOTES

1. Eugenio Tornaghi (1844–1915) was for decades the deputy, assistant manager, confidential clerk—and scapegoat—of the House of Ricordi. To date, however, his correspondence with Verdi, his wife, Boito, Puccini, and other prominent personalities is almost the only reliable trace of Tornaghi's inconspicuous existence. According to a death certificate obtained from the registry of the City of Milan, he was the pensioner Eugenio Tornaghi who died in that city on 15 January 1915 at the age of seventy-one. When, after thirty years of loyal service, his position was threatened by changes in the firm's administration, Tornaghi appealed to Verdi in two letters, on 30 October and 7 November 1887, and Verdi intervened on his behalf.

2. Presumably a loan from the House of Ricordi to acquire land for the Casa di Riposo. (See Phillips-Matz, p. 702.)

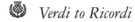 *Verdi to Ricordi*

St. Agata, 27 August 1889

Dear Giulio,

Welcome back[1] and good health!

Your telegram[2] brings all my plans to a standstill,[3] and now I don't know if I'll come to Milan tomorrow. Later today . . . no . . . tomorrow after 12 I'll wire you *yes* or *no*.

I'll write you, then, where to send the sum that is ready.[4]

In haste addio ad.

Your

G. Verdi

Faccio was here yesterday! In vain . . . and I knew it beforehand.[5]

NOTES

1. From Bayreuth, where Ricordi and Faccio had attended a performance of *Die Meistersinger von Nürnberg*, and from Levico.

2. Missing.

3. See the following letter from Verdi to Piroli.

4. See Verdi to Tornaghi, 24 August, n. 2. Instead of writing, Verdi obviously wired and canceled the trip.

1889

5. Faccio's refusal to accept Verdi's and Boito's advice to become director of the conservatory in Parma. (See Verdi to Boito, 18 August, and Boito to Verdi, 20 August.) Verdi recalled this last visit from Faccio in his letter to Boito of 6 October 1890.

🌼 *Verdi to Giuseppe Piroli*

St. Agata, 28 August 1889

[. . .] I received your last letter and send my deepest apologies for not answering you immediately, as I should have done, because of some troubling affairs—some friction in my little hospital[1] between the president, the nuns, and their director, head of the institute of the nuns. They should really mind their own business, but the priests poke their noses into everything.[2] [. . .]

Addio, my dear Piroli. Get ready, and come soon, for we await you with open arms. [. . .]

NOTES

1. Verdi had quietly opened this hospital for his peasants, at Villanova sull'Arda near St. Agata, on 5 November 1888. Problems with its administration concerned him for the rest of his life.
2. "Verdi restored order himself, introducing new regulations at the meeting of his hospital commission. A few minutes before they all sat down, Sister Maria Broli [heading the staff] spoke to Verdi about [president] Boriani's meddling. He reassured her, saying he wanted 'only peace and charity' to prevail. At the table he seated her beside him. Sister Maria reported to [Monsignor Agostino] Chieppi that Verdi 'always spoke very sweetly' and 'seemed like a father surrounded by his children.'" (Phillips-Matz, p. 699.) Her successor later wrote to Verdi: "Others admire your artistic genius, I have always had occasion to admire your genius for charity." (Mingardi, *Verdi e il suo ospedale 1888–1988,* p. 33.)

🌼 *Ricordi to Verdi*

Milan, 31 August 1889

Illustrious Maestro,

I am really very sorry to have unintentionally upset your plans; but the signature of such a statement is of the kind that requires the approval of my associates. [. . .]

Enclosed herewith is the check from the Banca Nazionale for the amount of L. 20,000, according to your instructions, and [deposited] in your account.

Do not think that we forget your very dear invitation!! . . . We are preparing our move . . . . [1] and when it is under way, I will write you to find out when we may have the honor of being the Signori Verdis' guests and destroying a few grapes! . . . . . .

Meanwhile we send you and Signora Peppina affectionate greetings and wishes, looking forward to telling you many good and beautiful, mediocre and ridiculous things we experienced during our quick trip in German style.[2] [. . .]

NOTES

1. Unknown.
2. On the occasion of his visit to Bayreuth.

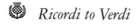 *Verdi to Giuseppe Piroli*

St. Agata, 24 September 1889

[. . .] I am very glad to hear that you are feeling better and wish you continued health . . . but in the meantime we missed your dear company![1] Be patient, I tell you, and we hope such a thing won't happen again!

I would like to do something for the Conservatory of Parma, but I don't know if I can succeed in doing something good. After Bottesini's death (he worked out so well) I turned to Faccio, but, alas, he doesn't have the courage to refuse or to accept. He's a poor man![2] I don't know any others who might have the necessary qualifications for that institute; and we must not deceive ourselves, it all depends on finding the *man!* [. . .]

NOTES

1. Unexpected illness prevented Piroli's visit to St. Agata.
2. See Verdi to Boito, 18 August, and Boito to Verdi, 20 August.

Ricordi to Verdi

Milan, 3 October 1889

Illustrious Maestro,

From the delightful, dear and congenial sojourn in St. Agata[1] I fell into long sessions with the attorney Panattoni!![2]. . An enormous jump, even fatal to peace of mind! . . But at least I find comfort as I think of the wonderful days spent at St. Agata, of the extraordinary pleasure of your and Signora Peppina's company, and of your exquisitely kind and courteous welcome.

Don't laugh, . . . Maestro: this is no perfunctory hyperbole. Certainly not;

1889

we returned from St. Agata truly moved, with enthusiasm and gratitude [. . .]

NOTES

1. In late September.
2. Carlo Panattoni, who represented the House of Ricordi in the suit against Bénoit in Paris. (See Ricordi to Verdi, 3 November, n. 5.)

✤ Verdi to Giuseppina Negroni Prati [1]

Busseto-St. Agata, 14 October 1889

Dear Signora Peppina,

This 76th [birthday] is over, too! Let's hope the others that must come will go by the same way. . . But who knows? . . Meanwhile, thanks, sincerest thanks.

Things of interest in Piacenza are: the Municipal Palace with its bronze horses.

In the cathedral: the frescos by *Guercino*[2]—and, better yet, other frescos by *Pordenone*[3] in the church of *La Madonna di Campagna*.

There also are two large modern paintings in *San Giovanni in Canale;* I say modern, because they were finished at the beginning of this century. The one is by *Landi,*[4] the other by *Camuccini.*[5] Two men of talent, but their era was not too conducive to painting, and, of course, one is aware of the era. [. . .]

NOTES

1. A Swiss-born Milanese aristocrat (1824–1909), the daughter of Verdi's close friend Countess Emilia Morosini (1804–75), and herself a friend to Verdi and his wife.
2. Actually Giovanni Francesco Barbieri (1591–1666), one of the leading, most-prolific Italian painters of the seventeenth century.
3. Giovanni Antonio de Lodesanis or de Sachis Pordenone (ca. 1484–1539) painted these frescos between 1529 and 1531.
4. Gaspare Landi (1756–1830) was born and died in Piacenza.
5. Vincenzo Camuccini (1771–1844).

✤ Verdi to Camillo Boito

[Presumably Milan, October 1889]

[. . .] Today I am sending to attorney Dina[1] the contract draft,[2] which he will then return to you as soon as he has examined it. I think there is nothing to comment on except one phrase "in order to start working as soon as possible," etc. . . , which I have marked in pencil.

So as soon as the attorney has returned the draft to you, you can have the contract drawn up in my name. After the 20th of this month the sum will be available, and you only give me 48 hours' notice to *be in Milan on such and such a day.* [. . .]

NOTES

1. Alessandro Dina (1837–92) was Verdi's as well as Ricordi's attorney. Upon his death, Verdi remembered "how capable and loyal he was." (Verdi to Ricordi and Boito, 12 February 1892.)

2. For the building of the Casa di Riposo, designed by Arrigo Boito's architect brother Camillo.

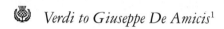 *Verdi to Giuseppe De Amicis*[1]

St. Agata, 22 October 1889
Busseto

[. . .] For three days I have been in Milan. . . Here it rains and rains.

We still haven't decided when we'll come to Genoa. Certainly not before that jubilee, etc., etc.[2] What madness! [. . .]

NOTES

1. See Preface, n. 7.

2. Events were also planned in Genoa, celebrating the fiftieth anniversary of the première of Verdi's first opera, *Oberto, Conte di San Bonifacio,* at La Scala on 17 November 1839.

 *Boito to Eleonora Duse*[1]

[Milan, 22 October 1889]
Tuesday

[. . .] I always followed you thinking of you, on land and sea. But I did my work every day,[2] yes, my love, as you did yours. And so I will do, and so you will do until the two celebrate a *brief reunion.* And when the work is accomplished, the accounts will be done living in peace. *It's our salvation.* You, too, understand it well by now, this great truth. Without work we would be ruined. [. . .]

I don't know when you will receive these words. The bad weather prolongs the sea routes and delays arrival of letters.

1889

Tell me all about you, your health and fatigue, and how much longer you will stay where you are.

In early November I will go for several days to that house you saw as a child, a house in the country you have seen and remember.[3] I will send you the address when I go there. [. . .]

NOTES

1. In Palermo.
2. On the *Falstaff* libretto.
3. St. Agata. Duse's mother had pointed out Verdi's villa to her.

 Eleonora Duse to Boito

[Palermo, 26 October 1889]
Saturday morning—26

[. . .] I am glad, so very glad that you go to the house in the country——
Passing through Genoa also this time, it was night, but through the smoke of the locomotives I made an effort to see *the Latin inscription*.[1]——
——I remember the house in the country very well . . .——My mama held me by the hand——Maybe it's a good omen!

Go to work!   Eleon. [. . .]

NOTE

1. Palazzo Doria, the Verdis' winter residence, was not far from the station. An antique Latin inscription is found on the wall of the medieval palace. (See *Carteggio* ii, p. 388.) Boito and Duse used to write "the one of the Latin inscription" whenever referring to Verdi.

 Boito to Verdi

Wednesday 30 [October 1889]
Milan

Dear Maestro,

I'll arrive next Monday (4 November) and if the 2nd act is not yet finished, I'll finish it during the week I will be staying at St. Agata.

That act has the devil on its back, and it burns when you touch it.

The theme of Alice's scene, as we arranged it in Milan,[1] no longer satisfies me. There is a shortcoming, and it is this: if Alice goes into the details of the jest, the jest loses interest.

I have drafted *the basket* scene and it seems to bode well.

But there is still a lot to be done.

So till we meet again Monday. I'll get off the train at Fiorenzuola at the usual time.

Many kind greetings to Signora Giuseppina and to you.

Many cordial wishes to Maestro Muzio.[2]

Farewell.

Your most affectionate
Arrigo Boito

NOTES

    1. In mid-October.

    2. Visiting at St. Agata.

 Eleonora Duse to Boito

[Palermo, 31 October 1889]
31 October 11 1/2 o'clock———

[. . .] *Go* to your GENTLEMAN of Sant'Agata.———That one *I trust.* He is the only one of your friends———who doesn't judge, for better or for worse, *other people's business.*—[. . .]

 Boito to Eleonora Duse

[Milan, 2 November 1889]
Saturday

[. . .] I will not leave tomorrow,[1] but no doubt the day after tomorrow, and will stay there seven or eight days.

You are so far, so far away that to explain that address I must see a map. When I go downstairs, I'll look it up and will then write. [. . .]

From the 10th to the 11th, yes, where you want. It just has to be.[2] [. . .]

Without having to consult maps, the best address is this:

Piacenza, Borgo San Donnino. Busseto.

NOTES

    1. For St. Agata.

    2. A brief rendezvous in Naples.

1889

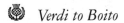 *Verdi to Boito*

[Telegram]   Busseto, 3 November 1889[1]

ARRIGO BOITO
MILAN
ALL RIGHT AND BRAVO
VERDI

NOTE

1. Presumably in answer to Boito's letter of 30 October. (In *Carteggio* ii, p. 376, this telegram is erroneously dated 3 November 1888.)

 *Ricordi to Verdi*

Milan, 3 November 1889

Illustrious Maestro,

For quite some time without your news, here I am asking for it, anxious to hear that it is excellent. For my part, I have various things to tell you, important and very important.

Meanwhile, I am informing you that in a few days the famous deed[1] will be duly registered, and thus everything will be in order. I could not do it earlier, because of the attorney Dina's, and then of the notary Strambio's absence; from the latter we had to get another deed to redraft the previous one for the registrar. At last, they both returned yesterday and reached an agreement.

The day before yesterday, as I entered the Café Cova,[2] I was told that Don Giulio Venino (I mention this name for your information) announced to an editor of the *Pungolo* that Maestro Verdi had acquired a site outside Porta Vittoria to establish a musical institute.[3] Of course, the editor of *Il Pungolo*[4] asked me for news; to that request I replied that I did not know a thing. Thereafter the news was not published; but I thought to inform you so that you might let me know how to act. [. . .]

We are engaged in an important suit against the publisher Bénoit in Paris,[5] who usurped some of Escudier's rights,[6] among them *Trouvère* and *Traviata*. You know that our agreements with Escudier excluded the right of *location du matériel* [rental of material] which has always belonged to our House. Escudier, with indecorous and dishonest subterfuges, did not respect our contracts and was up to mischief all the time, not only renting out the scores on his own, but even selling them. Bénoit would like to continue along this road; called into court, we won a full victory in the 1st instance; Bénoit appealed, and we considered ourselves sure of victory in the appeal as well, when he suddenly pulled out a letter from Verdi, which—as I am told—authorized Escudier to rent out the material. Whether this is true or not, I do not know, but our attorney in Paris, Pouillet (a celebrity), fears that this will make us lose. The matter is of the utmost importance for us, and we would be dealt a severe blow. Therefore I must urgently beg you to remember if such a letter was actually written; if Escudier skillfully extorted it from you, who knows with what lies, with what crafty arts, the reason might be found in Escudier's letters. Our own contracts with Escudier leave no doubt that he never had the right to dispose of our material in any way; always excluded, of course, are the *droits d'auteur* [author's rights] which have nothing to do with the present suit.

If this were not a matter of the greatest importance, I would certainly not have bothered you; but I need not add any words to express the extreme gravity of the matter, or to excuse myself for giving you this trouble.—

Awaiting your answer, I also hope to learn that your coming to Milan is not too far away. We are eagerly anticipating the great pleasure of seeing you again, which will be a true feast for us.

Meanwhile, cordial, affectionate regards to you and Signora Peppina from   Your always most grateful
                                                                                          Giulio Ricordi

NOTES

1. Regarding land Verdi bought in Milan for the construction of the Casa di Riposo.
2. Elegant café and restaurant in Milan. (See *Otello* i, p. 277, n. 3; and *Otello* ii, p. 717, n. 3.)
3. See n. 1.
4. Leone Fortis (1824–98) founded this newspaper in Naples in 1859, with editions in Rome and Milan. A writer, playwright, and librettist, he was haunted for years and driven into temporary exile by the Austrian police. Fortis edited *Il Pungolo* [The Goad] for some thirty years. For a while he also staged operas at La Scala. He disliked Wagner and vigorously promoted Boito's *Mefistofele*. In an article for Ricordi's *Gazzetta musicale di Milano*, Fortis expressed his admiration for the aged Verdi's physical condition as much as for his art. In April, at the train station in Genoa, Fortis unexpectedly met the Maestro; a Frenchman mistook him for Verdi's son! (See Conati, pp. 231–3, for this little episode.)
5. Fréderic-Jean Bénoit (1805–88) had two sons: Jules-Édouard (1839–1913), who took over his father's firm and owned *Le Trouvère* and *La Traviata*, as well as works by Auber and Meyerbeer, and Émile-Claude (1843–97). Emanuele Muzio had Verdi's power of attorney to deal with both sons. Verdi offers a short explanation of the complicated suit in his letter to Giuseppina Negroni Prati of 15 March 1891.

1889

6. The prominent Parisian music publisher and producer Léon Escudier (1821–81) was associated with Verdi for many years. Together with his brother Marie (1819–80) he founded the weekly *La France Musicale,* a valuable source of information about Europe's musical life in the nineteenth century. Léon Escudier's early success turned to failure when, against Verdi's advice, he managed the Italian Theatre in Paris. His reluctance to pay royalties led to the end of their friendship. (See *Aida.*)

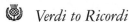 *Verdi to Ricordi*

St. Agata, 4 October [November] 1889[1]

Dear Giulio,

In spite of this always terrible season our health is good!—
The havoc wreaked by the Po is grave for all!

As to the *Venino* news, I have bought, it is true, three thousand square meters of land not outside *Porta Vittoria* but *Porta Garibaldi.* Just as at other times, when I had money at my disposal, I bought stocks, etc., etc., I have bought this site now, when the occasion presented itself; but without a firm idea what I will or could do with it. It is money put to use, for better or for worse, but without a project.[2]

The Escudier affair surprises me, and it seems impossible to me that I should have given him the authorization you mention! It is true, however, that when one had to deal with a man like Escudier, who, as you say, *didn't respect contracts and was up to all kinds of mischief,* any kind of subterfuge is possible. I do not remember that letter; I can give you no clarification, nor can my papers reveal anything pertaining to the matter. It would be good, however, to examine that letter, the *original,* if it exists, and to guard it well.

I am sorry I cannot tell you any more. Keep me informed on what is happening. In a hurry addio ad.

Your
G. Verdi

P.S. I add:

When I translated *Trovatore* for the Opéra, I bought the orchestra score for France from your father, then sold it again later on . . . And then? Could the authorization you fear possibly be in this resale? I further add . . . Muzio left St. Agata a moment ago.[3] He is at the Hotel di Francia [in Milan]; talk with him. Who knows if he might not be able to give you some clarification.

NOTES

1. Obviously in answer to Ricordi's letter of the previous day.
2. The project became the Casa di Riposo per Musicisti [House of Rest for Musicians] in Milan, which Verdi called his "favorite opera."
3. As Boito arrived.

 *Boito to Eleonora Duse*

[Milan, 4 November 1889]
Monday

Another greeting.———

I leave in two hours[1] and tell you about it as if I were going far away, which is not the case.

In four hours I'll be several kilometers nearer to you. But then I have to stop.

I don't know why I feel you are sad, so I write you these lines again, imploring you not to be.

Tell me how you are. Tell me that you make every effort to conquer the sadness. Escape from the loneliness, help yourself. In a few days you will be in another city,[2] and then you too will be a bit nearer.

Listen. I love you so much. I have said it. And I see you from far away. Take heart. Hold on.———

Your Your
Arrigo

NOTES

1. For St. Agata.
2. Messina.

Ricordi to Verdi

Milan, 7 November 1889[1]

Illustrious Maestro,

Here is the registered deed,[2] and I am happy to have been of use to you in fulfilling your wishes, and without burdening you with a heavy tax, thanks to the attorney Dina's skill.

I thank you very much for your kind and prompt attention to the important Paris affair; today I will discuss it with Muzio, and we shall see what might be done. It would be truly painful to be victims of too much good faith. [. . .]

NOTES

1. In answer to Verdi's letter of 4 November.
2. For the site of the Casa di Riposo.

1889

 *Verdi to Giuseppe De Amicis*

St. Agata, 10 November 1889

Dear De Amicis,

I am happy about the decision of the City Council of Genoa,[1] and I thank them most cordially.

As soon as the usual business here is done, we'll go for a few days to Milan; then we'll come to Genoa. That might be a good time for the medal with which the City kindly wishes to honor me.

Please give the Mayor my regards.

Ever your most affectionate
G. Verdi

NOTE

1. To limit the celebrations of the fiftieth anniversary of Verdi's first opera to the solemn presentation of a gold medal. (See Verdi to De Amicis, 22 October.)

 *Boito to Eleonora Duse*

[Milan, 10 November 1889]
Sunday

As I was arriving,[1] (my Bumba), your telegram[2] was running to reach me and reached me an hour later. You are very, very good.

The two letters, I hope, will be forwarded to me from the country. The last one from Palermo came Thursday evening while the coffee was served; a sweet, sweet, sweet letter and sweet coffee. I liked your excursion to Monreale;[3] beautiful things gladden one's thoughts. While I was in the country, when I looked out of the window of my room, I saw the gate before the house, and in the distance I saw the postal route and the open plain; and I thought of a mama holding a little girl by the hand, telling her to take a good look at that house and to remember having seen it. And the little girl remembered it.[4] [. . .]

NOTES

1. Returning from St. Agata.
2. A missing telegram from Palermo, apparently announcing two letters Duse had addressed to St. Agata.
3. The Benedictine monastery at Monreale near Palermo. The adjacent cathedral is

one of the most splendid medieval churches in all of Italy, famous for its mosaics by twelfth-century Byzantine and Sicilian artists.

4. See Boito to Duse, 22 October, n. 3.

 *Verdi to Boito*

Monday [St. Agata, 11 November 1889][1]

Last night a letter arrived here for you.[2] I immediately forwarded it to Milan; but I'm afraid I put the wrong address on it . . . Principe *Umberto* instead of Amedeo.

The letter will reach you anyway . . . but I thought I should advise you of it.

GV

NOTES

1. Postmark: BUSSETO 11/11/89.
2. From Eleonora Duse.

 *Boito to Verdi*

Tuesday [Milan, 12 November 1889][1]

Dear Maestro,

Thank you; I properly received the letter you were kind enough to send me.[2]

The address was not wrong.

The voting for the elections,[3] which forced me to leave the pleasant life of St. Agata, is announced, with good promises for the moderates.[4] Tomorrow we shall have definite news.

I have gone back to work.

I haven't seen anyone but Giacosa;[5] thus no one has told me about the notice in the *Figaro*.[6]

Please, dear Maestro, give Signora Peppina my best regards.

Until we meet soon in Milan.[7] A good handshake from

Your most affectionate

Arrigo Boito

NOTES

1. Postmark: MILANO 12/11/89.
2. On 11 November.
3. To the City Council of Milan.

1889

4. This seems to have pleased Boito, notwithstanding his Bohemian past.

5. See Biographical Sketch.

6. In the Paris daily newspaper; not ascertained, probably discussed at St. Agata.

7. Between 23 November and 6 December, in Milan, on the Verdis' way from St. Agata to their winter home in Genoa.

 *Boito to Eleonora Duse*

[Milan, 12 November 1889]
Tuesday

To you——Nothing got lost.[1] [. . .] A strong hand that knows how to make the pen obey deleted and added the address of the white street.[2] For fear that all those postal indications might be confusing, he followed it up with a letter of his own informing me that he had forwarded the letter. You see, Buscoletta, that your writing is in good hands.

And the address I gave you[3] is far less extravagant than you had thought. Oh Buscola! [. . .]

NOTES

1. Verdi to Boito, 11 November.

2. Principe Amedeo 1, Arrigo and Camillo Boito's home in Milan.

3. On 2 November. Duse had written to Boito on 5 November: "The address you gave me seems strange to me, three towns in one—but so be it." (Radice, p. 586.)

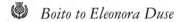 *Boito to Eleonora Duse*

[Milan, 14 November 1889]
Thursday

[. . .] The one of the Latin inscription[1] has worked three days in a row changing addresses. A lion's paw on a swallow's wing. Those hasty and strong characters (Buscoletta is also strong) united are nice to see. [. . .]

NOTE

1. See Duse to Boito, 26 October, n. 1.

 *Verdi to Ricordi*

[Busseto] 17 November 1889

[. . .] I am sorry that I could not send the letter Mme. Pouillet[1] had asked for. I could not ignore the fact that Duprez[2] had translated *Traviata* as he had *Rigoletto,* etc., etc., before then, and that he consequently *stressed* author's rights; I also knew that Dumas for *Traviata* and Victor Hugo for *Rigoletto* had their *Droits d'auteur.* I never cared to know in what proportions, and this is so true that when Victor Hugo claimed all the musical and poetic rights, I turned everything over to the Society of the Authors and gave it no more thought. But the question is this: whether by selling the [orchestral] parts did you or did you not lose the [whole] property?

I know that Escudier always told me "J'ai acheté tel et tel partition etc., etc." [I have bought that and that orchestra score, etc., etc.] I repeat that I am sorry I couldn't send the letter requested of me. [. . .] But I don't want to talk of or confirm things about which I am not certain, and which happened so long ago that I don't remember. [. . .]

NOTES

1. Apparently the wife of the French attorney mentioned in Ricordi's letter to Verdi of 3 Nov. 1889.
2. Edouard Duprez, brother of the famous French tenor Gilbert Duprez (1806–96).

 Verdi to King Umberto I

[Telegram]   Busseto, 17 November 1889[1]

DEEPLY MOVED I THANK YOUR MAJESTY FOR HONORING THE ARTIST WHOSE ONLY MERIT WAS HIS LOVE OF FATHERLAND AND ART [. . .]

NOTE

1. In answer to the King's congratulatory telegram commemorating the fiftieth anniversary of Verdi's *Oberto, Conte di San Bonifacio* at La Scala. Umberto I, King of Italy (1844–1900), was the son of Vittorio Emanuele II. He was crowned in 1878 and assassinated in Monza on 29 July 1900. He was a truly enlightened monarch, a dedicated and courageous *pater patriae.*

 Verdi to Giuseppe De Amicis

Milan, 24 November 1889
[. . .] I thank you for forwarding the telegrams[1] (in hopes that no more may arrive), but we are glad that our servants arrived [in Genoa] without getting lost in the fog.

As for ourselves, nothing has been decided. I read in the papers about a demonstration, etc., etc. . . . If this is so, I would prefer to escape to Florence or Naples.—Tell me something about it. [. . .]

Decisively, without pose and false modesty, *I cannot take it anymore.*

I entreat you to help me.

Greetings from Peppina and a handshake

from your G. Verdi

NOTE

1. On the occasion of the fiftieth anniversary of Verdi's first opera.

 *Verdi to Giosuè Carducci*[1]

Milan, 3 December 1889

Until now I have not had the courage to address a word to you . . . to you, our greatest poet!

But now I can no longer resist the wish and the obligation to thank you for the letter you sent to Ugo Pesci.[2]

I would never have dared hope that you could remember my name with such benevolent and splendid words.

I bow to you and thank you with profound admiration.

Most devotedly,
G. Verdi

NOTES

1. The son of a liberal country physician and a patriotic mother from Tuscany, Carducci (1835–1907) glorified Italy's past. One of her most admired nineteenth-century poets, he was an early Nobel Prize winner. From 1860 to 1903 he taught Italian literature at the University in Bologna, where he died. Together with his young companion, Annie Vivanti, Carducci paid a visit to Verdi in Genoa on 14 March 1891. (See Giuseppina Verdi to Marietta Calvi Carrara, 14 March 1891, which documents the correct date of that visit. See also Phillips-Matz, pp. 707–9.)

2. On the occasion of the fiftieth anniversary of Verdi's *Oberto, Conte di San Bonifacio* at La Scala, Carducci had sent the following letter to Ugo Pesci, a collaborator on Ricordi's *Gazzetta musicale di Milano*:

> Dear Cavaliere Pesci,
>
> Giuseppe Verdi portended and foretold the rise of the fatherland with the first throbbings of his youthful art. What unforgettable and sacred songs for all who were born before 1848!
>
> Giuseppe Verdi, with the flower of his enduring art, honors and elevates the reborn fatherland in the sight of all nations.

Glory to him, who is immortal, serene and triumphant, as the ideal of the country and art.

Dear Signor Pesci, I am religious. Before the Gods I worship and am silent.

Your
Giosuè Carducci

Bologna, 14 November 1889.

A facsimile of this letter appeared in *Gazzetta musicale,* No. 1, 27 November 1889. (*Copialettere*, p. 354, n. 1.) Other congratulatory messages from King Umberto and the mayor of Milan, Gaetano Negri, as well as Verdi's acknowledgments, are also published in *Copialettere*, pp. 354-5.

 *Verdi to Giuseppe De Amicis*

Milan, 3 December 1889

Dear De Amicis,

Thank you for the news about the jubilee. . . Since they wanted to do it, it was better like this; at least they avoided the theatrical fuss.[1]

It's all over . . . and I am very happy about it.

We still haven't set a date for our arrival [in Genoa] . . . but I'll write it to you later on. [. . .]

NOTE

1. Torch processions in the streets of Genoa, etc., on the occasion of the fiftieth anniversary of Verdi's first opera. (See Verdi to De Amicis, 22 October.)

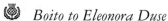 *Boito to Eleonora Duse*

[Milan, 3-4 December 1889]
Tuesday night[1]

[. . .] Lovely Signora—You say there is some woman at the [Hotel] Vittoria.—I have some fellow at the [Hotel] Nobile, permanently.—So another place must be found.[2] [. . .]

But another case must be foreseen.—The one who lives at the Latin inscription is here.[3] I don't know when he leaves.—If he should leave Monday night, I would have to take the other, longer route[4] and would arrive at the station not at 6:44 but at 9:55 the same evening. [. . .]

NOTES

1. In answer to a telegram Duse sent from Catania. (Tuesday was December 5.)

2. For a secret rendezvous in Naples from 10 to 11 December.
3. Verdi, who returned with his wife to Genoa on Friday, 6 December.
4. Via Bologna-Florence rather than on the Verdis' train via Genoa.

 *Ricordi to Verdi*

Milan, 12 December 1889

[. . .] I just received a telegram from Paris: We have lost the Bénoit suit!![1]
As I said, I'm having a run of bad luck!! . . . and it is time to apply a bit of
philosophy . . . . . . so as not to completely lose my health!— Suits have been
made, and won, and lost! . . . all the better!—but when you see rogues
triumphing . . . . . it breaks your heart. [. . .]

NOTE

1. Presumably at the first stage of the proceedings.

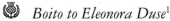 *Boito to Eleonora Duse*[1]

[Nervi, 22 December 1889]

[. . .] To avoid too many arrivals and departures at home,[2] I'll stay here until
the day when I'll be on the way again to my love. Besides, the work that now
occupies me[3] is enough to fill up the time it will take to arrive at that day.
[. . .]

NOTES

1. In Alexandria, Egypt.
2. From and to Genoa for working with Verdi on *Falstaff*.
3. *Falstaff*.

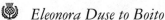 *Eleonora Duse to Boito*

[Alexandria, 23 December 1889]
Monday 23 Dec. 89 Morning

[. . .] you think that I am stronger than I am—and I for one don't see that—
to see each other once a year, and woe to complain——

But let's not talk about it! You close yourself at home, and the door
remains closed to me [. . .]

E.

Ricordi to Verdi

Milan, 29 December 1889

Illustrious Maestro,

Giuditta had a very dear letter from Signora Peppina, and we hoped to write you that finally everybody was healthy . . . . and that there was hope of beginning the new year quite well; however . . . . . the *influenza* has visited us. — I was in bed for 8 days; at the same time, *six* others: Tito, Manolo, Gigi,[1] Giuditta and two servants!— Giuditta felt better, but yesterday the fever returned; today Giuditta, Ginetta,[2] and Manolo are in bed.— I am fairly well, but forbidden to leave the house! However, this influenza isn't serious for any of us; the only problem is the convalescence, which requires the greatest care.—All of this is nothing, Maestro, in comparison to our distressing grief over a terrible misfortune!— My dear nephew Pippo Brentano, whom we have always cared for and loved like a son, is dying of typhus and pneumonia! . . . At the moment all hope seems lost!! A horrible fate, beyond words!— And none of us is able to help him.— We are going through real affliction!—

Please console me and my family by writing us that both of you are well, really well!! . . and accept the warmest wishes from our most grateful hearts. A happy New Year, then, and keep your good will toward us as ever.

Your most affectionate
Giulio Ricordi

Our best wishes also for Muzio.[3]

NOTES

    1. Sons of Giulio and Giuditta Ricordi.
    2. The Ricordis' daughter.
    3. The Verdis' guest for the holidays.

 Boito to Eleonora Duse

[Nervi, 31 December 1889]

Lenor—The last hour of the year. Here is the one who loves you. It is he who bends your will (you say), it is he who follows yours. In a week he will return to his home, because you, Lenor, like it this way. He would go there tomorrow if the work[1] weren't keeping him. [. . .]

Good night and a good year. I am tired and cheerless. [. . .]

NOTE

    1. With Verdi on *Falstaff* in nearby Genoa.

1890

I am having fun writing the music . . . [1]

F ranco Faccio's fatal disease and its consequences hang over Verdi and his friends throughout the year. In January and February, at Genoa's Palazzo Doria, Verdi is drafting the music for the first act of *Falstaff*.[2] From 3 to 8 March and again from 12 to 16 April he is absent from Genoa to look after his affairs at St. Agata. On 8 March he thanks Boito for the completed libretto of "this stupendous *Falstaff*." On 17 March he writes Boito that "the first act is finished." Faccio's worsening illness, however, seems to contribute to Verdi's ensuing lack of creative activity. Between about 28 April and 3 May, on their return from Genoa to St. Agata, the Verdis meet Boito and the Ricordis in Milan. In his letter to Boito of 23 May, the Maestro admits not having "done a thing" for the Potbelly, apart from minor corrections. Verdi and Giuseppina see their friends again in Milan, en route to their annual cure in Montecatini in late June.[3] They return to St. Agata via Milan in mid-July. In August Verdi appears relaxed and in good humor until he begins to worry about Muzio, who is ill in Paris with a liver ailment. In November one blow follows the other: Piroli dies in Rome on the 14th, Muzio in Paris on the 27th, and Verdi's problems with the hospital at Villanova increase. Between 17 November and 1 December the Verdis are again in Milan, on their way to Genoa for the winter.

Ricordi, amid frequent illnesses, his demanding work for the publishing house, and his family obligations, remains perturbed by the continuing Bénoit suit. The entire House of Ricordi is honored by a visit from King Umberto I on 24 May. Nevertheless, Ricordi mentions his not infrequent depression to Verdi the following day. "The decline of moral standards" in his business weighs on his mind, as he confesses on 10 June, while he declares on 5 July that "the art of music is killing itself with the most cynical and vulgar triviality." Pork shoulders the Maestro sends from his farm help to restore Ricordi's good humor, and in mid-September the Ricordis again enjoy the Verdis' hospitality at St. Agata. The publisher is in the dark about Verdi's collaboration with Boito on *Falstaff* until 26 November, when Boito reveals the secret at a dinner in Milan. Upon learning the sensational news, Ricordi swings into action.

Until 10 March Boito stays at the Hotel Eden in Nervi to finish the *Falstaff* libretto, which he discusses with Verdi during several visits to nearby Genoa. Meanwhile he hopes in vain to welcome his sick friend Faccio in Nervi, while on 20 February Duse arrives in Barcelona from Egypt. Boito is caught between his concern for Faccio's condition and Duse's irritation about his long silence. On 11 March he is home in Milan. On 31 March he arrives in Barcelona for a brief disappointing reunion with Duse. Faccio's worsening illness torments Boito and necessitates several trips to the Conservatory of Parma, where he becomes acting director for his friend. Following his first appointment in Parma, 28 to 31 May, he sees the Verdis on 1 and 2 June at St. Agata and, probably, again in Milan at the end of that month. His reaction of 11 June to Duse's enjoyment of a bullfight illustrates his deep regard for all life and his disgust with human pride and cruelty. On or about 7 July he meets Duse in Turin, and he is back in Parma on the 12th. Duse joins him at San Giuseppe on the 14th and departs in late August for another season in Barcelona. On 10 and 11 September Boito sees to Faccio's affairs in Milan. On the 12th he is at Villa d'Este. He returns to San Giuseppe, and on 2 and 3 October, he helps once more to settle Faccio's estate in Milan. On 12 October he is present at the opening of the academic year at the Conservatory of Parma, and then visits St. Agata. After another reunion with Duse in Turin at the end of October, Boito is home in Milan on 5 November. On the 26th of that month, the eve of Muzio's death in Paris, he attends a dinner with the Verdis and Ricordis in Milan. To comfort Verdi over the loss of his friends, and to motivate him to proceed, Boito toasts the *pancione* [potbelly], revealing the secret of *Falstaff*. Two days later, he briefly sees Duse, who has meetings with her agents in the city. Boito's idea of a short rendezvous in Verona, combined with his next appointment from 17 to 20 December in Parma, remains a dream; but the frustrated couple still hope to have a few hours together, which apparently comes about in Venice over Christmas. At the end of this particularly restless year Boito is at home in Milan.

NOTES

    1. Verdi to Gino Monaldi, 3 December.
    2. See Hepokoski, p. 35.
    3. *Carteggio* ii, p. 400, para. 2.

 Verdi to Maria Waldmann[1]

Genoa, 1 January 1890

Dearest Maria,

    It is a joy for me to receive your letters! For a moment I forget my many years and in my thoughts return to those joyful, happy times which you, despite the splendor of your present position,[2] have not forgotten. This trait commends those of your qualities that I have always so highly appreciated.

    Those stormy times of agitation, fears and hopes are gone . . . yet so longed for and so dear! And you have not forgotten the old Maestro, who wishes you all the best that is possible and clasps both your hands with deepest affection.

Your
G. Verdi
with greetings and good wishes from Peppina.

NOTES

    1. The Viennese mezzo-soprano (1844–1930) appeared under Verdi's direction in the European première of *Aida* (1872) and the *Requiem* (1874). Verdi loved her like a daughter. (See Biographical Sketch.)
    2. As the Duchess Galeazzo Massari of Ferrara, to whom Verdi addressed this letter.

 Boito to Eleonora Duse

[Nervi, 1 January 1890]
1-1-1890

    A good year. A good one. Eight o'clock in the morning. Blessings from this side of the sea.[1] [. . .]

    Yesterday I spent the day at the Latin inscription;[2] I had dinner there and

also stayed for the evening. And now I'm returning there. I'll stay in the city until the evening. [. . .]

NOTES

1. To Duse in Cairo.
2. See Duse to Boito, 26 October 1889, n. 1.

 *Giuseppina Verdi to G. De Sanctis*[1]

Genoa, 2 January 1890

[. . .] *Don Quixote, Romeo and Juliet,* and *King Lear*[2] are sleeping the sleep of the just! . . . Let the journals and the journalists sing, for from time to time they need material to fill their columns. [. . .]

NOTES

1. Giuseppe De Sanctis (1858–1924), a painter in Naples, was Verdi's godson.
2. Subjects for operas Verdi considered but abandoned.

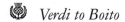 *Verdi to Boito*

Genoa, 6 January [1890]

Dearest Boito,

My servant has been dismissed. Another one, a certain *Vittorio Falsetti* (ugly word, Ford would say[1]) has presented himself, having been for many years in the service of the Marquis Gropallo.[2] If the Marquis would tell you confidentially something about him . . . especially whether he was dismissed somewhat suddenly, he would do me a real favor. Falsetti also knows Don Marco Sala.[3] You understand? I await an answer from you, then; and it should reach me by Wednesday morning.[4]

Excuse me.

Our affectionate greetings.

G. Verdi

NOTES

1. Referring to "le corna" [the cuckold's horns] in *Falstaff* II. i.
2. Unknown.
3. A popular composer (1842–1901) and friend of Boito.
4. We have no record of Boito's reply.

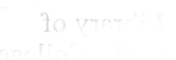

1890

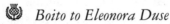 *Ricordi to Verdi*

Milan, 7 January 1890

Illustrious Maestro,

I never had the courage to write you during these days, although I felt an immense desire to do so; I am so bewildered and dejected that I am still unable to collect my thoughts. For 25 days I have been locked up at home, and thus the sad hours are even more interminable; today a little sun appeared, however, so I hope for [the doctor's] permission to go out—now that all the sick ones, including Ginetta—the last to pay her tribute—are finally out of bed! You can well imagine how frustrated I was, unable to take care of business at the very end of the year! [. . .]

I was glad to see our friend Muzio, who with real joy brought your excellent news, which I expect you to confirm! . . . There is hope that the weather, which is nice and fresh again, may finally liberate us from that uncomfortable epidemic, which, although not dangerous, is spreading enough to cause most serious harm to the economy.

Muzio told us, too, how much you shared our mourning![1] . . . and in this we see more evidence of that golden heart and noble soul, which are not the only gifts which make us love and adore Giuseppe and Giuseppina Verdi. [. . .]

NOTE

1. Presumably for Ricordi's nephew. (See Ricordi to Verdi, 29 December 1889.)

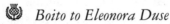 *Boito to Eleonora Duse*

[Nervi, 10 January 1890]
Thursday night

[. . .] I have decided to stay where I am until the day I leave for Naples.[1] By now it's too late for me to go home; after three or four weeks I would have to travel again.[2] Here I have work that is still keeping me for several days;[3] here it is easier for me to leave again without having to worry about a hundred eyes watching me. So I stay. [. . .]

NOTES

1. To meet Duse there on her return from Egypt.

2. From Milan to Genoa to work on *Falstaff* with Verdi.
3. The *Falstaff* libretto.

 *Ricordi to Verdi*

Milan, 11 February 1890

Illustrious Maestro,

Please give me your news so I may have the pleasure of knowing that it is excellent.— Our health is enjoying a favorable period at this time, although a Siberian cold wave has returned, with menacing snow; but we forge ahead. Those who don't are the theatres!!— This cursed epidemic, taken lightly in the beginning, has brought even greater harm than the aftermath of the cholera.— Thus the year has had a bad start, and it continues in this vein.— We must arm ourselves with courage and patience.— During this time I also had such distressing moments concerning Faccio that I decided to see his doctor to find out what is going on. The doctor, one of the foremost in Milan,[1] confirmed the absolute need for a month or two of complete rest; this can restore Faccio's health; he is physically well, but in such a state of depression that its persistence would be dangerous for him and harmful for the theatre. During a long talk, which I had to keep in a joking tone, I persuaded him to again consult his doctor, whom he saw yesterday, and who confirmed the above. Faccio will probably decide to request a leave of absence; he should go to the Riviera, maybe to Nervi—what do I know—for a complete physical and mental rest. This is the only way to rescue his position in the future, since with each passing day he is losing whatever authority he has in the theatre. Painful as it is, I thought to inform you immediately of what is happening. During his *leave* he will, of course, be replaced by Coronaro,[2] and I also hope to have arranged with the City for him to receive his full salary for the season.

When he recovers, he must touch heaven with a finger, as the saying goes, to find the position in Parma he owes to you!— This is the lovely news . . . . . . and I think it's about time to change the tune and jump from minor key to the most brilliant of all the majors!— I hope this will happen in another letter of mine. Meanwhile, I express to Signora Peppina and to you my feelings of deepest gratitude.

Most devotedly,
Giulio Ricordi

NOTES

1. Professor Levis.
2. Gaetano Coronaro (1852–1908), Faccio's pupil at the Milan Conservatory and a friend of Boito, had been the First Assistant Conductor of La Scala since 1879. After the third performance of *Die Meistersinger* (in Italian), Coronaro took over all of Faccio's assignments during this season.

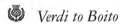 *Verdi to Boito*

Saturday [Genoa, 15 February 1890][1]

Dear Boito,

Do you have more immediate news about Faccio? Read this little article in the *Pungolo!*[2]

What must be read between those few lines?

There is certainly something which I do not wish to define.—

Addio. 'Til we see each other.[3]

Your
G. Verdi

NOTES

1. Postmark: GENOVA 16/2/90.
2. Verdi attached the enclosed:

THEATRICAL COURIER

Maestro Faccio has asked the City and the management for a two-week leave of absence in order to restore himself completely from a brief, yet not negligible, indisposition he suffered last month. Thus he obeys the urgent recommendation of his distinguished physician and friend, Professor Levis.

During the brief absence of Faccio, who will spend the 15 days on the Ligurian Riviera, [probably together with Boito in Nervi], the direction of musical performances at La Scala is, naturally, entrusted to the excellent substitute, Maestro Coronaro.

We do not believe the news, therefore, that *Edgar* [Puccini's second opera, which Faccio had premièred at La Scala on 21 April 1889] could be conducted and directed by its author, Maestro Puccini.

Until Faccio's return, the rehearsals and the direction of this opera also remain entrusted to Maestro Coronaro.

Thus we do not believe the news wired to [the newspaper] *Il Resto del Carlino* of Bologna, that Maestro Puccini is among the competitors to succeed Faccio next year. The latter, as is known, will take over the direction of the Conservatory and the Teatro Regio in Parma.

3. Frequently visiting Verdi in Genoa from nearby Nervi, Boito apparently answered this letter in person.

Boito to Eleonora Duse

[Nervi, 17 February 1890]
Monday

My Love—

Neither the great distance nor the long silence has power over the two [of us]. No letter from down there has missed me. I have not written you for ages. Now we are closer.[1] [. . .]

A great sadness weighs upon me. A friend of mine (a friend for so many years) is very sick.[2] I am awaiting him here. If he comes, I will stay a little longer in this town, which has saved me from the calamities of the city and which, I hope, would be good for him, too.[3]

In a week I will have finished that work which I had hoped to finish in three months.[4] Then, if my friend arrives, I'll stay here for another week. But next month I'll be back home. [. . .]

NOTES

1. Duse arrived in Barcelona from Egypt on 20 February, via Marseille.
2. See Ricordi to Verdi, 11 February, and Verdi to Boito, 15 February.
3. Boito's hope was in vain.
4. The *Falstaff* libretto.

 Eleonora Duse to Boito

[Barcelona, 21 February 1890]
Barcelona—21 February—

Arrigo——

Arrived yesterday——I found THE letter[1] upon arrival.—I hope and wish that your anxiety may have been dispelled. I hope and wish—all the best—for you—and those you love.

Yesterday I searched all over Barcelona for Italian papers and found them. *La Piemontese* confirmed, even *completed*, your news; it mentioned the name of your sick friend and the plan to take him to Nervi, near you.

[. . .]

NOTE

1. Of 17 February.

1890

🌀 Ricordi to Verdi

Milan, 23 February 1890

Illustrious Maestro,

I thank you for your letter,[1] and when I have the pleasure of writing you, I at least want to be as little annoying as possible; unfortunately, however, this '90 is so far a lousy year. Our home still functions as a small hospital. [. . .]

And now let's talk about poor Faccio: It was absolutely impossible for him to continue the season, even conducting only the first two operas he had produced; in the last performances he did not move the baton for several beats and was unaware of it. The matter is more serious than we thought, as proven by the fact that the doctor did not let him leave but instead submitted him to a rigorous cure. Since yesterday Faccio is better and could take a little walk; if he continues like this, there is hope that he can depart[2] in a few days.

Above all, absolute rest and complete calm are necessary. [. . .]

NOTES

    1. Missing.
    2. For Nervi.

🌀 Boito to Eleonora Duse

[Nervi, 25 February 1890]
Tuesday morning

Bumba, be good.

Be good to yourself and fair toward others. Believe the one who believes you.[1]

If you did not receive letters down there [in Egypt] from someone who loves you, the reason is simple: your letters arrived precisely the day after the answers had to leave. And your moves were so uncertain that, at that distance, any correspondence was impaired. The fault is the sea's, my child; the sea has many faults but it doesn't drown souls. [. . .]

My friend delays his arrival.[2] In three days I will have done everything I had to do here.[3] And to remain here without work, idling, will bother me. In three days I'll decide and write or wire. [. . .]

your your
Arrigo

NOTES

    1. In answer to Duse's bitter complaints about Boito's long silence.

    2. Faccio never arrived.

    3. See Boito to Duse, 10 January and 17 February.

 *Boito to Verdi*

[Nervi] 1 March [1890][1]

Dear Maestro,

Here is the latest news about Faccio. It is good, and I hasten to give it to you.

The good Fortis's letter[2] reached me just this minute.

In three or four days at the latest I will have finished *Falstaff*.[3] The third act isn't turning out as short as I had hoped, but it is the most varied of them all.

Many cordial greetings to Signora Giuseppina and to you.

'Til we see each other Tuesday or Wednesday.

Your affectionate
Arrigo[4]

NOTES

    1. Apparently, Boito wrote from Nervi, where Verdi answered him the following day.

    2. Missing.

    3. See Boito to Duse, 10 January, 17 and 25 February.

    4. This is the first of the extremely rare occasions when Boito signs a letter to Verdi using only his first name.

 *Verdi to Boito*

Genoa, 2 March 1890

Dear Boito,

Thanks for the better news you give me about the poor man's health. I'll be happy when I know that he is completely restored, as I hope with all my heart.

The Potbelly [libretto], then, is almost finished! Evviva! . . . I don't fear its length, because I am certain that there will be nothing useless in it.

1890

You said that you will be in Genoa on Wednesday. Delay a couple of days. I leave for St. Agata in the morning, and I won't be back until Saturday.— As soon as I arrive, I will wire you.

Greetings from Peppina. I clasp your hands.

Affectionately,
G. Verdi

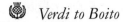 *Verdi to Boito*

Genoa, 8 March 1890

Dear Boito,

Accept this[1]..... not as compensation, but as a sign of gratitude for your having written this stupendous *Falstaff* for me.

If I should not be able to finish the music, the poetry of *Falstaff* will remain your property.

I shake your hand—

Thank you again. Addio.

Affectionately,
G. Verdi

NOTE

1. Presumably a generous check, the sum of which has not been ascertained.

 *Verdi to Boito*

[Telegram]   Genoa, 9 March 1890

ARRIGO BOITO
EDEN HOTEL—NERVI
HAVE RETURNED[1]—GREETINGS
VERDI

NOTE

1. From St. Agata.

 *Boito to Verdi*

9 March [18]90
Genoa[1]

Dear Maestro,

Thank you with all my heart and the utmost gratitude. The compensation you give me is too much; to accept it and to feel that I deserve it, I must think that I have worked for you spurred on solely by my affection for you, and that the splendid compensation you give me derives from your recognition of this affection.

Now, Maestro, again in Shakespeare's name, give to art and to our country another completely new victory.

An embrace.

Your
Arrigo Boito

NOTE

1. Boito sent these lines—addressed only "Giuseppe Verdi"—presumably through a messenger to Palazzo Doria. He probably greeted the Verdis there on his way to Milan on 11 March.

Boito to Eleonora Duse

[Nervi, 10 March 1890]
Monday morning

[. . .] Yesterday I finished that work I had to do. I leave today. I'll be in the city [Genoa] during the day, and tomorrow I'll be home, in the little room in the white street. [. . .]

The two [of us] will do this—

They'll meet at the Hôtel in Marseilles where you landed. You'll tell me the name of the Hôtel. Answer me right away. You will decide the day. We'll meet. We'll cut the journey in half. Thus we shall save time and distance. From where you are [Barcelona] to Marseilles, the trip is not far. From where I'll be tomorrow [Milan], my journey won't be longer than yours.

I'll arrive in Marseilles, at the Hôtel you wish, at 4:43 in the morning. You'll tell me the time of your arrival.[1] [. . .]

NOTE

1. This meeting did not come about.

1890

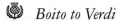 *Eleonora Duse to Boito*

[Barcelona, 11 March 1890]
11 March

Your other letter[1] said: *"In three days I shall wire or write whether I leave or stay."*

14 days have gone by, and today I receive a letter of yours.[2] [. . .]

In the great silence of all these months you make a big drumroll——Trrrrrr—— "Let's cheer up! We'll meet again in Marseilles!" [. . .]

One ought to be stronger, and less broken by waiting, less tortured by loneliness, to be contented with this. [. . .]

You have driven me so far away from everything that consoled me. I want to go back right away *over there,*——*over* there—beyond the sea——

And then—the thread holding us has become so thin—and it doesn't even cross your mind that it might break——[. . .]

Lenor

NOTES

1. Of 25 February.
2. Of the previous day, apparently by express mail to Milan.

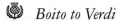 *Boito to Verdi*

Thursday. Milan [13 March 1890][1]

Dear Maestro,

I still have not been able to see Faccio. Twice I have gone to his home, and both times the porter's wife did not let me in. The doctors' order is that he not see anyone, to spare him the effort of conversation and keep any excitement from him.—I insisted a bit, trying to disregard the order, but then I understood that the prohibition was very strict, and therefore I limited myself to writing my name on the visitors' list.

However, the news at the porter's lodge is good; our friend is better, but in need of complete mental rest. Dr. Levis continues to hope.—Let us then hope with him.

Remember, dear Maestro, that whenever you find something to change or to modify in the libretto of *Falstaff,* I am always most ready to listen to you and to make the change immediately. I am rather slow in writing, but very fast in correcting what has already been written. When a work of art goes well as a whole, it is quite easy to perfect its details.

I still haven't seen Giulio.

Most affectionate greetings.

Your
Arrigo Boito

Many cordial wishes to Signora Giuseppina.

NOTE

1. Postmark: MILANO 13/3/90.

 Boito to Eleonora Duse

[Milan, 14 March 1890][1]
Friday

Lenor—I love you. You don't understand. There is nothing to be clarified, nothing, nothing. All your thoughts are directed against me. My unfair Love—The work[2] besieged me, I wanted to free myself; I freed myself, I wrote you, I proposed a plan to you; you deride it. [. . .] Peace, peace, my Love. If there is no peace between us, we will not have it inside us.—So it is.—Destiny is not to be remade. The knot will never be untied and, deep in our hearts, it will never be broken. [. . .]

NOTES

1. In answer to Duse's letter of 11 March.
2. On *Falstaff*.

 Boito to Eleonora Duse

[Milan, 15 March 1890]
Saturday morning

Lenor—Give me a good word, a word of ours. I have no more peace.

I have read and reread it.[1]—It's monstrous—Never have you talked like this to me. It is a nasty blow. My blood still boils. And it is the first real sorrow that comes to me from you. [. . .]

I was distracted by work, a work not my own and so far from pain;[2] I was distracted and worried by the commitment I had undertaken, a victim every day of the illusion of completing my task the next day. You know how I deceive myself in those calculations, hoping to take up the pen for you every morning. And in the meantime I hoped for a word from you, which

1890

did not come. And thus the silence whiled away the silence, and the days went by. My Love. Look at me. Believe me! [. . .]

Arrigo

NOTES

  1. Her letter of 11 March.
  2. *Falstaff.*

 *Boito to Verdi*

Sunday [Milan, 16 March 1890][1]

Dear Maestro,

    I have seen F. twice; I left him half an hour ago at the home of a lady-friend of ours, where we arranged to take him in order to talk with him quietly about his business affairs without the presence of that brother-in-law of his.[2]

    I found F. much better than I had expected. I'd even say, much better than when I saw him four months ago. The cure to which he has submitted is beneficial.

    One of the reasons for his illness is a blood infection which is treated with mercury injections. There is reason to hope that once this infection is conquered his health can greatly improve or be completely restored. He no longer regrets having accepted the Parma business; and when he attempts to regret, it is because of old sentimental habit rather than because of a painful emotion. In fact, today when I joked about these attempts to whine, I made him laugh so heartily that no healthy man would have laughed more or better than he did.

    Yet he speaks haltingly (however, he always did) as you know; in conversation he searches a bit for a word, but finds it precisely. I have never heard him confuse one [word] with another.

    The inflection of his voice and accent is his natural inflection. His eyes look straight ahead and see well.—So I have hope, then. He will soon go to Gratz, where there is a most effective treatment for this kind of illness.[3] He will go there with his brother-in-law.

    When I was informed of this, I wanted to know something positive about the security of his savings before letting him leave.

    His savings are most secure; they are deposited at the savings bank in the form of bonds in his name; these are in the custody of an employee of the same institution, a person of exemplary probity who has kept them for him for many years. The securities issued in his own name are automatically safeguarded. So there is no fear that they will be taken from him. If his illness, instead of turning out well, should turn out badly, and if F.'s savings could somehow be threatened through a lien imposed by a person possessing the legal right to request it, I would consult the attorney Dina to ask for advice. But I hope, but I believe, that by God's grace we shall not arrive at these extremes.

On the other hand, our poor friend has gone through horrible bitterness, too revolting to be recalled.

Affectionate greetings to you, dear Maestro, and to Signora Giuseppina.

Your most affectionate

Arrigo Boito

NOTES

1. Postmark: MILANO 17/3/90.

2. Piero Fabricci from Trieste, the husband of Faccio's sister Chiarina (1846–1923), a soprano who had a brief career. Her marriage had alienated Chiarina from her brother and his friends.

3. In Graz, Austria, Faccio hoped to cure his dementia, the result of latent syphilis, which was diagnosed later on. (See Boito to Verdi, 25 March, n. 3.)

 *Verdi to Boito*

Genoa, 17 March 1890[1]

Dear Boito,

Let's hope then . . . but the [doctors'] order, being so strict, alarms me! When I was in Milan,[2] I found him away from home, and a few days later he accompanied [Signora] Pantaleoni[3] to the railroad station. And now? . . . Let us hope, let us hope. Tell me something about it when you can.

The first act is finished without any change in the poetry, exactly as you gave it to me. I think the same will happen with the second act, except for some cuts in the concertato, as you said yourself. Let's not talk about the third at this time; but I think there won't be much to do in that one either.

And you? . . . I say this *sotto voce: Work.* And I say this not only in the interest of art but also a bit in my own interest, because when, sooner or later, it becomes known that you have written *Falstaff* for me, they will vent their anger against me, because I have made you lose time. Of course, we'll let them scream, but if you *grab them by the throat* (as Otello says) and stifle their screams, it will be better.

On the word *Falstaff* do you want the accent on the first or on the second [syllable]? It makes no difference to the verse; but which is better?

I greet you from Peppina and shake your hands.

Affectionately,

G. Verdi

NOTES

   1. In answer to Boito's letter of 13 March.
   2. From 23 November to 6 December 1889.
   3. Faccio's mistress, the soprano Romilda Pantaleoni (1847–1917). She had a notable career, but was disappointing as Desdemona in the première of *Otello*. (See *Otello*.)

 *Boito to Verdi*

Thursday. Milan. [20 March 1890][1]

Dear Maestro,

I wanted to let San Giuseppe[2] go by without writing you, in order not to add one more letter to the hundreds you will have had to read yesterday. And I answer.

Above all, a first *Evviva* for the news you give me that you have finished the 1st act of *Falstaff.*

Falstaff, like all English disyllabic names, is accented on the first [syllable]. Ask Signora Giuseppina if I am right or wrong. I cannot remember a single English surname of more than one syllable with the accent on the last. Only the French, who are incorrigible distorters of foreign surnames, pronounce it Falstáff.

I also believe that the episode of the *basket* and the *screen* must be shortened. I leave the scissors, dear Maestro, to you. Cut where it seems necessary and where it pleases you. I have purposely been generous so that you may cut the piece from that large amount of material in your own way and with greater leisure. In the development of the ensemble the needs of the music cannot be foreseen; therefore it is better to have plenty of verses.

Don't worry about me. I'm working.[3] Today the Cortis[4] came to see me, and I repeated the promise I gave them last summer, certain to keep it.[5]

They restrained their curiosity and asked me no indiscreet questions about the work at Palazzo Doria.[6]

Yesterday I saw Faccio again in his home, and in his presence I had an appointment with his accountant, who is a highly respectable person. Our friend's money is altogether safe. — I know that you must have received a letter from him for San Giuseppe's Day,[7] and this pleased me, too. I repeat my impression: it's a tired brain, but not a mind that is burning out. His rest will make him healthier than he has been.

Remember me cordially to Signora Giuseppina.

An affectionate greeting

from your
Arrigo Boito

NOTES

1. Postmark: MILANO 20/3/90.
2. Giuseppe and Giuseppina Verdi's saint's day, the 19th of March.
3. On *Nerone*.
4. The brothers Cesare and Enrico Corti managed La Scala from 1876 to 1882, 1885 to 1887, and 1888 to 1891.
5. Presumably to finish *Nerone*.
6. On *Falstaff*.
7. Missing, if sent.

 *Verdi to Maria Waldmann*

Genoa, 21 March 1890

Dearest Maria,

Thanks, my dearest Maria, to you and the Duke, in my and in Peppina's name, for your good wishes. San Giuseppe's Day is *lovely,* as you say, but alas, it also means . . . one more year. . . and I have accumulated so many already!!

So you have been and still are a little ill?! This cursed *influenza* we laughed about in the beginning has been rather serious for so very many, and for some extremely serious! . . . Let's hope that the good season[1] may restore matters and that there may be no more talk of misery! We have skipped this *influenza* and hope it won't visit Palazzo Doria.

Thank you so much for your most beautiful portrait, which I will keep with fondest memories.

Give the Duke our very best. Get completely well, and soon. A good handshake from the old, very old

friend
G. Verdi

NOTE

1. The coming of spring.

1890

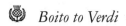 *Boito to Verdi*

25 March [1890]
Milan[1]

Dear Maestro,

Our poor friend left last night for Gratz. It cost me a great deal of trouble to have him delay his departure by a couple of days. It would have been impossible to keep him from going—not on account of the opposition his brother-in-law would have raised, but because of the desperate excitement I would have aroused in the patient, which would have aggravated his illness. Faccio has boundless faith in the cure at Gratz, and he rushes there with the impatience of a man sure of finding recovery.

I forced him to delay his departure, as I wanted Todeschini[2] to visit him, and so it was. I called for a meeting of the physicians with me, and that took place yesterday.

Before letting him depart, I wanted to know my friend's exact physical condition. Our Todeschini proved once again that the nobility of his heart equals his talent. The meeting took place yesterday in his home, in my presence, after he had visited the patient on the previous day, with indefatigable kindness. Present were Todeschini, Levis, the doctor in charge, and De Vincenti, specialist for diseases of the brain.

The result is this: *There are grave reasons to suspect a cerebral paralysis.*

It is advisable that the name of the threatening disease not be known by the public.

If within four or five months our friend can realize a consistent improvement from the cure in Gratz, then he is safe; if not, it is worse for him than death. Until this period has passed, I shall find a way to mark time with Parma; the doctors themselves have given me this advice.

A thread of hope exists, but it is very slim.

The doctors left me with these words: *Let us hope*; but not in the tone of true hope.—Todeschini and Levis are a little more confident than De Vincenti, whose confidence is extremely slight. The fact is that in the whole world there is no more appropriate cure than in Gratz.

De Vincenti, who knows that establishment, having seen and studied it, spoke with outright enthusiasm of Dr. Krafft-Ebing,[3] who directs it; and he does not hesitate to proclaim this scientist on a par with Charcot.[4]

The same Dr. De Vincenti promised me to write to Krafft-Ebing, whom he knows personally, in order to have frequent news about our friend.

Between Milan and Trieste, between Milan and Gratz, there is no lack of communication. [Signora] Pantaleoni's brother[5] has a friend who goes to

Gratz every month and will take care of the essentials. I myself can make an excursion there if it should be necessary.

Sad days, dear Maestro.— The first impressions I received of the sick man were good, for in those days I always saw him in the afternoon. But then, when I saw him in the morning—and evening—hours, I was scared. I would never have imagined such a change.

Yesterday was the last evening. I found only two friends in his home: *Orsi*[6] and *Alcèo Pantaleoni,* who always came twice every day. On the other days I found *Countess Dandolo*[7] and a close lady-friend of [Signora] *Pantaleoni*—I am sorry not to remember her name. I did not accompany him to the station, in order to spare him any further pain; I said goodbye one hour before his departure yesterday evening at ten o'clock.

He was so good and so genuinely honest.

We had studied together.

Dear Maestro

A handshake

Your
Arrigo Boito

NOTES

1. Postmark: MILANO 25/3/90.
2. The dates of this well-known physician, who also treated the Verdis, and those of his colleagues in Milan are no longer on record.
3. Richard Freiherr von Krafft-Ebing (1840–1902), distinguished psychiatrist and pioneering sexologist, taught in Strassburg, Graz, and Vienna, and was a teacher of Sigmund Freud.
4. The French neurologist Jean Martin Charcot (1825–93), at whose Salpêtrière hospital in Paris Krafft-Ebing studied, as did Sigmund Freud.
5. The conductor Alcèo Pantaleoni (1839–1923).
6. Probably Romeo Orsi (1843–1918), first clarinetist of La Scala and inventor of the bass clarinet in A for *Otello*. (*Carteggio* ii, p. 394.)
7. Ermellina Dandolo was born into a family of patriotic martyrs. Boito and his friend the writer Emilio Praga (1839–75) had frequented her salon.

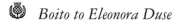 *Boito to Eleonora Duse*

[Milan, 29 March 1890]

Saturday   around evening

[P.S.] I am leaving tomorrow night.———[1]

Try to get rid of all business—I'll arrive at noon. We shall see each other at the hour you wish. I'll leave a note for you.

NOTE

1. For Barcelona.

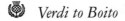 *Verdi to Boito*

Genoa, 31 March 1890

Dear Boito,

Thank you for the news you give me about the health of our poor friend! It's not the sort I would have wished, but I know that, unfortunately, it expresses the truth! Of course, I never had such close relations with him as you; yet the misfortune of this outstanding artist, this most honest man, grieves me deeply! Strange things! And they will know it at La Scala later on.

Let us hope, let us hope; and don't hesitate to let me know about it from time to time.

You spoke of Parma! If you have written already, never mind; but not to write is perhaps better. To [Signora] Pantaleoni, who was of the same opinion, I said that, better than we, she could, informally, write either to Count Sanvitale[1] or to the mayor.[2] I think she has done so.

I greet you in Peppina's name and cordially shake your hands.

Your
G. Verdi

NOTES

1. Stefano Sanvitale (1838–1914), President of the Commission of the Teatro Regio in Parma. (*Carteggio* ii, p. 394.)
2. Giovanni Mariotti (1850–1935), historian and politician, member of parliament, senator and mayor of Parma from 1889 to 1914.

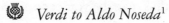 *Verdi to Aldo Noseda*[1]

Genoa, 1 April 1890

Dear Signor Noseda,

I have never been so tenderly attached to my things as to keep them in my portfolio to fondle and admire!— Everything I have done has been published.

But .... I correct myself! .... About 60 years ago, before I came to Milan, I composed some choruses from Manzoni's tragedies[2] and the *Cinque Maggio*.[3] (They shall never see the light.) Then, lately, I set a few notes to a *distorted bass* which I found in the *Gazzetta Musicale.*[4] Nothing worth mentioning.

It's Easter, and I thought to make a general confession. I have no other sins in my portfolio!

I am happy along with you, Signor President, about the Orchestral Society, to which I wish the very best of luck.

Yours as ever,

G. Verdi

NOTES

1. Aldo Noseda (1852–1916), under the pen name *Il Misovulgo* [The enemy of the vulgar] was for many years music critic of *Il corriere della sera* in Milan. He was president of the *Società Orchestrale* of La Scala.

2. Three choruses (about 1840).

3. Ode on the death of Napoleon Bonaparte (1836) to words by Alessandro Manzoni (1785–1873).

4. Verdi to Boito, 6 March 1889, and Boito to Verdi, 7 March 1889. (*Otello* ii, pp. 366–7.)

 *Ricordi to Verdi*

Milan, 3 April 1890

Illustrious Maestro,

I have been too long without your news, and now I am asking for the most ardent pleasure of receiving an excellent report. These last weeks I have been in over my head with work, and, unfortunately, always with . . . . . attorneys! [. . .]

This morning I was glad to hear that Signora Stolz has taken an apartment near our own; so there is a congenial neighbor.

I send you best wishes for the Easter holidays, feasts of peace, of calm, of colors and hopes; and thus may the year continue for both of you, always pleasant and serene. [. . .]

 *Boito to Verdi*

Monday. [7 April 1890]
Milan[1]

Dear Maestro,

I should tell you so many things, but time is pressing and the letter will

1890

be short.— Poor Faccio returns to Milan tomorrow morning. The doctor in Gratz did not want to admit him to his establishment and has advised taking him back to Milan and placing him in an asylum.— In the last few days he has gotten worse.

Here I am again on the *via crucis* of doctors and attorneys for him. Still I am glad that he is returning to us.

It is not true at all that his sister[2] has come to Milan. At Faccio's home I was assured that she had not been seen, even for an hour. His home is exactly the same today as it was when he left. So much the better. Our suspicions were exaggerated. Dina, with whom I spoke yesterday, offers his full support. Regarding material interests, nothing is to be feared any more.

Let's talk about something else.— Last night I heard *Don Pasquale.* — All right. I seem to have recognized a good Ford and a good merry wife in the one who sang the part of Norina.—The bass[3] has a nice voice, sound, solid and young. This individual seems intelligent; he will have to rid himself of the old traditions of Italian *buffos* that go well in *Don Pasquale* but for Ford would be a curse.—

And now I ask you for a favor: Today or tomorrow a certain Signor Rouillé-Déstranges[4] will arrive in Genoa; he is a Frenchman, but one of the good ones, who gave me examples of the most selfless cordiality when *Mefistofele* was given in Nantes.[5] I don't know him personally, but only through letters; and through his letters I became aware of the man's quality. This gentleman fervently desires to know you, that is, to be admitted for a few minutes to the drawing room of Palazzo Doria.

By now a hundred persons must have asked me for this favor; I have denied them all. But I don't have the heart to deny this good Frenchman. He has nothing to request, he only wishes to offer his respects to you; I don't know whether he is a musician, but I know that he thoroughly and fully understands matters of art.— Please let me know either by a telegram or a card if you will allow me to inform Signor Rouillé-Déstranges that the favor he requests is granted.— In this case I would wire the good news to the Hôtel de la Ville (where he will be staying today or tomorrow).— I think he will remain in Genoa for a few days.—

Many good greetings to Signora Giuseppina.

An affectionate handshake.

Arrigo Boito

NOTES

1. Postmark: MILANO 7/4/90.
2. See Boito to Verdi, 16 March, n. 2.

3. Boito seems to refer to the baritone part of Malatesta.

4. The music critic Etienne Déstranges (1863–1915). He wrote, *inter alia*, *L'évolution musicale chez Verdi: Aida, Othéllo, Falstaff* (Paris: Fischbacher, 1895).

5. In late April 1887.

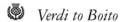 *Verdi to Boito*

Genoa, 8 March 1889 [8 April 1890][1]

Dear Boito,

Unfortunately, my forebodings have not deceived me! The refusal in Gratz, I think, is grave! It's a condemnation! . . .

Poor friend! So good and so honest! . . .

Just send the Frenchman when you wish.[2]

Addio, addio.

Affectionately,
G. Verdi

NOTES

1. Verdi confused the date of this answer to Boito's preceding letter.

2. Verdi granted a most lively interview to Etienne Déstranges, who published it in *Consonnances et dissonances. Études musicales.* (Paris: Fischbacher, 1906). See *Carteggio* ii, pp. 395–8; also Conati, pp. 212–18.

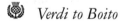 *Verdi to Boito*

[Telegram]   Genoa, 10 April 1890

ARRIGO BOITO

PRINCIPE AMEDEO I — MILAN

THINK I SHOULD INFORM YOU THAT SATURDAY I LEAVE FOR S. AGATA FOR THREE OR FOUR DAYS

VERDI

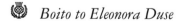 *Boito to Eleonora Duse*

[Milan, 10 April 1890]
Thursday

Lenor—If you knew in what grief and what horror I am living, you would spare me your angry words and your suspicions.[1]

1890

My sick friend has returned,[2] in worse shape.— There is no more hope. It's frightful to see him. I am spending my days, all my hours, at his side. He came back two days ago. Down there, where he had hoped to be cured, they did not want him. There is no more hope for the poor one. It's a horrible thing. I will continue to be near him as much as I can; I hope to get used to this sacrifice. And you, love me well if you can, and not badly as you do.

Let's pray to God that He may always keep us in the clear light of reason. For goodness sake, for pity's sake, let's pray for this.

Any other punishment, never that of insanity. My Love, be good with me, if you can. I have given you all.

Good, Lenor, good.

Arrigo

NOTES

1. In a missing letter.
2. From Graz.

 Eleonora Duse to Boito

[Madrid, 14 April 1890]
Monday—14th 1 P.M.

Arrigo! Poor Arrigo! Since yesterday I have had your letter and wanted to write you at once, and I couldn't; and I am still feeling the impact of your letter.

Poor Arrigo! I understand so well your grief for your poor friend! When one *loves,* really loves a friend, it's the best part of ourselves that lives in him!

And then, the poor man's illness is so terrible. It's better to die—Yes— and your poor friend perhaps no longer realizes that the *decisive moment* is still in his hand.

In less than a year,—there is———a friend you love—and for my part the complete loss of another person I loved so much![1]———

Yes! Let's hold each other tight! How *dangerous* is life!———

I don't know how to write you, Arrigo! But I put my arms around your neck.—I wish you calm and courage———You will need them———more than ever.——— I ask you to forgive me, to forgive me a thousand times, that I wrote you in anger the moment I arrived here.———The *few* hours in Barcelona had *estranged* me.———Too few hours!———Now I have gotten over it—and go ahead!

May God help you and give you everything, everything that is good. [. . .]

NOTE

1. Matilde Acton, who committed suicide in July 1889. (Weaver, p. 79.)

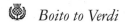 *Boito to Verdi*

[Milan] 15 April [1890][1]

Dear Maestro,

Our poor friend is lost. There is no further hope of saving him.

It is better to die.

I spare you the details of his condition, so as not to renew our grief by talking of them.

The papers, in their impatient impudence, have reported the whole misfortune, although I had entreated them to be silent.

In a few days we shall transport him to a house in the country, very well chosen near Monza, isolated and tranquil.[2] We hope that he may remain there until the end, and that the end may come soon. He will be very well attended by his good and skillful maid, also by a skillful man who is attending him very well at this time, and by an honest and very efficient male nurse.

Yesterday the governor of the Conservatory of Parma came to the home of the sick man to talk with me. I did not hide the truth from him. Meanwhile, his [Faccio's] stipend is accumulating in Parma, and in order to take advantage of it, he must sign a paper. I don't know if he will be able to sign it. I am awaiting the return of the attorney Dina, who is away, in order to arrange a family council to proceed to a declaration of incompetence, now inevitable, and to elect a guardian for him.

Our poor friend has safely invested his two hundred thousand Lire, the sacred fruit of ceaseless work throughout his life and conscientious saving!—The irony of human providence!

I thank you, dear Maestro, for the telegram you sent me to let me know of your departure for S. Agata. I think this letter will find you in Genoa. I also thank you for kindly having received the person I commended to you.[3]

Many good, most affectionate greetings to you and the good Signora Giuseppina.

Most cordially your
Arrigo Boito

NOTES

1. Postmark: MILANO 15/4/90.

1890

2. The nursing home Villa dei Boschetti, about half an hour by train from Milan.

3. Etienne Déstranges (Boito to Verdi, 7 April).

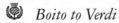 *Verdi to Boito*

Thursday [Genoa, 17 April 1890][1]

Dear Boito,

Upon my arrival[2] last night I found your letter.

Unfortunately, any word is useless by now.

It is better to die!

About the Parma business, I suppose, there is something to say. It's a rather delicate matter. We'll talk about it soon in person when I come to Milan.

Addio. I greet you from Peppina and take your hands.

Cordially,
G. Verdi

NOTES

1. Postmark: GENOVA 17/4/90.
2. From St. Agata. (See Verdi to Boito, 10 April.)

Boito to Verdi

Friday [Milan, 18 April 1890][1]

Dear Maestro,

In Faccio's name and for Faccio I have accepted from the governor of the Conservatory of Parma only that part of his check which represents the stipend from the Ministry, and I have refused the one which represents the stipend from the City of Parma. I have done this after having repeatedly assured myself that the money I accepted for my friend was rightfully his own; and I was urged to accept it by the insistence of the governor of the Conservatory. It is a stipend for three semesters, that is, one and a half thousand Lire accumulated from the Ministry in the Conservatory's fund.

Have I done right or wrong? If I have done wrong, let me know; there is still time for a remedy.

Affectionate greetings

from your
most affectionate
Arrigo

P.S. I hear that the *Lombardia*[2] has taken from a paper in Parma[3] an answer of mine to the governor of the Conservatory, in which there is a word of hope for the health of our friend. I advise you that my reply was in an official capacity and that, therefore, I did not intend to let the whole truth be known.

I told the governor the whole truth when I saw him and also encouraged him to go to Dr. De Vincenti to find out more exactly about Faccio's illness by consulting the doctor in charge.[4]

NOTES

1. Postmark: MILANO 18/4/90.
2. A newspaper in Milan.
3. *La Gazzetta di Parma* of 17 April.
4. In his letter to Verdi of 25 March, Boito mentioned Dr. Levis as the doctor in charge and Dr. De Vincenti as a specialist.

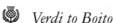 *Verdi to Boito*

Genoa, 20 April 1890

Dear Boito,

It is an opinion of mine! Nothing else . . .— It seems to me that poor Faccio is no longer entitled to the stipend in Parma. As long as the doctors had not pronounced that tremendous sentence, he, as the appointed director, although not in office, could *request*; but not now, it seems to me. I do not speak of rights; it is a delicate matter, and besides, I repeat, it's only my opinion.

I have seen your letter! But, my dear Boito, in the future speak in your own name and leave out the family, the principal, if not the only, cause of the great misfortune.—

Last night I went to *Orfeo.*[1] Har[2] . . . (Orfeo) has talent; uneven voice with twenty registers; and without *charme*. The second act is truly beautiful. While hearing it, I could not help confirming to myself that the Germans must remain Germans, and the Italians Italians. Even at the time when only melody was made in the theatre, or better said, melodic phrases, the German was more successful in instrumental music, despite the poverty of the orchestras at that time. In this same second act, the chorus of the demons and the dances are powerful; but the notes Orfeo sings as he accompanies himself with the lyre are deficient. He [Gluck] did not know how to find the calm, broad, and deeply felt melody that was needed. Instead, tormented and cold phrases based on modulations of that time.—

1890

'Til we see each other again soon in Milan we send our greetings.

Addio, addio.

G. Verdi

I haven't finished.

I told you about the talk I had with Maurel![3] Well then, he didn't waste time; he addressed himself to *Coquelin*,[4] who immediately sent him a sketch of an opera taken from . . . *Shakspeare* ! When I read this name in his letter, I had an attack of the shivers!— Fortunately, it didn't deal with *Falstaff* . . . The very extensive sketch is taken from *The Taming of the Shrew*. — It's not done badly; they have omitted the prologue and given important parts to *Catherine* and *Petrucchio*, that is, to the tamed and the tamer.— It's no equal to *Falstaff*; I wouldn't dream of it.

Excuse the long letter.

NOTES

1. Gluck's *Orfeo ed Euridice* at the Teatro Carlo Fenice in Genoa.

2. The American mezzo-soprano Helene (Elena) Hastreiter (1858–1922), from Louisville, Kentucky.

3. We do not know when and where this talk occurred and on what occasion Verdi told Boito about it.

4. Either to the famous French actor Constant-Benoît Coquelin (1841–1909) or to his brother, the actor Ernest-Alexandre-Honoré (1848–1909).

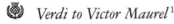 *Verdi to Victor Maurel*[1]

Genoa, 21 April 1890[2]

My dear Maurel,

I have read the manuscript you sent me. Superb! It's taken from a Shakespeare comedy: *La Megère apprivoisée* [*The Taming of the Shrew*],[3] omitting the prologue, out of which a little act could also be made. The French poet[4] has ably reduced it. It is most amusing. It's a real Italian *opera buffa*. Lucky the musician who will put his hand to it! But this comedy would call for the composers of the end of the last century, or of the beginning of ours: Cimarosa, Rossini, Donizetti, etc., etc. Today's composers are too harmonically and orchestrally oriented—excuse the expression—and don't have the heroic courage to *s'effacer* [keep in the background] when necessary, and even more, not to make music when it isn't necessary. Today they make harmonies and orchestral sonorities above all and—with great exceptions— forget the right accent, the sculpture of the characters, and the power of true dramatic situations. As to myself, all I can tell you is: alas, too late! . . . I return the manuscript to you.

Thank you.

G. Verdi

NOTES

1. Verdi probably wrote this letter in French, like others he addressed to Maurel, but Gino Monaldi gives it in Italian, p. 188.
2. See Verdi's preceding letter to Boito of 20 April, n. 3.
3. Obviously Maurel imagined himself in the leading role of Petrucchio.
4. Anonymous.

 *Boito to Eleonora Duse*

[Milan, 1 May 1890]
May   nine o'clock in the morning

[. . .] It's raining, the city is quiet,[1] cold and all wet. I'll stay home all day; I am tempted to light the stove, what joy! [. . .]

The one of the Latin inscription is in Milan. I am reassembling my life as best as I can. I leave the city only twice a week[2] and return in the evening.

[. . .]

NOTES

1. In spite of the usual May Day demonstrations.
2. To visit Faccio.

 *Verdi to Giuseppe De Amicis*

St. Agata, 8 May 1890

Dear De Amicis,

The offer of the House of Érard[1] is certainly kind and gracious, and I am most grateful for it. But I would really have preferred to pay for the job; for this reason I did not want to write them directly and asked Maestro Bossola[2] to do so in my behalf. Now that it's done, I can only thank the House of Érard for all its kindness. . . There is an additional problem, however, in that I have another piano here at St. Agata that is even more in need of repair than the one in Genoa, . . . and now I would no longer have the courage to send it to Paris! Never, never!! So much the worse! It will be a further nuisance I'll be forced to cause Maestro Bossola, who will have this piano adjusted as well as can be by any old tuner, by a carpenter, a bricklayer, etc., etc. . . . by whomever he wants. [. . .]

With my thanks to Bossola, I beg you both to forgive me for everything, and I shake your hands.

Affectionately,
G. Verdi

P.S. We have been here for four days, and we are working, or rather everyone is working but me, to put a lot of things in order.

Peppina sends you many, many regards.

NOTES

1. Founded by the French piano and harp manufacturer Sébastien Érard (1752–1831), the Paris firm enjoyed the highest worldwide reputation. They offered to repair, without charge, the piano in Verdi's apartment in Genoa.

2. Giuseppe Bossola, a musician and helpful acquaintance of Verdi in Genoa.

 *Ricordi to Verdi*

Milan, 9 May 1890

Illustrious Maestro,

The moment I received your letter,[1] I gave the *Pungolo* your new address; please let me know if the paper arrives now as it should. Otherwise I will repeat the order a hundred times. [. . .]

I have taken note of the dimensions of the billiard table, and am now awaiting your instructions to inform Della Chiesa[2] when the workman should come, at a time that is convenient for you.

We are very happy about your excellent news. In our thoughts we follow you on your morning walks in the fields and the beautiful verdant garden; and we see Signora Peppina very busy with the peacocks and ducks . . . . . . and I assure you that we are longing for as much peace and tranquillity!!

[. . .]

NOTES

1. Missing.
2. Billiard firm in Milan.

 *Boito to Eleonora Duse*

[Milan, 10 May 1890]
Saturday

[. . .] In about ten days I'll make an excursion to Parma to take care of business for my poor friend; I must stay in that city for three or four days. I'll wire you from Milan three days before I leave [. . .] .

I have so much studying and work to do, and also so much worry about other people's business, that the days go by in a flash. [. . .]

Boito to Verdi

[Milan] 21 May [1890]

Dear Maestro,

The day before yesterday I was hit with a bolt out of the blue by a letter from Commendatore Mariotti announcing my nomination (already signed by the King) as honorary director of the Conservatory of Parma. Who would have expected anything like it?— I bowed my head under the blow. He who bows his head says yes. I accepted. Mariotti explains to me in his letter how things transpired.— That distinguished and most amiable Mariotti is a torrent, not a man; his impulse conquers everything.— Well then, the sudden deed was done like this:

It seems that there were renewed pressures in Parma to appoint that Neapolitan maestro you know.[1] At the first sign of this threat Mariotti departed for Rome and persuaded the minister to add to the statutes of the Conservatory of Parma an article allowing for an honorary director; he pronounced my name, had the decree extended, and informed me when all was done.— Besides, I had already planned to pay a cautious visit to that institute, but I realize that this appointment will oblige me to pay more than one, and thus every once in a while, to somehow stand in for poor Faccio; his stipend (and also on this point the good Mariotti was impetuous and deaf) will be continued.— In the meantime, the threat of the Neapolitan maestro has been averted.

I'll be in Parma on Monday; and before next week (that is, the coming week) is over, I'll spend a day at St. Agata on my return from the visit to the Conservatory.

Well then, dear Maestro, 'til we see each other again soon; prepare something new for me to hear, something new from the enormous Potbelly!

By the way, the necessary variant in the final fugue is still missing. See if the one I'm transcribing on the back of this letter will do.

Tutto nel mondo è burla	[Everything in the world is a jest.
L'uom è nato burlone.	Man is born a jester.
Nel suo cervello ciurla	In his mind, his reason
Sempre la sua ragione.	Is wavering always.
Tutti gabbati! Irride	All mocked! All mortals
L'un l'altro ogni mortal,	Taunt one another,
Ma ride ben chi ride	But he laughs well who has
La risata final.	The last laugh.}

Affectionate greetings to Signora Giuseppina and to you. Till we see each other again; I shall wire you on which day I will arrive.[2] Where must I get off: Fiorenzuola? Alseno?

> Your most affectionate
> Arrigo Boito

P.S. Look at the humbug in the papers: The *Tribuna* in Rome says that *you* had repeatedly offered me the direction of the Conservatory of Parma, and that I refused.

Those journalists cannot write anything correctly.

But the *Perseveranza*, which is an enlightened paper, has sent me now (at this moment) the news already prepared, from the *Tribuna*, so that I could check it. I have deleted the error again in the proofs. Once more

> Your most affectionate
> Arrigo Boito

NOTES

1. Paolo Serrao (1830–1907), composer and conductor, had been a professor at the Conservatory of Naples since 1863. On 30 March 1873 he conducted that city's first *Aida* at the Teatro San Carlo under Verdi's direction.

2. No such telegram has been located.

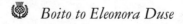 *Boito to Eleonora Duse*

> [Milan, 22 May 1890]
> 22 May Thursday

The papers blow everything up. If one of these days you should happen to see a piece of news regarding me, I want you to know that this news is incorrect, not false but incorrect.— The reader may think that I would have to move my home elsewhere to assume a task which would tie up my time and my freedom.— Never——

I have taken it upon myself to provide (by name rather than in actuality)[1] for the poor friend, and I have done this to save him money, because in his condition life at that villa[2] is extremely expensive.— But this task is accomplished by the very few excursions I will undertake to the place where he would have been active.[3]

I leave on Monday, will be away from home for five days, and will return to the white street[4] by the end of next week. Perhaps I will (if I want to) make another short excursion there next month. You see that this matter amounts to very little time.

The very first day of July (this is certain) you will see me on the mountain.[5] [. . .]

NOTES

    1. I.e., in name only. (See Boito to Verdi, 21 May.)
    2. Villa dei Boschetti, a nursing home near Monza.
    3. The Parma Conservatory.
    4. His home in Via Principe Amedeo 1 in Milan.
    5. At San Giuseppe in Piedmont.

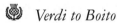 *Verdi to Boito*

St. Agata, 23 May 1890

Dear Boito,

You have done very well! You will help art and our poor friend, and you have prevented something bad at the institution. About your initial refusal, let the papers say all the humbug they want. It's their business and, besides, it's of no importance.

As to the Potbelly, oh dear, oh dear! I haven't done a thing!! . . . *"L'uom è nato poltrone"* [Man is born lazy][1] except for a few periods and commas added or changed in what had already been done. But we will talk about it in person at St. Agata.

The most convenient train from Parma is the one leaving at *12* and arriving at Alseno[2] at *12:56*. The trip is a bit longer by train, but you save about half an hour of coach [to St. Agata]. Write or wire me the day before you come to St. Agata, so you will find the coach at *1:56*[3] at the station in Alseno.—

1890

Addio, addio . . . No, no *sans adieu.*
'Til we see each other again!

Affectionately,
G. Verdi

Peppina has just entered my room and wants me to greet you. Amen.

NOTES

1. A play on the text of the final fugue in Boito's letter of 21 May.
2. Small railway station between Fidenza and Piacenza.
3. Verdi no doubt meant 12:56.

Boito to Eleonora Duse

[Milan, 24 May 1890]
24.

[. . .] Yesterday I wired you that I postponed the departure and short stay[1] to Wednesday. I'll be gone until Sunday, will then be home. [. . .]

NOTE

1. In Parma.

Ricordi to Verdi

[Milan], 25 May 1890

Illustrious Maestro,

Yesterday morning I received your esteemed letter and regret, to my greatest embarrassment, that yesterday I was unable to go to Chiesa. The other night at 11 I was informed that the King would visit our establishment at Porta Vittoria! . . . So I had to work from 6:30 in the morning until 2 P.M., and then accompany the King until . . . . . then . . . . dead tired I went home. Today and tomorrow are holidays; first thing Tuesday morning I'll go to Chiesa and wire you the date of the workman's arrival.— And now, Maestro, forgive my truly unintentional negligence. It was my fault to be too sure of my strength, when I planned to carry out your errand after the King's visit. He is a very good man and an able politician; you should have seen him talking with the workers, who gave him an enthusiastic ovation when he left.—

As I write, I receive another esteemed letter of yours with the bill;[1] I am turning it over to the bookkeepers. It will certainly be all right, and I thank you for your kind attention.

You exclaim: Oh! . . the attorneys . . . the composers! . . and with good reason . . . . . . Oh! what an ugly business this has become! I find myself in a real and very grave *moral* depression. Wouldn't it be better, Maestro, to side with the enormous mass of *rogues* . . . . who are the masters today? . . . I am really asking myself what honesty is worth at this time . . . . . . and if it's of any use? [. . .]

NOTE

1. Unknown.

 Boito to Eleonora Duse

[Milan, 26 May 1890]
Monday

[. . .] Today I am yet again sending you a short sign of life, before leaving for the country,[1] where I'll spend the day, returning in the evening. If I don't go there, no one does. Abandonment takes over quickly in great misfortunes. People come in crowds the first day for painful curiosity's sake, then fade away.

My Love—Be blessed by all my thoughts. Work, earn, and run away. Art isn't worth a tear. It is the great enemy of life. [. . .]

NOTE

1. To visit Franco Faccio.

 Boito to Eleonora Duse

[Milan, 3 June 1890]
—3 June—

Bumba—Last night I returned.[1] [. . .] After the Croce Bianca[2] I spent two days in that house in the country which little Lenor had seen. I spent these days so well, in such complete peace, that it felt painful to leave. [. . .]

NOTES

1. From Parma and St. Agata.
2. Hotel in Parma.

1890

 Ricordi to Verdi

Milan, 3 June 1890

Illustrious Maestro,

I am returning the account you kindly sent me; all goes well, and we have taken note that in the future the half-yearly tax for the loan[1] will amount to 681.50 Lire, and I conclude with warmest thanks. [. . .]

Has the billiard table been repaired? [. . .]

NOTE

1. See Verdi to Tornaghi and Ricordi, 24 August 1889.

 Giuseppe De Amicis to Verdi

Genoa, 7 June 1890

Dear Maestro,

At the end of May the piano was sent to Paris,[1] after the necessary documents had been obtained to avoid problems entering and leaving the respective frontiers. [. . .] Since the matter is not urgent, the transport is being handled at slow speed, in order to economize.

Everything possible was done for the good outcome of these operations under Bossola's particular care.

Here there is nothing new, while the time of my usual trip to Montecatini is approaching. I shall wait to hear from you when I should leave.

Addio from the heart.

Your most affectionate
Giuseppe De Amicis

NOTE

1. Cf. Verdi to De Amicis, 8 May.

 Giuseppe De Amicis to Giuseppina Verdi

Genoa, 7 June 1890

Dear, good Signora Peppina,

From your kind letter[1] I learned with pleasure your good news, except about your dental trouble, which was passing, I hope, since in that respect you are still among the fortunate ones. [. . .]

Matters in Africa continue to look rather unfavorable [. . .].[2]
Everything is in good shape in your apartment [. . .].

Your most affectionate
Giuseppe De Amicis

NOTES

1. Missing.
2. Italy's protectorate of Abyssinia had suffered a military setback when the natives rebelled.

 *Boito to Eleonora Duse*

[Milan, 9 June 1890]
ninth day

[. . .] I wrote you on the sixth, that I had quietly and calmly gotten back to my work.[1]

Had I never said it.

The next day a disaster came crashing upon my shoulders. For two days now I have been running to doctors and lawyers on behalf of the poor friend. But this time everything will be settled for his estate, and I'll find peace again. I have led a dog's life these months. [. . .]

NOTE

1. Presumably *Nerone*.

 *Ricordi to Verdi*

Milan, 10 June 1890

Illustrious Maestro,

On your instruction I have paid the billiard man the amount of 200 Lire. You will find the bill with the usual semiannual papers.

You cannot believe the tempest of questions, letters, and even telegrams that silly Mascagni anecdote[1] has caused!! However, I had the great pleasure that almost no one believed you!—But . . . at what point have we now arrived, and what decline of moral standards do we experience every day!! I am absolutely terrified . . . and I understand that this era is no longer mine. This upsets me greatly, as I reflect upon the enormous responsibility entrusted to me, upon which my own and my family's future will ultimately depend. It is really frightening to watch this slime rising more each day, to read this filthy publicity bought for so much per line, and to realize that instead of gentlemen there are trained gangsters all over. I cannot say that I am dissatisfied with the business, despite the strenuous and difficult times for commerce and industry; but how to resist the flood of swindle and dishonesty?. . . Can one go ahead on a . . . . straight and honest road? I for one would be unable to resort to subterfuges and shady transactions . . . . . and do I take good care of the future this way, or do I make it an even more difficult one?. . . *To be, or not to be* . . is always the arduous question . . . . . and I feel absolutely nauseated! . .

Forgive me, illustrious Maestro, for boring you with these lamentations . . . but I am in one of those moments of moral and physical fatigue, which make others feel gloomy, too. Just send me to the devil, and even to hell if you want . . . . . and let's talk about it no more.

The King's visit has given me great pleasure; his kindness with everyone, including the workers, was without parallel; it seemed that he was really very interested, since even third parties confirmed to me that among all the establishments the King has visited, ours impressed him the most favorably for its cleanliness and the arrangement of the premises. [. . .]

I am happy about the good news concerning your health. . . You mention only one illness . . . old age!!! . . . Blessed be your old age; let most of *us*, who are moral and physical failures, talk the way you do!!!

[. . .] I pass over the *idiotic irreverence* of the Mascagni story!!. . One has to be a real animal! (Excuse me!) [. . .]

NOTE

1. Unknown. Pietro Mascagni's (1863–1945) *Cavalleria rusticana* had been premiered in Rome on 17 May.

 *Boito to Eleonora Duse*

[Milan, 11 June 1890]
Eleventh day of June

[. . .] The next time you write *manana* watch out that you write it as I did.[1]
I love you.

Well then, you had sworn never to go back to *los toros*, and you went back. And this second time you left the circus enthusiastically, full of admiration, glad to have been there and vowing to return. Isn't it so?—It is so. But you won't go back. One of the first sweet, sweet impressions I had of your hand was when I saw it caressing the good long, gentle, suffering snout of a cabby's horse.—Poor animals! They drag their load until they die; like us under a burden. But in that cruel Spain eager and anxious for pain, they find an even more horrible death. They die disemboweled, smelling the imminence of horror, bandaged, dragging their bowels before the mob. Poor animals. And this to excite a bull (who without that slaughter would quietly return to his stable) and to tire him enough to be mocked by a man, almost all the time without endangering the man.—Who, if it were not like this, would run through half a dozen *espadas* [swords] for each horn, like little birds on a spit.

I don't know of a more degrading spectacle than a glittering, hopping dancer triumphant in the semblance of courage over a stupid, tired beast. [. . .]

NOTE

1. *Mañana.*

 *Boito to Eleonora Duse*

[Milan, 15 June 1890]
[. . .] I had a lot of worries and business not my own.[1] Now I'll have a few days of respite. Toward the end of the month there is still going to be some difficulty, and then all will be in order.

NOTE

1. Concerning Faccio.

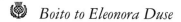 *Boito to Eleonora Duse*

[Milan, 25 June 1890]
25 Monday [Wednesday][1]
[. . .] I decided to leave for Parma tomorrow night to travel when it is cool. I'll arrive at midnight; the trip is short, I'll go to the Hôtel I mentioned to you. I'll come home Monday at the latest, will spend a day where you wrote me last autumn.[2] [. . .]

NOTES

1. 25 June 1890 was a Wednesday.
2. At St. Agata. However, the Verdis were on their way to Montecatini at that time.

1890

🏵 *Verdi to Emanuele Muzio*

Milan, 30 June 1890

Dear Eman. Muzio,

What do you want me to say?![1] I am thunderstruck, and it seems impossible that what you tell me has really happened!

Unfortunately, it is true that when one has to deal with cheats (and such smart ones!), it's almost impossible not to be duped: I, who am so very reluctant to be concerned with numbers. Because of this reluctance I never looked at Escudier's accounts [. . .].[2]

I want all of it to be arranged without courts and attorneys, and if M. Roger should intervene, he would do me a real favor.

Addio. I am leaving for Montecatini.

Greetings

Your
G. Verdi

NOTES

1. In answer to a missing letter about the Bénoit affair.
2. Here follows a lengthy and detailed account concerning French translations and royalties involving *Il Trovatore*.

🏵 *Ricordi to Verdi*

Milan, 5 July 1890

Illustrious Maestro,

[The existence of] magnetic current can really not be denied!!—I was just at my desk, with pen in hand to write you, hoping for your news. . . . and here comes the delivery man with the mail, and immediately I have the pleasure of discovering your handwriting and reading your good news.[1] [. . .]

Our health isn't bad; the two boys[2] are always busy with their exams, and my wife does vocal gymnastics from morning to night to make them study. I do gymnastics of patience . . . . and philosophy in the midst of tedious business, while musical art is killing itself with the most cynical and vulgar triviality. Going on like this . . . . . I see myself walking the streets with a hurdy-gurdy! . . . . and . . . . long live Italy!! [. . .]

NOTES

1. Missing..
2. Tito and Manolo.

Verdi to Teresa Stolz[1]

St. Agata, 12 August 1890

Together with this letter you will receive by rail a box containing two *spallette*[2] San Secondo style; we are sending one for you and one for the Ricordi family. Choose the one you want. Mind you, to cook the *spalletta* well, you must:

1. Put it in lukewarm water for about 12 hours to remove the salt.[3]

2. Then put it in cold water and boil over a slow fire, not letting it boil over, for about 3 and a half hours, perhaps 4 for a larger one. To test if it is done, prick the *spalletta* with a toothpick and, if it enters easily, the *spalletta* is cooked.

3. Cool and serve it in its own broth. Pay attention above all to the cooking; if it's hard, it's not good, if it's cooked too much, it becomes dry and chewy.[. . .]

NOTES

1. The Bohemian soprano (1834–1902) appeared under Verdi's direction in the European première of *Aida* (1872) and the *Requiem*. She became his intimate friend and companion until his death. (See Biographical Sketch.)

2. *Spallette di maiale* [pork shoulders].

3. Obviously the pork shoulders had been cured in salt, like a ham.

Ricordi to Verdi

Milan, 22 August 1890

Illustrious Maestro,

Really . . . . you are most successful in everything! . . . . even in the little pork shoulders. I am pleased to inform you that yesterday it was solemnly introduced amid general enthusiasm! . . . And the *bis* [second helpings] were innumerable!— To tell the truth, I found the bill rather . . . . high; *mais à tout Seigneur, tout honneur!* [but honor to whom honor is due!]. In view of the exquisite quality of the piglet roast I didn't want to bargain for a lira more or less!! . . . .

So I paid the bill at once as per the enclosed receipt!—[1]

Nevertheless, I repeat my warmest thanks for the consignment.

Yours most respectfully and devotedly,
Giulio Ricordi

NOTE

1. Jokingly, Ricordi filled out a pretend bill he had had printed, addressing it to himself in the amount of 100,000 Lire received by G. Verdi.

🏵 *Verdi to Giuseppe Piroli*

St. Agata, 31 August 1890

[. . .] Excellent, excellent![1] Alseno is all right. We assume you will arrive at Alseno at 8:33 in the morning. Send me a telegram the day before, and you will find the usual coach at the station. [. . .]

NOTE

1. In answer to a letter or telegram announcing Piroli's visit to St. Agata.

🏵 *Verdi to Giuseppe Piroli*

St. Agata, 6 September 1890

[. . .] Although both of us are saddened by your decision, we must resign ourselves to the disappointment of not seeing you here, since your health is at stake and you must regain the strength you have lost. We ardently hope to see you in Genoa, flourishing and perfectly recovered. But allow me to tell you again that you have worked, and are probably still working, too hard. I, too, understand this conscientious devotion to duty; but the moment you had to take a coach to go to and from the Council, you could have in good faith stayed at home.

Muzio has been sick for some days (not the heart, but the liver), and quite seriously. Yesterday he wrote me that he feels better,[1] with three doctors around! I say three! . . . Even if the illness is not grave, it will certainly become so.

Give me frequent news, and console me by saying *"I am perfectly fine!"* [. . .]

NOTE

1. The letter is missing.

Boito to Eleonora Duse

[Milan, 11 September 1890]
Wednesday evening[1]

[. . .] Tomorrow I will be in the house of other people, in the same house as last year.[2] I know you don't like it. What to do? [. . .]

The first of October (in twenty days) I'll go up again to the mountain, will open our house and stay there the whole month, and for a while in November, too. [. . .]

You are my little one—Yes—I feel you close to me—I feel you as part of myself. We shall conquer everything—and the promised days will come. [. . .]

NOTES

1. 11 September 1890 was a Thursday.
2. As the guest of Donna Vittoria Cima at Villa d'Este.

Verdi to Giacomo Persico[1]

St. Agata, 11 September 1890

Esteemed Mr. Mayor,

Thank you for the interest you are taking in matters that are very close to my heart and, at the moment, causing me rather grave worries.[2] But after serious and sound deliberations, I don't think it advisable to make overly radical decisions. Perhaps it must come to that later on, but for now, I repeat, it does not seem advisable to me.

I thank you again and remain

Sincerely yours,
G. Verdi

NOTES

1. The new mayor of Villanova, who was following the internal conflicts at the Villanova Hospital involving the doctor Giuseppe Torre, the parish priest Don Luigi Mari, the nuns, and Salvatore Boriani, "who, although no longer mayor, was still the president. Hoping Boriani would resign, Verdi adopted a wait-and-see attitude. [. . .] From 1890 on, Persico, to whom Verdi wrote more than 100 letters and notes, remained his trusted mediator and confidant in many of the crises that followed." (Phillips-Matz, pp. 693, 704–5.)

2. Not only "at the moment." (See Verdi to Piroli, 28 August 1889; also Verdi to Boriani, 16 January 1889, in *Otello* i, pp. 377–8; and *Carteggi* iv, pp. 296–307.)

1890

 *Verdi to Giuseppe De Amicis*

St. Agata, 27 September 1890

[. . .] When you see Maestro Bossola, please tell him that since winter is approaching, I ask that he write to Érard to send the piano so that I may find it upon my arrival in Genoa.[1]

As you know, according to the papers, I must write *half a dozen* operas. . . Well then . . . the piano, for God's sake!

We are getting older and still doing all right!

Greetings from Peppina.

Ad[dio] Ad. Ad.
G. Verdi

NOTE

1. See De Amicis to Verdi, 7 June.

Ricordi to Verdi

Milan, 28 September 1890

Illustrious Maestro,

It is impossible to be more ill-mannered than . . . . this humble writer!! . . . . After one of those dear, kind, unforgettable invitations that exist only in Villa Verdi . . . . to wait eight days after departing before sending a thank-you note! . . . This is a bit too much, isn't it? . . . And therefore I implore forgiveness from you, the most courteous of hosts.

Upon my return, I was obliged to leave again immediately; back in Milan, I find urgent need for transactions regarding property we are renting. This doesn't leave me a free minute! . . . . . And therefore? . . . Therefore I must appear as ill-mannered as all that.

But I have taken care of your request; I wrote to Paris for exact news about poor Muzio, and asked our agent to find the physician Vio Bonato and then write me. Last night I had a telegram saying no imminent danger, but condition critical; and now I am awaiting a letter. Pisa (our agent in Paris) has instructions to see to anything that might be needed, as if a member of the family were involved.

Your watch is already on the way;[1] I talked about the piano[2]—will write you in detail regarding this, and I will also write you about the *Cavalleria rusticana,* which I heard in Florence.[3] But today. . . . . today I am asking for forgiveness for my sins: I ask you, Maestro, and Signora Peppina to accept our thanks for the dear, lovely sojourn you let us enjoy at St. Agata! With repeated, infinite *thanks* I remain, full of boundless gratitude and devoted affection,

Your most devoted
Giulio Ricordi

Our cordial greetings to Signorina Barberina[4] and Signora Stolz. Gina and her kidnapper[5] will finally be back the day after tomorrow!

NOTES

1. Probably a watch Ricordi had taken along to Milan for repair.
2. See Verdi to De Amicis, 27 September.
3. No such letter appears to exist.
4. Barberina Strepponi (c. 1828–?), Giuseppina Verdi's younger, unmarried sister, was a gifted artist. Many of her sketches can be seen at the Museo del Seminario in Cremona. She tutored children in that city, a couple of hours by horse carriage from St. Agata across the River Po, but she spent much time with the Verdis at St. Agata. Although she was ailing throughout her life, apparently from tuberculosis, she outlived Verdi by some fifteen years.
5. Luigi Origoni, the husband of Ricordi's daughter Gina.

 *Ricordi to Verdi*

[Milan] 28 September 1890

Most illustrious Maestro,

In addition to my letter of this morning, I am transcribing what I received this very moment from Paris:

"I am terribly sad that I must give you rather bad news about Signor Maestro Muzio; as I already wired, there is no immediate danger. But it is to be feared that he will never again be able to return to Italy; his stomach and his legs have become very swollen. Yesterday, Dr. Vio Bonato consulted an important Parisian specialist. Their opinion is that the illness can last a month, a year, or forty-eight hours, according to the progression of the water toward the heart; but in any case it is incurable. For eight days Signor Muzio has been at S. Jean de Dieu; let us hope that the physicians may be wrong, as can occur even among the most eminent ones.

"I have sent the box that Signor Muzio handed over to me, packed with greatest care, to Signora Verdi."

If you have instructions to give me, it goes without saying that our representative in Paris is completely at your disposal.

I remain always most gratefully,

Your devoted
Giulio Ricordi

1890

 *Giuseppe De Amicis to Verdi*

[Genoa] 2 October 1890

Dearest Maestro,

Following your kind letter,[1] I went to see Maestro Bossola, who had heard from Érard about your piano and assured me that it would be returned to its place in your apartment before the end of this month.

Dear Maestro, on this occasion I would like to convey, in anticipation of your approaching birthday, the most fervent wishes for your good fortune that a heart could express with sincerest veneration and affection. I hope that I may be able to repeat these wishes to you as well as to the dear Signora Peppina for many years to come. [. . .]

NOTE

1. Of 27 September.

 *Boito to Eleonora Duse*

[Milan, 2 October 1890]
Thursday   White street

My Love—

I arrived this morning.[1] The poor friend's affairs keep me in the city all day long today and tomorrow.

I hope I can go up to the mountain the day after tomorrow; I'll know for sure in an hour, after I have attended a meeting. [. . .]

NOTE

1. From Villa d'Este.

 *Boito to Verdi*

3 October [1890]
Milan[1]

Dear Maestro,

It's been a century since I've had news from you or from Signora Giuseppina, and from Potbelly.

I will come to get it myself in a couple of weeks. I'll be at St. Agata on the 18th of this month; I'll arrive *from Parma* on the train that arrives at Alseno at *one o'clock and 59 minutes,* as I did the last time.[2]

Now I am staying in Milan for a couple of days because of poor Faccio, who is going from bad to worse. The day after tomorrow I'll return to *Ivrea* (San Giuseppe) where I shall stay until the twelfth of this month. Then I must go to Parma, and from Parma, as I said, I'll stop at St. Agata to breathe a bit of air and serene art.

This world is a heap of sadness; the condition of our friend is becoming graver all the time; his old father threatens to die; he is very sick. . .[3] Let's try to stay healthy, dear Maestro, as much as we can, and to forget life while we work.

'Til we see each other again on the eighteenth.

I shall send you a telegram from Parma to reconfirm.

Affectionate greetings to Signora Giuseppina and to you.

Your most affectionate

Arrigo Boito

NOTES

1. Postmark: MILANO 3/10/90.
2. See Verdi to Boito, 23 May 1890.
3. Franco Faccio's father, who also suffered from syphilitic dementia, was in the same nursing home, but father and son could no longer recognize each other. He survived his son. Romilda Pantaleoni visited her companion behind the doctors' backs and desperately resented not being allowed to assist him.

 *Verdi to Boito*

St. Agata, 6 October 1890

Dear Boito,

Heavenly! 'Til we see each other again, then, on the 18th, and we'll talk about lots of things!

I have worked little, but I have done something.

The sonnet in the third act tormented me; and to pull this thorn out of my flesh, I put the second act aside; and beginning with that sonnet, jotting down one note after another, I have come to the end.——

It's only a draft! And who knows how much will have to be redone! We'll see later on.[1]

Mondo ladro, Mondo rubaldo. Reo mondo! . . . [Thieving world. Rascally world. Evil world! . . .] He says!

I know it, and, unfortunately, I knew it thirty years before you.

That poor Faccio! Not a year has gone by since he came here,[2] and,

1890

walking in the garden late in the day, I spoke to him frank, sincere, and perhaps also somewhat harsh words, for which I now reproach myself. . .

Mondo ladro! . . . .

'Til we see each other again soon.

I greet you from Peppina and affectionately take your hands.

Your
G. Verdi

NOTES

1. See Barblan, "Spunti rivelatori nella genesi del *Falstaff*."
2. See Verdi to Ricordi, 17 August 1889.

 Emanuele Muzio to Verdi

[Paris, 22 October 1890][1]

My dearest Maestro and friend Verdi,

There is a little trouble with my will; please do as I say.[2] I shall soon depart for the other world, full of affection and friendship for you and for your good and dear wife. I have loved you both, and remember that ever since 1844 my faithful friendship has never diminished.

Remember me sometimes, and till we see each other again later on in the other world.

Many kisses from your faithful and affectionate friend

E. Muzio

NOTES

1. This date is based on two notes in *Copialettere*, pp. 359 and 361. (See *Otello* i, p. 375.)
2. Muzio had named Verdi the executor of his will.

 Verdi to Giuseppe Piroli

St. Agata, 24 October 1890

[. . .] First of all I am asking for news about your health, which concerns me the most.

Then, when you have time, please take a look at the papers I am enclosing.

The municipality of Villanova, together with those of Busseto and Castelvetro, would like me to contact the Ministry of Public Works to fulfil their request. But before causing a fiasco (fiascos in the theatre I tolerate with great serenity), I want to ask you whether it is possible or not.

In my opinion, based on common sense, the matter in question is just; because the community of Villanova must, at its expense, maintain roads and a large bridge across the Ongina [river], which mainly serve the transports going to Cremona. This year has been a real inferno. Day and night there are large cargos as well as the enormous weight of the grapes obtained by the Lombards in the province of Parma. This leads to worn-out roads and the bridge broken again, and expenses on top of expenses for the community. [. . .]

I stop, feeling true remorse for asking you to occupy yourself with this business, you who have so much on your mind, etc., etc.

Excuse me, excuse me a thousand times! [. . .]

G. Verdi

 *Ricordi to Verdi*

Milan, 24 August [October] 1890[1]

Illustrious Maestro, ˙

If I had the *impudence* . . of some modern . . . . artists, I could say: the geniuses meet! . . . because when this morning's mail gave me the pleasure of a letter from you,[2] I just wanted to please myself by writing to you!—But I certainly don't have this *impudence*, and it was the long silence that prompted me to ask for your news, which is always so dear to us.

Several reasons caused me to remain silent for some time. A cold heavy enough to keep me in bed for 4 days, with a coda threatening bronchitis; the weather being splendid at that time, I went to the Erbas[3] on the lake,[4] and 5 days of good air wiped out all the illness. Then, just for a change, meetings with 3 (I say three!!) attorneys!—If you feel for me . . . . I'll be consoled! But you know, this publishing business is an ugly thing, where one must deal solely with gangsters, thieves, both the two-faced and three-faced kind. . . . and with attorneys . . with their *personal fees*, which every decent man would dread!—Finally, a big budget meeting with my partners . . which means eight days of work on the provisional report, and eight days of anxiety, since you never know what kind of mood these good people are in!! Imagine reading a report lasting a good three quarters of an hour. . . . . received with an icy silence . . . . . which meant to say, of course, ... that I was an *ass!*— The silence didn't last long and, fortunately, meant to say the opposite, so that . . . . . I was congratulated by everyone. Such a moment, however, costs me 6 months of my life!!—But the *via crucis* is not over; the budget is approved, but in the meeting next month, I will have to hear all the wishes, advice, etc., etc.—and accept them with the greatest pleasure. Good people they are, these partners, but for them the ideal manager would be that famous ass who ate straw. . . . and gave money in return!—They may not be wrong, and it would be better for me, too.—I am so glad that you are satisfied with the watch—the bill is all right, don't worry about it—and since last month I have a note concerning the piano; I shall send it to you, so you can see what is to be done.—

But . . . . there must be some nuisance from time to time. And always on account of that infamous Bénoit in Paris; he has already robbed us of some thirty thousand francs!! And now he starts all over again!—Please be so kind as to read the enclosed statement,[5] and see if you can find something in writing to trim the claws of that consummate thief, to spare our House another great loss.—

Last week, Pisa[6] gave me better news, actually hopeful, about Muzio; yesterday, however, I had a letter from Muzio himself,[7] which seems rather sad. Pisa has already been told to treat Muzio as a member of the family; today I must write him and will ask him again to keep me informed.

I can't tell you what a consolation it would be for us to know that you and Signora Peppina are in good health. Still . . . . with November approaching . . . . we hope to see you fairly soon in Milan,[8] and those are days of true contentment.—

Ginetta is well; now she is in the country near Milan, at the Negris.[9] She will definitely return in a day or two, so much the more since a wintry cold has set in.—As to Ginetta I fear . . . . that she is already paying the consequences of matrimony!! . . . and as natural as this is, ... it amazes me!—As usual, she is always joking in her frequent letters, even with the first sufferings of motherhood! To sum it all up . . . . our home seems a desert to us . . . . and philosophy is meager consolation!—

And now that I have bored you for so long, you may prefer my silence; in any case, I prudently stop immediately, sending you our most affectionate greetings, and reiterating that feeling of true gratitude, which time does not weaken, but strengthens forever.

Your most devoted
Giulio Ricordi

NOTES

1. The contents of this letter and other circumstances definitely imply that Ricordi wrote it in October not August.

2. Missing.

3. Carlo Erba was Giulio Ricordi's father-in-law and the grandfather of the director and scenic designer Luchino Visconti (1906–76). (Phillips-Matz, p. 691.)

4. On Lago di Como or Lago Maggiore.

5. A lengthy document, involving infinite details and raising more questions than Verdi could possibly answer.

6. Ricordi's agent in Paris.

7. Missing, but probably in the Ricordi archives.

8. On the Verdis' annual journey to their winter home in Genoa.

9. The family of Giulio Ricordi's schoolmate Gaetano Negri (1838–1902). He was a writer, a politician, the mayor of Milan from 1884 to 1889, and a senator from 1890 until his death.

 *Giuseppe De Amicis to Verdi*

Genoa, 25 October 1890

[. . .] Yesterday the piano happily arrived in Genoa, having been sent from Paris on the 6th of this month.[1] [. . .]

NOTE

1. See De Amicis to Verdi, 2 October.

 *Ricordi to Verdi*

Milan, 29 October 1890

Illustrious Maestro,

I got your letter of the 26th,[1] and this morning those of the 27th and 28th.[2] I thank you very much for the first one, sorry to have disturbed you again with Bénoit's latest roguery. I shall hear (alas!) from the attorney in Paris . . . . and what will be, will be. *Fin de siècle* of the thieves!!

I am awaiting news from Pisa; he wrote me what I had the honor of letting you know. And I have already written to Pisa (city), where we have a good correspondent, who will certainly give me exact and detailed information,[3] better than a physician in Milan. As soon as I have an answer, I will communicate it to you. Let us hope that poor Muzio will be able to endure the fatigue of the journey; he has a great desire to come to Italy!

Most happy about your good news and about seeing you fairly soon!! Meanwhile, we send affectionate greetings with everlasting gratitude.

Your most devoted
Giulio Ricordi

NOTES

1. Missing.

1890

2. Both of these letters are missing.

3. About a nursing home in Pisa, which Verdi tried to find for Muzio. (See Verdi to De Amicis, 2, 22, 25, 26, and 28 November.)

 Verdi to Giuseppe Piroli

St. Agata, 30 October 1890[1]

[. . .] I am surprised and, moreover, distressed to hear bad news about your health.

I have received no more letters from you since the one of early September in which you told me that you would not come to St. Agata! Delays or losses of letters are quite frequent (shame on our mails), and if you wrote me after that, the letter was lost.

I hope and wish that, after such a considerably long time, your health may have taken a turn for the better, and that you may be able to write me *"I am well."* This will be a real consolation for me and Peppina, who sends you the most affectionate greetings. Meanwhile, have patience, courage, and good humor (good humor is a great medicine), and the whole illness will go away very fast.

Don't tire yourself by writing me at length; I will be content if you send me even a single word.

Courage, then, and all the good wishes you can imagine.

G. Verdi

P.S. Don't go to any trouble with the papers I sent you . . . they'll wait!

NOTE

1. Verdi's last letter to his friend.

 Ricordi to Verdi

[Milan] 1 November 1890

Illustrious Maestro,

I hasten to reply and to send you the program I just received from Pisa [city].

From Paris:

"I used to see Maestro Muzio every Sunday; he is again in poor condition. The day before yesterday I could not enter his room; the doctor had given him an injection which caused a fever. Dr. Vio Bonato told me that the liver had become very hard, and that there is very little hope!"

Sad news.—Needless to say, we are at your service.

We hope to see you soon!— Meanwhile

Your ever devoted and grateful

Giulio Ricordi

 Ricordi to Verdi

[Milan] 2 November 1890

Illustrious Maestro,

Very sad news about Muzio!—I don't think I should withhold the truth from you, and so I am enclosing Pisa's letter.[1] In case you wish to give specific instructions, we are at your disposal.

I am truly desolate!!

Always your devoted

Giulio Ricordi

NOTE

1. Missing.

Verdi to Giuseppe De Amicis

St. Agata, 2 November 1890

[. . .] I don't know if you know that our poor friend Muzio is gravely ill with dropsy, causing complications of the liver, etc., etc. . . . in Paris. They gave him a first injection and extracted 14 1/2 liters of fluid! And now the fluid has returned! He would like to come to Italy, and the physicians suggest the climate of Pisa. He would go to a clinic in Pisa; I know of one [run] by a Dr. Calderai[1] [. . .] but I would like to have more information from a number of sources.—Could you ask someone among your acquaintances? [. . .]

Write me as soon as possible, and let's change the all-too-painful subject!

Now that the piano has been adjusted by the House of Érard, and the House of Érard knows that it belongs to me, I am obliged to write them a word of thanks.

Do me the favor of asking Maestro Bossola to let me have the address, name and street number, of the House of Érard.

A thousand thanks, then, to Maestro Bossola until I myself will thank him before long!—

Please excuse the many, many troubles I am causing you. Yours as ever

affectionately,

G. Verdi

A thousand greetings from Peppina.

1890

NOTE

1. Unknown.

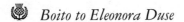 *Boito to Eleonora Duse*

[Milan, 6 November 1890]
Thursday 5.11.[1] Little room upstairs
[. . .] To work, to work, that is my salvation.[2] But today I must go to that
poor friend outside the city.[3]

NOTES

1. 6 November.
2. Probably again on *Nerone*.
3. Franco Faccio.

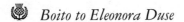 *Ricordi to Verdi*

[Milan] 7 November 1890
Illustrious Maestro,
I got your esteemed letter.[1] This very moment I received news from Paris:
"Dr. Vio Bonato informs me that Maestro Muzio is slightly better . . . .
but . . . . ."—
Since yesterday Giuditta has been in bed, suffering from one of her usual
throat inflammations . . .which means six or seven tormenting days! . . .
Ginetta, poor girl,[2] came early this morning, and so I could go to the office.
But . . . . we are ever more missing our Gina, who thank Heaven is well
and always the Gina . . . . she was.
Good health to both of you always, and till we see you soon . . . . but we
hope not for too short a time!—
Your ever devoted and, from the bottom of my heart, most grateful
Giulio Ricordi
P.S. Wrote immediately to Paris in accordance with your letter men-
tioned above.

NOTES

1. Missing. Probably regarding Muzio.
2. Presumably a servant.

 *Verdi to M. Érard*[1]

[In French]   Busseto—St. Agata, 7 November 1890
Monsieur Érard,

A few months ago Monsieur Bossola in Genoa was requested on my behalf to send one of my *pianos,* which was in need of repair, to the House of Érard in Paris.

I hear that this piano has been returned to Genoa perfectly restored— Maestro Bossola has just written to me—and I also understand that the House of Érard has refused to be compensated for its expenses and labor. I am embarrassed, and at the same time deeply grateful for this exquisite kindness. This work was rather lengthy and substantial, and my gratitude to the House of Érard is equally keen and lasting. [. . .]

NOTE

1. Descendant of the French piano and harp manufacturer Sébastien Érard (1752–1831). See Verdi to De Amicis, 8 May.

Ricordi to Verdi

Milan, 12 November 1890

Illustrious Maestro,

To your esteemed letter of the 8th:[1] Giuditta had her bad throat inflammation, with all the trimmings, which made her suffer a great deal; since last night she has been a lot better, and I hope she will leave her bed soon.

I immediately sent instructions to Paris to pay Muzio what you ordered.— Poor Muzio! . . . so accustomed to great activity!!— If he were only in condition to come to Italy— [. . .][2] but there is very little hope!

Sad news.— Needless to say, we are at your disposal!—

We hope to see you soon!—

Meanwhile, ever Your

devoted and grateful
Giulio Ricordi

NOTES

1. Missing. Apparently concerning Muzio.
2. A few words are missing in the photocopy of the autograph.

1890

 Verdi to Giacomo Persico

St. Agata, 16 November 1890

Esteemed Mr. Mayor of Villanova,

I could neither see the President nor the Vice President of the Hospital, as they were away; but if you, Mr. Mayor, can issue a certificate of poverty, the Ferretti woman[1] will be admitted.

As I think back to our last conversation of the day before yesterday, though at a sad time,[2] I repeat after serious consideration what I told you then: If you think that the contribution for the maintenance of the Hospital is a burden to the community of Villanova, you have only to issue the necessary documents to release it from this obligation. I assure you that there will be no objection whatsoever on my part.

I am leaving tomorrow.[3]

With kind regards, I remain

G. Verdi

NOTES

1. An unknown peasant.
2. Giuseppe Piroli had died in Rome on 14 November; Emanuele Muzio was dying in Paris.
3. For Genoa via Milan.

 Verdi to Giuseppe De Amicis

Milan, 22 November 1890

Dear De Amicis,

Today my servants will arrive, so do me the favor of asking Giuseppina[1] to immediately call the usual *heating man* to find out if the stove needs some adjustment. If so, she should ask him to do it right away before our arrival.

Please also let me have another prospectus of that establishment in Pisa (of that doctor, whose name I do not recall). Muzio would like to have it, because he hopes to come to Italy and go directly to Pisa. May Heaven allow!

Hold on to this prospectus until my arrival in Genoa.

'Til we see each other soon, and greetings from the two of us.

Affectionately,
G. Verdi

NOTE

1. A servant.

 *Verdi to Giacomo Persico*

Milan, 23 November 1890

Esteemed Mr. Mayor,

There can be no bad feeling whatsoever between us on account of our discussions the last time I had the pleasure of seeing you. They could have been of great importance, or of none at all, but I really think that they are of no importance!

The friction at the Hospital[1] certainly displeases me a great deal; but it is not yet serious enough to warrant an irritating and radical decision.

For the time being, then, let us leave things as they are, and let us hope that time may calm and straighten out what is wrong.

With all esteem, I remain

G. Verdi

NOTE

1. Cf. Verdi to Piroli, 28 August 1889.

 *Verdi to Giuseppe De Amicis*

Milan, 25 November 1890

Dear De Amicis,

I am very sorry about the inconvenient delay in the servants' arrival, above all for you, who have gone to so much trouble.

Thank you for the letter you wrote to Pisa; on that subject Muzio writes me[1] that he hopes to be in Pisa on the *9th or 10th* of December. May Heaven allow! He wants a *large room facing the south on the ground floor,* etc., etc.

When I'm in Genoa, I myself will write to the director of the establishment to obtain what he [Muzio] wants. Upon his departure [from Paris] Muzio himself will then wire the day and the hour of his arrival in Pisa, in order to have a covered carriage sent to the station, etc., etc.

We'll talk about it all in Genoa.

Greetings, and till we see each other soon.

Affectionately,
G. Verdi

1890

NOTE

1. In his letter of 23 November. (Gaspare Nello Vetro, *Emanuele Muzio*, pp. 262–3.)

 *Verdi to Giuseppe De Amicis*

Milan, 26 November 1890

Dear De Amicis,

Today again I write to tell you that yesterday poor Muzio had to undergo a second operation (more than 17 liters of fluid) and says that he will come to Pisa next week! I am quite surprised that he can have the strength to make such a long and tiring journey. In any event, we must be ready, if what he says should come about. [. . .]

As planned, we'll be [in Genoa] Saturday (and I am sorry that my affairs don't allow me to arrive before then). Tell Giuseppe[1] to prepare dinner for us.

We arrive at 6:10 P.M. and ask you to keep us company, if the late hour doesn't disturb you!

Also tell Giuseppe to inform the mailman on Saturday morning not to forward any more letters that may arrive; because on Saturday or Sunday morning one from Paris might arrive. Excuse all these troubles; have patience and till we see each other.

Affectionately,
G. Verdi

NOTE

1. A servant.

 Verdi to Giuseppe De Amicis

Milan, 28 November 1890

Dearest De Amicis,

The telegram[1] will have brought you the most distressing news![2]

Poor Muzio! Poor Muzio!!!

This misfortune compels me to stay here a few more days, and thus we won't be in Genoa until Monday evening.

I'll write you again.—

I am utterly devastated!—

Affectionate greetings

G. Verdi

NOTES

1. Missing.
2. Muzio's death in Paris on 27 November.

 *Verdi to Giuseppe De Amicis*

Milan, 28 November 1890

Dear De Amicis,

The moment I received your letter[1] I wired Muzio, who replied immediately with these distressing words: *"Most indisposed cannot leave at this time. Muzio."*

He underwent two operations, and in the last one they extracted more than 17 liters of fluid!

I am devastated!

Please inform Dr. Calderai that for the time being everything is suspended.

Tomorrow evening at 6:10 we'll be in Genoa.

Ad [dio]. Ad.

G. Verdi

NOTE

1. Missing.

 *Ricordi to Verdi*

Milan, 3 December 1890

Illustrious Maestro,

Again I am writing you from home, as I still don't have the doctor's permission to go to my office; first he wants me to be completely rid of the cough. Otherwise I am doing all right, since I am a lot better and hope to get back to work tomorrow or the day after tomorrow. In the meantime, I was deprived of the pleasure of accompanying you to the station . . . just so that a little drop of bitterness should not be missing in the sweetness of the last days. [. . .]

I find also Franchetti's letter[1] most natural! . . .Doesn't it also seem so to you?. . . And don't you think it's such a good letter that it deserves a favorable reply?. . . . On this occasion he belies the fame that surrounds him!—Besides . . . . these days you have upset the whole world.[2] [. . .]

We are very happy to hear that your journey was excellent[3] [. . .]

NOTES

1. A missing letter by the composer Baron Alberto Franchetti (1860–1942), who wrote nine operas in a mixture of Meyerbeer and Italian *verismo* styles. His wealthy family allowed him prolonged studies in Italy, Munich, and Dresden, and lavish productions of his successful operas.

2. On 26 November Verdi had invited Boito and the Ricordi family to dinner at the Hotel Milan. During the dinner, Boito—probably with Verdi's prior consent and to cheer him up—proposed a champagne toast to the Potbelly, Falstaff. Ricordi was puzzled until his wife turned to Giuseppina Verdi and asked, "A new opera?" Giuseppina nodded assent. Under the headline "A new Opera by Giuseppe Verdi," Milan's *Corriere della sera* of 27 November revealed the secret that Verdi, his wife, and Boito had kept until then. (Hepokoski, pp. 19–21, and Phillips-Matz, pp. 705–6.)

3. Ricordi did not learn this from Verdi. (The Verdis returned on 1 December to their winter home in Genoa.)

 Verdi to Gino Monaldi[1]

Genoa, 3 December 1890

What can I tell you? For forty years I have wanted to write a comic opera, and for fifty years I have known *The Merry Wives of Windsor*; yet . . . . . the usual *buts,* which are everywhere, always kept me from fulfilling this wish. Now Boito has dissolved all the *buts* and created a lyric comedy for me unlike any other.

I am having fun writing the music to it, without any [other] projects of the kind; and I don't even know if I will finish it. . . . I repeat: I am having fun. . . .

Falstaff is a rascal who commits all kinds of wickedness . . . . . but in a jolly way. He is a *type!* There are so many different kinds of types! It's a completely comic opera!

Amen. [. . .]

NOTE

1. The Marquis Gino Monaldi (1847–1932), scion of an ancient noble family referred to by Dante, was a writer, biographer of Verdi, critic, impresario, and composer. He was a friend of Boito and frequently met Verdi at Montecatini. From 1890 to 1893 Monaldi rented the Argentina and Costanzi opera houses in Rome.

 *Verdi to Maria Waldmann*

Genoa, 6 December 1890

Dearest Maria,

Your letters, my dearest Maria, are always a consolation to me; but the last one has been solace and balm at this very sad moment. Within about two weeks I have lost my two oldest friends!

Senator *Piroli*, a learned, frank, sincere man of unequaled rectitude. A friend, constant and unchanging for sixty years! *Dead!!*

Muzio, whom you knew as conductor of *Aida* in Paris. Sincere, devoted friend for some fifty years. *Dead!*

And both of them were younger than I!!

Everything ends!! A sad thing is life!

You can imagine the grief I felt and feel! And so I have little will to write an opera I have begun, but with which I haven't gone far.

Pay no attention to the chatter in the papers. Will I finish it? Won't I finish it? Who knows? I write without plans, without goal, without aim, just to pass some hours of the day. [. . .]

Boito to Verdi

Tuesday, Milan [9 December 1890][1]

Dear Maestro,

I recognize that name.[2] It's my Lily, my old Lily whom I, too, took for a man the first time she wrote me, ten years ago, asking me for a seat at the first performance of *Nerone!!!*

The name of that little English dog has remained in my memory. Lily, correspondent of the *Daily News*, daughter of a wolf of the race of Israel, lived in Naples at that time as well.

I answered *Monsieur Lily* (!) granting him the seat that in so much haste had been requested from me. Thereupon Lily wrote me a second time to thank me and to reveal her sex and her age (mature) and her situation. It seemed that she wanted to enter into a lifelong correspondence with me.

I said: *Enough*, and didn't answer any more.

It's best not to answer.

They turn to you, dear Maestro, and take advantage of your name to further their own publicity and the publicity of the paper for which they are writing.

1890

Mondo ladro! Reo mondo!

I return Lily's letter to you.

I'll delay my excursion to Nervi, I'll postpone it until the middle of January. For that time I promise myself a great delight, which will be hearing the entire 1st part of the Potbelly's 2nd act.

Affectionate greetings to Signora Giuseppina and to you.

Your
Arrigo Boito

NOTES

1. Postmark: MILANO 9/12/90.

2. See the following letter, written in English, which Verdi forwarded to Boito with the writer's calling card and some lines of his own, which are missing:

Naples, Nov. 5th 1890
La Favorita
Parco Grifeo

Illustrious Sirs,

It would be a great honour and immense gratification to me, if I could be the first to publish *a resumé* of the libretto of the comic opera "Falstaff" previous to its being brought out on the stage. I mean the first to publish it in a *London* paper, where, on account both of the great genius of the two collaborateurs, and of the source from which the libretto is taken, it is sure to excite the greatest interest. That our great poet should be so well appreciated by two distinguished Italians as to inspire them with the masterpiece "Otello" and now again with an entirely different work is, of course, very gratifying to our English feelings.

My request will not, I hope, seem presumptuous; for *outlines* of many great works are often published before they actually appear. The *time,* of course, rests entirely at your disposition. My paper is one of the highest character in London, the "Daily News," and I always strive to serve it well and truthfully in all that concerns Italy.

Enclosing my card, I beg you to accept the assurance of the highest esteem and admiration on the part of

your obedient servant
Lily Wolffsohn

 *Ricordi to Verdi*

Milan, 19 December 1890

Illustrious Maestro,

Signora Peppina left me the note regarding the newspapers, and all the subscriptions have already been renewed accordingly.

The weather here is fit for doomsday!! . . But if Milan is crying, Genoa doesn't laugh!— All the better that we enjoy good news about your health, and this is the best.— [. . .]¹

NOTE

1. The rest of this note, written by Ricordi on a card, is missing.

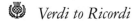 *Giuseppina Verdi to G. De Sanctis*

Genoa, 28 December 1890

[. . .] I could not make you the gift (as you say) of any detail regarding *Falstaff.* To relax from his activities and to amuse himself, Verdi sought and longed for a subject for an opera buffa (not buffona), and his choice fell on *Falstaff.* Boito, the master-poet, to whom he had mentioned it, presented it to him in the shape, proportions, and conditions required for an opera, and Verdi is writing it. Will he finish it, will he not? Will he give it, will he not? It's a future possibility, but no one could say, not even he himself. The idea was to occupy himself having fun; Verdi occupies himself and is having fun.

Moreover, in spite of his 77 years he is well and younger and faster than many youngsters who are old at twenty, twenty-five years! [. . .]

Verdi to Ricordi

Genoa, 28 December 1890

Dear Giulio,

The Marquis Gino Monaldi was here and will come to you tomorrow.

He spoke to me about a rather serious business, as you will hear.

He also spoke to me of *Falstaff,* but about that I answered him with these precise words:

"Falstaff is not done . . I don't know if I will finish it . . No project is acceptable {to me} at this time. . . But {there is} no obstacle to perform it, once it is born, in a theatre that can provide all the means which are needed; and if the Costanzi[1] should be the one, that must be {it}, there will be no problems."—

I only forgot to tell him not to use those words of mine, neither in conversation nor, much less so, in writing.

We are having a devilish wind and tremendous cold. [It has been] like this ever since we arrived, and if it continues, it's better to come to Milan.

Greetings to all and addio—addio.

G. Verdi

NOTE

1. The most prominent opera house in Rome.

1890

 *Verdi to Maria Waldmann*

Genoa, 29 December 1890

Dear Maria,

Your news is always, always most dear to me, and you must not think that I don't care about everything that concerns you; if I don't always write you at length, attribute it to time, of which I never have too much. Besides, I have never forgotten *Amneris,* nor our most pleasant artistic excursions for the *Mass.* Beautiful times . . though a bit far removed!—.

Thank you, my dear Maria, from me and from Peppina. Both of us wish you all the best that is possible—

A good handshake from your

G. Verdi

P.S. Here we have Siberian cold. The sky is very dark. Perhaps a good snow in the morning!

What a year!!

Verdi to Giuseppina Negroni Prati

Genoa, 30 December 1890

[. . .] *Falstaff!?* Almost nothing is done! What can one do in this cold! And then the holidays! And the misfortunes that have *boulversé* [upset] me for a long time![1] [. . .]

NOTE

1. Faccio's terminal illness, Piroli's and Muzio's deaths.

Verdi to Eugenio Checchi[1]

Genoa, 30 December 1890

What can I tell you? Everything has been said about *Falstaff,* and even more than the truth. The truth is this: Boito has written me a funny, comic libretto, the way they like it. It's very funny, and I enjoy tormenting it with notes. Little, almost no music is done. When will I finish it? Who knows? Will I finish it? Perhaps!! This is the true, the real truth. [. . .]

NOTE

1. An aggressive journalist, critic, librettist, and biographer of Verdi, Checchi (1838–1932) was tolerated by Verdi and Boito. (See Phillips-Matz, p. 733.)

 *Ricordi to Verdi*

Milan, 30 December 1890

Illustrious Maestro,

Today I am sending you the accounts for the second half-year; I am sorry that they are not as brilliant as I would have wished! . . . but the country's economic conditions are so sad that everyone feels the calamity, and the theatres above all!— Let's hope that a little peace and general well-being may return . . which would be truly providential! Besides, lately I have had a succession of troubles compared to which the torture of San Sebastian is nothing . . . . and, to top it off, I add that Giuditta and Manolo are in bed with sore throats!! . . . So I can't tell you how much fun there is at home as well. It seems, however, that it's not a serious thing for either of them, so I hope they will soon be well.

Yesterday morning I received your esteemed letter of the 28th, and later on, as you announced, Monaldi's visit; he related to me the whole state of his affairs with the Costanzi, and what he had to tell you in that matter. Therefore, in regard to the most longed-for Potbelly (good health to him and long may he live!), I have always been very careful not to disturb you and not to mention all the requests which I answered as best I could; namely, that the opera is not finished, that the opera belongs to Maestro Verdi and to no one else, and that therefore I could not give any answer to such requests. But I must inform you that, as soon as he got the news, the first to telegraph was Canori[1] for Rome; then came D'Ormeville;[2] to Canori I answered always, always in the same way. Monaldi's plan—provided, of course, that all the circumstances come about (*God* willing . . . . and *Verdi*, too!!)—pulls the rug out from under poor Canori. But Monaldi has taken the direct approach: he spoke directly with you! Today Monaldi was here again, and also D'Ormeville, who, of course, presented Canori's priority with drawn sword; but then, in light of my completely evasive answer and declaration that it was not up to me to enter into any commitment, he understood that this could not be upheld. But in my desire to reconcile everyone, I suggested that whenever the Maestro should decide to allow the opera to be performed, his permission might be obtained for Canori, in a big theatre, to do the first revival after the première, followed by Monaldi at the Costanzi. It goes without saying that I proposed all this only hypothetically, as I declared to the one as well as to the other that definite arrangements were by no means up to me. Monaldi seemed to be satisfied with this arrangement, which, on the other hand, is always subject to the conditions mentioned in your letter. And he seemed satisfied because he wants to remain on good terms with Canori. It's easy to understand that Monaldi would buy out the Costanzi for no other reason than to give *Falstaff* "once he is born," as you write me; (take care of the midwife). And therefore he turned to you, for otherwise he would not have risked such an affair! In light of your letter and the repeated conferences I had yesterday and today with Monaldi, please tell me how to proceed, this also in order to calm the souls of the two rivals . . . . so that good may not turn into evil.

In order to calm Canori and Monaldi, is it all right, then, for me to say that whenever *Falstaff* may be performed, the proposed arrangement can perhaps be realized, always assuming the author's consent?

Monaldi has left for Rome and anxiously awaits an answer there, which is rather difficult for me . . . . but which, if I use the very phrases in your letter, does not commit me.

Do you think that a *quid simile* [something like this] would go well?

"To your request concerning the opera *Falstaff* by Maestro Verdi, we must reply that we are not authorized to enter into any commitment, because, as is known, the opera is not finished and, naturally, belongs to the author.

"In regard to your proposal for the Teatro Costanzi, we believe that Maestro Verdi will have no objection to having the new opera revived at the Costanzi, provided the theatre can offer all the necessary elements. Of course, we are telling you this without any assurance on our part, because, we repeat, we do not consider ourselves authorized to do this."

I am sorry to cause you this trouble . . . . what shall I do? . . I am trying to spare you all the troubles, or almost all, and I am quiet . . . . perforce, but quiet! Now, however, because of your letter, I could not help asking you to let me know how to proceed, being involved in a special case like Monaldi's.

It's also cold in Milan . . . but there is no wind!!. . And see how bad I am! . . I hope for storms and cold wind in Genoa to make you escape for a little while to Milan! Oh, what consolation, what a feast!! . .What a pleasure!

I really don't want to anticipate the good wishes today! . . . For a good start of the year, my first wishes will go to you and Signora Peppina!!— Today I limit myself to greeting you with a most grateful heart.

Your most devoted   Giulio Ricordi

NOTES

1. Guglielmo Canori (1842–1912) was the impresario of the Teatro Costanzi in Rome (1885–87). In 1887, he brought the Scala production of *Otello* to the capital.

2. Carlo D'Ormeville (1840–1924) was an influential Italian dramatist, librettist, critic, and theatrical agent. As a stage director at La Scala, he also staged the première of *Aida* in Cairo; as a theatrical agent in Milan, he organized the first great opera companies for Argentina and represented prominent Italian artists abroad. Many letters from Muzio to D'Ormeville bear witness to the latter's influence on the world's opera houses, including Covent Garden and the Metropolitan.

 *Boito to Verdi*

[Milan] 31 December 18[90]

Dear Maestro,

The new year must begin with a smile, and therefore I am sending you a letter from the good Zorzi in Vicenza, which I received this morning; he informs me that his historic stick is always in order.[1]

Good and happy wishes to you and Signora Giuseppina.

Your most affectionate
Arrigo Boito

NOTE

1. Count Andrea Zorzi of Vicenza had the titles of all Verdi works, from *Ernani* onward, engraved in the silver handle of his walking stick. (*Carteggio* ii, pp. 403–4.) His letter is missing; Verdi probably threw it away.

1891

The Potbelly goes forward . . . but very slowly[1]

The sad events of 1890 have for months prevented Verdi from working on the new score, and his paralyzing involvement in Ricordi's suit against Bénoit results in endless letters to the publisher. An undated draft in Ricordi's handwriting refers to Verdi's satisfaction with Camillo Boito's construction of the Casa di Riposo. From about 9 February to 7 March, the Verdis see their friends in Milan, with no apparent progress on the new opera. Finally, on 19 March, a water color of Falstaff Ricordi wisely sends to Genoa[2] wakes up the "Potbelly," and Boito helps to "warm up the engine again."[3] In mid-April Verdi is alone at St. Agata and returns to Genoa after a day or two; on the 28th he and Giuseppina leave Genoa together for St. Agata. The choice of Faccio's successor at La Scala and, later on, at the Conservatory of Parma is of major concern. Verdi and Boito agree on Edoardo Mascheroni,[4] and the young conductor wins the nomination in Milan. Verdi's resentment toward the impresario Piontelli jeopardizes the *Falstaff* première at La Scala. Nevertheless, Verdi's letter to Boito of 12 June and Boito's reaction of 14 June reflect an outright creative explosion. Between mid-June and 2 July, in Milan on the way to Montecatini, Verdi is interviewed by Ricordi for an article in the publisher's own *Gazzetta Musicale* of 5 July.[5] Upon their return to St. Agata from Montecatini on 22 July, the Verdis learn of Faccio's death. While the composition of *Falstaff* is progressing, the casting of Quickly begins to concern Verdi more than that of any other role. On 3 September Boito engages Verdi's support for the appointment of Giuseppe Gallignani[6] as director of the Parma Conservatory. At the same time, Verdi orchestrates all the *Falstaff* music he has sketched thus far.[7] Between mid-November and 8 December, on the way from St. Agata to Genoa, the Verdis enjoy some rest in Milan. In the comfort of their hotel the Maestro works "with pleasure and profit" on his score.[8] On 5 December Anton Rubinstein[9] and Alfredo Piatti[10] give an impromptu recital in Verdi's salon at the Grand Hôtel et de Milan. Boito and Ricordi are among the select audience.

In mid-January Ricordi visits the Verdis in Genoa. As litigation continues with Bénoit in Paris, Ricordi wins a legal battle against his competitor Edoardo Sonzogno[11] in Milan. On 6 June he begins to persuade Verdi to present the *Falstaff* première at La Scala. In August he attends two performances at Bayreuth.[12] From 11 to 18 September the Ricordis, together with their twenty-six-year-old son, Tito,[13] visit St. Agata and are permitted to read the *Falstaff* libretto. Giulio's letters at this time speak mainly about the irksome journey to Bayreuth, illness in his family, and worries about his own health; but *Falstaff* at La Scala looms as his major concern.

Boito spends most of the year at his home in Milan.[14] On 9 February, he probably attends Duse's Italian première of Ibsen's *A Doll's House* in Milan, prior to her departure for Rome and Russia.[15] In the spring he is a member of the commission to appoint a successor to Faccio as principal conductor of La Scala. In mid-May he fulfills administrative duties at the Conservatory of Parma, and on the 21st he visits St. Agata. On that occasion he reads his libretto for *Nerone* to the Verdis, and the Maestro praises it in a letter to Ricordi on the 25th. In June Boito rekindles Verdi's enthusiasm for *Falstaff* and suggests a possible Quickly. Faccio dies on 21 July; on the 24th, Verdi attempts to console the late conductor's closest friend. Boito declines the offer to become permanent director of the Conservatory of Parma; his letter to Mariotti of 4 September documents his integrity and need for freedom. On 3 October Boito informs Verdi from Rome that Giuseppe Gallignani has finally been named director of the Parma Conservatory. While Boito may have visited the Verdis at St. Agata on his return from Rome, he no doubt sees them frequently in Milan between mid-November and 8 December. He is apparently at home in Milan as another trying year comes to an end.

NOTES

1. Verdi to Ricordi, 2 June.
2. Ricordi was aware of Verdi's need to visualize particular characters such as Falstaff and Iago. (See Verdi's correspondence with the painter Domenico Morelli in *Otello*.)

3. See Boito to Giuseppina Verdi, Ricordi to Verdi, Verdi to Ricordi, 19 March; Verdi to Boito, 21 March.

4. See Biographical Sketch.

5. See Ricordi to Verdi, 22 May. In addition to mentioning Verdi's retirement home for musicians, Ricordi's interview quotes the Maestro as follows:

> *Falstaff* is not completed, and I am confirming what I have already declared. At my age artistic obligations are not held to a definite deadline; I am working for my own entertainment, because Arrigo Boito's merry libretto cheers me up, because every once in a while it makes me break into the most agreeable laughter. Could I bring *Falstaff* to completion? . . . Who knows! Even less can I say if and where I shall have it performed; I am afraid that the ambience of La Scala may be too vast for a comedy in which the rapid flow of the dialogue and the play of facial expressions are the principal features. But I can tell you nothing certain about this, because I haven't yet given it any definite thought. [*Carteggio* ii, pp. 412-3.]

"*Falstaff* is finished but not orchestrated," Gino Monaldi quotes the composer as saying: "Today the orchestration of this opera is for me a matter of care and labor: of care because of today's orchestral importance in opera, and of the *significance* I intend to give to it; of labor, because I am old and my eyes and hands don't serve me as before." (Monaldi, p. 264.)

6. Boito to Verdi, 3 September, n. 1.

7. Verdi to Boito, 10 September. (See Hepokoski, p. 39.)

8. Verdi to Boito, 23 January 1892.

9. The eminent Russian pianist (1829–94), celebrated all over Europe and America, composed works for the piano, operas, oratorios, chamber works, and orchestral music. (See Boito to Verdi, 28 May, n. 3.)

10. The famous Italian cellist (1822–1901) studied at the Milan Conservatory, played with Liszt and Clara Schumann, and enjoyed great popularity in London. He also composed concertos and solo pieces, as well as variations and songs.

11. Ricordi to Verdi, 12 April, n. 2.

12. Ricordi to Verdi, 21 August, nn. 1–4.

13. Verdi to Boito, 15 September, n. 3.

14. Since only seven letters between Boito and Duse survive from this year, and only one from 1892–93 (all of them written by Duse), we know less than before about Boito's innermost feelings, his thoughts, and even his whereabouts.

15. "From Milan, Duse and company went to Rome, their last Italian engagement before leaving on the bold Russian tour. [. . .] Before then, in early March, Duse writes to Boito: 'That other bore la Oppenheim one morning brought me *your* (of *your* CIRCLE) Velleda Ferretti.—Well!—I didn't much like her—if I were to see her again I'd be bored, and if I were to see much of her, in the end I would hate her as I hate everything that surrounds you. . . .' Duse's words were prophetic. She was, indeed, to see much more of Velleda, and the dislike remained. Boito had known Velleda since her childhood (she was five years younger than Duse); eventually she was to take Lenor's place in his life and remain close to him—or rather, at a comfortable, faithful distance—until he died." (Weaver, pp. 86–7.)

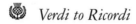

Verdi to Boito

Genoa, 1 January [18]91

Dear Boito,

Let's laugh, then!

That poor Zorzi is decidedly crazy! He considers the Potbelly something done to put on his curious stick,[1] which by now must be completely infested by termites.

Also to you (from Peppina, too) good and happy wishes, and I add a single word . . . .

Finish![2]

The Potbelly isn't moving. I am upset and distracted. The very sad last months, now the cold, the holidays, etc., etc., have thrown me off balance.

Your affectionate

G. Verdi

NOTES

1. Boito to Verdi, 31 December 1890, n. 1.
2. *Nerone.*

Verdi to Ricordi

Genoa, 1 January 1891[1]

Dear Giulio,

Tomorrow or the day after I'll return the accounts, etc., to you.

I am sorry that Giuditta and your son are confined to bed, but if the illness is not serious, they will have recovered by now, and you will all be united to celebrate this very cold year.

And now we come to *Falstaff.* I really think that all the plans are foolish, truly foolish! Let me explain. I began to write *Falstaff* simply to pass the time, without preconceived ideas, without plans; I repeat, *to pass the time!* Nothing else! Now the talk about it, the propositions you get, no matter how vague, and the words they extort from you become obligations and commitments which I absolutely do not wish to assume. I told you and I repeat: *I am writing to pass the time.* And I told you that about half the music is done . . . . but let's understand each other well: "one half is sketched," and in this half most of the work is yet to be done, redoing and adjusting the vocal ensembles, apart from the instrumentation, which will be very tiring. In short, to say it all in one word: the whole year 1891 will not suffice to finish.— Why, then, make plans and enter into commitments, even without specific terms? And then, if I felt in some way, even in the smallest way, tied down, I would no longer be *à mon aise* [at ease] and could not do anything good. When I was young, even when ailing, I could stay at my desk for *10,* even *12* hours, always working,[2] without taking a breath. Then I had command of my body and time.— Today, alas, I do not.—

Let us conclude: The best thing to do for now and later is to tell everybody, everybody that I neither can nor wish to make the slightest promise regarding *Falstaff.* If he will be, he will be; and he will be what he will be!—

The *Perseveranza* said that for the 1st of the year they would publish a supplement about *Falstaff.* The supplement has not arrived here. Do me the favor of sending it to me. A lot has already been said about this *Falstaff,* and not very well! Who knows if the *Perseveranza* may not have found something good to say.

Greetings and health. Good year!

a [ddio ?]

G. Verdi

P.S. I received the *supplement* which the management of the *Perseveranza* sent me. Thanks all the same.——

NOTES

1. In answer to Ricordi, 30 December 1890.
2. In his draft of this letter, Verdi inserted at this point: "and more than once I worked from 4 in the morning until 4 in the afternoon, with only coffee in my stomach. . . ." (*Copialettere,* p. 713.)

 *Verdi to Gino Monaldi*

Genoa, 11 January 1891

Whenever I decide to finish *Falstaff* and to have it performed, you may later have it performed at the Teatro Costanzi in Rome the first time it is to be *re-produced*, always on the condition that, in my judgment, there exist all the necessary elements for an excellent performance. [. . .]

 *Ricordi to Verdi*

[Milan] 18 January 1891

Illustrious Maestro,

Two lines to tell you that the attorney Panattoni[1] will be in Paris today, and that I shall hasten to inform you as soon as we hear from him.

Then, also to tell you what a *very great* pleasure it was to see you and Signora Peppina in such excellent health.

Then, to thank you for your most courteous welcome! ...[2] But this, to tell the truth, is nothing new on the part of the Signori Verdi, ... but so dear to us that it always feels unique!—

It's as cold as Siberia . . . . . so we must take care of our health; for which the quick excursion to Genoa was most beneficial—a welcome moral jolt worth more than any medicine.

Again I repeat my gratitude as ever—

Most devotedly your
Giulio Ricordi

NOTES

    1. Representing Ricordi in his suit against Bénoit.
    2. During a short visit Ricordi paid the Verdis in Genoa.

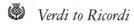 *Verdi to Ricordi*

Genoa, 19 January 1891

Dear Giulio,

I received your dear letter and am very glad that the journey[1] didn't bother you.—

I think, and think again, and think all over again about the well-known [Bénoit] affair, unable to understand anything.— [. . .]

Let's hope that the attorney Panattoni will give us some explanation that may free me from this very sad affair.

Greetings—

Your
G. Verdi

P.S. Ginetta is here.[2] She is a ray of sunshine that warms and comforts us, physically and spiritually.

NOTES

    1. Return to Milan.
    2. Ricordi's daughter.

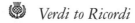 *Verdi to Ricordi*

Genoa, 20 January 1891

Dear Giulio,

Here is the receipt for the last 6 months, and thanks for everything.

III

1891

Today I went out for the first time in about 20 days. Alas, my legs don't work too well.

Peppina has been up for two days; and we hope that if the weather continues to be as beautiful as today, we'll be better.—

Addio! In haste,

Affectionately,
G. Verdi

 Verdi to Camillo Boito[1]

[Presumably Genoa, January 1891]

While I am expressing my complete satisfaction to you for the building you conceived with so much skill, I thank you also for the vigilant care you have shown during the construction of the building, the care I hope you will continue until the completion of the *House of Rest for Musicians*.

Desirous to pay the bill which you sent me upon my request, I enclose a check from the Bank of Italy [in the amount of thirty thousand Lire],[2] asking you to sign the receipt on the attached bill and to kindly return it to me.

I am pleased, dear Commendatore Boito, to reaffirm my heartfelt and friendly esteem.

NOTES

1. Undated draft in Giulio Ricordi's style and handwriting.
2. Struck out.

 Verdi to Ambroise Thomas[1]

[In French]   Genoa, 23 January 1891

My dear Maestro,

Away from Genoa for a few days, I did not hear of the lamented death of Delibes[2] until my return.

Aware of the interest you took in this valiant artist, I turn to you, Sir, to express my sincere condolences. The loss of this composer is doubly regrettable, for in addition to his brilliant abilities he did great honor to French musical art. [. . .]

NOTES

1. Best known for his operas *Mignon, Hamlet,* and *Roméo et Juliette*, Thomas (1811–96) was a distinguished professor at the Paris Conservatoire and its greatly respected director from 1871 until his death. He thanked Verdi for his condolences on 27 January. (*Copia-lettere*, p. 365.)

2. Léo Delibes (1836–91) wrote *Lakmé* and other operas, operettas, and ballets, including *Coppélia*.

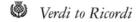 *Verdi to Leone Fortis*

Genoa, 26 January 1891

Dear Signor Fortis,

I have partly reread these *Conversazioni,*[1] which I was honored to receive from you. I was pleasantly surprised, and I thank you.

For a long time I have known your works, which I have always admired. You have the talent—rare among Italian writers—to express yourself in an interesting manner, treating our affairs and today's society with profound insight, discovering qualities and faults, discussing art and all things; and always in a correct, attractive, discerning, incisive style.

It is a fine book, a pleasant and useful book. I repeat: I thank you for having sent it to me, and remain with all esteem

G. Verdi

NOTE

1. L. Fortis, *Conversazioni 1883–1890,* 2 vols. (Milan).

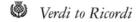 *Verdi to Ricordi*

Genoa, 27 January 1891

Dearest Giulio,

Here, as far as I can recall, is a bit of the history of *Trouvère* at the Opéra.

Late in 1854, during the *Vespri* rehearsals at the Opéra, the management of the Teatro Italiano invited me to attend the rehearsals of *Trovatore* with Frezzolini,[1] Borghi-Mamo, the mother,[2] and the baritone Graziani.[3] The success inspired the director of the Opéra to sign Borghi-Mamo and Graziani to present *Trovatore* in French. [. . .] *Vespri* opened at the *Opéra* in June 1855, I believe,[4] and immediately thereafter they thought about a translation of *Trovatore*. At that time Escudier brought out Pacini's translation.[5] I, without inquiring about the price, took a shortcut and said that if Pacini, in addition to doing the translation, were ready to make the adjustments, the inevitable changes for the Opéra, leaving me his *Droits d'auteur,* I would pay him fr. 3,000. The next day, or a few days later, Escudier told me that Pacini had accepted. Thereupon I consigned the fr. 3,000 to Escudier to give to Pacini, probably asking for a receipt. What happened thereafter? One day after another, time went on, and I either didn't have the courage to ask for the receipt, or perhaps, careless as usual, forgot the whole thing.

The height of carelessness, you will say!! And, alas, that is true; but, unfortunately for me, now as then, when business and numbers are involved I always try to dispatch them as fast as possible, as if I were getting rid of a nuisance; and when I am not on the *qui vive* I never watch exactly what I am doing, and so it's easy to surprise or cheat me. [. . .]

But now it's useless to talk much longer. Now, my dear Giulio, I can only call upon your friendship to do everything possible to reach a settlement, any agreement whatever.

My many years don't leave me time to await the result of such a complicated suit!

My many years don't leave me the strength to endure these oppressive troubles!

Addio Ad.

Affectionately,
G. Verdi

P.S.—You may send this letter to the attorney Panattoni.

NOTES

1. Erminia Frezzolini (1818–84) sang the first Violinda in Verdi's *I Lombardi* (1843) and the title role in *Giovanna d'Arco* (1845).

2. The mezzo-soprano Adelaide Borghi-Mamo (1826–1901) appeared all over Europe, including Paris and London. Her daughter Erminia (1855–1941) sang Margherita and Elena in Boito's revised *Mefistofele* at Bologna in 1875.

3. Francesco Graziani (1828–1901) had "one of the most beautiful and mellow voices of the last century, but apparently little artistry [. . .]" (*Oxford Dictionary*.)

4. On 13 June 1855 as *Les Vêpres Siciliennes*.

5. The prolific composer Giovanni Pacini (1796–1867), "il maestro della cabaletta," inspired by Rossini, wrote several successful operas, but was eclipsed by Donizetti, Bellini, and Verdi.

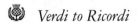 *Verdi to Ricordi*

Genoa, 28 January 1891

Dear Giulio,

I add to my letter of yesterday and ask:

Whether Escudier had the right to make a French translation of *Trovatore*? If he had this right, was this translation to have been made before my negotiations with the Opéra, perhaps in view of the performances in the provinces, for the scanty sum of fr. 500 which was given to the translator?[1]

At the Opéra they would never have used this translation without my authorization, especially since I then resided in Paris, where I stayed for almost three consecutive years.

But when it came to *Trovatore-Trouvère* at the Opéra, I don't understand why Pacini, who had made all the changes, additions, modifications required by the demands of that theatre—assisting at the rehearsals, asked by one, tormented by the other—didn't say to me or to the director Royer,[2] his friend, more or less these words: "This is no longer any old translation made for 500 fr.; but a work of great importance, being presented in the leading theatre of France" (which he had never hoped for); "I think it fair that I should also enjoy a part of the *Droits d'auteur*, etc."

Now, this would have been only fair, of course, and would have clarified a lot of things. Addio.

G. Verdi

NOTES

1. See Verdi to Ricordi, 30 January.
2. Idem.

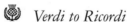 *Verdi to Ricordi*

Genoa, 30 January 1891

Dear Giulio,

I am returning the Panattoni memorandum to you; it seems excellent, clear, and straightforward to me.— At the end of the 1st page are the words "The elder Royer . . . "; perhaps Panattoni thinks that Royer is the father of the present agent of the *Droits d'auteurs*?[1] No! [Alphonse] Royer was once the director of the *Opéra*, a distinguished poet, author of *La Favorita*,[2] who translated *I Lombardi* into *Jérusalem* for me. If he had [then still] been the director, he might have translated *Trovatore* for me. How many troubles would have been avoided!

Getting back to the *Memorandum*: This is all well and good, but I still think we should come to an agreement. We must act and move in a world where all is hostile. An agreement would give us peace and quiet, good for everyone, but especially for me, and for my nearly 78 years!— Oh peace!

Addio, addio.

Your
G. Verdi

1891

P.S. If you don't mind, send this page to Signor Pisa in Paris to let the Italian Consul read it.

NOTES

1. Agent of the Société des Auteurs et Compositeurs Dramatiques in Paris. His name was Roger.
2. *La Favorite*, opera in four acts by Donizetti to a French libretto by Royer and Vaëz.

 Verdi to Ricordi

Genoa, 3 February 1891

Dear Giulio,

Here is a letter for Panattoni.[1] Read it, and if it is all right, put on a stamp and mail it.— If it's no good, correct and return it here, and I shall mail it myself.—

Woe is me! Woe is me! You say, "It is a principle, only a principle." The attorney says, "One should have no illusion about a quick solution," etc. Ugly words!

Woe is me! Woe is me! Meanwhile, the time is passing sadly for me, being idle, thinking and meditating about far from merry things!!

An agreement would be a good thing for you, too, in view of my present disposition and while I am still alive! I close, as always, repeating "Let's come to an agreement!"

Addio addio

Affectionately,
G. Verdi

NOTE

1. Missing.

 Verdi to Ricordi

Genoa, 5 February 1891

Dear Giulio,

Out of necessity there existed a contract between me and the directors of the *Opéra* to translate and perform *Trouvère* in that theatre. But where do I find it after almost 40 years?—

If I am well, I'll go Saturday to St. Agata and rummage through my papers again . . . . but with little hope.—

Perhaps Roger could be useful to us in this, if he would introduce the attorney Panattoni to Nuitter,[1] who is the archivist at the Opéra; I am enclosing a note for him, convinced that Nuitter himself will offer to search for this contract.

Do you think it convenient to write to Panattoni in this vein? If you think so, do it, and I will be most grateful to you.

In case Roger could not or should not have time, Pisa himself could introduce Panattoni to Nuitter.

I think, though, Roger would be better.

Addio, addio.

Affectionately,
G. Verdi

NOTE

1. Charles-Louis-Étienne Nuitter (1828–99), anagram of C.L.É. Truinet, wrote numerous librettos of operas, operettas, vaudevilles, and ballets. He also translated Italian and German operas, including some by Verdi and Wagner, into French. Nuitter also wrote several scholarly books and an article on the rehearsals and first performances of *Tannhäuser*. In 1866 he was appointed archivist of the Paris Opéra, whose library he catalogued and enriched with innumerable acquisitions at his own expense. At his death Nuitter left one million francs to the artists of Paris and half a million to the library of the Opéra. (*Otello* ii, p. 847.)

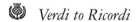 *Verdi to Ricordi*

Genoa, 7 February 1891

Dear Giulio,

Read the note[1] that Panattoni sent me, and then return it.—

Read my letter in reply and mail it, if it's all right.[2]

Oh yes! Oh yes! I still think we should come to an agreement. Even with all the arguments in the world, before a French court we shall always be wrong!

Keep very well in mind, my dear Giulio, that the French—I have known them since 1847—have never liked us; on the contrary, we have always had the honor of their contempt! In better times they spoke of us as "Un peuple de chanteurs et de brigands" [A nation of singers and brigands]!! Today they not only despise us but fiercely hate us; Crispi's fall[3] is not going to make them any gentler toward us when they find out that, even after Crispi, we cannot leave the Triple Alliance.—

Therefore, and for a thousand other reasons, I want an agreement! You are young and could endure these impediments better than I!!— Still, peace and tranquillity are good for everyone! At my age I cannot wish for more than this blessed tranquillity, so I may return quietly to the occupations I like, and to my studies.

Addio addio

Affectionately,
G. Verdi

P.S. I was writing this letter when I got your telegram, which I answered immediately.[4] If my suggestion is all right, we will certainly see each other at the Hotel Milan Friday evening at 10.—

NOTES

1. Missing.
2. Missing.
3. Francesco Crispi (1818–1901), adventurous patriot, controversial politician, prime minister from 1887 to 1891 and from 1893 to 1896. (*Otello* i, pp. 417–8, 818.)
4. Both telegrams are missing.

 Verdi to Giuseppe De Amicis

Milan, 3 March 1891

Dear De Amicis,

I had hoped to be able to tell you *tomorrow we'll be in Genoa*, but, alas, the attorney Panattoni will be here only Thursday, and return to Paris on Friday. (You know that I am involved in a very serious lawsuit in Paris concerning *Trovatore.*)

If nothing else interferes, we'll be in Genoa on Saturday at 6:04. Since that is not too late an hour, I hope you will stay for supper with us.

Excuse me, and accept our thanks and affectionate greetings.

Your
G. Verdi

[. . .]

 Verdi to Giuseppina Negroni Prati

Genoa, 8 March 1891

Dear Signora Peppina,

We arrived here fairly well last night.[1] Peppina suffered a great deal of very intense pain in her knees, but with the cure prescribed by Todeschini I hope the acute suffering will pass and she will be at least the same as before.

And you, too, are in distress? What can one say? Sorrows are the daily bread of life; but when we have reached a certain age, they grow with astonishing force.

You should bear them and take courage, they say; but . . . . at the moment I am also well provided with them, and they are big and grievous! I have read *Job* again to find strength to bear them, although he, too, swore very well. . . .

Courage, then, and let's go on as long as we can. [. . .]

NOTE

1. From Milan on 7 March.

 Giuseppina Verdi to Marietta Calvi Carrara[1]

Genoa, 14 March 1891

[. . .] I believe you know already that we have spent a winter full of painful upsets! Verdi really does have the qualities you mention in your letter;[2] unfortunately, however, good faith, loyalty, and generosity are too often like a well-set table out in the open air, loaded with all the gifts of the gods, but not watched carefully enough, and therefore subjected to all kinds of thievery, deceit, and tricks. . .[3]

I stop writing because at this very moment *Carducci*[4] is arriving, with another poet, . . and, being very curious, I am running to see him . . . and the young poetess, too! . . .[5]

This moment they left. Carducci is short and ugly, simple, almost shy. He has the most expressive eyes, which alone suggest his enormous intelligence! He is a Tuscan, and speaks Tuscan, of course, very rapidly, in short bursts. The poetess is 22; Carducci has issued her a passport to enter Parnassus, and, as you can imagine, this passport is of great value!! [. . .]

NOTES

1. Wife of Angiolo Carrara (1825–1904), Verdi's notary in Busseto. Their son, the lawyer Alberto Carrara (1853–1925), married Verdi's adopted daughter Filomena Maria (1859–1936) in 1878.

2. Missing.

3. In reference to the Bénoit affair. (See the following letter from Verdi of 15 March.)

4. See Verdi to Giosuè Carducci, 3 December 1889, n. 1.

5. Annie Vivanti (1868–1942), whose father was an Italian political exile and whose mother was German, was born in London. She lived in England, Italy, Switzerland, and the U.S.A. She studied singing in Italy and made her operatic debut in New York. On her return to Italy she became Carducci's friend, and he wrote an introduction to *Lirica* (1890), her first collection of poetry. She was the successful author of novels, plays, and short stories

1891

of a semi-autobiographical nature, which portrayed extraordinary events and passionate yearnings. Vivanti described Carducci's visit to Verdi in London's *Daily Graphic* on 4 January 1893. (See Conati, pp. 228–42.)

 Verdi to Giuseppina Negroni Prati

Genoa, 15 March 1891[1]

[. . .] As to my personal troubles, nobody can offer a remedy. They concern property rights to some of my operas to which a French publisher pretends to be entitled. Therefore there is a fight between *Verdi-Ricordi* on the one side, and the French *publisher* on the other. An agreement wasn't possible. To carry on a lawsuit at this time in France is an ugly business for us Italians! As to myself, winning or losing means little to me. Losing, I would pay.— I'll always have enough to keep on going to the *end*. What bothers me are the conferences, the letters, the lack of peace, and, consequently, the ill humor. [. . .]

NOTE

1. In answer to a missing letter.

 Boito to Giuseppina Verdi

[Milan] 19 March [1891]

Dear Signora Giuseppina,

My best wishes for this day to you and the Maestro,[1] to the Maestro and to you, distributed in exactly equal parts.

I had your news from Giulio Ricordi and learned that upon your arrival in Genoa you did not want to be carried in a sedan chair, and this news did not surprise me. I know that your aversion to physicians kept you from consulting one, and this news didn't surprise me either.

Today I am writing you for two reasons; first of all because I like to write you, and also in order not to burden the Maestro with yet another letter. But I beg you, I earnestly beg you, not to answer me: otherwise my precaution would result in a new error if it were to bother you.

I have seen the watercolor,[2] which by now should have arrived in Genoa. It seemed masterfully executed; Falstaff's character is very close to what I had imagined, except that I would like him even more robust, with less white in his beard and hair.[3] I don't know whether the Maestro is of the same opinion. Please greet him kindly for me as I am greeting you with all my heart.

Your most devoted
Arrigo Boito

NOTES

    1. On San Giuseppe, their saint's day, the 19th of March.

    2. The rendering of Falstaff by Adolf Hohenstein (1854–1928). Born in St. Petersburg, he designed and painted posters for the House of Ricordi, a large portrait of Arrigo Boito, and numerous scenic designs and costumes. For the première of *Falstaff*, he studied on location in Windsor and at the British Museum. Hohenstein was also the first designer for Puccini's *Manon Lescaut* and *Tosca*, and he produced a famous group of drawings of Verdi on his deathbed. He spent the later years of his life in Düsseldorf and Bonn, where he died.

    3. Hohenstein apparently had Shakespeare's text in mind. In *King Henry IV,* First Part II. iv. 509, Prince Henry calls Falstaff "that old white-bearded Satan," and Falstaff says of himself in the same scene, 513–5: "That he is old, the more the pity, his white hairs do witness it." Boito and Verdi obviously imagined a more youthful character.

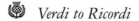 *Ricordi to Verdi*

Milan, 19 March 1891

    To the most exalted Verdi, to the dear Maestro, best wishes from all of us.

    In these wishes, which include those for Verdi's glory and a new triumph for the great Italian art, there is also something else! . . Namely, that the Maestro amuse himself by writing, and that the Maestro, together with his dear companion, enjoy excellent health.

Evviva from the heart to Giuseppe and Giuseppina Verdi!
Giulio Ricordi

    Verdi to Ricordi

Genoa, 19 March 1891[1]

Dear Giulio,

    Oh dear, oh dear, oh dear! What a surprise! The *Potbelly?*[2]—

    For over four months I have had no news from him! In the meantime, beastly drunk, he will have been asleep the whole time!—Let him sleep!—

    Why wake him up?— He might commit some great mischief to scandalize the world! And then?—But!—Who knows——

    Meanwhile, my compliments to the painter-musician-poet![3] But where do you find the time?

1891

Peppina and I thank you for your and your family's wishes, and may there be *health, good cheer,* and *all the best* also for you.

Peppina is better on her legs.

Addio, addio.

Affectionately,
G. Verdi

1. Supposedly in answer to Ricordi's lines of the same date.
2. Ricordi seems to have enclosed Hohenstein's watercolor mentioned by Boito to Giuseppina Verdi on the same date.
3. In reference to a performance of marionettes Ricordi produced at his home and described to Verdi in his letter of 31 March. Verdi must have heard in advance about this event.

 Verdi to Boito

Genoa, 21 March 1891

Dear Boito,

Thank you for your wishes, and I thank you also for Peppina, in case she doesn't answer you; you have given her this permission.

I have received Falstaff (the watercolor). It is nice, it is in character, but you are right to say that he should be a bit fatter (not too much) and have less white in his beard and hair. I add that with those sleepy eyes he gives me the impression of a rotten drunkard. Falstaff, who always has so much wit, must not be an obese drunkard. Furthermore, the waistcoat and that style of trousers are not three centuries old; they are too modern. But these observations are pointless at this time; we'll have plenty of time to talk about them! Unfortunately, we shall have time! How much I have lost! I still haven't been able to warm up the engine again!

Tell me in the meantime if on the word *Vindsor* you want the accent on the first or on the second [syllable]!

E.g., in the verse

> *Cè a Vindsor una donna . . .*[1]
> [There is a woman in Windsor . . .]

the accent seems to be on the first.

In this other verse

> *Gaje Comari di Vindsor! È l'ora!*
> [Merry Wives of Windsor! The hour has come!]

the accent seems to be on the second; unless you want the eleven-syllable verse with the accent on the seventh.

You decide as you wish.

Addio. Always your

Affectionate
G. Verdi

NOTE

1. *C'è a Windsor una dama* in the final text (II, i). Cf. Shakespeare, *The Merry Wives of Windsor,* II.ii. 198: "There is a gentlewoman in this town."

 Verdi to Ricordi

Genoa, 21 March 1891

[. . .] I thank you again for Falstaff,[1] whom I find beautiful and masterful, as Boito says. Since I had to write to the latter,[2] I made some observations about this Falstaff, that is, that the eyes are too sleepy and too much those of a drunkard, and without Falstaff's spirit. Also the belly and the trousers are not three centuries old. [. . .]

NOTES

1. Adolf Hohenstein's watercolor.
2. See the preceding letter.

 Boito to Verdi

Sunday [Milan, 22 March 1891][1]

Dear Maestro,

Wíndsor. Like this:

Gáje comári di Wíndsor è l'ora, etc.

It's precisely as you say, an eleven-syllable verse with the accent on the seventh, and the word Windsor is correctly accented in this way. I don't think that in the entire English language there is a word accented on the last syllable; ask Signora Giuseppina if one can establish this rule, which I have not seen in any grammar but which I believe to be right.

And here I must confess that in your libretto I have once transgressed this rule; only once, and in a verse not very far from the one cited, where Falstaff says:

1891

quand'ero paggio
Del Duca di Norfolk ero sottile, ecc. ecc.
[when I was a page
Of the Duke of Norfolk I was slim, etc., etc.][2]

The nature of this verse would put the accent on the sixth, whereas the word Nórfolk is accented on the first syllable like Wíndsor and Fálstaff, etc.

I have tried several times to correct this verse, but when I adjusted the accent, I ruined the verse, and between the two evils I preferred to falsify the accent of the word.

Meanwhile, I take note that you have already arrived at the music for the verse *Gaje comari di Windsor è l'ora*, and this comforts me with the idea that the engine is already beginning to warm up again; a few pages later you will see that the engine will boil, and then: Forward! *à toute vapeur!* [full speed ahead!] And then the four months[3] lost will be regained in one week. I am most certain of this.

Your observations about the watercolor agree fully with mine.

Most cordial greetings to Signora Giuseppina; I hope that rest may be the best cure for her knees.

To you, dear Maestro, a good handshake

from your
Arrigo Boito

P.S. Here we have had all hell break loose because of Chiarina Faccio, who wanted to take her father to Trieste. We prevented it.

NOTES

1. Presumably Boito answered Verdi by return mail as usual, and this time was particularly eager to help him "warm up the engine" without delay.

2. Cf. Shakespeare, *King Henry IV*, First Part II. iv. 362–5: "When I was about thy years, Hal, I was not an eagle's talon in the waist; I could have crept into any alderman's thumb-ring."

3. Boito probably knew of Verdi's letter to Ricordi of 19 March, in which Verdi mentioned having done no work on *Falstaff* for over four months.

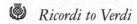 *Ricordi to Verdi*

[Milan] 31 March 1891

Illustrious Maestro,

What will you ever say about my silence? . . . And what will you say when you know what was partly the reason for it?— Nothing less than a performance of . . . . marionettes . . . . . with this grey beard and with those few troubles on my shoulders? . . . . What a shame! It all began when we laughed while dressing old marionettes brought over by a friend of ours . . . and it ended when they had me write nothing less . . . . than a drama with battles, live fire and bayonets . . . , etc., etc., with musical intermezzos, a great production! . . . In short, for a whole week we and friends as old as we are . . . . became children again! Thus, in the midst of life's miseries, we found a way to laugh a bit . . . . even if *risus abundat in ore stultorum*.[1] Finally, the other night the *grrreat* performance took place! . . . There seemed to be lots of laughter, and that's that.[2] Let's now be sensible again.

I thank you very much, illustrious Maestro, for the kindness with which you accepted the watercolor. It is the work of a distinguished aquarellist, Hohenstein. I also read your observations with interest, but to tell the truth, Hohenstein did not want to make the theatrical costume, except for the jacket of dark beige velvet, which is traditional. But . . . you write me that Falstaff is asleep!! . . . . This is the worst news you can give me. . . There is a remedy, though . . . . . wake him up, wake him up, Maestro! For heaven's sake, don't tell us anything like this again. It's like a *knife* in the heart! . . I don't believe you are such a cruel man!! To pierce that vital organ with a *knife*! [. . .]

NOTES

 1. Unidentified Latin quotation: "laughter overflows in the mouths of the stupid."
 2. See Verdi to Ricordi, 19 March.

 *Ricordi to Verdi*

Milan, 5 April 1891

Illustrious Maestro,

An eye? . . . He has opened an eye?[1] . . . Evviva!! . . . . evviva! . . . You, Maestro, are not a man to leave a one-eyed Potbelly! . . . Now he has opened one . . . . . . and then he will open the other! . . . . and little by little he will laugh in our faces . . . . and we will repeat a never-ending Evviva! . . . .

Colossal fiasco, Samara's opera last night at La Scala![2] . . it hardly made it to the end amid boos and laughter. I have never heard music like this, with neither rhyme nor reason! I will soon write about something else; meanwhile . . . . . I think about the eye . . . . . . and am enjoying it no end just for myself.

Affectionate greetings to Signora Peppina, who I hope and pray is in excellent health like you, Maestro, too, and assuring you of my eternal, warmest gratitude.

Your most devoted
Giulio Ricordi

1891

NOTES

1. Boito might have mentioned the good news to Ricordi.

2. *Lionella* by the Greek composer Spiro Samara (1861–1917) in its only performance at La Scala.

 *Ricordi to Verdi*

Milan, 12 April 1891

Illustrious Maestro,

Thank you for your note.[1] Well then, on the 10th or 11th our suit against Sonzogno[2] was discussed in the Court of Appeals. Our 3 (I say three!) attorneys consider themselves certain of victory . . . and those of the adversary will say the same! . . . . It might take at least another month to pronounce the sentence!! . . . . and this is the fun. The many attorneys involved in the proceeding all agreed that Sonzogno's defense lawyers were not very efficient, and that one of them was downright unscrupulous, whereas ours are highly praised. But eloquent words count little in the minds of the appellate judges . . . . . who now have a nice entanglement to unravel and lots of documents to digest.

Enough . . . . . now let's await this famous sentence!—

We are having bad weather, rainy and cold; also, my wife's mother is perpetually in a very grave state of health, so that for some ten days everything has been upside down!

None of the news from here is very cheerful, as you see; but good news can always reach me from Genoa!! . . . . . . all the more so as it is connected with the news of your excellent health!—

Meanwhile I am happy to reassure you of my continuing warmest gratitude, and remain with the most affectionate greetings

Your most devoted
Giulio Ricordi

NOTES

1. Missing.

2. Edoardo Sonzogno (1836–1920) founded a music-publishing house in Milan in 1874. A writer himself and the proprietor of the newspaper *Il Secolo*, he also opened a theatre of his own, the Teatro Lirico, in Milan. Sonzogno primarily published French works and inexpensive editions of Italian *verismo* composers. In 1883 he introduced a competition for a one-act opera, which Pietro Mascagni won with *Cavalleria rusticana*. From 1894 to 1897 Sonzogno even managed La Scala. Eduard Hanslick describes him as an "ash-grey little man with a black look and the clever face of a banker or broker. No one would have guessed that he had anything to do with music." (*Aus meinem Leben* ii, p. 277.) The reason for this particular lawsuit might be found in the archives of the House of Ricordi.

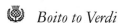 *Ricordi to Verdi*

Milan, 24 April 1891

Illustrious Maestro,

When several days go by without your news, I find myself out of sorts; therefore, here I am knocking on your door, asking "May I?" . . . and upon the friendly "Come in" I shall inform myself of your and Signora Peppina's news and health.

As for myself, I have gone through an alarming week due to a threatening visit by my annoying skin ailment, exquisitely called *exema rubro!!* But the doctor's immediate care and the pleasant burning of the ointments finally freed me, more or less, from the malady.

I am still anxiously awaiting the sentence of the Court of Appeals . . . . but it looks as if it's going to take another month!! . . . and so amid expectations, weariness, and troubles, the time is pleasantly going by! . . . . and it would really be a dog's life if every once in a while one didn't have the good fortune to spend some precious days in your company.

Ginetta is well . . . . . and the moment is approaching when she will make me a grandfather!! . . . . To our great comfort, she remains ever cheerful, and except for her maternal roundness, she looks like the Ginetta she used to be.

My wife is, as ever, her mother's nurse!!—

Having thus emptied the bag of news, I send you, from all of us, affectionate greetings and wishes; and I cannot finish better than by expressing my undying gratitude. Your most devoted

Giulio Ricordi

Boito to Verdi

Saturday. Milan [25 April 1891][1]

Dear Maestro,

If, on the way to St. Agata, you were to stop for a day in Milan, the conductor of La Scala[2] would be born on that day and our beautiful theatre would be saved. I would take our friend Bazzini[3] to the Hôtel Milan, and among the three of us, conversing in perfect agreement, the question that is so urgent, and the most important of all, regarding the reorganization of La Scala would be solved.

The municipal commission is so convinced of the supreme importance of this problem that it would like to see it resolved in the best possible way.

The best possible way is the one I am proposing to you: a conscientious discussion among you, Bazzini, and myself.—

Negri, a skillful man, as you know, strongly insisted that I should write you along these lines.

Any other arrangement would be inadequate.

If a *competition* were announced, only the mediocre ones would participate.

To leave the choice of the conductor to the management would be an imprudent decision, and worse than imprudent.

The theatrical commission does not have the artistic competence required to deliberate on such a grave question.

The same applies to the City Council.—The publishers must not become involved. Who, then?

And that is why I had to write this letter to you.

Fondest greetings to you and all the best to Signora Giuseppina.

Your most affectionate
Arrigo Boito

NOTES

1. Postmark: MILANO 25/4/91.
2. Faccio's successor.
3. Antonio Bazzini (1818–97), violinist and composer championed by Paganini. He toured Europe as a violinist, lived in Paris from 1848 to 1852, and was a friend of Schumann and Mendelssohn. In 1873 he was appointed professor of composition, and, in 1882, director of the Milan Conservatory, where Puccini was one of his pupils. His many compositions include the opera *Turanda* (1867), based, like Puccini's last opera, on Gozzi's *Turandot*. Bazzini also wrote a symphonic poem, *Francesca da Rimini* (1890), overtures to *King Lear* and Alfieri's tragedy *Saul,* sacred and chamber music, and songs.

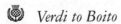 *Verdi to Boito*

Genoa, 26 April 1891

Dear Boito,

I must go to St. Agata right away to see to my affairs and could not come to Milan at this time. We are in the midst of packing; tomorrow morning the servants will leave, and the day after tomorrow we shall leave at 7 o'clock in the morning, in order to be at St. Agata by about 3 P.M.

Besides, I couldn't be of much use to you for the nomination of a conductor at La Scala. Since I rarely go to the theatre, I don't know the best conductors . . . neither the two Mancinellis[1] nor Mascheroni.[2] Anyway, I would never be in favor of a competition. A conductor is judged on the *podium*.

I'll write you again tomorrow if I have a little time, or as soon as I arrive at St. Agata.—

I greet you for Peppina and affectionately clasp your hands. Addio.

Cordially,

G. Verdi

NOTES

1. Luigi Mancinelli (1848–1921) was "the most important Italian conductor between Faccio and Toscanini. [. . .] Boito called him the ideal conductor of *Mefistofele*." (*Oxford Dictionary*.) His brother, Marino Mancinelli (1842–94), conducted the first Italian performance of *Der fliegende Holländer,* in Bologna in 1877. He committed suicide in Rio de Janeiro when a theatrical venture went bankrupt.

2. Edoardo Mascheroni (1859–1941) was named Faccio's successor; he conducted the first *Falstaff* productions and became Verdi's friend. (See Biographical Sketch.)

Verdi to Boito

[Genoa] 27 April 1891

Dear Boito,

. . . Well then, as I wrote you yesterday, not knowing the best conductors, I can't talk about them. The two Mancinellis and Mascheroni have the best reputation.

I think we must give up on Luigi. . .[1] Of the two others, I would choose Mascheroni, who, in addition to his other qualities, I am told, is a hard worker (an indispensable quality at La Scala), a conscientious man without favorites and, better yet, without antipathies.

The conductor must be completely independent of the management and be given all the musical responsibility before the commission, the management, and the public. He must choose the chorus master, to whom should be entrusted not only the musical but also the dramatic instruction. Furthermore, either the chorus master or his assistant should be obliged to put on a costume at the performances and sing with the chorus.

La Scala absolutely must have a stage director of great capability. There has never been one in that theatre, but today's scenic demands urgently require one.

Finally, a clear, decisive repertory must be planned, and the operas must not be chosen haphazardly, as has been done in the last few years, and not just with any singer who comes along.—Either singers for the operas; or the operas for the singers. Stable and complete companies for the whole season;

and two operas prepared for the opening, etc. Thus the public's ill will would be avoided—ill will which then lasts throughout the season.

All would go well, but . . . there is always the *but*. . . Everything depends on finding THE MAN!

Don't make a big thing of what I have told you, because I told it only to you. Write me at St. Agata, where I shall be tomorrow at three.

Addio, addio.

Affectionately,

G. Verdi

NOTE

1. Mancinelli pursued his international career at Covent Garden in London and at other leading opera houses.

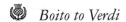 *Boito to Verdi*

29 April [1891]

Milan[1]

Dear Maestro,

Since you cannot take part in the commission that will elect the conductor of La Scala's orchestra, the authority it lacks due to your absence should be supplied by numbers.

The commission will be composed of five maestros: Bazzini, Martucci,[2] Catalani,[3] Gomez,[4] and myself.

I will do my best to let Mascheroni win the nomination, but I cannot guarantee (one against four, if the other four do not agree with me). I cannot guarantee the outcome of the election.

You should give me your permission to read the following words of your letter to the commission:

"*I would choose Mascheroni, who, in addition to his other qualities, I am told, is a hard worker (an indispensable quality at La Scala), a conscientious man without favorites and, better yet, without antipathies.*" These words, which I have transcribed from your letter, read at the right time, could tip the scales in favor of Mascheroni.

But if you do not give me your permission to say them, I shall not say them; but then I shall lack a most powerful weapon to win.—

I want the Potbelly to find La Scala organized in the best possible way.

The reorganizing commission has worked well, and our work fully conforms with the ideas of your letter.

The elimination of the boxes in the 5th tier is an excellent decision.

This liberates the theatre from a faction of the audience which is, by old tradition, distracted, bored, and disruptive, and replaces it with a large gallery of middle-class spectators who will pay little and enjoy themselves much as soon as the occasion arises.

The audience in the gallery is today the best audience at La Scala, and from now on, the boxes in the 5th tier having been removed, this audience will be twice as large.—I am still waiting to hear from you.

To my mind the Potbelly must be getting very fat in the quiet of the country. Affectionate greetings.

Your
Arrigo Boito

NOTES

1. Postmark: MILANO 29/4/91.

2. Giuseppe Martucci (1856–1935) studied at the Conservatory of Naples and became its director in 1902, after serving as director of the Conservatory of Bologna. Martucci conducted *Tristan und Isolde* in Bologna in 1888, wrote chamber music and symphonic works, and edited Bach's orchestral suites for pianoforte. Arturo Toscanini often included Martucci in his symphonic programs.

3. Alfredo Catalani (1854–93) studied composition at the conservatories of Milan and Paris, and became Ponchielli's successor as professor in Milan. Between 1875 and 1892 he wrote six operas, including *La Falce* [The Scythe] to a libretto by Boito, *Loreley* (1890), and his most successful *La Wally* (1892), whose première his friend Toscanini conducted, and after which he named one of his daughters. Attracted to Germanic subjects, "Catalani attempted to express Italian lyricism in a harmonic language which was patently influenced by Wagner." (Marek, p. 107.) However, "when tuberculosis killed the thirty-nine-year-old Catalani in 1893, he had not yet produced a work mature enough to enter the mainstream repertory [. . .] ." (Harvey Sachs, *Opera News*, October 1993.)

4. Antonio Carlos Gomes (1854–93), Brazilian composer in whom Verdi recognized "true musical genius," was sent by Emperor Pedro II to study in Milan. Gomes later became director of the conservatory in the Brazilian city of Pará (now Belém). He composed several operas, some based on South American plots. *Il Guarany* was premiered at La Scala with great success in 1870. Boito and Emilio Praga (1839–75) wrote the libretto for Gomes's *Maria Tudor*, whose première, conducted by Franco Faccio at La Scala on 27 March 1879, was a complete failure.

 *Verdi to Boito*

St. Agata, 1 May 1891

Dear Boito,

There is nothing wrong with reading my four lines to the commission, stating, however, that I only know these conductors personally and by name; and that I do not intend, therefore, to pass judgment. I repeat again that since Luigi Mancinelli cannot be had, the better of the other two, especially for La Scala, is Mascheroni.

The decision to do away with the 5th tier is very good. The audience in the gallery, which is the one that lets itself be impressed and sincerely manifests its impressions, is the real audience. The other one, adopting a *blasé* pose, playing the *savant*, judges and talks of the future, of today, of idealism, of realism, of the classic, etc., etc., etc. . . Oh, for the love of God! And now also program music?! . . . But all music must have a program, that is, it must produce sensations in the people who listen to it, according to age, period, and nationality (and therein lies the true power of music).

Music that does not have this program is bad; but music that *imposes* a program is even worse!—Oh, how much chatter!!

The Potbelly? Poor fellow! Since that illness which lasted 4 months he is scrawny, scrawny! Let's hope to find some good capon to reinflate his belly. . . It all depends on the doctor! . . . Who knows! Who knows! Good health and greetings.

Affectionately,
G. Verdi

 *Boito to Verdi*

[Milan] 2 May [1891][1]

Dear Maestro,

Thank you for the permission you grant me; I will make the most convenient use of it, and it will help.

And in answer to what you further say in your letter, I will add that those who impose a program on music do not appreciate the divine essence of the art.

Around the middle of the month I will go to Parma; then, as usual, I will drop in at St. Agata, and that will be toward the twentieth or, more likely, the twenty-first.

If the weather is nice and if you feel like it, we'll make an excursion to that beautiful old cloister Mariotti told me about.[2]

Well then, till we see each other again soon, with many kind greetings to Signora Giuseppina, and an affectionate handshake for you.

Your most affectionate
Arrigo Boito

NOTES

1. Postmark: MILANO 2/5/91.
2. Probably the twelfth-century Abbey of Chiaravalle della Colomba, not far from Busseto.

 *Verdi to Boito*

St. Agata, 5 May 1891

Dear Boito,

Very well! And till we see each other again on the 21st.—You will tell me later if I shall have you picked up at *Borgo*[1] or at *Alseno*[2] or at *Fiorenzuola*.[3]

Greetings from Peppina and a handshake from your

Affectionate
G. Verdi

NOTES

1. See Verdi to Piroli, 16 July 1889, n. 2.
2. See Verdi to Boito, 23 May 1890, n. 2.
3. Verdi traveled most frequently from and to this little station. A station master's memorial tablet commemorates the Maestro's departures with his music into the world, and his glorious returns.

 *Ricordi to Verdi*

Milan, 9 May 1891

Illustrious Maestro,

If you send me your news and, of course, good news, it will be a real gift.

No good news from here; my mother-in-law is still in a very serious state, and so my wife and sister-in-law are alternately keeping watch every night!—A most beautiful and saintly thing, but in the meantime both of them are in danger of becoming ill because of their great fatigue and their state of mind.[1]

NOTE

1. The rest of the letter is missing.

1891

 Ricordi to Verdi

Milan, 22 May 1891

Illustrious Maestro,

I got your most welcome letter,[1] with the good news of your health, but, unfortunately, with less gratifying news of Signora Barberina; however, since this excellent lady even performs miracles, I hope to hear that another miracle has happened!—[. . .]

The papers bring great news about you;[2] what line shall I take?. . Must the *Gazzetta musicale* be completely silent?. . . . In the meantime, for my part . . . . I'm keeping quiet, so as not to say too much.

I am ever anxiously awaiting the verdict of our appeal!![3]. . It looks as if it will take 7 or 8 more days!!!—

I can tell you nothing new or good . . . . . since something new and good could only come from St. Agata!!—Here the weather is awful and life is wretched—improved by a bit of *spleen*! That's all I can say about us. . . . . . However, at least Ginetta is very well!! . . . Even though by now she resembles a rubber ball, which is always a joy to behold.—[. . .]

NOTES

1. Of 21 May. (*Otello* i, p. 377.)
2. Concerning the Casa di Riposo.
3. In the Sonzogno suit. (Ricordi to Verdi, 12 and 24 April.)

 Verdi to Ricordi

St. Agata, 25 May 1891

Dear Giulio,

In answer to your letter of the 22nd.

1. Barberina is here, and I am not too sure about her. But to her, it's really true; so many miracles have happened that we hope for another one!

2. [. . .] What you read in the *Corriere* is true.[1] Over two years ago I bought, with Camillo Boito's advice, 3000 square meters of land outside Porta Magenta,[2] intending to erect there a building to house about *80* or *100* poor ailing artists. It remains to be seen if after my death the necessary funds will be left to me!!—I would have liked this to be a secret . . . but it's remarkable that nothing leaked in over two years!—

Other more important news! On his return from Parma, Boito stayed here for about 48 hours and read the libretto for *Nerone* to me!! I don't know if I do well to mention this to you, but he did not ask me to keep it a secret; and so I'm telling you—certain that you will be glad to hear this—that the libretto is splendid. The period is masterfully and profoundly drawn; five characters, one more beautiful than the other, and despite his cruelty, Nero is not odious. A deeply moving fourth act; and the whole thing is clear, neat, theatrical in spite of the greatest bustle and complication.

I won't speak of the verses, you know how Boito can make them; but these seem to me the most beautiful of all he has made until now. Long may he live then, and addio.

Affectionately,
G. Verdi

P.S. I am happy about the improvement in your mother-in-law's health, also for poor Giuditta's and her sister's relief.

NOTES

1. Concerning the Casa di Riposo.
2. See Verdi to Camillo Boito, October 1889.

 Boito to Verdi

[Milan] 28 May [1891][1]

Dear Maestro,

I have been to the *terrybile* Mr. Terry,[2] who promised me he would dedicate all the learning of his most delicate hands to Signora Giuseppina and to you. I advise you, however, that appointments for treatments by the illustrious dentist must be made several days in advance. I, for example, had to make a reservation yesterday for next Tuesday, as if for a Rubinstein concert.[3]

The manager of La Scala is Piontelli; I would have preferred the Cortis.

The conductor will be Mascheroni, under contract for one year; if he does well, as is hoped, the contract will be extended.

I have no other news to give you.

I hope that the devil may ride at St. Agata on the bow of a violin,[4] and that you, dear Maestro, may be very busy with the laundry basket.[5]

Finally, today the sun promises to last; that gives me hope that Signora

1891

Barberina may recover her health and go down into the garden; please greet her warmly for me and also give Signora Giuseppina my best.

To you, dear Maestro, a firm handshake and till we see each other soon.

Your most affectionate
Arrigo Boito

NOTES

1. Postmark: MILANO 28/5/91.
2. An "American dentist of great reputation," as Verdi had written to Opprandino Arrivabene on 1 May 1885.
3. A concert by the Russian pianist and composer Anton Rubinstein (1829–94) was a sensation in the musical life of that time. (See Chronological Sketch for 1891, n. 10.)
4. Boito quotes from Falstaff's line in II.ii of the opera: "Il diavolo cavalca/Sull'arco d'un violino!!" [The devil rides/On a violin's bow!!]. Cf. Shakespeare, *King Henry IV*, First Part II.iv.534–5: "*Prince*—Heigh, heigh! The devil rides upon a fiddlestick. . ."
5. In II.ii of the opera.

 *Boito to Verdi*

[Milan] 29 May [1891][1]

Dear Maestro,

Today I am writing to tell you that I received a letter from the good Vellani,[2] full of the warmest gratitude for the autograph you donated to the library of the Liceo Musicale in Bologna. Vellani, an ingenuous and most simple soul, cannot muster the courage to thank you directly; he is afraid to bother you by obliging you to read the expressions of his gratitude. And so he charges me to act for him, which I do with the greatest pleasure. But to Vellani's thanks I add mine, too, because you have been so prompt in granting my request that I can only thank you.

Yesterday, too, I wrote you a letter which, like this one of today, needs no reply.

You must not lose time unnecessarily with correspondence, you have to attend to the laundry.[3]

Dear Maestro, 'til we see each other again soon, with affectionate greetings to everyone,

Your
Arrigo Boito

NOTES

1. Postmark: MILANO 29/5/91.

2. Federico Vellani was secretary of the Liceo Musicale in Bologna and a collector of musicians' portraits. (*Carteggio* ii, pp. 410–1.)

3. Referring to *Falstaff* II.ii.

 *Ricordi to Verdi*

Milan, 31 May 1891

Illustrious Maestro,

I intended to reply at once to your esteemed and very kind letter of the 25th, but have gone through days of such intense anxiety that I felt incapable of gathering my thoughts! . . . You must know, therefore, that last Monday I was informed that the Court of Appeals would pronounce the famous sentence!! . . . I waited from hour to hour . . . sent messengers to the court; later on, the answer was that a legal hearing expected to finish earlier was still going on, etc.! . . . and so Monday went by . . . and so Tuesday and Wednesday!—On Thursday, a holiday, the court was closed; the sentence will be read Friday morning! . . . And Friday morning at 10 I sent word: nothing . . . . it will be read at 3 because of a further debate. And while I'm fretting away, a young attorney friend of mine enters the office, out of breath, panting and shouting "Victory!! victory!" showing me the verdict on a little piece of paper. [. . .] But do not believe, Maestro, that this means the end of the troubles and *expenses!!* Sonzogno will go to the Supreme Court of Appeals . . . . If the verdict is reversed on account of some procedural error, it will start all over again . . . . . . Anyway, another suit will now be brought to cover the losses! And so the attorneys' good luck will continue . . . . . expenses of many tens of thousands of Lire . . . . . and this is the fun that even follows victory!! [. . .] But let's leave these miseries alone . . . . and come to something better, that is, to your deeply appreciated letter.

I hope with all my heart that Signora Barberina may overcome this latest crisis, as she has done before, and that she may regain the good health she has enjoyed over the last years. [. . .]

With the greatest interest I read what you write me concerning the plan the journalists were discussing.[1] . . . I am in awe, but not surprised, that Verdi's heart is as great as his mind, creating a true miracle of moral and physical balance! . . . Just let me tell you, Maestro, that you are great in everything; moreover, who knows this better than I, who have had proof? . . . . .

Judging from the tenor of your answer, I don't believe I am authorized to handle this like the *Gazzetta*, to correct the news printed by the political papers. I believe it would be all right, but please tell me if I should do it.

1891

I am certainly delighted by the news you kindly give me of Boito's *Nerone!*[2] Finally!!! .... I repeat, I am delighted .... but by no means as much as I would be by certain other news .... which you know .... which I don't know ..... but about which I am always, always thinking!! ....

Just for a change, so that there's never any peace at home, Giuditta is in bed with a sore throat!! ..... I hope it won't develop into the usual inflammation ..... imagine, with her mother, who is always in need of help ... and with Ginetta, who very suddenly may need her mama!!

Lots of cheer!—

In all events, however, your news will be most precious to us, and since the weather seems averse to any more nasty tricks, it will be good also for your health and will brighten the appearance of the fields.

Our affectionate greetings to all. To you, Maestro, I repeat the always warmest expression of devotion and gratitude.

Your most affectionate
Giulio Ricordi

NOTES

1. Concerning the Casa di Riposo. (Verdi to Ricordi, 25 May.)
2. Verdi's impression of Boito's libretto to *Nerone*. (Verdi to Ricordi, 25 May.)

 *Verdi to Boito*

[Memorandum]   [May–June 1891?][1]

Ask BOITO

1. After *Fals.* lines

> I love you and it's not my fault
> If I have so much vulnerable flesh

Add two	Ah!
lines for	But the sighs of love
Alice	*Swell and the heart*

Fal.

> When I was a page
> Of the Duke of Norfolth I was slim! / *period.*
> U _ _ U _
> _ U _ _ _ U _ _ _ U _
>
> Lout!
> Poltroon!
> Paunch

	Drunkard	
	Rogue!	
	On your knees	
Further on	Glutton!	
	Paunch	Change, so as
	Drunkard	not to repeat
	Pardon	

Possibly after the line	*And spirits*
add two more	. . . rits
	. . . rits[2]

NOTES

1. Verdi's undated memorandum, which he left among his papers at St. Agata, might have been written at the time of his meetings with Boito while he was working on II.ii and III.ii of *Falstaff*. (See *Carteggio* ii, p. 507.)

2. The first part of this memorandum concerns II.ii. In the final text, the corresponding lines read:

FALSTAFF   Chi segue vocazion non pecca.
                   T'amo!
                   E non è mia colpa . . .
ALICE (interrompendolo e scherzando)
                   Se tanta avete vulnerabil polpa . . .

[FALSTAFF   He who follows his vocation doesn't sin.
                   I love you!
                   And it's not my fault . . .
ALICE (interrupting him and joking)
                   If you have so much vulnerable flesh . . .]

The "two lines for Alice" were not added. Verdi, of course, meant the "Duke of Norfolk" rather than the "Duke of Norfolth." The unusual word *Gorgion* in the second part of this memorandum could not be found in any Italian dictionary; Boito replaced this apparent product of his fantasy, evidently derived from the word *gorgia*, a literary word for *throat*, with *Ghiotton* [Glutton]. Except for his remote allusion to Shakespeare's text (Boito to Verdi, 22 March, n. 2), all of Verdi's quotations from the libretto are Boito's invention.

 Verdi to Ricordi

St. Agata, 2 June 1891

Dear Giulio,

I did not answer your telegram immediately because I was awaiting the promised letter, which arrived last evening.[1]

1891

I am happy about the outcome of the suit; and I am particularly happy for you, since all the operas of the Ricordi archive were found to be in perfect order. And if the Court has not definitely ruled on the operas by Cottrau [2] and on *Favorita,* it has nevertheless acknowledged the property rights—and this is a victory. Let's hope that the Supreme Court may have nothing to repeat, and that everything may go from good to better. And otherwise?!! That one there!![3] God forbid!! We can speak in person about the news printed in the *Corriere* when I come to Milan en route to Montecatini, which I hope will be before long.

The Potbelly goes forward . . . but very slowly. You well understand, he is so fat that he cannot and must not take long walks! And yet he ought to be able to take two more—long, long ones, and labor a lot!—

I read that Piontelli will be the manager of La Scala! I regret this for the theatre, because he is not a good manager; but personally I am almost pleased, because he relieves me of a great embarrassment, or to put it better, of some indecision. I was not much inclined toward performing *Falstaff* at La Scala, too large a theatre to adequately hear the words and see the faces of the artists. I was inclined toward the Carcano.[4] Piontelli's appointment makes me decide to think no longer of La Scala. I do not personally *know* the man; but even without our knowing each other, the relations between us have been so impolite and rude on his part that it is impossible for me to be in contact with him and set foot, so to speak, in his house!—I'll tell you everything in person.[5] In the meantime, don't mention it to anybody, to avoid any sort of idle talk. Even if negotiations were proposed, there is a most plausible answer: "The theatre is too large."

Unfortunately, it is true that one can never stay calm! You are surrounded by illness, and I am, too! Barberina is always in bed except for two or three hours a day, and runs a fever at night. It's painful for everyone and especially for Peppina . . . who also exerts herself too much, walking up the stairs two or three times!! I wish we could leave as soon as possible.[6]—

I hope [her sore throat] will have been a false alarm for Giuditta, to whom you will give our very best. I greet you all from my heart, also for Peppina, and till we see each other, I hope, soon.

Affectionately,
G. Verdi

NOTES

1. See Ricordi's preceding letter of 31 May.
2. Apparently Giulio Cottrau (1831–1916), popular composer of Neapolitan songs like his French father, Guillaume Louis Cottrau (1797–1847), and his brother Teodoro (1827–79). Giulio Cottrau also wrote two successful operas.

3. Presumably Sonzogno.

4. The Teatro Carcano, which opened in 1803, was the scene of the first Milan performances of Verdi's *La battaglia di Legnano* in 1859, of the first concert of Wagner's music given in Milan under Faccio in 1883, and of the first Italian performance of Massenet's *Manon,* in 1893. The premières of Donizetti's *Anna Bolena* in 1830 and Bellini's *La sonnambula* the following year were also given there.

5. See Verdi to Ricordi, 31 January 1892, n. 3.

6. For the annual cure at Montecatini in July.

 *Ricordi to Verdi*

Milan, 6 June 1891

Illustrious Maestro,

I received your esteemed letter of the 2nd, which brings me good and bad news; above all, it brings me the very good news of your forthcoming arrival, which, I hope, will be soon; also because this will mean that Signora Barberina is in better health.

The Potbelly goes forward, but slowly!! . . but he who goes slowly, goes safely and far!! . . . and as long as he is walking . . . . long may he live. I also note that slowness is a relative matter, e.g., slowness in Boito's style is measured in tens of years, and Verdi's, if not measured in minutes, is measured at most in days. And then . . . the Potbelly will greatly profit from the purifying cure of Montecatini, which once had prodigious effects on that gentleman of the chocolate![1] So I repeat: Long may he live!—

I am really very sorry about what you write me regarding La Scala and Piontelli; if I could have foreseen this, I would have mentioned it to the mayor, without compromising anything. But it must also be noted that Piontelli was the only competitor, and that no one else applied. When I say that I am sorry, it goes without saying that it's not just for the management, but for poor La Scala, which we are attempting in every way to keep going against the democratic storm! . . . Certainly, the theatre will be dealt a severe blow . . . . a most severe one, worse than remaining without a subsidy!! . . . You tell me that it is impossible for you to set foot in a theatre of Piontelli's!! . . . But if you were to deal exclusively with the directors of the theatre, or with City Hall, eschewing any and all personal contact with the management? . .

But we shall speak about it, as you wrote me; please excuse me for having brought it up at this time, moved by my great love for our Scala!—

My wife has recovered and we are still waiting until Ginetta decides to make us grandparents!!—

I hope to receive good and comforting news, and I hope to see you shortly: a true joy for us!—

1891

Always most grateful and devoted, I remain

Your most affectionate
Giulio Ricordi

NOTE

1. *Otello.*

 *Boito to Verdi*

[Milan] 9 June [1891][1]

Dear Maestro,

Last night I heard a real alto voice at the Dal Verme in *La Cenerentola*, a certain *Guerrina Fabbri*,[2] student of Galletti.[3] Extensive range, in tune, sonorous without effort, and in the middle register beautiful enough to recall Alboni.[4]

Fair *comédienne* and vivacious when called for; musical accentuation fair; pronunciation fair. This singer must not be judged by *La Cenerentola*, because she appears ignorant, completely ignorant, of Rossini style.[5] But I believe that she could become a very good Quickly. When you come to Milan, you will hear and judge and perhaps find in that Dal Verme company some other element worthy of consideration.

Yesterday Giulio showed me part of a letter from you, and it gave me the deepest joy.[6] When in matters of art and life I have your approval, dear Maestro, I am sure not to make a mistake and do not ask for any other reward.

Camillo left for Rome before I had time to read the libretto[7] to him, because I wanted to read it to him nicely copied, and with the two cuts you suggest. The cut in the 2nd act goes well, it is made and is very useful. I am abbreviating the fourth[8] a little.

Giulio tells me that Signora Barberina keeps running a fever, and this news saddens me. Please give her my best regards.

Many affectionate greetings to you, dear Maestro, and to Signora Giuseppina.

Your most affectionate
Arrigo Boito

NOTES

1. Postmark: MILANO 9/6/91.

2. The contralto Guerrina Fabbri (1868–1946) excelled in coloratura roles, but she also became a successful Quickly in later *Falstaff* performances under Leopoldo Mugnone (1858–1941) and Arturo Toscanini.

3. The soprano Isabella Galletti Gianoli (1835–1901) sought in vain to appear in the première of *Aida* in Cairo in 1871. She became a successful voice teacher after a short career.

4. Marietta Alboni (1823–1894), celebrated nineteenth-century contralto, sang the role of Carlo V in the first performance of *Ernani*, at London's Covent Garden in 1847, when the baritone engaged for the part found it too high. Her physical proportions prompted Rossini to call her "the elephant that swallowed a nightingale."

5. According to the *Oxford Dictionary* and other sources, however, the young Guerrina Fabbri was "a coloratura of the Supervia type renowned for her *Cenerentola* and *L'Italiana in Algeri.*"

6. See Verdi to Ricordi, 25 May.

7. The libretto for *Nerone.*

8. Actually the third act.

 *Verdi to Ricordi*

St. Agata, 9 June 1891

You are joking, my dear Giulio! . . and I am glad to see you in a good mood!—

Why? Six or seven months ago nobody thought of *Falstaff*, or of the *Venerable Old Man* of St. Agata. The theatre went on all the same between boos and successes (few of the latter) . . . And now you want to tell me that the theatres would be better off without a subsidy!!

Forget the jokes. This is not the time to talk of *Falstaff,* which is going very slowly; still, I am more convinced than ever that the vast size of La Scala would harm the effect. In writing *Falstaff*, I had neither theatres nor singers in mind. I wrote to amuse myself, just for myself, and I think it should be performed at St. Agata instead of La Scala.—

I repeat, we'll talk about it in person.—

I am going to Cremona, but will be back tonight.

Addio, addio.

Affectionately,
G. Verdi

 *Ricordi to Verdi*

Milan, 12 June 1891

Illustrious Maestro,

No, illustrious Maestro! . . I am not joking, nor am I in good humor!! . . . In the universal misery reigning in Italy, the theatres are going to the dogs . . . . . and only upon the shoulders of the giants of art can they be saved!—Look at one more great theatre sunk in the economies of bad municipal administration! . . No more subsidy for the San Carlo in Naples, and good night!! . . And, just as by walking with a limping man you learn to limp, so by staying with the attorneys (oh! . . poor me!) I have learned (at my expense!) to harangue!! . . . . .

When the good Potbelly was locked up in the most secret cell . . . . . . who could have hoped for the good fortune of seeing him emerge into the light? . . . . And won't it be a great fortune for that theatre to be the first to have the honor of witnessing his triumph? . . . . and if La Scala were deprived of this fortune, isn't it clear as daylight that it would be a true artistic disaster for that house? . . . . Hence declining prestige, immediate and lasting damage. If it is a matter of what you wrote me in regard to the management, I venture to tell you that it would not be difficult to sever any and all contact!! . . . But it is always understood that when artistic considerations are involved, we can only tip our hats to our great Maestro, who is also truly "maestro di color che sanno" [master of those who know].[1]

Yesterday Mascheroni signed his contract with City Hall; I am glad, because he certainly is a conscientious artist, inspired by great zeal, and above all a hard worker.

Boito went to hear *La Cenerentola* and was quite satisfied; I think he has written you concerning two of the performers: the alto with a marvelous voice, and the excellent baritone with a very beautiful voice and much talent.[2] [. . .]

NOTES

1. Dante, *La divina commedia: Inferno*, Canto IV, verse 131, which refers to Aristotle.
2. In his letter to Verdi of 9 June 1891, Boito had mentioned only Guerrina Fabbri, the alto.

 *Verdi to Boito*

St. Agata, 12 June 1891

Dear Boito,

If you have discovered a good *Quickly,* I am the happiest man on Earth. That part gave me much to think about, for aside from the dramatic interest, the music has a very low tessitura. I could not do otherwise. There being four parts for women, one at least must be low.

The Potbelly is on the road that leads to madness. There are days when he doesn't move, sleeps, and is in a bad mood; at other times he shouts, runs, jumps, rages like the devil. . . I let him sober up a bit, but if he persists, I'll put a muzzle and a straitjacket on him.

Barberina is better; she has been getting up and eating with us for three or four days.

Peppina greets you and I embrace you warmly.

Your
G. Verdi

 *Boito to Verdi*

[Milan] 14 June [1891][1]

Dear Maestro,

Evviva! Let him have his way, let him run, he will break all the windows and every piece of furniture in your room; never mind, you will buy others. He will smash the piano, never mind. You'll buy another one; let everything be turned upside down! But the *big scene* will be done! Evviva!

Go! Go! Go! Go!

What pandemonium!!

But pandemonium as bright as the sun and dizzying as a madhouse!!

I know already what you will do. Evviva!

I guarantee Quickly to you. Down to the *low G* her voice is excellent, and the middle register is beautiful.

I am so glad to hear that Signora Barberina is better; give her my best regards, together with Signora Giuseppina.

A firm handshake

from your most affectionate
Arrigo Boito

NOTE

1. Postmark: MILANO 14/6/91.

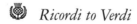 *Ricordi to Verdi*

Milan, 16 June 1891

Illustrious Maestro,

This very moment the Court of Appeals delivered the verdict in the Verga versus Sonzogno-Mascagni suit.[1] Verga has been accorded 25% of all box-office receipts, obliging Sonzogno to submit the accounts within 2 months. [. . .]

1891

NOTE

1. Concerning non-payment of royalties for *Cavalleria rusticana*, based on the novel and play by Giovanni Verga (1840–1922).

 *Verdi to Boito*

Montecatini, 5 July 1891

Dear Boito,

I am returning *le Rêve* [The Dream][1] to you and I thank you.—There are good intentions in it . . . but the road to hell is paved with good intentions, as the saying goes!

In this opera there are neither spoken dialogues, repetitions of words, *couplets*, reprises of motives, or many other formulas so much in use, especially at the *Opéra-Comique!* All of this goes well; but it doesn't go so well when all the action is locked in and strangled by the circle of three or four, I won't say motives, but orchestral phrases running and rerunning throughout the opera, without the relief of a little vocal line. And in the drama, which may not be altogether suitable for music, moments were not lacking to do this. On page 28 there are six verses spoken by the Bishop . . *Heureuse heureuse enfant* etc., etc., and further on, in a scene between the Bishop and Angelique . . . and in another one between the Bishop and her son; and in still others, to which sincere, dramatic, simple music could have been made, without so many orchestral tricks that aren't pleasing and, worse yet, are unnecessary. Besides, there is in the entire opera a continuous use of slurring, which must have a rather monotonous effect. Furthermore, an awful abuse of dissonances which make you feel like Falstaff shouting, "un breve spiraglio" [a brief respite][2] of a true chord! How much chatter!

Here all goes well. The *orage* [storm] of yesterday has refreshed the air, and today one lives well. . .

Peppina greets you and I take your hand.

Affectionately,
G. Verdi

NOTES

1. Opera by Alfred Bruneau (1875–1934), Parisian composer, musicologist, critic, and admirer of Verdi. His friend Emile Zola (1840–1902) wrote the libretto for *Messidor*, Bruneau's best-known work.

2. In the final text (III.ii): "Un poco di pausa" [A bit of rest].

 *Verdi to Ricordi*

St. Agata, 23 July 1891

Dear Giulio,

We came back to St. Agata yesterday morning,[1] and the moment we arrived we were distressed by the sad news about Faccio![2] Although his death had been foreseen for a long time, I was deeply upset! Poor Faccio! So able and so good! . . And he was still young!!! [. . .]

NOTES

1. From Montecatini.
2. Franco Faccio had died on 21 July.

 *Verdi to Boito*

St. Agata, 23 July 1891

Dear Boito,

He too is gone! Poor Faccio!

Yesterday, on arriving at St. Agata, we were all moved by the sad news we found in the *Corriere!*[1]

No matter how much his artistic intelligence might have vanished, and with it the other qualities of his good soul, I imagine the heartache you must have felt at this loss!

Poor Faccio was your schoolmate, companion, and friend in the stormy and happy times of your youth. . . (And he loved you so much!) —In the great misfortune that struck him, you rushed to him, giving him solemn, admirable proofs of your active friendship. You should be content with yourself, since you have deserved all the praise of honest people!

Poor unfortunate Faccio! So gifted! So good!

Addio.

Affectionately,
G. Verdi

NOTE

1. The Milan daily *Corriere della sera.*

1891

 *Boito to Verdi*

24 July [1891]
Milan[1]

Dear Maestro,

It's all over. Our friend rests in peace and has returned to the eternal law of souls and matter. Only death could heal him, and death has truly healed him. In his face reappeared, after life had ended, the noble expression of the human mind.

I wired you the sad news at Montecatini the morning of the 22nd, but the telegraph office there advised me in the evening that you had left.

Today your very kind letter comes to console me; thank you, dear Maestro, thank you. And today I repeat to you what I wrote you in the spring of last year: *better so.*

Again many thanks, and give Signora Giuseppina my affectionate regards.

To you a grateful handshake from your

most affectionate
Arrigo Boito

NOTE

1. Postmark: MILANO 24/7/91.

 *Ricordi to Verdi*

Milan, 26 July 1891

Illustrious Maestro,

After 8 days this is the first moment when I am, literally, able to take pen in hand. I was at risk of dying, visited by sudden and terrible indigestion, which has reduced me to a bundle of rags. The cause? . . . Who knows!! . . . perhaps excessive anger, the doctor says! . . . Briefly, my family, Boito, and Dina, who kindly came to see me, insist that I go for a short cure to Levico for at least fifteen baths. Overriding all considerations of my affairs in general (and my finances!! . .), I decided on this cure, which has always done me much good and, I hope, will do me good this time, too. If I continue to feel better, I shall leave tomorrow; and if I have no trouble during the trip, I'll go to Bayreuth, where, unfortunately, I hope to, and must, conclude the current business with the attorney for Wagner's heirs; by now it is all arranged with the publishers and only requires the approval of the attorney. Ah! . . . that Wagner contract has given me much to do . . . . and has made me bilious!! . . . Maybe the composer of the future wanted to avenge himself thus upon a rather mediocre admirer like . . . . this writer.

Poor Faccio has ended this wretched life, and one can say: better for him and his friends. I was very sorry that I could not pay him a final tribute!!

Tornaghi informed me of your telegram regarding the bonus for the semi-annual account;[1] as kind as ever, you took this trouble, too. I thank you very much.

Giuditta is accompanying me, and we shall be back between the 10th and the 12th of August. We send you our most affectionate and reverent greetings, and we hope to have your excellent, most excellent news upon our return.

I hope that I shall be able to write . . . . "I came back not rejuvenated!! . . (not even Levico does that much) but the same as I was a week ago" . . . . because at this time I feel as if 10 years had suddenly leapt upon my shoulders, so harsh was the blow I received.

Ginetta is in the country, near Varese; the young mama and her little daughter are very well, and Manolo and Gigi left today for a bit of country life with their sister.

If need be, you can always write to me in Milan, since at the office they will know of my whereabouts day by day, whereas I cannot inform you ahead of time, not knowing whether I'll be able to travel in one stretch or two, or whether I must rest somewhere.

In confidence I tell you, Maestro, that a principal motive of my going to Levico . . . . . is the prospect of an excursion to St. Agata [. . .].

NOTE

1. Missing.

 *Ricordi to Verdi*

Milan, 21 August 1891

Illustrious Maestro,

Here I am back in the *alma parens* [in the bosom of my family] . . . . and here I am writing you immediately, most anxious to have your news, which I seem to have lacked not for days, but for years!—You will say: "Well now, couldn't you have written me sooner?" . . . Let me tell you, then, Maestro, that the excursion to Germany was a continuous tossing about on the railway! . . . After a delayed departure because of my indisposition, we made a quick trip to the famous Bayreuth! . . . and there, mysterious news from Milan about the health of my mother-in-law made us return in worry to Munich, and from there to Trento, where alarming telegrams obliged Giuditta to go straight to Milan . . . . ; and so I went alone to the baths of Levico, always on the *qui vive*! . . restless in my fear of having to rush to Milan. Therefore, I took a short, very rapid cure with 2 baths per day, which, fortunately, I was able to endure; for all that, the cure, even like this, has helped me immensely, and now I am glad I decided to take it. Our life here is now very sad: my wife and my sister-in-law are staying with their mother all the time! . . . It is a pitiful case, which has now lasted for nine months; and while feeling sorry for the poor sick lady, I am even sorrier (allow me to say so) for her daughters!! . . but . . . they do right, they are doing very well; . . only it pains me to see this spectacle enduring without any hope!! . . . . . There are days of great alarm, then respite, and so on! . . .

But . . . . forgive me for entertaining you with such sad things; proceeding to cheerful ones . . . . I must tell you that I heard an abominable performance of *Parsifal*[1] and a good one of *Tannhäuser*,[2] as far as the artists are concerned, excellent regarding orchestra and chorus in a stupendous *mise-en-scène*. But when the singers are inadequate . . . . . it's the same the world over!! . . . And even in Bayreuth they don't make them any better; those in *Parsifal*, with the exception of the baritone,[3] were absolutely unbearable.[4] [. . .]

NOTES

1. Conducted by Hermann Levi (1839–1900), a rabbi's son, who ignored Wagner's anti-Semitic slurs. Therese Malten (1855–1930) alternated with Amalie Materna (1844–1918) as Kundry in this production.

2. Conducted by Felix Mottl (1856–1911), with Pauline de Ahna (1862–1950), Richard Strauss's future wife, as Elisabeth.

3. Theodor Reichmann (1849–1903) alternated with Karl Scheidemantel (1859–1923) as Amfortas and Wolfram von Eschenbach.

4. At a Bayreuth performance of *Parsifal*, G. B. Shaw asserted that the "bass howled, the tenor bawled, the baritone sang flat, and the soprano, when she condescended to sing at all, did not merely shout her words, but screamed." (Frederic Spotts, *Bayreuth* [New Haven: Yale University Press, 1994], p. 105.)

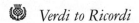 *Verdi to Ricordi*

St. Agata, 23 August 1891

Dear Giulio,

I am very happy about your good news, and very happy to hear that Levico has been good for you even this time. Evviva!

But poor Giuditta! These daughters do well, very well, to do what they are doing, but if I were in charge up above, I would have a little pity for them.

And when are you coming to St. Agata? And will Giuditta be able to? We hope so. When you come, you will be received with open arms; and the sooner the better. You only have to write or wire these words: "We shall arrive at Fiorenzuola on the day . . . hour . . . ."

Our health isn't holding up on its foundations. Peppina's legs have been in bad shape for several years, my own since last summer when we came to Milan on the way to Montecatini. The rest is well . . . but let's understand each other: by the *rest* I mean the stomach and the head . . . . nothing else!

Ah! The Potbelly? His legs are also in bad shape; he moves slowly and I'm afraid he sings like a drunkard!

And now addio. Stay healthy always. Greet Giuditta and tell her that both of us await *both of you* with *open arms* . . . Ah!—I said it already.

Affectionately,
G. Verdi

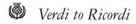 *Verdi to Ricordi*

St. Agata, 30 August 1891

Dear Giulio,

Returning from Levico you wrote me a nice letter, which I answered immediately, saying that we await you at St. Agata with open arms, Giuditta and you . . . *the sooner the better.*

I am again writing you these two lines for fear that that letter of mine might have been lost, etc., etc. . .

In a hurry . . . greetings, greetings, and once again *till we see each other!*

Affectionately,
G. Verdi

 *Ricordi to Verdi*

Milan, 1 September 1891

Illustrious Maestro,

From day to day I hoped to answer and tell you: "Thank you, we are coming!" . . . And so from day to day I delayed in vain hope!—My mother-in-law is still in the very same state! . . . . which means that neither my wife nor my sister-in-law can leave Milan. [. . .]

As to certain news[1] . . . . I am like St. Thomas—seeing is believing!—And since my nose is already long enough, you will not be so cruel as to make me add another inch. [. . .]

NOTE

1. Unfounded rumors regarding the completion of *Falstaff*.

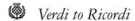 *Verdi to Ricordi*

St. Agata, 3 September 1891

Dear Giulio,

I deeply regret your many enduring and cruel discomforts. There is nothing else to be said other than patience and courage.—

Imagine! You can come on the 10th or 12th or whenever you want, alone or with Giuditta, and you will always be welcome in every way. [. . .]

 *Boito to Verdi*

3 September [1891]
Milan

Dear Maestro,

It has been a century since I had the pleasure of writing to you.

Gallignani[1] now offers me the occasion; he wants to be accompanied to St. Agata by a letter of mine. Here it is. Mariotti, a month ago, offered me the directorship of the Conservatory of Parma; I did not accept, but he would not admit defeat.

He returned ten or twelve days ago to repeat his invitation; I did not accept, but Mariotti would not admit defeat. He went to Rome with a plan that Gallignani will tell you about, and does not admit defeat.

Meanwhile, Mariotti's reluctance to accept my refusal can facilitate action from other influences which Mariotti himself greatly fears, and this would be a disaster.[2] To prevent this disaster, Maestro Gallignani must be helped to become director of the Conservatory of Parma.

Gallignani will ask you, dear Maestro, for a letter to Commendatore Mariotti; I shall write him another one in which I will clinch my refusal with a final and decisive stroke; let us hope that Maestro Gallignani will thus be appointed director.

Many, many greetings to Signora Giuseppina and to you, dear Maestro, and till we meet again in October.[3]

Your most affectionate
Arrigo Boito

NOTES

1. Giuseppe Gallignani (1851–1923) was primarily a composer of sacred music. He was *maestro di cappella* at the cathedral of Milan from 1884 to 1891, when—with Verdi's and Boito's considerable support—he was named director of the Parma Conservatory. Three years later, Verdi pleaded in vain with Gallignani to admit his coachman's son to that institution. (See Verdi to Gallignani, 20 June, 29 October, and 4 November 1894.) In 1897 Gallignani became director of the Milan Conservatory and recommended Toscanini's engagement at La Scala. Because of alleged abuses in the administration of the Milan Conservatory, Gallignani threw himself out of a window, a victim of Fascist persecution. "Toscanini's grief was only equalled by his anger." He sent a telegram of strong protest to the Ministry of Public Education, and at the funeral he grabbed the minister's wreath and threw it away. Then he grabbed the notes of a would-be Fascist speaker, "threw them to the ground, stepped on them, and shouted: 'No, you will not speak!'" (Harvey Sachs, *Toscanini*, p. 163.)

2. The nomination of Paolo Serrao. (See Boito to Verdi, 21 May 1890, n. 2.)

3. At St. Agata.

 *Verdi to Giovanni Mariotti*

St. Agata, 4 September 1891
Commendatore Mariotti-Parma

Boito wrote me recently that he can in no way accept the position of Director of the Conservatory of Parma.

Thus I can only repeat what I told you in person here at St. Agata about twenty days ago, about the merits of Maestro Gallignani. He seems to me in every respect the most suitable and appropriate man for that office.

I trust that his appointment will be advantageous to the Conservatory and an honor for everyone.

Set your tireless energy in motion, dear Signor Mariotti, and have him nominated. You will be content, as are, in anticipation, Boito and your devoted

G. Verdi

 Boito to Giovanni Mariotti

Milan, 4 September [1891]

Dearest Signor Mariotti,

I know that tomorrow you will be back in Parma; I am writing you, therefore, certain that this letter will be read tomorrow. I repeat what I told you in person; I repeat it after having reconsidered the question that caused you so many troubles, and me the painful worry of finding no way to satisfy you. I really cannot take over the directorship of the Parma Conservatory, and hope that the ministry will not offer it to me so that I need not be obliged to refuse. I cannot accept this directorship as a sinecure; my conscience forbids it. And I cannot accept it as a genuine and demanding task to fulfill; my work forbids it. If during our hurried talks my words might have betrayed some emotion that weakened the strength of the refusal, it came from the regret I felt in being opposed to your kind offers; it also came from the sympathy binding me to the young Parma Conservatory, and from my gratitude for the benefit it gave poor Faccio. But feelings do not change circumstances of affairs and persons; my circumstances are such as to impose this refusal.

I am comforted by the certainty that under the most worthy Maestro Gallignani's direction the Parma Conservatory will continuously proceed on the high road of art.

With all my devoted friendship and profound gratitude to you,

Your most affectionate
Arrigo Boito

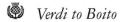 *Verdi to Boito*

St. Agata, 5 September 1891

Dear Boito,

Gallignani, as you will know, did not encounter Mariotti in Parma; he couldn't find out where he was. He left my letter to be given to him when he returns.

Now Gallignani asks me for a letter to the minister. This would, in my opinion, be a wrong move! Mariotti would be excluded in this way; that would be bad. On the other hand, I am convinced that when Mariotti finally persuades himself that you do not accept the director's position, he will not be opposed to our (your and my own) proposal.—In the end, Mariotti will then write me, and we shall see.

From the letter Gallignani wrote me last night[1] I see that he is quite upset and nervous. Try to calm him and tell him that in this matter there is nothing, so far, to be alarmed about.

Many, many greetings from Peppina and myself. 'Til later . . . and then 'til we meet again in October.

Affectionately,
G. Verdi

NOTE

1. Missing.

Boito to Verdi

8 September [1891]
Milan[1]

Dear Maestro,

What restless and impetuous people!! Mariotti is a tornado and Gallignani an earthquake. I am caught in the midst of these two wild furies unchained by nature, and don't know how to save myself.

I wanted to read to the earthquake the letter you wrote me, and he promised to calm himself and to await quietly the course of events. In the event of extreme danger, you will be asked to write to the minister; only in the event of extreme danger.

Nobody knows Mariotti's whereabouts; Gallignani is in the presbytery of the cathedral,[2] where he is *quietly* and feverishly awaiting news from Rome at any moment.

We shall see.

Meanwhile, I have heard that *Falstaff* is finished.[3] Evviva! I can't wait until October to pat his belly.

So long, then, for not too many days.

Many greetings to Signora Giuseppina and Signora Barberina.

An affectionate handshake.

Your
Arrigo Boito

NOTES

1. Postmark: MILANO 8/9/91.

2. As *maestro di cappella* at this time.

3. A rumor spread by several papers, which Giulio Ricordi sharply denied in the *Gazzetta musicale* of 20 September. (*Carteggio* ii, p. 416.)

🟣 *Giovanni Mariotti to Verdi*

Rome, 9 September 1891

Illustrious Maestro,

I thank you warmly for your very kind letter.[1] To tell you the truth, I have not yet received it (since it is in Parma, where I shall arrive tomorrow); but I know the contents already from what Gallignani has written to me.—I did not fail to discuss it immediately with the ministry, where everyone welcomed your recommendation with the greatest deference.—Here, today as always, your advice and desire is law for all. [. . .]

1891

NOTE

1. Of 4 September.

 *Ricordi to Verdi*

Milan, 9 September 1891

Illustrious Maestro,

After my return[1] I received your letter of the 3rd of this month—as always, both great and kind! . . . .

In view of my mother-in-law's health, we must seize the opportunity and profit from a moment of calm. Our plan would be the following: Arrive at Fiorenzuola the day after tomorrow, Friday, at 9:11 A.M. All that must be said [to the conductor] is "please stop" . . . . and I am sorry to arrive at an hour that does not correspond to your customary breakfast time; but . . . . it's the timetable's fault! . . .

We cannot enjoy your dear hospitality as at other times, because Giuditta cannot be absent for more than 3 . . . 4 days at the most, since her sister would be unable to withstand the strain of caring for her mother alone.

But . . . . . I would like to tell you something . . . . and find it so embarrassing that I don't know how to begin . . . . I take courage and come forward! If instead of 2, 3 of us were to arrive? . . . . . Good Lord, how impertinent!—Softly, softly I whisper in your ear that Tito, too, is dying to pay you a visit!! [. . .]

Please be so kind as to wire me as soon as you have received this letter.[2]
[. . .]

NOTES

1. From Levico.
2. No such telegram has been located.

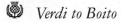 *Verdi to Boito*

St. Agata, 10 September 1891

Dearest Boito,

Only one word:

I correct:

It is not true that I have finished *Falstaff*.[1] I am working to put all I have done into the orchestral score, because I am fearful of forgetting some passages and combinations of instruments. Afterwards I'll do the first part of the third act . . . and then amen! This part is shorter and less difficult than the others. . . But Falstaff's first recitative and the passage where the wives are leaving must be worked out with care. . . Here there should be . . . I must say, a *motive* that would become ever softer, losing itself in a double *pianissimo*, preferably with a single violin above the stage. Why not?—If orchestras are put into the cellar today,[2] why could a violin not be put into the attic!!? . . . If I were a prophet, my apostles would say . . *"Oh, the sublime idea!"* . . . *Ha ha ha ha!* What a beautiful world this is!!

Peppina and Barberina thank and greet you. I [. . .][3]

NOTES

1. See Ricordi to Verdi, 1 September, and Boito to Verdi, 8 September.
2. Wagner's idea practiced at Bayreuth. (See Verdi to Mascheroni, 8 December 1893.)
3. Verdi's final words and signature are missing in the autograph.

 *Verdi to Boito*

St. Agata, Tuesday. . . [15 September 1891][1]

Dear Boito,

Here you have Mariotti's letter.[2] Return it to me after having read it to the *earthquake*.

You know already that Giuditta, Giulio, and Tito[3] Ricordi are here. Giulio asked me to let him read the libretto of *Falstaff*. I gave it to him, and in his room, I believe, all three of them read it. . . Nothing wrong. The impression was very good. . .

. . . 'Til we meet again.

Your
G. Verdi

NOTES

1. Postmark: BUSSETO 15/9/91.
2. Of 9 September.
3. Tito Ricordi II (1865–1933), Giulio and Giuditta's eldest son, was named after his grandfather. He studied engineering at this time, but he succeeded his father as head of the House of Ricordi from 1912 to 1919. He left no heirs. "He lacked Giulio's tact and business sense (he even quarrelled with Puccini over the publication of *La Rondine*), and the direction of the firm eventually passed to people from outside the immediate family." (William Weaver and Simonetta Puccini, eds., *The Puccini Companion*, p. 381.)

1891

 *Boito to Verdi*

16 September [1891]
Milan[1]

Dear Maestro,

I have already taken Mariotti's letter to Gallignani. Gallignani has read it, is now at ease, and asks me to convey to you his warmest thanks.

I knew that the Ricordi family was at St. Agata, and I imagined that they would ask to read the libretto of *Falstaff*; I am glad that this reading has made a good impression.

I am here, still a slave to the affairs poor Faccio has left upon my shoulders.

In a few days a new family council must be formed for the guardianship of the father; then one must proceed to a new inventory and other legal formalities.

On account of this business I couldn't go to the country this year, and if I succeed (as I hope, as I wish and believe) in finding refuge at St. Agata, it won't be for the long sojourn I had planned. But in any event I will arrange matters so that at the very beginning of October I can enjoy a bit of liberty. As soon as I am able to fix the date of my arrival, I'll wire you.

At this point I have become more knowledgeable about courts, magistrate's courts, and official papers than violins, clarinets, and trumpets.

Many good greetings to all the inhabitants of St. Agata.

A firm handshake

from your most affectionate
Arrigo Boito

NOTE

1. Postmark: MILANO 16/9/91.

 *Ricordi to Verdi*

Milan, 19 September 1891

Illustrious Maestro,

Although my absence was short,[1] I found a pile of stuff on my desk, so that despite writing all day long, and even all evening at home, I still haven't been able to catch up. But having taken care of urgent matters, I said to myself: *now stop* —and here I am, finally, in higher spheres, as I enjoy writing to our great, dearest, and kindest Verdi. If an old proverb doesn't lie, you and the most gracious Signora Peppina must have felt your ears ringing a bit! . . . for between me, Giuditta, and Tito, we do not cease talking about the very beautiful days we spent at St. Agata. [. . .]

I am particularly grateful to you for the favor of letting me read the libretto of *Falstaff!!* . . . Ah! . . if I had had the courage . . . . to ask a certain Maestro!! . . . perhaps I might have had the delicious gift of hearing a bit of music; . . . . but before a certain person I became (as the Milanese say) *on fiffon numer vun* [a number-one coward]! Will I have a little courage on another fortunate occasion? . . um! [. . .]

And now, finally, I close in the hope that both of you may remain in such good health! . . . . Truly, there is that business . . . . . of the legs . . . . but dear God, our Maestro is too . . . . . too *sedentary* . . . . and this *lack* of exercise might be the cause of this regrettable inconvenience!! . . . . . Jokes aside, as Verdi is a marvelous artist, so is he a marvelous man . . . Yes, marvelous, marvelous. . . Long may he live . . . . and I allow my fantasy to render me so swellheaded as to consider composing a fugue on this subject:

What do you think of it? . . Is it a good subject? . . . . Or do you find it bad? . .

Always your devoted and most grateful

Giulio Ricordi

Have written immediately to Paris for the music paper. As soon as it comes, it will be sent to you.

Our regards to Signora Stolz.

NOTE

1. During his visit with his wife and son at St. Agata. (Ricordi to Verdi, 9 September.)

 *Ricordi to Verdi*

Milan, 2 October 1891

Illustrious Maestro,

I hope that after my letter [to Paris] you received the paper for the orchestral score that I sent you the moment it arrived from Paris. [. . .]

1891

🌣 *Boito to Verdi*

3 October [1891]
Rome[1]

Dear Maestro,

Gallignani has finally been named director of the Conservatory of Parma. That took some doing!

The minister convened the music council[2] to consider this and other questions, and that's why I am here, hurtled to Rome by the earthquake Gallignani.

But it's finally over!

I hope to leave again tomorrow, when the other questions Villari has submitted to us have been resolved. I will then tell you all about it in person.

In the meantime, I amused myself yesterday by watching the very funny hunt for the pilgrims.[3]

Today the whole city is quiet and it is raining.

For the time being I will return to Milan, where I am called by the interests of Faccio's father. I hope to rid myself soon of that nuisance, and then, God willing, I'll spend a few days with our friend Falstaff at St. Agata and will have fun with him.

I shall let you know my arrival time from Milan.

Many kind greetings to you, dear Maestro, and to Signora Giuseppina.

Your most affectionate
Arrigo Boito

P.S. The council has nominated Gallignani unanimously, without even discussing the candidate; the vote was taken based *only* on the letter which you, Maestro, wrote to Mariotti. So it had to be. Maestro Marchetti (who is a man of common sense) was the first to speak, and he guided the vote in this direction.

NOTES

1. Postmark: ROMA 3/10/91.

2. Pasquale Villari (1826–1917), an historian from Naples and, from 1891 to 1892, the minister of education, had called Boito, Antonio Bazzini, and Filippo Marchetti to Rome.

Marchetti (1831–1902) composed *Ruy Blas* (1869) and other, less successful operas. From 1881 to 1886 he was president of the Accademia di Santa Cecilia in Rome, and from 1886 to 1902 he directed the Liceo musicale in the same city.

Bazzini writes at the top of the first page of this letter: "On my feet again, I profit from my friend Boito's hospitality to send the illustrious Verdi the warmest and most affectionate greeting. His most devoted admirer A. Bazzini."

3. On 2 October, a group of French pilgrims had desecrated the tomb of Vittorio Emanuele II in the Pantheon.

 Verdi to Ferdinando Resasco[1]

St. Agata, 21 October 1891

Dear Signor Resasco,

I have nothing unpublished to offer you for the single issue of *Genova-Iberia*. But since you speak of agriculture, in which I am but a simple amateur, I would like this most noble science to be widely fostered by us. What a source of wealth for our fatherland!

A few less musicians, lawyers, physicians, etc., and a few more farmers: This is the vote I cast for my country. [. . .]

NOTE

1. Ferdinando Resasco, president of the *Genova-Iberia* committee, had asked Verdi for a contribution to this special publication for the benefit of flood victims in Spain.

 Verdi to Giuseppina Negroni Prati

St. Agata, 26 October 1891

[. . .] Let us be clear. You say: beyond the 70s . . . far more than *beyond!* . . . 78 years rang in several days ago.[1] I couldn't care less . . . and let it be. Meanwhile, to pass the time, and when I feel like it, I still scribble a few notes; and it doesn't tire me, because the genre amuses me and between me and myself I sometimes laugh out loud.

Concerning our health, Peppina and I, too, are doing fairly well, apart from legs that are slower and getting ever slower, like the *tempi* in tenors' arias. [. . .]

NOTE

1. Verdi's birthday, on 9 or 10 October, on which his friend had congratulated him.

 Verdi to Ricordi

St. Agata Busseto, 6 November 1891

Dear Giulio,

Thank you for sending me the score of *Fritz*.[1]

1891

In my life I have read many, many, very many bad librettos, but I have never read a libretto as *foolish* as this.

As to the music, I read on a bit, but I soon got tired of so many dissonances, of the false key relations in modulations, of all the suspended cadences, of all those tricks, and moreover . . . of so many tempo changes in almost every bar. All the most arresting things, which, however, offend the sense of rhythm as well as the ear.

The word-accent is good in general, but it never hits the truth of the situation. It isn't difficult to hit the target a bit high or a bit low; but it is difficult to hit it in the middle (as Manzoni said), and thus the characters are not well drawn. The music may be beautiful in any case! I consider things from my point of view . . . but I am old and set in my ways . . . that is, old, yes, but not so set in my ways.

I hope that your health may be excellent, as I will find out myself in a few days in Milan.—When? I don't know yet.

Greet your Giuditta from the two of us.

Yours as ever,
G. Verdi

NOTE

1. *L'amico Fritz*, opera by Pietro Mascagni.

 Verdi to Bramanti

Milan, 14 November 1891

Sir!

. . . . *Remedy an inconvenience* . . . . you say? But which? . . . *Inconvenience,* because I have not sent my donation for Dante's monument?[1]

Dante by himself has raised such a monument, and of such a height that no one can reach it. Let us not devalue him with manifestations that put him on a level with so many others, even the most mediocre ones.

To that name I do not dare raise hymns; I bow my head and worship in silence.

Devotedly,
G. Verdi

NOTE

1. We know nothing about Signor Bramanti or his letter to Verdi, who had probably been asked for a monetary contribution or a hymn for a monument to be erected in Ravenna.

Verdi to Giuseppe Gallignani

Milan, 15 November 1891

Dear Gallignani,

I regret having been unable to attend your concerts of sacred music.[1] I know they went well, and I am glad.—I am particularly glad for the performance of Palestrina's music: the true Prince of Sacred Music, and the Eternal Father of Italian Music.

Palestrina can no longer compete with the bold harmonic inventions of modern music, but if he were better known and studied, we would write in a more Italian spirit and be better patriots (in music, of course). [. . .]

NOTE

1. Referring to concerts in early November in Milan's Church of San Antonio during a congress on sacred music.

Ricordi to Verdi

Milan, 15 December 1891

Illustrious Maestro,

With the greatest pleasure I read your confirmation of the good news which Origoni[1] brought us the same night he returned [from Genoa]. Evviva then! [. . .]

We do not accept your thanks, ... since we are the ones to thank you, because during your sojourn here[2] we took over almost half the Verdi domicile!! [. . .]

In secret: say two sweet little words to the dear Potbelly . . . . . who has winked his eye a bit at me . . . . . but too briefly! [. . .]

NOTES

1. Luigi Origoni, Ricordi's son-in-law, Ginetta's husband, apparently had reported on the Verdis' good health.
2. On the Verdis' annual move to Genoa from 17 November to 8 December via Milan.

Ricordi to Verdi

Milan, 29 December 1891

Illustrious Maestro,

I am enclosing two lines to my letter of today[1] to tell you that the year is ending dismally for us!!—My mother-in-law is dying, and her two poor daughters are staying with her *night and day*; thus, in addition to their emotional pain, their physical exhaustion is pitiful! . . . No matter how involved in my work, I cannot forego running up there every 10 or 15 minutes, feeling so sorry for them. It is far, far too prolonged a spectacle!!— The influenza reigns in Milan, and how! Fortunately, we are still all right.

Please give me your news, Maestro! To know that you are in the best of health will be a real bonus to our morale and a true joy!! . . . . I send you and Signora Peppina our best wishes; you can imagine how we send them with all our hearts, and how we bless these two dear, beloved, good people! Evviva for both of you, as '92 is being born! The best of health and joys . . . . . . and . . . . . and . . . . another evviva . . . . to His Majesty Potbelly!!— With all affection, with all gratitude

Your most devoted
Giulio Ricordi

NOTE

1. Missing.

1892

Divos and Divas[1]

T
he year begins with Verdi concerned by an influenza epidemic which affects not only him and his wife in Genoa but also their friends in Milan. "I haven't worked on it [*Falstaff*] for three months," he informs Monaldi on 18 January. Internal strife at the Villanova Hospital preoccupies its benefactor throughout the year and requires his frequent intervention. He postpones a visit to Milan because of an unexpected revival of *Otello* at La Scala, of which he disapproves. Between late February and 21 March, however, he contemplates the casting of *Falstaff* with Boito and Ricordi in Milan, keeping busy at St. Agata in between. Ricordi persuades him to return to Milan on 7 April to conduct the Prayer from Rossini's opera *Mosè* at La Scala on the 8th, in observance of the centenary of Rossini's birth. The Maestro is back in Genoa on 11 April and finds an amazing letter from Hans von Bülow awaiting him. In spite of these interruptions, he finishes orchestrating the first act of *Falstaff* by the middle of the month.[2]

In early May the Verdis are "half sick because of the horrible journey" on their annual return from Genoa to St. Agata. The Maestro's correspondence with Ricordi in the summer reflects his increasing involvement with his final opera. His long "rigmarole" of 13 June, in particular, reveals many of his ideas and intentions concerning production. Much time is wasted on account of the tenor Angelo Masini, who cannot accept the role of Fenton because of prior engagements in Russia. In June Verdi takes his fragile Giuseppina to nearby Tabiano on the 18th, returns to St. Agata on the 20th, and comes back to the little spa on the 23rd or 24th. From there the couple travels to Milan on or about July 2 and arrives with Teresa Stolz in Montecatini on the 5th.

1892

Giuseppina Pasqua presents herself to the Maestro at the spa on the 10th and is offered the role of Quickly. On the night of 20 July the Verdis experience another fatiguing journey to St. Agata. From 25 to 27 July Verdi is in Genoa on business. In Milan between 28 and 31 July, he auditions Emma Zilli for the part of Alice and decides with Boito and Ricordi on the première of *Falstaff* at La Scala during the following season. The serene tone of his letters changes abruptly when "the Divos and the Divas spread not their wings but their claws," as Verdi declares to Tornaghi on 17 August. Victor Maurel's[3] acceptance of the title role had been taken for granted, but his exorbitant demands, conveyed by his wife, put the entire project in jeopardy. "Cancel everything!" Verdi explodes, and he and Ricordi succeed in bringing "the Divo" to his knees. Maurel rushes to St. Agata on 7 September to "clear up the misunderstanding," and he leaves in peace. On the 15th Verdi hands over the orchestra score of the third act to Giulio's son Tito at the railway station in Piacenza, having entrusted the first act to Giulio himself at St. Agata on 27 August. Verdi is still "meticulously examining the second act," as he writes to Boito on the 20th, and apparently sends the autograph to Ricordi in early October.[4] On the 13th of October he accompanies his wife to visit her sister Barberina in Cremona and proceeds immediately to Milan to discuss the *Falstaff* production in detail with Ricordi, Boito, and the designer Alfredo Hohenstein. He is back at St. Agata on the 16th.

On 24 October the Verdis move directly from St. Agata to Genoa, where the Maestro, Ricordi, and probably Boito, too, hear several artists engaged for *Falstaff* in Franchetti's *Cristoforo Colombo*. With a sore throat, and worried about the young tenor assigned to the role of Fenton, Verdi personally coaches the singers at his apartment in Genoa. On 7 November he surprises Pasqua with the insertion of Quickly's narrative in II.i.[5] and tells her how to perform portions of it. The following day he cautions the highly intellectual Maurel, with admirable psychological insight and diplomacy, against overdoing his part. Casting questions and endless corrections of the orchestra and piano-vocal scores fill his almost daily correspondence with Ricordi until the end of the year.

In January, while upset about the effects of the "devastating influenza," Ricordi is favorably impressed by the young Edoardo Mascheroni, Franco Faccio's successor at La Scala. In early February Ricordi is distressed by the sudden death of his attorney and friend Alessandro Dina. With his wife, Giuditta, he visits the Verdis in Genoa in late April. In May, an informative trip to the Music Exhibition in Vienna[6] impresses and enlightens him. Unforeseen casting and other production problems concern Ricordi all summer and into autumn. A younger son is seriously ill in the country. For the weekend of 27 August Ricordi comes to St. Agata to accept the autograph orchestra score of the first act of *Falstaff*. The excessive demands of Maurel and Pasqua require infinite patience and particular diplomacy, while Ricordi constantly strives to maintain a delicate balance between Verdi's wishes and Piontelli's management. Between 28 October and early November he sees the Maestro in Genoa. Back in Milan, Ricordi, in the dual role of publisher and producer, is overburdened with critical deadlines, rehearsal schedules, problems concerning orchestra and technical personnel, translations, a complicated American copyright application, public relations, and almost daily changes in the proofs of the piano reduction.[7] In addition, the Bénoit affair has still not been resolved. On 28 December he receives Verdi's supposedly final corrections. The end of the year finds him enthusiastically anticipating Verdi's arrival in Milan and the rehearsals for the new production.

Boito, after recovering from influenza at home, goes to Turin for a performance of *Die Walküre* in Italian on 23 January. Two weeks later he plans to be in Nervi and hopes to have a long chat with the Maestro in nearby Genoa. He travels to Sicily in February to inspect the Palermo Conservatory, but is back in time for *Falstaff* talks with Verdi and Ricordi in Milan. Boito apparently stays in the city for much of the summer and meets Verdi there on various occasions as well as at St. Agata on 17 June. A personal confession about a "very sad moment" in his life may allude to his impending separation from Duse.[8] Intense work on *Nerone* compels him to forego a promised visit to St. Agata, but on 27 September he sends Verdi a few more changes in the text of the third act. On 11 October Ricordi summons him from Villa d'Este to the city for a conference with Verdi and Hohenstein.[9] In late October Boito is again in Nervi, dines often with the Verdis at Palazzo Doria, and probably also sees Ricordi in Genoa. In early November he moves to the Villa Rosten, in nearby Pegli, where he works on *Nerone* and on the French translation of *Falstaff*.

NOTES

1. Verdi to Eugenio Tornaghi, 17 August.
2. Verdi considered it "completely ready" only in August. (Verdi to Ricordi, 14 August.)
3. See Biographical Sketch.
4. See Tito Ricordi to Verdi, 30 September. (See Hepokoski, p. 45.)
5. See Hepokoski, p. 42; and Hepokoski, "Pasqua," p. 248.
6. Verdi to Bülow, 14 April, n. 1.
7. "Verdi altered over 300 passages and kept Ricordi informed of these changes in almost daily correspondence. His work on the score during these two months may be followed and dated with precision. Not only do we have the highly informative (and still

1892

largely unpublished) letters of Verdi and Ricordi, but the proofs themselves, with Verdi's corrections, are also available for study in the library of the Milan Conservatory. Only slightly over half of the revisions are simple corrections of printing or reduction errors. Well over 100 were compositional revisions of either text or music." (Hepokoski, p. 45.)

8. In the absence of any Boito-Duse letters from this year, we have no clue concerning this remark. (See Boito to Verdi, 9 August, n. 2.)

9. By telegram addressed to Villa Cima, Cernobbio: "MAESTRO WILL BE HERE THURS-DAY AT THREE-THIRTY AND LEAVES AGAIN SUNDAY."

 *Boito to Verdi*

1 January 1892
[Milan][1]

Dear Maestro,

I want these first words, which I am writing today, to be addressed to you, dear Maestro, with affectionate good wishes for you and Signora Giuseppina.

Good health and good work.

Your most affectionate
Arrigo Boito

NOTE

1. According to all indications, Boito wrote these lines at his home.

 *Verdi to Boito*

Genoa, 2 January 1892

Dear Boito,

Thank you for your kind words.

We are a little *marotti* (as they say in Genoa).[1] Peppina is in bed with catarrh and nausea; I am plagued by a bad cough that is upsetting my stomach.—Let's hope for later!

If you have begun the year well, continue so until the end. Together with Peppina, I wish this for you with all my heart.

Affectionately,
G. Verdi

NOTE

1. "Sick" in Genoese dialect.

 *Verdi to Maria Waldmann*

Genoa, 3 [January] 1892

Dear Maria,

Peppina and I are a bit sick. She has been in bed for several days with an upset stomach and nausea; I with a bad cough that gives me no rest. And thus we ended the old year poorly, and poorly began the new one! [. . .]

 *Ricordi to Verdi*

Milan, 4 January 1892

Illustrious Maestro,

Once again December 31st brings bereavement to my home[1]. . . . at least my poor mother-in-law need suffer no longer! . . . . However, for her daughters the grief is still the same, no matter how long they had been prepared!!—

On top of this sorrow I learned that you and Signora Peppina are ill! . . . . . You can well imagine how upset we are. This morning I had better news about you, kindly sent me by the excellent Signor De Amicis, and I hope to hear from you yourself soon that both of you are completely recovered.

Regarding La Scala, I know little these days! But having been at the rehearsals and the 1st performance,[2] I can tell you *de visu et auditu* that Mascheroni surpassed my expectations; he is really an excellent acquisition: good memory, quick in rehearsals, secure in his tempi and his beat, and extremely calm before the audience. Of course, any of those who had either desired his position or had had a conductor of their own in mind will fight him ferociously!—Mascheroni is a bit dismayed by this!! [. . .]

NOTES

1. See Ricordi to Verdi, 29 December 1889 and 7 January 1890, concerning the death of Pippo Brentano (?–1889).

2. Of *Tannhäuser*, which had opened the season on 29 December; the illness of several artists forced postponement of the traditional opening date of 26 December.

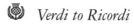 *Verdi to Ricordi*

Genoa, 7 January 1892

Dear Giulio,

The doctor says it probably isn't serious, but in the meantime Peppina

1892

and I have not moved out of the house for about 12 days and stay in bed for about 18 hours a day!—

I still have not been able to take a look at the papers you sent me,[1] but as soon as I can I will look at them and we'll arrange the rest. I can tell you nothing else, stuck in the house and in bed as I am—

Tell me about all of you and stay well.

Addio, addio.

G. Verdi

NOTE

1. Unknown.

 *Ricordi to Verdi*

Milan, 8 January 1892

Illustrious Maestro,

You can well imagine how very pleased we are to receive a letter from you to me, and another one from Signora Peppina to Giuditta.[1] This pleasure, however, was quite diminished when we learned that you are still indisposed and obliged to stay in bed for part of the day! . . . It's a nuisance, really an awful nuisance, but your doctor is a very brave man to oblige you thus; it is the only sure remedy against any serious consequence of that strange and mysterious influenza! [. . .]

What news do you expect from Milan that isn't full of sadness? We are definitely surrounded by this devastating influenza! . . . . The sky is foggy, the sick number in the thousands, the dead in the hundreds! . . . and among them are many friends and acquaintances. [. . .]

NOTE

1. Missing.

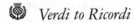 *Verdi to Ricordi*

Genoa, 9 January 1892

Dear Giulio,

I return the papers to you. All right . . .

Do me the favor of sending a check to the bank for the *20th* of this month. I hope that by then I shall be able to leave the house to get some cash. . . My health is a bit better, although the cough is quite tormenting, especially at night. But Peppina is still in the same state. No fever, but most violent coughing and nausea. The worst is that she doesn't eat. [. . .]

Ah, what an ugly start to the year!

Give me your news and stay healthy. Addio

G. Verdi

 *Ricordi to Verdi*

Milan, 11 January 1892

Illustrious Maestro,

We are sorry, very sorry that we still don't have the news we so ardently desire . . . to know that you and Signora Peppina are completely liberated from any and every kind of influenza!!—May the devil take it once and for all!! . . . and [to know] that we need not talk about it anymore, ... since it is really a universal disaster!—In the summer . . . . . it's the threat of cholera, ... in the winter the visit of influenza, and so we live in a truly pleasant world! . . . The theatres, in particular, feel the effects. La Scala, too, which this year appeared to have made a good start, thanks to excellent administrative reforms, is poorly frequented at this time; about 100 boxes of the leading families are empty because of mourning!!—When, I repeat, is this fun going to end? . . . . I also would have liked to give you news about the rehearsals of Catalani's new opera,[1] which it is my duty to attend, though I do so with little desire. I only wanted to give you this news to let you know that quite a number of the singers really have the qualities for . . . . other operas as well.[2] [. . .]

NOTES

1. *La Wally*, premiered at La Scala on 20 January, had thirteen additional performances in that season.

2. Virginia Guerrini, Adelina Stehle, and Arturo Pessina all appeared in *La Wally* and later in *Falstaff*. The repertoire of Virginia Guerrini (1872–?), mezzo-soprano, included Fidès, Ortrud, Dalila, and Amneris; she was the first Meg in *Falstaff*, but sang Quickly on tour in 1893, and in a production conducted by Leopoldo Mugnone (1858–1941) at the Teatro Dal Verme in 1895. The Austrian-born Adelina Stehle (1863–1945) studied at the Milan Conservatory and began her international career as a light lyric soprano at Bologna in 1888. Between engagements in Chile, Peru, and Rio de Janeiro, she appeared at La Scala in 1890–93. In the role of Nannetta, her pure, delicate voice gave particular delight. She developed into one of the first great *verismo* singers, and together with her second husband, Edoardo Garbin (1865–1943), sang *Bohème, Fedora, Adriana Lecouvreur*, and *Manon Lescaut* throughout Europe. Arturo Pessina (1858–1926) was a highly esteemed bass-baritone, whose repertoire encompassed Germont, Rigoletto, Amonasro, Wolfram, Hans Sachs, and Wotan. His noble and elegant phrasing won greater praise than his acting.

1892

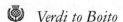 *Verdi to Gino Monaldi*

Genoa, 18 January 1892[1]

No, no, no . . . Don't commit yourself to artists for *Falstaff* at all! I have
done a lot for this opera . . . and a lot is still to be done; I haven't worked on
it for three months! I have been and still am indisposed, and so is my wife!
Imagine if I can think about *Falstaff* . . . and who knows if I will be able to
think about it in the future! [. . .]

NOTE

1. In answer to a missing letter.

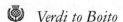 *Ricordi to Verdi*

Milan, 19 January 1892

Illustrious Maestro,

From Tito I heard, with the greatest pleasure, better news about you but,
with the greatest regret, not what we would like to hear about Signora
Peppina; the latest news Tito gave us, however, indicated an improvement,
and we hope her progress is rapid. Boito also had the influenza, with fever
and severe pain in the back of his neck and in the kidneys. Yesterday I went
to see him: he is better, is beginning to get up, but keeps the cough as a gift.
. . . for which I recommended patience and prudence as always! . .

Milan seems to have returned to normal . . . but the weather is awful!—
and we cannot as yet declare victory.—Many, many thanks for your kind
hospitality to Tito! . . . . Well, . . . on the subject of the Verdi home we are
at a loss for words!—

Always your most grateful

Giulio Ricordi

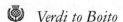 *Verdi to Boito*

Genoa, 23 January 1892

So you, too, were ill! Ah, this cursed influenza!—Giulio tells me, however, that you are better, and that only a slight cough is left.[1] Watch out
though; these dry, hacking coughs last forever. We know this from experience. From the last days of December onward we were confined at home,
almost all the time in bed. Peppina got up only two or three days ago; and

I went out of the house in a coach only three or four days ago! Therefore, take very, very good care of your cough!—

But what an ugly year! How badly it has begun! Almost two months lost! And to think that in Milan I worked with pleasure and profit![2] I hoped to continue so here, too! . . . But no!

Get well, then, soon, and get a change of air as soon as you can— Addio, addio.

Affectionately,
G. Verdi

NOTES

1. See Ricordi to Verdi, 19 January.
2. Between mid-November and 8 December 1891.

 *Boito to Verdi*

[Milan, 23 January 1892][1]

Dear Maestro,

The good news about Signora Giuseppina is beginning to arrive, and I am pleased and pray that it may get better all the time.

I know that you, dear Maestro, have been up for several days and have been getting out of the house.[2]

The storm is over. I have also been ill with the influenza. One week in bed, and one week shut in the house. Camillo has been sicker than I, but has completely recovered and is also going out. I have gone out for three days and am feeling so well that in a couple of hours I shall leave for Turin to hear *La Valchiria*.[3]

I am curious what my impression will be, and how much a staged performance may correct an artistic monstrosity of a great genius, or make it appear more beautiful. We'll see. In two weeks I'm going to Nervi and will turn up in Genoa, and we'll have a long chat.

My best greetings to Signora Giuseppina and to you.

Your most affectionate
Arrigo Boito

NOTES

1. Postmark: MILANO 23/1/92.
2. He apparently heard this from the Ricordis (see Ricordi to Verdi, 19 January).
3. The first Italian performance of *Die Walküre* had taken place at Turin's Teatro Regio on 22 December 1891.

1892

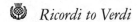 *Verdi to Giacomo Persico*

Genoa, 23 January 1892

Esteemed Mr. Mayor,

I am very happy that you remain Mayor of Villanova.

It is a good thing for everyone! I understand that it might be a sacrifice for you; life, however, is but a continuous sacrifice! On my own behalf I am most grateful to you.

It is not quite true that we are enjoying perfect health. Since the end of last year we have been imprisoned at home by the most terrible cough. Only two days ago was Peppina able to leave her bed and I to leave the house. If we continue in this vein, we shall soon be recovered.

I think that it is absolutely necessary to put a damper on the priest's exuberance.[1] The newly arrived doctor is putting up with it for the moment, but later it will bother him, and then the gossip, the friction will start as in the past . . . and the resentments, the grudges, etc., etc.

So this must be foreseen and remedied immediately. Everyone should do what he must do to the best of his ability, nothing more. Therefore the priest's visits to the doctor are entirely out of place. The priest must cure the soul, not the body, of the sick!

You, as President of the Hospital, should see to it (and in my name, if you wish) that this blessed priest remain in his place. He should come to the beds of the sick only when called.

Pay a visit every once in a while, but do not assume tasks that must not be yours. And if anyone should want to interfere with acquiring a 4th sister, just tell him that this is none of his business! [. . .]

NOTE

1. See Verdi to Piroli, 28 August 1889.

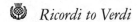 *Ricordi to Verdi*

Milan, 25 January 1891 [1892][1]

Illustrious Maestro,

I wanted to answer your letter of the 20th right away, but man proposes, and nuisance . . . . disposes!—I wanted to write you immediately to tell you how joyously we received the news with which you favored us [. . .]. This damned influenza has manifested itself this year in the oddest fashion. . . . Apart from making us tremble with fear for the health of our family and friends, it ruins commerce and industry . . . . . . and first and foremost the theatres! Why can I, of all people, not possess the good fortune to see some tranquil years? . . . . After a good start, the theatres are being ignored: illnesses of artists, the audience staying away, grave lamentations!! . . . Shouts and supplications from the impresarios, ... since the operas that were planned can no longer be presented, and only half the rental fee can be paid, if anything at all! Patience, then . . . and philosophy, if possible, and *adelante con juicio!*[2] . . . .

Catalani's opera[3] had a well-deserved success; oh God . . . . it is not the fruit of genius . . . . and where are the geniuses *except for Mascagni?* . . . But it's really a pleasing work, with three out of four successful and quite interesting acts. Darclée[4] had the greatest success; certainly the best soprano voice for pleasant timbre, secure and easy sound, combined with more than sufficient intelligence, which stands out even further because of her personal charm and tasteful dress. All in all, she is truly an artist to be taken seriously. In a small but treacherous comic character role, Cesari[5] greatly distinguished himself. The others all right. [. . .]

NOTES

1. Without doubt, Ricordi absentmindedly misdated this letter 1891.

2. Spanish for "forward with prudence."

3. *La Wally.* (See Boito to Verdi, 29 April 1891, n. 3; and Ricordi to Verdi, 11 January, n. 1.)

4. Hariclea Darclée (1860–1939) was a Romanian soprano of extraordinary versatility. She made her debut as Marguerite in *Faust* at the Paris Opéra in 1888, was engaged in St. Petersburg, and, in 1890, for the first time at La Scala. In 1900 Darclée was Puccini's first Tosca. She appeared in many Verdi, Wagner, Puccini, and Mascagni roles, as well as in the *bel canto* operas of Bellini and Donizetti; she even sang Carmen and the Marschallin. After retiring from the stage in 1918, Darclée lived for some years at Verdi's Casa di Riposo; she died penniless in Bucharest.

5. Pietro Cesari (1847–1922), buffo-baritone and impresario, active in Italy and South America, was first engaged at La Scala in 1892.

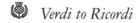
Verdi to Ricordi

Genoa, 31 January 1892

Dear Giulio,

Again *Otello* at La Scala?!!!![1] After its massacre the last time,[2] it should have been left alone for ten years before being taken up again!

But that manager of yours[3] imposes himself and imposes . . . also disposes of your property without even saying "Hello!!" At least punish him for such boldness! . . If I were the proprietor of *Otello*, I would have asked for 100,000 Lire (I say one hundred thousand) for renting the material, just to make true the insolent remark that one of his clerks hurled behind my back in the lobby of the Carlo Felice: "To Maestro Verdi we pay hundreds of thousands of Lire to rent the material; so let him pay for his servant's ticket"; and this because my servant had permitted himself to look into the auditorium through the glass in a door.

It was a scandal! [. . .]

Our health is as usual! . . . . Little improvement!!—Peppina and I had decided to go to Milan for a few weeks to have a change of air and to get away from this environment, which is now so sad for us. But *Otello* puts an obstacle in our plans. [. . .]

NOTES

1. On 29 January Ricordi had informed Verdi about the sudden plan to revive *Otello* at La Scala in February. (See *Otello* i, p. 380.)

2. In a second production, in February and March 1889.

3. Luigi Piontelli.

⚜ *Ricordi to Verdi*

Milan, 1 February 1892

[. . .] Your esteemed letter of yesterday distresses me greatly, above all because of the announcement that a probable trip of yours to Milan would now be delayed. [. . .][1]

NOTE

1. See *Otello* i, pp. 381–2.

⚜ *Verdi to Ricordi*

Genoa, 2 February 1892

[. . .] What I am now anxious to know is when will you be rid of *Otello*. [. . .]

As far as I am concerned, I only want it to be performed soon, since I need to get myself going, to have a change of air, and to take care of and conclude many affairs in Milan.

So then, when will it happen? [. . .][1]

NOTE

1. See *Otello* i, pp. 382–3.

 *Ricordi to Verdi*

Milan, 5 February 1892

[. . .] I am advising you that *Otello* will not be ready to be performed until the 12th or 15th of this month [. . .].[1]

NOTE

1. See *Otello* i, p. 383.

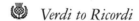 *Verdi to Ricordi*

Genoa, 9 February 1892

Dear Giulio,

A letter every day! Heaven, what a bore, you will say, and if you sent me to that country [hell] (of course, I wouldn't go there), you'd be right!

Do me the favor of sending someone to get me two boxes of *Di Celso Pills* at the Valcamonica & Introzzi pharmacy, Corso Vitt. Emanuele across from the Beati shop . . .

Send them to me by mail at once. . Excuse me and addio

Greetings and good health.

Your
G. Verdi

 *Boito to Verdi*

Wednesday [Milan, 10 February 1892][1]

Dear Maestro,

The last card you wrote to Giulio[2] does not mention your health; I hope that this may be a good sign, and that every trace of that most aggravating *influenza* may have disappeared, and that Signora Giuseppina may no longer be suffering from nausea, which is the worst of all ills.

I have delayed my arrival on the Riviera[3] because I could not avoid Villari's assignment to inspect the Palermo Conservatory (as much as I put it off). Thus I will allow my excursion to Sicily to follow my sojourn on the

Riviera in March. But before then, dear Maestro, it seems that we must see each other in Milan;[4] so much the better.

Last night, when I went to the *Megère apprivoisée*,[5] I ran into Maurel; he has gained weight, wonderful![6] And I am told that he has never been in better voice than he is this year. I said that I went to the *Megère apprivoisée*, and I add that I enjoyed myself very much, even though in that botched Parisian rendition, Shakespeare's most lively picture had been pretentiously and stupidly repainted by a highly mannered *boulevardier* painter. In the first act there are *six* witty remarks in the text (I counted them); the rest are by the adapter. Six witty remarks are few; nevertheless they suffice to create that admirable character of Petrucchio, splendidly interpreted by Cocquelin.

In the following acts, there is more of the [original] text, and the unfortunate additions by the French adapter aren't enough to ruin it. All in all, the reduction is well planned, and if the adapter had respected the dialogue, there would be little to criticize.

Give my very best greetings to Signora Giuseppina, who I hope is again completely recovered.

'Til we meet again soon.

Your most affectionate
Arrigo Boito

NOTES

   1. Postmark: MILANO 10/2/92.

   2. On 8 February, concerning an article in the *Gazzetta musicale.*

   3. See Boito to Verdi, 23 January.

   4. See Verdi to Ricordi, 31 January.

   5. *La mégère apprivoisée* is the French title of Shakespeare's *Taming of the Shrew.* (See Verdi to Maurel, 21 April 1890.)

   6. For the role of Falstaff.

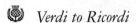 *Verdi to Ricordi*

Genoa, 10 February 1892

Dear Giulio,
   What a fate,
Poor Giulio!
A letter every day!

Go ahead and pay the property taxes,[1] etc., etc., from my account, according to the bill.

As for La Scala, I think the reduced prices will ruin it (you say so yourself) unless a damper is put on the manager's greed! For one thing, the commission ought to be able to oblige the manager to give only one performance at reduced prices for each production after the 10th performance, and whenever a production has great success, a second performance could be allowed after 20 performances.

I am just saying this, and addio addio.—Greetings and health.

Affectionately,
G. Verdi

[. . .]

NOTE

1. Presumably on the land purchased for the Casa di Riposo.

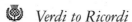 *Verdi to Ricordi*

Genoa, 12 February 1892

Dear Giulio,

In the grief I feel, I imagine how great your sorrow must be for the loss of a friend and a gentleman, who took such an interest in our affairs. Poor Dina! I myself needed his advice several times and could only admire his capability and his loyalty, as I now deplore his loss.[1] [. . .]

NOTE

1. See Boito to Verdi, 16 March 1890, n. 4.

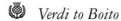 *Verdi to Boito*

Genoa, 12 February 1892

Dear Boito,

Giulio writes me in desolation about Dina's sudden death.[1] Certainly, Giulio has lost a friend, an intelligent man and a man of honor. I myself needed his advice several times, and I know how capable and loyal he was. Poor Dina!

We no longer talked about the *influenza,* that's true, but we still feel it: I myself through a very great weakness that keeps me from any work lasting more than half an hour; and Peppina through an absolute lack of appetite. I can't wait to have a change of air, even to a harsher climate, as long as I can rid myself of this damned wind that splits my brain and puts thorns in my throat.

So you found *Mégère* fairly well cut? In the *brouillon* [rough draft] they sent me, the flaw of the dialogue was less obvious. But I know for that matter what the French usually do. *In diebus illis* [in those days] I have heard in Paris 8 or 10 of *Shaespeare's* most powerful dramas, all of them frightfully altered. In the dialogue I felt as though I were witnessing a conversation either on the boulevards or in the lobby of the old Opéra. That even in the reduction of *Hamlet* by Dumas père! Imagine!

To the French, beauty exists only in their own works:

Cela ne va pas. . .	[That doesn't go. . .
Ce n'est pas pour nous. . .	That isn't for us. . .
Ce n'est pas de bon goût.	That's not in good taste.][2]

These are their sacramental phrases. And with this *bon goût* of theirs they permit themselves to alter everything and to take away the character and originality of the products of other countries!

So you are going to Palermo? Do good if you can. . .

'Til we meet again soon, I hope. Peppina greets you and thanks you for your concern. I shake your hands.

Addio, addio.
Affectionately,
G. Verdi

NOTES

1. This letter is missing.
2. See Verdi to Camille Du Locle, 8 December 1869. (See also *Aida*, pp. 4–5.)

 *Ricordi to Verdi*

Milan, 16 February 1892

Illustrious Maestro,

Forgive me if I briefly follow up on my telegram[1] and confirm to you that everything[2] went really well, well, well. [. . .][3]

NOTES

1. Missing.
2. *Otello* at La Scala on the previous night.
3. See *Otello* i, p. 384. With the first performances of the *Otello* revival over, Verdi and his wife left for Milan at the end of the month. There the Maestro met with Ricordi and both Boitos concerning *Falstaff* and the Casa di Riposo. Apparently he did not attend a

single one of the *Otello* performances that were still running, conducted by Mascheroni, with Maurel as Iago.

 *Verdi to Giuseppe De Amicis*

Milan, 16 March 1892

Dear De Amicis,

I arrived last night from St. Agata, and it's a miracle that I am not mad with rage. Imagine that I was kept prisoner at home[1] all day Sunday and Monday because of the huge amount of snow that had fallen. Auff!!

And so we cannot be in Genoa for San Giuseppe.[2] [. . .]

NOTES

   1. At St. Agata.
   2. On 19 March, their saint's day.

 *Verdi to Maria Waldmann*

Genoa, 22 March 1892

Dear Maria,

I regret not having answered your dear letter right away; since you sent it here, it was forwarded to me in Milan, and again from Milan back here, where I received it last night upon my arrival.

Peppina and I thank you for your good wishes,[1] more precious than so many others, for we know that they are sincere and affectionate.

I am very sorry about your husband's illness and can only hope that he may be on the way to recovery. Poor Maria! I imagine your distress!

As I just told you, we were in Milan and returned here yesterday. We found our friends there in good health, with Signora Stolz having put on a lot of weight! Sign of good health [. . .]

NOTE

   1. On the Verdis' saint's day.

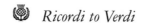 *Ricordi to Verdi*

Milan, 25 March 1892

[. . .] As soon as Puccini[1] is back, I will get the exact information about Signora Pasqua from him.[2] I saw Maurel and gave him your message.[3] [. . .]

1892

NOTES

1. Giacomo Puccini's (1858–1924) first opera, *Le Villi,* was premiered at Milan's Teatro Dal Verme in 1884, thanks to Boito's recommendation. Puccini's second opera, *Edgar,* failed at La Scala in 1889, but its revision fared better in Madrid, where Giulio Ricordi had sent him, on 19 March.

2. Giuseppina Pasqua (1855–1930) made her debut at age fourteen as Oscar in *Un ballo in maschera* in her native Perugia. Having appeared as a soprano throughout Italy, Pasqua followed Maria Waldmann's advice to shift to such mezzo roles as Azucena, Eboli, and Amneris, in which she was admired from Moscow to Lisbon. There was hardly any opera house in Italy and Spain where she did not appear; and there was not a prominent role in the Italian mezzo repertoire which she did not interpret. Verdi apparently liked Pasqua's Eboli at La Scala in 1884. Eight years later, he asked Ricordi to obtain Puccini's impressions of her in Madrid. (See Ricordi to Verdi, 30 March and Verdi to Ricordi, 31 March.) Eventually, Verdi enjoyed coaching Pasqua in the contralto role of Quickly so much that he added the little aria "Giunta all' Albergo della Giarettiera" for her; and by all accounts she brought an inimitable sparkle to each performance of *Falstaff.*

3. While Maurel was appearing as Iago at La Scala, Ricordi may have conveyed to him Verdi's thoughts about casting the role of Falstaff.

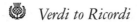 *Verdi to Ricordi*

Genoa, 26 March 1892

Dear Giulio,

What shame!

I'm the one who should have written to you the very moment we got here!![1]

And you had reached me before then! Shame, shame, shame! Oh, these *composers,* other than notes, never do anything right! . . Oh, no, no . . . . I'm correcting *"the notes"*! When they do them right. *Rara avis* [rare bird].

The box and cake, almost half of which we ate (not the box), have arrived. Thursday we celebrated a second San Giuseppe,[2] with De Amicis and Prof. Igola,[3] and we drank a glass of Champagne to the health of our good friends in Milan, whom we bothered so much, Peppina says, during our stay in the capital.———

We arrived in good shape and feel almost as well as in Milan.————Give us your news, and give many, many greetings to all, in Peppina's name, too—

Your
G. Verdi

P.S. Peppina also shouts

Shame Shame Shame

for still not having written to thank you————————

NOTES

1. On 21 March, returning to Genoa from Milan.
2. The Verdis had celebrated their saint's day, San Giuseppe, on 19 March, in Milan.
3. Unknown.

 *Ricordi to Verdi*

Milan, 30 March 1892

Illustrious Maestro,

I talked with Puccini:[1] Pasqua feels the rigors of her years;[2] for the demands of a rather dramatic part with a high tessitura, she is no longer the same as she was years ago; but her low notes are as *good* as ever, the voice is *pleasant.* Her artistic qualities are known, and there is no need to discuss them. All in all, for a contralto part that does not go high, she still is excellent. [. . .]

NOTES

1. Upon his return from Madrid. (See Ricordi to Verdi, 25 March, notes 1 and 2.)
2. "Pasqua [in the part of Tigrana] has adjusted herself, but what is not in order is her incredibly tired voice," Puccini had written to Ricordi during the rehearsals of *Edgar* from Madrid on 8 March. At only 37 years of age, "she was still far from her sunset; but the part of Tigrana was probably too high for her. At the launching of the opera at La Scala in 1889, they understandably entrusted this part to a soprano, Pantaleoni [Verdi's first Desdemona], albeit with some transposition." (Eugenio Gara, *Carteggi Pucciniani*, p. 69.)

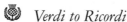 *Verdi to Ricordi*

Genoa, 31 March 1892

Dear Giulio,

Thanks for the *Mignon*[1] and thanks for Puccini's news, which is not what I hoped for!—Although the low notes are still good, it is always to be feared that the voice prefers the descending line.—

The part is low, and for me these notes would suffice

from

Ask Puccini again if these notes are still good and robust, and above all if she can sing *in that area* without getting tired.[2]

1892

I am again stuck at home for three days because of the bad weather; today it's nice and I'll go out . . .

Peppina has been nauseated for 48 hours, unable to take food . . . ah, what a world!!

Greetings to all—addio addio.

G. Verdi

NOTES

1. Presumably Ricordi had sent Verdi a vocal score of Ambroise Thomas's opera.

2. During Verdi's forthcoming stay in Milan, Ricordi and/or Puccini himself might have convinced him in person that Pasqua could fulfill his demands.

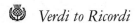 *Verdi to Ricordi*

Genoa, 2 April 1892

Dear Giulio,

The Committee for the Commemoration of Rossini has invited me (you will certainly know this) to conduct the Prayer from *Mosè*.[1]

That is a bolt out of the blue! I would like to get out of it, but don't know how to go about it.

I could not bring up my age, or inability to conduct, or my health, etc., etc.

Could you find a way to spare me this *exhibition*, this *spectacle* that doesn't please me at all?

Could you have a talk with those gentlemen to excuse me?

Could you tell me your frank, clear, decisive opinion? . . .

Wire me at once, and addio

Your
G. Verdi

P.S. The letter is signed by Messrs. Cambiasi,[2] Bellini,[3] D'Ormeville, Mascheroni, Nappi,[4] Zorzi.

NOTES

1. This powerful excerpt from Rossini's opera *Mosè in Egitto* (1818) was to be performed at La Scala during the centenary of his birth.

2. Pompeo Cambiasi (1849–1908) wrote theatrical chronicles and published, *inter alia, La Scala: Note storiche e statistiche, 1778–1906.*

3. Unknown. (The composer Vincenzo Bellini died in 1835.)

4. G. B. Nappi succeeded Filippo Filippi as music critic of *La Perseveranza*. (See Abbiati iv, p. 361.)

🏵 *Ricordi to Verdi*

Milan, 3 April 1892

Illustrious Maestro,

While I am writing you in answer to your esteemed letter of yesterday and am confirming my telegram of this morning,[1] an agitated hand and mind are certain to keep me from writing you calmly. In the very first sessions of the committee, the idea of asking Verdi *himself* to conduct the Prayer from *Mosè* was put forward by Cambiasi and Mascheroni; you were even to be proclaimed Honorary President. You can imagine how much I insisted that . . . . . Verdi be left alone. As the reason for your absolute reluctance to appear in public, I mentioned your work, which is now certainly absorbing your time and thoughts, etc., etc. You can imagine the opposing answers, Maestro; among them, this one: that Verdi had twice made an exception: for Manzoni[2] and for a national disaster.[3] Perhaps Verdi could make yet another exception: for Rossini!—However, thanks to my fervent entreaties, things seemed to have settled down—so much so that nothing more was said.—But it was not so; to my face there was silence, but the idea was *boiling, boiling,* which was natural. They talked to Negri,[4] and he came to see me just yesterday morning for a long conference. For many political and administrative reasons, Negri would not agree to speak in public at this time; he told me, however, that he had been informed of what I had done in the matter.—"You understand," Negri said to me, "if Verdi accepts, it is a different matter; for me and for everyone else there would then no longer be any political, senatorial or administrative consideration. The invitation to speak about Rossini excites me! . . . However, for the above-mentioned reasons, I could not do so in public at this time. But with Verdi's presence these motives disappear!! Then it becomes a *national* event; it becomes one of the greatest artistic solemnities of the century; and I will speak briefly, for I don't want to give a lecture, I am not a musician! But I will address Rossini in the name of Italy!"—

This is where we stand. It is a *blow,* that is true; a serious *blow*—an inconvenience, even a nuisance (as I said to the committee at the first session: "You cause Verdi displeasure whether he accepts or not!"). And yet . . . . . how to stop an idea . . . . unique and great? And can its existence be denied? . . . . Actually, I am writing you with such emotion that tears come to my eyes! . . . .

What can I tell you, Maestro, ... after all of this? . . . .

Either you wish to make such a *grave* personal sacrifice of conviction and sentiment for Rossini and for Milan . . . . and then . . . . one can literally only *kneel* before the Great Man called *Giuseppe Verdi*; or the matter is absolutely repugnant to you, and then . . . . take pen in hand for a reply to the committee; some plausible reason is easily found, and you would have many!! It would suffice to say that you join in the commemoration with your heart.

As good and kind as you always are with me, would you stop to ask for my frank, candid opinion? . . . . An opinion of mine to Verdi? But I am unable to explain it. I will say that I *feel* this way in my heart: for nothing on earth would I have wanted you to be bothered even with the slightest nuisance.—But Verdi in Milan at La Scala . . . . for Rossini . . . . for our Italian art? . . . Oh! merciful God . . . . what can I say? . . . . Nothing, because I would end up in an insane asylum!!

The [date of the] commemoration will be decided upon tonight, but it will probably be on Friday the 8th of this month, since some artists leave on the 9th or 10th.—Will you wire me as soon as you receive this letter? . . . This means that I won't shut an eye the whole night!! . . . . Please also wire me Signora Peppina's news.—Ever your devoted and grateful

Giulio Ricordi

The first ensemble rehearsal with the chorus was stupendous; today second chorus rehearsal, tomorrow orchestra rehearsal [of the Prayer].

NOTES

1. Missing.

2. Conducting his *Requiem Mass*, composed in honor of the poet Alessandro Manzoni (1785–1873), on 22 and 25 May 1874 in Milan, and several times thereafter in other cities.

3. Conducting the same work in Milan at a benefit concert for flood victims on 29 June 1879.

4. See Ricordi to Verdi, 24 October 1890, n. 9.

 *Verdi to Ricordi*

Genoa, 4 April 1892

Dear Giulio,

I could not have been asked to make a greater sacrifice!!

This exhibition of myself (sprinkled with sugar as much as you like) is still a spectacle, a real show that is utterly revolting to me!

But I swear, adjure, and swear again (as there are no two Rossinis) that I shall never again make similar sacrifices for anybody, for nothing in the world, for no country whatsoever.

I'll arrive in Milan on Thursday either at 9:55 or after *two twenty*.—

I would like to arrange at least two rehearsals for myself, either during the day or at night. One with the singers and chorus combined; the other with the singers, chorus, and orchestra. I would like to have at least 4 harps. Is that possible? Choose the soloists well. The text of the Prayer is short, but sublime. It must be sung sublimely.[1]

Tomorrow I'll write or wire the Committee. Inform them in the meantime. Addio

Your

. G. Verdi

Peppina is not sick, but has no appetite at all.

NOTE

    1. The commemorative concert took place at La Scala on Friday, 8 April 1892 (*Carteggio* ii, p. 420). Among the participants were the conductor Edoardo Mascheroni and the singers Virginia Guerrini and Arturo Pessina, who both appeared later in *Falstaff*. Gaetano Negri gave the oration, and Verdi conducted the Prayer from *Mosè* to end the festive program.

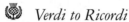 *Verdi to Ricordi*

Tuesday evening [Genoa, 5 April 1892]

Dear Giulio,

    Since there will be no rehearsal until Thursday at 3:30, I can also arrive at 2:20, although that's a long journey on a local train.

    I hope no one will be at the station, and I ask you yourself to await me at the hotel. All the rest remains as you said.

    'Til Thursday

Affectionately

G. Verdi

P.S. Make my excuses to the Committee that I have not yet replied . . . but now I will reply in person.

 *Hans von Bülow to Verdi*

Hamburg, 7 April 1892

Illustrious Maestro,

    Deign to hear the confession of a contrite sinner![1]

    Eighteen years ago the undersigned was guilty of a great—great journalistic *bestiality*—toward the last of the five kings of modern Italian music. He has repented, he has felt bitter shame, oh how many times! When he committed that sin (perhaps your magnanimity will have completely forgotten it) he was really in a state of insanity; allow me to mention this, so to speak, extenuating circumstance. My mind was blinded by fanaticism, by ultra-Wagnerian "Seide."[2] Seven years later—gradually came the light. The fanaticism has been purified, has become enthusiasm.

Fanaticism = kerosene; enthusiasm = electric light. In the intellectual and moral world light is called: justice. Nothing is more destructive than injustice, nothing more intolerable than intolerance, as the most noble Giacomo Leopardi[3] has said.

Finally having reached this "point of enlightenment," how much can I congratulate myself, how enriched has my life become, how much has it been enhanced by the most precious of joys: the artistic joys! I began by studying your latest works: *Aida, Otello,* and the *Requiem,* of which, recently, a rather weak performance—moved me to tears; I have studied them not only according to the letter, which kills, but according to the spirit, which renews life! Well then, illustrious Maestro, now I admire you, I love you!

Will you forgive me, will you avail yourself of the sovereign privilege of grace? However that may be, if only to set an example for the lesser mistaken brothers, I must confess past guilt.

And faithful to the Prussian motto *Suum cuique* [to each his own], I ardently exclaim: Evviva VERDI, the Wagner of our dear allies!

Hans von Bülow

NOTES

1. In 1870, the German pianist and conductor Hans von Bülow (1830–94) made such a deep impression in Milan that La Scala considered appointing him as its leading conductor. Aware of Bülow's well-known addiction to Wagner, Italy's most influential critic, Filippo Filippi (1830–87), warned Bülow that in the event of such an appointment, Giulio Ricordi threatened to withdraw all of his firm's material from La Scala. What Ricordi feared were the amicable relations between Bülow, a renowned conductor of Wagner's music, and Ricordi's competitor Francesco Lucca, Wagner's publisher in Italy. This situation may have contributed to Bülow's malicious review of Verdi's *Requiem* in 1874. (See *Allgemeine Zeitung,* Nos. 148 and 152; also Hans von Bülow, *Musikalisches aus Italien* in *Ausgewählte Schriften* iii, pp. 340–1.) Bülow's friend Johannes Brahms, however, having leafed through the pages of the *Requiem*, was quoted as saying: "Bülow made an incredible fool of himself; only a genius can write such a thing." (Josef Viktor Widmann, *Erinnerungen an Brahms,* p. 164, n. 14.) This judgment may have influenced the ailing Bülow's radical change of mind and precipitated the above letter, which he wrote in Italian, to settle his debt before his death on 12 February 1894. (Marie von Bülow, *Hans von Bülow,* p. 187.)

2. The German noun *Seide* [silk], which Bülow uses in his Italian letter, might refer to Wagner's notorious love of luxury.

3. Count Giacomo Leopardi (1798–1837) was considered the greatest Italian lyric poet since Petrarch (1304–74).

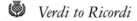 *Verdi to Ricordi*

[Milan] *Friday* [8 April 1892][1]

Send me the orchestra score again and a printed piano-vocal score of the Prayer from *Mosè* . . . Take care of the letter you know to the[2] . . .

"Constant admirer of Rossini's genius, I have acceded to the invitation of your Committee, although my presence will be as useless as Donizetti's was useful when he conducted the *Stabat* for the first time in Bologna. Pleased, nevertheless, to have paid this tribute of admiration, I have the honor . . ."
[. . .]

Season this with salt and pepper, and with all the ingredients you want.
[. . .]

NOTES

1. Verdi appears to have sent this message to Ricordi on the day of the commemorative concert.
2. Committee for the Commemoration of Rossini.

Verdi to Ricordi

Genoa, 11 April 1892

Dear Giulio,

Here I am again, safe and sound despite a bit of fatigue I felt yesterday . . . If the thing[1] went well, I am happy and *Amen.*

Peppina has received your letter[2] and asks me to thank you, sorry that she didn't have the courage to face a bit of fatigue by coming along to Milan. She will answer you later on. [. . .]

And now be amazed, be amazed! Be amazed! . . . . and be amazed again! *Hans de Bulow* sends me the letter I am enclosing and which you will return to me as soon as you have read it. . .

He definitely is mad! How can he think that I, *I* of all people, could have such a letter printed!?[3] If he is repentant and in torment, has confessed and taken communion, he himself should have it printed, or at the most, should have written to you directly, asking you to publish all he liked. But . . then he is mad!! Meanwhile, I shall answer him that I forgive, had forgiven, and will always forgive, the more so as he might have been right at that time. . . .

1892

Addio. Greet everybody and return the letter. Show it to Boito, who will laugh about it.——

Ad. ad.

Your
G. Verdi

NOTES

1. The commemorative concert at La Scala on 8 April.
2. Missing.
3. Bülow did not suggest this in his letter of 7 April, but Ricordi published Bülow's letter, together with Verdi's answer of 14 April, in *La Gazzetta musicale* of 7 August 1892. (See *Carteggio* ii, pp. 420–2.)

 Giuseppina Verdi to Ricordi

Genoa, 14 April 1892

Dearest Signor Giulio,

If only I had a tenth of your talent, of your strong will, of your incredible energy, I would feel richly endowed by Mother Nature! I am, however, . . . what I am! A body that appears robust but is really weak, always tired, worn out! If it weren't so, I would have come to Milan, as Verdi had wanted, and I would have enjoyed that great, ineffable emotion that had you all electrified and that would have done me so much good to the point of making me ill!

Instead, I remained in Genoa, alone, in a very sad mood, always thinking, however, with feverish agitation of the unique and moving spectacle the beautiful Scala must have presented; it must have been teeming with people of every class, enthusiastically evoking the memory of Rossini's enormous genius, while Verdi bowed with infinite tenderness. May God keep him in the love of his friends and the glory of Art!

I would have answered your beautiful and dear letter[1] sooner, but endless occupations—all of them simple, but pressing—prevented me.

I answer now, Signor Giulio, with many, many, many thanks!!

Happy to hear that I can see you, with Signora Giuditta, I hope, before our departure for St. Agata, and with my regards to everyone, I remain

Yours most affectionately,
Peppina Verdi

NOTE

1. Missing.

Verdi to Ricordi

[Genoa] 14 April 1892

Dear Giulio,

I have written to Roger, and we shall see how he has come to terms with Tamagno, who paid a high rental fee.——[1]

Tomorrow I shall write to Bulow. I will then send you a copy of the two letters so that if Bulow should have them printed in German translation, you could have them printed in the original language.——[2]

'Til we see each other then. We will stay here until about the 28th.

What the devil has taken hold of the Rossini Committee to have medals struck!

Wouldn't it have been better to save that money for a rainy day?

Addio to all.

Affectionately,
G. Verdi

NOTES

1. Francesco Tamagno (1850–1905), Verdi's first Otello, had arranged for the first *Otello* production (in Italian) in France, which was performed at Nice in February 1891. (See *Otello* i, p. 376 and *Otello* ii, p. 858.)

2. See Verdi to Ricordi, 11 April, n. 2. Bülow refrained from publishing the two letters in German translation.

 Verdi to Hans von Bülow

Genoa, 14 April 1892

Illustrious Maestro Bülow,

There is not a trace of sin in you!—and there is no need to speak of repentance and absolution!

If your earlier opinions were different from those you hold today, you were quite right to express them; and I would never have dared to complain. Besides, who knows . . . . , perhaps you were right at that time.

In any case, this unexpected letter of yours, written by a musician of your stature and your importance in the artistic world, has given me great pleasure! And this not because of my personal vanity, but because I see that truly superior artists judge without prejudice regarding schools, nationalities, and time.

If the artists of the North and South have different inclinations, let them

1892

be *different.* They should all hold on to the particular *character of their nation,* as Wagner has said so well.

You are fortunate still to be the sons of Bach! . . . And we?. . . We, too, the sons of Palestrina, once had a great school. . . . our own! Today it has degenerated and threatens to go to ruin!

If it were only possible to return to the beginning!

I regret being unable to attend the Music Exhibition in Vienna,[1] where, apart from the good fortune of meeting so many illustrious musicians, I would have enjoyed the particular pleasure of shaking your hand. I hope that the gentlemen who so kindly invited me will consider my old age and forgive my absence.

Your sincere admirer,
G. Verdi

NOTE

1. The International Theatre and Music Exhibition in Vienna from 7 May until 9 October 1892.

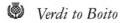 *Verdi to Boito*

Genoa, 15 April 1892

Dear Boito,

I have answered Bulow . . . and already today have sent Giulio Bulow's letter and a copy of my answer; if Bulow were to publish these letters in German, then it would be well for Giulio to publish the two original letters in Italian.[1]

I have also written to Roger.[2]

These singing celebrities bother me a bit! For Nannetti there would only be the part of Bardolfo,[3] if it's not a little too low. But this is not so bad. . . When we get to the rehearsals, what is he going to say when he finds out that almost all the others have a better part? That causes ill will, and then and then . . . We'll see! . . .

And now, before I lock up the complete orchestration of the first act, tell me if these two verses remain:

Bel costrutto!—L'onore lo può sentir chi è morto?
No. Vive sol coi vivi?—Neppure, perchè a torto et. . .

[Fine benefit!—Can one who is dead feel honor?
No. Does it live only with the living?—Not even, because wrongly, etc.]

I greet you from Peppina and cordially shake your hand.

Your
G. Verdi

NOTES

1. See Verdi to Ricordi, 14 April, n. 2.
2. Ibid., n. 1.
3. Verdi confused Bardolfo's tenor part in *Falstaff* with Pistola's bass part, for which Romano Nannetti (1845–1910) was too prominent.

 *Boito to Verdi*

[Milan] Easter [17 April 1892][1]

Dear Maestro,
Bel costrutto! L'onore lo può sentir chi è morto?[2]
No.—Vive sol coi vivi?—Neppure, perchè a torto
Lo lodan le lusinghe, lo corrompe l'orgoglio,
Lo ammorban le calunnie.—E per me non voglio!!
[Fine benefit!—Can one who is dead feel honor?
No.—Does it live only with the living?—Not even, because wrongly
Flattery swells it, pride corrupts it,
Slanders infect it.—And, for myself, I want none of it!!]

This way, I think, it goes better and is more faithful to the text. I have changed the feminine articles to masculine ones, because the subject has become masculine. Thus, ceasing to prolong the image deriving from the word *aria,* we return to the word *onore* and the conclusion becomes clearer and stronger. I found myself compelled, therefore, to modify a word in the penultimate verse, and wrote:

a torto
Lo lodan le lusinghe.—

You can lock up the 1st act and go on to the 2nd. I have read the reply to Bülow; Giulio has shown it to me. Bravo, Maestro. It is very noble and very beautiful.

You possess the secret *of the right note at the right time,* which is the great secret of art and life.

All the best to Signora Giuseppina.

Your most affectionate
Arrigo Boito

1892

NOTES

    1. In 1892 Easter was on 17 April. Presumably Boito was in Milan.
    2. Cf. Shakespeare, *King Henry IV*, First Part, V.i. 130–41.

 *Ricordi to Verdi*

Milan, 26 April 1892

Illustrious Maestro,

    The hours spent in your company have flown like minutes![1] [. . .]

    Today I am awaiting from London various designs and engravings which I shall examine with Boito and the painter Hohenstein; if we find something good and useful, we will submit it to you.

    This trip to Vienna[2] really comes at an inopportune moment, when I have many other things on my mind!! . . . But I hope to rid myself quickly of that business, too; and then I will again assume the office of your Number One bore! [. . .]

NOTES

    1. Referring to a recent visit the Ricordis paid the Verdis in Genoa.
    2. No doubt in connection with the Music Exhibition. (See Verdi to Bülow, 14 April, n. 1.)

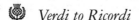 *Verdi to Ricordi*

Genoa, 27 April 1892

Dear Giulio,

    Received your letter. To give thanks? *Il n'y á pas de quoi!!*

    Before leaving for Vienna, please ask Signor Finzi[1] to send my pianoforte to

Maestro Verdi
Borgo. S. Donnino.

    I will see to it that the men at the station are informed to send it on to my home. We shall return to St. Agata either Monday or Tuesday, unless a bit of dynamite blows us up on Sunday.[2] As soon as we arrive, I'll send you a telegram to inform the usual workman, who will come to set it up. He must leave Milan at 7:05 in the morning, and I'll have him picked up at *Borgo, Fiorenzuola*, or *Alseno*. The telegram will inform you.—

Good health to you, to Giuditta and everyone in Peppina's name and mine.

Affectionately,

G. Verdi

P.S. Please pay Signor Finzi's *bill*.

NOTES

    1. Unknown.

    2. During May Day demonstrations.

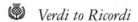 *Verdi to Ricordi*

[Genoa, April 1892]

What a nuisance! What a nuisance! you are going to say . . . . and you have a thousand reasons. Again Bulow's letter with my reply. If Bulow should have my letter or both letters printed in German, you will do me the favor of having both letters printed in their original Italian.[1]

Health and greetings—

G. Verdi

NOTE

    1. In light of Verdi's intense dislike of any kind of publicity, this repeated request suggests the importance he himself attached to Bülow's letter of 7 April, and his reply of April 14.

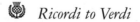 *Ricordi to Verdi*

Milan, 1 May 1892

Illustrious Maestro,

    Up to this moment (noon) all is quiet as I am writing! . . . We are a bit worried for tonight, but hope the calm may continue.[1] We hope that you will have had an excellent journey,[2] and that you may find yourselves happy in the dear and tranquil St. Agata, and in excellent health. If nothing interferes, I shall leave with Giuditta for Vienna Tuesday night. [. . .]

A handshake to the dear Potbelly, whom I think about day and night!! . . You see how attractive these rascals are! [. . .]

NOTES

   1. May Day demonstrations.
   2. Returning with his wife from Genoa to St. Agata, via Voghera instead of Milan.

 *Boito to Verdi*

[Milan] 9 May [1892][1]

Dear Maestro,

When Giulio went to Genoa,[2] he was to have brought a message I had given him for Signora Giuseppina; I don't know if he did so. He was to tell her that the price of the *Dictionary of the Ancient and Modern Terminology of Medical Science* is thirty Lire. If he didn't say so, I say so now.

The painter Hohenstein is working on the costume sketches and the scenic designs for *Falstaff*; I gave him the information I knew, but it would be good for him to have the scenic descriptions as they are in the libretto. And therefore it would be helpful if you would take the trouble to transcribe them, as I don't have a copy of my manuscript.

Engravings illustrating the figure of Falstaff were sent from London; some of them might be useful, others not. It is absolutely necessary that you see them; when Giulio returns to Milan, I'll have him send them to you. In our characters' costumes the *too beautiful* will have to be avoided, since the *too beautiful* is very rarely associated with the *picturesque*. Pistola and Bardolfo must wear clothes that seem worn out; at last we want to see something on the stage which they never dare to show, that is, *real rags*, picturesque rags of a style and cut that make Pistola and Bardolfo become two figures from a painting. If Murillo[3] could lend us his, it would be ideal!

The women's costumes, of simple but elegant cut, can perhaps be found in the engravings that were sent from London.

It is good that the painter is working; this way there will be more time to correct and to think and do well.

Many greetings to Signora Giuseppina; and you, dear Maestro, work well and accept a firm handshake from

Your most affectionate
Arrigo Boito

NOTES

1. The year is inferred from the contents of the letter. Presumably Boito wrote from Milan.
2. See Ricordi to Verdi, 26 April.
3. Bartolomé Esteban Murillo (1618–82), "the Spanish Raphael."

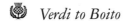 *Verdi to Boito*

St. Agata, 11 May 1892

Dear Boito,

We have been here for almost eight days, still half sick because of the horrible journey from Genoa. Imagine! A stopover of almost 3 hours (I say THREE HOURS!!) at Voghera!

With that cold!

With that wind!

And in that place![1]

Giulio told Peppina the price of that dictionary, and she thanks you.

Too soon, too soon to think of costumes and scenery for *Falstaff*. And first of all,

Will it be given?

Where will it be given?

Who are the singers going to be?

Which theatre?

Which impresario?

And then . . . will I finish what remains to be done? . . . At this moment I feel so tired, so listless that it seems impossible that I will finish the work that remains to be done! When Giulio comes back, we'll talk about it! . . .

Well then!—A little rest for now, then we shall see—.

Peppina greets you and I shake your hand.

Affectionately,
G. Verdi

NOTE

1. See Ricordi to Verdi, 1 May, n. 2, and *Carteggio* ii, p. 423.

 *Eugenio Tornaghi to Verdi*

Milan, 14 May 1892

Illustrious Signor Maestro,

I am in possession of your most esteemed letter of the 12th.[1] Cova[2] will send you the 20 bottles of Marsala the excellence of which has been guaranteed to me. The House of Ricordi will pay the bill from your account.

Need I repeat to you that you honor me with your instructions? . . Let me add that when I have the good fortune to receive some word or instruction from you, I feel rejuvenated. [. . .]

NOTES

1. Missing.
2. Elegant restaurant in Milan. (See *Otello* i, p. 277, n. 3; and *Otello* ii, p. 717, n. 3.)

 Verdi to Carlo Panattoni

[Calling card][1]

[Undated][2]

I have never owned the parts of *Trouvère*. I consigned the finished orchestra score to the directors of the Opéra, and thereafter I have seen neither the score nor the parts again.

I am glad that you are in Paris, and I hope that a solution will be found.

With highest esteem,
G. Verdi

NOTES

1. In answer to a question from Ricordi's attorney concerning the suit against Bénoit.
2. Postmark: GENOVA 24/5/92.

 Verdi to Eugenio Tornaghi

[Calling card]

[Undated][1]

I have written to Panattoni. Let's hope for a solution . . . And when does he arrive?

Greetings

NOTE

1. Postmark: GENOVA 24/5/92.

 Ricordi to Verdi

Milan, 30 May 1892

Illustrious Maestro,

Finally I am back,[1] after an absence three times longer than I had believed it would be. I worked like a slave and had countless troubles!! . . because, as usual, our government is always impossible and was created especially to discredit poor Italy! . . Thank goodness things went fairly well to make amends as much as possible for its many blunders! . . . But as I hope to see you soon, I shall bore you with my chatter at that time instead of imposing on you with a long letter today.—For now I will only say that the Viennese people's interest in music is extraordinary. The Archduchess Elisabeth, mother of the Queen of Spain,[2] as well as the Archduke Victor, brother of the Emperor,[3] had a great deal to say about you. The latter had made a special trip to Milan for the first night of *Otello,* and he is a true enthusiast!!—As you can imagine, this Archduke wants to come for the first night of the *Potbelly,* and he, like all the other personages I met, besieged me with questions about *Falstaff,* so I had a hard time being on guard against committing some involuntary indiscretion that I would later see in print. . . The Emperor remembers perfectly the famous nights of the *Mass* and *Aida,*[4] and the audience you had with him; and he expressed great hope to see you again in Vienna.

But . . . . . enough of this; here I am entirely available for your instructions! . . . I await them, and many! . . . and don't tell me, for heaven's sake, that you have none to give me! . . . . for then you would have the trouble of seeing me at St. Agata!! . . . and then, for the impertinence of boring you, you would be obliged either to evict me with a stick or . . . . to do something else!—

I wired your answer to Paris;[5] it seems to me that you are right—but, really, lawsuits, courts, attorneys are the worst misfortune that can befall us. And perhaps it is better to be robbed than to demand our due.

Roger still seems not to have understood anything about the matter of the librettos, and the thing, it seems to me, can be understood as follows: if the libretto is in Italian, the rights go to Ricordi; if it is in French, all rights go to Maestro Verdi. Have you written him again? . . . Has Roger taken care of the accounts? [. . .]

NOTES

1. From Vienna.

2. Archduchess Elisabeth (1831–1903) married Archduke Karl Ferdinand (1818–74) in 1854, one week before the wedding of Emperor Franz Joseph I of Austria (1830–1916), whom she was supposed to have married. Her daughter Maria Christina (1858–1929) grew up at the Emperor's court and married King Alfonso XII of Spain in 1879. When he died in 1885 at the age of 27, Maria Christina became regent of Spain. The following year, on the day their only son was born, she proclaimed him King Alfonso XIII of Spain. Maria Christina's highly respected regency ended upon her son's ascent to the throne on his

sixteenth birthday. After his loss of the Spanish-American War and many other misfortunes, he was deposed in 1931 and died in 1941.

3. Archduke Ludwig Victor (1842–1919), nicknamed "Luzivuzi," was the youngest brother of Emperor Franz Joseph I of Austria. His arrogant behavior and homosexual tendencies embarrassed the imperial court. After having approached a young man in a public bath, causing a major scandal, he was exiled from the court to a castle at Klesheim near Salzburg. In 1915, "Luzivuzi" was declared insane and placed under guardianship.

4. Verdi had conducted the *Requiem* and *Aida* at Vienna's Hofoper in June 1875. (See *Aida*, pp. 383–4.)

5. An unknown opinion regarding the Bénoit suit, which Verdi was prepared to lose.

Verdi to Ricordi

St. Agata, 1 June 1892

Dear Giulio,

Welcome home, I repeat, and I congratulate you on everything. . . I congratulate you as the artist, the man of the firm, and what a firm!! So, long may you live!—

You forewarned me by saying *"awaiting your instructions . . . and don't answer me that you have none to give me! . . ."*

But is that really the case? I have no instructions to give . . . and if you mean to speak of *Falstaff,* then one must first and foremost begin from the beginning and decide

1. Who will be the impresario? (You know that I don't want to have anything to do with Piontelli![1])

2. Which theatre?

3. Which singers?

Let's discuss this and settle something; then we shall see if it is advisable to present the opera . . . and this not only in my interest, but also in yours. . . . I will not hide from you that the more I go forward, the less I see clearly, and—worse from one day to the next—I get more and more confused when I think of *Falstaff.*—

You will never be a bore (understand that).—Thank you in haste. Always

Your
G. Verdi

P.S. The business with Roger is settled and he will send me a statement to collect.

NOTE

1. See Verdi to Ricordi, 31 January, n. 3.

🏵 *Ricordi to Verdi*

Milan, 5 June 1892

Illustrious Maestro,

I could not answer your esteemed letter right away because of one of those indispositions that suddenly and mysteriously hit me one or two times a year. My remedy consists of 48 hours of absolute fasting!—And since a fasting man writes poorly and reasons worse, I waited until I felt better— and here I am, entirely yours today.

In your above-mentioned letter you again ask me three questions which I had hoped would be resolved when I had the pleasure of greeting you in Genoa,[1] and after we had talked at length and discussed the Potbelly. Thus I returned to Milan, happy as a king, even three kings, to get the ball rolling by procuring books, designs, and costume sketches from London, and by preparing many other matters which I don't have the courage to tell you about at this time.—But proceeding in order, I return to your three questions [. . .]

1. "Who will be the impresario?" We have talked a great deal about this; I also told you that during the three times you were in Milan, Piontelli wanted to present himself to you, completely confident of being able to beg your forgiveness. But realizing how much you still resent his fatal offense,[2] and fearing that Piontelli's presence might irritate you, I persisted in persuading him not to carry out his idea. Have I perhaps done wrong? . . . Would it have been better if this had come about? . . I really do not know what to say. However, upon my return from Genoa, Piontelli reminded me again of his great desire to present himself to Verdi, and even to make a quick trip to St. Agata; he continues to insist that it is incredible to suppose that he committed, or knowingly allowed to be committed, an insult against Maestro Verdi. At that time, however, I was preparing for Vienna, and therefore made the accused abandon his idea once again. Now Piontelli is in Ravenna, where *Otello* was presented, but I think the season is over, or almost over, and he will certainly come to me right after his return. What line shall I take? What is the solution? . . . .

Not to have anything to do with Piontelli is easy. Whenever you came to La Scala, you never signed a contract with any management whatsoever; it was always our House which, acting in accordance with your wishes, stipulated each of the usual contracts with the management. Therefore, Maestro Verdi never had anything to do with any impresario. But by virtue of the contract stipulated between impresario and publisher, he arranged for

1892

everything as he thought best. [. . .] Ultimately, the Gordian Knot would be cut by admitting Piontelli to your presence and hearing his excuses.—I certainly understand how difficult and delicate this would be, but it would be a definite solution.—As you certainly will have noticed, I find myself in a painful position, not toward Piontelli, but toward you; being fully aware of the whole fatal offense, I would, if I followed my impulse, forbid any business with this impresario, no matter how capable and clever he may be. [. . .] The conclusion is that since you told me what had happened, I should have had the strong and natural desire to do no more business with Piontelli. But must Piontelli really prevent us from giving *Falstaff* under all the favorable circumstances we enjoy at this time? . . . In that case I would truly feel enraged enough to throw a stick of dynamite between the legs of this Signor Piontelli!! . . . Well, either this or some other solution should be found.

2. "Which theatre?" Didn't we discuss this at length in Genoa? And in which other theatre are the resources of La Scala to be found?. . . .And even the orchestra, since I have now heard the famous Viennese orchestra several times, conducted by the famous Hans Richter!![3] . . We have made progress, Maestro, great progress, taking giant steps! . . because . . . . . (*sotto voce*, so that the scholars and the good Viennese may not hear me) opera and concerts are now performed a hundred times better by us!! . . . However, my trip to Vienna enabled me to see several splendid productions at the Opera, and an enormous number of *maquettes* built in major European theatres; reduced to a small size, such sets could be most effectively employed for *Falstaff*. I had talked earlier with Stannich,[4] the excellent technical director of La Scala, and the problems you mentioned seemed solved; for example, in the garden scene where the singers must not be far from the footlights, though somewhat separated in the middle of the stage. In regard to lighting effects, all you want can be obtained, and as for acoustics, no other theatre can compete with La Scala. In Milan, then, I see no other possible theatre; rejecting La Scala, another city must be chosen—Rome?. . . What then?

3. "Which singers?" You told me that Italian artists are required for the female roles, intelligent ones, good singers, agile onstage, and amenable. Well, I believe that an excellent ensemble of 4 pleasant voices, 4 young artists, and, miraculously, all 4 of them Italian, could be arranged. That is: Colonnese,[5] Brambilla,[6] Guerrini, Fabbri.—Actually, you heard her [Fabbri] at the Dal Verme, and while you found her contralto voice stupendous (nowadays she is, unfortunately, the only true contralto in existence!), you did not consider her an intelligent actress. However, Maestro, you happened to come to the Dal Verme on a rather unfortunate night, when

things were falling apart and everything washed out.—By chance, I met Fabbri the other day and was surprised to find a young, most pleasant personage, animated, sparkling, and intelligent; in short, I am sure that she would do what you require for the character she is to interpret. I told you about Colonnese and Brambilla in Genoa; thereafter I obtained detailed information from Rome, where they both sang in the last Carnival season; and I heard they were excellent as singers and as actresses.

Maurel goes without saying; Paroli has your approval. Tenors: Masini[7] or Valero.[8] Another baritone: Pessina. Then a choice must be made between Pini-Corsi[9] and Cesari for the other scoundrel. It seems to me, then, that you would have a homogeneous, pleasing ensemble, suited to meet all your requirements, vocally and dramatically!—When I think of the radical changes you have made for either poorly coached artists or blockheads, I am really confident that from a company of this kind you would get a truly effective performance.

But meanwhile . . . . . . time is passing! . . Here I am on tenterhooks, because the good artists involved can sign other contracts from one moment to the next . . . . and we would absolutely be beside ourselves if, upon the *Potbelly*'s completion, the interpreters were no longer available! [. . .] Also, there is much to be researched for the costume designs, for making and remaking them if necessary; all the *maquettes* of the sets must be built, because we must not be satisfied with colorful designs alone, but must judge the effect from the model. All of this requires a lot of time, and nothing can be done without at least one copy of the libretto!—

But as you say so well, we must begin from the beginning . . . . . . and the real beginning can only begin with you, Maestro [. . .]. May that ray of pure light, which can come from nobody but you, at last shine again!! . . . . Only from you!! . . . . for, as Giusti (another Peppino!)[10] says:

> *Oh . . . che non ha a venire*   [Oh . . . may the day
> *Il giorno del giudizio? . . .*   Of judgment not come? . . .]

Always your most grateful and devoted
Giulio Ricordi

NOTES

1. See Ricordi to Verdi, 26 April.

2. See Verdi to Ricordi, 31 January.

3. Austro-Hungarian conductor (1843–1916), particularly distinguished as an interpreter of Wagner and the German classics in a career which spanned forty years. Richter assisted Wagner from 1866 to 1867 and copied out the score of *Die Meistersinger* for the printer. He conducted operas and concerts in Munich, Budapest, and, from 1875 to 1900, in Vienna. At Bayreuth, where he appeared from 1876 to 1912, he led the first cycle of the

1892

Ring, and in London the first *Tristan* and *Meistersinger* in 1882. As a former French horn player at the Hofoper in Vienna, Richter spoke the language of his musicians, who enjoyed his good humor.

4. Stannich or Stanrich, whom Ricordi had praised in a letter to Verdi of 8 February 1889: "[. . .] he is from Trieste and has studied a lot at the theatre in Vienna; excellent not only as a stagehand, but also on account of the new lighting [. . .]." (*Otello* i, p. 359.)

5. Elvira Colonnese (c. 1860–?), daughter of the Neapolitan baritone Luigi Colonnese (c. 1835–?), was a successful lyric soprano. She sang and taught in Buenos Aires, and probably died there.

6. Presumably related to the soprano Teresina Brambilla Ponchielli (1845–1921), wife of the composer Amilcare Ponchielli (1834–86), or her aunt Teresa Brambilla (1813–95), who was Verdi's first Gilda.

7. The particular success of Angelo Masini (1844–1926) as Radames in Florence, in 1874, was noticed by Verdi and led to his engagement for a European tour of the *Requiem* and performances of *Aida* under the composer's baton in Vienna in June 1875. Masini was known as "il tenore angelico" because of the purity of his *mezza voce*.

8. Fernando Valero (1854–1914), Spanish tenor.

9. Antonio Pini-Corsi (1858–1918), Verdi's first Ford, was a short, squat baritone. He made his debut as Dandini in *La Cenerentola* at Cremona in 1878, and had a distinguished career with a large and varied repertoire. Verdi heard him in Franchetti's *Cristoforo Colombo* in Genoa in 1892. As one of the last *buffi cantanti* of the Rossini period, Pini-Corsi was particularly acclaimed in roles such as Don Bartolo, Don Pasquale, and Leporello. His real war horse, however, was Ford; he appeared in that role on the world's leading stages, including Covent Garden and the Metropolitan. "A fine musician," as Verdi called him in his letter to Ricordi of 20 November, Pini-Corsi was also self-assured to the point of stubbornness. (See Harvey Sachs, *Toscanini*, pp. 45–6.)

10. The Tuscan poet Giuseppe Giusti (1809–50), ardent patriot and a pioneer of the Risorgimento, ends his poem "La terra dei morti" with these words. (*Le poesie di Giuseppe Giusti,* Verona, 1877.)

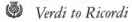 *Verdi to Ricordi*

St. Agata, 7 June 1892

Dear Giulio,

I shall answer your last letter in detail; but tell me in the meantime: Did you ever think about the ballet Manzotti[1] must give? Two important productions in the same season are not possible!! They are not possible in the interest of the management, which must maintain public interest and the quality of performance, unless Manzotti were not to open on St. Stephen's.[2] Simultaneous rehearsals are always harmful. The stage must be completely free for the rehearsals of the ballet; and equally so for the rehearsals of the opera.

Addio addio

Your
G. Verdi

NOTES

1. Luigi Manzotti (1835–1905) was a celebrated mime and the choreographer of La Scala's spectacular ballets, the sets and costumes of which were designed by the fashionable Alfredo Edel (1856–1912). Edel, an Italian painter and illustrator of Alsatian origin, had designed the costumes for the first *Otello* at La Scala in 1887.

2. 26 December, the traditional opening night at La Scala.

 *Ricordi to Verdi*

Milan, 9 June 1892

Illustrious Maestro,

Honored by your letter of the 7th of this month, I am pleased to answer you in detail, since the negotiations and discussions regarding the new ballet took place in my office, as Manzotti himself had requested. The new ballet will not be ready for next season, because the management wanted Manzotti's absolute assurance that it would be performed on St. Stephen's night, or at the latest before the 3rd of January [. . .] so that the stage would be completely free for any other productions. Evidently Manzotti had no time to have all his materials ready to begin rehearsals [in the autumn]; therefore it has all come to naught.

Meanwhile, the management wants to find an elegant little ballet, but not a spectacular one. So they asked me to see a few ballets in Vienna. I think the *Puppenfee*[1] would be good—small but charming, and only 40 minutes long. But until now I have refrained from talking about this or anything else—also, before deciding on the repertoire . . . . . I would like . . . . . to know quite different matters, in order to make the whole thing hinge on a major goal, making sure that no opera or ballet rehearsal gets in the way.

This is the answer, then, Maestro, to that which you wish to know; and it seems to be a completely favorable one. I await your instructions most anxiously and meanwhile remain, with the most affectionate regards,

Your most grateful and devoted
Giulio Ricordi

NOTES

1. Ballet in one act by Josef Hassreiter (1845–1940) and Franz Gaul (1837–1906), music by Josef Bayer (1852–1913), Austrian composer of operettas and ballets. *Die Puppenfee* was actually performed at La Scala after *Falstaff*.

1892

 *Verdi to Ricordi*

St. Agata, 10 June 1892

Dear Giulio,

After receiving your letter, I replied with two words[1] to ask you if Manzotti would give the ballet.—If this point is not clarified, it is useless to discuss the rest. So say a word . . . .

I don't know if I wrote you that the Roger business is settled.[2]

And the Bénoit suit? What is going on? . . Greetings

Your
G. Verdi

NOTES

1. Presumably in a missing telegram.
2. See Verdi to Ricordi, 1 June.

 *Ricordi to Verdi*

Milan, 11 June 1892

Illustrious Maestro,

I am in receipt of your esteemed letter of yesterday, and I hope you will have received my answer regarding Manzotti's new ballet.[1] Therefore I confirm what I wrote you.

It is only natural that the new program must be established according to the situation. I am awfully sorry to give you the impression of being a pig-headed bore! . . . But, e.g., for costumes and sets, much time is needed, and it can also happen [. . .][2]

He is full of hope!![3] . . . . Let us hope his guess is correct. Therefore I am enclosing a report on the first hearings; it certainly is convincing, and the defense most skillful. Please return it to me.—The attorney Panattoni sends kind regards; he leaves again for Paris tomorrow, where on the 14th of this month the 2nd hearing will take place. [. . .]

NOTES

1. See Ricordi to Verdi, 9 June.
2. Part of this letter is missing, and the conclusion is unsigned.
3. Presumably Panattoni, regarding the Bénoit suit.

🏵 *Verdi to Ricordi*

St. Agata, 13 June 1892

Dear Giulio,

It would have been better if Manzotti had given his ballet: that would have spared us a serious embarrassment for everyone, and a most serious one for me!

Under no circumstances whatsoever do I intend to meet with the impresario, nor do I wish to have direct contact with him. I am convinced that the insult was committed, and on purpose, but I don't want idle talk, nor do I want to call upon the living or the dead as witnesses. It is no use to say that he is too intelligent to have indulged in such an act. But wait a minute!— He was convinced that I would do nothing after *Otello*; and so he could indulge in such an insult to avenge himself for my demands and pretensions! His reasoning could have been right . . . but he didn't think that I could still say . . . *Finished; and da capo!*

I don't want to have anything to do with the Commission, either; and if the many, many difficulties could be overcome, you, I say you, would be my temporary manager (and mind you, it won't be easy this time), and I would turn to you for everything, reserving the right to withdraw the score if I am ever unsatisfied with the performance on musical or dramatic grounds.—

You talk to me about sets, about sending painters to London (what for?), about costumes, about machinery, about lighting! To make sets for the theatre, theatre painters are needed: painters who, above all, have the vanity not to exhibit their vanity, but to serve the drama. And for God's sake, let's not do it the way it was done for *Otello*, when, in wanting to do too much, *too much of a good thing was done*. Rather, get the costume designs for the *Wives* from London (with Downing's help),[1] as they are executed in London. I, too, have received—I don't know from whom—photographs of German designs; a few of them are very nice, but they will be of no use.

For the machinery, little need be done, apart from the *basket* scene, which, however, involves no problems at all, as long as there are no unnecessary complications.—

There is no need for lighting effects, just for a bit of *darkness* in the park scene; but let's understand each other well, *darkness* in which the faces of the artists can be seen. Not the kind of lighting effects as in the last act of *Wally:* very nice, if you want; but they completely ruined the dramatic effect, and the opera ended cold!

As for the orchestra, *something is rotten in Denmark.* You see that the

1892

management has also installed at La Scala, as in other places, its accomplices who aren't worth a thing. Also, the first violins sound thin, because they don't all play. Let's not even talk about the *seconds!!* The woodwinds aren't worth very much, apart from the two old musicians who are better than all the others. The new ones are unprofessional, can't attack . . . and what lousy playing! The horns are no good; the trumpets can't *tongue.* The trombones are better, but don't know how to play softly. . . But Mascheroni must straighten everything out, because this way it does not work.—

Let's now come to the most serious matters. Alas, the problems grow and grow and suffocate us!—

Fabbri, with her lovely, agile voice, can be successful in *cantabile* pieces such as *La Cenerentola,* etc., etc. But the part of *Quickly* is something else. It calls for singing and acting, much aplomb on the stage, and the right emphasis in her diction. She does not have these qualities, and we run the risk of sacrificing a part which is the most individual and original one of the four.—

The part of Alice requires the same qualities, plus even greater vivacity. She must be full of the devil. *She stirs the brew.*

Guerrini is good for the part of *Meg,* but I am sorry that the part isn't more important.

Nannetta must be extremely young and sing beautifully, and be a very brilliant actress, above all in the two little duets with the tenor, and especially in the one that is very vivacious and comic.[2]

You see, it isn't easy to find what is needed! Do Colonnese and Brambilla have these qualities? . . And how could they be heard?

For the male part [Fenton] there is no one better than Masini, but I fear his bad temper when he realizes during the rehearsals that the parts of *Falstaff, Alice, Quickly,* and *Ford* are much more important than his own.— Valero no; he is too whining! What is this Moretti[3] like?—

Pessina is a good artist, but more singer than actor, and he is a bit stodgy for the part of Ford, who, in a towering outburst of jealousy, roars, screams, jumps all over, etc. . . Without this, the finale of the second act would be sacrificed. All the attention is turned to him and to Falstaff's face bumping up and down in the basket.

In this part [Ford], Pini-Corsi would be better, if his legs could be changed.[4]

Paroli good for Dr. Cajo. *Cesari* is too much for the part of Pistola. But if he is content with it, it could be enlarged by giving him a few of Bardolfo's phrases; we'll talk about that with Boito.

Also, for Bardolfo a very free and easy actor is required, one who knows how to carry his nose[5]. . .

So you see how hard it will be to find all that is necessary. I add that the piano and stage rehearsals will be long, because it won't be too easy to perform it as I want—and I will be very demanding; and not as I was for *Otello,* where, out of regard for this or that person, and to *pose* as a serious, worthy, and venerable man, I endured everything. No, no: I shall again be the bear[6] of old, and all of us will benefit from it. . . The music is not difficult, but will have to be sung differently from other modern comic operas and from the old *buffo* operas. I wouldn't want it to be sung, for example, like *Carmen,* and not even like *Don Pasquale* or *Crispino.*[7] There is need for study, and that will take time. Our singers, in general, can only sing with *big voices;* they have neither vocal flexibility nor clear and easy diction, and they lack phrasing and breath.—*Excusez du* [illegible word].

What rigmarole!—I have written very poorly about everything . . but excuse me . . . . it would take too much time to rewrite . . . addio, addio

G. Verdi

I still haven't had time to read attorney Panattoni's report. I shall return it to you tomorrow.

NOTES

1. Probably referring to Ricordi's representative in London.
2. In I.ii.
3. Unknown despite his supposedly successful career.
4. He was bowlegged.
5. "Quel tuo naso ardentissimo/ Mi serve da lanterna" [That most glowing nose of yours/ Serves me as a lantern], Falstaff says to Bardolfo in I.i.
6. In earlier times Verdi frequently compared himself to a bear, threatening to behave like one when things did not go his way.
7. *Crispino e la Comare,* "melodramma fantastico giocoso" in three acts by F. M. Piave, music by L. and F. Ricci.

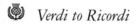 *Verdi to Ricordi*

St. Agata, 14 June 1892

Dear Giulio,

I return Panattoni's report. As you say, it is certainly "convincing and the defense most skillful," but in Paris the lawsuit will be lost. . . Oh yes, oh yes . . *in Paris* we shall lose in spite of everything.—But if we must capitulate, let's at least do so quickly. For *15* or *16* months this suit has tormented and distracted me; and, to tell you the truth, for my part I would rather lose it than remain in such turmoil; and even more so today, for if *Falstaff*, unfortunately, had to be performed, I would require the utmost calm. I said "unfortunately"! I repeat this word, because the saying goes that misfortunes are like cherries, they never come alone; and thus the suit lost and the fiasco of *Falstaff* would be the pair. Watch out!

You will have received my rigmarole of yesterday. One could not write or talk in a worse manner, but mind you there are good reasons for it . . . Addio, addio

G. Verdi

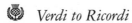 *Verdi to Ricordi*

St. Agata, 15 June 1892

Dear Giulio,

The other day I wrote you a 12-page letter![1] I say *12*!!!! Yesterday another one!

Today yet another one!!!!!!!!!!

This morning Du Locle wrote me about the *Droits d'auteur* for *Othello*. That is already settled between me and Roger, and you can withdraw your share of the Italian *Otello* presented in Nice whenever you wish.—It seems that the terms of the declaration, made through the French consul (which was useless for Roger), are not clear, and that they must be modified as Roger himself will indicate.—

I haven't finished!!

Do me the favor of submitting this application form for the subscription to the works of G. Carcano.[2]— Go ahead and pay the entire cost of the works for Peppina and for me, as follows

for Peppina	*L. 30*
for me	*L. 30*
Total	*L. 60*

Also charge *L. 300* to my account for the bust to be made of poor Faccio.[3] Please excuse me very much!

Your
G. Verdi

NOTES

1. On 13 June.

2. Giulio Carcano (1812–84), poet and novelist, worked for some forty years on a complete translation of Shakespeare. Verdi's copy of his *Opere di Shakespeare* is preserved at St. Agata. One of the volumes contains the personal dedication to "his friend on 19 March 1875."

3. In the Museum of La Scala.

🏵 *Ricordi to Verdi*

Milan, 15 June 1892

Illustrious Maestro,

To your honored letter[1] I will say right away that *two* things frighten me!
. . . I will say it even better: one thing saddens me, for with my long letters
I rob you of precious time, obliging you to give long answers; the other
thing frightens me, because you charge me with a *managerial* responsibility
which will flatten me, so to speak, like a cake. *Mais qui veut la fin, doit vouloir
les moyens!* —And the end is so beautiful and great that the means must well
be sought. I pass over Piontelli, since I would truly go too far wishing to
show you that perhaps not all your assumptions are correct. For simple love
of brevity and truth, I must tell you only that Piontelli has put together an
excellent orchestra, having replaced at least 30 musicians; and if he was
unable to fulfil all your demands, it was because of great pressures from all
sides! . . . Mind you, it was the management's and Mascheroni's first year. [. . .]

As to the costume designs, I already received the necessary material from
London; and for the sets, to avoid serious blunders, *maquettes* must definitely
be built as a sure guide to allow for those changes and improvements which
cannot be made once the sets are under construction.

The great *problem* lies in putting together the company you need!—You
understand, of course, that I talked at length with Boito about the things
you wrote me. I called him in today. And the *problem* of *problems*, to my feeble
mind, lies in the *Quickly!*—Neither Boito nor I, Maestro, have any doubts
about Fabbri!!—Excuse the boldness of this affirmation, but we really are
persuaded that you can get all you want from this artist. The basic material
is there: a truly splendid contralto voice; think of the changes you had an
artist make when you could work with a real voice. In *Quickly*'s case there are
two possibilities:

Either a true contralto voice is required as the foundation for the three
other female voices—and, unfortunately, the only true and powerful contralto voice today is Fabbri's; it is for you to mold the voice and the artist
according to the demands of the music. You will say that this takes half a
miracle, but you make whole miracles, and have made many.

Or you absolutely do not want to use Fabbri, and see then only one artist:
Pasqua. And her voice? . . Can it function as the double-bass in the
ensembles? . . . . Will it have the necessary timbre in the low notes?—That
is the big question.

Guerrini: good, then, for *Meg*.

For *Alice* and *Nannetta* I suggested Colonnese and Brambilla; these artists are still young, but have already made excellent careers: they move well onstage, have attractive and elegant personalities . . But others could also be proposed, e.g., Bellincioni,[2] most intelligent—Calvé[3]—Stehle—Zilli,[4] not beautiful, to tell the truth, but an excellent actress and elegant onstage.

With *Falstaff* and *Dr. Cajo* we are all right. What kind of voice is needed for *Bardolfo?* . . . .

For *Ford*, Boito likes Pini-Corsi best. I had suggested Pessina to you, however, because he made such an excellent impression on you in his short phrase in the *Preghiera di Mosè*. He is a most industrious artist, very intelligent, an excellent actor, and in the future, I think, he will be one of the best Falstaffs after Maurel; that is why it would be good to have him at La Scala. But, I repeat, these are just my ideas.

Let's move on to *Fenton*. Your observations regarding Masini are so right; but once we tell him what it is about, it's all over. If he accepts, I believe that as a good Romagnolo[5] he will cause no trouble! If he doesn't accept, we will be at his mercy. It will certainly be difficult to find another tenor as long as you consider Valero not entirely suitable. Moretti is an excellent artist, but has no great voice; you heard him in the ensemble pieces of the *Stabat Mater*.[6] He has been successful in all the theatres where he has gone. Another good tenor is De Lucia.[7]

Getting back to *Bardolfo:* If he is a bass, there are two excellent artists: Silvestri[8] or Nannetti.

As for the way to hear the singers you don't know, I offered, if you recall, to find out if in some theatre an opera might be performed *ad hoc*. But so much time has gone by, and I fear that some artists may already be engaged for the autumn; so I don't know if my idea could be easily realized at this moment. But if you could be in Milan, Boito and I believe we have found the way to enable you to hear some artists without compromising you; my idea of a performance might not have kept the reason for it secret, to say nothing of your presence at a performance! . . . I also think that in order to spare you excessive fatigue, and, moreover, to have all the necessary time, it would be useful to begin the coaching soon, in autumn even!—But, then, Maestro . . . . . . the music must be prepared . . . . the reduction must be made and the parts extracted! . . . etc., etc. How to do it all? . . . .

All the preparatory work must certainly be decided upon before the end of this month; but it also seems wrong to me to waste your time with letters and the necessary long replies.

If you think my coming to you could be useful, and, better yet, along with Boito, I am at your disposal; possibly, I can also come to Tabiano, because I will be busy through Sunday, and I believe you are going there only during these days.

Just this moment I received another registered letter from you, with Panattoni's report; I will answer you about it tomorrow; now I finish, before reaching twelve whole pages, which are really too much! . . .

Always your grateful and devoted

Giulio Ricordi

NOTES

1. Of 13 June.

2. Gemma Bellincioni (1864–1950), Giulio Ricordi's choice for the role of Aida, was particularly admired by Massenet and Richard Strauss. (See *Aida*, p. 159n; and *Otello* i, pp. 185, 192, 193n., 194, 196, 197, 199n., 200, 207-10, 305-7; *Otello* ii, p. 809.)

3. The French soprano Emma Calvé (1858–1942), a famous Carmen, had appeared at La Scala and other Italian theatres since 1886.

4. Emma Zilli (1864–1901), the first Alice in *Falstaff*, had been a pianist and began singing only after her marriage to the painter Giacomo Zilli, in 1882. Five years later, at Ferrara, she made her operatic debut in the soprano role of Paolina in Donizetti's *Poliuto*. Thereafter she appeared throughout Italy, in Spain, and in eastern Europe. Puccini admired her as "an exciting singing actress," and she frequently performed his Manon Lescaut. In mid-career she died of yellow fever in Havana, while on a South American tour.

5. Masini was born near Forlì in Umbria, not in Romagna.

6. At La Scala on 8 April, in observance of the centenary of Rossini's birth.

7. The Neapolitan Fernando De Lucia (1860–1925) was a master of *bel canto*. He appeared at London's Drury Lane, Covent Garden, and the Metropolitan.

8. The bass Alessandro Silvestri (1851–1922) was known to Verdi from his performance as Filippo II in *Don Carlo* at La Scala in 1884.

 *Ricordi to Verdi*

Milan, 16 June 1892

Illustrious Maestro,

I continue my letter of yesterday to answer you about the business in Paris. Oh! . . . you are so right, Maestro . . . . . . the hearings lead to material and moral ruin, whatever the outcome; and having learned the hard way, I understand the intense annoyance you must endure. [. . .] I am in ill humor these days, above all on account of administrative troubles and bitterness over being deprived of peace and health. I shall see if I can regain a bit of the philosophy which has sustained me so far; aging makes people become selfish, they say!! . . But the opposite is happening to me, which tortures my soul and upsets my mind, which perpetuates the torture. But what a bore, am I not? . . . That bore is ever your most devoted, most grateful, albeit boring

Giulio Ricordi

1892

🏵 *Ricordi to Verdi*

Milan, 16 June 1892

Illustrious Maestro,

I don't know what to do! . . . I propose not to bother you . . . and instead here is one letter after the other! One yesterday, one this morning, and now another one. Forgive me for all three of them at once.

Today Mascheroni was in Milan, and, of course I talked with him about the orchestra. Meanwhile, and in Mascheroni's name, I confirm the radical changes that were to be made last year, but will no doubt be made this year, in the 1st and 2nd violins—changes already decided upon last season; because of certain circumstances these will be even more radical. Also, the singers were discussed, and especially the contraltos. I consider it my duty to relate Mascheroni's opinion to you. As to vocal timbre, he, too, believes that none is better than Fabbri; he also thinks that much could be done with her as an actress, if she were well directed. But he also deems Pasqua an excellent choice; her intelligence and dramatic art are without question. I told Mascheroni about Puccini's impression of her; he fully agrees, but remarks that the part in Puccini's opera is eminently dramatic and high; and since Pasqua can no longer pretend to be young, the role of Tigrana would no doubt have been hard for her.[1] Mascheroni taught Pasqua the part of [Gluck's] *Orfeo* last year and was very content. If in *Falstaff* comic action and pointed phrases are involved, he thinks that Pasqua's present capabilities are more than sufficient.

That is Mascheroni's opinion; I would think, then, that with your permission, the simple thing to do would be to consult Pasqua herself. You once jotted down the range of Quickly for me; if I remember correctly, it's like this

—but then I don't know whether with the $B\flat$ you meant to indicate the highest note or the particularly necessary part of the scale.

Pasqua is an artist to whom one can write frankly, of course. I could do so to obtain information for myself before making any mention of it to you. Otherwise write her yourself, Maestro, as you know how to write, and I would forward the letter, being unable to give you her address, which I don't know at this time!—Anyway, it must be done right away, so that we are not left in the lurch by either Pasqua or Fabbri, or by both of them.

And since you do not mistreat the bearer of bad news, I must inform you of the following: Boracchi the impresario[2] represents Baron Franchetti, Sr.[3] He asked me if it is true that *Falstaff* will not be given at La Scala, and I replied that I knew nothing.—Thereupon Boracchi told me that Baron Franchetti is putting the theatre of Reggio Emilia completely at our disposal, giving Maestro Verdi *carte blanche* to assemble the company, orchestra, and chorus, under whatever conditions he may wish.

Of course, I observed that I could not give any reply; Boracchi then asked me to mention Baron Franchetti's project to you, which, of course, I could not refuse to do.

I take a step back. For the tenor, if a *clear* agreement can be arranged with Masini, nothing would be better. But in another letter you mentioned De Lucia.[4] Mascheroni gave me an excellent report about him today.

For today, I have emptied the sack . . . it was about time.

Excuse me once again, with my feelings of devoted affection.

Your most grateful
Giulio Ricordi

NOTES

1. See Ricordi to Verdi, 25 March, nn. 1 and 2; and 30 March, nn. 1, 2, and 3.
2. Unknown.
3. The wealthy father of the composer Alberto Franchetti. (See Ricordi to Verdi, 3 December 1890, n. 1.)
4. Mentioned by Ricordi himself in his letter to Verdi of 15 June, n. 6.

 *Verdi to Ricordi*

St. Agata, 17 June 1892

Dear Giulio,

The more we proceed, the more complicated things become. First and foremost, do not think about the music of *Falstaff* either for the end of this month or the next. Also, in the finished pieces I am redoing some bars here and there; also some pages, and I'm not making progress.

But what need is there? And what need to think now about costume designs, about sets, etc., etc.? . . Let's not look for too much! One of the two: either a *mise-en-scène* after the *Opéra* fashion (they cost from 2 to 3 hundred thousand francs), or an unpretentious *mise-en-scène* (which is better) after the fashion of, for example, *La forza del destino,* which in my staging was better than in other productions that came later! And tell me if it isn't true that

1892

despite all the fuss nothing more shabby and unworthy of a great theatre could be imagined than the *Fuoco di gioia* in *Otello;* and even more so the garden scene, which rendered unintelligible even such a plain and clear text?[1] No, no: in Italy things must be done conveniently, but without pretense, and without looking for *midi à quatorze heures.*[2]

Besides, my dear Giulio, it is better to say things right away: *I shall not tolerate anything which does not convince me.—*

As for the orchestra, Piontelli will have replaced, or will replace, the musicians in order to spend less, as he has always done in Genoa and elsewhere. Just one example: Why did he replace the excellent oboist with a very mediocre one? With this system he will replace the good musicians who still remain at La Scala!

But the great *problem* lies, as you say, in assembling the cast! Greatest difficulty regarding the three women!

Pasqua, according to Puccini's report,[3] is frightening; nevertheless, could you write her and tell her plainly that here the chips are down, and to dispense with the sentimentality.[4] It's a comedy; no cantabile music, notes and words, bustling about the stage and lots of vivacity.

And the other two?

Bellincioni most intelligent, but too sentimental.

Calvé no.

Better Stehle. Her voice is too thin, but for Nannetta it might go well if, in addition to vivacity, there is a little feeling. In the third act there is a very delicate, poetic song to the Fairies, which ought to be rendered well.

But Colonnese and Brambilla? You suggested them yourself? Is there no chance to hear them? Not in a room! I confess that I don't understand and cannot judge an artist in a room, and not even in an empty theatre without costume and headdress. I don't think Pessina is a great actor, but [he is] altogether an excellent artist. Better for the part of Falstaff than Ford.

Bardolfo is another tenor. ⎫
Pistola is a bass. ⎭ musically not very important.

Moretti or De Lucia if . . the Divo [Masini] causes problems.

Ugh, what a mess!

Quite difficult to clean up!

Tomorrow I go to Tabiano.

I'll return here on Monday.

After three or four days I'll return to Tabiano, and from there we shall come to Milan for two or three days. Take care of everything and clear up the

216

difficulties if possible.—About *Falstaff* in Reggio I can't say anything but *it's not possible* for so many, many reasons too long to explain.

In haste addio, addio
G. Verdi[5]

Alice	?
Quickly	Fabbri (doubts that I do not have)
Meg	Guerrini (good)
Nannetta	?
Falstaff	Morel . .
Ford	Pini-Corsi (to me excellent)
D. Cajo	Paroli (good)
Pistola	Cesari (too good)
Bardolfo	?
Fenton	Masini (none better)

NOTES

1. Verdi repeatedly expressed his dismay on this subject. (*Otello* i, pp. 293–4, 303–4, 380–1.)

2. Verdi used this French saying, which means not to complicate matters by thinking too much, on various occasions, as in a letter to Léon Escudier on 8 February 1865: "Sometimes, trying to multiply effects ends up with each one killing the other." (Franz Werfel and Paul Stefan, eds., *Verdi, the Man in his Letters*, pp. 237, 239.) See also *Aida* and *Otello* letters.

3. See Ricordi to Verdi, 30 March, and Verdi to Ricordi, 31 March.

4. Of predominantly dramatic roles.

5. Attached to this letter are Boito's casting thoughts in his own handwriting.

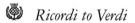 *Ricordi to Verdi*

Milan, 17 June 1892

Illustrious Maestro,

What are you going to say about my letters if you find one of your own excessive, one that amounts to less than half of mine? . . . . Do I have to tell you again what pleasure your letters give me, whether they contain 2, 4, 8, 12, or 20 pages? . . .

I took note and carried out your instructions.[1] Thanking you, I renew my greetings and warm feelings from the most grateful heart of

Your most devoted
Giulio Ricordi

I just received the following telegram from Paris:

"Yesterday's objections opposing attorney insignificant—Pouillet happily

summed up my notes—Lamoureux's[2] opinion most impressive verifying musical differences—Republican prosecutor will conclude 23 August—Wishing triumph—Panattoni."
Do you have hope, Maestro!?![3]

NOTES

1. See Verdi to Ricordi, 15 June.
2. Charles Lamoureux (1834–99), prominent violinist and conductor, was the founder of the concert society in Paris named after him, and a devoted Wagnerian.
3. Two words in Italian, "Spera, Maestro?!?" are written, here evidently in Tornaghi's hand.

 *Ricordi to Verdi*

Milan, 21 June 1892

Illustrious Maestro,

I received your latest esteemed letter.[1] Everything you write me is fine. Above all, I find no words to tell you how pleased I am by the announcement of your next visit. Therefore, I do not want to disturb you with more long letters; in your presence we will attempt to solve all the problems, and I will be the faithful executor of your instructions. God willing, I will be fortunate enough to say: *Verdi is content!*

I am writing to Signora Pasqua. I hope that your trip was a most pleasant one, and that Signora Peppina is comfortable in Tabiano, and that it will do her good.

I hope, then, to see both of you shortly and in good health, which will delight

the always grateful and devoted
Giulio Ricordi

NOTE

1. Of 17 June.

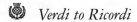 *Verdi to Ricordi*

Montecatini, 12 July 1892

Dear Giulio,

Journey good; health good. Herewith the 4 words, to which I add *suffocating heat!!!*

Pasqua came here 2 days ago. I read her much of the libretto and had her sing a few phrases from the third act, which I had with me. In her heart of hearts she might have wanted some piece in which to stand out alone, but, intelligent as she is, she understood what it's about, and she will be content to do that role, which she will do well.—I also noticed (I alone) that at some points in the third act *Quik* is onstage for too long without saying anything; and I think that without hurting the comedy, some phrase or some words can be taken from *Alice* or Meg and be given to *Quik* without sacrificing anything in the performance. I'll write Boito about it myself when I've gone over the third act; meanwhile, if you see him, mention it to him.—

Everybody tells me that Masini will be content to sing, whatever the part may be! Ready, aim, and try to hit well.—

I was told about Garulli, a bit stocky, but nice voice and good singer.[1]

And Alice? Here is the trouble. Usiglio[2] told me about Tetrazzini, not the one who does Desdemona so well, but the other one, who supposedly eloped with the bass Cesari to America.[3] Is she returning? Are they staying there? But isn't Cesari at La Scala? In my opinion he could be replaced with the bass who did *Montano* in *Otello*.[4]

And Paroli, who must do Dr. Cajo?

And Bardolfo? . .

I leave you because I'm burning up from the heat—

Greetings to you and everybody

[Illegible]

G. Verdi

NOTES

1. The tenor Alfonso Garulli (1856–1915) was known throughout Italy and Europe in operas such as *Carmen, Mignon, La Favorita, Lohengrin, Cavalleria rusticana, Manon,* and *Werther*.

2. The conductor Emilio Usiglio (1841–1910). See *Aida*, pp. 250n., 331, 333, 340–1, 370n., 377, 378n., 408n.; and *Otello* ii, pp. 796, 840n., 860.

3. Luisa Tetrazzini (1871–1940) studied with her sister Eva (1862–1938), who was the first Desdemona in America. Luisa Tetrazzini ("had a brilliant voice above the stave, and a phenomenal coloratura technique. [. . .] She barely attempted to act,") earned millions, and had a chicken dish named after her, but died in poverty (*Oxford Dictionary*).

4. Napoleone Limonta appeared at La Scala in 1881–82, 1885, and, as the King in *Aida*, in 1886–87.

 *Verdi to Ricordi*

Montecatini, 12 July 1892

Dear Giulio,

If you think so, send Masini the enclosed card, together with a nice letter from you telling him everything I didn't say, and well.[1]

1892

They tell me all the time about this Garulli, who must now be singing in Pesaro!——

And Alice? That is a very important matter! . . . Let's hope for this *Colonnese* or for *Busi*.[2] We are doing well here in the heat. Greetings and health. Write me as soon as possible about Masini.

Your
G. Verdi

NOTES

1. Both these communications are missing.
2. Unknown.

 *Ricordi to Verdi*

Milan, 14 July 1892

Illustrious Maestro,

It is really superfluous to tell you how pleased we are to receive your excellent news! [. . .]

And now to the Potbelly! . . . to the Potbelly! in answer to your two esteemed letters, which reached me almost simultaneously. I am very happy that you write about Pasqua; I have already talked with Boito, who says that what you say about *Quick*'s part is *very good*. In fact, he thinks it is better that you find the most suitable places; to let *Quick* say them instead of the others won't take anything away from the comedy. Of course, if need be, you can also modify a verse or two; but after all, that is easily done.

Garulli for the tenor? . . . But I believe he is utterly impossible! . . . better a beginner! Garulli has already sung at La Scala; he is certainly not an insignificant artist, but he has the bad quality of being extremely disagreeable to the audience! . . . Moretti would be a thousand times better.

Tetrazzini (sister of the good one engaged at Madrid) is a sister, and nothing else; her range is limited, she is almost a mezzo-soprano and certainly no artist for La Scala.[1]

Cesari, a bass, is engaged at La Scala, and there is no reason to think that he would give up his contract; if that were to happen, it would be very easy to replace him.

Paroli is engaged.

Pini-Corsi is engaged.

For the other tenor there is Pelagalli-Rossetti,[2] who is one of the best *Cassio*s.

We always return to *Alice!!* . . . Well then, Colonnese was not in Naples, but in Paris, and just three days ago she was in Milan on her way to Naples. I caught Colonnese, I caught Boito . . . . . . and an audition was arranged: *Nothing*. She doesn't sing badly, she has a certain expressiveness, but in her desire to perform parts that are too strenuous for her kind of voice, she has spoiled its freshness; it has become heavy, and on the G, A, B following the high F we are in trouble!! . . . . . You need not bother to hear her, just as I don't think it worth your while to hear Busi; after a long discussion I had yesterday with Boito and the management, it appears that this audition would be useless; but, of course, whenever you want the audition, it will be arranged. In summary, Zilli still remains the best. I seem to hear you exclaim: *Woe is me! What misery!* . . . And yet, see how bold I am. . . . I am firmly convinced that you can reduce Zilli's part as you wish. The other singers you heard[3] you either did not know or had heard at the beginning of their careers. Zilli is another kettle of fish; I heard her last September in the theatre; her voice is secure and she is an excellent actress. As to the interpretation of a part . . . . where are the artists who can do it today, unless directed by good conductors? . . . And where are the good conductors? . . . There's the rub. Maybe the only one who felt, knew, and could was Patti![4] . . But the others, even with voice and talent, were, and certainly are, no *spontaneous* interpreters! . . .

Enclosed in your other esteemed letter I received that very beautiful note! . . . I shall ascertain at once Masini's whereabouts; some people say he is in Forlì, others, at the Abetone in Tuscany; but I still haven't found out with certainty where he is. So I shall send for information as to where he is staying and write him immediately. But another little note from you would be needed for the other star, Maurel, a splendid artist, but an impossible and intractable fellow. But since he at least shows correct and proper deference toward you, two lines from Verdi will really help to prevent difficulties with his contract.

As I had asked you, please advise me in time regarding the payment of the semiannual account so that I may withdraw the appropriate sum from the bank. Up to now I have spoken of beautiful things; there must be a few ugly ones, too. However, I think it indispensable to provide you with a copy of the Paris attorney's letter addressed to Panattoni.[5] Certainly, all they say is very nice . . . but that is a meager consolation! . . .

However, to return to more breathable air, let us turn again to the *Potbelly!* Yesterday, I once again warmly recommended to the management that it undertake the formation of the orchestra. It will draw up the lists in accordance with Mascheroni, and I will see them, too. The good news goes without saying . . . . that the repertoire also is to be settled so that

1892

everything may run smoothly and so that you may be in complete command of the singers and the theatre altogether.

So Franchetti's *Colombo*[6] will be given!! . . . . . City Hall in Genoa, at least, has been assured of this. The mayor would like to open the season with *Otello*. But it isn't easy to form a good company! . . . and I don't know where to start.

But I make you lose time with my chatter.

Have a good cure, good health, and *au revoir* soon! . . . .

With our most affectionate greetings and devoted gratitude,

Yours ever,
Giulio Ricordi

NOTES

1. This seems to have been the general opinion about Luisa Tetrazzini before the start of her sensational career at San Francisco in 1904.

2. Paolo Pelagalli-Rossetti was cast for the role of Bardolfo. Otherwise unknown.

3. Apparently two weeks earlier in Milan on the way to Montecatini.

4. The famous soprano Adelina Patti (1843–1919), whom Verdi had admired as early as 1862. (See *Aida*, pp. 13–4n., 130, 141n., 166n., 352n., 357, 381, 403, 407–10; *Otello* i, pp. 30, 192, 305, 349; ii, 820, 840, 846–8.)

5. Missing letter regarding the Bénoit suit.

6. *Cristoforo Colombo* by Alberto Franchetti (1860–1942) was commissioned by the City of Genoa. It was premiered there on the four hundredth anniversary of the discovery of America and was to open the 1892–93 season of La Scala on 26 December. This opera, Franchetti's second, "has more than moments of power and sweep, partly because Franchetti's training in Germany led him to write choral music especially with contrapuntal ease. The solo music tends toward limpness, except for Columbus' Act II aria—indeed, Act II is the work's highlight, culminating of course in the first sight of the New World. Act III, including a love story with native Americans, is weak, and the epilogue [. . .] is overlong." (Patrick J. Smith, *Opera News*, October 1992.)

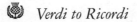 *Verdi to Ricordi*

Montecatini, 14 July 1892[1]

Dear Giulio,

Tomorrow I'll talk about *Lassalle*[2] with you; today we talk *Falstaff*.

Woe is me, woe is me! Paroli is lost?![3]

Pini-Corsi is lost!![4] I am very sorry about him, because no one will be able to do that part, which is of supreme importance.

Pessina? Regarding him I told you "good singer, perhaps good actor," but not in a furiously hot-headed part like that of *Ford*.

For the moment let's not talk about the tenor, but what makes me despair is the artist for *Alice!* Nothing, then about *Colonnese* and *Busi!*

Zilli better than all of them?—Poor us!

I realized, too, that there was something good in her voice, but when I heard the excerpts from *Aida*, her *war-horse*, that was the rub. Still, if we succeeded in finding all the rest, another experiment might be made with Zilli. I could have two excerpts from the opera copied; I myself would study them with her a couple of times, or three or four times, and then decide! . . What do you say to this?—We will stay here until the middle of next week; then we'll go to St. Agata, where I want to rest two or three days. I would then go to Genoa on business and return via Milan, where I would hear Zilli; I would confer with Boito, and it would be decided if there is a chance to present the opera. All right? Meanwhile you will have news from Masini.—

Write me here right away.

Addio, addio

Your

G. Verdi

P.S. I shall write to Maurel.[5] Of him, I think, we are certain——

NOTES

1. Presumably in answer to a missing communication.

2. Unknown Frenchman involved in the Bénoit suit.

3. In his letter of the same date, which Verdi had not yet received, Ricordi had informed him about this artist's engagement.

4. Ibid.

5. No such letter seems to exist. Verdi's letter of 8 November appears to be the first he wrote to Maurel concerning *Falstaff*.

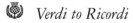 *Verdi to Ricordi*

Montecatini, 17 July 1892[1]

Dear Giulio,

All the better if Paroli and Pini-Corsi are at La Scala. Let's now hear about Masini; then we'll see if Zilli is a possibility.——

We shall leave Montecatini Wednesday evening (the 20th) and will be at St. Agata at 6 in the morning on the 21st. I will rest there for three or four days, then go to Genoa. If you can send me the usual *bank check* to Busseto for the 23rd or 24th, I would cash it in Genoa around the *25th* or *26th*.— If it is too early, I will delay my departure. In any case, please send me the *check* at Busseto, St. Agata.——

I am returning the Lassalle copy.[2] You know my opinion, and I strongly confirm it after reading this report.[3] The attorneys do their job . . . and with much talent, very much . . . but I have no faith.—This morning I, too, received from the attorney Pilastre[4] the copy of the judgment in Paris. Tomorrow I shall reply that I agree with the decision of the House of Ricordi.

You still have time to answer me here briefly about everything.—Addio, addio

Affectionately,
G. Verdi

The best I forgot.
As I told you, I can hear and, in a certain way, and up to a certain point, judge Zilli in the way I suggested to you.——

Well then   *Garulli* no?
          And Gabrielesco?[5]
          And Cremonini?[6].

NOTES

1. In answer to Ricordi, 14 July.
2. See Verdi to Ricordi, 14 July, n. 2.
3. Supposedly a pessimistic one as to the outcome of the suit against Bénoit.
4. Unknown.
5. The Romanian tenor Gregorio Gabrielesco appeared in Italy, Spain, and South America between 1887 and 1894. He was most successful in *Edgar, Gioconda, Rigoletto, Aida, Tannhäuser, Les Huguenots,* and, particularly, *Otello.* Basically a lyric tenor, he over-taxed his uniquely beautiful voice, thus considerably shortening his career.
6. The tenor Giuseppe Cremonini (1866–1903) sang in secondary Italian theatres until his breakthrough as Turiddu in Bucharest in 1891. He was heard in London (1892), Buenos Aires (1893), Madrid, and in other major cities until a few days before his death in his native Cremona.

 *Ricordi to Verdi*

Milan, 18 July 1892

Illustrious Maestro,

In answer to your most esteemed letter of yesterday, I shall send you the Banca Nazionale check to St. Agata on the 22nd of this month. In order to avoid additional transactions I shall send you the entire sum of your account for the half-year. [. . .]

At La Scala a small army is ready and engaged: *Women*: Stehle, Guerrini, Brambilla, Colonnese, Ricetti,[1] and, I think, others, too.

Men: Cesari, Paroli, Pelagalli-Rossetti, Pessina, Moretti, etc.

From this group, the dead wood has already been eliminated. Pasqua and Maurel are still to be signed; to the first I shall write today; to the second a letter of yours will be providential.

During all this time I have also searched everywhere for Masini without ever finding him. I don't want to write him *without being sure that he will personally receive my letter;* I am informed that he is in Forlì at the moment, so I wired him immediately.

Your proposal of another audition for Zilli is the most *practical* and *positive* solution.

Garulli, I repeat, is impossible. Gabrielesco is engaged for Madrid, if I am not mistaken, and he isn't suitable either. Cremonini, who is better than both of them, is engaged for Turin. Boito had very good information from Gallignani about Moretti, who sang in Parma last winter, and we know that the Parma audience is the toughest in Italy! . . .

Ah! . . . How right you are, Maestro, about lawsuits and lawyers!! . . but . . . . how to endure bowing the head before the wicked sentence?[2] . . .

Bon voyage to all of you.[3] On the 26th or 27th, then, I will have the pleasure of seeing you here! Evviva, Maestro, from your always devoted and most grateful

Giulio Ricordi

NOTES

1. Unknown.
2. See Verdi to Ricordi, 17 July.
3. Presumably including Teresa Stolz, who frequently accompanied the Verdis to Montecatini.

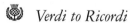 *Verdi to Ricordi*

Montecatini, 19 July 1892

Dear Giulio,

Our departure is still planned for tomorrow, the 20th—the 21st at St. Agata.

Your suggestion for the half-year is all right.

Today I shall write Maurel to wait,[1] and I am convinced he will wait.— He will answer me, and then we shall settle.

I know that Moretti is good—but the voice?!—

Write me immediately about Masini.

Oh, these attorneys!!

Good people . . with much talent! And the more they have . . . the worse it is!

Addio . . 'til we see each other, and let's hope that my visit may be useful.

Affectionately,
G. Verdi

NOTE

1. See Verdi to Ricordi, 14 July, n. 5.

 *Ricordi to Verdi*

Milan, 19 July 1892

Illustrious Maestro,

Welcome back to St. Agata. Just two lines to tell you that I did well to wire to Forlì, where I finally dug up Masini! Here is his return telegram just received:

"Will be in Milan next week—Will give myself the pleasure of greeting you—We shall talk about illustrious Verdi affair—Masini."

Always your devoted and grateful
Giulio Ricordi

 *Ricordi to Verdi*

Milan, 20 July 1892

Illustrious Maestro,

I confirm my letter of yesterday and acknowledge receipt of your esteemed letter, also of yesterday. Having arrived there you will already know about Masini; thus I look forward to your deciding everything the next time you come, and I hope you will also have an answer from Maurel. [. . .]

 *Verdi to Ricordi*

St. Agata, 21 July 1892

Dear Giulio,

I am at St. Agata—a bit tired. Twenty years ago I wouldn't have been this way! But!! We spent an infernal night in the mountains of Pistoia[1] . . . with the [Gran] *Sasso* in view.—

We'll hear, then, about Masini. I have faith that Maurel will not fail. [. . .]

NOTE

1. On the train.

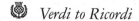 *Verdi to Ricordi*

St. Agata, 22 July 1892

Dear Giulio,

Perhaps you mailed your letter of the 19th too late, because it arrived in Montecatini after I had left.

Masini's telegram does not present itself to me in a favorable *allure.*

As I told you, I'll go to Genoa Monday or Tuesday, and on the way back I could be in Milan on Thursday. Could Zilli be in Milan on Thursday or Friday? Write me once again.—You will be in time.

Your
G. Verdi

Please have this [enclosed] bill of Peppina's paid in Paris as soon as possible.

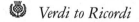 *Verdi to Ricordi*

St. Agata, 23 July 1892

Dear Giulio,

I have received the check drawn on the Banca Nazionale in Genoa for L. 34,827.03 as the balance of my account for the first half-year of 1892. I am sending you the enclosed receipt herewith.—

I will leave for Genoa Monday, the 25th. I'll stay there for two days and will be in Milan the morning of the *28th.* You can make the appointment with Signora Zilli for the same day at two or three P.M. at your home. I want to hear the excerpts from *Aida* again. 'Til we see each other—addio.

G. Verdi

 Giuseppina Verdi to Ricordi

[Calling card]

St. Agata, 4 August 1892

Dearest Signor Giulio,

Knowing him, I already suspected that my Priam, since he wanted to be thought of as a young Cupid, would be up to mischief!!!—I thank you for having honestly confirmed it to me with your letter of the 1st of August![2]

. . But I shake and shudder when I think of all these disruptions and of those to which he will succumb next Carnival![3] . . .

A certain blond Maestro, however, had better think about his *Nerone* before one by Mascagni may come into this world![4] . . I add that a certain publisher of great talent, but a false friend, would do a good deed by not inciting him, together with the above-mentioned blond Maestro, to too fatiguing disruptions!

I, poor Hecuba, instead of avenging myself, am compelled to watch my knees to avoid frequent *tumbles!* I shall close one eye and even two in order not to see too many things that can hurt him and make me suffer!

A greeting in haste to all of you from your most affectionate

Giuseppina Verdi[5]

NOTES

1. The plans for the *Falstaff* première.
2. Missing.
3. At the time of the *Falstaff* première at La Scala.
4. See Verdi to Boito, 6 August. Boito's slow creative pace regarding *Nerone* was so well known that Puccini, among others, declared he was not a *neronione*. (Eugenio Gara, *Carteggi Pucciniani*, p. 222.)
5. Signature in ornate Victorian printing.

 Ricordi to Verdi

Milan, 5 August 1892

Illustrious Maestro,

I could not write you even last night, since I had to finish a most urgent task! Now I am writing you this morning to tell you that the moment I read your letter to Bülow in the *Corriere,* I arranged for the publication of the 2 letters, remembering your wishes in this matter.[1] Please tell me if I should return the original to you.

Well then, Masini came to see me for quite a while. [. . .] He confirmed that he has a contract with Petersburg and Moscow; for this reason he did not want to present himself to you, being extremely sorry to have to tell you that he is already engaged. [. . .]

What shall I do? . . What shall I say? . . . how shall I act? . . . For Masini, of course, asked me to write you.—Certainly it's not up to me to say something in the matter; it seems to me, though, that if you were to drop a line to Masini, you would make him happy. [. . .]

But what a fool I am! . . . . . I didn't want to say one word . . . and now

I've said too many!—But I haven't finished: Hohenstein is already in London and will go from there to Paris in a few days; would you send me a line addressed to Nuitter, recommending Signor A. Hohenstein to him? . . . I'd like to tell you many other things concerning the dear Potbelly; but for now I think it is enough!!—

Greetings to you and Signora Peppina. With all devotion,

Gratefully,
Giulio Ricordi

NOTE

   1. Verdi to Ricordi, 11 April, n. 2, and 14 April.

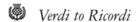 *Verdi to Ricordi*

St. Agata, 5 August 1892

[. . .] I am always of the same opinion about Masini.[1] With him nothing is certain, and now we have no more time to hesitate.—The matter is most embarrassing; I neither can nor should write him, for if I told him, "Free yourself from Petersburg and come to Milan to start the rehearsals on the 2nd or 3rd of January, etc.," and then, for whatever circumstance, there were a delay of 15, 20, 30 days, I would feel remorse over having made him lose the contract with Petersburg. I also add: "Too many celebrities, too many Divos!!" Too much of a good thing creates the bad!

Hohestein in London and Paris?!! This, too, is a bit too much! He will derive very little from it!

Nevertheless, I am sending the letter for Nuitter. In Paris they will, perhaps, show him the costume design for Falstaff in the *Songe d'une nuit d'été* [Midsummer Night's Dream][2] at the Opéra-Comique, which is awful! Another print in the *Illustration* 8 or *10* years ago!! The same. The two nicest costume designs (for me) are those in the inexpensive English edition![3]

And I am not finished! Something else: Our county engineer asks me to take an interest in a nephew of his, *Bontempi Augusto,* a very gifted designer. Could you employ him "if not" (so he writes me) "as a substitute for Edel, at least in some other way that may give him a chance to apply himself to art, for which he feels special aptitude" . . . . It is for his daily bread!, says Biagio da Vigginto.[4]

Answer me with a word. As ever

Your
G. Verdi

NOTES

1. Verdi had not yet received Ricordi's preceding letter of the same day.
2. Opera by Ambroise Thomas.
3. Unknown.
4. Unknown.

 *Verdi to Boito*

St. Agata, 6 August 1892[1]

Dear Boito,

I don't think I have ever been among the very indiscreet people who talk to you too often about *Nerone*.—

But after the article in the *Secolo XIX* of Genoa that I am sending you,[2] I think it is my duty to tell you, in the name of my friendship and esteem for you, that now you must no longer hesitate. You must work day and night, if need be, and see that *Nerone* is ready for next year; indeed even now, you ought to have announced: *"This year at La Scala* Falstaff, *next year* Nerone. . ."* This will appear to you to be an answer to the impertinence cited in the paper in Genoa. It is true! But there is no remedy and, in my opinion, nothing else can be done.—

If I haven't said it well, if I have said too much . . . let it be unsaid! . . . You know that old people are *bavards* and grumblers,—

Addio, addio.

Affectionately,
G. Verdi

NOTES

1. See Giuseppina Verdi to Ricordi, 4 August.
2. Verdi attached a nasty article, which mentioned that Pietro Mascagni had boasted to Genoese students about a *Nerone* of his own, for which "the esteemed Maestro Boito is still leaving me plenty of time." Alessandro Luzio affirms that Mascagni kept a promise to renounce his claim to that subject. (*Carteggi* ii, p. 143, n. 2.) At La Scala on 16 January 1935, however, Mascagni conducted a *Nerone* of his own, which soon fell into oblivion.

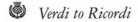 *Verdi to Ricordi*

St. Agata, 8 August 1892

Dear Giulio,

I sent a telegram this morning.[1] You will have read my letter to Bulow in the *Corriere*. They rewrote and corrected it. I am grateful to these masters, but since I did not wish for that letter to be printed and have no literary reputation to sustain, it should either not have been printed or have been left as it was.

Now I ask you to print both of them. You can add a feather to your cap by saying that "you knew those letters since the month of . . . (look up the dates), but that they were not published in accordance with the Maestro's wish. Now you are publishing them, taken from the originals," etc. Have them published at the same time, if you can, in the *Corriere*, in the *Perseveranza*, and in any papers you want.[2]

I hope that your Gigino is completely recovered. I had a good trip and without suffering from the heat![3] Yesterday I worked like a dog to put my things in order so I will be able to work on the Potbelly today or tomorrow!

I am very content with *Masini!* [4] I hope you wrote to *Maurel*. As for *Zilli*, write her in particular that she should not forget what I told her, to keep her voice *steady and to unglue her tongue* and enunciate clearly. Furthermore, she should, of course, plan to be in Genoa from approximately the middle of December until the hour of departure for Milan.—This way one can perhaps (I say perhaps) succeed at something good; if not, no . . .

Addio, addio

Your
G. Verdi

NOTES

1. Missing.
2. See Ricordi to Verdi, 5 August.
3. Returning from Milan to St. Agata.
4. See Ricordi to Verdi and Verdi to Ricordi, 5 August.

 *Boito to Verdi*

Tuesday [9 August 1892]
Milan[1]

My dear Maestro,

I assure you that the article in the *Secolo XIX* has left me neither hot nor cold, and that, for its sake, I would not speed up the completion of the opera by one day; but the good, strong letter that accompanies it has shaken me so much that if I don't start running now, I shall never run again.

I promise you, for all the devotion I feel for you, that I will make every effort to complete the work in time to perform it the year after *Falstaff*. I will make every effort, I promise you; a promise made to you is binding, I know. It is given.

1892

If I succeed, I shall owe you this immense benefit. Your letter has been like a firm handshake that has put me back on my feet; it reached me at a very painful moment of my existence.[2] Enough. Among men no more is said.

I thank you with deepest affection.

Many kind greetings to Signora Giuseppina.

An embrace

from your
Arrigo Boito

NOTES

1. Postmark: MILANO 10/8/92.

2. Possibly caused by Eleonora Duse. However, even Piero Nardi, Boito's biographer, does not know the reason for his sorrow. (Nardi, p. 590.) Boito's concern about the supposedly terminal illness of his mysterious friend Fanny, who died three years later (Nardi, p. 424), might have contributed to his distress.

 *Ricordi to Verdi*

Brescia, 12 August 1892

Illustrious Maestro,

Although a bit indisposed, I had to make a mad dash to Brescia, urgently summoned there because the tenor Durot[1] fell ill!! [. . .] But not wanting to delay my answer to you any longer, I am writing you from here, where I'll stay for another day or two until everything is on the right track. Thus, Maestro, you can answer me in Milan.

You are right, as always, in regard to Masini; but perhaps I did not make myself clear. I did not mean that you should drop him a line that might be interpreted in any way as an invitation or a commitment. Masini would be the happiest man in the world to receive a line from you, and isn't it prudent to keep a door open . . . . if a suitable tenor should really not materialize? . . . Oh! . . . I know, too, what a great burden *divinity* entails! . . Pasqua, Maurel . . . . Masini! . . It makes you wonder! I still have faith in Moretti! . . In fact, the management, very cleverly, is having him sing in *Rigoletto* in Genoa this autumn, so you can hear him.—Yesterday I immediately asked Mascheroni about Garulli: $0 \times 0 = 0$—a hunchback's voice that doesn't *ring out!*

Do not be surprised by Hohenstein's trip; he didn't go to London for the costume designs—there are more than enough designs for *Falstaff,* as indicated by you; but the sets had to be studied, not to indulge in unnecessary luxury, but because we could find absolutely nothing regarding the architecture. In Windsor, perhaps, some old house, some tavern can be found; at any rate, there will be designs in the academies. In Paris, a visit to the *maquettes* will also be most useful. Besides, everything will be submitted for your approval.

My health leaves a bit to be desired these days; for 3 years I haven't had a day to catch my breath!!—Alas! . . . age 52 is approaching! . . . and the years make themselves felt. The doctor absolutely wants me to breathe at least 8 days of good mountain air; I shall see if I am able to obey him . . . . but first . . . . . I would like to see everything under way pertaining to His Majesty the Potbelly!! How can I keep calm? . . . . .

When do you think, Maestro, that you could send at least one act? . . . It will take time to do the reduction with the necessary care. I have the best of all arrangers already lined up and will lock him in my studio . . . in prison!! . . . .[2]

If Durot is better today, there can be a rehearsal; so I shall hear Zilli and see if she confirms the good impression she has already given me in the theatre.—I think you wrote me that you would like her to come to Genoa in November?

As soon as I return to Milan, which will be tomorrow or the day after, if nothing goes wrong, I will at once take care of the recommendation you gave me.[3]

I had a very dear letter from Signora Peppina;[4] please give her my warmest thanks.

Excuse the long chatter, Maestro, and accept my most affectionate greetings, with the expression of my lasting gratitude.

Your most devoted
Giulio Ricordi

NOTES

1. The French tenor Eugène Durot (?–1908), a student and friend of Emanuele Muzio, was acclaimed mainly in Italy. Durot sang Puccini's *Edgar* in Brescia, where Emma Zilli's verve in the role of Fidelia was to delight the composer. (Eugenio Gara, *Carteggi Pucciniani*, pp. 87–8.)

2. Carlo Carignani (1857–1919), composer, conductor, and Caruso's voice teacher, made the reductions (piano-vocal scores) of *Otello* and *Falstaff*. A friend of Puccini's ever since their boyhood days in Lucca, he did the same work for several of the younger master's operas. (He should not be confused with Ricordi's chief engraver Caregnani, whose name Ricordi himself misspelled occasionally as Carignani.)

3. Probably concerning *Augusto Bontempi*. (See Verdi to Ricordi, 5 August.)

4. Of 4 August.

1892

🏵 *Verdi to Ricordi*

St. Agata, 14 August 1892

Dear Giulio,

What a mountain!

What mountain air!

The air of St. Agata a bit heavy, it's true; but free from the poisonous emissions of the great centers, it is the best air in the world! And then we also have the mountains!! High above sea-level, that is, above my puddle . . . 5 1/2 meters! I say five and a half!!! So pack your bags and come here, but without work and without the nuisance of letters, and I assure you that eight days thereafter you will be completely restored. You need only send me a telegram saying "on such and such a day and time I will be at Fiorenzuola" and do it soon. Mind you that the most comfortable train is the one that leaves Milan at 7 and arrives in Fiorenzuola at 9:13.

Boito told me that he would come here in August. Come together . . . but no; maybe it's better you come alone. He will come a little later! . . But, do as the two of you wish, after all.

I have gone over the instrumentation, and, alas, at every turn I find some note, some bar, some phrase to redo! That notwithstanding, the first act will be ready, completely ready, in three to four days. How to send it?! But if you come here, you will take it with you.

Masini? Oh!!! "An open door!!" you say!! But watch out! And if you were to have both doors closed?!! It seems to me that, if he had good intentions in view of my letter, he should have said: "As things now stand, I am writing at once to cancel the contract with Petersburg, and if I succeed, I will be at your disposal from the day, etc. . ." This is what men of good will do. . . .

All right if Moretti sings in Genoa! And in which month?

My concern is Zilli. She needs to study more than all the others, and I would really like to have her study in Genoa in November.

For the rest . . . nothing else. Addio, addio. And if you have sense, you will come to take the cure here.

Your

G. Verdi

I have received the 200 kilos of manure from the Sazza firm, and today they are writing me concerning the way to apply it. . . All right. Has it been paid for?—

 *Eugenio Tornaghi to Verdi*

Milan, 16 August 1892

Illustrious Maestro,

Giulio has gone to Brescia for the final rehearsals of *Edgar,* which should have been performed on Sunday the 14th. By sitting in a draft after the dress rehearsal, Giulio caught a fever and a cough, so he left Brescia right away to get well at home. Fortunately, it was a little thing; today he will be on his feet again. He asked me to thank you for your letter and your very kind invitation. He will write you very soon.

Signora Zilli made a very fine impression on Giulio, by acting and singing in a truly distinguished fashion. Unfortunately, the performance could not yet take place because of Durot's indisposition! . .

Signora Pasqua, who led us to hope she would be easy to deal with, has asked for 25, I say twenty-five thousand Lire. I have not yet told Giulio about it in order not to upset him. Oh, the *divas* . . And Maurel writes that "la conclusion du contract pour les représentations de *Falstaff* est une chose assez delicate et qui ne saurait pour la tranquillité respective être traité par lettres, ni conclu hatiement. ." [The conclusion of the contract for the performances of *Falstaff* is a rather delicate matter, which for mutual tranquillity should not be treated by letters or concluded hastily. .] He adds that, instead of his *business representative,* he will send his wife to deal with Giulio. . . [. . .]

🏵 *Ricordi to Verdi*

Milan, Wednesday 17 August 1892

Illustrious Maestro,

I write you briefly from my bed to thank you a thousand times for your kind letter![1]—But how can I say "kind"? . . . . Maestro, you are so gracious and so good to me that I am moved to tears!—

My trip to Brescia was *unfortunate.* Durot, who appeared to have recuperated, fell sick again!! . . . So the opera still could not be performed!—And I, sweating as I left a rehearsal, caught a sudden draft: extremely high fever at night! . . . I decided to leave at once, horrified by the idea of remaining sick in a poor hotel.—And I did well!—At home I could at least take care of myself and be taken care of, averting the danger of more serious pneumonia!—Now I am a lot better; oh! . . how I could profit by the gracious Verdi invitation!—But I won't be up to it for eight or ten days; and if I am not imposing, I will come for a couple of days, to return with a *most precious* cargo!!² . . . Evviva! . . evviva!

I am pleased to confirm to you my good impressions of Zilli; her faults . . . . you know them; but she is as easygoing onstage as she is secure. Keeping in mind the present misery, I honestly believe that no one better could be found. Signora Zilli will be at your disposal, if this is useful to you, in 16 or 20 days, right after Brescia, or after Venice, and, I think, at the end of November. In a word, it will be arranged at your utmost convenience.

Excuse my bad handwriting³ and accept my good intentions. The most devoted greetings to you and Signora Peppina from

Your most grateful
Giulio Ricordi

NOTES

1. Of 14 August.
2. The "completely ready" orchestra score of the first act of *Falstaff*, as Verdi wrote Ricordi on 14 August.
3. Impeccable as ever.

 Verdi to Eugenio Tornaghi

St. Agata, 17 August 1892

Dear Tornaghi,

I am glad to hear that Giulio's illness is minor, and I still hope to see him here to restore himself! I have sent the letter for *Boncompagne.*¹ Alas! Time lost and money wasted!!!!

Ha, ha! The Divos and the Divas² spread not their wings but their *griffes!* [talons] Well then! I would send them all you know where!!

For this purpose I am transcribing here a few lines I wrote on 30 December 1885 to Maurel in answer to a letter from him regarding Iago:

" . . . . . . The conditions in our theatres are such that the impresario, even when achieving a success, must always suffer a loss due to the exorbitant expenses for the artists and the *mise-en-scène.* Therefore I do not want to feel remorse for causing anyone's ruin with one of my operas. So things remain suspended, etc., etc."—³

And I wrote to Tamagno in more or less the same vein.

This is what I said at that time.

This is what I say now, and I wish all of this to be repeated in a loud voice, without hesitation, without diplomacy . . . so that everyone knows it.

Maurel wrote at that time: " . . . . . *pour cette circonstance mes pretentions*

*pécuniaires seraient simplement de tout autre chanteur tenant l'emploi de Bariton.
. . ."* [. . . . . in this case my monetary demands will simply be those of any
other singer engaged as a baritone. . . .][4]

Besides, whether *Falstaff* is performed or not, is completely irrelevant to
me . . . but it must not, under any circumstances, be said that "*Falstaff* was
uninteresting."

Please, esteemed Tornaghi, say all this to Giulio. As ever

Your
G. Verdi

NOTES

    1. Unknown.
    2. Maurel and Pasqua, among others.
    3. *Otello* i, p. 188.
    4. Ibid., p. 190, para. 4.

 Verdi to Ricordi

[St. Agata][1] 19 August 1892

Dear Giulio,

Has Mme. Maurel arrived?

Why is she coming? . .

I am expecting something peculiar, for her coming seems strange to me—
Pay attention to everything, and do not tolerate anything. Keep me posted
on everything. And Pasqua?!!!!!!

'Til we see each other. Addio

G. Verdi

NOTE

    1. Postmark: BUSSETO 19/8/92.

 Eugenio Torgnaghi to Verdi

Milan, 20 August 1892

Illustrious Maestro,

I have received your esteemed letter of yesterday.[1] Giulio is a bit better,
but not really well. He is also quite preoccupied about Gigi[2] in the country,
ill with a high fever. God grant that it is a passing thing!

I have forwarded your letter to Giulio. We have sent a telegram to

1892

Signora Pasqua, attempting to lead her toward more reasonable terms. We also wired Madame Maurel, giving her an appointment for the end of next week, because if Giulio is better, he would spend three or four days with his family in the country. He would then have to postpone for another week the pleasure of seeing you. [. . .]

NOTES

1. Tornaghi appears to refer to Verdi's preceding letter to Ricordi of 19 August.
2. See Verdi to Ricordi, 8 August.

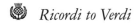 *Ricordi to Verdi*

Barasso,[1] 21 August 1892

Illustrious Maestro,

Briefly I would like to tell you about my Odyssey during these days. Well then, I escaped from Brescia running an extremely high fever and threatened by pneumonia or pleurisy, whatever! . . . But through an intensive and immediate cure I got away with only 5 days in bed.—But in the meantime our Gigi had a relapse of an infection, along with a very high fever and the threat of typhoid. Thus Giuditta had to return here to be an anxious nurse to me and Gigino! . . .

Today I came to Barasso to see my son and to revive a bit, being rather worn out. Gigi is still running a high fever, but up to now there are no threats of complications: time, patience, and major treatments day and night! . . .

I remain here until Thursday, then return to Milan, since I cannot afford to be away any longer. Therefore, I am now asking the most illustrious Verdis if the undersigned were to arrive there on Saturday or Sunday morning . . . . . would he be a nuisance? . . . Please tell me frankly if this should conflict with other arrivals. Anyway, I could enjoy your kind hospitality only for a day or two at the most before returning to Milan . . . . . with, I hope, a lovely, precious cargo, as you wrote me.[2]

In case you wish to let me know anything, it is always best to write to Milan.

I hope to leave Barasso completely reassured that all the others are well, including Giuditta, who is wearing herself out day and night! [. . .]

NOTES

1. Village between Varese and Laveno (Lago Maggiore).
2. On 14 August.

Ricordi to Verdi

Barasso, 22 August 1892

Illustrious Maestro,

My letter of yesterday will have given you our news. Today I received a note from you[1] asking me for news of the divos and divas. Here is the latest bulletin: Madame Maurel will be in Milan next Saturday!!—which disturbs me, since it might delay my excursion to you.—On Saturday I shall hear at last what she wants!—With Pasqua, there is close combat and lively fire; but this will also be settled, after all. It isn't worth your while to think about these miserable things. . . . . I will be sure to keep you posted on everything.

I am better . . . . but I would regain my health sooner if it weren't for the worry about Gigi!—His sickness is typhoid, after all: benign, without complications; but even so, it is always a serious matter. [. . .]

NOTE

1. Of 19 August, forwarded by Tornaghi.

Verdi to Boito

St. Agata, 22 August 1892

Dear Boito,

In Milan[1] you told me in person that you would come here in August . . . August is about to end . . . . but never mind! Come when you like, and you will always be welcome!

I am writing and working like a dog, but I never finish——

Greetings from Peppina.

'Til we meet again.

Affectionately,
G. Verdi

NOTE

1. Between 28 and 31 July.

Verdi to Eugenio Tornaghi

St. Agata, 22 August 1892

Esteemed Signor Tornaghi,

Has Madame Maurel arrived? How strange this visit is . . . very strange!!! What does it mean?

1892

If we were dealing with someone else, I might believe it to be a childish prank, a useless thing . . . . but Maurel is no simpleton . . . and much less, far less Madame Maurel!

Enough: Make things really clear, twice as *clear*, and manage to avoid friction at the rehearsals.

And Pasqua? Tell me something as soon as possible, also for my . . . *musical* information.

When Giulio comes, he will always be welcome. I wish him all the best and excellent health.

Addio to you . . . . .

G. Verdi

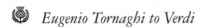 *Eugenio Tornaghi to Verdi*

Milan, 23 August 1892

Illustrious Maestro,

I received your esteemed letter of yesterday. Giulio wrote me with better news of himself and Gigi. He added that he was planning to write you, although he had no news. We are waiting for the manager of La Scala to settle the Pasqua matter and, we hope, also the Maurel affair, since Madame Maurel will be here next Friday or Saturday. It will be our duty to keep you informed about everything. [. . .]

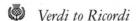 *Verdi to Ricordi*

St. Agata, 23 August 1892

Dear Giulio,

I wrote to Tornaghi yesterday, and there is nothing left to tell you except to come when you like and when you can; sorry about your discomfort and Gigino's illness.

Inform me 24 hours before your arrival here[1] so you will find a Bucefalus[2] of mine at Fiorenzuola. Courage and health.

Your
G. Verdi

NOTES

1. No such communication has been located. Presumably Ricordi spent the weekend of 27–29 August at St. Agata, and returned to Milan with the orchestral score of the first act of *Falstaff*. (See Hepokoski, p. 43.) "I went to Verdi's for one day on business," Ricordi

wrote to Puccini on 19 September. "That man is a marvel. I know it and yet I cannot get over it, with the years. It will give you pleasure to know that both Verdi and his wife have interested themselves in you, asked me news about *Manon*, if you will have good performers, etc., etc. They wish you success." (Marek, *Puccini*, p. 122.)

    2. Bucephalus, warhorse of Alexander the Great.

Boito to Verdi

23 August [1892]
Milan[1]

Dear Maestro,

    The regimen of work[2] to which I have subjected myself would make me a very uncomfortable guest; that is why I had to forego, at this time, the pleasure of coming to St. Agata. If in September I have managed to obtain from my reluctant brain as much as I have resolved to, I'll come to you, dear Maestro, to rest for a week.

    Milan is rather propitious for work this season: everybody is on vacation; the house where I live is entirely empty. I can play, sing, and dance without bothering anyone, turn night into day, and pay no attention to the customary hours for sleeping or eating. All these advantages keep me in the city. If only four or five hours of work could suffice for me, I would come to St. Agata right away; but you have pushed me (it was you) on this accelerated drive,[3] and the best I can do for now is not to change the conditions in which I find myself.

    I imagine that the orchestration of *Falstaff*, if it isn't finished, will be reaching the last drops of ink.

    Lucky you! I greet you affectionately, together with Signora Peppina.

Your
Arrigo Boito

P.S. If you need some verses or some retouching of the kind that is noticed when a work is finished, write me, and in a wink it will be done. For you I can work fast. Now I remain in the hope of seeing you in September.

NOTES

    1. Postmark: MILANO 23/8/92.
    2. On *Nerone.*
    3. See Verdi to Boito, 6 August.

1892

Verdi to Ricordi

St. Agata, 30 August 1892

Dear Giulio,

In this morning's telegram[1] I told you "Cancel everything!" I now repeat the same words: "Cancel everything" . . . not one time, but twenty!—

The coming of Madame Maurel alarmed me, and I expected something enormous; but I did not believe that he would go so far as to pretend (in addition to everything else) to be the only "first interpreter in certain first-class theatres," and thus in a certain sense take possession of our opera! And we? . . . Who are we? . . And he! Who is he! . . Nothing like this has ever happened to me in 50 years in the theatrical galley![2] It is a monstrous pretension, which permits no discussion!

In dangerous matters the worst thing is hesitation! Here we must not hesitate, but publish Maurel's pretension at once, and also my telegram, and add, "therefore *Falstaff* cannot be performed."

You will find this a bit strong! . . I think it is the only useful course of action that can be taken under the present circumstances. *One thing leads to another,* and who knows . . . perhaps such a decision can lead to other ideas, other arrangements.

Don't be afraid.—Talk with Boito and go forward along this road. . .

Cards on the table—No compromise!—

When things have gotten to such a point, one must even smash the pieces!

Addio, addio

Your
G. Verdi

NOTES

1. Missing.
2. Verdi used to call his early years, when he had to compose under pressure in order to make a living, "his galley years."

Ricordi to Verdi

Milan, 30 August 1892

Illustrious Maestro,

It pains me greatly that my telegram[1] upsets you, as your answer suggests,[2] an answer that caused deep regret, but which I perfectly understand!—Could I, on the other hand, keep all these matters from you?—

Yesterday was a day of furies!—The train to Milan was 1 hour and 10 minutes late!—As soon as I arrived, I was informed that Signora Maurel was waiting for me, and so I ran to her at once, without even going home.—I exercised patience for 1 hour and a half, always replying with only a few words for fear of blowing up and making a scene. Finally, the conditions with which I was presented were as follows:

— 4,000 fr. per performance.
— 10,000 fr. for special compensation for the rehearsals.
— An extensive number of performances assured.
— 16,000 fr. paid at once in Paris.
— 8 *consecutive* days of sick leave, without being liable for replacement by the management; in case of prolonged indisposition, permission for a substitute, with the right to reassume the part at once. In any case, the guaranteed performances would always be paid.
— A *dressing room* (!) new and especially for him.
— Assurance that Maurel will be engaged for the principal theatres, especially London, Madrid, Paris, North America!—

This is it!! . . . I won't tell you about the endless arguments and my patient and prudent replies in order not to upset the applecart! . . . but with such indigestion that I couldn't even go to bed that night!—This morning, anticipating that in a second conference I might not possess the necessary diplomacy, I wrote the enclosed letter No. 1.[3]—

Signora Maurel replied with a foolish tittle-tattle letter, saying that it had already been anticipated in London that *I did not want Maurel*, out of antipathy to the French!!!!—and because I am under the influence of the impresarios!!, etc., etc.

I thought it best to reply with letter No. 2, which I am enclosing.[4]—I would be quite relieved if you, Maestro, would approve these letters of mine and the line I have taken. An explosion was to be expected there, but an outright charge of dynamite, no!—

Of course, I informed D'Ormeville as well as Madame Maurel of the receipt of your telegram;[5] and I am refraining from further negotiations until I receive your new instructions.

With all of this, I know that the management continues to negotiate with Signora Maurel, and that they hope to arrive at a reasonable fee, with the guarantee of 30 performances between Milan and Rome.—Faithful to the order given me, I am not showing my face!—I also know that Signora Maurel said that if she were assured that the opera would be given in

1892

London, Paris, Madrid, and North America with Maurel, the contract with La Scala might be facilitated at once. But I am not showing my face!—

I went to see Boito this morning to inform him of the situation! . . . I never saw him with such a gloomy face, the likes of a rabid Nero! . . . but if I had looked at myself in the mirror, I, too, might have been a Caracalla with liver disease!—You think I'm joking? . . . No, Maestro! I'm joking so as not to cry about the level to which human bestiality has sunk! [. . .]

NOTES

1. Missing.
2. In another missing telegram.
3. Copy [in French].

Milan, 30 August 1892 1st

Madame Anne Maurel

Milan

In my office I found your kind invitation for this morning. But I think I need to write you beforehand. I have thought a great deal about the proposed contract of which you were obliged to inform me; and I have also thought a great deal about the interview I had the honor to have with you yesterday, Madame. Above all, I assure you that M. Maurel's personality is entirely beside the point; this concerns business, so let us talk business.

When all is said and done, I do not think it possible to arrange this affair; the size of the fee exceeds by far the resources of our theatres. While a great interpreter is needed for the protagonist, another *nine* artists are needed, all of them for absolutely leading roles, raising the expense by an enormous degree.

As to my own person, I cannot allow my hands to be tied in advance, and even less can I commit myself to a kind of engagement contrary to my business convictions. M. Maurel knows from experience that he has always been given preference on great occasions. But this time he demands an absolute assurance, and this is not possible, for two reasons:

1. This way, it is M. Maurel who, for a certain period of time, would become the virtual owner of the work.

2. The work belongs to Maestro Verdi; it is up to him alone to dispose of it. I shall inform him promptly of the situation, and he will decide whether or not it is convenient to have his opera performed.

In view of all these considerations, I believe, Madame, that my presence at the meeting to which you invite me this morning with Signor D'Ormeville is utterly useless.

If, in one way or another, you should find a way of arriving at a perfect understanding, I could not be happier. In this case I would be completely at your disposal if you should judge my intervention to be of use.

In the meantime, Madame, be assured of my most attentive regards.

Yours most devotedly,
signed   Giulio Ricordi

4. Copy [in French].

Milan, 30 August 1892 2nd

Madame Anne Maurel

Milan

Permit me, Madame, to speak with you in all frankness!—Your reply to my letter of this morning offends me to the highest degree!—You must know that I yield to no influence whatsoever, neither to M. Maurel, nor God Almighty, nor the devil! Thank heaven I am still of sound mind, and my honesty has no need to call to witness 34 years of work!—I believe, Madame, that after what you wrote me concerning M. Maurel's *French* quality, concerning the encounters in London, and the influence of Piontelli, who is not even in Milan, it is completely useless for you to give me the honor of intervening. You must see Signor D'Ormeville—you can very well make arrangements directly with him.

But as I must follow the path you prescribed, I think you will find it quite natural that M. Verdi, who wrote the work, demands a million for it; that M. Boito, who created the libretto, claims 300,000 francs, and that, finally, the undersigned, the publisher, wishes to be paid 100,000 francs for the lease [of the material]. Everything is relative, and the best thing to do is to close the theatres, which are already headed in that direction.

I pass over your other, also most offensive, assertion, Madame, that I could lend myself to the exploitation of Monsieur Maurel, only to throw him into the wastebasket later on.—Dreaming of the role of Iago, there truly is an affirmation based on the truth!—

I deeply and immensely regret what is happening; I have always been a fervent admirer of M. Maurel, and a loyal friend!—In order not to change this, it is better to keep me out.—Again with the assurance of my esteem, Madame,

Yours devotedly,

signed   Giulio Ricordi

[Both letters were copied by Tornaghi.]
5. See n. 2.

 Verdi to Ricordi

St. Agata, 31 August 1892

Dear Giulio,

Do not hesitate for a moment to break off all negotiations. My self-respect is too offended by Maurel's proposals. Imagine!! . . . A singer, whoever he may be, comes to my study to take possession of my not-yet-completed opera, saying ". . I will perform your opera, but afterwards I want to be the first performer in the leading theatres . . . . London, Madrid, etc."

I do not accept the salary conditions either, [although] it will be said that this doesn't concern me, because I don't want them to say that the management has lost money on a new opera of mine. Maurel has known my thoughts for a long time! . .

I do not accept the 10,000 Lire for the rehearsals, either!! *C'est trop fort!* What a *precedent!!* And that for the rehearsals of *Falstaff!!?* But this is horrible. . .

Enough, though. . . Do not waste time. To hesitate is worse. Break off everything!! I give myself leave, after all, to still be the owner of my opera!! *I firmly declare that I cannot accept, nor do I accept, any of Maurel's proposals.* Say this frankly to D'Ormeville and to whomever you wish, and let's not talk about it any more!—And then? You tell me!—I don't know anything; but I do know that I feel humiliated dealing with this business. . . Come what may. . . .

I said already, "One thing leads to another" . . . . . and if you agree with me and make up your mind, this *one thing* can ruin everything. What I wrote yesterday, I think, also holds for today.

Addio

G. Verdi

P.S. The letter is very good; however, I wouldn't have written the second one—[1]

NOTE

1. See Ricordi's preceding letters to Madame Maurel, whose copies Verdi returned to him with this letter.

 *Ricordi to Verdi*

[Telegram]   Milan, 31 August 1892

HOPE YOU RECEIVED MY LETTER[1] — BELIEVE MANAGEMENT WOULD AGREE GENERAL TERMS CONVENIENT TWO THOUSAND PER NIGHT FORTY AS-SURED PARTLY SCALA PARTLY OTHER THEATRES — IF THERE ARE NO IM-POSSIBLE ADDITIONAL CONDITIONS THIS MATTER CAN BE CLOSED — BUT ALL THIS SUBJECT TO MY SIMPLE FRIENDLY LETTER ASSURING FIRST PRO-DUCTIONS LONDON PARIS MADRID NORTH AMERICA — DIVO WILL HAVE PREFERENCE AS LONG AS HIS CONDITIONS AGREE WITH THOSE DIRECTORS IN ORDER NOT TO PREVENT CONCLUSION OF CONTRACTS — I DECLARED I HAD NO BUSINESS DOING THIS — PLEASE WIRE ME IF YOU WISH TO AUTHO-RIZE ME TO WRITE MORE PRUDENT LETTER ADDING THAT RIGHT OF PERFORMANCES IN THE THEATRES IS ALWAYS RESERVED BY THE AU-THOR — OTHERWISE HOW TO CONDUCT MYSELF — CANCELLING PERFOR-MANCE WOULD BE TREMENDOUS CATASTROPHE BECAUSE PUBLIC WILL ACCEPT NO OTHER PROGRAM — TALKED WITH BOITO POSSIBLE SITUATION

WITH PICCORSI[2] FALSTAFF PESSINA FORD—IF AGREEABLE SUCH ADVICE
SHOULD NOT BE REFUSED DUE TO PRETENSION OF ONE PERSON—PLEASE
WIRE INSTRUCTIONS—CORDIAL GREETINGS

GIULIO

NOTES

1. Of 30 August.
2. Pini-Corsi.

 *Ricordi to Verdi*

[Telegram]   Milan, 1 September 1892

BOITO ALSO THINKS NEWS RELEASE WOULD BE PREMATURE SINCE MANY
ARTISTS EXPRESSLY ENGAGED WOULD BE FREE AND WHENEVER YOU
THINK OTHER CASTS POSSIBLE THEY COULD NO LONGER BE PROVIDED—
I ALSO THINK PUBLICATION PRIVATE CONTRACT NEGOTIATIONS DANGER-
OUS GIVING CAUSE FOR CLAIMING LOSSES—BUT SINCE WE BOTH FIND
YOUR FEELINGS AND RESOLUTIONS JUSTIFIED WE PROPOSE FORMAL COM-
MUNICATION TO MANAGEMENT BY A TELEGRAM FROM YOU READING THUS
WITH YOUR APPROVAL: I DECLARE ALL NEGOTIATIONS SUSPENDED AND
CUT OFF—UNFORTUNATELY SOMETHING I FEAR WILL LEAK TO PUBLIC
PROVOKING GENERAL INDIGNATION—AWAITING YOUR INSTRUCTIONS—
CORDIAL GREETINGS ALSO FROM BOITO

GIULIO

 *Ricordi to Verdi*

Milan, 1 September 1892

Illustrious Maestro,

I received your esteemed letter and went to Boito, and then wired you.
Later on I received your telegram[1] announcing a letter to be forwarded to
Signora Maurel, which I shall do the moment I receive it.

What can you say! I am entirely of your opinion; it is indescribable, the
action of an outright procurer! . . . In my telegrams I refrained from
expressing my thoughts, but I really suffered, thinking of the indignation
you must have felt.—But why?? . . a man who for 6 years pursues his career
blessed by the role of Iago!—Who now glimpses an unexpected fortune
. . . . and dares to issue an emperor's edict! However, Maestro, you are a rare

and unique judge, and thus you will see what is really for the best. I am expressing this sole fear more clearly than I indicated in my telegram: Unfortunately, something has transpired, as much as the secret was guarded; already many people have anxiously questioned me whether it is true that because of Maurel *Falstaff* will no longer be given. What they are saying must be heard; and what anger is erupting against Maurel! Of course, I reply that I do not know a thing, and that this is the usual gossip of the theatre world! [. . .]

But leaving aside this most miserable aspect of the matter, let me tell you that I have examined some twenty pages of the 1st act reduction; it seems well done, clear and not too difficult. You will see then, Maestro; whatever may happen, if good fortune should let you decide in favor of the performance, the time is short for preparing the reduction and the parts. Could you begin, a little at a time, to coach several of the performers? But with what material?

Meanwhile, as I already wrote you, the orchestra score is locked in the safe, and only to the arranger do I hand a few pages, which I lock up again as soon as he has reduced them.—If they arrive early enough, it would be a good idea to have *all* the orchestra parts engraved, thus saving much time. But you will tell me: "Slowly! slowly! slowly! What castles are you building in the air right now?"

What can you say! . . The Potbelly is giving me fits, thanks to Signor Maestro Giuseppe Verdi, so that I am about to trim 4 to 5 kilograms off my own belly. [. . .]

NOTE

1. Missing.

 Verdi to Ricordi

St. Agata, 1 September 1892

Dear Giulio,

We are losing time with these letters and telegrams!!

Permit me to tell you that you are all a bit mad and out of your minds. I am not out of my mind, and I will not allow anyone to deprive me of my property; and so I repeat once again:

1. There is no obligation to give *Falstaff* where it suits others.

2. There will be no exorbitant fees for the artists.

3. There will be no paid rehearsals.

Regarding no. 1: . . . Supposing that after the performances at La Scala I deem it advisable to make a few changes, could I allow an artist to come along and say to me, "I have no time to wait, and *I will* do this opera in Madrid, in London"? By God, that would be too much!!

Regarding no. 2: I do not wish the management, despite a success, to lose money on one of my *new* operas!

Regarding no. 3: That would be a disastrous precedent!!—A precedent tailor-made for the rehearsals of *Falstaff!!*

I told you from the beginning that you are all out of your minds, and I tell you now that Maurel, too, is out of his mind. Doesn't he see that if the libretto of *Falstaff* is good and the music tolerable, and that if he presents this role in superior fashion, he will be in demand without having to be pretentious, which does him no good and offends others?!

Madame Maurel, who is so intelligent and who just now is a bit irritated and nervous, will say that I am wrong; a month from now she will be saying: *"Le Maître avait raison!"*

Let's put things in order.

I demand simply that I be master of my property, and that I bring harm to no one.

If I were faced with the dilemma of either accepting these terms or burning the score, then I would light the fire at once, and I would lay Falstaff and his belly on the funeral pyre myself.—[1]

Addio, addio

Your

G. Verdi

P.S. Permit me to tell you that in this matter you have gone a bit too far wearing *kid gloves*. At once, at once one should have had to *casser les vitres*[2] and break off negotiations. Then it would have been easier to find a solution. Now, on the assumption that things are to be resolved, I am quite alarmed for the rehearsals. . . I won't say I have no confidence, but I consider it advisable to take all measures to protect myself against any surprise.

NOTES

1. See *Aida,* pp. 261–2.
2. Break the windows, i.e., kick up a row.

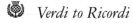 *Verdi to Ricordi*

St. Agata, 2 September 1892

Dear Giulio,

If Madame Maurel has left, we may assume that the negotiations have been broken off. That would be very good; and if they had been broken off

1892

four or five days earlier, it would have been better. The theatre could have thought about something else, and the Pasqua business would be decided by now; now it can't be settled except by not engaging her for *Profeta, Trovatore,* etc., without guaranteeing *Falstaff.*

We have lost much time, after all, without settling a thing! Too bad!—

Addio for now—
G. Verdi

 *Ricordi to Verdi*

Milan, 2 September 1892

Illustrious Maestro,

I received your letter of the 31st, and yesterday's arrived just this moment, so I shall forward it at once to Signora Maurel.—This stupendous letter of yours deserves to be engraved in gold; it is a full portrait of the artist and the man: the first lofty, the latter kind!—*Such is Verdi.* I shall hear what Signora Maurel decides.—[. . .]

(Mme. Maurel left last night for Aix-les-Bains. I am sending you a telegram to learn if I should forward a copy of the above-mentioned letter to her.)

The management will negotiate, of course, but certainly will not sign a contract without authorization. As I informed you, Pasqua wired, authorizing me to settle her contract as I thought best. Under a pretext I have taken my time, but the days go by and I don't want my silence to offend her. If, on the other hand, you have reason to be annoyed, your name always has a magical influence: Pasqua settled for reasonable terms, less than the Divo! All the others are too honored and too happy to throw a monkey-wrench into the works, including the kind Pessina, who, though aware that he was not chosen for the lead, has turned down far more lucrative offers for the privilege of learning how you want his character to be interpreted. And yesterday, I also noticed another very beautiful thing: Maestro Carignani, in charge of the *Falstaff* reduction, was offered a fine engagement to conduct in America; he turned it down, telling me that not for all the gold in the world would he forego the honor of working on the reduction of this opera. Maybe these are little things! . . . but all in all they crown Verdi's great name! . . . So, long may he live!

Hohenstein has returned, having addressed a letter to me in care of you, who then forwarded it to Milan. In this letter he asked me to pay his respects to you and thank you for the letter to Nuitter, who showed him exquisite courtesy.[1] Hohenstein found many good things, especially in London and

Windsor, more useful for the sets than for the costumes. But in the British Museum he also found details for costumes of the Henry IV era. He has already begun his work.

If you recall, the payments to the artists have been calculated, but since I did not know them exactly, I have verified them; there are some minor and some major figures, especially Moretti and Cesari. Here they are: Zilli: 10,000—Stehle: 9,000—Guerrini: 4,500—Pini-Corsi: 4,000—Paroli: 3,000—Pelagalli: 3,000—Cesari: 4,000—Moretti: 15,000. In toto, 52,500.—2 more artists must still be engaged. The management observed that with a maximum of about 4,500 or 5,000 remaining per night, they would be content, so much the more so since approximately 20 performances are planned, and even 2 or 3 additional ones might be possible, which would greatly increase the gain. I also observe that not all the fees could be calculated, since—without disturbing the rehearsals or performances of *Falstaff*—one or more artists could profit from 4 or 5 nights in another opera, thus reducing the expense. So we are in good shape, as you desire, which means that the [artistic] success should be crowned by a financial one.

That's enough for now, unless I must again torment you today with some telegram! . . . . I hope not—and asking you to forgive the nuisance which I am causing without meaning to, I repeat my feelings of most grateful devotion.

Your very affectionate
Giulio Ricordi

NOTE

1. See Ricordi to Verdi, 12 August. Nuitter probably gave Hohenstein particular advice regarding his research for Puccini's *Manon Lescaut*, as evidenced by a letter Giulio Ricordi addressed to Puccini on 5 August 1892: "[. . .] Hohenstein is already in London (to study Windsor Castle for the scenery of *Falstaff*). He will remain there six or seven days, then he will go to Paris for the necessary research for *Manon*. [. . .]" (Marek, p. 120.)

 *Ricordi to Verdi*

[Telegram]   Milan, 2 September 1892

MADAME LEFT FOR AIX—PLEASE WIRE WHETHER TO SEND HER IMMEDI-ATELY COPY OF HER LETTER—IF YOU THINK I COULD MEANWHILE SET-TLE PASQUA BUSINESS WHICH AWAITS REPLY—KIND REGARDS

GIULIO

1892

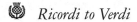 *Ricordi to Verdi*

Milan, 2 September 1892

Illustrious Maestro,

Under separate cover I am sending you by registered mail 2 bundles containing the reduction. Please examine them and see if they are all right. It goes without saying that Maestro Carignani, the arranger, is on tenterhooks for fear of not having adequately translated your ideas. From what little I can judge, having had, in addition, the keen pleasure of hearing you play it, the reduction is clear and easy to execute, while preserving the essential elements of the orchestra score. As of now, no stage directions have been entered; I will put them in later on, transferring them from the orchestra score and the libretto.

Again I repeat my affections,

Your most devoted and grateful
Giulio Ricordi

Ricordi to Verdi

Milan, 3 September 1892
6:30 A.M.

Illustrious Maestro,

I am going on a short trip to see Ginetta, who is celebrating her wedding anniversary and wants me to be with her.—I got your telegram late yesterday.[1] I went at once to the hotel to obtain precise information: Signora Maurel left before receiving your reply, but had left instructions to forward letters and telegrams immediately to Aix. Hence I thought it appropriate to send her a copy of your letter (minus the postscript), in order not to lose any more time. If you should need to wire me, or need anything else, feel free to write to Milan, from where they will contact me immediately. I will be back on Monday, always ready for your instructions, and with Boito, who, if necessary, would come to St. Agata with me whenever it might suit you.

With all devotion,

Giulio Ricordi

NOTE

1. Missing.

 *Victor Maurel to Verdi*

[Telegram, in French]   Aix-les-Bains, 5 September 1892

JUST RECEIVED COPY LETTER YOU SENT RICORDI[1] — SERIOUS MISUNDER-
STANDING WE SHALL CLEAR UP IN PERSON AT ONCE — IF YOU DO NOT SEND
COUNTER-ORDER HÔTEL LOUVRE AIX LES BAINS WILL DEPART BUSSETO
THIS MIDNIGHT

MAUREL

NOTE

1. On 1 September.

 *Verdi to Ricordi*

St. Agata, 5 September 1892

Dear Giulio,

Madame Maurel writes me from Aix these exact words:

". . . *Nous sommes en règle. Monsieur Piontelli a accepté 40 répresentations à
donner en 3 mois et 1/2 à la Scala, à Rome, à Florence . . . etc., etc.*" [We are
in agreement: Mr. Piontelli has accepted 40 performances to be given in
3 1/2 months at La Scala, in Rome, in Florence. . .]

If this is true, I have nothing more to tell you except to return the 1st act
of *Falstaff* and not to talk about it again. We are agreed then, my dear
Giulio, — — — I shall never, never, never accept these conditions. I told
you from the beginning in a telegram that I would never pass below these
Caudine Forks.[1]

I replied to Madame Maurel[2] that I am opposed to all her demands——

Wire me a word to tell me if what Madame Maurel has written me is
true.

Addio, addio

Your
G. Verdi

NOTES

1. This telegram is missing. At the Caudine Forks, two narrow passes in the southern
Apennines, the Roman army was defeated by the Samnites in 321 B.C. and suffered the
humiliation of having to file below a yoke. (*Aida*, p. 5, n. 2.)

2. In a missing letter.

253

1892

 Verdi to Ricordi

St. Agata, Wednesday [7 September 1892][1]

Dear Giulio,

I am returning the letter![2]—The darling! I thought she was smarter! . . A lost illusion.

I'm expecting the Divo any moment! What's going to happen? Some big affair, or a concession?

Anything is possible!————

I'll write you two more words if I can—It's 4 o'clock and the Divo has arrived. I'll wire and write you————

In any event, to avoid the nuisance of talking about the score, I'll tell him that it is no longer in the composer's but in the publisher's hands.—

Addio, addio [Unsigned]

NOTES

1. Postmark: BUSSETO 7/9/92.
2. From Anne Maurel in Aix-les-Bains (in French and undated) to Carlo D'Ormeville in Milan. Apparently upset, Madame Maurel wrote:

> The Maestro is right. To a man of his genius, engagements, money, problems must not be mentioned. The business aspects exasperate and irritate him, as I had told you, my dear D'Ormeville. He is going to become so annoyed that he will withdraw Falstaff. There was no need to send him a telegram pointing out Maurel's conditions! That business was to be handled, to be discussed between us; but a man who lives in the starry heavens of his artistic dreams must not be pulled abruptly out of his heaven and down to earth. I wrote him a very nice and affectionate letter. Moreover, I sent for Victor, who will go to Busseto. Since they both speak the same language of the heart and of mutual esteem, they should come to an understanding. [. . .]

Madame Maurel's letter to Verdi is missing.

 Verdi to Teresa Stolz

St. Agata, 9 September 1892

[. . .] I have spent an infernal week because of Maurel. His demands were so outrageous, exorbitant, incredible, that there was nothing else to do but send it all to the devil. Four thousand lire per night! Paid rehearsals at ten thousand lire! The exclusive right to perform Falstaff in Milan, Florence, Rome, Madrid, America, etc., etc.!

Then I extended my claws and said: "The opera is mine, and I do not give up rights to my property. I will not grant you the right to be paid for rehearsals, something that has never been done; I do not want a management, not even Piontelli's, to be ruined by an opera of mine." [. . .][1]

NOTE

1. Teresa Stolz, who meanwhile had become Verdi's intimate friend, had caused very similar problems before her appearance in the first *Aida* at La Scala in 1871. (See *Aida*, pp. 124–33, 139–40, 143, 145, 149–53.)

 *Ricordi to Verdi*

Milan, 10 September 1892

Illustrious Maestro,

In response to a telegram I sent him last night, D'Ormeville arrived this morning from Genoa, talked with Maurel, drew up the contract with him, and returned to Genoa. The contract is altogether as intended; but as usual, Maurel tacked on some appendices which, though actually not changing the general concept, could injure the feelings of the management; but I hope they will let it pass, and so the thing will be done. [. . .]

If some time next week you should wish to turn over the 2nd act, please wire a day in advance to Milan, indicating the hour and the station; Tito will come, or our chief copyist, a trustworthy person. [. . .]

 *Boito to Verdi*

11 September [1892]
Milan[1]

Dear Maestro,

Yesterday I received a letter for you from Rome and have forwarded it to you.

It is a letter from that certain person who wanted to come to St. Agata, sent by the officials of the Columbian Exhibition in Chicago.[2] I spared you the visit but could not spare you the letter.

Maurel is still in Milan to tie up the loose ends of his contract. Let's hope that this business will soon be concluded and not be talked about any more.

Today I have nothing else to tell you but to greet you affectionately, together with Signora Giuseppina.

Your
Arrigo Boito

1892

NOTES

1. Postmark: MILANO 11/9/92.
2. On the occasion of the four hundredth anniversary of the discovery of America.

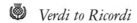 *Verdi to Ricordi*

St. Agata, 13 September 1892

Dear Giulio,

I hope first of all that your Gigino is on his way to a full recovery, for your and everyone's peace of mind.——

I won't be able to send you the *second act* so fast, but I can send you the *third*. Actually, I plan to finish the few things that are still to be done, and to take the score myself to Piacenza on Thursday the 15th.[1]

I will be in Piacenza, then, the day after tomorrow at *9:25*. If you send Tito or someone else to Piacenza, departing at 7:05, he will arrive before me. He should wait for me at the station, and I will hand the score over to him; if he wants to, he can return immediately to Milan on the 10:10 train.

Is that all right?

If so, send me a telegram with your approval.

In case I am unable to come to Piacenza, I'll send a telegram tomorrow night to spare you the trouble of sending someone to Piacenza. If you do not receive anything, I'll be in Piacenza at *9:25*.

Send me the bundle containing the original score where Falstaff says

In quest'addome	[In this paunch
Sta un migliajo di lingue. . . .	There are a thousand tongues . . .][2]

3

I don't recall if it's harmonized or in unison. I need to examine and, perhaps, to modify it.——

Addio
G. Verdi

NOTES

1. Verdi took the same precaution with the delivery of his *Otello* autograph score. (See *Otello* i, p. 237, and Hepokoski, p. 45.)

2. In I.i (PV p. 22, 4/2) the libretto reads: ". . . in quest'addome / Cè un migliaio di lingue."

3. I.i. See bass clef in PV p. 23, 1/1.

 *Ricordi to Verdi*

Milan, 17 September 1892

Illustrious Maestro,

Tito gave me your good news, which makes me very happy. I also received the 3rd act, and the reduction has begun. Today I sent you the last bundle containing the 1st act reduction. Thus everything proceeds under full sail. Later on I hope to wire you that Pasqua's contract is also signed. [. . .]

I am really desperate, illustrious Maestro! My son has been sick for 7 weeks and is still in bed,[1] and there is no one in the house any more! Even the last servant left to me was recently stricken by typhoid and became so ill today that I had to have her taken to the hospital! Thus disinfecting and related nuisance! This thing is getting to be alarming, for since I haven't found the real cause of this typhoid infection, I cannot let my family return to the apartment. My very upset wife cannot abandon Gigino and, therefore, can't come to Milan, regretful as she is about leaving me here alone, all alone! And I can't leave, because I must also take care of the business! In short, we're pursued by bad luck . . . and I wonder if it isn't time to change the tune! But meanwhile I am changing it, having bored you enough with these miseries great and small. Please excuse me.

I forgot the best part! Since July, the management of La Scala, as stipulated by its contract, had to present to City Hall the definite program of next season's performances. Out of regard for you, the city administration and the directors of the theatre did not pressure the management, but waited until all the necessary elements were at Maestro Verdi's disposal. Now that with Pasqua's engagement everything is finally settled, please authorize me to assure City Hall and the management regarding *Falstaff*, which everyone is longing for. Of course, I shall do this as correctly as you think best; and, of course, I shall submit the contract with the management to you, so you may see if I have put in all the appropriate *caution* and *reservation*. But since it is getting late and the contractors[2] must be alerted that they will soon be receiving orders, I must again have your official authorization; otherwise I would be without the necessary mandate, so to speak. In a few days the plans for the sets will be ready for all your comments; this way, the trouble with the *Otello* sets, which were planned too late, will not be repeated.[3]

1892

Do you think, perhaps, that just a few words in the *Gazzetta musicale* might suffice, announcing simply that the company performing *Falstaff* has been completed and fully approved by Maestro Verdi? . . . That might also suffice for City Hall, without a special letter. I await your instructions, then, in which you will tell me the proper way to proceed with this most important affair.

The management has notified me that [the following artists] will be in Genoa around mid-October: Guerrini—Moretti—Paroli—Pini-Corsi. Later on Stehle will arrive from America and can remain in Genoa for a few days; and later on Zilli. The management has also charged me to ask you— before definitely casting Paroli—to hear the other tenor, Pelagalli-Rossetti, whom they believe to be better. Pelagalli-Rossetti is probably also in Genoa, and so you yourself can judge whether he is better suited to Bardolfo or Dr. Cajus, and, vice versa, Paroli.

As you see, everything is cooking and boiling. It's up to you to say: *Fiat lux!!*

You will have seen the 1st act proofs of the libretto; the typographical problem of the many simultaneous strophes seems to have been solved quite well without distorting them.

And now I have actually finished, enjoying the pleasure of sending you and Signora Peppina the most devoted and affectionate greetings, remaining always with the warmest gratitude,

Your most obedient
Giulio Ricordi

NOTES

1. At Barasso. (See Ricordi to Verdi, 21 August, n.1.)
2. Carpenters, painters, costume shops, etc.
3. See *Otello* i: Verdi to Ricordi, 14 March 1887; Ricordi to Verdi, 15 March 1887; Verdi to Ricordi, 19 May 1887; Verdi to Ricordi, 1 January 1889; Ricordi to Verdi, 8 February 1889; Verdi to Ricordi, 9 February 1889.

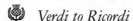 *Verdi to Ricordi*

St. Agata, 18 September 1892
Dear Giulio,

I am returning the reduction, with some comments, and the libretto, too.

There are a few mistakes in the score, which I beg you to mark so that I can correct them.

The libretto looks even nicer now that it's printed. On page 20, the verse *Giungi in buon punto* [You arrive at a good moment][1] is missing . . . and it is there in the reduction! On page 21, they omitted the word *t'offro* [I offer you][2] . . . perhaps because I forgot to write it in, but it must be there. Tell Boito.

You ask a few questions about the *entrances* and *exits* of the actors.[3] Nothing is simpler and easier than this staging, if the painter makes the scenery I had in mind while I was composing the music. No more is needed than a large and real garden, one with paths, and here and there groups of shrubs and plants, so that one can hide wherever one wishes and appear and disappear as the play and the music require. For example:

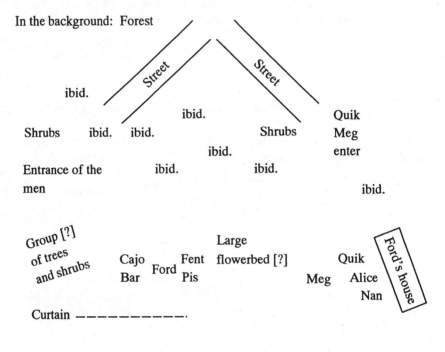

N.B. Just put in as many large and small groups of trees and shrubs as you like. But there must be empty spaces, too, and an open area for the action.

Also for the women an open area that is large enough for their action.

Prompter

In this way, the men would have their place apart, and later, when the women are no longer onstage, they could also take their place. Thus, at the

1892

end of the act, the women could occupy the place where the men had stood. Tell no one about my scribblings (not even Boito) but be careful that Obestein's [Hohenstein's] ideas are more or less in agreement with my own.—

Tito told me that Obestein proposed to place the screen at the far side of the stage "since it is natural and logical that a screen should lean against the wall."—Not at all.—What we have here is a screen that, so to speak, takes part in the action, and therefore it must be placed where the action requires it; all the more so as Alice is saying in a certain passage, *più in quà, più in là, più aperto ancora* [more here, more there, still more open], etc., etc.[4]

The set for the second act finale should be almost entirely open, so that one can move about and the main groups are clearly visible: the one at the *screen,* at the *basket,* and at the large window:

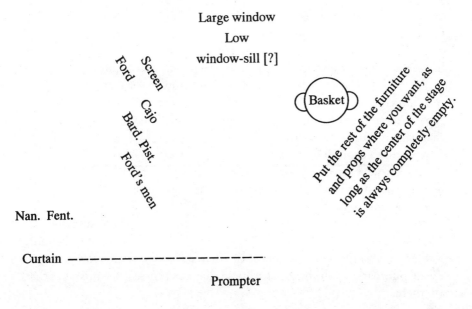

I repeat: Tell no one any of this, for I don't want to impose on anyone, and I'm hoping that others will find something better. . . On the other hand, I will not approve anything that does not totally convince me.

I was about to mail this when your letter of the 17th arrived.

I am truly saddened, as is Peppina, by the misfortune in your family,[5] and we share your and Giuditta's sorrow. There is nothing else to be said than to be patient and brave.

In regard to *Falstaff,* I have no desire to commit myself to anyone, but *I promise to the publisher Ricordi* to give *Falstaff* at La Scala during the Carnival season of 1892–93, provided the cast agreed upon is complete; I reserve the right to replace anyone whom I may find inadequate during rehearsals. *Falstaff* may be given in early February if the theatre is placed entirely at my disposal as of 2 January 1893.

The rehearsals will be handled the same way as they always have been. Only, the dress rehearsal must be different this time. Never have I been able to obtain a dress rehearsal at La Scala as it ought to be in that theatre. This time I will be unrelenting. I won't complain, but whenever something displeases me, I will leave the theatre, and then you will have to withdraw the score.

Let's leave Paroli where he is. The role of Bardolfo is perhaps more important than that of Cajo.

For the flute, there is only a small detail involved: *D flat* with *E flat* [trill]. Look up the *Honor* scene in the score.

The bass clarinet in *A* also appeared in *Otello.* In *Falstaff,* it is particularly important in the third act, when the women sing that litany of theirs:
            Domine fallo casto [Lord, make him chaste], etc.

A hunting horn is also needed; a real *hunting horn*, one without valves and capable of producing a low *A flat.* The instrument should have a certain size; that way, it will be easier to play.—

And that's enough for now.

Has Pasqua been engaged?—And how about Cesari?—As far as I know, he isn't coming to La Scala this year. Let me know.

Addio, addio

Affectionately,
G. Verdi

I am enclosing the reduction of the first act, along with a few changes. Please put marks in the original score so that I can correct the mistakes that are there.

NOTES

    1. Alice to Meg in I.ii (PV p. 49, 1/4).

    2. Meg's "amor t'offro" [I offer you love] in I.ii (PV p. 53, 2/4).

    3. Missing.

    4. In II.ii (PV p. 204, 2/1) Alice actually says, "Apriamo il paravento" [Let's open the screen] and "Bravissime! Così!/ Più aperto ancora" [Very good! Like that! / Still more open].

    5. The death of Giulio and Giuditta Ricordi's little grandson, Giulio.

1892

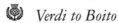 *Verdi to Boito*

St. Agata, 20 September 1892

Dear Boito,

Imagine, just last Thursday Tito Ricordi gave me a little package with 25 Lire inside, sent by your brother for rental of land. . . And I have never written or sent a receipt!—Horrible!

I gave Tito the third act of *Falstaff*. Yesterday I returned the libretto and the piano reduction of the first act, with a few observations of little importance about the *mise-en-scène* and the reduction.[1]

Now I am meticulously examining the second act, but no matter how careful I am, some wrong notes, many ♯s and ♭s always escape me. The reducer[2] and Giulio will think about it.

Addio then, and till we meet again who knows when. Greetings from Peppina.

Affectionately,
G. Verdi

NOTES

1. See Verdi to Ricordi, 18 September.
2. Carlo Carignani. (See Ricordi to Verdi, 12 August.)

 *Ricordi to Verdi*

Milan, 24 September 1892

Illustrious Maestro,

I received your esteemed letter of the 18th and have carried out your instructions regarding the reduction and the libretto. This morning I went with Boito to Hohenstein to see the set designs. He will immediately make the *maquettes*, which will give an exact impression and which we shall submit to you. I believe that Boito is going to write you a proposal;[1] therefore I am adding nothing else. But I was already in agreement with Hohenstein regarding the instructions you had given me. I hope all will go well.

Yesterday I sent you another part of the reduction. There are wonders upon wonders!! . . . . What grace, what life, what exquisite vivacity. . . . . We are astounded!—Excuse the outburst, Maestro, which is out of line with Verdi.—I had promised myself to keep my mouth shut . . . . but it wasn't possible.

I cannot find words to thank you for what you write me concerning *Falstaff* at La Scala; you give me such great honor that . . . . . that I am literally overwhelmed! [. . .] I will look up the contract for *Otello*,[2] and when the new one has been drafted by the management, I shall, together with you, see if modifications and additions are needed so that you may remain perfectly content.—

Pasqua accepted the general conditions, but then ruined everything with other impossible appendices! . . . I tried to reduce the damage by half; the management accepted, and all is finally settled. The management wrote some time ago about Cesari in order to stamp out the persistent rumors;[3] the reply will come soon. To tell you the truth, however, I wouldn't mind being without Cesari; the excellent Carbonetti[4] can replace him very well and is already being discussed. [. . .]

NOTES

1. See the following.
2. See *Otello* i, pp. 278–9.
3. Probably about his alleged elopement with Luisa Tetrazzini to America (see Verdi to Ricordi, 12 July).
4. Federico Carbonetti (1854–1916) was a *basso buffo*, writer, journalist, and librettist. He was particularly suited to such roles as the Sacristan in *Tosca* and Beckmesser, which he sang in the first *Meistersinger* in Italy at La Scala in 1889.

Boito to Verdi

Sunday [25 September 1892] Milan[1]

Dear Maestro,

When shall we meet again? In eight or ten days at the latest. We'll descend upon St. Agata, Giulio and I, with the little theatre in the hand-bag,[2] in order to show you all the *maquettes* for *Falstaff*, with all the *cutouts* and *platforms* in place. This way, we will be able to see and judge exactly even the smallest scenic detail, and thus we shall no longer have any unpleasant surprises at the stage rehearsals.[3]

Today I'll see the proofs of the third act (libretto) and we will send them to you after I have made corrections.

Many warm greetings to Signora Giuseppina, to Signora Barberina, and to you.

'Til we meet soon again.

Your most affectionate
Arrigo Boito

1892

NOTES

1. Postmark: MILANO 25/9/92.
2. Models of the set in a miniature theatre.
3. As in the case of the first *Otello* production at La Scala. (See *Otello.*)

 *Boito to Verdi*

27 September [1892]
Milan[1]

Dear Maestro,

I propose the following variants for Act III: Instead of having Meg say:

Ho nascosto i folletti *dietro al* fosso
[I've hidden the sprites *behind the* ditch]

have her say

Ho nascosto i folletti *lungo* il fosso
[I've hidden the sprites *along* the ditch].[2]

Instead of having Falstaff say:

Sono le Fate. Chi le guarda è morto.[3]
[It's the Fairies. Whoever looks at them is dead.]

have him say

Sono le Fate. Chi le *guarda* è morto.[4]

After the verse:

L'arguzia mia crea l'arguzia degli altri
[My cleverness creates the cleverness of the others]

everybody shouts *mò bravo!* That *mò* [now] is a form of dialect I don't like.
I propose to replace it with the two words: *Ben detto!* [Well said!][5]

And finally, I propose to modify the third and fourth verses of the fugue in this way:

Tutto nel mondo è burla.	[Everything in the world is a jest.
L'uom è nato burlone;	Man is born a jester;
La fè nel cor gli ciurla,	Faith in his heart is wavering,
Ciurla la sua ragione.	His reason is wavering.][6]

Or else: La fede in cor gli ciurla,
                 Gli ciurla la ragione.

You look at it, and decide.
The original verses are:

Nel suo cervello ciurla
Sempre la sua ragione.

The musical accents, I think, would not be disturbed by adopting this version:

"La fede in cor gli ciurla,"
"Ciurla la sua ragione"

and the two verses, I think, would work out better.

I await your opinion[7] and greet you affectionately, promising myself to see you again soon at St. Agata.

All the best to Signora Giuseppina.

Your
Arrigo Boito

NOTES

1. Postmark: MILANO 27/9/92.
2. Verdi agreed (III.ii PV p. 339, 2/2).
3. III.ii PV p. 351, 1/1.
4. Cf. Shakespeare, *The Merry Wives of Windsor*, V.v.51-2: "They are fairies; he that speaks to them shall die." Inadvertently Boito wrote the same words of the final text twice. His original version might have been "Chi le *parla* . . . ," as in Shakespeare's text. (See also *Carteggio* ii, p. 428.)
5. In III.ii (PV p. 406, 2/1) Verdi decided on "Ma bravo!" [Why, good for you!].
6. See Boito to Verdi, 21 May 1890. Verdi chose not to modify the original third and fourth verses. The libretto reads "La fede in cor gli ciurla / Gli ciurla la ragione."
7. Probably expressed in person.

 Verdi to Ricordi

[St. Agata] Tuesday [27 September 1892]

Dear Giulio,

I am returning the corrected reduction of the first part of the third act. How many mistakes, little ones and big ones, must there be in the orchestra score! Make a little mark wherever I have indicated, and I'll find some time to correct them. The reduction is not difficult—it's all right.

I am finishing the second act. When do you want it to be ready?

I am glad that your Gigi is doing better. Greetings to all.

Addio, addio
G. Verdi

Do me the favor of paying Monsieur Virgile, Coiffeur de Dames in Paris, 14 Rue de Hanovre, fr. 115 for the pomade from Signora Verdi's account.

I am sending only the 1st part of the libretto.

1892

🏵 *Ricordi to Verdi*

Milan, 30 September 1892

Illustrious Maestro,

Yesterday morning, by registered mail, I received the bundle containing the reduction, and the corrections and alterations indicated were made at once.

As to the second act, please indicate, Maestro, when it will be convenient for you to have it picked up, so you won't be disturbed.

One important matter: the marks in the orchestra score have been made, and now you should insert everything which corresponds to them; but . . . . . . this is urgent, since [otherwise] the parts cannot *be extracted.*

Do you think that when we turn over the 2nd act to you, we might bring the rest of the orchestral score along? . . . In that case there would be enough time to mark the corrections right in Piacenza, so that we would return with the 1st and 3rd acts in order. . . The chief copyist is pressuring me to have the parts extracted in time to be engraved, which is of great advantage for the orchestra rehearsals. Therefore, please give me your instructions as to what will be most suitable for you.

Boito will have written you regarding the sets,[1] and I believe he will have warned you about a forthcoming pilgrimage of ours down there, with Hohenstein and a little theatre. But won't we be disturbing you? . . . for we will have to stay for an entire day!! In short, it's up to you, Maestro, to command our vanguard, which must carry out strategic movements.[2]

Sunday I *must* go to Genoa for the dress rehearsal of *Colombo,* hoping for the 1st performance on Tuesday!—I say *I must,* because I go there reluctantly, having until now avoided going to other rehearsals!—I am ill at ease in that ambience of fools . . . . and of . . . . sodomites, speaking with all due respect!! Enough!—I must swallow this, too—

You wrote me, "I am sending only the 1st part of the libretto."—I have not received anything. . . . . *

I had the bill paid in Paris, as you instructed Please write to Milan, and if you should have instructions concerning the 2nd act, Tito will come.

Excuse the haste—I hope to see you soon. [. . .]

* It's here! . . . I had overlooked it among the pages.

NOTES

1. On 25 September.
2. This discussion of the models took place only between 13 and 16 October in Milan. A note Verdi jotted down concerning this might be attributed to that period: "*For the stage.*

In this scene [III.ii] Falstaff remains stretched out on the ground in an uncomfortable position for over five minutes! This can be difficult! . . . However, let's leave things as they are for now, but provision must be made.—The *maquettes* must be made so that a remedy may be found when we're at the stage rehearsals." This note is preserved at St. Agata within the pages of Boito's autograph of the libretto. (*Carteggio* ii, p. 428.)

 Tito Ricordi II to Verdi

Milan, 30 September 1892

Most Illustrious Maestro
    G. Verdi
        St. Agata

Papa wrote you this morning informing you that I would come to Piacenza one day next week to receive the orchestral score of the 2nd act of *Falstaff*.[1] But as I already told you the last time, I would like to have the pleasure of coming to St. Agata, thus saving you an unnecessary trip. Furthermore, since I am bringing along the orchestra score of the 1st and 3rd acts, you can look over at leisure the points already marked in the reduction, so that on my return to Milan I will also carry with me the corrected 1st and 3rd acts.

Please give my regards to Signora Peppina and Signora Stolz, and accept the expression of my deepest respect.

Most devotedly,
Ing. Tito Ricordi

NOTE

    1. Writing in haste, Giulio Ricordi either forgot or decided to delay informing Verdi of this arrangement.

 Verdi to Ricordi

Busseto St. Agata, 9 October 1892

Dear Giulio,

Thank you for your wishes for the 79!![1] Peppina will go to Cremona on Thursday;[2] I will accompany her and go straight on to Milan, where I shall arrive at 3:30. Arrange everything so I can leave again on Sunday; on the day of my arrival we can work from 4 to 6, if only to go over the libretto and compare it with the music; make the slight adjustments, and establish the number of choristers and extras, whom I want to be very few. Friday and

1892

Saturday we could apply ourselves to the sets, to the bowings, to the harpist, and other things. . .

All right?—

Should you not wish that the orchestra score be brought to the hotel at the time of my arrival, I could come to your office. In any case, do not come to the station but await me at the hotel.—

In any event, I'll confirm my arrival by telegram, which I will send on Wednesday. Then you can inform Signor Spatz[3] that I will arrive Thursday at 3:30 all by myself, and that I'll stay in Milan 48 hours.

Addio, addio

G. Verdi

Ah, Franchetti loves spectacular productions?[4] Unlike me, who detest them. That is what is needed, and nothing else. With these big productions, they end up always doing the same thing. . . Much ado—lots of people . . . and goodbye to drama and music!! They become secondary matters.—[5]

NOTES

1. Verdi's 79th birthday. (See Verdi to Clara Maffei on 9 October 1885, in *Otello* i, p. 182.) Ricordi apparently sent a letter or a telegram, which is missing.

2. 15 October.

3. Giuseppe Spatz, presumably of Swiss origin, was the owner of the Grand Hôtel et de Milan; in 1896 his daughter married the composer Umberto Giordano (1867–1948). See *Carteggi* iv, pp. 106–7.

4. Verdi seems to have read this in the press, if not in missing communications from Ricordi or others.

5. Cf. Verdi's letter to Arrivabene of 12 February 1884: "Good operas have always been rare; now they are impossible. Why? you will say.—Because one makes too much music; because one searches too much; because one looks in the dark and overlooks the sun! Because we exaggerated the dressings! Because we do *big* things, not great things! And the *big* leads to the small and the bizarre!" (*Copialettere*, p. 629.)

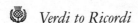 *Verdi to Ricordi*

St. Agata, 10 October 1892

Dear Giulio,

As I wrote you yesterday, I repeat that I will be in Milan almost certainly on Thursday at 3:30.—I am confirming what I said, and I add that it would be a good idea to make the reduction of the first part of the second act right away.

I'll be in Genoa around the 25th and could have Pini-Corsi study the duet and *Ford*'s monologue; these are his most important pieces.

I'll wire tomorrow.

Thank you for the very beautiful congratulatory remarks in your paper.[1]

Your

G. Verdi

NOTE

1. In the *Gazzetta musicale*, on the occasion of Verdi's 79th birthday.

🏵 *Verdi to Ricordi*

St. Agata, 21 October 1892

Dear Giulio,

Time permitting, the servants will go to Genoa tomorrow, and we'll go on Monday. We shall arrive at 6:05 in the evening. And so there will be a whole week to hear *Colombo*[1] and *Rigoletto*.

And now pay attention: *No presentations and no ceremonies*. I say even this: the ceremonies would spoil everything . . . because I wouldn't go to the theatre.

As I have always done when going to the theatre, I'll take a box and tickets with my own money. And when I see one or the other of these operas announced, I'll plan to hear them, without being asked "How do you do?"

If you're counting on coming to Genoa, as you said, bring along the bundles containing the original orchestra score. That is . . . in the second act, 1st part, the bundle Ford[2]

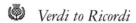

In the second part, the bundle[3]

Farther on in the same scene[4]

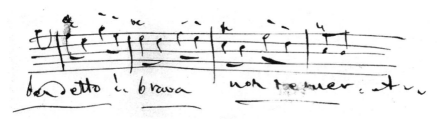

And bring or send the pieces for Ford in the second act.

If there are objections to these great [illegible word], I'll write or wire you.

Ad[dio] ad[dio]

Affectionately,

G. Verdi

NOTES

1. Verdi apparently attended a performance of Franchetti's opera at the Teatro Carlo Felice, together with Ricordi during the latter's visit in Genoa, and probably with Boito, too.

2. Ford-Falstaff duet (PV p. 163, 1/3). Since Verdi's musical example is not entirely correct, it seems to be only an indication for Ricordi to identify the bundle in question. So, too, with the other musical examples in this letter.

3. PV p. 193, 3/1, beginning of Quickly's narrative.

4. PV p. 202, 1/1, Quickly, Meg, and Alice.

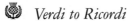 *Verdi to Ricordi*

Genoa, 4 November 1892

Dear Giulio,

I have received the three bundles and have examined one on which was written: See from p. 69 onward.

I corrected these, which you will find as you turn the page . . . some I will correct in the score. If that is not enough, I will send the reduction.—

I'll look over the rest.—

Meanwhile, arrange to have sent to me: the pieces for Pini-Corsi; and: the pieces for the tenor . . . I don't have the entire score.—

Tell me if you sent something to Maurel.———

Tell me where Pasqua is now.———In haste

ad[dio] ad[dio]

G. Verdi

In the 1st act, correct Page 72.[1]

1st act Page 78 . . . in *due* pa—[2]

ibid. Page 87[3]

[?]   Page 93[4]

[?]   Page 87[5]

[?]   Page 98 second bar—Al.[6]

1892

[?]   Page 107 1st bar: Quik.[7]

Page 105 Fals. 2nd bar[8]

ibid. 122 Fals. 2nd bar[9]

Page 111 Meg 1st bar[10]

Page 120 Meg 1st bar[11]

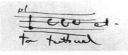

Page 130 Chorus sopranos 2nd bar[12]

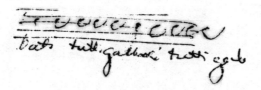

Page 93 In the cembalo, 2nd page, 3rd bar[13]

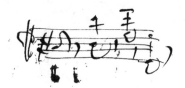

Page 95 1st bar[14]

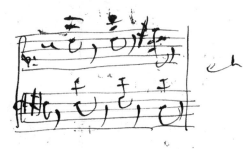

P.S.

In the first part of the 3rd act page 5, 2nd bar: take out the indication *urlando* [shouting].[15]

Page 10 2nd bar[16]

Page 11 Cembalo right hand[17]

NOTES

1. I.ii (PV p. 70, 1/2 to p. 74, 1/1).
2. I.ii (PV p. 76, 2/4), Pistola's text "In *due* parole."
3. I.ii (PV p. 83, 2/2).
4. I.ii (PV p. 91, 1/3).
5. III.ii (PV p. 416, 2/3).
6. Alice in III.ii (PV p. 427, 1/2).
7. III.ii (PV p. 436, 1/1).
8. III.ii (PV p. 434, 1/2).
9. III.ii (PV p. 451, 1/2).
10. III.ii (PV p. 440, 1/1).
11. III.ii (PV p. 449, 1/1).
12. III.ii (PV p. 459, 1/2).
13. III.ii (PV p. 422, 1/3).
14. III.ii (PV p. 424, 1/1).
15. Presumably Falstaff in III.i (PV p. 294, 4/1).
16. Falstaff in III.1 (PV p. 300, 4/2).
17. Ibid. (PV p. 301, 3/1).

 Boito to Ricordi

[Genoa?] 5 November 1892
Hôtel du Parc

[. . .] The Verdis are very well. We dine together every day, but in three or four days I'll be at my retreat.[1] [. . .]

NOTE

1. At the Villa Rosten in nearby Pegli.

 Ricordi to Verdi

Milan, 6 November 1892

Illustrious Maestro,

Alas! . . . alas! . . alas! I ask myself if the most beautiful days spent in Genoa were a dream! . . . .

The moment I came back I found myself drowning in the *mare magnum* of business, nuisances, troubles, and even sorrows! I don't know whether there is so much rubbish in any other industry!—Anyway, mine is a real dog's life, where honesty is detrimental . . . . . I agree with Falstaff! . . . *Honor?* . . . . to the devil with honor! . . .[1]

But let's come to important matters and proceed in order.

1. I received your letter with the various corrections, and the copy of the orchestra score page with your observations.[2] Everything is all right. But don't tire yourself at this time with corrections, since not all of the printed pages you have are corrected. When the engraving is finished, I'll send you a complete and corrected copy, on which I ask that you make the definitive revision.

2. Some days ago, we sent Maurel what has thus far been engraved of his part. I'll send him the rest as soon as it is ready.

3. I wired to find out where Pasqua is; as yet I have had no answer, but will let you know as soon as I get it. If it were possible to decide on the famous breathing in the 4 bars,[3] it would be most helpful in completing the engraving of the reduction and the orchestra parts, which are still being delayed.

4. You request the parts of Fenton and Ford, but the reduction of the 2nd act was turned over only last Tuesday; the engraving takes time and will require several more days, even though it's being done by 6 engravers. For Fenton as well as Ford you already have the 2nd part of Act I and all of Act III. Do you want another copy of this? The handwritten part of the duet was given to Pini-Corsi, and also his solo in Act II. I have ordered handwritten parts of the 2nd part of Act II for Fenton and Ford, and in a couple of days I can send them to you. I hope that in the meantime you can use these; as soon as a portion of pages has been engraved, I'll send them to you at once, at once. Unfortunately, the engraving of music takes a lot of time.

5. Signora Stehle is on her way back. It seems that she will arrive in Genoa between the 15th and 20th of this month; I have already written to her family to find out if she can stay in Genoa for 5 or 6 days.

6. I had the guitar part examined by a good player; altogether, it goes very well. A few notes can be removed, but the chords still remain complete. For example:

the *C* cannot be played.

This instead goes well.

A single step is quite difficult and therefore not very clear, namely the little groups:

If they could be played like this

it would be easy. See then, Maestro, how you think you want to do it.

Tomorrow: meeting at the theatre with Hohenstein and the scenic artist to determine the arrangement of the sets, which will be started at once, at once so they'll be ready when you want them to be.

I also spoke with Maestro Calcagnini[4] about the box for Signora Peppina: The directors are most honored to place the best available box at her disposal, which is the one above the directors' own box. So this is in order, too.

One last thing (at least for today): Tornaghi, despite the best intentions, is unable to face a trip of 2 or 3 hours, as he is suffering from an inflammation of the kidneys. So my plan for Genoa or Novi is out.[5] But permit me to observe that the *Otello* contract was also settled at the very end, when you came to stay in Milan [for the rehearsals]. Do you wish to do the same again? . . . At such time you will tell Tornaghi the conditions you desire, for Verdi does not discuss contracts, but establishes them. [. . .]

This seems to suffice for today. Tomorrow I will plead with them as much as possible to finish the work on Act II.

Boito wrote me giving me your excellent news.[6] I am very happy about it.

Once again, my thanks to you and Signora Peppina, always in the hope of seeing you again soon, and with all my gratitude.

Your most devoted
Giulio Ricordi

NOTES

1. Three years later, on 14 August 1895, Ricordi would write to Puccini: "[. . .] Don't pay any attention to the unsavory manure which is heaped upon our poor art! I, too, have my moments of anger in which I ask myself whether I ought to take art so seriously. But then I reflect and I am content with what I do. Honesty in art is rewarded in the end. You may be certain of that! [. . .]" (Marek, p. 154.) For related expressions of Ricordi's distress see his letters to Verdi of 25 May and 10 June 1890, 28 and 30 November 1892.

2. See Verdi to Ricordi, 4 November.

3. See Verdi to Pasqua, 7 November.

4. Unknown.

5. Presumably, while in Genoa in late October, Ricordi suggested sending Tornaghi to see Verdi in Genoa or Novi (a town 54 km west of Genoa on the Ligurian coast) about the contract for *Falstaff* at La Scala.

6. See Boito to Ricordi of 5 November.

 *Ricordi to Verdi*

Milan, 7 November 1892

Illustrious Maestro,

Just this moment I wired you Signora Pasqua's address.[1]

At the end of the last part of Act III, if you remember, Boito added a *Si* [Yes] to Meg and changed a word of Ford's. I am sending you the corresponding page so that you may correct it as you wish, having marked these words in pencil only.

I am also enclosing a correction you indicated to me, but I am unable to find it on pages 36 and 90.[2]

Again and always

most gratefully and devotedly your
Giulio Ricordi

NOTES

1. See Hepokoski, "Pasqua," p. 248, n. 30: "Confermando mia lettera ecco indirizzo Pasqua. Piazza Aldovrandi 10 Bologna. Cordiali ossequi." [Confirming my letter, Pasqua's address is Piazza Aldovrandi 10 Bologna. Cordial regards.]

2. Apparently Verdi indicated this correction to Ricordi in Genoa at the end of October. Ricordi misread page 36 for page 86, as Verdi points out on 8 November.

 *Verdi to Giuseppina Pasqua*

Genoa, 7 November 1892

My dear Signora Pasqua,

As promised, I am sending you the first proofs of *Falstaff*,[1] which I ask you to return to me as soon as you have read them.

In the second part of the second act, there is a *solo*[2] which causes some problems before the music is printed. It ought to be performed *prestissimo, a mezza voce, con un solo fiato, sillabando chiaro e netto* [very fast, in mezza voce, in a single breath, articulated clearly and distinctly]. I am sending you the few bars,[3] and I ask that you tell me something about them. With my regards to your husband, I remain most respectfully [. . .]

NOTES

1. Apparently according to a verbal commitment.

2. A surprising gift to the artist. (See Verdi to Ricordi, 12 July.) Verdi probably asked Boito for the additional lines in Milan at the end of July. (See Hepokoski, "Pasqua," pp. 246–50.)

1892

3. Verdi transcribed II.ii (PV p. 196, 1/1) as:

Infine, a farla spiccia,	[Finally, to make it brief,
Vi crede entrambe	He believes both of you
Innamorate cotte	Madly enamored
Delle bellezze sue.	Of his beautiful qualities.
E lo vedrete	And you will see . . . .]

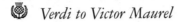 *Verdi to Victor Maurel*

Genoa, 8 November 1892

My dear Maurel,

By now you will have received, from the House of Ricordi, a few numbers of *Falstaff;* you will get the rest soon.

I admire study in general, and your study of Falstaff's character in particular. Mind you, however, that in art a predominant tendency toward reflection is a sign of decadence. In other words, if art becomes science, the result is something that is overdone, which is neither art nor science. To do well, yes; to overdo, no! In France you say: *"Ne cherchez pas midi à quatorze heures!"*[1] That is absolutely true.

Do not strain your voice to the extreme limit, but be satisfied with the one you have.

So don't overexert yourself to perfect your voice, and be content with the one you have. With your great talent as a singing actor, with your accentuation and enunciation, Falstaff's character will become a perfect creation once you have learned it, without racking your brain and indulging in studies that might be harmful to you. Study a bit, and let's see each other soon.

G. Verdi

NOTE

1. See Verdi to Ricordi, 17 June, n. 2.

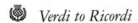 *Verdi to Ricordi*

[Genoa] Tuesday [8 November 1892][1]

The mistake you didn't find is on page 86, 1st act, 2nd part. It's in the duettino between *Fen.* and *An.* in *D flat*, ninth bar.[2] A bit farther on is the second mistake at the entrance of *Alice with the others*, page 90, eighth bar.[3]

As you will see, I made a correction where Boito changed *Si—non temer*

[Yes—do not fear].[4] Yesterday I sent the libretto and that little passage to Pasqua so that she might tell me something about it.—

If *Stehle* could stay here for a couple of days, it would be nice if you could send me her printed part; I don't have the entire orchestra score, but only the pieces involving her.—

This goes also for the parts of *Cajus* and the [other] *tenor.*—These two I haven't called yet, first because I have a bad cold, and further because I would like to have the respective parts.—

I have bad news about the bass;[5] he is said to be small fry, a blockhead . . . Find out again. You know that Pistola's part is very lively——

Addio for now.

Affectionately,
G. Verdi

Correct again

first act page 72 [illegible word]

ibid.: pg. 86 cembalo *9th bar*[6]

pg. 90 to the violins *8th bar*[7]

What I said yesterday, I repeat today: send me *Ford*'s and *Fenton*'s parts as soon as possible. Never mind if there are errors in the engraving. Then I can call for *Corsi* and *Garbin*[8] to review and teach them their parts.—

Ad. Ad.

Affectionately,
G. Verdi

1892

P.S. In the 1st part 3rd act page 21, correct 8th bar[9]

NOTES

1. Postmark: GENOVA 9/11/92. In answer to Ricordi, 7 November.

2. Fenton and Nannetta (not Annetta). See n. 6.

3. I.ii (PV p. 88, 4/1). See n. 6.

4. In II.ii (PV p. 202, 1/4), Alice says only *Non temer* [Do not fear].

5. Caused by an apparent misunderstanding. See Ricordi to Verdi, 2nd letter on 10 November, n. 3.

6. I.ii (PV p. 84, 2/1).

7. I.ii (PV p. 88, 3/2).

8. After Masini's engagement had not materialized, Edoardo Garbin (1865–1943), later Adelina Stehle's second husband, was cast in the role of Fenton. He had made his debut as Don Alvaro in *La forza del destino* at Vicenza in 1891, and Verdi heard him in Franchetti's *Cristoforo Colombo* under Arturo Toscanini's baton at Genoa in late October. Outside of Italy, he appeared in London, South America, France, Poland, and Russia. Toscanini engaged him for *La Traviata* and *Falstaff* in Busseto in 1913. Garbin's good looks and inspired acting, refined by his wife's advice and example, compensated for his apparent lack of musicianship.

9. III.i (PV p. 311, 4/1).

 Ricordi to Verdi

[1st Letter]   Milan, 8 November 1892
Illustrious Maestro,

Signora Stehle's husband[1] writes me that his wife departed from Rio de Janeiro on 28 October, and that she will arrive in Genoa after the middle of this month. He is certain that immediately upon her arrival she "will be most honored to follow the instructions of the supreme Maestro."

Under separate cover I am sending you a few pages for corrections;[2] please return them to me.[3]

Last page: Instead of *"Ancor"* [Again] Fenton says *"Sì"* [Yes], as has been corrected in the libretto.—Leave *"Sì"* in the libretto and *"Ancor"* in the music?[4]

On the sixth, seventh and eighth page Pistola [Bardolfo][5] says *"astuto e cauto*" [astute and cautious] instead of *"ardito e scaltro"* [bold and sly]. The first word was changed immediately, the second calls for one more note.[6]

In the libretto, *Alice* says to Nannetta: *"Evita il tuo periglio"* [Avoid your danger].[7] In the music, it is Quickly.—Change the indication in the libretto or in the music?

Confirming my preceding letters to you, I repeat the most affectionate greetings and remain, with all my gratitude,

Your most devoted
Giulio Ricordi

[. . .]

NOTES

1. Her first husband.
2. These pages, like other corrections, seem to be missing.
3. See Verdi to Ricordi, 9 November.
4. Ibid.
5. Ibid. Ricordi confused the roles of Bardolfo and Pistola. (See Ricordi to Verdi, 15 June, and Verdi to Ricordi, 9 November.)
6. See Verdi to Ricordi, 9 November.
7. III.ii (PV p. 371, 1/3). See Verdi to Ricordi, 9 November.

✿ *Ricordi to Verdi*

[2nd Letter]   Milan, 8 November 1892
Illustrious Maestro,

I haven't finished! Look at Act III first part—Falstaff scene:

che giornataccia nera [what a bad, black day.][1]

Segue    In the orchestral score the

viola and double bass do not have the C♯, but B natural.

1892

I think it's an error in the engraving.
Kindly let me know.

> Again your most devoted
> Giulio Ricordi

I am sending the 2 extracted parts of Fenton and Ford.

NOTE

1. III.i (PV p. 299, 4/2).

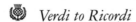 *Verdi to Ricordi*

> Genoa, 9 November 1892

Dear Giulio,

I am returning the corrected proofs received today. You will see that I
have *corrected* the *Si, due baci* [Yes, two kisses][1] on page 92 of the bundle you
sent me. I corrected the 4th *D*.

astuto e cauto [astute and cautious][2] are all right, but only two notes for *cauto*,
as also for *lauto*, which comes afterwards—

It's all right for Alice to sing the words I had written for Quik;[3] only a few
notes must be corrected, as you will see—*lesti* [quick] is all right.[4]

Mark everything so that I can make the corrections in the orchestra
score.—

I forgot to answer you about the guitar part. It doesn't matter if a few
notes in the middle are omitted, as long as the bass and the melody remain.
It is all right, and it's better to reduce the appoggiatura to triplets like this[5]

I have also received the parts for *Fenton* and *Ford* . . but up to now I have
called neither *Pini* nor *Garbin;* first, because I have a sore throat, which has
lasted for several days, and I have almost no voice; and then, because so little
is understood in these parts (which I myself don't understand) that in
explaining and making oneself understood, more time is lost than in
learning the part. And so I will call them as soon as you can send me the
parts.——

Send something to Maurel as soon as possible.—
Addio for today.

Your
G. Verdi

It's 4 P.M. and I just received your card——the $C\sharp$ stays.[6]
Besides, it goes very well in the printed reduction.

NOTES

1. I.ii (PV p. 83, 3/2). See Ricordi to Verdi [1st], 8 November.
2. Bardolfo in I.ii (PV p. 104, 2/2). See Ricordi to Verdi, 1st letter of 8 November, n. 4.
3. III.ii (PV p. 365, 1/3). See Ricordi to Verdi, 1st letter of 8 November.
4. Falstaff in I.i (PV p. 44, 2/1 and/or p. 45, 1/1).
5. See Ricordi to Verdi, 6 November, para. 6.
6. See Ricordi to Verdi, 2nd letter of 8 November.

 *Ricordi to Verdi*

Milan, 10 November 1892

Illustrious Maestro,

I am very sorry to hear that you have the unpleasant visit of a sore throat!
. . I hope it will be a passing thing, and that you will write me soon that you
are very well.

I have made all the indicated corrections in the orchestra score; so
everything is in order. *Tomorrow the printing of the 1st and 3rd acts will
begin!!!!! . . . . . . Evviva!*

On Saturday the 12th, I will send you 3 copies of the 1st and 3rd acts. As
to the 2nd, last night the engraving of the 1st part was finished, and today
I will send you a copy. The second part, if you remember, I myself took to
Milan; the engraving began on the 4th of this month—it consists of 110
pages. With all the engravers at work, even on Sunday, the engraving will
not be finished until the 15th. I'll do my utmost to send you 3 copies at
once, uncorrected, of course.—With Tito, I have studied all the means
of gaining a day or two, but it is absolutely impossible; I regret this
very much, because I would have liked to send you the whole 2nd act, as
you wish! . . I beg you to be patient; meanwhile, if you so desire, you
can have the entire 1st and the entire 3rd, which Garbin as well as Pini-
Corsi can study, with important scenes such as the 2nd part of the 1st act
and the 2nd part of the 3rd. For Pini-Corsi you now also have a completely
engraved part, in addition to the handwritten part of the duet and scene
in the 2nd act.

1892

Now I am studying the American *bill*[1] which is designed expressly to drive you mad. . . . . and maybe to trick the foreigners!! It appears that nothing less is required than:

1. Copy of the libretto written by hand. It must be written and printed in America. 2 printed copies must be submitted the same day they are submitted in Italy.

2. 2 handwritten copies of the title pages, also 2 printed copies of the opera to be submitted in Washington the same day as in Italy.

3. A handwritten copy of the orchestra score, before the opera is performed.

You see how much work and expense is required for this famous *American copyright*. So many formalities are frightening; actually, it seems to be some kind of a trap. Anyway, I will take care of everything, and let's hope that something will come of it. The copy of the handwritten orchestra score cannot be ready before the end of December; but even allowing for about twenty days, it will arrive punctually in Washington before the performance.

All these transactions and deliveries are communicated by telegram. If necessary, it would be worthwhile to postpone the 1st performance by a day or two in case the telegram from America is not received.

But I don't want to bore you with this anymore. I am anxious, however, to learn whether you are completely recovered. Remember that after the 15th of this month, I will be completely at your disposal; in case a trip to Genoa is required, it would be no trouble at all but, on the contrary, the greatest pleasure you could give me.

With the most cordial greetings to Signora Peppina and to you, and with the expression of my immense, abiding gratitude,

Most devotedly your
Giulio Ricordi

Falstaff for voice and piano will be a volume of *494* pages!

NOTE

1. Copyright application.

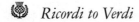 *Ricordi to Verdi*

Milan, 10 November 1892[1]

Illustrious Maestro,

Rushed as I was in writing you about the American *bill,* I forgot Pistola.[2]

The bass about whom I told you[3] is not short; on the contrary, he is a handsome man with big eyes and the shoulders of a grenadier. I heard him in *Cristoforo Colombo;* he has a fine, well-placed voice, he did the short but difficult part of a pilgrim; many times he has sung one of the brigands in *Fra Diavolo*, which calls for plenty of characterization. This is the information I can give you. I think Pini-Corsi knows him, and in that case you can be even better informed; as to his voice, I know that it is secure to the low F and even E.

Again, Maestro, I remain

Your most devoted
Giulio Ricordi

NOTES

1. In answer to Verdi's letter of 8 November.
2. See Verdi to Ricordi, 8 November 1892, n. 5.
3. Vittorio Arimondi (1861–1928), probably in person. While already embarked on a career in business, Arimondi studied voice and made his debut as a *basso profondo* in Gomes's *Il Guarany* at Varese in 1883. In the course of an international career he appeared at the Metropolitan Opera in 1895–96; at Hammerstein's Manhattan Opera House from 1906–10, and in Chicago. His imposing stature and thunderous voice contributed to his particular success as a gigantic, violent Mephisto in Gounod's *Faust.* After his retirement from the stage, he taught at the Chicago Music College until his death.

 *Tito Ricordi II to Verdi*

Milan, 10 November 1892

Illustrious Signor Maestro
Giuseppe Verdi

Genoa

Today I sent you, by registered mail, the uncorrected proof of the 1st part—2nd act of *Falstaff;* on Tuesday the 15th, I can also send you the 2nd part of the 2nd act. On Saturday the 12th, three complete and corrected copies of the 1st and 3rd acts will be ready, and I shall send them to you at once.

I hope you may soon get over the sore throat Papa mentioned this morning.

With my kindest regards to Signora Peppina,

Yours most devotedly and affectionately,
Ing. Tito Ricordi

1892

🏵 *Verdi to Ricordi*

[Genoa] *Thursday* [10 November 1892][1]

More corrections
3rd act 2nd part page 47
   in the second bar in the chorus tenors correct[2]

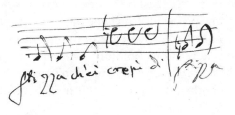

Also on page 80 of this second part in the pianoforte [reduction] a *D* is missing, which may also be missing in the orchestra score
   1st bar[3]

In the orchestra score it must be put into the violas as double-stops[4]

Whenever I find errors, I shall indicate them to you.
   I have received the first part of the second act. This copy will do for me. . . But couldn't you have sent me by now the pieces that have been printed so far to hand over to *Pini-Corsi* and *Garbin*?
   My sore throat and hoarseness won't go away.—

I had written to Corsi to come to me, but it is now two o'clock, and he hasn't come. . .

So much the better, or so much the worse.

Your
G. Verdi

P.S. It was three o'clock when Corsi arrived here after the orchestra rehearsal of *Fritz*.[5] We went over his two pieces, and I gave him the libretto and the first part of the second act. . . As I mentioned above, it would be good if you could send me all the pieces for Corsi and all the ones for Garbin.——

I just received your note.[6] I shall ask in minute detail about Roger.[7]

I also received a letter from Boldini,[8] who tells me that he wrote you about a seat for the *Falstaff* première. You didn't answer him, and he thinks you don't want to bother. Tell him, or tell me, about it. His address: 41 Boulevard Berthier, Paris. Addio.

NOTES

1. Postmark: GENOVA 11/11/92.
2. III.ii (PV p. 377, 1/2).
3. III.ii (PV p. 410, 3/1).
4. Ibid.
5. *L'amico Fritz* (1891), an opera by Pietro Mascagni, was performed at Genoa's Teatro Carlo Felice (see Verdi to Ricordi, 6 November 1891).
6. Missing.
7. The agent responsible for *Droits d'auteur* in Paris.
8. The painter Giovanni Boldini (1842–1931) was the prominent son and student of a less successful painter. His father sent him from his native Ferrara to Florence in 1865, where he soon became one of the *macchiaioli*, Florentine impressionist painters. In 1869 he was welcomed in London by a friend of Garibaldi, the Duke of Sutherland, who introduced Boldini to the English aristocracy, from whom he received important commissions. In 1872 he moved to Paris, where he painted Verdi in 1886. In 1877 Boldini visited Spain, where he was inspired by Murillo and Velazquez. In the 1880s he undertook long journeys through England, America, Austria, and Germany; while in Germany he formed a lasting friendship with the German painter Adolf Menzel (1815–1905).

 *Ricordi to Verdi*

Milan, 14 November 1892

Illustrious Maestro,

In regard to your most recent esteemed letters: In the 3 copies we sent you, some corrections are actually missing, because all the corrections will not be finished until tonight. So I am in time to add those you indicated to me in your letter of yesterday, and I have also noted them in the orchestra score.—Now I must really beg you to return to me, as soon as possible, the pages of the orchestra score, copies of which I am sending you today, so that you can correct them, if need be. You wrote me, "Hurry up with the printing, otherwise I'll make more changes!"[1] Well then, Maestro, we must really start by Wednesday, or Thursday, at the latest; otherwise the edition will not only not be ready, but the orchestra parts will not be engraved, since we really have hardly, hardly enough time. Therefore it is absolutely necessary that you write me, "It's all right, go ahead."

Tomorrow I will send you 3 copies of the 2nd act, but I warn you that *they have not been corrected;* it may suffice for you to correct only those errors [you will find] in the vocal part when you go over it with the artists. I will then send you a corrected copy, and that is the one I ask you to review for the final correction of errors.

Meanwhile, please give me your answer in regard to the following matters:[2] In the 1st part of Act II, of which I believe you have a copy, I need these clarifications: Quickly, when saying *Povera donna* [Poor woman] has, in the orchestra score, sometimes 2 Cs, at other times D, C, that is:

Assuming that it must always be the same, please indicate if D, C or C, C is all right.

Have you also decided on the *M'inchino* [I bow]? . . . Are you leaving it like this or are you changing it, as I think you later said?

Pasqua's silence surprises me![3] She was in Bologna; has she already left?. . Do you want me to find out? For I am in a great hurry to know your decision on those undecided bars; without them, the printing of the edition could not be arranged.

I have made further inquiries about that bass Arimondi.[4] It was confirmed to me that he is good, that he has a far better voice than Cesari, and that he is an excellent Don Basilio; he was engaged almost constantly by Ferrari[5] and Ciacchi[6] in Rio de Janeiro and Buenos Aires.

It seems that Franchetti will do little or nothing to the 4th act!![7] That's a pity . . . . but who can reason with madmen?

I got a long letter from Souchon[8] about the ill-omened Bénoit affair; Souchon gave it great effort, as he had promised me, and he seems to be quite confident about forcing Bénoit to a settlement. I am answering him today that a direct intervention seems premature to me; but if it must be, and if you, too, think it useful, I am ready to make a quick trip to Paris. You can imagine how glad I would be to finish this business, which has caused you so much trouble and grief.

What? . . . still the sore throat? . . . It's about time to give it the boot!— What a shame! . . . Meanwhile, you could have done something with the two artists who are there, especially with Garbin! But I hope to hear that you are completely recovered, which will be the best news you can give me. [. . .]

NOTES

1. No such letter has been found.

2. See Verdi to Ricordi, 16 November, nn. 4 and 5.

3. She still had not answered Verdi's letter of 7 November.

4. See Verdi to Ricordi, 8 November; Ricordi to Verdi (2nd letter) and Verdi to Ricordi, 10 November; Ricordi to Verdi, 17 November; Verdi to Ricordi, 18 November.

5. Angelo Ferrari (1830–79) was "The King of Impresarios" in South America, where he promoted the building of the new Teatro Colón in Buenos Aires, which was inaugurated in 1908.

6. Unknown.

7. Of his opera *Cristoforo Colombo*. After its première in Genoa in October, Ricordi considered the 4th act in need of improvement for the opening of the Scala season on 26 December.

8. Attorney in Paris.

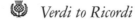 *Verdi to Ricordi*

[Genoa, 14 November 1892][1]

In the 3rd act page 21
Quik[2]

1892

ibid. page 41 Qui[3]

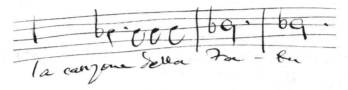

ibid. page 353[4]

ibid. page 354 Fal.[5]

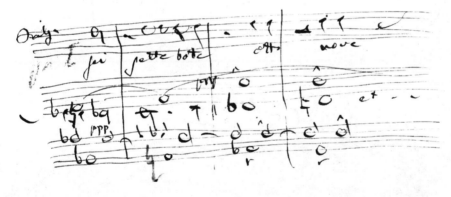

ibid. page 357 sixth bar *Falst.*[6]

ibid. page 367 *Nan.*[7]

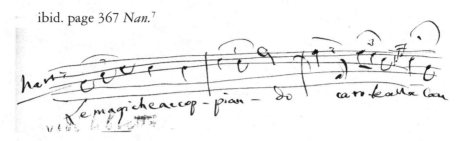

ibid. page 369 sixth bar at the cembalo F[8]

ibid. page 371 6th bar *Nannetta*[9]

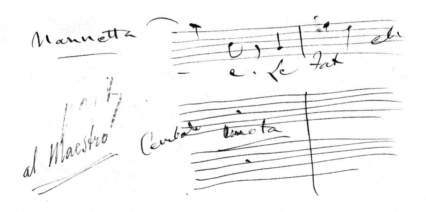

ibid. page 377 6th bar *Nan.*[10]

1892

ibid. page 389 2nd bar Chorus tenors[11]

ibid. page 429 7th and 8th bars Fals.[12]

ibid. page 432, 5th bar *Fals.*[13]

ibid. page 462, 1st bar *Meg* G instead of E^{14}

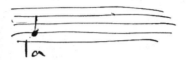

ibid. page 469 3rd bar Fen. ♯ to the F^{15}

Enough for now.
addio.

G. Verdi

NOTES

1. Postmark: GENOVA 14/11/92.
2. III.i (PV p. 311, 4/3). The two notes in the second bar are circled and questioned by the engraver. (See Ricordi to Verdi, 17 November.)
3. III.i (PV p. 329, 4/1).
4. III.ii (PV p. 341, 1/1).
5. III.ii (PV p. 342, 1/1).
6. III.ii (PV p. 345, 3/1).
7. III.ii (PV p. 355, 3/3).
8. III.ii (PV p. 354, 2/2).
9. III.ii (PV p. 359, 3/2).
10. III.ii (PV p. 365, 2/3).
11. III.ii (PV p. 377, 1/1).
12. III.ii (PV p. 416, 2/3).
13. III.ii (PV p. 419, 2/1).
14. III.ii (PV p. 449, 1/1).
15. III.ii (PV p. 456, 1/2).

1892

🏵 *Verdi to Ricordi*

Genoa, 16 November 1892

Dear Giulio,

May God grant that Sauchon free me from that nightmare, from that torment, from that infernal Bénoit affair!——

Pasqua wrote me[1] that she can reach those notes; so correct[2]

The accompaniment stays as is.

I am sending you by *registered mail* the little bundle containing the 3rd act Sonnet.—I changed a few harmonies in it: I added a few instruments and took out a few, etc., etc., etc., such as the accompaniment of the English horn to the words *unir chi lo disuna* [unite that which disunites it] . . .[3]

In a word, this whole passage must be examined bar by bar.[4]

Always *D C* on the word *don-na*, although at first I had written *C C*.—[5]

The sore throat hasn't left me, and so we have done very little work with the artists; I regret this, for Garbin is in great need of it; he has no experience and doesn't know a bit of the music! He doesn't know how to handle the final Fugue; you will tell me that since he has learned other roles, he will learn this one, too! But wait: almost all the operas written until now are orchestrated so that the violins, trumpets, and horns always go together with the voice; so he goes along, and with magnificent high notes he squeezes applause from audiences that are too kind. . But *Falstaff* is something else. The notes and syllables must be sung in a different way. Furthermore, he has that damned fault of opening the last vowels of the word . . . for example . . . in *la nota che non è più sola* [the note which is no longer alone] he doesn't put the accent on *sòl* but on the *a*. In this way he manages to deform and change the timbre of the voice. This is a most serious fault, which is hard to cure.—Enough . . . we shall see . . . but I am a bit worried.

This morning Boito settled down at *Pegli*, Villa *Roustan*.[6] A most beautiful site.

Ad [dio] ad[dio]
G. Verdi

P.S. You never told me anything more about Luigino Ricci?[7] Have you done something about this? Is there hope? I would be so glad to do this little favor.[8]

NOTES

1. In a missing answer to Verdi's letter of 7 November.

2. Quickly, in II.ii (PV p. 196, 1/1).

3. See Barblan, "Spunti rivelatori nella genesi del *Falstaff,*" pp. 18–21, and Hepokoski, pp. 46–48.

4. Quickly, in II.i (PV p.132, 2/3 and PV p. 139, 1/2). In III.i (PV p. 308, 1/3) the word *donna* is written under two eighth notes on *C*. PV p. 132, 2/3 and PV p. 139, 1/2 in II.i reflect Verdi's wishes. (See Ricordi to Verdi, 14 November.)

5. Quickly, in II.i (PV p. 143, 1/2). See Ricordi to Verdi, 14 November.

6. See Boito to Ricordi of 5 November.

7. Luigino Ricci (1852–1906), a composer of operas and operettas, was an illegitimate son of the Neapolitan composer and voice teacher Luigi Ricci (1805–59) and the singer Francesca Stolz, a sister of Teresa Stolz. Luigi Ricci was legally married to Ludmilla Stolz, another sister. With his brother Federico (1808–77), Luigi Ricci collaborated on four operas, including *Crispino e la comare,* which was performed as *Docteur Crispine* at the Metropolitan Opera in 1919. By himself, he wrote twenty-six operas, which were moderately successful. His adventurous life ended in an insane asylum in Prague.

8. Apparently at the suggestion of Teresa Stolz, Verdi tried to find work and to obtain Italian citizenship for her relatives Luigino Ricci and his son Rienzi, who were born Austrian citizens in Trieste. As such, Rienzi was subject to serving in the Austrian army.

1892

A few months later, however, the problem was solved. (See Verdi to Mascheroni, 10 August 1893, nn. 8 and 9.) Luigino became the heir of his celebrated aunt and died as Luigino Ricci-Stolz in Milan.

 *Ricordi to Verdi*

Milan, 17 November 1892

Illustrious Maestro,

I owe you an answer to your letter of the 15th,[1] but as much as I tried to write you yesterday, I was unable to do so.

As to your letter of the 16th—and in answer to both your letters—I am firmly bolting the door and sending all the more or less tiresome people to the devil!—

Well then: in the corrections you sent me in your 1st letter [14 November], I find a few about which I must ask for some explanations:

3rd act, page 21

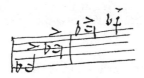

I am afraid you wrote the notes of the 1st bar in the violin clef, and the other two in the soprano clef, because those in the violin clef, that is, E flat and G flat,[2] go well with the chord underneath, but those in the soprano clef do not.—I think, therefore, that the correction to be made is definitely to put the 4 > that are actually missing, like this:

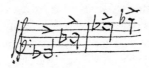

All right?

Splendid, your revision of the chords on the hours!![3] As beautiful as they were before, now they are really delightful, as natural and as new as they are!! Ah! . . . Verdi! Verdi! But let us go on:

Act 3, page 371, 6th bar

In the orchestra score there is a chord on the 1st quarter note; is it understood that it is deleted from all the instruments in the orchestra score as well as in the reduction?[4]

To your letter of yesterday [16 November]:

All right about the Quickly passage. I am putting it into the reductions and the parts, and am annotating it in the orchestra score.

All right, the *"Povera donna"* [Poor woman].

All right, the *"M'inchino"* [I bow].

I note what you write me about Garbin; just as I was reading your letter, Piontelli dropped by my office, telling me, among other things, that Garbin had written him, very happy to have seen the Maestro, but at the same time utterly mortified, as he knew so little of the music; so awestruck that he could not hit a single note. Therefore he wrote, being desperate and frightened that he didn't have the courage to insist on having his part at home, where he could study the notes by himself, without anyone else, just the notes; this way, the Maestro could better instruct him as to the dynamics and the expression he should give.—I didn't say a word, but thought I should write you as above. In fact, Garbin knows rather little about music; reading something new in a new style, and having his faults corrected . . . I understand why he loses his bearings! Therefore, if you will consider letting him study the music (alone, of course), you will have far less toil and trouble.

Have you found out about the bass Arimondi?. . . At the opening of the new Teatro Verdi at Carrara, just recently, he performed Sparafucile in *Rigoletto*. I have had excellent reports.

I have written at length to Souchon about the Bénoit affair; you can well imagine, Maestro, that I want, with all my heart, to succeed in arriving at a solution that, in the end, may rid you of so many troubles!!—

I have written to Boldini[5] that as soon as the subscription opens, I shall reserve the seats he wants.

1892

I have not forgotten about Maestro Ricci;[6] as soon as the occasion arose, I recommended him warmly to Mantua, where they want to give *Tannhäuser*. The trouble is his prolonged absence, which means he is little known; the management accepted Ricci right away, but the directors did not; they submitted the names of other conductors, one of them a good one. As late as yesterday, I was still insisting that Ricci is the Maestro who enjoys the greatest confidence of the House [of Ricordi].—

I haven't finished: See the enclosed little sheet;[7] the words *"Che avviene?"* [What's happened?] are missing for Alice. . . Do you wish to add them?. . . It would be better if you could . . . . . . leave them in the same bar with the syllable *cordia* . . If it isn't possible, never mind, we'll make a new plate.— I believe that's enough. With all my gratitude,

Your most devoted
Giulio Ricordi

Postscriptum!
There even is a postscriptum.
Have you thought about the translation, Maestro? . . . The law and international treaties impose time restrictions.—The translation of *Falstaff* will be difficult and long. Would you, in the meantime, see to one, the German one? . . . *Otello* was well translated,[8] and the same person could be engaged; even while, prudently, waiting to send him the material for the translation, I could find out whether he will accept the engagement, how much time he will need, etc., etc.,—and then act accordingly.

NOTES

1. Ricordi clearly refers to Verdi's letter of 14 November. Verdi did not write him on the 15th.
2. B flat, according to the above musical example.
3. See Verdi to Ricordi, 14 November, and Hepokoski, pp. 49–52.
4. Verdi to Ricordi, 14 November, n. 9.
5. See Verdi to Ricordi, 10 November, n. 8.
6. See Verdi to Ricordi, 16 November, nn. 5 and 6.
7. The enclosure, pertaining to II.ii (PV p. 229, 1/3), is missing. Verdi might have discarded it upon making the appropriate correction.
8. Verdi, though, had reservations. See his letter to Ricordi, 22 January 1888 (*Otello* i, pp. 336–7). Nevertheless, Max Kalbeck (1850–1921) wrote the first German translation of *Falstaff* (Ricordi plate no. 96370).

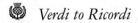 *Verdi to Ricordi*

Genoa, 17 November 1892

Dear Giulio,
    I have received the second act. Several days ago I sent the corrections for the first part, which have not yet been made.

Tomorrow I shall correct the second part, and I'll send it as soon as possible.—

I am writing to Boito that he should come to examine this second act with me.[1]

In haste addio.

G. Verdi

NOTE

1. No such message has been located, but Boito's frequent visits from nearby Pegli might explain the absence of written communication.

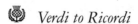 *Verdi to Ricordi*

Genoa, 18 November 1892

Dear Giulio,

The notes for Quik 3rd act go like this[1]

In the Nannetta scene the bar must be empty for all; the chord has already been heard in the last fourth of the preceding bar.

In the 2nd act *solo* of Quik: Just write, for the oboe also, the notes it does not have. They will say that I don't know the range of the instruments. So what![2]

Let's go ahead with Garbin, as you say. . . But watch out, we could find ourselves in big trouble in the end! He has come to me three times . . . no progress at all! Yesterday he didn't come! He doesn't feel well! He is singing here too much anyway . . . and they'll also make him do *La forza del destino*, a most demanding part!

I am sending you the *Che avviene?* [What's happened?][3]

They didn't speak well of Arimondi? . . I'm afraid he needs heavy parts, but in *Falstaff* he must run!

Thanks for Sauchon. . .

Thanks for Boldini. .

Thanks for Ricci, whom once again I warmly recommend.

Go ahead, then, with the German translation... But you know that I reserve the French translation for myself. . . . What can be arranged to guarantee your rights?. . The French translation could not be done unless *Falstaff* were to be performed, for example, at the Opéra-Comique!

Yesterday I sent you a part of the Sonnet with adjusted instrumentation.[4]

Today I will correct what you sent me, that is, the second act.—

Addio Your

G. Verdi

P.S. Just tell me: Instead of giving the artists the whole piano-vocal score, why not give them only the pieces in which they sing?

For instance: It's useless to give the music of the first scene of the 1st act to the four women, to *Ford* and *Fenton*, etc., etc., and to the others, too.—

Boito is here. Regarding *Re di Lahore*[5] I shall return [two illegible words].

NOTES

1. III.i (PV p. 311, 4/3). See Verdi to Ricordi, 14 November, n. 2.

2. See Hepokoski, "Pasqua," p. 249.

3. II.ii (PV p. 229, 1/3). See Ricordi to Verdi, 17 November, n. 7.

4. See Verdi to Ricordi, 16 November, n. 2.

5. *Le Roi de Lahore*, an opera in five acts by Jules Massenet (1842–1912), so impressed Ricordi at its Paris première in 1877 that he arranged for an Italian translation and productions in Italy, which significantly contributed to Massenet's international reputation. *Il Re di Lahore* was presented twenty times, Verdi's *Don Carlo* twenty-one times at La Scala in 1879. (See Irvine, *Massenet,* pp. 95–6, 103, 109–10.)

 Ricordi to Verdi

Milan, 19 November 1892

Illustrious Maestro,

In regard to your esteemed letter of yesterday, I proceed in order:

All right for Quickly's notes.

Ibid.—for the open Nannetta bar.

Ibid.—for the oboe.

Ibid.—for *Che avviene?*

As to what you wrote me about Garbin, I immediately called Piontelli, who told me that Garbin is engaged for 12 performances, of which he must have done at least 10. Therefore it seems impossible for him to sing *La forza del destino*, since he would have only 1 or 2 nights left before the end of his contract.—This would be a good thing, for if Garbin were free and could stay there 5, 6 or 7 more days, it would really be convenient for you to get a clear and precise idea. Piontelli, I believe, will go to Genoa on Monday, and will certainly talk with Garbin.

As to the translation, the German translator will be all right, and I thank you.—As I wrote you, to retain the property, the translation must be published within a certain period of time; this does not imply the obligation to perform it, as indeed was the case with *Otello*. Therefore, in preparing and publishing the French translation, too, you can always reserve the right of the 1st performance, just as in the case of *Otello*. With all these blasted complications of laws and international agreements, it is prudent, however, to prepare the various translations—French, English, German, Spanish— in order not to risk that the thieves, who already steal hand over fist, will do even worse! . . . . Therefore it is a good thing for you to see to the translations.

I have received the bundle containing the instrumentation of Fenton's Sonnet.—

So-called extracted parts are no longer made; whenever one was missing, there was confusion at rehearsals, and the artists, without the sequence of the pieces before their eyes, did not know where to come in. Therefore, these parts were abolished and are no longer made, except for very minor roles of a few bars. In the 1st part of the 1st act, many characters, of course, do not enter; but by not printing it we risk sending copies without it to Pistola, Bardolfo, etc., etc. If, in a special case, you think it useless to include the 1st part in the bundles we sent you, I would ask you patiently to delete the useless pages; they are not completely corrected, anyway, and it doesn't matter if they are of no further use.

Meanwhile, I am taking care of the German translation, and if you think it best, of the English one, too. In the meantime, give some thought about what to do with the French one; actually, I will tell you that Boito seemed to want to do it himself; has he never mentioned it to you?—No doubt the translators will have a tough nut to crack! . . . .

I think I have exhausted all that mattered today. I always fear that I annoy you with so many letters of mine obliging you to make so many replies.

With a most grateful heart,

Your devoted
Giulio Ricordi

1892

🌼 *Verdi to Ricordi*

Genoa, 20 November 1892

Dear Giulio,

I have received your letter of the 19th. Garbin will not do *La Forza del destino.* He can stay here, even when his performances are over; but the trouble is that, with my esteemed sore throat, I cannot show him the music as I would like. Garbin would need a good coach to teach him the notes and how to enunciate distinctly and *in tempo.*

He comes to me almost daily, and we do what little we can. If *Pini-Corsi* didn't have to sing in all the operas, he could work with him and teach him his part, as he knows how it must be sung. . . Pini is a fine musician, after all.—Here there is no one to be entrusted with this task. Garbin could come to Milan toward the end of the month, and there, instead of a *voice teacher*, a coach would have to be found to thoroughly teach him the *notes*, the *tempo*, and distinct and clear *enunciation*. Furthermore, he should not allow him to open the final vowels. *For example,* if he has to pronounce *"che gli risponde colla sua parolaaa"* the *a* is open to such an extent that the voice changes and appears to be someone else's. This is a most serious fault, above all in *Falstaff*, where many things are said without the support of flutes and clarinets. *Falstaff* is very difficult for the others, too, more so than I thought, and I scratch my head when I think of the *mumbling* of the men and women in the 1st act, in the finale of the second act, and in the final Fugue!!!!! . . . . !!!!

The French translation bothers me a lot! I regret having talked about it to Boito, because I don't want to distract him from his work!!—[1] But tell me—couldn't a quick and easy translation be made for the sole purpose of protecting the property? Then, if *Falstaff* is to be performed at the Opéra-Comique, make a good one with Boito and someone else, with my assistance? The case of two translations isn't new.—*20* or *30* years ago, *Rigoletto* was translated by Duprez and performed I don't remember in which theatre in Paris, then in the provinces. When it was to be given at the Opéra, the directors wrote me that Du Locle and Nuitter had made a new translation, which I could have used if I had wanted to.—Well then, well then, at a later date, an excellent translation could be made, but now, so fast, I think it makes no sense.—

When you send me the corrected edition you mentioned to me, I will return it to you at once; but in the meantime, I can't stand two little things that must be changed. For one of them, *alas!*, a new plate must be

made. (Did you receive the notes that come before the Sonnet?) Addio for
now.

G. Verdi

NOTE

 1. On *Nerone*. (See Giuseppina Verdi to Boito, 4 August; Verdi to Boito, 6 August; and
Boito to Verdi, 9 August.)

 *Ricordi to Verdi*

Milan, 21 November 1892

Illustrious Maestro,

 I am answering your esteemed letter of yesterday and confirming my
telegram[1] informing you of Signora Stehle's arrival in Genoa. You will
probably have seen her already, and I am anxious to know your impression
of her, which I hope and pray is excellent. Thus . . . . . the Palazzo Doria is
becoming a branch of La Scala, and my thoughts are there at all times.—
Toward the end of the month, the bass Arimondi finishes his engagements;
on his way to Milan he will pass through Genoa and could remain there 4
or 5 days. So you would see and hear him to decide if he suits you, and thus
another matter will be taken care of on time. Kindly tell me if this is all
right so that I may inform Arimondi, who, I hope, will make a good trio
with Paroli and Pelagalli-Rossetti. The idea concerning Pini-Corsi is excellent! . . . Shall I really tell him? It had occurred to me, too—also because
there are . . . . . no good coaches, unless you run into a rogue who brags about
knowing *Falstaff et similia!* Even though he sings frequently, I think that
Corsi will be very happy about such an assignment, all the more so because
I believe he has the best relationship with Garbin.—Thus you would save
yourself a bit of hard work, would fatigue your throat less, and in no time
regain your voice . . . . just like Tamagno!!—

 No doubt, the *mumbling,* the basket finale, and the fugue . . . are tough
nuts to crack; but on the other hand, everything is so obvious, so clear and
so bright that, once the difficulty of *memorization* has been overcome, I think
everything will run like clockwork, assuming the orchestra's able help.

 With reference to your comments about the French translation, permit me
some observations. I understand the very delicate, noble, most beautiful
feeling that is causing your uncertainty in regard to Boito; but it cannot be
difficult to reconcile matters without distracting Boito too much from other
work, when there is a person around in whom Boito would have absolute

faith. A provisional translation could be made, as you say, but it would turn out to be a piece of roguery; for if *Otello* was hard to translate for 10, *Falstaff* will require 100. Furthermore, all these laws and agreements supposedly protecting literary rights always make me quite afraid. Might not some rascal profit from various translations? ... And those dear Americans, could they not find a pretext by saying, "But the first one is different from the one being sung; so let's appropriate it!" .... Currently, in fact, I am preparing all the material to be submitted in America; one can sweat bullets making sure that all the formalities are observed! ... And that one makes no mistakes! .... For this reason, too, it is urgent that the reduction be printed and mailed in a few days in order that it be published at the right time.—Tomorrow I shall send you the corrected 2nd act; the sooner you can send it back to me, the better.— The printing of the 1st act has already begun; I suspended the 3rd because of the changes in the Sonnet, the proofs of which I will send you so that thereafter the work can continue at full speed. If a few plates of the 2nd act should then have to be remade .... don't worry; a couple of engravers can even work at night, and so no time will be lost.—I repeat that if a visit of mine down there should be useful to you, also to correct the proofs of the second act, don't let it worry you!—First of all, I would be very happy to see you, to wish Signora Peppina a good day, to receive your instructions, etc., etc.—but if it is not necessary, I will limit myself to greeting you from here, and remain always your devoted and grateful

Giulio Ricordi

NOTE

1. Missing.

 Verdi to Ricordi

Genoa, 21 November 1892

Dear Giulio,

Each time I must put my name on a *legal document* I get the shivers. But tell me! What do I have to do with all this business about old operas? And how is the income calculated?

Is my signature necessary? And tell me what the result of this *declaration* of mine is going to be?[1]

I am sending you the first bars of the Sonnet in the first part of the reduction.—[2] In about an hour the *Falstaffians* will arrive. If I have time, I'll write you later.

I have no more time; it is 5 o'clock. I ask only that you correct the first act on page 111: *Bardolfo* instead of *Barbaldo.* Ibid. page 115.

D. Cajo[3]

ibid. page 128[4]

NOTES

1. See Ricordi to Verdi, 25 November, and Verdi to Ricordi, 28 November.
2. See Verdi to Ricordi, 16 November, n. 3.
3. I.ii (PV p. 113, 1/2).
4. I.ii (PV p. 121, 2/1).

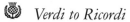 *Verdi to Ricordi*

Monday [Genoa, 21 November 1892][1]

Dear Giulio,

Who promised the part of Alice to Stehle?[2] Or at least led her to believe she would do that role? This is a bit of mess we could have done without.—

1892

Send me, as quickly as possible, the second part of the second act for Stehle. If it's upside down, never mind . . *but quickly.*

In haste addio

GV

Useless to tell you that Stehle was here and has gone over her part somewhat.

NOTES

1. Postmark: GENOVA 21/11/92.
2. She was engaged for Nannetta.

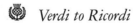 *Verdi to Ricordi*

Genoa, 23 November 1892

Dear Giulio,

I am returning your little sheets of music paper with the corrected notes.—

About Stehle nothing more needs to be said. She comes every day and is learning fast . . . but not so Garbin. He has a short part and no difficulty except in the grumbling ensembles and in the final Fugue. The finale of the basket is nothing for him. Enough, I don't know what to say. Tomorrow I hope to send you all the rest of the second act. . . . I sent the first part today.

Addio a[ddio]

GV

Many errors have been corrected. Many others are to be corrected.

I will send the second part soon.

 *Ricordi to Verdi*

Milan, 24 November 1892

Illustrious Maestro,

I am in receipt of your letter with the corrections and the bundle containing the corrected 1st part, 2nd act. I have marked the changes you indicated with pencil in the orchestra score; but since one of them calls for a chord change, I will not risk making a mark. I am transcribing the two bars[1] as they are and, below,[2] how they might be with your correction. Kindly examine and return them for the correction of the orchestra parts.

I am glad that nothing else need be said about Signora Stehle, and I hope that, thanks to your patience, Garbin is also coming along.

I inform you that the bass *Arimondi* will be in Genoa toward the end of this month.

Today I won't disturb you with a long epistle! . .

Always your devoted and grateful

Giulio Ricordi

NOTES

 1. On a missing separate sheet.
 2. Ibid.

 *Ricordi to Verdi*

Milan, 25 November 1892

Illustrious Maestro,

Do not be alarmed by the legal document[1] enclosed with this letter! Please sign your name on it (both copies) below the name of our firm, and sign your full name, that is: *Giuseppe Verdi*. You are ridding yourself of any nuisance, as had been agreed. At issue, again, are those contracts of your operas which were not registered, and which I think ought to be put in order; this is perhaps a necessary procedure, one which has tormented me for 2 years, not to mention the thousands of Lire already swallowed up by taxes, and additional Lire they are still trying to swallow! . . . Decidedly, the honor of being an Italian is a great burden, and I am thinking of becoming a Turk if it doesn't get any better . . . . even though the idea of a harem cannot be attractive at this time!—I beg you, then, to return to me the enclosed copies, signed, by registered mail, and forgive the disturbance.

While on this *diapason*, let me tell you that the famous Bénoit affair is still brewing, and that Souchon is applying himself diligently to it; unfortunately, we have to deal with an obstinate man, whose claims are enormous, since in addition to *Trouvère* he intends to take possession of *Traviata!!* . . . . and then? . . . It seems certain that Bénoit has bought Escudier's entire correspondence!! . . . and that he pretends it also contains compromising letters concerning *Traviata*. That is surely impossible!—I have used up rivers of ink with Souchon!—We'll see what concrete proposals he can obtain. I need not repeat that this business occupies and preoccupies me more than my own.—

I now close this regrettable subject and acknowledge receipt of your esteemed letter of yesterday containing some corrections, which I shall mark immediately.

I see that Signora Stehle is coming along all right, but to tell you the truth . . . . . I would have sent her to the devil after the foolish remarks she made concerning her part!!²—I still haven't swallowed them!!—

Boito will write me as you inform me, and I will see to what he tells me in his letter;³ everything is all right.

Another very important matter: Last night there was a long session at La Scala with Mascheroni, the directors, the management, the mayor, and the humble undersigned, in order to come to a definite agreement on the program. First I must tell you that, having seen the young mayor⁴ in the fire of his first theatrical session, I can give him 10 points for good conduct!— There were many difficult problems to be solved, and after 4 hours of discussion the program was established as follows:

Falstaff, of course, being of major concern, the rehearsals must start on the 2nd or 3rd of January; in accordance with the Maestro's wishes, the stage must be entirely free by the 15th.

The need to open with productions offering a guarantee of success⁵ [. . .] poster, then we go ahead as needed with *Colombo, Borgia,* and the ballet.

The management also noted that in the 3rd and 4th acts of *Colombo* it would like other artists to replace Paroli and Pini-Corsi, who, since they appear only in the Pilgrim scene of the 1st act, could also participate in the [*Falstaff*] rehearsals on the evenings when *Colombo* is performed.

This project was welcomed and completely favored by the directors, the management, and the mayor, who observed that the principal purpose was to organize the rehearsals in a way that fully satisfied the wishes of Maestro Verdi, leaving him complete freedom of action. He asked me expressly to inform you of everything.

And therefore I am writing you in detail, to fulfil the mayor's request as well as my duty.

The interpreters of *Rigoletto* would be *Stehle, Moretti,* and *Pessina,* a good group; and perhaps it will be a very useful opera to follow *Falstaff,* assuming (let's hope it won't happen!!) that some indisposition might prevent a performance of *Falstaff*.

I regret having to torment you with endless epistles!! . . . and in order not to go on too much longer, I tell you that I have also carried out Boito's instructions regarding the French translation.—I am sorry to read what you write me about your voice; but . . . . don't you tire yourself too often? . . . . I know that you do!! . . . .

Always your grateful and devoted

Giulio Ricordi

NOTES

1. See Verdi to Ricordi, 1st letter of 21 November.
2. See Verdi to Ricordi, 2nd letter of 21 November.
3. No such letter is known to exist.
4. Filippo Vigoni.
5. At this point Ricordi started writing on another page, which is missing.

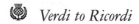 *Verdi to Ricordi*

Genoa, 25 November 1892

Dear Giulio,

Send the bass Arimondi here as soon as he is free. The sooner the better, since in early December I must hurry home and be back here again around the *8th* for Zilli.—If Arimondi could be here by the 2nd or 3rd at the latest, it would go well. I'll be finished with him in one day, because all I need to hear is the range of his voice and a simple phrase.—

And now to *Falstaff:*

I have seen Boito here; he will write you himself about the translation.[1]

In the bundle sent yesterday, 2nd act, page 129, the words in bar 13 are wrong[2]

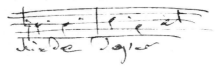

On page 139[3]

the fermata always on the syllable *Po*—and thus at all times.
Again on page 168 2nd bar: all the accents on the *A*.[4]

also in the orchestra.
page 182 *8th* bar[5]

Enough for today. I hope to send you the remainder of this act tomorrow evening.

Stehle and Garbin come here every day. We study, but make little progress; not because of Stehle, who is a good musician. It's true that my throat is still a little bad, so I can't shout as I am used to doing; and I can't accompany well without the finger which is still hurting me.——Oh, this damned convalescence!

Ad[dio] ad[dio]

G. Verdi

NOTES

1. Missing.
2. Bardolfo in II.i (PV p. 129, 3/3).
3. Quickly in II.i (PV p. 139, 1/2). See Verdi to Ricordi, 16 November, n. 4.
4. Ford in II.i (PV p. 168, 1/2).
5. Ibid. (PV p. 182, 4/1).

✿ *Verdi to Ricordi*

[Genoa, 25 November 1892][1]

If the *D* of the violins is not in the orchestra score, it's all right to add it. Thus:[2]

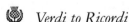

Also correct that *E in Falstaff's solo* . . . and further on, Ford's *quanti guai* [how many troubles][3]

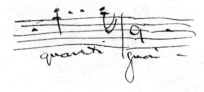

Agreed on Arimondi.

We study and make little progress, not because of Stehle but because of Garbin.

I hope to send you the corrected second act today.
  Ad[dio]

G. Verdi

I found another error on the page . . . where Falstaff says *L'astuzia mia crea l'astuzia degli altri* [My shrewdness creates the shrewdness of the others].[4]
All answer—*ma bravo* [Why, good for you].[5]
Nannetta must be omitted, however, since she is not onstage.
Will send 2nd act tomorrow.

NOTES

　　1. Postmark: GENOVA 25/11/92.
　　2. Unidentified.
　　3. II.i (PV p. 78, 1/1).
　　4. Verdi slightly misquotes Boito's text. (Cf. Boito to Verdi of 27 September.)
　　5. III.ii (PV p. 406, 2/1).

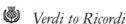

Verdi to Ricordi

Genoa, 27 November 1892

Dear Giulio,

I had no time to finish my letter yesterday,[1] so I am finishing it today.

Colombo, Borgia, Rigoletto. Too many irons in the fire! In the end, neither one nor the other will be done well; but I remind you once more:

1. . . . that *Falstaff* is far more difficult than is apparent from reading the score; and the difficulties will grow with the stage rehearsals.

2. . . . that Garbin is singing too much in the theatre here and has no time to study as he needs to. It was a mistake to allow him to sing in additional performances! He gets tired and doesn't study.—And if he doesn't bring himself to study the role? How are we to handle Maurel's performances? Think about that! . . I repeat again, do as you wish; but I again declare that, even if it means the end of the world, I will let no performance go on as long as the opera is not done my way.—

And something else:

An enormous, stupid, unforgivable oversight. A composer who does such things should be shot!

In the next to the last scene of the third act,[2] after Falstaff says, *Incomincio ad accorgermi/D'essere stato un somaro* [I begin to realize/That I was an ass], I have everybody shout *E un cervo, un bue e un mostro raro* [And a stag, an ox and a rare monster] . . without thinking that Nannetta, *Fenton, Bardolfo,* and *Cajo* are no longer onstage! . . . I have adjusted the solo and choral parts. The orchestra and piano [scores] both remain as they are.—I am sorry on account of the new plate that will have to be made! I repeat . . . *Shoot me!*

Send this score back to me as soon as you have put the parts in order and have made the corrections, since I don't have any other copy . . . and I would like to have this very one, with my own corrections.—

Addio addio

Today no one with me . . . Stehle left for Recoaro at noon; performs at night! Garbin came this very moment (1:30 P.M.), but was very hoarse and I sent him home.—

I received your telegram.[3] If Arimondi comes here at the end of the month, it's all right. I'll have time left to copy what is involved. Send him my address and let him come to me right away.—

Greetings   G. Verdi

P.S. Today I am sending the corrected third act by *registered* mail, with the variants mentioned above.[4]

NOTES

1. The day before.
2. III.ii.
3. Missing.
4. See Boito to Verdi, 27 September.

 Ricordi to Verdi

Milan, 28 November 1892

Illustrious Maestro,

I have received your esteemed letter of yesterday, and, having *shot you!!*, I inform you that I am noting all the corrections in the 3rd act; if I can manage, I will send them back today; otherwise tomorrow without fail.

In regard to the bass Arimondi, I sent a telegram confirming that he will be in Genoa the day after tomorrow, Wednesday; I am awaiting an answer.

As to the repertoire, we shall treasure your observations, but however it may be, you will be the absolute master, to let the performance take place when you judge it to be opportune; and I am not worried about the business of 20 performances, because it will be easy to plan them.

I don't understand why Garbin should be so busy and tired; the management here has not allowed him to sing more performances than those in his contract, nor to sing *La Forza del destino*. And I am quite alarmed by the news that he is making little progress . . . . . what a pity!

Permit me to make one suggestion: Don't you think that, in an absolutely confidential manner, you might let Moretti see the part and study it?. . He doesn't have Garbin's voice, but he is a musician, free and easy onstage. He has many faults, which can be remedied by making him study a new part the way it must be studied. Moretti will always be a good tenor for productions of *Falstaff;* no time will be wasted, and if needed he will be ready.—Is my idea stupid? . . . . Then drop it immediately; if it isn't, and if you think it is better to plan ahead, I'll think about the best way to keep a good reserve without jeopardizing anything.

I wish you a good trip to St. Agata and a safe return to Genoa, where in a few days Zilli will be headed—and Pasqua? . . . didn't she have to go there, too? . .

Lately, Maestro, I am having so many troubles that I am nauseated and don't know how I have the wits to write you; if I were assured of a mouthful for me and my family, oh! . . . how gladly I would retire to plant cabbage in the country!! . .

Forgive the outburst. As always,

Your most grateful and devoted
Giulio Ricordi

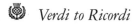 *Verdi to Ricordi*

Genoa, 28 November 1892

Dear Giulio,

Again today Garbin did not come, because he is indisposed.

They make him sing too much! His obligation to sing here until the 10th of December was a mistake, because he will have no time to learn his role in *Falstaff*.—After the 10th, or soon thereafter, he must go to Milan, and then I shall no longer study with him except at the ensemble rehearsals, and these rehearsals are not enough for him.—Watch out—

Another gross, enormous error, but of no great harm to the plates: At the end of the first part of the first act, Falstaff sings [notes] that don't fit the harmony——Adjust . . .—Page 43[1]

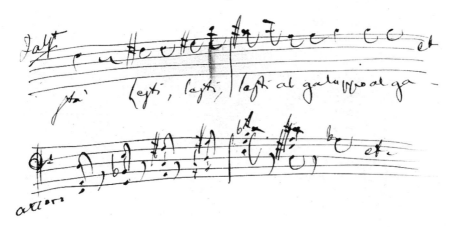

And so be it.

Monday [Genoa, 28 November 1892][2]

Correct if not yet corrected:
2nd act page 239, last bar
   Pianoforte[3]

and directly thereafter in the following bar, page 240[4]

In the little Duet, which comes a bit later on page 246, 2nd bar[5]

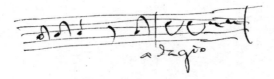

Further on same page, 8th bar
Pianoforte left hand[6]

Further on at the *Andante* page 253, 4th bar
   D. Cajus[7]

Further on, page 278
   Quickly[8]

Further on, page 285, I have adjusted a few notes for *Fenton*'s breathing
   Fen[9]

on page 289
   Nann:[10]

1892

Who knows how many other errors will crop up.
Meanwhile, addio.

GV

I sent the two papers *signed* and registered.[11]

NOTES

1. Falstaff in I.i (PV p. 45, 1/1).
2. Postmark: GENOVA 28/11/92. Continuation of above letter on the same date.
3. II.ii (PV p. 239, 3/4).
4. II.ii (PV p. 240, 1/1).
5. Nannetta in II.ii (PV p. 246, 1/1).
6. II.ii (PV p. 246, 2/4).
7. II.ii (PV p. 253, 2/1).
8. This and the following example (n. 9) do not appear in the PV, since the section involved was cut after the first performances in Milan. (See Verdi to Ricordi, 7, 8, 10, 11, 14, 16 March; 1, 5, 27 April; 23 May 1893; Ricordi to Verdi, 9, 11, 13, 15 March 1893.)
9. II.ii. See n. 8.
10. II.ii (PV p. 279, 1/1).
11. See Verdi to Ricordi, 21 November, and Ricordi to Verdi, 25 November.

Verdi to Ricordi

Tuesday [Genoa, 29 November 1892][1]

1st act, page 87 and [or?] 85, 6th bar
Pianoforte[2]

Ibid. page 83 and [or?] 4th bar[3]

1st act: In the Honor scene some notes must be adjusted for the sake of enunciation[4]

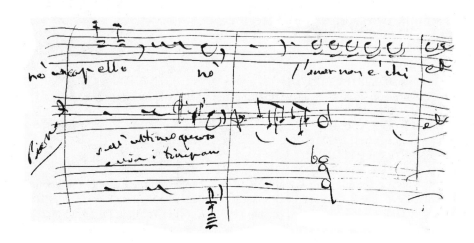

Further on, at the end of this passage, a bar is missing that can perhaps be added on the same plate. First, however, I would like to see Maurel. And when must he be in the city?

I know nothing about Pasqua! And this while she is obliged to be in the city?

Getting back to Garbin, it would be so good if he had no other obligations here, and if his engagement were over; but the fact is that he is singing all the time, and that he told me he is under contract with this management until the 11th of December; thus, if *La Forza del destino* doesn't go well tonight, he will sing again who knows how many times.

I will tell you nothing about your ideas. . .—I say only that Garbin's voice is good, but that I'm not sure he will learn the role. With such lack of experience, he should have been left free. By this time he ought to know the role, at least the notes! By going to Milan for the rehearsals of Colombo, he'll no longer learn a thing.

It's all right for Arimondi to come tomorrow; so at the end of the week I will go to St. Agata and will be back here the evening of the 7th or the 8th, awaiting Zilli.

Courage! . . And brace yourself well to face your many troubles! Who is causing them? Your associates?—Probably! There is nothing to say . . . but patience and courage!

Greetings and addio.

G. Verdi

1892

More !!!

1st act, page 67, 4th bar
Meg[5]

Final Fugue, page 98
Bardolfo[6]

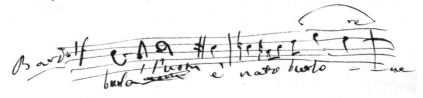

Ibid. page 105
Pist.[7]

It is true: I still haven't finished correcting the second act. But there are not too many mistakes.

NOTES

    1. Postmark: GENOVA 29/11/92.
    2. I.ii (PV p. 83, 2/3).
    3. I.ii (PV p. 79, 2/1).
    4. I.i (PV p. 40, 3/1).
    5. I.ii (PV p. 65, 2/1).
    6. III.ii (PV p. 427, 1/1).
    7. III.ii (PV p. 433, 1/2).

Ricordi to Verdi

Milan, 29 November 1892

Illustrious Maestro,

I acknowledge the corrections marked in your letter of yesterday. Kindly tell me:

Act 2, page 246—Pianoforte[1]

This is the correction. Must it also be made in the orchestra score for the clarinet?

Again

Yours gratefully,
Giulio Ricordi

NOTE

1. II.ii (PV p. 246, 2/4). See Verdi to Ricordi, 28 November.

Ricordi to Verdi

Milan, 30 November 1892

Illustrious Maestro,

In answer to your esteemed letter of yesterday: Have made the indicated corrections. And now . . . . excuse me for reminding you that I already wrote you that the printing of the 1st act had begun. Otherwise the edition cannot be ready for this country or arrive in time to be submitted in America.[1] Thanks to a fortunate coincidence, the corrections noted in your last letter arrived in time, since they were on two as yet unprinted sheets. The serious problem would now be the addition of that bar; could you await Maurel to decide on this matter? If you should add it, would you object to having the correction made in the reprinting of the edition? . . . The score will then have to be resubmitted in America to avoid the appearance of a change! . . but that is not so bad.—

The corrections for the third act are going very well, as it will not be printed before next week. Now we are awaiting the 2nd act with your corrections. Don't tell me: oh! . . what a bore!! What a bore!!—Unfortunately, the engraving, correcting, and printing of music are very lengthy operations!!—Books are another matter; one can even wait until the last moment, because they are printed very fast. Just send me to the devil, and even to hell, for I know I am tormenting you too much!!—

It seems to me, Maestro, that my idea of preparing Moretti did not meet with your approval. But . . . . if Garbin absolutely does not manage to learn his part in the appropriate time, what to do?. . . . I can ask Moretti to study it with a view to some production after La Scala, without hinting in the least at something else. But certainly I shall abide by whatever wishes you express.

I'll find out when Maurel must arrive, but I believe he has been called for the end of December; so has Pasqua. Actually, just today I saw Signor Giacomelli,[2] who came to Milan to secure lodgings for her. In a few days Pasqua leaves for Vienna, where she will sing the *Messa da requiem* of Giuseppe Verdi; that explains why she cannot come to Genoa. Signora Pasqua earnestly begs the Maestro to let her have her part during her absence; since she need not study anything else, she would have time to learn the whole role by heart; thus, in a couple of special rehearsals with you, she would be able to perform it in accordance with the Maestro's instructions. It goes without saying that she promises to let no one see the part. I think that an artist of her nature can be trusted; if you approve, then, I will hand over a corrected part to her.—Giacomelli also said that he regretted the delay, but wired the very moment he received the libretto. Signora Pasqua, after merely reading the libretto, is enthusiastic about Quickly's role—so, so happy.

I thank you, Maestro, for the good and kind words you have for me! They are inestimable, coming from such a Man!!—I am putting on the armor,[3] but it has been exposed to blows for so long that it is beginning to crack. Certainly, I do not spare myself in what little I am able to do; I have no regrets, and there is not a day or night that I have no work to do. But . . . . I am naive, and in modern life to be naive is to be asinine!—Certain arts I do not know, and I do not want to know them; and kowtowing to others is revolting to me. But is the world really made for the rascals? . . .

> "*Oh! che non ha a venire*   [Oh . . . may the day
> *Il giorno del giudizio? . .* "   Of judgment not come? . .]

says the great Beppe Giusti!![4]

Period

and not *a capo*, not having a Meg who flutters in my head.[5]

Again (and always!!!) a thousand thanks. Have a good trip to St. Agata.

Always your most devoted

Giulio Ricordi

Hohenstein is working. His costume sketches can be examined between the 15th and 20th of December.

NOTES

1. See Ricordi to Verdi of 10 and 21 November.

2. Pasqua's husband.

3. *La corazza dell'indifferenza* [The armor of indifference], as Verdi called this method of self-defense on various occasions. (See also Ricordi to Verdi, 6 November, n. 1.)

4. Ricordi repeats this quotation from his letter to Verdi of 5 June, n. 10.

5. Presumably Ricordi refers to Meg's line *Un flutto in tempesta / Gittò sulla rena . . .* [A wave in a storm / Cast on the beach . . .] in I.ii (PV p. 61, 1/3).

 Verdi to Henri Heugel

[In French]   Genoa, [?] November 1892

My dear M. Heugel,

Most flattered and honored by your request,[1] I infinitely regret being unable to reply as you wish.

Falstaff has been promised long ago, and for all countries, to my publisher, M. Ricordi.

There is no need to tell me that in your House I would have found all the security that can be desired; but I repeat again that I no longer possess the rights to my work.

Please accept my thanks and warm regards, dear M. Heugel, together with my regrets.

G. Verdi

NOTE

1. On 8 November the Parisian music publisher Henri Heugel (1844–1916) had expressed to Verdi his hope of publishing *Falstaff* in France and Belgium.

 Verdi to Ricordi

Genoa, 1 December 1892

Dear Giulio,

I have sent, by *registered mail,* the 1st act completely finished, even with the

1892

added bar in the *Honor* monologue.—In Milan I'll orchestrate it and correct the entire orchestra score. Therefore, these first editions corrected by me must be kept.—A reduction for piano must also be sent to me, because I gave one of the two that had been sent to me to Garbin, and the other to Pini-Corsi. The part for *Arimondi*, who came to me today, must also be sent to me.

Tomorrow I'll send the second act.

Garbin is engaged at the Politeama right up to the 10th. You are free to give the part to Moretti to study for another theatre. For La Scala, I myself gave the part to Garbin, and he must sing it, unless he is unable to learn the part.

You can give Pasqua her part as soon as Garbin, Corsi, and Maurel have theirs.

For the time being I'm not going to St. Agata, because the trip is rather hard with my usual sore throat.

Nothing else for today.

Addio ad.

G. Verdi

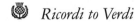 *Ricordi to Verdi*

Milan, 2 December 1892

Illustrious Maestro,

Took note of Falstaff's *Onore* [Honor][1] and immediately returned Act I to you; also, 2 copies of the 1st and 3rd acts, one for you, the other for Arimondi. You have the only copy of the 2nd act for the corrections; when we receive it, it will be returned to you at once. But . . . . . I must ask you a favor; and that is to send me the change you made in the 1st act instrumentation, which I will put into the original orchestra score; I need this change most urgently to correct the orchestra parts, since the 1st act of the orchestra parts is already completely engraved, and the new plates could not be made in time for your arrival.—Excuse the trouble I am causing you.

Again yours most gratefully,

Giulio Ricordi

NOTE

1. See Verdi to Ricordi, 29 November, n. 4.

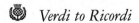 *Verdi to Ricordi*

[Genoa, 2 December 1892][1]

New discovery

2nd act Finale
  page 278   Nan.

in octave[2]

                                        Fent.

Further on page 280
Ford[3]

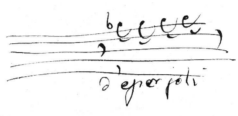

b to *C*.
  Sent this morning? 2nd act.

G. Verdi

NOTES

1. Postmark: GENOVA 2/12/92; not dated by Verdi. The postmark of this short letter was misread as 2/12/94 by Maffeo Zanon, who compiled Verdi's letters to the House of Ricordi. This particular one was unquestionably written in 1892.

2. Verdi refers to the proof of the original piano-vocal score. This passage in II.ii was part of the section he cut after the première in Milan. Therefore it does not exist in any subsequent scores (see Hepokoski, pp. 56–61).

3. Ibid.

🏵 *Verdi to Ricordi*

Genoa, *Monday* [5 December 1892][1]

Dear Giulio,

Received second act.[2] Correct again on page 194, eliminating the *G♯* in the first fourth; the ♯ must be added to the 4th quarter, like this[3]

1892

On page 256, first bar[4]

Do me the favor of sending me right away the second part of the second act for Arimondi . . . since he hardly knows the music and needs time to learn this little role. It's a loud voice, and he lets it roar without thinking; all his syllables are wrong, his voice completely lacks support, and for example, instead of an *a,* he pronounces an *i;* instead of an *e,* an *o,* and so on the other vowels, too. And then, he is the kind that cannot *sing the word* and the *note* in *tempo without the help of the orchestra??!!* It seems a joke!! But what pain! And what effort! And then, I don't know if in the end we shall succeed!—

Addio ad.   G. Verdi

NOTES

    1. Postmark: GENOVA 5/12/92.
    2. Corrected by Ricordi over the weekend. (See Verdi to Ricordi, 1 December; and Ricordi to Verdi, 2 December.)
    3. II.ii (PV p. 194, 1/1).
    4. II.ii (PV p. 256, 1/1).

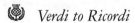 *Verdi to Ricordi*

Genoa, 7 December {1892}

Dear Giulio,

The program for La Scala is in the *Caffaro.*[1] That is bad from every point of view! Bad and offensive to me if it is for publicity!—

It is bad to announce the artists and to christen them *High Sopranos,* or *Dramatic* Soprano . . . that doesn't exist, etc., etc.—

It is bad to announce either a revival of *Tannhäuser* or *Falstaff* after the *Borgia.* No, no . . . either one or the other! Decide immediately, because neither must yield to the other.

It is bad, very bad to announce the première for *8 February.* Never, never! . . I don't want these anniversaries;[2] they are utter nonsense! The rest is bad, all is bad.

It would have been much better to have left Garbin free to study, in liberty; and I am not sure that he will learn to sing the role as I want.

It would also have been better for Pini-Corsi to sing less here. The other night, for his benefit, he added on to the *Forza* a little farce by Ponchielli, *Il parlatore eterno* [The Eternal Talker], in which, all alone, he continuously shouts himself hoarse and screams for three-quarters of an hour. Tonight another performance . . . what fun!

After all, I repeat, and you should take this very seriously: I am not sure that Garbin will manage to learn his role; that Arimondi will manage to learn his role, either, nor that Zilli, precisely because she is a dramatic artist, will manage to do well in her role, the most brilliant of all. . .

I am not at all sure of anything, nor am I tranquil. So much the more so because of so many indecisions that can only create trouble.

Addio ad.

G. Verdi

Greetings from Boito, who just arrived at 4 :30.[3]

NOTES

1. A newspaper in Genoa.

2. The 21st anniversary of the European première of *Aïda*, at La Scala, on 8 February 1872. Verdi had dreaded the jubilee commemorating the fiftieth anniversary of his first opera *Oberto, Conte di San Bonifacio*, which premiered at La Scala on 17 November 1839, ever since it had been planned. (See, e.g., in *Otello:* Verdi to Ricordi, 9 November 1888, 5 February 1889; Ricordi to Verdi, 8 February 1889; Verdi to Boito, 17 February 1889; Boito to Verdi, 20 February 1889; Verdi to Boito, 21 February 1889; Boito to Verdi, 7 March 1889. A number of Verdi's letters in that book express his growing distaste for public spectacle.)

3. In Boito's own handwriting on a separate sheet of paper.

🌐 *Verdi to Ricordi*

Thursday [Genoa, 8 December 1892][1]

3rd act, page 450, 2nd bar
Quik[2]

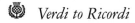

Received telegram.[3]

Still, there must be some truth to that article!

But let's forget about it . . . and be careful not to do foolish things in the future.—

1892

Now tell me if it would be a serious problem to change the engraving, that is, to transfer to *Ford*'s part what is now in *Falstaff*'s part, for only two bars? Like this, on page 459[4]

All this only to let the theme [of the fugue] stand out more clearly, etc.
  All right for Zilli.

On page 463, 2nd bar:
  Alice[5]

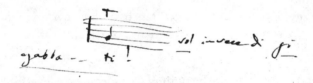

Another little mistake in the 1st act, page 121, 6th bar
  Alice[6]

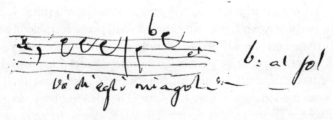

Garbin tells me that he is called to La Scala, I believe, for the 10th. Now that things are beginning to become clear, I would need a few more days [with him]. *All three* of them[7] would go to Milan the morning of the *12th*, leaving here at 9:00 o'clock on that day and arriving at twenty past one.
  Send me a telegram tomorrow morning giving me authorization.[8]
  Addio ad.

G. Verdi

NOTES

1. Postmark: GENOVA 8/12/92.
2. III.ii (PV p. 437, 1/2).
3. Following his complaint in the preceding letter to Ricordi, Verdi received this apology from the management of La Scala:

Milan, 8 December 1892

MANAGEMENT TEATRO SCALA REGRETS INCORRECT NEWS CAFFARO PAPER.

4. III.ii (PV p. 446, 1/2).
5. III.ii (PV p. 450, 1/2).
6. I.ii (PV p. 121, 2/2).
7. Presumably Garbin, Pini-Corsi, and Arimondi.
8. To delay, in the name of La Scala management, the three artists' arrival in Milan until 12 December.

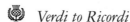 *Verdi to Ricordi*

Genoa, 9 December 1892

Dear Giulio,

I thought it better not to ask Franchetti for anything, so tomorrow Garbin and Arimondi will be in Milan; not Corsi, I think, because he is indisposed!

Too bad! Now that they are beginning to understand a few things, they are going away; and so what has been done is lost! Garbin, especially, who also has so much to do with a new number in *Colombo*, will forget everything I have taught him. I hope that *Pini-Corsi* may soon come to Milan, as I would like Garbin to stay with him; and for the management, whether or not obliged, to send him a little pianoforte to make Garbin study. I spoke about this, in passing, with Corsi, who agreed with great zeal; having been quite useful to me here, he will lend a helping hand in Milan, too. You, my dear Giulio, appear not to be persuaded by the doubts I expressed to you in another letter; but watch out, this is nothing to joke about at all, not at all.

It is not a good idea to give *Rigoletto!* The idea to give *Colombo* first, and then *Lucrezia* [Borgia], was better. The night of the *Lucrezia* performance, my singers were free; not so with *Rigoletto* . . .

After all, things are limping a bit and not going as I would like. We may find ourselves in serious trouble later on.—

Addio for now.

Your
G. Verdi

1892

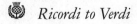 *Verdi to Giacomo Persico*

Genoa, 9 December 1892

Esteemed Mr. President,

I had actually hoped to drop in at St. Agata,[1] but I had no time, and even now I don't know precisely when I will be able to do so.

Meanwhile I am glad that the friction between nun and doctor is over. You have done very well in asking for explanations. Crisp and clear matters always produce good results. The doctor, from what you said to me yourself, is not the man we wanted. It seems that these blessed doctors want to pose for us as great minds, while lacking the talent and the self-confidence to tolerate those who do not think as they do; and these great minds do not know that tolerance is a great, maybe the greatest, virtue.

What is wrong with the nuns being attached—maybe a bit too much— to religion? And furthermore, what right do the others have to disapprove? These censors do not realize that their disapproval is not the fruit of liberty but of tyranny and, worse yet, of childishness.

Furthermore, these nuns are disciplined; they are sweet, gentle, full of charity for the sick... Just imagine, Mr. President, if instead of the nuns we had some of our servants or peasants at the Hospital, without breeding, ignorant, gossipy, dirty, etc., etc. God help us! The poor Hospital and, even more, the poor sick!!

Well then, dear Mr. President, bear all this nuisance with patience, and with your tact you will succeed in applying the brake and straightening out the confused heads. You will be worthy of the poor folk and have the gratitude of your

G. Verdi

NOTE

1. See Verdi to Ricordi, 1 December.

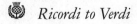 *Ricordi to Verdi*

Milan, 10 December 1892

Illustrious Maestro,

I owe you answers to several letters! ... But .... in the midst of having a discharge of bile,[1] it was literally impossible for me to answer you immediately, as I was most anxious to do.—As I wired you yesterday,[2] the management would have been most happy to allow the artists, who have nothing to study for *Colombo*, to remain in Genoa; for not even Garbin has any new number; only the 4th act finale was changed, precisely as you suggested, and ends with Columbus's arrest. In addition to that, a few cuts were made, and nothing else! . . Whether even these will be kept [is questionable], since when dealing with a madman like Franchetti, no one ever knows what he wants. Therefore the management is not running the risk of letting the artists be absent, realizing with whom it is dealing! [. . .]

Franchetti is now crazier than ever. . . and I say crazy so as not to say anything worse; but since my goal, as well as the management's and Mascheroni's, is to make things go smoothly, smoothly, we are letting him get away with all the insanities he wants, just so we go ahead with the rehearsals and ensure the opening of the season!! . . . I assure you that I am exercising my patience in a unique way, because many times I have come close to telling Franchetti that he and his *Cristoforo* should go to the devil!! . . . But I haven't done it . . . . . . always having the enormous *Falstaff* before my eyes!! . . . . and, therefore, the need to avoid any obstacle or perhaps even a scandal. And so we all are working toward that goal.

The ballet is well along. No artist engaged for *Colombo* is singing in *Rigoletto*. You do not much approve the choice of *Rigoletto;* but as I wrote you, another opera had to be ready to be given along with the ballet—and this opera should in all probability be a success. This was not the case with the *Borgia,* in the absence of a bass! [. . .] Assuming the good success of the ballet, there is no need for frequent performances of *Colombo*, and so you can finish coaching the artists. All of this has been discussed, evaluated, and studied with the mayor, with Mascheroni and the management, expressly to lay the groundwork for the *Falstaff* rehearsals, and to have the theatre completely free at the right time.

As to the poster, rest assured that all the news, even that given in the Milan press, is the product of fantasy!! Nobody knows a thing; artists have been mentioned who are *not even engaged at La Scala!* Furthermore, apart from the fact that the management will sign nothing without consulting me, the little poster which is to be distributed is printed at our own press, and thus the manuscript was given to me 6 days ago!!—Imagine how, reading the news in the *Caffaro*, I could not help laughing about the usual journalistic nonsense.[3]

What I really regret are the two lost days in Genoa, which you had considered so very useful!! Moreover, I really regret the patience you had to muster to shape so much raw material!! However, you foresaw these problems. . . . but they may have exceeded your expectations!! . . . It does not surprise me! Who knows music nowadays?. . .Who knows how to sing?. . . Who knows how to phrase?. . . Who knows how to enunciate?. . .

But let's leave the comments aside and get on with practical matters, and thus with the way to organize everything regarding the "Potbelly"!

The management wired Zilli its consent for the 12th. You can keep this artist as long as you wish, even until the end of the month, because she has nothing else to study or to sing.

You told me that, if necessary, you would sometimes reverse Nannetta's and Alice's parts. How did you like Stehle? . . . She came to see me most content and happy with her part. So this matter, too, is under control.

The management is also at your disposal to send you Guerrini. You told me you had no need of her, her part not being among the more important ones. But won't she lose the time for learning the music, while almost all the others will already know something? . . . . The garden scene, the basket scene, the final fugue are also difficult for Meg! . . . . I would appreciate hearing your decision.

The 2 tenors, Paroli and Pelagalli-Rossetti, I can take care of with Mascheroni; just so they at least know the music and the words, so that when you come, you need not start all over again from *b-a, ba*!

Pini-Corsi will get the piano. He and Arimondi have very little to do in *Colombo;* Garbin has what he had.[4] With a bit of goodwill they can always find a couple of hours per day to study, since the *Colombo* rehearsals and performances at the Politeama certainly won't tire them!

By the way, if I had imagined that Ponchielli's farce[5] was intended for Pini-Corsi, I certainly would not have sent it!!. . But no one thought of it, and by request of the management it was sent. But also Pini-Corsi, what need did he have to shout himself hoarse? . . . They're all alike, these singers, to make money on those odd, really stupid nights!! *Honor?* . . . Maybe Falstaff is right.

For the German translation I got Max Kalbeck, the one who translated *Otello* quite well;[6] he is one of the best German poets.

I am negotiating, too, for the English translation, also with one of the foremost poets[7]—foremost also in financial demands, since he aimed for an absolutely incredible sum! . . . I'll see if I can bring him down to a still respectable, but reasonable amount!! . . . .

The 1st act is in print; but I arrived in time for Alice's B flat. The 2 plates of the final fugue are being remade; then the printing of the 3rd act will start.

Fervet opus! [The work is brewing] . . . . . and my only ardent wish is that everything may go smoothly and securely. You tell me that I do not share your doubts!!! . . . Why not? . . . For the sole reason that the Great Sorcerer is involved . . . who draws blood even from turnips!!—If I had no remorse when I consider the patience you have already exerted, and will have to exert, Maestro, I would have nothing to worry about.

I left you alone for 3 days! . . . But today I bombarded you with an endless tirade.

Be kind enough to answer me about the important points I have mentioned to you.

With devoted, affectionate greetings, I remain

Your most grateful
Giulio Ricordi

NOTES

1. It is unclear whether Ricordi refers to a physical or an emotional situation.
2. This telegram is missing.
3. See Verdi to Ricordi, 7 December, n. 1, and Verdi to Ricordi, 8 December, n. 3.
4. The same role in *Cristoforo Colombo* he had before.
5. See Verdi to Ricordi, 7 December.
6. See Ricordi to Verdi, 17 November, n. 8.
7. Unknown. The first English translation (plate no. 96342) was by W. Beatty Kingston.

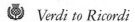 *Verdi to Ricordi*

Genoa, 11 December 1892

Dear Giulio,

To your letter of the 10th: I am glad to hear that Garbin has no new pieces and need not tire himself, since he still has a lot of work to do for *Falstaff*.

Pini-Corsi, it seems, will give him a room with a pianoforte in his house. Pini will make him study. This way we can manage. And you, my dear Giulio, will see to it that this arrangement works out. I have no doubts about Pini, who gave me his word that he would take care of it. Remind him of this promise.—As to Arimondi . . . . he'll be all right. He has a big voice, but uncertain rhythm . . . ! *But who knows music these days?*

You tell me: *Who can sing?*

I would be content this time if they knew how to enunciate. But let's forget these miseries and hope above all that *Pini-Corsi* will succeed with *Garbin*.

2nd. All right for the 2 tenors. To tell the truth, you could do the same with Guerrini. It is not true that the [2nd act] finale is difficult. It is exhausting only for *Pini-Corsi*, but never fear for him. Yes, the final Fugue is difficult, but less so than they think; more difficult is the *a capella* quartet in the 1st act.—

So do as you please about Guerrini. If you send her, all right; if you don't send her, it's all right, too.—

Pini-Corsi has again sung the *Parlatore eterno* for two more nights, because the management said it would give him, in fact has given him, a few more pennies. He was worn out, but now he is well. I saw him yesterday. He sings *Forza* tonight and will depart for Milan at 3:00 A.M.——

Everything else is all right.

And now, if there is still time to make a little correction: In the second act finale something calls for another shooting![1]—

Attention!! It's not because I have qualms about the two octaves, but because the bass isn't nice!

If you can, correct 2nd act, page 257 this way[2]

Then, too, Bardolfo's note would have to be adjusted like this[3]

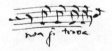

There might also be some different seating for the orchestra.

Addio ad.

G. Verdi

If Zilli comes tonight, we shall begin to *study right away* in the morning.

Just received letter from Berlin—they're also doing the *Mass* there![4] They really want me![5]

NOTES

1. See Verdi to Ricordi, 27 November.
2. II.ii (PV p. 263, 1/1).
3. Ibid.
4. The German composer and conductor Friedrich Gernsheim (1839–1916) had sent Verdi the following letter in French (*Carteggi* iv, pp. 34–5):

Berlin, 7 December 1892

Illustrious Maestro,

Permit me to send you the program of the last concert of the *Stern* Choral Society, whose director I have the honor to be; we had the great artistic joy of performing your immortal *Requiem*, which had not been heard in Berlin for a number of years. This masterful, so deeply inspired work made the most profound impression upon the large audience; and I cannot refrain from personally expressing my boundless admiration, illustrious Maestro, for this work. It is and will forever remain one of the greatest revelations of a genius such as yours. The chorus, the orchestra, the soloists were all carried away by the beauty of your music and have done their best to perform it in the most dignified way possible.

Allow me, illustrious Maestro, to thank you, also in the name of my friends Max Bruch [German composer and conductor, 1838–1920] and Moritz Moszkowski [Polish pianist and composer, 1854–1925], for having given the world of music this incomparable work, and be assured of the profoundest veneration of

Your most devoted
Prof. Fr. Gernsheim

5. Verdi seems not to have forgotten Giulio Ricordi's failure to include Berlin in the 1875 tour of the *Requiem*. (*Aida,* pp. 375, 383.) Bülow's letter to Verdi of 7 April may have contributed to the revival of the *Requiem* in the German capital.

🏵 *Verdi to Ricordi*

Monday [Genoa, 12 December 1892][1]

Dear Giulio,

I just this moment received the piece of music for Alice.

As I suppose you are still correcting plates, I mention on page 122, 5th bar[2]

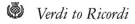

1892

On page 367, third act, 5th bar adjust the words . . . like this[3]

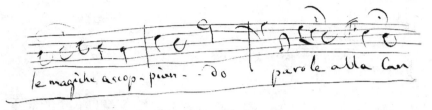

On page 59[4]

I have gone over the first act with Zilli. I can't say anything, because she hardly dared to sing out.

'Til tomorrow.

No need to reply.

G. Verdi

NOTES

1. Date derived from contents of this letter.
2. I.ii (PV p. 122, 2/2).
3. Nannetta in III.ii (PV p. 355, 3/1). Verdi writes "Le magiche accoppiando *parole* alla Canzon." The PV score says "carole."
4. Alice in I.ii (PV p. 59, 1/1).

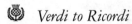 *Verdi to Ricordi*

Genoa, 13 December 1892

Dear Giulio,

A few days ago I sent you a little sheet with some corrections that had not been made, as I see from the three copies of the 1st and 3rd acts just received.—

1st act, on page 87 or 83

Cembalo[1]

Ibid. page 72[2]

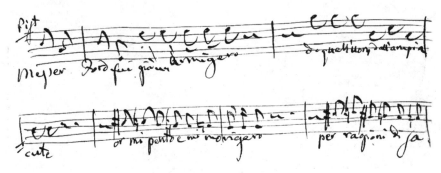

Now on to others—my fault:
1st act, page *15*

Cajus[3]

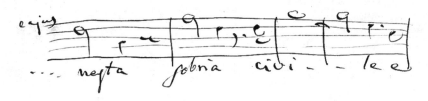

1st act, page 27
Fals.[4]

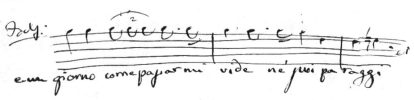

1st act, page 29, 2nd bar: Cembalo left hand: the ♯ is missing on the F[5]

1892

1st act, page 59 or 61
Alice[6]

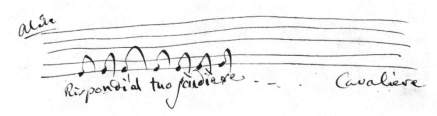

1st act, page 69. In the part of *Cajus*, *sia* instead of *è* must be put in *all three times*[7]

1st act, page 82 and [or?] 84, correct the words
Ford, seeing Alice[8]

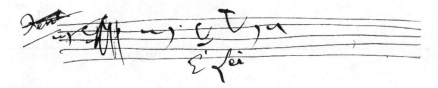

And that's enough for today, and I greet you—addio.

G. Verdi

I can't get rid of my sore throat . . and can't explain myself to the artists.—5 or 6 days ago I sent the libretto and those four bars to *Pasqua!* No answer at all!

Looking over the third act, I saw that in wanting to adjust the first harmonies of Fenton's Sonnet, I made it worse than before.[9] Do me the favor of sending me yet another little sheet with the first two verses in the orchestra score:

Dal labbro il canto estasiato vola   [From the lips the song flies in ecstasy
Pei silenzi notturni e va lontano   Through the nocturnal silences,
                                      and goes far]

Another correction page 412[10]

NOTES

   1. I.ii (PV p. 83, 2/2).
   2. I.ii (PV p. 70, 1/2).
   3. I.i (PV p. 15, 3/3).
   4. I.i (PV p. 27, 3/2).
   5. I.i (PV p. 29, 2/2).
   6. I.ii (PV p. 59, 1/1).
   7. I.ii (PV p. 69, 1/2). *"All three times"* seems to refer to the orchestra score, piano-vocal score, and the vocal part.
   8. I.ii (PV p. 82, 1/3).
   9. See Verdi to Ricordi, 16 and 21 November.
   10. III.ii (PV p. 399, 3/1).

 *Ricordi to Verdi*

[Telegram]   Milan, 13 December 1892

MASCHERONI TAKING CHARGE OF GUERRINI PAROLI PELAGALLI—THEY WILL BASICALLY KNOW PARTS WHEN YOU COME TO INSTRUCT INTERPRETATION AS YOU WISH—WE HAVE MADE PROGRAM FIRST PERFORMANCE SO THAT MONDAY TWO JANUARY AND ALSO WEDNESDAY FOUR ENTIRELY FREE MORNING NIGHT AT YOUR DISPOSAL—PLEASE WRITE ME IF ALL RIGHT—CORDIAL GREETINGS

GIULIO

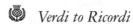 *Verdi to Ricordi*

Genoa, 14 December 1892

Dear Giulio,

   With the new program, I understand, the theatre will not be free right after the first of the year, as had been agreed.

I shall arrive on the second, and never mind an ensemble rehearsal on the third. I can ask Maurel and Pasqua to come to my place[1] to go over their parts with me; and afterwards, when everything is arranged so that my rehearsals will not be interrupted, we can begin with *Falstaff*.

Also see to it that the bass Arimondi, who always sings his notes with great uncertainty, rehearses with Paroli, Guerrini, and the other tenor. Let me remind you that Paroli must do the role of *Dr. Cajus*.—

Still two minor errors: on page 331 Nannetta, not Alice, must say the words *e canterò parole armoniose* [and I shall sing harmonious words][2]—

On page 341, 8th bar Pianoforte[3]

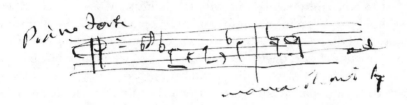

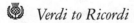

Addio for now.

G. Verdi

NOTES

    1. Verdi's suite at the Grand Hôtel et de Milan.
    2. III.i (PV p. 320, 4/2).
    3. III.ii. Verdi writes "the ♮ is missing on the E."

Verdi to Ricordi

Genoa, 16 December 1892

Dear Giulio,

Today I sent you the first act, which I now believe to be most accurate.—

Inter nos: You had been told and assured of a good, very good second bassoonist, who was in America a short while ago, and is now here, but he has not been engaged at La Scala.

I repeat again, to avoid friction, that I shall not endure bad players when good ones can be had. In haste

G. Verdi

Answer me regarding everything I have written.

🏵 *Ricordi to Verdi*

Milan, 19 December 1892

Illustrious Maestro,

At last, at last! . . . today I am writing you . . . . by lamplight, not because it is late . . but because it is early morning, and if I go to that (truly infernal) hell of the office, I shall not have a moment of peace! You cannot believe, Maestro, how far the troubles and worse—ugh, have gone . . . . I really couldn't take it anymore if it weren't for . . . . . the one who you know is the star of my thoughts. *Laboremus,* then!

At La Scala, the pot is boiling with much fire, so we are well ahead with everything; the supreme goal is to have the first productions go well, in order not to spoil the *Falstaff* rehearsals with some catastrophe. Taking one of your observations to heart, the *Borgia* was cancelled, so we will not bite off more than we can chew. *Colombo*, I think, will have a good success; *Rigoletto* should have no less; the only unknown quantity is the ballet, which can be judged only at the dress rehearsal! Let us hope it will go well. And so the season will be on its way; many performances must be given right away, since the carnival season is rather short; having delivered a certain number of performances, all the dark nights you consider necessary can be arranged. Mascheroni has already started with Paroli; the day after tomorrow with Rossetti, then Guerrini and Arimondi; they will know their music and words when you come. I am enclosing a schedule for you, subject to change in case of unforeseen circumstances! . . As you see, 10 performances would be given within a few days; we also hope to replace Stehle immediately in *Rigoletto* and Guerrini in *Colombo;* with the cuts that were made, her part is now much reduced.— Bearing in mind what you wrote me, Mascheroni will continue to rehearse with the others, while you take Pasqua and Maurel, who must be around for the 1st. I sent Pasqua her part a few days ago. If you so desire, Maestro, you can assemble the whole company on the morning and evening of the 4th.

Our program is planned until the 8th. When you come to Milan, you may give Mascheroni your instructions to establish the definite rehearsal schedule; if necessary, 4 dark nights can be arranged per week.

To plan ahead, I think we shall need:

— A grand piano for you at the Hôtel.

— A small upright piano in the little rehearsal room for whatever you will want to rehearse.

— A good grand piano in the rehearsal room, since the one belonging to the theatre is mediocre.

1892

Since *Borgia* is not being done, you will have two maestros at your disposal: Mascheroni and Nepoti.[1] Please tell me if this is all right, because I would reserve the pianos immediately so as not to get stuck with some old guitar!—

Apart from the usual business, I also have the rehearsal schedule for *Colombo!!* I would gladly have managed without wearing myself out at the stage rehearsals, but I was anxious for the first production to go as well as possible; I swallowed the pill and put aside my disgust, only to find myself under contract with that very odd Franchetti! Oh! . . what a madman, what a madman!! I will tell you about it some time.

Hohenstein will soon finish the costume sketches, which we shall submit for your approval.

I asked the mayor himself to take an interest in the sets, not trusting my own recommendations; this matter is so very close to his heart that he went personally to the painters. I am even enclosing his letter.[2]

I am very glad about what you write me regarding Zilli; she wrote me, too, that she is trying her best to satisfy the Maestro, who, she says, is so kind that she feels she is having the most beautiful dream of her life! She is happy with the part. The same goes for Stehle, Garbin, Pini-Corsi, and Arimondi!! . . . But where has that certain *Bear*[3] gone!! What do you say? . . . . . I think I hear myself answer: Wait, everyone!! . . he will leap forth.— But I hope there will be no reason for this to happen. You will find everybody not only at your command, but literally at your feet!—At this time, everybody in the theatre is already in a state, and I have my hands full keeping things smooth and serene—*Falstaff, Verdi, Verdi, Falstaff* . . . . . are the order of the day.

I have also noted the names of various female and male choristers who at the rehearsals seemed to be the best in voice and intelligence. Thus, little by little, definite decisions will be made regarding *Falstaff*—. The orchestra seems good to me; the woodwinds much, much improved—I like the trombones less, will hear them again. Do not worry about the bassoons: there are 3 excellent ones, and for this reason Silva,[4] who is also excellent, was not engaged; but there are no operas with 4 bassoons.—The second violins incomparably better than in former years. Magnini[5] has marked the cellos and basses. De Angelis[6] has already handed out the 1st and 3rd acts, which were done with great accuracy; in a few days he will give me the 2nd.

I think I have emptied the whole bag of news.

And as everybody is in a state, so . . . . . am I, too, thinking that the day you will be among us is not far off!! The blessed day!! Evviva! Evviva!! . . .

I await your reply about the pianos.

Devoted and affectionate greetings to Signora Peppina and to you from the always most grateful

Giulio Ricordi

Garbin has made an excellent impression at the rehearsals [of *Cristoforo Colombo*].

NOTES

1. Unknown, unless he was the Lodovico Nepoti who appeared in the tenor role of Carlo Körner in Franchetti's *Germania* under Toscanini at the Metropolitan Opera in 1910.
2. Filippo Vigoni to Ricordi

> City of Milan
> Office of the Mayor   12 December 1892
> Most worthy Friend,
>   *Falstaff* is so close to my heart, as is . . . my friend Giulio Ricordi, that I wanted to run immediately to the theatre to obtain precise information. I am glad to tell you that this time the Devil may not be as evil as you think. Work on the *Falstaff* sets had to be suspended for a few days, since the sets for *Rigoletto* needed to be finished in a hurry. Of the five [*Falstaff* sets], however, one is complete; a second one is partly painted, a third one already designed; and with this [information], Zuccarelli promised me that by the 15th of January he will be ready without fail.
>   Let us hope he will keep his promise. Anyway, in a few days I shall make a fresh attempt [to ensure timely completion of the *Falstaff* sets].
>   With a handshake
>
> Filippo Vigoni

The scenic designer and painter Giovanni Zuccarelli (1846–97) executed Adolf Hohenstein's designs for the first production of *Falstaff*. He also designed and painted sets in Cairo, Brescia, and Milan, including the sets for *Don Carlo* at La Scala in 1884 and for La Scala's revival of *Otello* in 1889.
3. See Verdi to Ricordi, 13 June, n. 7.
4. See Verdi to Ricordi, 16 December.
5. Unknown.
6. Unknown.

 *Verdi to Ricordi*

Genoa, 21 December 1892

Dear Giulio,

Oh yes . . . just wait . . . the *Bear* will leap forth . . who knows against whom! Perhaps against the Divos!!!

Zilli will leave tomorrow. She knows her role by heart, one can say. She has a *fierce will* to study and learn. If in the theatre she has a *smattering of knowledge* to hurl in the face of the learned . . . and famous! . . . she will be successful.

I imagine Garbin at an orchestra rehearsal! But these successes[1] are fatal! He certainly has a good attitude, but doesn't know a thing, and will also know little later on, because he doesn't have Zilli's *fierce will*.—When he can skip a rehearsal, he is completely happy. . .—On the last day of his stay down here, he led me to believe that Franchetti had added a large duet for him! A stupid lie . . . to make me let him off sooner! You may as well know that he knows very little of his role; and therefore I ask you to call upon Pini to make him study and become at least sure of the notes. . . A great deal more is needed for the rest, and I worry about the Sonnet; not because the piece is very important to me, since *à la rigeur* one could also, from a dramatic point of view, do without it; but because this passage adds a new color to the musical composition, and rounds out Fenton's character.—

Your program is all right; but if instead of *Rigoletto*, which will be neither warm nor cold, you had planned another opera, the result would have been the same, and there would have been the advantage of leaving Stehle free.

Substituting Guerrini in *Colombo* is unimportant. With that *poitrine* [bust] she won't tire herself singing very short roles.

The pianos are all right. Only I won't be able to play them very often, since the little finger of my left hand still hurts. I regret this, because by playing it's easier to explain myself as to the coloring, and to repeat when the singers are wrong. Also have a little well-tuned upright piano, to which I will keep the key, put in the little hall. This little piano will then serve for the stage rehearsals. For myself at the hotel I want an upright piano. I'll write you which day it must be delivered.—

I shall probably arrive on the second (I don't know the hour yet), and on the third I might have a partial rehearsal with Pasqua and Maurel; one at a time. On the *4th,* rehearsal with all.

Speaking of the orchestra, you tell me nothing about the horns, which in *Falstaff* have a lot to do . . ugh—ugh.

Addio ad. Merry Christmas
G. Verdi

I am keeping here the second act of Zilli's part for corrections. Do me the favor of giving her a copy of this second act.

NOTE

1. At *Cristoforo Colombo* rehearsals. (See Ricordi to Verdi, 19 December.)

🌼 *Verdi to Ricordi*

Genoa, 22 December 1892

Dear Giulio,

Further, to my letter of yesterday . . Make sure that the pianos are fairly bright, since for the rehearsals they are better than those which have a rounder sound. . . If possible, the *little piano* and *mine* at the hotel should have a good keyboard. . I have a hard time playing with my left hand. I play with three fingers! What fun! . . What fun to get old. . . And that's enough for today.—Addio, add.

G. Verdi

🌼 *Verdi to Ricordi*

Genoa, 23 December 1892

Dear Giulio,

I am also sending you the second act of *Falstaff.* Thus you will have the whole opera, but without the hope of the corrections being complete.

You will find a few little errors, and two minor changes: one for the metronome markings, the other in Ford's part in the Finale.

The worst of it is that there are still two minor errors in the last act.

On page 85 it is *Meg* who must say *Ford è geloso?* [Ford is jealous].

On page 112

Quik[1]

In the unaccompanied quartet of the *wives,* Nannetta will have the highest part . . . but for this we'll have time at the first rehearsals.

I am confirming my letter of yesterday.

And make Garbin study!!   Enough for now.

Addio—happy holidays to you and your entire family at home and away from home. I say the same in Peppina's name.

Your   G. Verdi

1892

NOTE

1. I.ii (PV p. 65, 2/2). Verdi's correction is not reflected in the PV.

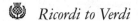 *Ricordi to Verdi*

Milan, 24 December 1892

Illustrious Maestro,

A very merry and most joyous *Christmas* to you and Signora Peppina—and infinite thanks for your kind and dear wishes.

I received the 2nd act with corrections and handed over a [copy of the] 2nd act to Signora Zilli, who isn't just in 7th heaven, but is at least in 14th.

I have secured the 3 pianos, choosing the most suitable ones. The horns are good, the 1st one very good. In a couple of days I will also have a low A flat horn, and I will have to find a good player to get used to playing it.

Until now everything at La Scala has proceeded without a hitch; I pray that it may continue like this, and that the schedule will not be disturbed.

I am counting the days that must still go by until your arrival . . . and it seems as if they will never pass! But in the meantime, I can at least finish with *Till we see you soon!* . . .

Always your most grateful

Giulio Ricordi

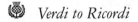 *Verdi to Ricordi*

[Genoa][1] 25 December 1892

Again ? °!!!

1st act, page 109, Ford[2]

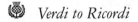

Again on page 117[4]

In the third act on the 9th little sheet, Quik (page 31)[5]

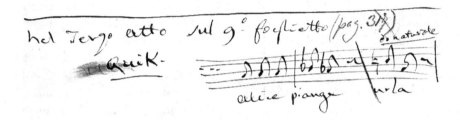

Ibid. second part, page 11 (page 355)
Left hand[6]

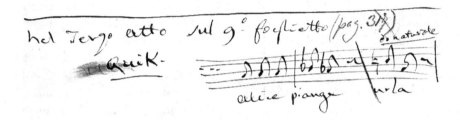

And that's enough for today.
'Til tomorrow perhaps!   GV

NOTES

1. Postmark: GENOVA 25/12/92.
2. "Page 109" in the engraver's handwriting.
3. I.ii (PV p. 109, 1/1).
4. I.ii (PV p. 115, 1/1). This is not reflected in the PV.
5. III.i (PV p. 307, 3/2). In the 2nd bar above the word *ur-la* Verdi writes "C natural."
Above these words, "page 314 [or 307]" appears in the engraver's handwriting. The slashes
across the staffs are also the engraver's.
6. III.ii (PV p. 343, 3/1); "page 355 [or 335]" appears in the engraver's handwriting.

1892

🌲 *Verdi to Maria Waldmann*

Genoa, 25 December 1892

Dear Maria,

It's true! I was sorry not to have seen a letter from you in such a long time; and I am remorseful, too, never having given a sign of life.

The excuse of having been very, very busy wouldn't be valid, unless you, as kind as you are, didn't have great indulgence.

And you, poor Maria, have been tormented by great misfortunes at home! I felt the deepest regret for you. Now I am glad to hear that your husband's illness is over, and that he is now in full convalescence. I hope soon to have news of his complete recovery.

As I already told you, I have been and am very busy. After the first of the year, we'll go to Milan, and my labors will become greater with the *Falstaff* rehearsals, which will begin right away. [. . .]

🌲 *Verdi to Ricordi*

Genoa, 26 December 1892

Dear Giulio,

I am fiercely furious, frenzied, fuming with you!!!![1]

Just this minute I received the panettone!!!![2] Oh! and why? Why?! Why?!

We must come to Milan in a few days, and, without disturbing anyone, you should have brought me a panettonino of about 1/2 kilo. Nothing more! We would have been happier! This way we aren't at all. . . . And moreover, it is my duty to thank you!!!

Calmati anima mia . . . (says the poet) . . .[3] But let's settle these things. When—not this time, but in the future—we come to Milan, you will, for your punishment, bring us a little panettone of about 1/2 kilo.—That will do; otherwise you'll make me flare up again. It is true that with age I have become quiet, patient, good, and calm. . . Let it be said that I haven't become unquiet *even once* with the singers of *Falstaff*. This doesn't mean that, as an exception, I won't again have some moments of fury, and of an obstinate fury, worse than at other times.—Watch out! Watch out! Watch out!!

In spite of everything, I wish you health and happiness. Write me or wire tomorrow morning tonight's outcome . . about Garbin above all.[4]

Your
G. Verdi

NOTES

1. Perhaps intentional Wagnerian alliteration in the Italian text: "Sono fieramente furioso, furente, furibondo con voi!!!!"

2. A Milanese pastry, Ricordi's annual Christmas gift to the Verdis.

3. Unknown.

4. Alberto Franchetti's *Cristoforo Colombo* was presented on the traditional opening night of La Scala's season with Garbin in the role of Guevara.

 *Ricordi to Verdi*

[Telegram] Milan, 27 December 1892

SEASON BEGAN WELL — OPERA AROUSED PLEASURE AND INTEREST — VARIOUS POINTS ACCLAIMED — ALL ARTISTS GOOD — ALTHOUGH EMOTIONAL AND SANG BETTER DRESS REHEARSAL GARBIN CONQUERED SYMPATHY ENTIRE AUDIENCE THROUGH VOICE AND APPEARANCE — TODAY POTBELLY IS STUDIED THROUGH AND THROUGH — THANKS FOR MOST DEAR LETTER CORDIAL AFFECTIONATE GREETINGS SEE YOU SOON

GIULIO

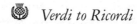 *Verdi to Ricordi*

Genoa, 27 December 1892

Dear Giulio,

Good good good!!

Good for the House [of Ricordi], for him [Franchetti], for the theatre . . . and also for me . . . I'll be able to rehearse with greater calm.—

Today, then, it's *Potbelly* through and through? For better or for worse?— It will be good if you limit yourself to the actual execution of the notes, for I would not want them to forget the corrections and suggestions made here regarding the syllables, accents, breathing, etc., and fall back into their old habits. Let this be said *inter nos* with no offense to anyone.—

Very good, however, is the study you are planning for *Meg*, for *Cajus*, for *Bardolfo*, and above all for *Arimondi*, whose attacks are always uncertain, and who enunciates so poorly that oftentimes an *e* becomes an *a* or an *o*, etc., etc.

Garbin must study only the final Fugue and the *mumbling* [ensemble] of the men in the first act.

And then? . . . Who knows!—

1892

I don't remember whether I sent you the correction of a badly executed bar, which is out of place. It would have been a *modern trait* in which, with almost 80 years on my shoulders, I cannot and must not believe.[1]

Correct, therefore, 2nd act page 236, 4th bar

Ford[2]

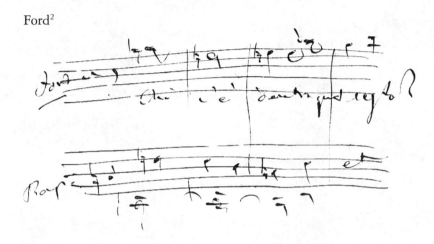

Addio

G. Verdi

NOTES

 1. Presumably an unpleasant dissonance.
 2. II.ii (PV p. 236, 2/1).

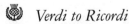 *Verdi to Ricordi*

Genoa, 31 December 1892

Dear Giulio,

 Happy New Year!

 We shall arrive Monday[1] (Boito will be with us) at *7:26* in the evening to have time before *10* to plan, etc., etc.

 Spatz has already been advised, and if on Monday, after your lunch, you pass by the Hotel Milano, ask if my apartment is ready; and if it is, have the piano brought up during the day.

 Don't mention the time of our arrival to anyone, so I can have a little peace at first, and also settle many things with you. And be sure not to come to the station. Wait for me at the hotel. We shall plan for *Maurel,* for *Pasqua* and for the rest.—

Maurel wired me from Paris that he is leaving for Milan tonight. We'll see each other in Milan.—Addio for now.

G. Verdi

NOTE

1. 2 January 1893.

 *Giuseppina Verdi to G. De Sanctis*

Genoa, 31 December 1892

[. . .] We are packing our trunks to leave on Monday for Milan, where Verdi will give his *Falstaff* at La Scala. [. . .]

1893

A real outburst of grace, power, and gaiety.[1]

On 2 January the Verdis travel with Boito from Genoa to Milan, where the rehearsals for *Falstaff*, under the Maestro's supervision, begin on the 4th. The première, conducted by Mascheroni, is hailed at La Scala on 9 February, but a certain passage in the second-act finale gives the composer no rest.[2] On 2 March the Verdis return to Genoa. On the 21st, on his way to St. Agata, Verdi attends the eighteenth *Falstaff* performance at La Scala. After four performances of the complete La Scala production at Genoa's Teatro Carlo Felice between 6 and 11 April, Verdi and Giuseppina leave with Boito for Rome on the 13th. La Scala's production—this time with a Roman orchestra—is enthusiastically applauded at the capital's Teatro Costanzi on 15 April. King Umberto I and Queen Margherita[3] invite Verdi to share the royal box at the theatre. Obviously relaxed after the exertions of recent months, the Maestro and his wife are accompanied by Boito on their return to Genoa on 20 April. On 6 May the Verdis are again at St. Agata, from where Verdi follows the events of the *Falstaff* tour under Mascheroni,[4] comments on Ricordi's reports about other productions, and reads the reviews. On 23 May he sends Ricordi "the last notes of *Falstaff*."[5] Four days later St. Agata is hit by a severe storm.

Verdi is anxious to pay off the Bénoit suit, which has been lost in Paris. His *Falstaff* royalties help to pay for the forfeiture of his old *Trouvère* royalties and the attorneys' fees. Meanwhile he comes to the assistance of the librettist for *Aida,* Antonio Ghislanzoni, who is on his deathbed. Farfarello, as the young, exuberant Mascheroni was nicknamed,[6] has problems during the tour, is consoled by the Maestro, and receives his fatherly advice.[7] The

Verdis plan to be in Milan by 24 June and arrive in Montecatini on 3 July. They return to St. Agata on the 20th for a continued period of relative tranquillity. Between early and mid-August Verdi has business in Genoa. Mascheroni conducts a brilliant *Falstaff* production in Brescia after the tour and comes for advice to St. Agata on 1 September. Boito arrives there on the 9th with the French *Falstaff* translation, and leaves again on the 14th. Congratulations from King Umberto and from all over the world are brought to Verdi at St. Agata on 9 October, his eightieth birthday, while he tends to his farm and peace reigns in the Villanova Hospital. On 1 November Boito answers his inquiry regarding costs for future occupants of the Casa di Riposo under construction. The Verdis again visit the site between mid-November and 2 December, on their customary journey to Genoa, which is delayed by an inconsiderate landlord.[8]

Falstaff rehearsals and performances at La Scala occupy Ricordi for months, while his concern about the première of Puccini's *Manon Lescaut* at Turin's Teatro Regio, one week before the *Falstaff* première at La Scala, is never mentioned in his letters to Verdi. Complicated preparations, meanwhile, for a *Falstaff* tour with La Scala's company require particular sensitivity and logistics regarding the Roman orchestra. In a mammoth letter of 4 April Ricordi pulls out all the stops to convince "Italy's most honored man" to go with his *Falstaff* to Rome. The Maestro's relentless wishes for further changes in the score add to Ricordi's pressures. Pasqua's illness and cancellation of her tour performances after Rome, plans for a *Falstaff* production in Brescia in August, plus the everyday direction of his expanding firm, demand all the fortitude the fragile man is able to muster. Verdi's own pessimism, reflected in his encouraging lines of 4 August, can scarcely have helped. Ill and overworked, Ricordi cannot accept Verdi's invitation for a short rest at St. Agata. Plans for new *Falstaff* productions and casts concern both men in September and October. In early November Ricordi is in Paris for discussions regarding the French *Falstaff* at the Opéra-Comique and *Othello,* also in French, at the Opéra in 1894.

After an intense period of close collaboration with Verdi at the time of the *Falstaff* rehearsals and performances in Milan, Genoa, and Rome, Boito returns to Milan on 26 April. On 13 June, along with Max Bruch, Tchaikovsky, and Saint-Saëns, he receives an honorary doctor's degree at Cambridge University. In the summer he works with Paul Solanges[9] in Milan on the French translation of *Falstaff*. He submits it to Verdi and goes over it with him at St. Agata from 9 until 14 September. On 12 November he witnesses the unsuccessful première, at the Teatro Dal Verme, of the opera *Signa* by Sir Frederic H. Cowen.[10] The unpleasant episode which ensues enrages him to the point of actual violence, worrying and upsetting

1893

his friends. Boito spends Christmas with the Verdis in Genoa. For New Year's Day he is back in Milan, where he receives a letter from Duse, the only one on record for 1893.

NOTES

1. Boito to Bellaigue, 16 February.

2. Verdi to Ricordi, 7 March, n. 1.

3. Margherita di Savoia (1851–1926), a highly motivated patron of arts and letters, was loved and respected in the difficult years following Italy's Risorgimento. Upon the King's assassination on 29 July 1900, she wrote a prayer for him, which Verdi unsuccessfully attempted to set to music.

4. After four performances at the Teatro Costanzi between 15 and 25 April, and one on 22 April at the Teatro Argentina in Rome, the complete Scala company—except for Pasqua, who because of illness had to forego the entire remainder of the tour—gave four performances in Venice (2–7 May) and four in Trieste (11–16 May). Two performances in Vienna (21–22 May) and four in Berlin (between 1 and 6 June) were presented with local orchestras. Pasqua was replaced by Guerrini and, in Berlin, Maurel by Blanchard.

5. Verdi to Ricordi, 23 May, n. 1.

6. Perhaps by Boito, after a little devil in Dante's *Inferno* (XXI 123, XXII 94–95), who also appears in Carlo Gozzi's (1720–1806) and Sergei Prokofiev's (1891–1953) *Love of Three Oranges*. See also Verdi to Ricordi, 15 March, n. 4. In William Weaver's English' libretto, *Farfarelli* is translated as "little butterflies."

7. Verdi to Mascheroni, 8 June.

8. See Verdi to De Amicis, 29 November.

9. French cavalry officer (1846–1914) who moved to Milan in 1873 and became a journalist and translator. He collaborated on the French versions of *Mefistofele, La Gioconda, Falstaff, Cavalleria rusticana,* and many Italian songs.

10. See Ricordi to Verdi, 14 December, n. 1.

🌼 *Verdi to Ricordi*

[Undated]

This, I think, would be the fair and convenient thing to do for the soon-to-be-born *Falstaff*:

1. The poet would sell the libretto to the composer to use for the music of the score and for the edition in print. The sum is to be established by mutual consent between poet and composer, etc., etc., according to the [illegible].

2. Except for the preceding, the libretto would always remain the property of the poet, who could [however] never prevent performances of the score or the sale of the edition; but he would always maintain the right to have his libretto printed.

3. Pay a sum for *rental fees* in these proportions: If the libretto is of his own

creation, establish 20% for him; if taken from a drama, comedy, or tragedy already existing, 10%.

> In the actual case of *Falstaff*
> As to paragraph   1: I have already paid a sum to Boito.
> As to paragraph   2: The poet, retaining the rights to the libretto, can sell it to the publisher, have it printed, etc., etc., etc.
> As to paragraph   3: . . . The right to rental fees, etc. —
> As to foreign countries, concerning France: *Droits d'auteur* are established by law: Half to the composer, half to the creator of the libretto, except for special arrangements ———
> For the other countries conforming to the current practices, which are for *rental* fees, more or less the same as with us.
> Examine this proposal; talk it over with Boito as far as it concerns him.— We'll settle later among ourselves. ———

 Ricordi to Verdi

Milan, Sunday [January 1893]

Illustrious Maestro,

I have to take care of two or three urgent matters and cannot allow myself the pleasure of coming over to say good morning to you before the rehearsal, as I am going to the theatre at 11:30. I am sending someone to find out whether you have instructions for me.[1]

NOTE

1. The remainder of these lines is missing.

 Ricordi to Verdi[1]

Milan, 28 January 1893

Illustrious Maestro,

Half an hour late and frozen like ice cream, here I am back again. After having taken care of a lot of very urgent business, I will come to you and hope to find you completely well. Meanwhile, not to lose time, I wrote the enclosed;[2] if it is all right, you only have to close it and hand it to the bearer for delivery.

Cordial greetings to you and Signora Peppina.

Most gratefully your
Giulio Ricordi

1893

NOTES

   1. At the Grand Hôtel et de Milan.
   2. Missing.

 Verdi to Ricordi

> Hôtel Milan
> Milan, 28 January 1893
> 10 A.M.

After receiving the enclosed letter from the management of La Scala,[1] I cancel this morning's rehearsal.

Inform Maestro Mascheroni at once.

Later on we'll think about what to do.

> G. Verdi

NOTE

   1. Missing.

 Verdi to Ricordi

> Wednesday [Milan, January–February 1893][1]

Dear Giulio,

Boldini, I repeat, has told me that he needs a single seat, but that he is prepared to pay for two,—

I, too, need only a single seat, but since I had ordered six, the other five will also, in this case, be charged to me.

Have the photographic portraits for the orchestra charged to my account.—

I left the score with the annotations,[2] etc., etc., in the theatre, but I don't know where. Have them look for it right away.—

For the *mise-en-scène* let's not find fault with everything. Now we must let matters run their course and not become embroiled in observations. I ask only for a bit of light in *Garbin*'s Sonnet.

And if possible, find a way for the Chorus of the Fairies not to look so much like *Vestals*—so they appeared to me.

However, this is also of no great importance.

> Your
> GV

NOTES

1. The contents of this letter suggest the final phase of rehearsals.

2. Apparently the galley proof of the first *Falstaff* piano-vocal score (PN 96000), in which Verdi noted his comments and corrections during the rehearsals for the première at La Scala. Verdi gave it to Mascheroni, who donated it to the Milan Conservatory in 1923. After World War II, Guglielmo Barblan discovered this unique score in the ruins of the Conservatory. (See Barblan, *Un prezioso spartito del Falstaff*.)

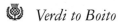 *Verdi to Boito*

[Milan, January–February 1893?][1]

If you can, come this evening at 6 to eat soup with us. Possibly a few minutes earlier for a little Falstaffian conversation.

NOTE

1. Verdi might have sent Boito this undated message at the time of rehearsals for the première of *Falstaff*. The Grand Hôtel et de Milan, where Verdi stayed while in Milan, and where he died, is only a short walk from Boito's home in Via Principe Amedeo 1.

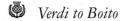 *Verdi to Boito*

Hôtel Milan—Monday
[Milan, January–February 1893?][1]

Dear Boito,

I have read, reread, and studied . . . the *Potbelly basket*.[2]

I have some doubts which I shall confess to you if, leaving your home after 4, you can come to me . . . and also stay here afterwards from six to seven, etc.

G. Verdi

NOTES

1. These lines, like the preceding ones, were obviously written during the preparation for the *Falstaff* première.

2. This episode in the finale of Act II was to preoccupy Verdi for quite some time.

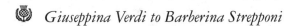 *Giuseppina Verdi to Barberina Strepponi*

[Milan, early February 1893]
[. . .] It is incredible, the work that Verdi has done and is still doing and will

do after the first performance of *Falstaff*, which, if illness or other obstacles don't intervene, will open, God willing, next week!

Add the infinite number of letters and requests of all kinds, which, in the midst of this mixture of unremitting physical and mental effort, come to besiege him and oppress him, and you will have an idea of Verdi's life during these days.

Tiresome people, admirers, friends and enemies—those who pretend to be real musicians—, true critics, backbiting gossips will flock from all parts of the world! Demands for seats continue as if the theatre were as big as a parade ground! I went to a rehearsal for the first time last night, and judging with my head, and on first impression, it appears to be a new genre, even the beginning of a whole new art of music and poetry! [. . .]

 Camille Bellaigue to Verdi

[In French]   [Paris] 3 February 1893
Dear and great Maestro,

We greatly regret that we are unable to attend your *Falstaff*, and I must tell you this: If we were not on the verge of becoming parents, my wife and I would have enjoyed seeing and hearing you.

It will be for your next masterwork. This time we think of you from afar, often rereading *Otello,* which does not age and always moves us. God be with you and give you success—and remind you that by sending a score with your signature to your humble and fervent admirer, you would somewhat soften these regrets.

Please remember me to Madame Verdi, and give an affectionate greeting to Boito, from whom I also await the *signed* libretto. For you, dear and great Maestro, all my respect, my admiration and friendship, which you have also bestowed upon me. [. . .]

 Journalists to Verdi

[In French]

Milan, 4 February 1893
Continental Hôtel Milan

Most illustrious Maestro,

The performance of *Falstaff* is an artistic event of interest to all of Europe, and Paris in particular, where the genius of the author of *La Traviata, Aida* and *Otello* is observed by an admiring public.

Thus the papers which we serve as critics have entrusted to us the task of judging your new work at its first performance. For this reason we have come to Milan.

As you know, dear and honored Maestro, the large Paris newspapers publish the reviews of new works the morning after their première. This practice has become an undeniable condition for their publication.

You do not, however, authorize anyone to attend an ensemble rehearsal,[1] and we have been informed that there will be no dress rehearsal.

This decision, the legitimate reasons for which we can perfectly appreciate, puts us in a most difficult situation. It forces us to judge an important work, worthy of all our intellectual endeavor, in haste, without sufficient reflection and meditation; furthermore, it betrays the legitimate hope of the papers that sent us to Milan in honor of this great artistic event.

Therefore, we earnestly beg you, most illustrious Maestro, to kindly rescind your decision for us, and to allow us to write our reviews conscientiously, in the interest of your work as well as of our own [. . .].

Should you not want to make an exception, we would then ask you to *ignore* our presence in the auditorium at one of the final rehearsals; we would attend discreetly, without being seen, and without in any way disturbing the work of the artists and the orchestra.

Please accept, most illustrious Maestro, the expression of our profound respect.

Henry Bauer (*Écho de Paris*)[2]
Charles Darcours (*Figaro*)[3]
Léon Kerst (*Petit Journal*)[4]
Alfred Bruneau (*Gil-Blas*)[5]

NOTES

1. *Une répétition d'ensemble* probably suggests a run-through or first dress rehearsal.

2. Henry Bauer (1851–1915), liberal journalist and critic. He was opposed to the Empire and was deported, but he returned to France in 1880. Bauer defended the *Théâtre libre* and left an autobiography, *Mémoires d'un jeune homme* (Paris, 1895).

3. Unknown.

4. A music critic also for *La Presse*. He wrote about the management of the Paris Opéra, and published a brochure entitled *L'Opéra et M. Halanzier* (Paris, 1877).

5. See Verdi to Boito, 5 July 1891, n. 1.

1893

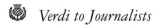 *Verdi to Journalists*

[In French]

Milan, 5 February 1893

Gentlemen![1]

I profoundly regret having to tell you that the customs and regulations of La Scala allow no one to attend rehearsals.

This is a rule of which I have always approved and which, above all, I could not rescind.

I am truly sorry and beg you, gentlemen, to kindly accept my regrets and apologies!

I am, with sincere regards,

Yours truly,
G. Verdi

NOTE

1. Verdi addressed this collective reply to Henry Bauer (*Écho de Paris*).

 Verdi to Camille Bellaigue

[In French]

Milan, 9 February 1893

My dear Monsieur Bellaigue,

I was very happy to receive your letter,[1] but at the same time I regret that you are not here tonight. Perhaps you are better off.

Tonight, then, *Falstaff!*[2]

I don't know if I have found the merry note, the right and, above all, the *sincere* note. Alas! Nowadays very beautiful things are done in music, and in certain areas (if one doesn't go too far) there is real progress . . . . . but, in general, people are not sincere and always do as their neighbors do![3] . . . .

But let's not talk politics! Tomorrow or very soon you will receive the score and the libretto.

I thank you for my wife, grateful for your kindly remembering her.

Clasping both your hands with all possible esteem and sincerest friendship,

G. Verdi

NOTES

1. Of 3 February.

2. See the original program below. As was customary at that time, the program does not list a stage director; Mascheroni and Ricordi acted as Verdi's assistants in this regard. Ricordi voices his honest opinion about the cast in a letter he wrote to Puccini on 12 October 1895:

> [. . .] Who talks to me about *Falstaff?* There was only one real artist in it, Maurel; all the others were almost mediocrities—including the diva Pasqua . . . including Pini-Corsi, who had a good voice but was a singer like a dozen others, and a trivial, second-rate actor. These and even that selfsame Maurel were *very bad* in their first interpretations.— It was the benison of our patient Verdi which gave them blood day by day, hour by hour, teaching them to pronounce the words, teaching them the sense of the words, all with that extraordinary patience which finally succeeded in obtaining a performance which was vivacious, lively, and persuasive.

George R. Marek, the translator of this letter, adds this comment:

> Ricordi's remarks on the première of *Falstaff* strike me as particularly significant. This performance, and similar historic performances, are now regarded in the light of retrospective sentimentality. We talk of the great singers of Verdi's time, we speak of Maurel as the supreme interpreter of Falstaff, we pay tribute to Tamagno as the one and only Otello. Yet when we read the accounts of reliable ear- and eye-witnesses—and I am convinced that Ricordi was a reliable witness—we begin to have doubts as to the infallibility of the stars of the golden age of opera. [. . .] When we read a letter such as this from Ricordi, [. . .] we realize anew that we must be careful not to let sentiment of the past run away with the present [. . .]. Marek, *Puccini*, pp. 156–7.

3. Cf. Verdi to Maurel, 21 April 1890.

 King Umberto I to Verdi

[Telegram]   Rome, 9 February 1893

UNABLE TO ATTEND FIRST PERFORMANCE OF FALSTAFF THE QUEEN AND I ANTICIPATE WITH BEST WISHES AND OUR FEELINGS OF ADMIRATION THE APPLAUSE WHICH WILL SOON WELCOME THE NEW MANIFESTATION OF AN INEXHAUSTIBLE GENIUS — MAY YOU REMAIN FOR MANY YEARS TO THE HONOR OF ART, IN OUR AFFECTION AND IN THE GRATITUDE OF ITALY WHICH EVEN IN SADDEST DAYS RECEIVED PATRIOTIC INSPIRATION FROM YOUR GLORY

UMBERTO

1893

MILANO
TEATRO ALLA SCALA
Impresa PIONTELLI e C.

Recita, 18 d'abbonamento.   Sera pari.

Giovedì 9 Febbraio 1893, alle ore 8 1|4 pom.

PRIMA RAPPRESENTAZIONE
della commedia lirica in 3 atti di ARRIGO BOITO:

FALSTAFF

Musica di GIUSEPPE VERDI.

PERSONAGGI

Sir JOHN FALSTAFF	Maurel Vittorio
FORD, marito d'Alice	Pini Corsi Antonio
FENTON	Garbin Edoardo
Dr CAJUS	Paroli Giovanni
BARDOLFO } seguaci di Falstaff	Pelagalli Rossetti Paolo
PISTOLA }	Arimondi Vittorio
Mrs ALICE FORD	Zilli Emma
NANNETTA, figlia d'Alice	Stehle Adelina
Mrs QUICKLY	Pasqua Giuseppina
Mrs MEG PAGE	Guerrini Virginia
L'oste della Giarettiera	Pulcini Attilio
Robin, paggio di Falstaff	N. N.
Un paggetto di Ford	N. N.

Borghesi e Popolani - Servi di Ford - Mascherata di folletti, di fate, di streghe, ecc.
Scena: Windsor - Epoca: Regno di Enrico IV d'Inghilterra
Commedia è tolta dalle ALLEGRE COMARI DI WINDSOR e da parecchi passi dell'ENRICO IV risguardante il personaggio di Falstaff.

Maestro concertatore e direttore d'orchestra EDOARDO MASCHERONI.

Farà seguito

DIE PUPPENFEE

Ballo comico in un atto di G. HASSREITER F. GAUL. Musica di G. BAYER -
riprodotto dal Coreografo CESARE SMFRALDI.

Biglietto per accedere ai Palchi L. 5 - Al loggione L. 5.

In platea non vi sono posti in piedi ed il piccolo atrio è chiuso al pubblico.
Allo spazio libero della galleria di V fila non potranno accedervi che le persone munite di tessera o di biglietto speciale dell'Impresa.
Ad evitare spiacevoli inconvenienti, i signori abbonati sono pregati di munirsi delle rispettive bollette d'abbonamento.
Il Teatro si apre alle ore 7 1|4 - Il loggiore alle TIP. LIT. ECONOMICA VIA FORI CHIRI S. MILANO

 *Verdi to Ferdinando Martini*[1]

[Milan, 11 February 1893]

I read in the *Perseveranza* that the title of Marquis is to be bestowed on me. I am turning to you, as an artist, so that you may do all you can to prevent this. My gratitude will be much greater if this nomination does not come about [. . .]

NOTE

1. Writer and politician (1841–1928), Italian Minister of Culture from 1892 to 1893.

 *Ferdinando Martini to Verdi*

Rome, 12 February 1893

[. . .] I wired you yesterday;[1] today I am repeating less briefly that the news revealed at first by the *Italie* and then by the *Perseveranza* has not, and never had, the slightest foundation. When His Majesty the King saw it in the papers, he laughed a little as if it were a fable of unknown origin; and he was also a little sorry, because he rightly thought that whoever believed it would offend the King himself as well as you.

Nothing more can be added to the nobility bestowed upon you by the purest glory increased with renowned operas and greeted by the entire civilized world for over fifty years. Even the slightest attempt to augment it would belittle you, or, at the least, display an unawareness of your greatness and perfection.

A King of Art in today's world cannot become Marquis of Busseto in Italy. His Majesty also expressed these thoughts to me this morning when I handed him your letter [to me], which he most greatly appreciated. [. . .]

NOTE

1. The telegram is missing.

 *Verdi to Camille Bellaigue*

[In French]

Milan, 12 February 1893

Thank you, a thousand times thank you, my dear Monsieur Bellaigue, for your telegram.[1] The audience was as indulgent about *Falstaff* as it was

1893

about *Otello*.[2] You will have received my letter, the *Falstaff* libretto and score.

I clasp your hands.

G. Verdi

NOTES

1. Missing.

2. *Falstaff*, however, would never become as popular as *Otello*. In fact, almost two years later, on 30 December 1894, Verdi wrote to Ricordi from Genoa during performances of *Falstaff* under Piontelli's management: "*Falstaff a fiasco!* But really a first-rate fiasco. Nobody goes to the theatre! The best of it is that they say that an opera so perfectly performed and so homogeneous has never been heard before! Then it must be said that the music is *cursed!*" And in another letter to Ricordi on 11 January 1895:

> Last evening at the Carlo Felice, *Falstaff* was reduced, not his belly, but his price!! I dare not say it! 1.50 Lire. Result? The same.
>
> If I were Piontelli, I would try something else. I would remove all the seats from the theatre. I would put in a large bar near the orchestra, with six or more barmaids, and four newsboys outside the theatre shouting: "Gentlemen, come in, come into the theatre gratis; performance gratis, chorus and orchestra gratis, everything gratis!! All you pay for is the beer, five cents a mug!!! Step right up, step right up, gentlemen!! A real bargain!!"
>
> With this trick Piontelli might see a few pennies in his box.

(See also Hepokoski, pp. 136–7.)

 Camille Bellaigue to Verdi

[In French]

Paris, 12 February 1893

Dear and admirable Maestro,

Yesterday I received your score, with gratitude and emotion. When I opened it, spring seemed to enter my home. What rays of light, what flowers, what life and what joy! I have read only the first scene so far, which is dazzling, and glanced at the rest. What verve, and what clarity! What a masterwork of classic *Latin* genius, which neither politics nor the Alps prevent (and never will) our two countries from understanding, loving, and sharing. But yours is the role of the old lion: *Well, old lion,*[1] as I already wrote you after *Otello*.[2] This time *well laughed,* and your smile, your laughter is that of a twenty-year-old genius. You are four times twenty, and this quadruples your prodigious youth. Be thanked, I should even say blessed, for this new masterwork, which you will allow me to discuss again when I know it better. I only wanted to tell you immediately about the first ray of my enthusiasm. I embrace you with all my heart, as I would have done had I been near you.

C. Bellaigue

What a modulation from A minor to F on

> *So che andiam la notte di taverna . . .*[3]

And the

> *Questo è il mio regno,*
> *Lo ingrandirò.*[4]

And the monumental *crescendo* propelled by the brass, isn't it . . . And the letter in the 2nd act![5] And the

> *Quando ero paggio*
> *del duca di Norfolk.*[6]

Come on, you are a miraculous man! I admire you and I love you. You see that I haven't aged!

NOTES

1. *"Well roared, Lion"* is Demetrius's line in *A Midsummer Night's Dream,* V.i.270.
2. See *Otello* i, pp. 295, 298; and *Otello* ii, pp. 690–701.
3. I.i (PV p. 20, 2/1).
4. I.i (PV p. 23, 3/2).
5. Bellaigue means Falstaff's two identical letters to Alice and Meg in I.ii.
6. II.ii (PV p. 222, 1/1).

 Giuseppina Verdi to G. De Sanctis

> Milan, 15 February 1893

[. . .] The first days of the *Falstaff* triumph are over, but the confusion of letters, cards, telegrams, visits, etc., has not yet ended. . . . Therefore, despite my determination not to write any more letters because of my age and [limited] physical strength, a few must still be written on this occasion. However briefly, I do so gladly for you, thanking you in Verdi's name for all the good and lovely things you say about *Falstaff* and its author. Without indulging in false modesty, Verdi really deserves them! It's impossible to possess greater genius and rectitude of character. [. . .]

 Boito to Camille Bellaigue

[In French]

> Milan, Thursday [16 February 1893][1]

I beg you, dear friend, to forgive me for what I cannot forgive myself, namely the delay of this reply to your charming letter.

If you knew the great joy it has given me, you would understand my silence even less, for it is really the height of egotism to keep for ourselves the good things others give us. I have an excuse for my shortcoming: ever since *Falstaff* has been on the stage, I have been the victim of all the bores who don't dare encounter the Maestro himself; and as prey to these vermin of success I am miserably wasting my days. . . Finally, here is a quarter of an hour of calm.

My dear Bellaigue, you ask for my impressions. . . . . what should I tell you? Where shall I begin? In your letter you touch with admirable clairvoyance and subtle intuition upon the very essence of the work. You say: *Here is the true modern and Latin lyric drama (or comedy)*. But you cannot imagine the immense spiritual joy this Latin lyric comedy produces on the stage. It is a real outburst of grace, power, and gaiety. By the miracle of sounds, Shakespeare's sparkling farce is returned to its clear Tuscan source of "Ser Giovanni Fiorentino."[2]

Come, do come, dear friend, come to hear this masterwork; come and live for two hours in the gardens of the Decameron, and breathe the flowers that are notes and the breezes that are sounds. Do come, we beg you; nothing bad will happen at your home during your short absence. If you arrive soon, Verdi might still be here; he will not leave before the middle of next week. You are going to hear a performance that still retains all the freshness and enchantment of things newborn. [. . .][3]

NOTES

1. De Rensis, pp. 317–8, erroneously attributes this letter to 1894.

2. Giovanni Boccaccio (1313–75). For additional information see Hepokoski, pp. 29–34.

3. Bellaigue was still unable to accept this invitation. (See his letter to Verdi of 3 February.)

 Verdi to Giuseppe De Amicis

Milan, 23 February 1893

Dear De Amicis,

I'll stay here a couple more days to arrange a few things for *Falstaff*, that is, the printing, the translations, and the tour being planned, etc., etc. . .

I read in the papers about a demonstration being planned upon my return to Genoa. . .[1]

Now do me the favor of going to see the Baron Mayor, to whom you will convey my kind regards, and beg him, entreat him, implore him to do all he can to spare me such a demonstration!

I am so tired, so weary that I cannot stand up anymore. . . I beg you, I beg you, I beg you! [. . .]

NOTE

1. After the triumphant première of *Falstaff* in Milan.

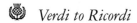 *Verdi to Victor Maurel*

[Late February 1893][1]

[. . .] Letters, telegrams, newspapers, and a bundle of other papers sent to Boito spoke of your successes, which gladden me. Alas, I am embarrassed that I still have not answered your kind telegrams!!! *Mea culpa . . . mea maxima culpa! . . .*

But consider all the business, little as it may be, that robs me of precious time; and then my age and, if you will, my laziness . . . and then you judge. When you come back to earth (I certainly will no longer be able to write either Iago or Falstaff for you), I will express to you in person all my esteem and admiration for you. [. . .]

NOTE

1. Abbiati iv, p. 497, gives this date, but the contents of these lines suggest that Verdi addressed them at a later time during or after the European *Falstaff* tour.

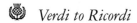 *Verdi to Ricordi*

Genoa, 3 March 1893

Dear Giulio,

Thank you for the telegram![1] Just as great is our regret at leaving Milan! Let's not think about it! Otherwise I'd fly to Milan in a balloon to ask my dear *Wives, Potbelly,* and the *accomplices* to start the rehearsals all over again!! Exactly two months ago today, on the 3rd, was the first rehearsal!!! Everything passes!! Alas, alas! . . . Too sad!! Too sad this thought!!!

I was in error . . Send all the packages, pictures, books, etc., etc., which you were to send to St. Agata, to Genoa instead.

Another nuisance . . . With the *Revue de deux mondes* the same thing is happening as happened last year. . They are sending two copies. Please inform whomever you wish. Address to Giuseppina Verdi — *à Josephine Verdi*.

Still another matter. But that is all. Peppina subscribes to the *Corriere della sera*, and I think they're not even sending it to St. Agata. Please ask them to send it here!

Oh, what a long letter! It's all Potbelly's fault! He made both of us lose incalculable time for over a year!! And it isn't over! . . . Why then? Bah!

1893

What fools!! All, all . . *He, they, she, you.* Tutto nel mondo è burla . . . . .
  Greetings to all, to all, to all.   Your
                                                                      G. Verdi

NOTE

  1. Missing.

 *Ricordi to Verdi*

                                                    Milan, 4 March 1893
Illustrious Maestro,

  I received your esteemed letter of yesterday. I had already informed
Hoepli[1] about the *Revue.* I am informing him again so that he may take care
of the matter. I'll have the *Corriere della sera* sent to you, and when the frames
for the portraits are ready, I shall send everything to Genoa.

  And now let me tell you again that your departure has been sad for
everyone, and saddest, naturally, for me! Gone are those very dear, most
enjoyable hours when life is all rosy, when we forget all the misery of the day.
I have returned to the same boring old rut, and it is a good day when I am
fortunate enough not to have some new and unforeseen aggravation!—
When I think of the two months gone by in an instant, my heart really
breaks. These last few days I have found myself in an indescribable state of
mind, so that I had neither the courage nor the strength to tell you all that
I wanted to tell you!—Just consider, Maestro, what I should have told you,
think of the feelings I wanted to reveal to you! . . . Think of the *Falstaff*
contract in these two months which passed so rapidly, and of the wretched
Bénoit affair, which embittered for me the last days of your sojourn in
Milan! Think then, Maestro, of what I owe you and how much gratitude I
feel toward you, the *only* person in the world from whom I received such
blessings!—And what must be the gratitude toward a benefactor when he
stands at the top of the ladder, when he is a Giuseppe Verdi? . . Truly, any
word is inadequate; so you may interpret what my heart's turmoil renders
me incapable of expressing. I hope that you may retain a very long and
pleasant memory of this Milanese sojourn, and think not only of your
artistic triumph but also of the great and reverent affection everyone has for
you, which manifested itself in true adoration.

  Thus my whole family wishes to be remembered to you and the kind
Signora Peppina; I will repeat this forever, aware of the great honor of
remaining your most devoted and grateful

                                                          Giulio Ricordi

NOTE

1. Ulrico Hoepli (1847–1935), distinguished publisher of Swiss origin in Milan. (See "Chronology of Boito's Life and Works," n. 45.)

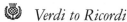 *Verdi to Ricordi*

Genoa, 5 February [March] 1893[1]

Dear Giulio,

Thanks for your telegram.[2] Amen . . . let's not think about it anymore!

In Paris there are two *bureaux* which amuse themselves by sending articles cut out from other newspapers and charging the poor artists, who don't have the courage to tell them to go to the devil. One of them calls itself *Courier de la* [illegible word], the other *Argus de la presse.* The articles in the first I sent back from Milan right away. But I don't recall whether I returned those of the *Argus* or if I threw them into the fire. The fact is that I can't find them. "He who does not seek shall not find." To avoid any trouble, do me the favor of having your representative in Paris pay the sum of 75 Lire (as you see from the letter from *Argus*), while I declare that never again, neither now nor in the future, will I pay a cent for all the twenty-five operas I shall write.

And tell Signor Pisa[3] to read my note to the gentlemen of the *Argus* . . .

Excuse the long letter and the trouble.— I won't bother you anymore!

Greetings to all.

G. Verdi

Just received your letter at 3:30. Thank you! I am moved by it!! Thank you, thank you. . . But let's stop it ! . . . With a white beard, the eyes must be kept dry. Greetings to all.

Addio, ad.

Send the *Gazzetta musicale* to me here.

NOTES

1. Postmark: GENOVA 5/3/93.
2. Missing.
3. Ricordi's representative in Paris. See Ricordi to Verdi, 28 September 1890.

 *Gino Monaldi to Verdi*

[Telegram]   Rome, 7 March 1893

MAESTRO VERDI GENOA

MAYOR OF ROME AGREES THAT BECAUSE NUMEROUS SOVEREIGNS COMING

1893

TO ROYAL SILVER WEDDING FALSTAFF BE PERFORMED ARGENTINA IN-
STEAD OF COSTANZI — PLEASE WIRE ME YOUR PERSONAL AUTHORIZATION
BEST REGARDS — MONALDI

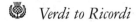 *Verdi to Ricordi*

Genoa, 7 March 1893

Dear Giulio,

Monaldi sent the enclosed telegram. I wired at once: *"Authorization does
not come from me. Address yourself to Milan."* One theatre or another, it makes
no difference to me.

Once more to *Falstaff*

I don't know if you know that when I heard the opera at an orchestra
rehearsal from the auditorium, I was so displeased with the [II.ii] *concertato*
that I said to all the artists gathered together: *"This piece doesn't work like that;
either you perform it more softly, totally sotto voce, and standing apart from one
another in groups, or it must be cut or changed."*[1] Nobody breathed, but these
words did not make a good impression, as they can tell you. The next night
they performed better and nothing more was said. But at the performances
I saw that on the stage this passage is long and too much of a *concertato.* I
wanted to change it in Milan, but I never had an hour of complete peace. I
say "change it," because I am an enemy of cuts. A passage that is cut is like
an arm, the belly, the legs, etc., etc., cut from a body. . . In pieces conceived
too broadly the cut becomes necessary, but it's always a monstrosity; it's a
body without head or belly, or without legs.[2]

In the *concertato* of *Falstaff* it was easy to cut and jump right away to
"Dolci richiami d'amor"; but the piece of music was no longer there, the belly
was missing. I have rewritten 6 bars, and the piece is shortened by 10 bars.
I'll send it to you tomorrow. . . I would like it to be done before the
performances at La Scala are over. . . And will you get it in time for the
second edition [of the piano vocal score]?[3]

It's quite easy to learn. Just a half-hour call for the singers (instead of
their going for a walk) will suffice, and 5 minutes will do for the orchestra
when it's assembled for another rehearsal.—

It can be done without Maurel . . . that is, if he should come too, his
parlandos could be redone; they are no longer in *tempo* and aren't musical
anymore. Ad[dio], ad.

G. Verdi

NOTES

1. See Verdi to Boito, January–February, n. 2; also Hans Gál, "A Deleted Episode in Verdi's *Falstaff*"; and Hepokoski, pp. 67–8.
2. Almost identical remarks are found in letters regarding *Aida* and *Boccanegra*.
3. Plate no. 96342, June 1893. (See Chusid, p. 69, and Hepokoski, p. 56.)

🏵 *Verdi to Ricordi*

[Genoa, 8 March 1893][1]

Here is the passage in the finale I wrote you about yesterday.— It's not a cut but a passage that ties in well with[2]

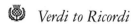

Ten long bars are saved. And that's a lot!

For the action this is better; for the music I don't know . . . , unless the reprise of the wives' phrase[3]

is good and if, moreover, neither the stomach nor the legs are missing in the piece.— Do with it as you wish.— Look it over with Mascheroni and Boito; actually, Boito may have to adjust a couple of verses.—

The singers know that I was not content with that passage, and so they won't mind coming to the *foyer* for half an hour. I will also be there, since (if advised half an hour before) I'll arrive posthaste.

When you decide to perform it, send me the original passage to be adjusted.—

Amen.

Greetings to all.

Addio

G. Verdi

Boldini has sent me an oil painting he did of me at the time of *Aida*.[4] I am writing him, but I don't have his address. Perhaps you have it. Put it on the letter addressed to him[5] and mail it.

1893

NOTES

1. Postmark: GENOVA 8/3/93.
2. II.ii (PV p. 278, 1/1). See Verdi to Ricordi, 28 November 1892, nn. 8 and 9.
3. II.ii (PV p. 253, 3/2) and n. 2 above.
4. Boldoni painted this well-known portrait in Paris on 9 April 1886, not at the time of *Aida*. (See Weaver, *Verdi: A Documentary Study,* plate 238.)
5. Missing.

 *Ricordi to Verdi* [1]

Milan, 9 March 1893

Illustrious Maestro,

Boito was just here for quite a while: he says that you are right as far as the progress of the scene is concerned, but he finds it highly regrettable to dispense with measures of enchanting music.[2] In any case, this new version ultimately gives the impression of moving too quickly toward the entrance of *Dolci richiami d'amor* and that one bar is missing; Boito says this not out of pedantry for the sake of the 8 measures, but because in a piece of such marvelous harmony the ear really needs them. It would appear that the final 2 new bars need to be developed into 3.— Boito has asked me to write you at once and present this impression to you before it goes into rehearsal; and thus I do. In order not to lose time, and so that you may have the entire matter before your eyes, I am returning the passage and the corresponding reduction that I have already prepared for the engraving of the parts.— Do not ask me what I think of it, for my opinion is absolutely worthless and anyway, the ensemble passage is too much in my ears; but I, too, felt a desire to hear an additional measure.—Meanwhile, I have let Mascheroni know, but he couldn't come because he had a rehearsal; however, as soon as the few new measures are ready and have been learned, I shall wire you and schedule rehearsals, first with the singers, then with the orchestra. This way you can have everything in order in half an hour. For my part . . . . I say only: Evviva!

Ever your most devoted
Giulio Ricordi

NOTES

1. In answer to Verdi's letters of 7 and 8 March.
2. Unaware of this correspondence, the composer and musicologist Hans Gál (1890–1987) objected to Verdi's cut for the same reason as Boito:

If Verdi had simply eliminated the whole episode, one might deplore it, but one could put up with it as with a sacrifice for higher reasons of unity and dramatic flow. But he seems to have felt the necessity for an oasis of music in that scene, as he left part of it. He replaced sixteen bars (1–16 of Example No.1) by a new invention of six bars, which have always given me an impression of something abrupt and inconsistent in the context. (See Example No. 2.)

In 1970, the present writer tried unsuccessfully to recover the original sixteen bars, which Verdi himself might have destroyed. Thereupon, Hans Gál made me the gift of his own orchestration, in his words "done with all the necessary piety and observance of style," but still waiting to be played. (See Hans Busch, "Apropos of a Revision in Verdi's *Falstaff*," in Thomas Noblitt, *Music East and West,* pp. 339–50.)

Example 1.

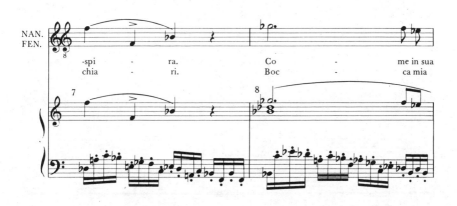

1893

Example 2.

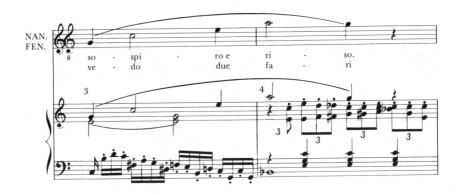

1893

🌼 *Verdi to Ricordi*

Genoa, Friday [10 March 1893][1]

Dear Giulio,

Since I had expected other observations, I was surprised that I should add a bar to the passage I sent you.—

Let's not talk of pedantry or of 8 bars . . . but here it really does seem to me that by adding a bar the phrase would be limping.

The musical movement goes in two-bar phrases:[2]

Thus the two-by-two phrase is right. By lengthening it, not one but two bars would have to be added, and it would become cold.

But perhaps there is a reason for you and Boito to be right. The little *cantilena* of the soprano and tenor above the movement of the basses requires a broader development in the last two bars; and if this phrase is shortened, it can work well like this:[3]

Anyway, rehearse it with the singers; and if, once it has been properly rehearsed, you still feel that a bar is missing, then let's talk no more about it and leave things as they have been until now.

Addio.
G. Verdi

NOTES

    1. Postmark: GENOVA 11/3/93.
    2. II.ii (PV p. 272, 1/2).
    3. II.ii (PV p. 276, 1/1).

🌼 *Ricordi to Verdi*

[Telegram]   Milan, 11 March 1893

I BREATHE AGAIN — RECEIVED[1] — DISPOSING — BUT AS SOON AS READY YOUR PRESENCE WILL BE INDISPENSABLE.

NOTE

1. Verdi's letter of 10 March.

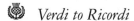 *Verdi to Ricordi*

Genoa, Saturday [11 March 1893][1]

Dear Giulio,

My presence indispensable!! What the devil! For such a little thing??— It would really be ridiculous for me to come to Milan to hold a rehearsal of *six* bars!!!! Oh Giulio, Giulio . . . how could you have said such a thing!!

If there is (how shall I say?) even the slightest disagreement, obstacle, etc., etc., then leave things as they are!—

I sent a photograph, promised in Milan, to Maestro Coronaro. I didn't know the address. Inform him!

When you write me, tell me the name of Zorzi, the one on the Committee.[2] Greetings and addio.

Your
G. Verdi

NOTES

1. Postmark: GENOVA 11/3/93. In answer to the preceding telegram. The date of 18 March given in *Carteggio*, p. 434, is in error.

2. Presumably Count Andrea Zorzi of Vicenza. (See Boito to Verdi, 31 December 1890.) Ricordi seems to have forgotten to answer Verdi's question.

 *Ricordi to Verdi*

Milan, 13 March 1893

Illustrious Maestro,

Last night the fifteenth performance of *Falstaff*: sold-out house, complete success!—

I have had the little parts distributed to the singers, and tomorrow a rehearsal will be held. But . . . . . how can you expect Boito, Mascheroni, and this humble writer to take the liberty, and also to assume the responsibility, of deciding whether the new version should be performed or not? . . .

Maestro, believe me, this is impossible, and it is far too obvious that you are the only judge, and an absolutely necessary judge, at that!— And there is even more to it: I have put off printing the edition as well as the orchestra parts in order to await your decision; this decision is especially important, even urgent, regarding the orchestra parts.

After all, I am only taking you at your word, since in your first letter, in which you enclosed the new passage, you really did say that you would, if necessary, make a dash for Milan!— It is a sacrifice, true; but earnestly consider whether the persons you were kind enough to designate are in a position to say yes or no . . . . ! *No, no, no, no! Better to be buried alive!*

In conclusion, it is a matter of real importance, which must definitely establish the form of a superb section of the opera.

In short, I will let you know by wire the day on which a full rehearsal is scheduled. Is this all right?—

That fellow Monaldi has been, and still is, up to mischief, and, what is more, is really driving me mad! . . . . By tomorrow I hope to have everything under control. Because of all of this, too, I would be very happy to see you and talk with you!!—

I repeat: I shall wire, and hope to have the joy of seeing you here; it will be a short excursion, but what a pleasure for us all!—

Please inform Signora Peppina that I am having all the things packed that were entrusted to me,[1] and that I shall send them to Genoa.

Always with all my gratitude,

Your most devoted
Giulio Ricordi

NOTE

1. Gifts to the Verdis on the occasion of the *Falstaff* première.

 Verdi to Ricordi

Genoa, 14 March 1893

Dear Giulio,

As I wired you,[1] if you think there is [too much] responsibility for you all (which I do not believe), then let's not talk about it anymore.— However, since you have written out the parts for the singers, hold a rehearsal for the singers only, maybe without Maurel, and you will see the result. Mind you, though, that this little rehearsal must be held onstage with the *screen* and the *basket* so that you'll be able to judge. The stage rehearsal must take place after they have learned their music.— With a little bit of good humor and goodwill you'll do it quickly and well. . . . In any event, there is always the supreme remedy: *Keep the original.* Addio, addio

Your
G. Verdi

NOTE

1. Missing.

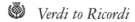 *Ricordi to Verdi*

Milan, 15 March 1893

Illustrious Maestro,

Your letter, which arrived this morning . . . . drives me to despair!—and after the hope you gave me in an earlier letter, what you write me can really give me no peace.

But now to the facts. Mascheroni tried the new version this morning; I couldn't go to the rehearsal, since I had a previously arranged meeting to attend. On Friday, the artists are to assemble onstage for a rehearsal at 12:30 and at 1:00 with the orchestra. I'll be there with Boito. Mascheroni told me that it works; of course, we will be better able to judge the effect on the stage. The rehearsal will not be tomorrow, since there is *Falstaff* at night, and we do not want to furnish pretexts for . . . . colds or whatever.

But . . . . I am an ass . . . . . and again I tell you, Maestro, that I, for my part, would never dare to decide; and I don't know if Mascheroni or Boito himself wishes to assume such a responsibility! But couldn't you make a dash here on Friday morning, attend the rehearsal, and return Saturday morning? . . .

"I have a bellyful of it.

I've had it up to my ears!"

This I hear you answer me; but why crucify all three of us? . . . And if we flipped a coin for yes or for no? . . . But do you want to compare our judgment with that of the one and only Verdi, with the author of *Falstaff* himself? . . . moreover, in a matter which you considered during the rehearsals as well as later on? . . .

Now I wish I had the overwhelming eloquence of Cicero; but since I don't . . . . I'll close by commending myself to divine providence, in the hope that it may grant me a telegram as follows:
"Agreed, I am coming."—

Ever your most grateful, most devoted

Giulio Ricordi

Last night, a magnificent full house.— As always, *complete* success.

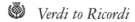 *Verdi to Ricordi*

Genoa, 15 March 1893[1]

Dear Giulio,

While looking again and again over that passage in the [II.ii] finale, I saw other bars that should be revised.[2] What's more, I have never cared for that mazurka-like ending of the first part of the third act . . . . and there I had a motive near at hand (*avrò con me dei putti*)[3] that, if well played and modulated, would have had a better effect; and it was also more fitting and musical. It was the continuation of the plan for the masquerade . . . *che fingeran folletti, spiritelli, farfarelli ecc.ecc.*[4] It was such an easy thing to do! . . Ah, what poor heads we have!!! It would be better to hurl them against a wall . . . . . and good night. . .

I received your two telegrams.[5] If you canceled the rehearsals, what good luck for the performers — but perhaps not so for the *Merry Wives.* Oh, no! I'm certain that they would have been ready and willing. You'll be able to let me know . . and greet them for me.

Addio

Your

G. Verdi

P.S. *Torno all'assalto*[6] . . . Let's make no changes in *Falstaff* for now. . . Later, who knows. . . Perhaps for a revival. .

So, a great success for Melba![7] . . . Also, *Noseda* says that. . . There is talk of a revival of *Rigoletto!!!* Oh, for God's sake, leave him in peace . . . you would do me a real favor . . . . and countless others, too!

NOTES

1. Postmark: GENOVA 16/3/93.

2. Probably the music under "Dolci richiami d'amor" and following bars.

3. Alice in III.i (PV p. 322, 1/2). For a complete analysis of these revisions see Hepokoski, pp. 68–76.

4. Ibid.

5. Missing.

6. Verdi quotes from Fenton's line in I.ii (PV p. 95, 1/1).

7. The legendary Australian soprano Nellie Melba (1861–1931) had sung Lucia at La Scala the previous night. Apparently Ricordi had informed Verdi of her success in one of the two telegrams mentioned above.

 Giuseppina Verdi to Ricordi

Genoa, 16 March 1893

Dearest Signor Giulio,

[. . .] I cannot but thank you from my heart for your kindness and for the great courtesy that did not send me to the devil in view of the troubles I have been causing you, in spite of the whirlwind of your wide-ranging activities!

I am glad to hear about the excellent state of your and your family's health. I cannot complain too much about my own. The so-called Great Old Man's health is absolutely flourishing! He is missing only the time spent with all of you and at the rehearsals in Milan; exhausting, noisy rehearsals, but full of harmony and fun! Well! Everything comes to an end, the good as well as the bad, and we must resign ourselves to the changes in life, with all its sorrows; nevertheless we try to make it last as long as we can!

To dear Giuditta and to your whole family, affectionate, cordial greetings! As for you, Signor Giulio, I consider myself always not only one of your oldest, but also most constant and sincerely affectionate friends

Peppina Verdi

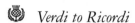 *Verdi to Ricordi*

Genoa, 17 March 1893

Dear Giulio,

I received your telegram.[1] It isn't possible for immediate reproduction.

Go ahead with your work, then, and let's no longer think of *Falstaff,* for the time being at least!

And by the way: I know nothing more about the *tournée!* Is it yes or no?

I hear that it's no longer going to be done in Rome.

I hear that you are negotiating with Vienna.

I hear that Maurel doesn't want to go to Berlin . . . that is, he would probably go if one were to beg him. . .

I hear also that for here nothing has been decided.

Would you believe it!!

I returned here over two weeks ago and have still not finished putting my papers in order. I found some papers that are yours, however . . the contracts for the last six months.— I'll return them to you.—

Addio for now.

Your
G. Verdi

NOTE

    1. Missing, but quoted in *Carteggio* ii, p. 434: "Not possible for immediate reproduction."

 *Verdi to Maria Waldmann*

Genoa, 18 March 1893

Dear Maria,

How much I would have enjoyed seeing you at the *Falstaff* première! It would have felt like a return to the days of *Aida*! Oh, many years have gone by! As young as you still are, they mean nothing to you, but to me!! However, you had a thousand reasons to stay away and assist your husband. I am so sorry about his illness! Give him my very best, and tell him to have courage and hope for the coming of spring, which will certainly do him good! [. . .]

 *Verdi to Giuseppe Spatz*

Genoa, 19 March 1893

Dear Signor Spatz,

You know that I am a serious man . . . .that I don't allow jokes when they go beyond certain limits! Well then, you have exceeded reasonable limits, and I cannot approve. But do you really think it proper to sacrifice so many old bottles!?[1] And why? Why? There is really no reason for it, and I can only judge and . . . sentence you! It's too much! It's too much!

The quality and perfection of the bottles is not to be doubted; we had proof of that in Milan, and here the proof will be renewed. [. . .]

NOTE

1. On the occasion of Verdi's saint's day, the owner of the Grand Hôtel et de Milan had sent him some excellent wine.

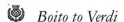 *Boito to Verdi*

[Milan] 19 March [1893][1]

Dear Maestro,

Good wishes to you and Signora Giuseppina, to Signora Giuseppina and to you.

Our good Milanese have all become citizens of Windsor by now, spending their life at the Garter Inn, in Ford's house, and in the park. I cannot remember, and I believe there has never been seen an opera which penetrated into the spirit and blood of a people like this one.[2] Art and the public must derive much good from this transfusion of joy, of power, of truth, of light, of spiritual health.

This regenerative cure must be extended elsewhere, too, and especially to those quite degenerate Romans of Rome.[3] Giulio and I are convinced that this time your presence at the capital would be most opportune, for many reasons. Giulio asks me to convey our opinion to you, and I need no urging to express it to you.[4] A very new art form like this *Falstaff* must not be abandoned by its author after a first experiment, in spite of its prodigious results. Today you are not only the composer, you are the physician (don't say this to Signora Peppina),[5] the physician of art. Today, Milan is entirely purged of any ultramontane fog.[6]

But after the healing of Milan we must proceed to the healing of the capital; and in order for the remedy to be perfectly effective, the doctor's presence is indispensable.

Falstaff will be presented in Rome in a new environment, with a new orchestra, and with two very important variants which must be arranged.[7]

Believe me, Maestro, your presence is necessary.

I didn't say this for *Otello*, but I say it now, because the presentation of *Falstaff* is still, and very much, greater than that of *Otello;* it is a true revelation, and the Roman public must not be neglected and abandoned before this work of art, which is so profoundly new. And then, many other considerations persuade me to ardently hope for your presence in the capital—considerations I won't mention here, but whose significance is just and eloquent in my mind.

The chatter is over.

The translation is progressing well,[8] much better than in the first act.

My affectionate greetings to you and Signora Giuseppina.

Your
Arrigo Boito

NOTES

1. Postmark: MILANO 19/3/93; presumably addressed to Genoa, which Verdi left on 21 March for St. Agata via Milan. Even Ricordi learned only at the last moment of Verdi's sudden decision to attend the eighteenth performance of *Falstaff* that night (*Carteggio* ii, p. 434).

2. See Verdi to Bellaigue, 12 February, n. 2.

3. On 15 April, Edoardo Mascheroni was to conduct La Scala's production of *Falstaff* at the Teatro Costanzi in Rome. Except for the orchestra, the company was the same as in Milan. On the way to the capital, the entire company gave four performances of *Falstaff* at the Teatro Carlo Felice in Genoa between 6 and 11 April.

4. Reluctantly, Verdi finally agreed to attend the first performances of *Falstaff* in Genoa and Rome.

5. Because of her aversion to physicians.

6. Fog from beyond the Alps, probably an allusion to *Der Fliegende Holländer*, which was performed in Italian, alternating with *Falstaff,* at La Scala in late February and early March.

7. In the II.ii finale and at the end of III.i. (See the entire Verdi-Ricordi correspondence between 7 and 17 March; also Verdi to Ricordi, 1, 4, 5, 27, 30 April, and 23 May.)

8. Boito's own French translation of *Falstaff*, with the assistance of Paul Solanges.

1893

🌼 *Verdi to Ricordi*

Genoa, 29 March 1893

Dear Giulio,

The *Falstaff* business in Rome is serious and ugly![1]

1. A management in bankruptcy!

2. A revolution in the orchestra!

3. The orchestra in Rome necessarily hostile!

4. An adversary, a powerful enemy who double-crosses us in every possible manner (and this, in my opinion, is the most logical way)!

And yet, despite all this, I still don't know positively and clearly how things are! — I don't know how the insolvency might have been settled! Nor am I clear about the controversy between orchestra and management.— The council says one thing, the management another; Mascheroni yet another, etc., etc.— Whom to believe? Perhaps the orchestra is at fault; but certainly the management has never treated them with *kid gloves.* And why not have them say they will not commit themselves until the *tour* has been set? The management will answer that the musicians were obliged by their contract to wait for two weeks? A tyrannical obligation! Why should they have to wait for two weeks after their engagements are over? And then . . Imagine how few of the poor devils know much about obligations!!!—

It would have been better to tell me everything, everything, everything quite frankly and clearly, without sugar-coating anything, so that no one could say *"It isn't true."* Then I, too, could have gotten a clear idea, formed an opinion, and made a decision! . . This way, it's chaos!!

And you want me to needlessly put myself in the midst of all that mess?!

Forget the interests of the publisher for a moment, and you yourself will say, *"The Maestro is right."*

Your

G. Verdi

P.S. I received your telegram[2] after I wrote this letter. I am sending the letter anyway, since the other problems still remain, even considering the excellence of the orchestra! . . . Still, 65 musicians are rather few!!

1st Violins	12
2nd	10
Violas	8
Cellos	8
Double basses	6

Flutes	3	
Oboes	2	
Clarinets	2	
Horns	4	
Trumpets	3	
Trombones	4	
Timpani	1	
Percussion	1	And Bass clarinet ?
Harp	1	And English horn ?

$$65^3$$

NOTES

1. During Verdi's impromptu visit to Milan on 21 March, Ricordi must have apprised him in person of the plans for the tour. (See Verdi to Ricordi, 17 March.) While attending to his affairs at St. Agata, and after his return from there to Genoa, Verdi seems to have had no news from Ricordi; but he may have seen Ricordi while passing through Milan between St. Agata and Genoa, or else been informed by others about the situation in Rome.

2. Missing.

3. Verdi failed to include the 2 bassoons.

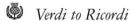 *Verdi to Ricordi*

Genoa, *Wednesday* [29 March 1893][1]

, Dear Giulio,

About the question of La Scala musicians, I read an initial letter from the musicians' council; a second one from Mascheroni, and now I am reading the names of the 27 non-contracted players. That is alarming, for these are actually the better ones. At the rehearsals I had noticed many of them; I asked for their names . . . and find them all engaged at the Dal Verme. For the tour the inferior strings will remain, just as I also see two or three of the better double-basses missing. And who will replace De Angelis?[2] Among the violins, two or three young men and a young girl will remain, who have neither attack nor sound. . . Watch out, Giulio! You have a *faible* for Piontelli, but this man is not to be trusted. . . . . If you have approved and are content, I cannot say anything . . . but the fact is that I am not content!

Addio

Your
G. Verdi

1893

P.S. I have seen *Falstaff* and *Manon*[3] announced in Brescia. That is a mistake! The one will kill the other! Give *Manon* alone. I need not make a career, and am glad if others profit by that.

NOTES

1. Postmark: GENOVA 29/3/93.
2. Unknown member of La Scala's orchestra.
3. Puccini's *Manon Lescaut* had been premiered on 1 February at the Teatro Regio in Turin.

 *Ricordi to Verdi*

Milan, 31 March 1893

Illustrious Maestro,

I received your esteemed letter of the 29th[1] and hasten to answer it. I delayed writing you in detail, since it was either not worthwhile to send you long stories of tittle-tattle or intrigue, or because I wanted to wait to give you positive and definite news. In any case, Maestro, you could and can be certain that I would never have committed myself to anything but clear-cut affairs. Unfortunately, all the difficulties, all the troubles were caused by Monaldi; I don't know whether he is more a rascal or an ass—perhaps both. It is well to establish the course of events:

The following is agreed upon[2] with Monaldi: 1st Rome, at once— 2nd Florence or Genoa—3rd Venice— 4th Trieste.

The moment he returns to Rome, Monaldi wires that it is necessary to employ the Rome orchestra. All the contracts of La Scala's orchestra are suspended, but are to be arranged later on for the other 3 theatres, in order not to leave our musicians without work for 15 days; Piontelli considers a performance in Florence during the run in Rome.—

All of a sudden, Monaldi goes to the mayor [in Rome] to arrange a gala performance, without consulting me.[3] This I learn from a telegram, and I send one to Monaldi at once, protesting his manner of acting without authorization—besides the fact that with those dates he upsets all the arrangements of the tour.

Now enter onstage: the court, mayor, prefect, etc., etc., declaring the immense desire that the artistic celebration of the silver wedding take place together with the supreme artistic event; it is noted that a refusal would be nothing less than an affront to the King and the Queen, etc., etc. In order to prevent possible offense and a bad atmosphere, a new schedule is studied:

No longer Rome, first, but Genoa; then Rome, to include this blessed 21st April!— Then Venice, then Trieste.— Starting with Genoa, the orchestra must be engaged directly; but then they must be employed in all the theatres, including Rome; the management prepares new contracts for 2 months and 4 theatres. Thereupon the Rome orchestra, in an uproar, goes to the mayor, declaring itself dishonored and offended; and that dolt of a mayor, who knows nothing about the theatre, to please the orchestra, promises that it will play!!—And the orchestra of La Scala already engaged? . . . More predicaments!!—During all this mess, Sonzogno plays one nasty trick after the other!!—And I wouldn't be surprised if, as I suspected on earlier occasions, he had an accomplice in the Milan telegraph office informing him of our telegrams. [. . .]

The elements chosen for this tour are all good; 3 mediocre or missing string players were immediately replaced by Piontelli, and have already played in the last performances.— This long account will give you an idea of past vicissitudes and nasty surprises. For over 10 days, I can tell you, I have neither eaten nor slept, because apart from my great responsibility toward you, you may well imagine the fury and the bile raised in me by the unceasing nefarious volleys worthy of convicts! . . But no!— Some people in prison are better than those outside.

Now then: The only problem that still exists is that of the "celebrated Rome orchestra," as they call it. During 3 days of rest [at La Scala], Mascheroni left for Rome to find a solution. He arrived there tonight, and I am awaiting telegrams with decisive news. Meanwhile I have even studied the commercial code and all its articles of bankruptcy; for if Monaldi were declared bankrupt, I would want to find out if he had forfeited all commercial rights. Then the right by which he boasts that after Milan *Falstaff* must be given in Rome would be annulled. But, unfortunately, it isn't so!! Because whatever right he had before his bankruptcy —founded or unfounded as it may be— is therefore a commission that cannot be taken away from the creditors!! . . . If this weren't so, everything would be decided. Good-bye to Rome!! . . and a good day to all!— [. . .][4]

NOTES

1. Apparently Verdi's first letter of that date to have been received.
2. For the *Falstaff* tour.
3. See Monaldi's telegram to Verdi of 7 March.
4. The continuation and end of this letter are missing.

1893

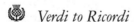 *Verdi to Ricordi*

Genoa, 31 March 1893

Dear Giulio,

I returned here yesterday evening very tired![1]

I am hoping for good news concerning the child.[2]——

I read that a committee has been established for a bust in memory of poor Todeschini.[3] Be kind enough to contribute for us

Giuseppe Verdi 100 Lire

Giuseppina Verdi 50 Lire.

If this is too little, put in more.

Addio in haste.

Your
G. Verdi

NOTES

1. Could Verdi have been so tired as to have forgotten that he returned to Genoa on or before the 29th? (This letter and his two previous ones to Ricordi appear to be clearly dated and postmarked in Genoa.)

2. Verdi had probably learned of a Ricordi child's illness while he was in Milan on his way to or from St. Agata.

3. See Boito to Verdi, 25 March 1890. The esteemed physician had also treated the Verdis.

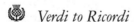 *Verdi to Ricordi*

[Genoa] 1 April 1893[1]

Dear Giulio,

For a long time, ever since the first orchestra rehearsals in Milan, I had planned to make two changes. Many nuisances distracted me; this morning, enraged by the latest events, I threw myself down to write.

I am sending you the passage (I don't know what it's like);[2] have the short vocal parts copied right away, and then I'll rehearse it here with the artists; not to have it performed in a theatre, either here or elsewhere, at least not for now, but for my own artistic satisfaction . .[3] Addio.

G. Verdi

NOTES

1. Postmark: GENOVA 1/4/93.

2. Missing (not included in the autograph).

3. See Hepokoski, p. 75.

Verdi to Ricordi

Sunday [Genoa, 2 April 1893][1]

Dear Giulio,

I received your telegram the moment I had sent my own.[2]

I saw Mascheroni . . . I am happy that everybody is happy. As for me, there is something in this combination[3] that isn't natural, that smacks of coercion; . . it no longer has anything to do with art. It has to do with an occasion.[4] . . . In haste addio, addio, addio.

G. Verdi

NOTES

    1. Postmark: GENOVA 2/4/93.

    2. Neither telegram has been located.

    3. *Falstaff* and the Royal Silver Wedding in Rome. (See Ricordi to Verdi, 31 March.)

    4. Averse to competing with other events, Verdi no doubt remembered the failure of the gala première of *Don Carlos*, which took place during the Paris Exposition, on 11 March 1867, with the Emperor and Empress of France in attendance.

Ricordi to Verdi

Milan, 4 April 1893

Illustrious Maestro,

I sent you a telegram the very moment I returned from the station, where I put the members of the orchestra, including De Angelis and Zamperoni,[1] on the train [to Genoa]. At 2:55 o'clock I shall see the artists and Mascheroni to the train, and then I'll strike up a glorious *Te Deum laudamus!* and take a deep breath after a month of continuous fights.

But these fights are nothing compared to one still remaining that I want to win, even if I risk being thrashed and losing some of my skin!!! The words "thrash me" never came at a better time than right now! But listen!—

You had the kindness, illustrious Maestro, to write me regarding several objections you had about Rome, from which I extract the two major ones:

1st. What am I doing in that mess?[2] . . . Let the publisher answer no.

2nd. This business of the Rome orchestra has all the aspects of pressure.[3]

The publisher, believe me, Maestro, has nothing to do with it; I, the publisher, will never pressure a man such as Giuseppe Verdi, the epitome of the most noble selflessness, not even about a matter of the greatest personal interest. It is quite a different feeling, a profound conviction that encourages me to speak up—a feeling and conviction felt just as deeply by another person with no publishing obligations: I mean Arrigo Boito.[4] While I cannot rival the highly distinguished, very rare qualities of his mind, I dare to rival his genuine affection, the unique respect we feel for the man and artist that is Verdi!!— I hope that Verdi will not reject these feelings of ours, for what else could explain the proofs of singular benevolence so often manifested in *moral* and *material* terms toward us?

Now, if you admit this, Maestro,—and you must admit it, because it is too clear and shining—how can you explain why we earnestly feel the need for your presence in Rome? . . Mind you, reasons of art and mere convenience could be brought up in abundance!—Yet, better than all of these, I base myself on all of Italy's quite fervent, almost inexplicably intense desire to see the most glorious of her sons in Rome, in the capital. You will perhaps object again, as if this looked like another caprice of mine! . . And why a caprice? . . . Why not acknowledge this universal sentiment as a new token of affection toward you on the part of the Italians? . . . . . In Rome! . . . a magic word that is now repeated for Verdi, quite naturally in view of all the extraordinary circumstances soon to be realized.—Two truly eminent persons, the King and the Queen, the Senate, the Ministry, look forward to seeing Italy's most honored man in Rome! . . . And you, Maestro, wish to remain insensitive to these voices, which emanate from Vittorio Emanuele's famous cries of pain?[5] — I will not stoop to the consideration of another aspect that I might mention to you; but you know what has been done to stop the immense *Falstaff*'s triumphant march!![6] . . . And does this great Potbelly, your beloved son, not deserve to present himself once again under the aegis of the great Jove, thus driving back into the dirt all the Titans of trash?—

As for the Rome orchestra, I think the saying might be applied, that people are taken for what they are. Ever since there was talk about *Falstaff* in Rome, consideration was given to the local orchestra, engaged by Monaldi at that time; and it was not possible to cite the case of *Otello*, for which the Milanese orchestra came, since the Apollo theatre was then open, with the Rome orchestra already engaged. These poor musicians suddenly find themselves before a closed theatre, with their wages in arrears, unemployed! How can we pretend that they should remain calm? Adding self-respect to the vital economic problem, you will see that they must be completely absolved. In artistic terms, then, Rome is the only city where a local orchestra has been formed; for better or for worse, this fact exists and is all the more remarkable since—due to the poor municipal finances—nothing is done anymore for the arts. Musically, Rome does not count but for its orchestra; to pass over it would be like a *coup-de-grâce*, a death sentence. The agitation was expressly supported by Milan, taking advantage of passions rather easily stirred. It was important to find out whether the Rome orchestra still contained good elements; regardless of Mascheroni's assurance, I thought it wise and useful to send him to Rome, to clarify everything as well as to ascertain that this orchestra would be capable of a performance worthy of that work. And now everything is in order—materially; in essence, however, everything is missing, that is, light, sun, and life!!—

I understand, Maestro, what your sacrifice would be, but you would make it for your son, who, no matter how corpulent, is a very good son. A kind of Pretorian Guard faithful to its orders would spare you much needless trouble. I offer myself as secretary, waiter, courier, ready to arm myself to the teeth, ready to devour alive all the pests.—A few days; one or two rehearsals, as you see fit—in short, we all will see to it that a heavy sacrifice will result in the least personal discomfort, and that you will be accorded all the respect due you. What if you should then object: But who asked me to come? . . . . I would answer you that your Pretorian Guard intercepted all invitations according to your wishes; otherwise you would have received a hundred invitations by this time. After all, art is involved, and not a regular season for which the orchestra can easily be changed without the composer's being present. It is a matter of unique performances under unique circumstances which, certainly, had not been foreseen, let alone warranted. Mascheroni is all right, but he is not the composer. And only the composer can embark on an eternal and glorious flight with his *Falstaff* from the Eternal City, Rome!! All of us feel this way; we have felt this so strongly for many days that it has been the topic of all my conversations and arguments with Boito, always leading to the conclusion that you . . . . you know, and I won't repeat!— There is more to it: I don't meet anyone who doesn't ask me with the greatest interest: "Verdi is going to Rome, isn't he?" . . . It's a kind of plebiscite. Maybe *"vox populi, vox asinorum!"* . . . , but it could also be *"vox populi, vox Dei!"* However it may be, doesn't it seem strange to you that something is now occurring that has never happened on other similar occasions? . . Good Lord, I know so well how tormented you have always been by official and officious invitations—that is more than natural. But until now, not even persons with the honor and the pleasure of approaching you more directly have prevailed upon you; none of them ever dared express a desire to you in this way, because they understood perfectly that it was not to be done. At this moment, this desire is all of Italy's; be assured that I do not exaggerate! The fear of seeming indiscreet, particularly toward you, stops me. Base, vulgar, and contemptible as the fights have been up to now—everything will disappear before your presence.—It is a

1893

genuine prayer which I dare make to you . . . blushing and with my heart pounding as I am beseeching you; but I take courage from the knowledge that I am a proper spokesman for all the people who love you for all those gifts that make you unique!

Oh, if only my words had the power of persuasion I wish they had, I would really call myself fortunate!! . . . . . and I say no more!— *Alea jacta est* [the die is cast].

The Wives and all the others are there!![7] And I am here, very sad as I think of the beautiful days gone by in a flash.— Everyone has left in good health except for Stehle, who sprained an ankle in one of the last performances; she is in need of rest, and I hope that Mascheroni will ask her to be seated during rehearsals, so as not to jeopardize the performance.

Most cordial greetings to Signora Peppina; and you, Maestro, magnanimous as you are, once again forgive that enormous pest who is

Your grateful and devoted
Giulio Ricordi

NOTES

1. Two important members of La Scala's orchestra, which was to play *Falstaff* in Genoa, but not in Rome. The telegram is missing.

2. Paraphrase from Verdi's letter to Ricordi of 29 March.

3. Ibid.

4. See Boito to Verdi, 19 March.

5. On 10 January 1859 King Vittorio Emanuele II declared in a historic address to parliament: "We are not insensitive to the cry of pain that calls to us from so many parts of Italy."

6. Jealousy and intrigue as on the part of Sonzogno.

7. In Genoa.

Verdi to Ricordi

Tuesday [Genoa, 4 April 1893][1]

Dear Giulio,

I was hoping to receive the written-out parts of the little passage[2]

this morning. Perhaps Mascheroni will bring them along tonight. . .

Also send me, as soon as possible, the newly written bars in the finale of the second act.

Addio in haste.

G. Verdi

P.S. I know that the musicians have already arrived.[3]

NOTES

1. Postmark: GENOVA 4/4/93.

2. III.i (PV p. 325, 2/3).

3. From La Scala for the *Falstaff* performances under Mascheroni at the Teatro Carlo Felice on 6, 8, 9, and 11 April 1893.

 Verdi to Ricordi

Wednesday [Genoa, 5 April 1893]

Dear Giulio,

I received your letter, which I can't answer at the moment.

Later, I received the parts of the altered passage. . . . . [1]

If you come tomorrow evening, bring along the part of the original [piano-vocal] score in which I made the change in the finale, so that I can orchestrate it.—[2]

Addio.

G. Verdi

NOTES

1. Verdi to Ricordi, 4 April, n. 2.

2. Both of these modifications were first performed together ten days later in Rome. (See *Carteggio,* p. 435.)

 Verdi to Ricordi

Genoa, 8 April 1893

Dear Giulio,

I hope you have calmed down,[1] and I hope I won't bother you too much by asking you whether you have paid, from my account, to the committee that is erecting a bust of poor Todeschini

for Giuseppe Verdi 100 Lire

for Giuseppina Verdi 50 Lire.

I wrote you about it *8* or *10* days ago. Excuse me; greet everyone in your family.

Affectionately,
G. Verdi

1893

NOTE

1. Apparently Ricordi had attended the first *Falstaff* performance in Genoa on 6 April. As the tone of these lines implies, Verdi's constant demands seem to have significantly added to the publisher's stress, and even caused some ill feelings.

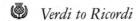 *Verdi to Ricordi*

Tuesday [Genoa, 11 April 1893][1]

Dear Giulio,

I have answered Minister Martini and the Mayor of Rome that I'll be present at the first performance of *Falstaff*.[2]

I'll leave Thursday *after* noon.

I hold you to your word: You have promised me that you will liberate me from all the nuisance in Rome.

I hope you won't fail me.

Till we see each other
G. Verdi

NOTES

1. Postmark: GENOVA 11/4/93.
2. The communications from the minister and the mayor are missing, as are Verdi's replies.

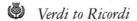 *Verdi to Ricordi*

Genoa, 11 April 1893

Dear Giulio,

I now hear that you are very embarrassed that you cannot free yourself from the promise to Berlin. . . But why is it that a year after I had told you that Pessina is impossible for Falstaff, you are so committed that you are unable to free yourself?! Permit me to tell you that you were very wrong. I will not create obstacles, but Pessina cannot go and jeopardize *Falstaff*.[1] But let's not talk about it anymore; I will not talk about it with you either here or in Rome. It will be what it will be.

I wrote you this morning, and at this hour you will have received the letter saying *"We shall leave* Thursday at *12:39."*[2]

Addio.

Your
G. Verdi

NOTES

1. Maurel's refusal to appear in the capital of France's old enemy caused Ricordi a serious dilemma.

2. Boito accompanied Verdi and his wife to Rome. King Umberto I and Queen Margherita were to receive Verdi at the Palazzo Quirinale and invite him (apparently without his wife) to share the royal box at the Teatro Costanzi on 15 April. (See Appendix II: Eduard Hanslick, "*Falstaff* in Rome.")

 Verdi to Edoardo Mascheroni

Genoa, 23 April 1893

Dear Mascheroni,

Ah! Ah! Ah! Ah! Ah! I, too, sang like the Wives upon reading your letter![1]

Poor Farfarello . . . . All those toils and troubles, and then the danger of losing 100 Lire![2]

Ah! Ah! Ah! Ah!

I wired Giulio immediately—who wired Nuti[3] immediately—who at this hour should have settled the debt. So be it! [. . .]

And we?. . . And art?. . . But why *we,* why *art!* We? Poor supers in charge of beating the drum until they tell us: *Be quiet! . . .!*

Tutto nel mondo è burla . . . . [Everything in the world is jest . . . .]

Ah ah ah ah. Greet everyone onstage who inquires about me! . . . . Perhaps you won't greet anyone for me.

I will not give you any compliments, because I already have. I won't say "Thank you," because I hope to cause you more trouble in the future.

Forgive me.

NOTES

1. A missing letter written after the Verdis' return with Boito to Genoa.

2. At the station in Rome, Mascheroni had lent Verdi 100 Lire for the purchase of the railway tickets to Genoa, and Verdi had forgotten to repay.

3. Ricordi's representative in Rome.

 Ricordi to Verdi

Milan, 26 April 1893

Illustrious Maestro,

Upon my return I was overwhelmed by such an avalanche of business

1893

and nuisances that I paid quite heavily for the dear and most beautiful days spent in your company! I would have liked to tell you an infinite number of things; in particular, I would have liked to thank you, Maestro, for all you have done! . . But can I find adequate words to say to the benefactor? . . . Absolutely not!!!— It is certainly true that in some cases silence is golden! . . . But there is silence and there is silence . . . . and sometimes it cannot be kept, even at the cost of appearing dull!— And any word of mine will seem dull compared with the gratitude I owe you, which I feel so deeply and am unable to express!— But you and Signora Peppina should not forget that there are many of us who always, always think of you!!—To think of that great kindness which is even more precious because of its simplicity!— We bless you with all our hearts.— At a later time I shall write at greater length; now you will make us happy by answering, "We are very well!". . Evviva then!

Ever your devoted
Giulio Ricordi

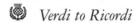 *Verdi to Ricordi*

Genoa, 27 April 1893

Dear Giulio,

I have corrected and am sending you . . Take a look at the oboes, which could also be wrong.—

I was hoping for a letter or a telegram from Farfarello but haven't received a thing. I was most anxious to know how things went between the *Divo* and the *others*[1] after my departure!

And now that I have nothing more to do for *Falstaff*, let's think a bit what must be done about Sauchon in the Bénoit affair. We talked about it earlier, but now it seems to me that we can no longer afford to let much more time go by. As far as I am concerned, do everything you deem suitable, and I will approve it immediately. Sauchon has done a lot for us, and I think we must show him our gratitude, the sooner the better.

Addio in haste.

Greetings —

Your
G. Verdi

Write me something about Sauchon and, I repeat, as soon as possible.

NOTE

1. During the remainder of the *Falstaff* performances in Rome.

🌀 *Verdi to Edoardo Mascheroni*

Genoa, 27 April 1893

Dear Mascheroni,

You are not the only privileged one! I, too, made a big fool of myself!!

Don't laugh, for I'm in danger of committing suicide!

Listen and be horrified!

For once in my life I wanted to do something nice, and it turned out wrong! . . . I sent a picture [of myself] to the owner of the [Hotel] Quirinale and addressed it: *"Al sig. Bruni proprietario dell'Albergo Quirinale,"* etc., etc.— Last night, when Boito left for Milan, he shouted with a voice in F♯: *"But Bruni isn't the proprietor of the Quirinale!"*

Ahhhh!

And who is? He couldn't tell me! . . . I was furious, grabbed a *revolver* (of chocolate) and shot myself in the mouth! . . .

And I'm still alive!!! Alas, alas!! AND I AM STILL ALIVE!!

E vi— vo an co— ra!!—

I throw myself into your arms: *Save me, save me!* . . . .

What can you do?

What must I do? . . . [. . .]

🌀 *Verdi to Ricordi*

Genoa, 30 April 1893

Dear Giulio,

Thank heaven!

The hubbub of Rome is over! It might have been better had it not happened!

Make it a rule: Never give new operas for great popular or royal celebrations, for expositions, etc., etc.[1]

It would have been better not to have given *Falstaff* in Rome at this time; and for me it would have been even better to have stayed in Genoa to rest! . .

Well! It's my own fault. Now it is done and we won't talk about it

1893

anymore! That poor Piontelli, how much he will cry! If he lost seven thousand Lire in Genoa, he'll have lost at least seventy thousand in Rome!

Poor fellow!

It is all right to redo the passages in the original orchestra score; but I'll do this little job at St. Agata.[2]

What you say about Sauchon is also all right; but explain to me your phrase "*I shall send also in your name.*"[3]

. . Since we had agreed to share the expenses, even with two-thirds coming from my account, the gift must come from both of us. Make sure that it is beautiful, well made, and not too cheap!

Addio, addio.

We'll hear how Potbelly fares in V[enice].

Affectionately,

G. Verdi

P.S. I received the telegram. *And it won't be the last!!*[4]

NOTES

1. See Verdi to Ricordi, 2 April, n. 4.
2. Ricordi's relevant letter is missing. (Verdi to Ricordi, 27 April.)
3. Missing. See Verdi to Ricordi, 17 [16] May, and Verdi to Tornaghi, 29 July and 1 August 1894.
4. Meaning unknown.

 Verdi to Edoardo Mascheroni

Genoa, 3 May 1893

Dear Mascheroni,

Thanks to you, to Piontelli . . . . to Piontelli, to you . . . . and to you and Piontelli . . . . (must I continue?) for the telegram you sent me.[1] So you all did well!

And Pasqua has recovered?[2] And what is the Divo doing, and what will he do? I don't believe in the alliance Pasqua-Maurel. For what purpose? To forgo performances? No, no, the few Lire please them, too.

But tell me something later on.

I cannot write more, because I'm putting my papers in order; I'm packing to go to St. Agata the day after tomorrow. Finally!! [. . .]

NOTES

1. From Venice, the first stop after Rome, to inform Verdi of *Falstaff*'s success in La Scala's production, with La Scala's orchestra, at the Teatro La Fenice on 1 and/or 2 May.

2. Verdi did not yet know that Pasqua's illness forced her to forego all remaining *Falstaff* performances on the tour after Rome. (See Ricordi to Verdi, 27 May.)

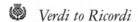 *Verdi to Ricordi*

Genoa, 5 May 1893

Dear Giulio,

The servants left for St. Agata this morning. We'll leave tomorrow.[1] We'll be in Fiorenzuola at two o'clock, and in St. Agata by about 4.

For over four months now I have been at the ball! Now the *Tarantella* is over. My greetings to your Giuditta and everyone in your family.

Addio, addio.

Your
G. Verdi

P.S. Do me the favor of having the *Corriere* change the mailing address to *Busseto*. As soon as you can.—

NOTE

1. Presumably a day later than planned (Verdi to Mascheroni, 3 May).

 Verdi to Edoardo Mascheroni

St. Agata, 7 May 1893

Dear Mascheroni,

I am at St. Agata and can breathe again! But what am I saying! . . Here, too, I will have so much to do before things are in order. It's my fate! Some people are predestined: one to be an infant all his life, one to be a cuckold, one to become rich or desperate; I, with my tongue hanging out of my mouth like a rabid dog, to work forever until the final blow!

And if you were predestined to put five thousand Lire into your savings every month? You would have to run to Rome every first of the month to be blessed by the *poor Papin* [Pope].

I have heard very little about Venice. I have received only two newspapers, sent by *Meg* and *Quik*, I believe,[1] and the telegrams.— If you think it useful to add the little instruments in the quartet,[2] as long as they aren't heard, go ahead; but take out the

in the oboes. The low B sounds too awkward in the oboes.

1893

Bon voyage to Vienna; I don't believe in the other bon voyage to Berlin. In artistic terms it was a mistake. I could have prevented it, but realizing how much Giulio had committed himself, I didn't want to cause him serious embarrassment; Giulio, however, was wrong to act too arbitrarily and with little artistic sense.[3]

Nothing better than to look *away!* New rows will be avoided! And how are the Wives? Have no rivalries come about between the old and the new ones?[4] But what lovely comedies always occur in the theatre and outside of it, too!—*Tutto nel mondo è burla!* And I greet you in earnest and go to work . . . not on music! No, no, no, no!![5]

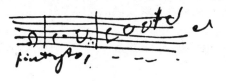

rather
Addio — ad.

G. Verdi

NOTES

1. If actually "sent by *Meg* and *Quik,*" Emilia Pini-Corsi as Meg and Virginia Guerrini as Quickly, replacing the sick Pasqua, were the senders. (See Verdi to Ricordi, 21 May.)

2. In the *a cappella* passage of the Wives in I.ii (PV pp. 65–7). In the facsimile orchestra score at rehearsal number 25, Verdi scratches out the oboe and clarinet parts, indicating that the entire quartet of the Wives is *a cappella* until rehearsal number 26. (See also Hepokoski, "Pasqua," p. 249.)

3. See Verdi's second letter to Ricordi of 11 April.

4. Regarding cast changes and tempers see Mascheroni to Verdi, 12 May; Verdi to Ricordi, 21, 23, 29 May, 18 June; Ricordi to Verdi, 27, 31 May, 18 August; Verdi to Mascheroni, 10, 16 August.

5. Unidentified quotation.

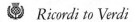 *Ricordi to Verdi*

[Telegram]   Milan, 12 May 1893

POTBELLY PURSUING HIS TRIUMPHANT WAY WENT SKY HIGH ALSO TRIESTE—HAPPY ANNOUNCING THIS—ONLY REGRET HAVING BEEN UNABLE TO SHARE SHOUTS OF VIVA VERDI—GREETINGS

GIULIO

🌼 *Verdi to Giuseppe De Amicis*

St. Agata, 12 May 1893

Dear De Amicis,

Thank you for the telegrams.[1] Thank you for the house.[2] Thank you for putting the picture from Turin in its place . . . But this embarrasses me a great deal, since I don't know whom to thank and how. In the last days in Genoa, I believe I received a letter announcing the arrival of this picture. . . but in the midst of so many papers and so much to do during those days, who knows where that letter is hiding. Please tell me if next to the name of the picture's creator there might be his address to say at least "Thank you" to him; or if you know of another way to find this blessed address!!

We are busy filing papers and putting a little order in this hut of ours. [. . .]

NOTES

1. Missing.
2. Presumably for taking care of the apartment at Palazzo Doria in the Verdis' absence.

🌼 *Edoardo Mascheroni to Verdi*

Trieste, 12 May 1893

[. . .] Another great triumph for *Falstaff.* You can imagine with what joy I am writing you this. By dint of conducting *Falstaff* I will end up like Maurel, thinking I have composed it myself. . . It was not merely what is called a success, but ecstasy, incredible enthusiasm, an apotheosis of your (for now) latest masterwork. I don't know how to describe last night's performance to you. All of us were moved. . . What evvivas, what shouting, what a madhouse!

The performance went fine: all the artists accurate, warm, spontaneous, but for a few little flaws unnoticed by the audience; my orchestra performed wonders and also had a great success. For the record: there were repeats of the little quartet, Ford's monologue, and, four times, of *"Quand'ero paggio."* Artists and conductor, the *Famous Mascheroni (that's me),* were called after each act. Really: they begin to call me famous, and in the long run I'll end up believing it. . .

Last night's success, yes, the triumph of *Falstaff,* has brought about the miracle of my reconciliation with Maurel. Really? Yes, really, and you will certainly be glad about this peace. This is what happened: I am staying on the same floor at the hotel as Maurel, in an elegant room on the second floor. Of course, that's where great gentlemen, famous artists, and conductors go. This morning about eight o'clock I leave my room for an urgent need, with a nice newspaper in hand, and in slippers and shirtsleeves set out to . . . where we are all equal before God and man; as I push the doorknob, in a certain haste to enter, out comes Maurel, holding his pants up, with the inspired face of one who has just relieved himself of a heavy burden; for a moment we stare at each other, he buttoning his pants, I balancing a bit on my left leg, a bit on the right. . . Finally, Maurel opens his mouth: "What a success, eh!" — "Colossal" — "I'm very happy" — "And I'm overjoyed." Finally, a firm handshake, an embrace, and laughter about the nice figure we cut; and peace was sworn at that sacred altar, not too well perfumed as it was. . .

I am told that tonight innumerable telegrams will go out to Vienna and Berlin with enthusiastic news about *Falstaff.* After this letter, I would like (if I am not too indiscreet) to find a couple of lines from you upon my arrival in Vienna: Hofoper or at the Grand Hôtel. [. . .]

 Verdi to Edoardo Mascheroni

St. Agata, 15 May 1893[1]

Dear Mascheroni,

Congratulations, congratulations, and more congratulations to you, the *third* author of *Falstaff!* Who will be the *fourth?*

Perhaps Pini-Corsi.

And the fifth?

The Wives.

In this regard, I received a very charming and, above all, a very good letter from Zilli.[2] Thank her, and tell her that I'll answer later on, since at the moment I'm extremely busy finishing an opera in *12* acts, including a prologue and a symphony which is as long as all the nine Beethoven symphonies together; then, still, a prelude to each act, in which all the violins, violas, cellos, and double-basses will play a melody in octaves, not in the *Traviata, Rigoletto*, etc., fashion, but one of those most beautiful modern melodies that have neither a beginning nor an end and hang in the air like Mohammed's tomb.

I have no more time to explain to you how the singers shall do the accompaniment, but I'm hoping for an inspiration about how to imitate the *tshak, tshak* of the cymbals with them. . . I'll tell you some other time. Addio.   Your G. Verdi

NOTES

1. Misdated "13 May" in Abbiati iv, p. 508.

2. Her name is deleted in the autograph but is legible in Verdi's handwriting. For no understandable reason, *Copialettere,* p. 633, and other transcriptions give Pasqua's name in error; illness had forced her to withdraw from the entire tour after Rome. Zilli's letter to Verdi is missing, as is his reply, to which he refers in his letter to Ricordi of 29 May.

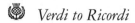 *Verdi to Ricordi*

St. Agata, 17 [16] May 1893[1]

Dear Giulio,

I approve of your proposal for the gift I should make to Sauchon.[2] I really don't know this renowned factory of Noah[3] . . . but if their object is marvelous, as you say, I approve, approve, approve.

I ask only that you do it quickly, and finish all the rest! Greetings. I may write you tomorrow.

G. Verdi

NOTES

1. Postmark: BUSSETO 16/5/93.

2. Ricordi's relevant communication is missing. (See Verdi to Ricordi, 30 April.)

3. "La fabbrica di Noé," Noah's ark, is to the Milanese a task that is never completed. Ricordi must have warned Verdi that obtaining this gift could take a long time. (See also Verdi to Tornaghi, 29 July and 1 August.)

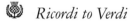 *Ricordi to Verdi*

[Telegram] Milan, 17 May 1893

FIRST ORCHESTRA RESHEARSAL VIENNA MASCHERONI MOST SATISFIED— ORCHESTRA GAVE HIM MANY OVATIONS—CORDIAL GREETINGS

GIULIO

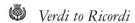 *Verdi to Ricordi*

Busseto St. Agata, 21 May 1893

Dear Giulio,

Do me the favor of sending from my account and as soon as possible to Ghislanzoni at *Caprino Bergamasco* the sum of two hundred Lire.—[1]

1893

I wanted to talk no more about *Falstaff* in Berlin, but I cannot deny Pini-Corsi a small favor. He tells me that the part of Meg is to be taken away from his wife?![2] . . But if it is true that she did that part quite well in Venice and in Trieste, as I was also told by two people from Trieste who came here, why make her suffer an unnecessary affront! . . Ah, there can be no great disaster in *Meg!* Give it some thought, and don't provoke unnecessary shocks.

I still have not been able to transcribe the few pages of the *Falstaff* orchestra score. I hope to do so today.

Addio, addio —   Your

G. Verdi

P.S. I am told that the impresario[3] doesn't want Pini's wife because 4 years ago she sang at the *Kroll Theater* [in Berlin]! But if it is true that in the space of a single month she sang in *Lakme, Barbiere, Ballo in maschera, Trovatore, Rigoletto,* that should be just the reason to accept her. . . But the motive will be that the impresario wants to present some big name, who will also ruin all the scenes of the wives. [. . .]

NOTES

1. Antonio Ghislanzoni (1824–93), Verdi's librettist for *Aida,* died at Caprino Bergamasco near Lecco on 16 July 1893. His friend the poet Ferdinando Fontana had gone to see him, along with a Dr. Caporali, who diagnosed a serious kidney disease, bronchitis, and arteriosclerosis. As Fontana wrote to Verdi from Milan,

> There is little hope, and if the sick man survives, he would be more like a vegetable than alive. . . While I tried on my own and through friends to provide for the urgent needs of the sick man, who is penniless, I asked the Signori Boito and Ricordi to intercede with you. . . They promised to talk about it with you when you come to Milan. But moved by today's sad news from the sick man, I pluck up my courage to write you. (Abbiati iv, p. 513.)

2. Emilia Pini-Corsi, Antonio Pini-Corsi's wife, sang Meg in Venice, Trieste, Vienna, and Berlin, when Virginia Guerrini, the original Meg, took over the part of Quickly from Pasqua, whose illness prevented her from joining the tour after Rome.

3. Canori (see Ricordi to Verdi, 31 May, n. 1).

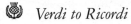 *Verdi to Ricordi*

St. Agata, 23 May 1893

Dear Giulio,

This morning I sent you the last notes of *Falstaff.*[1] Peace be to his soul!! —

I have heard nothing more about Pasqua. Up to now I thought she was still sick in Rome; but I heard that her husband was in Milan a few days ago!

Then she is not sick!! What happened? Perhaps it's one of the usual tricks, or, better said, deceits which all too often happen in the theatre![2] Give me some news, so that I can answer knowing the cause, should she write me about it.—

Darclée, who is now at the Hotel Milano, writes me that she has plans to do Desdemona in France! But where? Anyway, let me know if she did that part well in our theatres, I believe in Bologna and Genoa, etc.[3]

I have to tell you so many other things, but today is a bad day. It's raining! Addio —

Affectionately,
G. Verdi

NOTES

    1. Final corrections in the orchestra score at II.ii (see Hepokoski, pp. 75–6).

    2. This was not the case. Pasqua was still sick (Ricordi to Verdi, 27 May).

    3. See *Otello* i, p. 385.

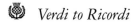 *Verdi to Ricordi*

St. Agata, 24 May 1893

Dear Giulio,

    I received the telegram.[1] I can imagine Mascheroni's joy!

    Yesterday I answered Sauchon's report. I received (oh no!) the two *Falstaff* passages, which I shall adjust right away . . . just to get it over with.—

    Finally, after all this time, I found an hour to open the boxes that came from Milan, from Genoa, from Rome . . . . . . I was badly disappointed!! I didn't find the drawings which the Artists' Society had made for me!!

    What happened?

    Haven't they sent them?

    Did they address them incorrectly?

    Are they lost?

Please let me know, and give me some word.

Your G. Verdi

NOTE

    1. A missing telegram about the success of *Falstaff* in Vienna on 21 and 22 May.

        It was billed as a *Performance by the entire solo contingent of the Teatro alla Scala, Milano*, conducted by Maestro Edoardo Mascheroni, but with the Vienna Opera orchestra. The Falstaff was Victor Maurel, the Scala's first Iago, whose fee was in proportion to the exorbitant cost of tickets; but he did at least sing his aria *Quand'ero paggio del Duca di Norfolk* three times. (Prawy, *The Vienna Opera*, p. 60.)

Virginia Guerrini appeared as Quickly and Emilia Pini-Corsi as Meg, although their roles were confused on the Hofoper poster. (Prawy, p. 57.)

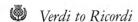 *Verdi to Ricordi*

Wednesday [St. Agata, 24 May 1893][1]

Dear Giulio,

I don't talk of music!! Please ask Tornaghi to send me the bill for the guano I bought from the Cantú firm last spring. [. . .]

Greetings
G. Verdi

NOTE

1. Postmark: BUSSETO 26/5/93.

 *Ricordi to Verdi*

Milan, 27 May 1893

Illustrious Maestro,

I am in your debt: . . . . oh, for so many, many things . . . . but now for owing you an answer to two esteemed letters of yours.[1] I received the extracts from the *Falstaff* orchestra score . . . . Alas! . . what a pity there is no more work to be done with the back and forth of reductions, of galley proofs . . . . . and so on and on! In short, I repeat: what a pity. Couldn't we start all over again? . . . . .

And now, here I am: the news from Pasqua is that she was most gravely ill; first in Rome, with a terrible allergic rash, then in Bologna, with jaundice. You can imagine the desolation; her husband[2] came expressly to Milan; he, too, was in despair, with tears in his eyes. He had hoped to go to Venice and had already wired Piontelli, who announced it; then, overnight, the jaundice developed. Now she is better; apparently she wants to go to Berlin; but can she risk such a journey, just now convalescing from such a long illness? It seems dangerous to me.[3]

I had exact news about Madame Pini-Corsi from a member of the orchestra: she is quite mediocre, as Mascheroni confirmed to me in his personal letter. Too bad, since the wife's engagement would have facilitated that of her husband, who had lately gotten quite pretentious, considering himself indispensable!! [. . .]

The French translation of *Falstaff* seems to be coming along very slowly!— All the others are already in preparation. [. . .]

I immediately sent Ghislanzoni what you ordered; he is in very poor health.

Here are the bill and the receipt for the guano; we don't need them anymore, since they have already been entered in your account; and now you can better see how the manure was divided up.

For your information, we have paid fr.100 to M. Pilastre in Paris, who was your attorney in the unfortunate Bénoit affair; I thought there was no need to ask you about this little sum.

This morning I saw Maestro Gallignani; I heard his news about your health with the greatest pleasure! Evviva, then, and may it always be so excellent.

Our most affectionate greetings to Signora Peppina and to you, with undying gratitude,

Your most devoted
Giulio Ricordi

NOTES

1. Of 23 and 24 May.

2. [?] Giacomelli, under whose name she also appeared. According to Phillips-Matz, pp. 732–3, however, she was the wife of the conductor Leopoldo Mugnone (1858–1941), and also Verdi's "inseparable companion" at Montecatini. (Ibid., p. 748.)

3. Pasqua could not go to Berlin, either. Abbiati's statement that she ". . . did her share to create disagreeable troubles by pretending to be ill" is in error and defames her character. (Abbiati iv, p. 508.)

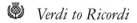 *Verdi to Ricordi*

Busseto, 29 May 1893

Dear Giulio,

Thank you for all the news you give me.

I am very, very sorry for Pasqua! What a calamity!

I answered Darclée;[1] must answer Zilli[2] but don't know where and how to address the letter. Send me her address.

I am in the midst of the tears and desperation of these poor peasants! Saturday a very long and severe storm destroyed everything: *Beans, crops, wheat, corn,* mulberries, grapes, meadows!! In short, everything, everything!

Nothing is left to us! Beasts and humans won't even have grass to eat, which doesn't exist anymore, just earth! . .

I'll write you again later about the matters in Paris, which I wish would end as soon as possible so that we will hear no more about them. .

Good-bye for now.   Your
                                                              G. Verdi

P.S. To save you the trouble of sending me Zilli's address, I'm enclosing my letter[3] in answer to hers, and ask you to address it.

NOTES

    1. See Verdi to Ricordi, 23 May, and *Otello* i, p. 385.
    2. See Verdi to Mascheroni, 15 May. (Zilli's letter is missing.)
    3. Missing.

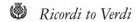

Ricordi to Verdi

Milan, 30 May 1893

Illustrious Maestro,

    No!— It isn't finished![1] Today I am sending you the 2nd part, act 1, of the French text, which Boito gave me so that you might be kind enough to look over the pages on which you will find markings. In the margin, there are red marks wherever a change was made to improve the verses. Boito desires your approval before the engraving.

    Please return this passage to me so I may send it on to the engravers.

    Meanwhile I have the pleasure of greeting you again and repeating that I am

Your most grateful and devoted
Giulio Ricordi

NOTE

    1. See Ricordi to Verdi, 27 May, para. 1. (See also Hepokoski, p. 77.)

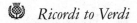

Ricordi to Verdi

Milan, 31 May 1893

Illustrious Maestro,

    I received your esteemed letter of the 29th and am quite distressed by what you write; I imagine the sight of desolation, not to mention the consequences . . . . in financial terms!!— And your garden? . . was it also hit and devastated? . . . In short, when there are nice times in this world, several ugly ones follow right after; perhaps it's a law of compensation . . . . but not at all a pleasant one.— And so, while I am going through certain bad days of *spleen* . . . . the hail at St. Agata confirms it to me . . . . for I like to get only good news from you!—

Just as I received your letter, I got a note from Signora Zilli giving me her address in Berlin, and so I have already sent her your letter.[1]

I have a note for the 8th of June about the payment of the 2nd *Falstaff* installment. Please tell me what to do, and whether it may perhaps be convenient for you if I send you a check from the Banca Nazionale for 40,000 Lire.

With regard to *Falstaff*, Canori,[2] before dissolving the Berlin company, plans 6 *popular* performances with the same cast at the Costanzi in Rome. He says that the majority of the public still has not heard the opera; that such a well-matched company can hardly be put together again, even the way it is now made up; that its return to Rome would be greatly welcomed and would crown the tour in a dignified manner, all the more so since the Rome orchestra is still assembled and, therefore, would be in readiness. What do you think about it? . . . Would you favor me with your revered opinion as soon as possible, before the company is dissolved? Hold off for the outcome in Berlin?. . As Falstaff, Blanchard,[3] who rehearsed with the orchestra in Venice, is making an excellent impression.

Awaiting your answer, I send affectionate greetings and am ever your most grateful

Giulio Ricordi

NOTES

1. Missing (see Verdi to Ricordi, 29 May, n. 4).
2. Impresario for the tour in Berlin (Verdi to Ricordi, 21 May, n. 3).
3. Ramón Blanchard (1865–1934), a versatile baritone from Barcelona, replaced Maurel, who refused to appear in Berlin (see Verdi to Ricordi, 11 April, n. 1). Soon after his debut at Barcelona in 1885, Blanchard was acclaimed as a singer and actor. He had earlier replaced Maurel as Iago in Verdi's *Otello* at La Scala in 1892. Among many other baritone roles, Blanchard's Falstaff, too, won international praise.

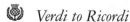 *Verdi to Ricordi*

[St. Agata] 1 June 1893

Dear Giulio,

Oh, just go ahead with *Falstaff* in Rome whenever and however you want . . . . better in Rome than in Vienna and Berlin! How much better it would have been to end the tour after Trieste!—

1893

I'll write you another time about the installment in June[1]—
Addio in haste

G. Verdi

P.S. Have returned 1st act *Fals.* translation [French] yesterday at once.

NOTE

1. See Ricordi to Verdi, 31 May, para. 3.

 *Edoardo Mascheroni to Verdi*

[Telegram]   Berlin, 2 June 1893

IMPERATIVE YOU WIRE COUNT HOCHBERG[1] DELIGHTED FALSTAFF TRI-
UMPH CONGRATULATING EXCELLENT ORCHESTRA — MASCHERONI[2]

NOTES

1. Hans Heinrich XIV, Bolko, Count von Hochberg (1843–1926), Prussian diplomat
and composer, was general manager of the royal theatres in Berlin from 1886 to 1903.
2. Mascheroni conducted four performances of *Falstaff* in Berlin between 1 and 7 June
at the end of the tour.

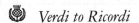 *Verdi to Ricordi*

St. Agata, 2 June 1893

[. . .] Read this telegram from Mascheroni . . . .
Imperative!!!
Why? If Count Hochberg had wired me, I would have replied; but in this
case I think I may be excused from sending a telegram.
According to the *Corriere* it was a partial success.

Addio, addio.
G. Verdi

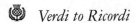 *Verdi to Ricordi*

St. Agata, 5 June 1893

Dear Giulio,
Here is my answer regarding the 2nd *Falstaff* installment. With this sum
and the other one of last December, I would like to pay all I owe and be done

with . . that ill-fated Bénoit affair!! Pay it all, all, all . . . so that I may never again hear about it, . . never again, never again. The sooner you do it, the better . . . for, if I should feel like dying, I wouldn't want to be obliged to live in order to pay bills to the living.

Don't think that I'm joking. No, no: I really wish to settle it once and for all!

Addio—

Your
G. Verdi

 *Verdi to Giuseppina Negroni Prati*

St. Agata, 5 June 1893[1]

[. . .] Do not for a moment believe in the peace of St. Agata! It's a big lie! I really ought to enjoy a little peace, but it isn't possible! Any bore on earth, or some desperate fellow comes here to seek me out, preferably in person, in my retreat; then letters, impossible projects, advice about what remains to be done and what I must do!! Ugh! And troubles, troubles upon troubles, and even disasters! A fierce hail has destroyed two-thirds and more of the entire annual produce for me and my neighbors: Hay, mulberries, wheat, corn, grapes. . . . Imagine the cries of these poor farmers! For them the damage isn't just material! These are the joys of life![2] [. . .]

We, my wife and I, are at an age at which such [travel] plans are impossible. We have arrived and must stay put! [. . .]

NOTES

1. In answer to a missing letter.
2. See Verdi to Ricordi, 29 May.

Verdi to Edoardo Mascheroni

St. Agata-Busseto, 8 June 1893

Dear Mascheroni,

I assure you that I have not received your letters from Vienna. Your last one was dated 12 May from Trieste! Thereafter I have heard almost nothing more about *Falstaff*, and I don't complain. Recalling my troubles, I can imagine your own: apart from all that labor, the gossip, the tantrums, and, as you say, also the *insults!!* . . . . This is bad, very bad . . . . but have no illusions. You will find these things under similar conditions in the future, too.

The theatre is and must be this way! . .

1893

When seasons are normal, they end quickly; one goes to the right, one goes to the left, and good night; but on a tour like this one, the artists are together too much, they know each other too well; they all think they're indispensable, that they're the only ones entitled to applause . . . their puffed-up heads are growing, growing, growing, and they end up believing, and believing themselves to be who knows what!— There is no remedy! At moments of major excitement one may try a shower of ice water on their heads . . . and it should also inundate the stage, the dressing rooms, and all the rest! . . . .

If you are waiting to come to Busseto for the performance of *Forza del destino*,[1] you will have to wait quite a while! Busseto's finances don't allow a theatre production. But even if we shouldn't see each other in Montecatini, the house at St. Agata hasn't moved and is always open for you!

Enough of this chatter—

I greet you from Peppina and take your hands.

Your
G. Verdi

NOTE

1. Mascheroni might have heard a rumor about such a plan.

 Verdi to Ricordi

St. Agata, 8 June 1893

Dear Giulio,

Mascheroni writes me from Berlin about the toils and troubles he had!![1] . . He tells me that he's leaving Berlin tomorrow, Friday; therefore, this letter of mine would not arrive in time. I'm sending it to you because you will know where to find him . . .

Take care of the Bénoit business! . . For God's sake! Addio.

G. Verdi

NOTE

1. In a missing letter.

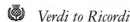 *Verdi to Ricordi*

St. Agata, 9 June 1893[1]

Dear Giulio,

Send the 316 kilos[2] to my address in care of the Borgo San Donnino station.

From now on, just as old Cato, upon leaving the Senate, shouted, *"Delenda Carthago,"* I will shout . .

   Deliver me from Bénoit.

When I pass through Milan on my way to Montecatini, please give me the *remainder* you owe me.

   Addio, addio

G. Verdi

NOTES

   1. This letter, without the first sentence, is published under the date 7 June 1893 in *Copialettere*, p. 710.

   2. Probably an agricultural product.

 Verdi to Ricordi

[Busseto] 14 June 1893

Dear Giulio,

Delenda Carthago!!

etc., etc., etc.

Do me the favor of having your Signor Nuti pay, from my account in Rome, for the subscription I am enclosing, and send it to Rome. [. . .]

   Boito is in London!! Hasn't the future *Doctor*[1] written you at all?—

   Addio, addio

Affectionately,

G. Verdi

NOTE

   1. On 13 June, along with Max Bruch, Camille Saint-Saëns, and Pyotr Ilyich Tchaikovsky, Boito received an honorary doctor's degree at Cambridge University.

 Verdi to Edoardo Mascheroni

St. Agata, 15 June 1893

Dear Mascheroni,

   I received your letter of the 13th[1] and share your joy in the ovations in Vienna and Berlin: solid ovations that prove to be facts, in view of the splendid offers Berlin and Hamburg have made you. And that is all very well.—

   You ask for my advice? And what advice? Who could give it?—

   It can be a serious error to say: *Go.* As it can also be to say: *Remain.*

1893

Conditions in our theatres are certainly deplorable. There is no security at all! Even the capital has no theatre!! Only La Scala is still holding on, but no one can be sure that it may not soon be closed. All the projects that had until recently been planned can hardly be realized. A firm repertoire is impossible with us and our audience! Give them [La Scala's audience], for example, this year's company for two consecutive years with the best operas in its repertoire, including Maurel in *Rigoletto, Hamlet*, etc., etc., and then tell me. Each country must be left to its innate character, and here we must every once in a while put up with indecent hullabaloo and stupid judgments! It's bad, but that's the way it is! These conditions are truly deplorable, and conditions at German theatres . . . . are better in many ways, particularly as regards the security of salaries and retirement [benefits] after ten years of service. On the other hand, they have a repertoire for which knowledge of their language is indispensable; hostility, if dormant at this time, will awaken later; and also the war of all conductors and non-conductors against *the Italian*. All that is inevitable! Will you have the courage to face all that baseness with the armor of indifference? It is the only sure and certain armor, but difficult to put on!

There is more to it . . You have said it yourself: the education of the children; a big problem to solve. Either you leave your family here in Italy for nine months and go alone; or you take the whole family with you, giving the children an education that will be neither Italian nor German. You will tell me that they are going to be educated as you wish. No, don't deceive yourself. Your children will breathe that air, and it will alter their blood and mind.—

And after this picture you want my advice!![2]

God help me!—

That's all for now; I'll tell you other things at another time. Now I greet you, also from Peppina, and take your hands.

Addio

G. Verdi

NOTES

1. Missing.
2. Mascheroni decided against a position in Germany.

 Verdi to Ricordi

[Busseto] Thursday evening [16 June 1893]

Dear Giulio,

Delenda Carthago!

The boxes have now arrived![1] Whom do I have to thank if I haven't already done so?

Tell me what I must do.

Addio

Your
G. Verdi

NOTE

1. See Verdi to Ricordi, 24 May.

 *Verdi to Ricordi*

St. Agata, 18 June 1893

Dear Giulio,

Delenda Carthago —

This weekend we'll be in Milan,[1] and I hope that *Carthage* will be destroyed.

[. . .] I've heard nothing more from Pasqua! Nobody said a word about it to me after you did. What's the matter? . .

'Til we see each other. Addio, addio

Affectionately,
G. Verdi

NOTE

1. The weekend of 24–25 June on the way to Montecatini, where they arrived on 3 July.

 *Ricordi to Verdi*

Milan, 20 June 1893

Illustrious Maestro,

well then, soon we will have the pleasure of seeing you! . . Evviva, evviva, evviva! . . It is a feast for all of us, and a real joy for me in particular, for when

I have the good fortune to see our great Verdi, I feel that I am gaining years of life, and the bad moods tormenting me, because I am tired, tired and weary, disappear! Ah! . . . If I were able—in even microscopic proportions—to follow your example and live in any little place in the country! . . . . But how to do this, with all these blessed children and grandchildren . . . . and Noah's entire Ark! I must drag the chains and live the life of a galley slave. [. . .]

Pasqua is recovered; it seems that she should also take the cure at Montecatini, having suffered a bad case of jaundice; I wrote her a few days ago asking for her news, but have had no answer.

I also haven't heard from Boito since his doctoral departure. . . . . He got lost in the gown and the mortarboard!! [. . .]

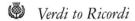 *Ricordi to Verdi*

Milan, 6 July 1893

Illustrious Maestro,

I hope you had an excellent journey in excellent health, and that you began the cure with excellent results, and that you again found the usual congenial company.

Giuditta renews her greetings, regretting not having seen you.

I am sending books and orchestra score to Busseto.

Always affectionately, with enduring gratitude,
Your most devoted
Giulio Ricordi

Verdi to Ricordi

Montecatini, 10 July 1893

Dear Giulio,

Thank you for the telegraphed news from Buenos Aires;[1] and even greater thanks for the good news from you and your family.

Here we spend our time drinking and eating, eating and drinking . . . . and eating too much! Not Peppina! . . she doesn't eat!

The heat has six ♯s in the key signature, but it's tolerable.

Wishing good health to everyone and lots of good things to you all . . . addio, addio

Affectionately,
G. Verdi

NOTE

1. A missing telegram concerning the first *Falstaff* at the Teatro de la Opera in Buenos Aires on 8 July 1893, conducted by Cleofonte Campanini (1860–1919), with Antonio Scotti (1866–1936) as Falstaff.

 *Ricordi to Verdi*

Milan, 14 July 1893

Illustrious Maestro,

I thank you for your kind letter, very happy about your good news.

Just for a change . . . . a nuisance, as you will see from the enclosed,[1] sent to me by Maestro Marchetti. As you can see, a portrait of you with your signature and a couple of words alluding to Mozart are desired for the Mozart Museum.[2]— So I am the envoy of the Embassy . . . . and am also sending you the portrait, to save time. You can send it on by registered mail to Maestro Filippo Marchetti — R. Accademia di Santa Cecilia — Rome.

Even down there . . . . . you are tormented . . . . but as the envoy of the Embassy, I should not bear the punishment. Meanwhile, this provides me with the pleasure of sending you cordial greetings and of repeating my feelings of warmest gratitude.

Your most devoted
Giulio Ricordi

NOTES

1. Informal and unsigned request, written by hand in French, from the Austro-Hungarian Embassy in Italy.
2. Presumably the Mozarteum in Salzburg.

 *Verdi to Giuseppe De Amicis*

Tuesday [Montecatini, 18 July 1893][1]

Dear De Amicis,

The letters bring good news: *"Distinct improvement continues. General condition satisfactory. Our hearts comforted."*[2] So they wire us. I hope you had a good journey;[3] we leave tomorrow evening. Greetings.

G. Verdi

NOTES

1. Postmark: BAGNI DI MONTECATINI 18/7/93.

1893

2. Leonello Sartoris, the editor of the Verdi–De Amicis correspondence, states in a footnote: "We have no precise information; however, we believe that this concerns the mezzo-soprano Giuseppina Pasqua, who in other letters, too, appears in this connection."

3. Presumably returning to Genoa from Montecatini, where they may have discussed Pasqua's illness.

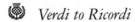 *Verdi to Ricordi*

Montecatini, 18 July 1893

Dear Giulio,

We leave tomorrow evening. Thursday morning around six o'clock we'll be in St. Agata. Write me there and tell me if for the end of the month the balance for the last half-year, ending in June, has been accounted for.

Addio, addio

Affectionately,
G. Verdi

 *Verdi to Eugenio Tornaghi*

Busseto St. Agata, 24 July 1893

Dear Signor Tornaghi,

From your most esteemed letter[1] I learn with pleasure that [Giulio] has decided to go to the country. The rest will do him good; he really needs rest.

I received the two contracts for *Forza del destino,* which I am returning *by registered mail,* together with the others I had in my possession.

The sum for the half-year at the end of the month is all right. I shall write you in a couple of days where to send it . . . probably to Genoa as before.

I greet you cordially.

[Illegible]
G. Verdi

NOTE

1. Missing.

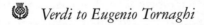 *Verdi to Eugenio Tornaghi*

St. Agata, 29 July 1893[1]

Dear Signor Tornaghi,

I am very happy that Giulio enjoyed the air in the country so much. I hope he will profit from it whenever he can.—

I beg you, then, to send the *check* here for the bank in Genoa (if you can, by Monday) so that I might go to cash it Wednesday or Thursday.—
Good health and greetings,

Your

G. Verdi

And the gift that I had to give to *Sauchon?!* It's taking too long.[2]

NOTES

1. In answer to a missing letter.
2. See Verdi to Ricordi, 17 [16] May, n. 3.

 *Ricordi to Verdi*

Comerio,[1] 31 July 1893

Illustrious Maestro,

My rather long silence is due to various reasons—not the least being my health, which is a bit shaken, either by physical indisposition, or by such grave and persistent depressions that it takes much will power not to give in to deadly despondency.— This is but one of the reasons that kept me from writing you; I didn't want to bore you with my miseries, which, as the years go on, persuade me of two things: that in business a gentleman and a dupe are one and the same, and that a gentleman does nothing good for the future of his family! And here I leave off and tell you that last week I accompanied the whole gang to this house . . . . deserted. But . . . . we are very close to Ginetta; her appearance is more than splendid, it is enchanting![2] [. . .]

I went to Milan again on business; then back here again for three days, to find out if in this good air my sick stomach would calm down. The day after tomorrow, I return to Milan, and next Sunday I'll be in Brescia for the stage rehearsals of the *Great Potbelly!!* Long may he live, and his creator, who brought him into the world. [. . .]

Read the article I am enclosing.[3] There are two or three mistakes, but it is essentially true. Sonzogno's attorney asked Tornaghi for a conference and more or less disclosed the project mentioned in the article. Tornaghi informed me of it, and a moment later Boito happened to come to my office. Of course, the first thing to do is to call upon you and to hear . . . . how this latest bomb hits you.—My own impression is negative, and so is Boito's; it's clear that Sonzogno would like to serve huge dishes to make us swallow his rancid sauces! But . . . . we may also be wrong; and therefore we must know your opinion. If Tornaghi, however, should have to reply right away, then I would ask you to kindly wire me upon receiving this letter.

If he is to give a negative reply, please wire: Very well.

In the other event, please wire: Wait—Will write.[4]
Whatever your reply may be, I shall convey it, of course.

And herewith I have managed to bother you even from out here! . . . It is my job.

Please send all telegrams or letters to Milan, where I shall be the day after tomorrow in the morning.

The offspring, big, little and very little, are all well. I would like to know that you and Signora Peppina are also well, and send you most affectionate greetings, renewing the keenest expression of immense and enduring gratitude.

Your most devoted
Giulio Ricordi

NOTES

1. Village between Varese and Laveno (Lago Maggiore).

2. During pregnancy.

3. "Italian Art Abroad," in the *Resto del Carlino*, a prominent newspaper in Bologna, regarding the idea of Ricordi's competitor Sonzogno for an Italian season at the Paris Opéra.

4. Below a postage stamp on the envelope, marking this letter's arrival on 2 August, Verdi scribbled these words, presumably the text of the requested (missing) telegram: "Received letter. Leaving for Genoa where will stay until Sunday. The idea is wrong, as I already wrote to Maurel [in a missing letter]. [. . .] Shall write about the rest."

 *Verdi to Eugenio Tornaghi*

Busseto St. Agata, 1 August 1893[1]

Dear Signor Tornaghi,

I have received the two checks for the Bank of Genoa, and am sending you the receipt.

Giulio has done well to go breathe different air from that of the Omenoni[2]. . . . and may it do him good!

Let's hope that the furnace will finally be hot enough to cook those damned plates for Sauchon.

The poet Ferdinando Fontana writes me for a contribution for a bust of poor Ghislanzoni! I don't like to contribute, but will offer two hundred (200) Lire for this purpose, as long as the project materializes.

Good health and greetings.

Your
G. Verdi

NOTES

    1. In answer to a missing letter from Tornaghi.
    2. Ricordi's office in the Contrada degli Omenoni, near Milan's City Hall and La Scala.

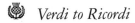 *Verdi to Ricordi*

Genoa, 4 August 1893

Dear Giulio,

Before speaking of business, I wish you a healthful vacation, begging you to take care of your body and, above all, not to let yourself be oppressed by sad thoughts. What are the miseries of life, after all! And what are the joys? . .

Zero, zero, and zero.—

I wired you about the *Opéra*.[1] You know that I am not very fond of that *grande boutique*, but it is a recognized theatre, after all; and to give one night a French opera in an expensive production, the next night an Italian opera in a cheap one, seems outrageous to me.

Othello in Belgium! If it were in Brussels it might work, but in the provinces I don't think so.[2]

If you go to Brescia, observe very carefully, and watch, watch, watch. The protagonist you have engaged doesn't have the talent to do Falstaff, after all.[3]

The day after tomorrow I leave for St. Agata, where I'll be at 4 o'clock.— Let me hear from you. . Good health and greetings.

Affectionately,
G. Verdi

NOTES

    1. See Ricordi to Verdi, 31 July, n. 4.
    2. See *Otello* i, p. 385.
    3. Arturo Pessina.

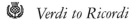 *Verdi to Ricordi*

Busseto, 8 August 1893

Dear Giulio,

In Paris they ask me, with a certain very annoying insistence, what the truth is about the Sonzogno business at the Opéra,[1] whether I'll go to Paris, etc., etc.

1893

I must reply . . . and at the same time don't want to reply! . . What to do? *I.e.:* If on your own behalf you were compelled to say a few words in the papers, you could express my opinion, too . . . that is, that I consider this an *outrageous* idea . . . ; then I would send the whole reply to the paper, but it would have to be done fast . . .

In a hurry addio.
G. Verdi

NOTE

1. See Ricordi to Verdi, 31 July, n. 4.

 *Ricordi to Verdi*

Brescia, 10 August 1893

Illustrious Maestro,

Further to my telegram[1] to give you more detailed news.— I attended a stage rehearsal and the first dress rehearsal—and as I wired you, it went very well; of course, this is based on the premise that we are dealing with a provincial theatre with a subsidy of 20,000 Lire!—Bravo, bravissimo our little Mascheroni, who in a few days performed miracles with a mediocre orchestra, obtaining liveliness, vigor, and elegance.— The majority of the artists . . . . . are known to you *lippis et tonsoribus*.[2] Let's move on to Guerrini, then, a good, attractive *Quickly*. Now to the dark horse: Pessina. To tell you the truth, my faith was shaken by such formidable doubts;[3] therefore I heard and watched him with great distrust; now I am happy to be able to tell you that he will be an excellent Falstaff. There certainly exists a line of demarcation between him and Maurel: certain details of refinement, partly due to vocal facility, partly to natural talent, but largely due to Verdi's unique, most subtle coaching, which Pessina did not receive—no! But he has many other good qualities: a firm secure voice, which gives many, many phrases greater clarity. Good in the entire first act; excellent in the duet with Ford; superior to Maurel in *te lo cornifico!* No Maurel in *Quand' ero paggio*, but better than good. Excellent in the third act monologue, and good in all the rest. Enunciation perfectly clear; he moves well onstage. His partners declare him far superior to Blanchard.— Excellent sets; today I'll see the costumes. This morning at 12 o'clock special stage rehearsal with the 3rd act chorus. Tonight dress rehearsal; tomorrow rest. Saturday 1st performance.

This dear *Falstaff* and his creator shall be forever blessed! Last night, in the dark auditorium, I had a delightful time, the first after many months of intense displeasures and afflictions!! I enjoyed it as if it were the first time.

What joy! What joy! What joy!

The good Bazzini,[4] living here in the country, has attended *16 rehearsals!!* . . and *hasn't missed* a single one! . . So great is his interest, so amused and excited is he!

Blessed be that great magician *Verdi!* I'll wire him further news. Sunday I'll be in Milan. In the meantime, I owe you even more gratitude: I repeat that after several months, three delightful hours last night have given me peace and tranquillity; and I found again the refreshing sleep which for many, many nights I had longed for in vain. So then, in certain cases: *Prescription: Falstaff!!!*

Let us hope that no indispositions may occur, and that everything may go *comme sur des roulettes*. [. . .]

NOTES

1. Missing.
2. Ricordi's Latin reference is to the Seventh Satire from Book I of Horace's *Sermones*. The line in the poem is "omnibus et lippis notum et tonsoribus esse" [known to all, both the sore-eyed and the barbers, i.e., to nearly everyone] (Horace. *Sat.* I.vii.3).
3. See Verdi to Ricordi, 17 June 1892, 11 April, and 4 August 1893.
4. See Boito to Verdi, 25 April 1891, n. 3.

 Verdi to Edoardo Mascheroni

St. Agata, 10 August 1893[1]

Dear Mascheroni,
   We are born to suffer!

And you think that composers and conductors can go without eating their heart out every day, a piece for breakfast and one for dinner, always reserving a bit for tomorrow!!!

I had imagined everything you tell me. I know big and little theatres only too well not to understand the problems you encountered; and you are lucky if you could overcome them, at least in part.

Certainly, certainly Pini-Corsi will end up having a golden statue made of himself!! He will be more grateful than anyone else for the favor you did him!!!! A true favor from a friend![2]

I say nothing about the protagonist;[3] you will tell me! . . . . After his first performance you will write me the real truth about how he is doing. . . . . Meanwhile, thank the artists who will remember me, and among the three Wives, give my regards to the good ones as well as the bad ones. I say *three*, because I don't know the new one;[4] the *fourth* I saw at Montecatini,[5] desolate because she couldn't finish the tour.—

Poor Catalani![6]

A good man and an excellent musician! It is a great pity! Please compliment Giulio upon the few and beautiful words he said about the poor man. Shame and reproach to the others![7]

My regards to the most illustrious Zanardelli;[8] and tell him that I remember most gratefully the favor for that poor youngster who might now be carrying an *Austrian rifle* on his shoulder instead of being a musician in your orchestra!![9]

And you? — You know that we are at St. Agata, and that you will always be welcome on any occasion, at any time, at any hour.—

Greetings from my wife and a handshake from

Your G. Verdi

NOTES

1. In answer to a missing letter from Mascheroni written between *Falstaff* rehearsals in Brescia. The young conductor seems to have complained particularly about Pini-Corsi's obvious arrogance and resentment that, in Brescia, his wife was not engaged for the role of Meg.

2. Apparently, Mascheroni had yielded to Pini-Corsi's demand to keep his wife in the role of Meg for the entire tour after Rome. (See Verdi to Ricordi, 21 May, and Ricordi to Verdi, 27 May.)

3. Arturo Pessina.

4. Emilia Pini-Corsi.

5. Pasqua.

6. The composer Alfredo Catalani had died in Milan on 7 August, following a violent hemorrhage he had suffered on a train in Switzerland.

7. Verdi alludes to the many who did not attend the funeral, perhaps including even himself. (*Carteggi* iii, pp. 94–5.)

8. Giuseppe Zanardelli (1826–1903), President of the Chamber of Deputies, had fought in the Risorgimento and been sent by Garibaldi to his native Brescia to promote that town's participation in the movement. He lived at this time in Brescia.

9. Thanks to Zanardelli's intervention with the Italian ambassador in Vienna, Luigino Ricci and his son Rienzi had gained Italian citizenship. (See Verdi to Ricordi, 16 November 1892, nn. 7 and 8.)

 *Verdi to Edoardo Mascheroni*

Busseto–St. Agata, 16 August 1893
"Well, that's done with,"[1]
said the fellow who had killed his father!! We haven't killed anyone;

nevertheless, we have fleeced the good audience a bit; but as long as they don't complain, it's not too bad! . . . Still, still, after the fifth or sixth performance you will tell me something about the box office. Anyway, my compliments to everyone, my . . . . . what shall I say? Well, I'll shout bravo, bravissimo to all the singers, and to you: *ten points!! Amen!*

I greet you from Peppina and clasp your hand.

P.S. Oh, I forgot to tell you that I am delighted to have been wrong about the protagonist![2] That is, I am delighted about his success! I hear, however, that his *make-up* was horrible! Oh, these Italian artists!! In their stupid vanity they don't care about such trifles and would rather do badly than do as others have done!

And there he had a model, who, particularly in this respect, could not be surpassed![3] [. . .]

NOTES

1. Referring to the first performance of *Falstaff*, following the tour, at the Teatro Grande in Brescia on 12 August.

2. I.e., Pessina.

3. Victor Maurel. Some two years later, Verdi's Ford, Pini-Corsi, committed the same error in his own interpretation of Falstaff, under Toscanini's baton in Turin. Pini-Corsi exaggerated the comic aspects of Falstaff's make-up and deportment in general. The young conductor, whose later performances of *Falstaff* became legendary, did not seem to object, at a time when conductors were responsible for the total production. (See Della Corte, *Toscanini*, p. 40.)

 Verdi to Edoardo Mascheroni

St. Agata, 18 August 1893

Dear Mascheroni,

I don't remember for certain if in the letter I wrote you yesterday[1] I asked you about things I must know:

1. How many performances will be given in Brescia?

2. What is the second opera?[2]

3. And when and on what day will the last performance be?[3] —

Addio ad.

G. Verdi

NOTES

1. Verdi means the day before yesterday, 16 August.

1893

2. See Verdi's P.S. in his letter to Ricordi of 29 March.
3. Mascheroni's replies to these questions are missing.

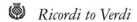 *Ricordi to Verdi*

Milan, 18 August 1893

Illustrious Maestro,
Al sommo Verdi sia gloria, onor! [Glory and honor to the supreme Verdi!]
Al Gran Pancione! al suo Autor! [To the Great Potbelly! To his Author!]

The music . . . . you will have to write yourself.— I believe Mascheroni has given you detailed news of the new, complete, and utter success in Brescia;[1] this success continued, even increased, each night, with great public acclaim. Everything went really at full tilt! The production is excellent; I preached gaiety!—gaiety!, and the performers threw themselves into it with a *verve endiablé* [devilish verve], which was a pleasure to see. Mascheroni good, very good.— But what atrocious heat! . . . the theatre illuminated by gas . . . . dressing rooms without windows . . . . delicious perfume of the most excellent choristers and illustrious extras! . . . I won't tell you about the artists you know; Guerrini as Quickly, good.— Pessina, very good 1st act; very good in the 1st part of the 2nd act, especially in the duet with Ford; adequate in the duet with Alice; very good in the entire 3rd act. He carries his belly with aplomb, moves well, enunciates crisply and clearly. The new Meg, nice, moves well.[2] The audience was amused all along, and the humble undersigned was, too!—

We are having an African heat; I am running to the country to restore myself with a bit of pure air; my whole family is very well, thank God, and that is a consolation. My health . . . *clopin-clopant!* [hobbling along] Perhaps my bones aren't destined to age too much! . . Perhaps the fierce troubles which upset me in the last months have shaken my system too much; so I hope I'll be able to recover . . . and so be it!— But this is needless melancholy! Joy returns to me the moment I read "Peppina and I are very well"!! And so evviva, evviva with all my heart from your devoted and grateful

Giulio Ricordi

NOTES

1. In a missing communication.
2. Probably Isabella Bentivoglio, an otherwise unknown artist (see Verdi to Mascheroni, 10 August, n. 1).

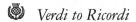

Verdi to Edoardo Mascheroni

[Telegram]   Busseto, 31 August 1893[1]

NOW I BELIEVE SUCCESS — PERHAPS IT WOULD BE MORE CONVENIENT FOR
YOU TO COME AFTER THE SEASON [in Brescia] — BUT IF YOU COME TOMOR-
ROW FRIDAY WIRE ME IMMEDIATELY — YOU LEAVE AT 7:18 CREMONA RAIL-
WAY — YOU WILL FIND MY COACH AT HOTEL DEL CAPELLO [in Cremona][2]

                                              VERDI

NOTES

    1. In response to a missing letter from Mascheroni that may also have answered Verdi's
questions of 18 August.
    2. Mascheroni came to St. Agata on Friday, 1 September.

Verdi to Ricordi

                             St. Agata, 2 September 1893
                             9 o'clock in the morning

Dear Giulio,

    Farfarello was here, as you know. He left for Brescia an hour ago. Then a
telegram arrived for him—I don't know whether from you or from
Brescia—which I sent on right away to the Teatro Grande.

    He spoke to me at length about everything that happened, about the
present and the future.

    The plan for the new tour doesn't appeal to me very much. There is
something common about it; and I now think that *Falstaff* ought to be
rented out[1] as best as can be, and that things should go as God wills. I add,
too, that the tour would go to small towns with few resources. Supposing
the receipts should not suffice and the management be compelled to *pack
up and get out!* That would be a rather black mark!! Better the other plan,
to find new artists and make up another, altogether different company.
This is a good idea. I have always thought, and still think, that *Falstaff* is
a very easy opera to produce; and one that, with a bit of instruction, almost
everybody can perform. The proof is that, despite their lack of talent, two
presentable Falstaffs in addition to the first one were found.[2] There are
twenty who can do Ford well (not, however, like Pini); and many who can
do the wives. But much attention must be paid to Alice's part. Alice is the

most important part after Falstaff. Zilli, who has much talent and who understands and acts well, doesn't have the flexible voice, however, or the free and easy deportment for that part. She is good, I repeat, but she doesn't render the part with the brio that is needed, as I also told you, if you recall, at the rehearsals in Milan. Alice is the most important part, after Falstaff. .

For Falstaff, don't meddle with artists who want to sing too much and express feeling and action by falling asleep on the notes. . .

I have spoken . . . and see that you do [for me].

Addio, addio

Affectionately,
G. Verdi

NOTES

1. The *Falstaff* material.
2. Blanchard in Berlin, and Pessina in Brescia.

 *Boito to Verdi*

4 September [1893]
Milan[1]

Dear Maestro,

We must think about doing another work together,[2] because otherwise, we who don't care for idle letters will end up writing each other upon every bishop's death.—[3]

Meanwhile, the French translation[4] has progressed to the final page; only fourteen verses are missing, which will be done in two evenings of work.

I will arrive at St. Agata this *Saturday* with the finished translation; I will take the usual train, which stops at Fiorenzuola at the usual time.

We will work together revising the translation; then I shall return to Milan to hand it all over to Giulio. But in October, my favorite month, I will come back to St. Agata for a longer stay.

Cordial greetings to Signora Giuseppina and to you.

Your most affectionate
Arrigo Boito

P.S. The publisher Gilder in New York[5] wrote me to obtain an article from you about Palestrina,[6] or at least a conversation of yours on the same subject—dictated to a *stenographer!!* I replied that this business seemed to me difficult to realize.

Till we see each other Saturday.

NOTES

1. Postmark: MILANO 4/9/93.

2. Among Boito's papers is a complete sketch of a libretto for *King Lear* in three acts. Supposedly, Boito once mentioned the sketch or the hope for another collaboration to Verdi, but Signora Giuseppina urged the librettist to give up the idea. (Nardi, pp. 593–4. See also Phillips-Matz, pp. 500–2.) Pietro Mascagni remembered Verdi's offer to let him have "a vast amount of material on that monumental subject (King Lear) [. . .] to make a heavy task lighter." When Mascagni asked Verdi why he himself had not composed *King Lear,* "Verdi closed his eyes for several seconds, perhaps to remember, perhaps to forget. Softly and slowly he then replied: 'The scene when Lear is alone on the heath terrified me!'" (Conati, pp. 313–4.)

3. Italian saying, meaning "very rarely."

4. Of *Falstaff*. (See Hepokoski, p. 77.)

5. Richard Watson Gilder (1844–1909) was editor of *The Century Magazine* in New York, and an influential figure in the cultural life of America during this time. His wife, Helena, was a close friend of Duse. (See Weaver, pp. 98–9.)

6. For the tercentenary of Palestrina's death, in 1894.

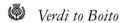 *Verdi to Boito*

[Telegram]   Busseto, 6 September 1893

AGREED — SATURDAY YOU CAN FIND COACH AT FIORENZUOLA AFTER THREE

VERDI

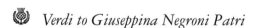 *Verdi to Giuseppina Negroni Patri*

St. Agata, 10 September 1893

[. . .] Our health is as good as can be at our tender age. I still feel the exertion of Rome. It was only eight days; but what days! I don't walk anymore at my former speed and tire immediately.

I am still working on *Falstaff.* Boito is here and we are putting the finishing touches on the French translation. It is useless work, since now we will certainly not go to Paris;[1] but this translation was begun and had to be finished, after all. [. . .]

NOTE

1. Because of growing political tension between France and Italy. (See *Otello* i, pp. 379, 386–8, 418, and *Otello* ii, p. 818.)

1893

 Ricordi to Verdi

Comerio, 10 September 1893

Illustrious Maestro,

Surtout pas trop de zèle! Your letter,[1] precisely because of the recipient's zeal, has twice gone from Milan to Comerio and back! . . It ran after me during my quick trips, without ever reaching me in time! . . . That is why I am unintentionally late in answering you.— A definite plan for another *Falstaff* tour has not come about; at most it was to be repeated in one or two cities in the autumn, but that was a vague proposition which is not going to happen. Besides, I am entirely of your opinion. For the forthcoming Carnival, two new companies have been almost completely assembled, and I hope they will be homogeneous, that is, Turin and Ferrara. Now I am negotiating for the Bellini in Naples, and that will be the third; but this one will be a bit more difficult, in view of the city's importance; however, we shall also succeed there, after all. As you see, all of this is linked to the ideas you have expressed.— In the autumn, the Pagliano in Florence should also be considered, with some of the artists from Brescia, along with some new ones.—Very well also regarding Zilli: I have already heard three or four![2] . . But, alas, just parrots, without spirit and brains; however, we'll discover some, after all. [. . .][3]

Mascheroni wrote me excellent news about your health! Evviva, then; this is really good news. My whole Noah's Ark is well, whereas my own health is a bit of a see-saw; when I am here for a couple of quiet days, . . . it isn't so bad. Then . . disturbance!—1 telegram . . . 2 telegrams—and it's back to Milan.

Most affectionate greetings from us all to you and Signora Peppina. Ever your devoted and grateful

Giulio Ricordi

NOTES

1. Of 2 September.
2. Candidates for the role of Alice.
3. See *Otello* i, p. 386 for continuation.

 Verdi to Ricordi

St. Agata, *Thursday* [14 September 1893]

Dear Giulio,

Boito has left and will tell you everything about the translation, which is excellent [. . .][1]

And you can think that your *customary autumn visit could disturb? Oh!!!* Addio, addio.

Your
G. Verdi

NOTE

1. See *Otello* i, p. 386 for continuation.

 *Verdi to Boito*

St. Agata, 15 September 1893

Dear Boito,

I hope that you arrived safe and sound in Milan;

that by now you have rested from the mad joys of St. Agata;

that you have handed over the beautiful translation to Giulio;

and that you also have given my watch to the watchmaker . . . which is very important to me![1]

Peppina beats her breast about a word that escaped her, quite contrary to her wishes, the moment of your departure! . . . *"That word shall be considered unsaid."*[2] So she told me to write you.

I greet you from her and myself clasp your hands.—

Your
G. Verdi

Barberina has left!

NOTES

1. Presumably the golden repeater timepiece that played a short musical phrase on the hour. Verdi left it and its chain to Dr. Angiolo Carrara (1825–1904), his notary in Busseto, in his will dated 14 May 1900.

2. Perhaps a reference to Boito's still uncompleted *Nerone*.

 *Boito to Verdi*

Sunday [17 September 1893]
Milan[1]

Dear Maestro,

The watch is in the hands of Signor Milani, the watchmaker of the Brera Observatory,[2] who (not the observatory, but the watchmaker) told me that in a couple of weeks (or a little longer) the watch will be returned to me in perfect condition, and I myself will take it back to St. Agata in early October, and this to prove that—even before you in your scrupulous kindness had informed me—I myself had interpreted Signora Giuseppina's leave-taking as being involuntary, and if I lie, *I want my belt to break.*[3]

And this is the longest sentence I have written in my entire life.

Well then, thank you so much, dear Maestro, for your good letter; and Signora Peppina should not beat her breast. We are born to understand each other very well, all three of us, even when the word betrays our thought.

'Til we see each other again in October.

To Signora Peppina and to you my affectionate greetings.

Your
Arrigo Boito

NOTES

1. Postmark of arrival: BORGO S. DONNINO 18/9/93.

2. The Palazzo di Brera in Milan, inaugurated as a Jesuit hostel in 1651, has been the home of the noted Academy of the Arts since 1776. In addition to a picture gallery and lecture rooms, the building houses a library, which was established in 1770, and an observatory.

3. Boito quotes Falstaff in the last scene of the opera: "voglio che mi si spacchi il cinturone."

 *Ricordi to Verdi*

Milan, 20 September 1893

Illustrious Maestro,

I had planned to write you yesterday to announce my arrival with Giuditta, and I had already begun to pack my suitcase . . . . . when the lawyer informed me that on the 25th, 26th, 27th, and 28th I have to attend 4 sessions for the arbitration of the suit brought by that delightful Signor Stragra, a nephew of dear Lucca!![1] . . . Therefore, a double pleasure; sessions with lawyers and the impossibility now of giving myself the pleasure of seeing you. But since, with or without arbitration, we don't want to relinquish this great pleasure, and since I am busy at the end of the month, I must ask the most obliging Verdis to allow us to postpone our customary excursion until the end of October, after the big day of San Donnino,[2] of course. You can imagine, Maestro, how much I regret this inconvenience, and how much I fear that the delay might be a disturbance to you! . . . . But I truly hope that, without any ceremony, you will tell me frankly: "You can come after whatever day of October without causing me any trouble at all!"— [. . .][3]

Today I received the entire French translation of *Falstaff*, which I am putting into production right away.

For Naples I hope to assemble a homogeneous company; perhaps I have found an Alice; I'll hear her next week. I am still without a Fenton. In the meantime, Maestro Toscanini is engaged, and also Pessina. Three wives are being considered who, I think, will do very well. And thus, as you wish, a new company is being formed; another one for Turin.

The plan for the Pagliano in Florence has gone up in smoke, thanks to the foolishness of the impresario; but there are new plans for November, though there is also trouble ahead, because of the lack of a good conductor! They are . . . . all impossible!!

From Boito I had your excellent news; need I repeat with how much joy I received it, and how glad we all are? That would be superfluous. My family is well—I am not ill, but am not well; it may be a physical problem, but also a state of mind, for troubles and misfortunes, too, should have a limit . . . . . which in my case does not exist; however, I am not made of iron.—I anxiously await your reply—and will count the days until we'll be able to say: Here we are!—Always with devotion and deepest gratitude,

Your most affectionate
Giulio Ricordi

NOTES

1. Verdi's first publisher, Francesco Lucca (1802–72), was, like Sonzogno, Ricordi's rival.

2. Patron Saint of the diocese of Fidenza and Busseto; his feast day fell on 9 October, which this year marked Verdi's eightieth birthday.

3. See *Otello* i, p. 386, for continuation.

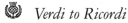 *Verdi to Ricordi*

St. Agata, 21 September 1893

Dear Giulio,

You will always be welcome at any time! [. . .]

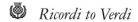 *Ricordi to Verdi*

Milan, 29 September 1893

[. . .]

As to what you write about the dear visit to St. Agata, I can only verify once again the height of the courtesy of the Verdis, and thank you, hoping to greet you soon in that delightful tranquillity.

And now let us turn to business—"ugly word," as Ford says, but it can't be avoided. [. . .]

The company for *Falstaff* in Naples is being completed; I hope to succeed in assuring a really good performance.

Remember me to the kind Signora Peppina, and let me happily conclude this letter by saying: "'Til we meet again quite soon." To this I am adding the expression of all my reverent gratitude.

Your most devoted
Giulio Ricordi

 *Verdi to Ricordi*

St. Agata, 2 October 1893

[. . .]

As to *Falstaff Opéra-Comique,* things are no longer of the same color as before.— Carvalho[1] used the same phrase with me in Milan as Grus[2] is using now, *"Je suis à votre disposition"* . . . ; at that time there was talk of Maurel, and now there no longer is. . Besides, not a word was said about the opera for eight long months. From this profound silence, I think I can guess Carvalho's intentions; and I think that with these *allures* he wants to say to his conductors and the respective cliques . . . *"Cet opéra s'impose . . . on en parle. . . il faut s'en debarrasser, nous la donnerons, quoi qu'il arrive, cela m'est egal . . . . ."* This attitude, these *allures,* this *sans façon* don't suit me at all!

In all earnest, I add that today I don't feel like burdening myself with great exertions! I will be told that someone else can relieve me. . . No, no, this isn't possible, especially in France.

So don't count on me; and if the interests of the firm and the translators require those performances,[3] I would tell you also with regard to *Falstaff* *"do what you think best,"* and permit me to finish by saying *"what good are fiascos or partial successes? What good can come of the poor showing in Stuttgard?"*[4]

Addio, addio.

Your
G. Verdi

NOTES

1. Léon Carvalho (1825–97), French baritone and impresario, was director of the Opéra-Comique at the time of the first French *Falstaff* in 1894.

2. Léon Grus (?–1902), music publisher in Paris.
3. Of *Othello* and *Falstaff* in France.
4. Of the first *Falstaff* production in German on 10 September.

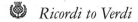 *Ricordi to Verdi*

Comerio, 10 October 1893

Most illustrious Maestro,

My health seems to be improving; but the doctor, who just now left, forbids me to work for another 5 to 6 days. Then I hope to return to Milan, and from there to make the longed-for visit to St. Agata.

In the name of all, I repeat the heartfelt wishes to our greatest, dear, blessed Maestro!![1]

I was to have written you to receive your instructions regarding the payment of 10,000 Lire owed you since the 8th of this month; but my indisposition prevented it; kindly give your instructions directly to Tornaghi.

Affectionate greetings to you and Signora Peppina from your ever grateful

Giulio Ricordi

NOTE

1. On the occasion of Verdi's eightieth birthday.

 *Verdi to Ricordi*

Cremona, 16 October 1893

Dear Giulio,

I am in Cremona, and by tonight I'll be back at St. Agata with Peppina . . . Our royal palace is thus at your disposal. Just let me know 24 hours before so I may send the coach to Fiorenzuola for you.—

Sans adieu till we see each other.

G. Verdi

Boito was to come to St. Agata in early October to . . . . *work,* I say *work!* . . . If he came now, along with you, there would be no more work! . . What a mess! . .

If he doesn't come, tell him to take care of my watch, which will be repaired by this time — pay the bill.—

1893

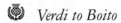 *Boito to Verdi*

1 November [1893][1]
Milan

Dear Maestro,

Camillo hasn't returned yet, and I don't know where he may be; all the people who would have given me detailed news about the Luoghi Pii[2] are still in the country, and this is the reason for my delay in writing you. But here is a card worth more than any verbal information:[3] it is the financial report of the *Luogo Pio Trivulzio*, where needy old people are lodged, and of two other charitable institutions. The average for each lodger at the Luogo Pio Trivulzio is, I believe, not very different from that of the *Albergo dei poveri di Genova*; it amounts to 345 Lire annually for each healthy lodger.—

Many kind greetings to Signora Giuseppina and to you.

I hope that Signora Maria[4] is getting better each day.

Giulio has left for Paris.[5]

'Til we see each other again soon.

Your most affectionate
Arrigo Boito

NOTES

1. This year is established by Verdi's reply, which follows immediately.

2. Charitable institutions, i.e., homes for the aged, which interested Verdi in connection with his founding of the Casa di Riposo.

3. Not located.

4. Filomena Verdi (1859–1936), daughter of a cousin of Verdi's father. The Verdis adopted her in 1867 and named her Maria. She married Alberto Carrara in 1878 and became the mother of Peppina Carrara Verdi (1879–1927), whose descendants still live in the villa at St. Agata.

5. Presumably to prepare the first French *Falstaff* at the Opéra-Comique on 18 April 1894.

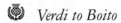 *Verdi to Boito*

St. Agata, 3 November 1893

Dear Boito,

A thousand thanks! Don't bother to get further information: What I have is sufficient; later we'll have time to talk about it.

Maria is getting better. . .

We are leaving St. Agata soon. . .[1]
Greetings from Peppina and myself.
'Til we meet again.

Affectionately,
G. Verdi

NOTE

1. In mid-November, the Verdis were in Milan, on 4 December in Genoa.

 Verdi to Camille Bellaigue

[In French]   Milan, 18 November 1893

My dear Monsieur Bellaigue,
Pardon, pardon . . . I should have written you long ago; but I wanted to
read and reread your fine book *Psychologie musicale*, and that took some time.
There are splendid and very true pages in this book: the XIIIth page of
the foreword,[1] pages 15, 16, 17 about *Palestrina*, pages 113, 114 about the
two incantations[2]—*perfectly true*—and many, many others. . . You made only
one mistake, namely, to have talked with indulgence of a composer whom
I have known, alas, for a long time. But I am too involved to forgive you
for such a sin. . . I absolve you, then, and I thank you. [. . .]

NOTES

1. Luzio notes (*Carteggi* ii, p. 303, n. 1): "The idea that beautiful music must be a *result*
rather than a *purpose*." (See Verdi to Ricordi, 3 September 1883, in *Otello* i, p. 145.)
2. Luzio also notes (ibid., n. 2): "In establishing the comparison between the blessing
of the daggers in the *Huguenots* and the oath of the Rütli in *Guglielmo Tell*, Bellaigue shows
that '*la qualité de la melodie est plus rare et la forme plus pure chez Rossini que chez Meyerbeer.*'"
[The quality of the melody is rarer and the form is purer in Rossini than in Meyerbeer.]

 Verdi to Giuseppe De Amicis

Milan, 29 November 1893

Dear De Amicis,
I am angry and furious! What is going on?—After all this time the
workmen are still in the house? . . .
But what good is this apartment to me, if in the few months I stay there
I must be plagued by odors and must freeze in the cold??!!
This indifference, this carelessness on the part of the owners is absolutely
intolerable.

1893

For many days I had planned to come to Genoa! I sent my servants ahead! My bags are packed, and I must postpone my move??

I am postponing my arrival until Saturday[1] 6 o'clock in the evening, but by that hour I demand that the painters and carpenters will have finished and left the apartment, because I come to Genoa to have peace and quiet.

I hope you will speak clearly to the agent and to whomever you think best.

Forgive also this nuisance . . . but I did not expect this ugly surprise.

Ad[dio]. Ad. Affectionately,

G. Verdi

NOTE

1. 2 December. According to Verdi's letter to Ricordi of 4 December, however, the Verdis arrived only on the 3rd.

 *Verdi to Ricordi*

Milan [Genoa], 4 December 1893[1]

Dear Giulio,

Here we are in Genoa about 20 minutes late. . Good trip, with Peppina a bit *gloomy*; and because of fog *10%* visibility from Milan to Pavia, *20%* from Pavia to Novi. After Novi a serene sky, with Venus shining splendidly before us, and a violent wind that persists. . [. . .][2]

And now, thank you for the kindnesses you extended to us; excuse us the troubles we have caused you, with the promise to cause you greater ones another time. . .

Peppina and I send our greetings to all.

Your

G. Verdi

NOTES

1. Postmark: GENOVA 4/12/93.
2. See *Otello* i, p. 389, for continuation.

 *Ricordi to Verdi*

Milan, 7 December 1893

Illustrious Maestro,

Your very dear and kind letter has moved us all, the more so since we are the ones who should be thanking the Verdis for the infinite courtesies coming one after the other without interruption. Your presence in Milan is always a real feast for us, one which passes too quickly.

We are happy about the news of your safe journey without any inconvenience.[1] Now we wish you a happy homecoming, and always the best of health.

For several days we have had splendid weather, a rare thing for Milan at this time of year. [. . .]

Hoping for the good fortune of seeing you again soon, I repeat all my gratitude to you and am ever

Your most devoted
Giulio Ricordi

NOTE

1. Cf. Verdi's contrasting view immediately above.

 Verdi to Edoardo Mascheroni

Genoa, 8 December 1893

Dear Mascheroni,

I received the *Lombardia*[1] you sent me; and in my opinion, you were wrong to have written that letter.

Let them do the talking, and you do what you must do within the limits of the possible. Invisible orchestra! . . . . It's such an old idea, which everybody, or at least many people, have dreamt of![2] I, too, would like the orchestra invisible in the theatre; but not only half the orchestra. I would like it *completely invisible!* The orchestra, part of an ideal, poetic world, playing in the midst of an applauding or booing audience, is the most ridiculous thing on earth. With the great advantages of the invisible orchestra one might tolerate even the inevitable loss of power and sonority, the nasal and weak sound that the orchestra with, so to speak, *sordini* would produce. But if the *completely invisible* orchestra is not possible—as proven not only by the Opéra, but also by many German theatres, including even Munich and Bayreuth—(I repeat *completely*) all the changes you will make are childish and have nothing to do with art. I think, alas, that 30 years from now people will laugh about these *discoveries* of ours.

For my part, I also think that your soundboard[3] underneath the orchestra pit is of no use whatsoever. With or without it, the sonority will be the same.

1893

I also think that the orchestra, whatever the case may be, should be well placed and distributed; I'm not saying that because I was the culprit who arranged it this way when I gave *Aida*,[4] but because the instruments mix well, with the strings surrounding and enveloping the wind section, the brass in particular. This would not be the case if you were to put all the double-basses in a single file next to the stage;[5] the brass would then be too open and their sound would, so to speak, be reflected by the theatre walls. By leaving the double-basses where they have been so far, the problem of the *sleeve* would be avoided. . . [6] But where will you put the harps, which are higher than that *sleeve?*

And the conductor up so high, with that *sleeve* always in motion, up and down, to the sides, all over the place?

The conductor will have to be abolished!!!

For God's sake! Don't we waste time with such questions?

Far from it, far from it! The question is simple and . . . *Amen!*

You devil of a Farfarello, you made me lose half an hour telling you all this useless nonsense!

Addio ad. ad.

Your

G. Verdi

NOTES

1. A newspaper in Milan that apparently had printed a letter to the editor from Mascheroni in which he advocated the idea of lowering the orchestra pit.

2. See *Aida*, p. 183.

3. Verdi writes "cassa armonica [sound box]."

4. See *Aida*, pp. 133, 151, 181, 183–4, 212–5, 218–9, 229, 237, 239–41, 262, 323, 356, 427.

5. See *Otello* i, pp. 353, 361.

6. The conductor's hand and sleeve protruding onto the stage.

 *Edoardo Mascheroni to Verdi*

[Milan, ca. 10 December 1893]

[. . .] With your permission, I did well to write that letter . . . about the *sleeve*, because it provided me with the welcome surprise of such an interesting, witty, authoritative letter of yours that, once and for all, eliminates all the useless and vicious discussions. Giulio laughed a lot about the conductor's *sleeve always held up* right and left, which you, with unheard-of subtle cruelty, would want to abolish!! Good Lord! So I would have to give up that sleeve, which gives me such lovely artistic satisfaction!! No, no, dear Maestro, I'd rather die!

I am still rehearsing *Walkyria* at all possible hours. There are those poor wretches, the 9 Walkyries, who must burst out with *"Hojotoho!! Hojotoho!! Hejaha . . ."* all the time.[1] I feel really sorry for them; once in a while I compensate them with caramels, and the poor darlings always bring me roses, carnations, and violets!

Giulio, to prove himself equal to the situation, still has not deigned to assist at a rehearsal; he actually shows a contemptuous and haughty indifference to anything that smells of Wagner; perhaps he is also frightened by those screaming, furious Walkyries! [. . .][2]

NOTES

1. Only 8 Valkyries appear in this scene at the beginning of the third act. Brünnhilde is the 9th.

2. *La Walkiria* opened La Scala's 1893–94 season on 26 December. See Ricordi to Verdi, 28 December, Boito to Verdi and Verdi to Mascheroni, 31 December, for the failure of that performance.

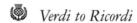 *Verdi to Ricordi*

Genoa, 10 December 1893

Dear Giulio,

I have been struck a blow and will let you have some of it, too!

I couldn't get out of receiving an American lady from Chicago, who has come to Italy to study singing and then make it her profession. She is a pretty *20*-year-old, casual manner, American face.* She wanted me to suggest a good voice teacher here or elsewhere. I replied that I don't know any voice teachers. So she asked me to refer her to a friend in Milan to find —ugh!—this blessed maestro. . . And here is your share of the blow. I gave her one of my cards for you. She'll come to Milan tomorrow; she will present herself perhaps on Tuesday, and you will do what you can, and pardon me. Mind you that I did not hear her and don't know what kind of a voice she has; she only told me that she sang the aria from *Semiramide,* *"Bel raggio,"* etc. By the time she left, I think I understood that she knows nothing or almost nothing about music. . . If this were so, it would be better to hand her over to a good musician rather than to one of the usual voice teachers . . . and in this regard Stolz's nephew[1] (should he be interested) came to mind.

Would you mind going to Stolz for five minutes to ask her this?— For that matter, is there nothing this Ricci[2] may hope for?

1893

Take care of everything. Excuse me, and don't waste time replying. Addio—

Affectionately,
G. Verdi

Greetings to all from Peppina and me.
*Her name is Miss Helen Ulrich.

NOTES

1. Luigino Ricci.
2. In his search for employment (see Verdi to Ricordi, 16 November 1892, n. 6).

 *Ricordi to Verdi*

Milan, 14 December 1893

Illustrious Maestro,

There are many fools in this world, but a bigger, more conceited fool than this Mr. Cowen doesn't exist! . . . . And of all people, he had to saddle Boito with this![1]—I know that Giacosa informed you of everything.[2] I almost never read the papers, and was informed of the *Secolino*[3] article very late Monday evening; Tuesday morning, Tito went to see Boito; but he came back home, saying that Boito had already left.[4] I regretted this very much, since I might have been able to give him some—perhaps not bad—advice in the matter. Anyway, his sudden departure is a most noble act; but I told our mutual friends right away that, even if the affair were to be settled in a duel, Boito must have gone through some upsetting moments, and worse.—I know with whom he has to deal; the real danger is that things might be protracted so that someone else might take Sonzogno's place!!— We wired Boito to keep calm, and in no way to go beyond the personal and direct question.[5] The telegram I received just now from our representative Clausetti[6] shows that my presentiments were correct: "Spent all night Boito's company; dispute not yet resolved because of Sonzogno's objection regarding seconds. Boito anxious to get it over with, most upset."

As you see, they are trying to drag it out; all this gains them time, and who knows what kind of tricks they will attempt!!—

Oh! what a rotten, disgusting, utterly disgusting world!!— You can imagine the anxiety in which all of us live! Clausetti will inform me by telegram of all that goes on, and I won't fail to let you know.—

I hope that your health is excellent; my own . . . . so-so! Work, troubles, this latest unforeseen event hurting a friend all worry me . . . . . and my stomach is caught in the middle of it. But I hope this abnormal situation, too, will pass.

I will be happy to receive two lines from you; to know at least that you are both well is the greatest consolation for someone who is ever grateful and devoted to you with all his heart.

Most affectionately,
Giulio Ricordi

NOTES

1. Sir Frederic Hymen Cowen (1852–1935), prominent British conductor and composer. His opera *Signa* had been unsuccessfully performed at the Teatro Dal Verme in Milan on 12 November 1893. Thereupon his publisher, Edoardo Sonzogno, broke their contract. Boito wrote disapprovingly of Sonzogno to Cowen in London. Cowen made the letter public, and Sonzogno learned about it, labeling Boito a "coward" in the press. Boito challenged him to a duel and on 13 December arrived in Naples, where Sonzogno was staying at that time. The seconds prevented the duel; Boito smashed the furniture at his hotel and returned to Milan in a rage. (*Otello* ii, p. 818.)

2. Ricordi refers to a long letter of 13 December in which Giacosa, greatly upset, informed Verdi in detail of the situation threatening Boito's life. (*Carteggio* ii, pp. 439–40.)

3. Ricordi's disparaging diminutive for Sonzogno's newspaper *Il Secolo,* which printed its owner's insult, prompting Boito's immediate departure for Naples.

4. For the intended duel with Sonzogno in Naples.

5. I.e., to avoid any mention of his own and Ricordi's intense dislike of Sonzogno.

6. In Naples.

 Frederick Cowen to Boito

[In Italian]   London, 14 December 1893

Dear Maestro,

I must thank you with all my heart [. . .].[1]

I have heard that Signor Sonzogno is furious about what you said in your letter.

Now I must confess that it was an indiscretion on our part (Thompson's[2] and mine) to publish that letter in the *Star*. We did it, I beg you to believe me, without thinking what result it might have. We were wrong, and all we can do is ask you to forgive us. I hope with all my heart that our indiscretion will have no *serious* consequence for you. [. . .]

NOTES

1. For the letter Boito wrote Cowen, disapproving of Sonzogno's breach of contract. (See Ricordi to Verdi, 14 December, n. 1.)

2. Herbert Thompson (1856–1945), for fifty years critic of the *Yorkshire Post,* and a friend of Cowen's.

1893

 *Verdi to Ricordi*

Genoa, 15 December 1893

Dear Giulio,

I, too, live in anxiety, just as all of you do.

Giacosa informed me of everything.—Your letter gives confirmation and adds the matter of the seconds.

Tonight I am sending a telegram about this to the *Caffaro*.[1]

Thus the duel is postponed!

Why do Bovio and Imbriani[2] refuse Boito's seconds?

You have done very well to advise Boito to keep calm and, above all, *in no way to go beyond the personal and direct question*. And it seems to me that Boito should not have worried about the seconds, but should only have given his own the authority to make all the arrangements, declaring that after the 24 hours he would have left, etc., etc. . . He need not have known about the refusal of the seconds; that didn't concern him. Nobody could accuse him of cowardice, since his immediate journey to Naples and the prompt dispatch of the seconds, etc., spoke in his favor. . . But perhaps I don't make myself clear. . . and I hope that all may be well in the future.—

Oh, that *Cowen* you can have lock, stock, and barrel! . . What an ugly thing!

Give me more news. A few words . . . . and I'll try to understand.

Greetings.

Your

G. Verdi

NOTES

1. The location of such a telegram has not been ascertained, nor has Verdi's reason for writing it.

2. Sonzogno's seconds.

 *Verdi to Emma Zilli*

Genoa, 15 December 1893[1]

Dear Signora Zilli,

It's true, it's true!

A year has gone by since the time of the *Falstaff* rehearsals, first in my home, then in the foyer of La Scala. A splendid time of enthusiasm, when we were breathing only Art! I remember the moments of happy emotion and also . . . Do you recall the third performance of *Falstaff?* I said farewell to you all; and you all were a bit moved, you and Pasqua, in particular. . . . Imagine what my greeting meant to say: "We won't see each other again as artists!!"

We met again thereafter, it's true, in Milan, in Genoa, in Rome; but my memory always brought back that third night, which meant:

It's all over!

You are fortunate still to have a long career ahead of you, and I wish that it may always be as splendid as you deserve. [. . .]

NOTE

1. In answer to a missing letter.

 Frederick Cowen to Boito

[In Italian]   London, 18 December 1893

Dear Maestro,

I was about to write you when your telegram arrived.[1] I am more than happy that all has ended well, and I am even happier that you forgive my indiscretion. [. . .]

NOTE

1. Presumably before Boito's departure from Naples.

 Verdi to Ricordi

Genoa, 20 December 1893

Dear Giulio,

I hope that by this time you will be completely restored and, when you go back to work, calm and collected. It does no good to worry. The world always has gone badly, and it always will!!

I have asked Origoni[1] to let me know what is new with Boito, and where I must send a telegram which arrived here for him three days ago!

And now excuse the trouble I am about to cause you. Ugh! Poor Giulio!

It concerns subscriptions to the following papers as of the 1st of next January:

1. To the *Corriere della sera* complete, i.e., with picture supplement
2. *Illustrazione Italiana* (complete).

3. *Italia Giovine* (Hoepli).

4. *Guerino Meschino*;[2] starting, however, from the 1st of this December, or better, pay the year 1894 plus the three months since this past October.

5. *Revue des deux mondes* / Dumelard.

Once again I entreat you to be calm and take care, which means complete health. To you, Giuditta, and everyone in your family, I send, and in Peppina's name, too, the most cordial wishes for the coming holidays.

Affectionately your

G. Verdi

P.S. I am glad about the judgment in Turin. And now . . . will it be over?[3]

Again!!!! Have Cova[4] send 20 bottles of Marsala here.

I reopened this letter to tell you that I received your telegram.[5] . . Oh dear! Oh dear! All four of you sick?!!! But I see that you are all recovered by now, and I'm glad about that.

NOTES

1. See Ricordi to Verdi, 28 September 1890, n. 5.
2. Satirical paper published weekly in Milan from 1882 until 1950.
3. Unknown.
4. See Ricordi to Verdi, 3 November 1889, n. 2.
5. Missing.

 Verdi to Ricordi

Genoa, 21 December 1893

[. . .] Last night I saw Boito at the station[1] for five minutes. He is quite changed; he did not want to stop here, as I would have wished, to talk with him at length and to calm him a bit. One may or may not be satisfied with this outcome, but now there's nothing more to be done. I still believe (though I am not a man who lives by the sword!) that the best thing would have been to say, *"I am here; have come expressly. These are my seconds. Arrange for everything within 24 hours . . . Then I return to Milan."* But I don't understand these things and am certainly wrong; but I certainly believe that the matter has been mishandled. Good health. Greetings. Salve.

Affectionately,

G. Verdi

NOTE

1. In Genoa, on Boito's return from Naples to Milan.

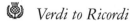

Boito to Verdi

[Milan, 21 December 1893][1]

Dear Maestro,

I received your telegram;[2] thank you.

Yes, *calm and again, calm;* I have found it again.[3]

I must make a change in my fine plan to spend a day in Genoa: That day will not be Christmas Eve, but the last day of the year.

Well then *till we see each other on 31 December.*[4]

Yesterday evening I heard from Origoni that you—having been informed I don't know by whom (I hadn't charged anybody with this) that I would be passing through Genoa and would like to dine at your home—had already gone to the station the previous day and had had to delay your meal at home.[5] I am terribly sorry about this inconvenience, which is like a final curse from Maestro Cowen. My intention was to surprise you, and not to inform you that I was passing through, all the more so since the day of my departure was uncertain.

Many kind greetings to you and to Signora Giuseppina.

Your most affectionate
Arrigo Boito

NOTES

1. The Milan postmark is illegible; the postmark of arrival shows GENOVA 22/12/93.

2. Verdi's telegram is missing, but it was obviously intended to calm his friend, who was still upset over events that might have cost him his life.

3. Boito's unusually hurried script appears to belie this affirmation.

4. Boito spent Christmas with the Verdis in Genoa after all. (See Verdi's telegram to him of 22 December and Boito to Bellaigue, 26 December.)

5. Verdi apparently wired Ricordi that he did not find Boito at the Genoa railway station on 19 December.

Verdi to Ricordi

[Telegram]   Genoa, 22 December 1893[1]

ALL RIGHT AS YOU PROPOSE AND AM MORE TRANQUIL — AWAITING BOITO THEN ON 27TH AND THOUSAND THANKS — GREETINGS — VERDI

NOTE

1. In answer to a missing communication from Ricordi.

1893

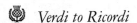 *Verdi to Boito*

[Telegram]   Genoa, 22 December 1893[1]

VERY WELL BUT ADVISE THAT CHRISTMAS EVE IS NOT SUNDAY BUT TOMOR-
ROW SATURDAY[2] — GLAD TO KNOW YOU TRANQUIL — VERDI

NOTES

1. In answer to a missing telegram.
2. Verdi's error.

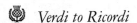 *Boito to Camille Bellaigue*

[In French]   Milan, 26 December 1893

[. . .] While I was in Genoa, I talked with Verdi about your work.[1] Verdi is
an admirer of Palestrina, and, among the masterworks of the "Principe
della Musica," he particularly admires the *Madrigali,* the *Improperia,* one of
the *Stabats*—the one beginning with the fifths, and the *Messa del Papa
Marcello,* of course.

Verdi loves Pergolesi, especially in his *Stabat Mater,* in the *Salve Regina,*
in the *Serva Padrona,* and in the *Olimpiade.* Among Benedetto Marcello's
works he admires only the *Psalms,* and he is quite right. Marcello's powerful
originality manifests itself only in the *Psalms;* the sonatas for viola da gamba
and the cantatas contain nothing that approaches them. [. . .][2]

NOTES

1. Bellaigue's book *Psychologie musicale,* which appeared in 1894 (see Verdi to Bellaigue,
18 November).
2. See *Otello* i, pp. 331–3.

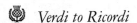 *Verdi to Ricordi*

Genoa, 26 December 1893

Dear Giulio,

This year, too, the panettone! . . . . But really, you'll never listen to reason!
Thank heaven that, though you're much younger than I am, you're not
a boy anymore!— How I would punish you!

Since you obviously could be my son two times over, never fear, I won't forget. You'll be aware of it the first time I return to Milan.

I received your telegram from Turin. .[1]All right . . But in such matters you are always a bit of an optimist. You'll tell me something about the receipts after the fifth or sixth performance.

Can you give me the address of Madame Maurel in Paris?—

I repeat my good wishes for everything — calm and health to you — ad. ad.

> Affectionately,
> G. Verdi

P.S. I am so mad that I forgot to thank you for the panettone! I thank you, but we'll have a return match in Milan.

AAhhh !!!. by God! by God! by all the Gods!!! Now I am really mad!! Just this moment I received a panettone from Mascheroni!!! He'll get a scolding when I have a little time!—This really makes no sense! With a *Walkiria* on his shoulders he thinks of panettoni?—And he doesn't think about the bolts of lightning that can hit him tomorrow? How senseless! How senseless!

NOTE

1. Missing. Presumably concerning Puccini's forthcoming *Manon Lescaut* at La Scala on 7 February 1894. Verdi appeared not to foresee the young composer's success with nineteen performances during La Scala's season.

 Verdi to Giuseppe Gallignani

Genoa, 27 December 1893

Dear Gallignani,

You really mean it? No, no, you're joking! You know well that I don't know, cannot, and must not do a thing without having myself committed to an insane asylum!! I can and shall send my contribution, and you'll do the rest.[1]

I highly praise the plan to honor the Eternal Father of Italian music.

I see that among the first on the Committee is Count Lurani.[2] He is supposed to be a passionate admirer of Bach . . . *exclusively* of Bach! I see he's been slandered! His membership on the Committee for Palestrina proves that he is a true musician with great ideas, without bias and prejudice. One can admire Bach and honor Palestrina, who are the *true and only* Fathers of the music of our time, from the 16th century onwards. Everything derives from them. [. . .]

1893

NOTES

1. Gallignani had asked Verdi to write a vocal composition on the occasion of tercentenary celebrations of Palestrina in Parma. (*Copialettere*, p. 634, n. 1.) See Boito to Verdi, 4 September, nn. 5 and 6.

2. Unknown.

 *Ricordi to Verdi*

Milan, 28 December 1893

Illustrious Maestro,

I received your esteemed letter[1] yesterday, and I beg you to forgive me for not answering you the same day; but despite all my good intentions, it was impossible.—For goodness sake . . . . let's not talk about the very modest panettone!—

The *Walküre* had a success of unspeakable boredom . . . as I foresaw—and I also foresaw that the famous Wagnerians, unable to beat the horse, would beat the saddle! . . Orchestrally and vocally, contrary to what is being said, the performance is magnificent!! . . but three and a half hours of colossal weight are really hard to swallow!— Meanwhile, much time, study, and money have been wasted; I fear the opera cannot last!— Meanwhile, poor Mascheroni has become the target of the angry Wagnerian apostles!— So goes the world.

Here is the address of Madame Maurel in Paris: 10, Rue Lesueur.

At my house, everybody has been visited by the influenza, one after the other—fortunately not seriously! Now that all of us are over it, there appear to be no other calamities.

I hope to hear that your health is as excellent as ever, and send affectionate greetings, with all my gratitude.

Your most affectionate
Giulio Ricordi

NOTE

1. Of 26 December.

 *Verdi to Maria Waldmann*

Genoa, 30 December 1893[1]

I am very happy to receive your news; and I am happy to stay with you as long as I can while I answer your most charming letter.

First of all, I am so glad to hear about the Duke's recovery. I wish him to keep well always and to renew the cure at Aix, if those waters have really been so helpful to him.

Well, by now you have a young man for a son? It seems like only yesterday that I still saw him as a little boy, very alert and sometimes maybe a bit rebellious! (Oh, how fast the time is going by!) And now, who knows what an example of grace and kindness he will be with the counsel of a mother like you!

We? . . Not too bad, but the years are heavy!

Peppina suffers a lot with her legs, and now only rarely leaves the house.

I also feel that I no longer have my former energy; work and fatigue weigh heavily on me. Early this year I labored a bit with the *Falstaff* rehearsals and afterwards really felt the effects. I must no longer risk overwork but must say *enough!* [. . .]

NOTE

    1. The autograph of this letter, published in *Carteggi* ii, p. 266, is missing.

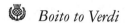 *Boito to Verdi*

[Milan] 31 December [1893][1]

Dear Maestro,

The conductor of the *Walkiri* in Turin was Vanzo;[2] he is now conducting in Trieste.

The Milanese press has thrown itself on Mascheroni like a rabid dog, holding him responsible for the infinite boredom this opera has produced, and that is unfair.[3]

The principal reason why the opera didn't please must be sought in the opera itself and in the system Wagner employed. Another reason is the vastness of the stage, which makes the whole structure of the drama seem pitiful. An insipid action that moves more slowly than a slow train stopping at every station, driving through an endless sequence of duets, during which the stage remains miserably empty and the characters stupidly immobilized. None of this is likely to please.

The ride of the Walkiri and their pleading [with Wotan], two sections that greatly impressed me in Turin, left me cold at La Scala. And the explanation is: for our enormous theatre, not just nine, but some thirty Walkiri would be needed, and then the effect obtained in Turin would be achieved.

I turned over the letter to Signor Campes, who was moved and thanks you with all his heart.[4]

Good wishes, best wishes to you, dear Maestro, and to Signora Giuseppina.

And a firm handshake

from your most affectionate
Arrigo Boito

NOTES

1. Postmark: MILANO 31/12/93.

2. Vittorio Maria Vanzo (1862–1945), a versatile musician and a Wagnerian, had conducted the first performance in Italian of *Die Walküre* at the Teatro Regio in Turin on 22 December 1891. (See Boito to Verdi, 23 January 1892.)

3. See Ricordi to Verdi, 28 December.

4. The letter is missing and the recipient unknown.

 Verdi to Edoardo Mascheroni

Genoa, 31 December 1893

Dear Mascheroni,

A few days ago I received the . . . . . .[1]

At the first moment I was surprised!

At the second moment I was in a towering rage!

At the third moment I calmed down and resolved to say "thank you," but on a condition I am borrowing from our father-confessors: *Ego te absolvo . . . nec amplius peccare* [I absolve you . . . but sin no more] . . . . .Unfortunately, it's true that people sin again, but you, I hope, won't do it again.

I heard about the poor success of the *Walküre!* Who knows if it may not recover later on. I think it's possible.

What the apostles said was to be expected! They were right, however, in saying that La Scala is too large, and that a curtain 9 meters away is wrong. I add that the two rows of boxes above the stage are horrible. But, alas, these things cannot be remedied. If a remedy had been possible, it would have been done at the time of *Aida,* or even before then.[2] But all these people who talk about the theatre know little about it, and with their ideals succeed in creating an atmosphere that isn't practical.—

Oh dear! All this chatter! Addio, addio. And all the best that is possible for tomorrow and the whole remainder of the year and the years to come.

Your
G. Verdi

NOTES

1. The panettone Verdi mentioned in his letter to Ricordi of 26 December.
2. See *Aida*, pp. 237, 239–41.

 *Eleonora Duse to Boito*

[Berlin, 31 December 1893]
Last night of 93 *First* of *1894*

And if it is the last day of the year I write—so be it. I regret little of it. 32 more days, and it is over.[1]

I had to gather my bread—I have done it, and [she] who will live after me[2] will find bread and a humble house—

They thought that I got lost—No—but it is a miserable thing that we can help one another so little in this world—

By oneself, and for oneself—there is a law!

But it is over! And tonight I have to *shout* that I have worked—and it's over! [. . .]

Whoever has lived in PRISON, he, yes, he can understand me! One who has lived in darkness, underground, without the oblivion of the dead, that one, yes, understands! It is over! [. . .]

This, and *nothing else,* I wanted to say—

Eleonora

If someone *steals* this letter, too—let death strike him—and that is no empty wish.

NOTES

1. Duse had decided to dissolve her company (see Biographical Sketch, and Weaver, pp. 108–9).
2. Her daughter, Enrichetta.

1894

I demand that Falstaff *be performed as I conceived it.*[1]

ayment of a bill to a Paris shirtmaker prompts Verdi to make resentful comments about the French at the start of the very year in which he is to receive France's highest honors.[2] In January he is still corresponding with Boito regarding corrections in the third act of *Falstaff*. From mid-February to 6 March the Maestro and his wife see Boito, his architect brother, Camillo, and other friends in Milan;[3] and then return to Genoa.[4] All pleas for the octogenarian's presence in Paris to oversee preparations for the French première of *Falstaff* encounter his customary resistance. Yet, after much persuasion, the Verdis arrive by sleeping car in Paris on 4 April for rehearsals and the first three performances of *Falstaff* in France, at the Opéra-Comique. Opening night on the 18th is a happy event, even for the dour Verdi. No one understands and enjoys the work better than his and Boito's friend the critic Camille Bellaigue.[5] On 25 April the Verdis return to Genoa via Turin. On 5 May they proceed to St. Agata, where they enjoy Boito's visit from the 17th to the 22nd. A letter to Ricordi of 10 May reflects the old composer's concern about being surpassed by the young Puccini. Tito Ricordi's euphemistic telegram from London of 19 May, regarding the first *Falstaff* in England, is contradicted by facts. From the end of May until early June Verdi is in Milan to confer with Ricordi and Pierre Gailhard, the director of the Paris Opéra,[6] regarding *Othello*. Scandalous goings-on at the Comique, where Maurel has made cuts and other alterations in *Falstaff*, dismay the Maestro during the first half of June.[7] The obligatory ballet music he must write for the Paris *Othello* preoccupies him throughout the summer.[8] Between 24 June and 1 July Verdi is again in Milan. He and Giuseppina go on to Montecatini and are home at St.

Agata on 19 July. They depart for Genoa on 18 September and arrive in Paris on the 26th. On the 29th Verdi congratulates the "Waltz King," Johann Strauss (1825–99), on the fiftieth anniversary of his career. On 12 October, close upon Verdi's eighty-first birthday, a glorious *Othello* at the Opéra crowns the composer's achievements. With Ambroise Thomas, Verdi attends a memorial service for Gounod at the Madeleine. He enjoys a lively performance of *Falstaff,* despite exaggerations, at the Opéra-Comique. This is his final visit to Paris; he leaves with his wife and Teresa Stolz on 22 October. The couple returns to Genoa on the 23rd. On 12 November Verdi goes alone via Milan to St. Agata for a few days on business. Between the 19th and the 21st he welcomes Massenet for a visit at Palazzo Doria.[9] On 3 December Verdi turns once more to Boito for help, this time with the text for *Pietà Signor,* a short prayer he composes to aid the victims of an earthquake in Calabria and Sicily.

Another influenza outbreak in January disrupts Ricordi's life and closes theatres in Milan, including La Scala. The first French productions of *Falstaff* and *Othello,* in the spring and autumn, respectively, dominate his activities for Verdi this year. Ricordi makes a special trip to Genoa on 22 March and finally succeeds in persuading Verdi to be in Paris during the rehearsals and initial performances of *Falstaff* at the Opéra-Comique. A few days later, Ricordi and his wife, Giuditta, join Boito in Paris for the event. By the end of April they are back in Milan. Ricordi's arrangements for the first *Falstaff* in conjunction with Puccini's *Manon Lescaut* at London's Covent Garden in May are a failure. Maurel's presumptuous tampering with the score of *Falstaff* at the Opéra-Comique in May and June requires more forceful action than Ricordi is able to obtain. Throughout the summer he helps Verdi by researching ancient dances for the ballet to be inserted in the third act of *Othello* at the Opéra. Verdi's corrections of the French *Othello* score and reduction take additional time. As the Maestro's publisher, secretary, personal representative, travel agent, and bodyguard, Ricordi shares the glory of the first French *Othello* on 12 October. Along with Boito, he is named Cavalier of the Legion of Honor.

In January, Boito, in the aftermath of the Cowen-Sonzogno affair, is at home still making changes in the French and, subsequently, even in the Italian version of the second scene of the third act of *Falstaff*.[10] He discusses these changes with Verdi in Milan in February and early March. His energetic letter to the old Maestro of 16 March adds strong support to Ricordi's attempt to secure Verdi's presence at the first *Falstaff* in Paris. In late March Boito attends the rehearsals at the Opéra-Comique and the opening night on 18 April. He remains in Paris until early May to work with Camille Du Locle on the French translation of *Othello* and to negotiate for the first *Othello* at the Opéra in the autumn. Duse arrives in Paris on 23 April in the midst of initial *Falstaff* performances, craving enduring love and protection. Boito can meet her only briefly and—as usual, in secret— prior to her departure for London on the 28th. He returns to Milan in May, and, between the 17th and the 22nd, he reports to Verdi at St. Agata on the progress of *Othello* in Paris. After a couple of weeks at home in Milan, he journeys back to Paris on 14 June to conclude the preparations for *Othello* and to meet Duse on the 15th.[11] Verdi asks to see him in Milan on 27 June,[12] but Boito apparently is away until early July. At the end of July, he attends the first performance of *Falstaff* at Aix-les-Bains with his and Duse's friend Luigi Gualdo.[13] In late August, following excursions in the Alps, Boito returns to Milan. In the autumn, he is back in Paris to take part in rehearsals for the first French *Othello* on 12 October at the Opéra. He probably spends a week at the end of the month at Villa d'Este.[14] Between 20 and 22 November Boito is in Parma, attending a Palestrina Festival and the Second International Congress for Sacred Music. He has reservations about the festival, but he raves to Verdi about the effect of seeing Correggio's painting "electrically illuminated" in the Church of San Giovanni in Parma.[15] A few days later, he sends Verdi his text for *Pietà Signor*.

NOTES

1. Verdi to Ricordi, 9 June.
2. Verdi to Ricordi, 11 January and 11 November.
3. Verdi to Bellaigue, 3 March.
4. Giuseppina Verdi to G. De Sanctis, 13 March.
5. See Boito to Bellaigue, 25 April, and Appendixes III and V.
6. Gailhard (1848–1918) was an outstanding French bass and singing actor as well as an opera manager. He introduced *Lohengrin* and *Die Walküre* to France.
7. See Bellaigue to Verdi, 27 May; Verdi to Ricordi, 1, 8, 9, 13, 14, and 16 June; and Verdi to Bellaigue, 8 June.
8. See *Otello* i, pp. 400–1, 403–13.
9. Boito to Verdi, 2 December, n. 3.
10. Boito to Verdi, 18 January, and Verdi to Boito, 19 January.
11. We do not know how much time they had for this encounter; Duse's next surviving letter to Boito was dated only "Ravenna—October 94." Weaver states (p. 114) that "Arrigo and Lenor did meet in Paris, and Enrichetta was also there. [. . .] The two did not seem to have gone to San Giuseppe or to another refuge that summer. They met in Milan in July, but later that same month Lenor was in Switzerland."
12. "In case you have finished the work with Gailhard, come to Milan quickly. [. . .] If you could be in Milan about 27 June, there would be time for us to examine the notes on the translation, and everything would be finished." (*Otello* i, pp. 404–5).
13. Count Luigi Gualdo (1847–98), an Italian writer of impressive facility who even

wrote two successful novels in French, led an elegant life between Rome, Milan, Paris, and London. Boito, Giacosa, Verga, and D'Annunzio were among his many literary friends. His major work, *Decadenza*, was republished in 1981 by Arnaldo Mondadori in Milan. (See Duse to Boito, 23 April, n. 3.)

14. Abbiati maintains (iv, pp. 563–4) that "Boito hurries to Germany and sends news about the magnificent success of *Falstaff* (not about the problematic success of his approaches to Lenor) from there." No one else, not even Nardi (p. 607), seems to have discovered any documentation to support this vague and cynical statement. The facts are partly revealed by Duse's letter from Ravenna in October, her telegram from Venice of 14 October, and her letter from Magdeburg of 22–23 October. If Boito had attended the German *Falstaff* at Berlin in the autumn (see Verdi to Ricordi, 7 November), he might have seen Duse in Berlin at the end of October rather than in Milan between 31 October and 3 November, as she proposed. However, her performances in Berlin might have been unexpectedly extended until 18 December. (Weaver, p. 123.)

15. Boito to Verdi, 2 December.

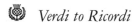 *Verdi to Ricordi*

Genoa, 10 January 1894

Dear Giulio,

Hold on to the enclosed semi-annual sum a little longer, as I am counting on coming to Milan any day now; and this day never comes!!!!

Boivin[1] informs me that he has sent the package with the shirts, and just two days ago I asked *Roger* and *Sauchon* for my semi-annual accounts. So at the moment I have no funds in Paris. You will have to do me the favor of paying for me the sum of fr.403 . . . after I have received the shirts, of course . . . and have let you know. I have no more paper!

Your
G. Verdi

NOTE

1. Shirtmaker in Paris.

 *Ricordi to Verdi*

Milan, 11 January 1894

Illustrious Maestro,

With greatest pleasure I received your honored letter of yesterday—and with even greater pleasure I see that you haven't given up the promised trip to Milan. Better delay it, however: We are having a spell of cold weather and much influenza; it is not serious, but it is enough to keep hundreds of people

1894

in bed. And yesterday La Scala was closed because the baritone Devoyod[1] and the alto Steinbach[2] were sick with the influenza; Mascheroni already felt it, too. Doses of quinine have kept me going so far. A real delight!! . . .

Bombs, revolutions, fear of cholera in the summer, influenza in the winter! What good fortune!!—

Affectionate greetings to you, to Signora Peppina from your always devoted and grateful

Giulio Ricordi

NOTES

1. The French baritone Jules-Célestin Devoyod (1841–1901) sang Wotan in *Die Walküre* at La Scala.

2. Emma Steinbach (1854–1937), of German or Austrian origin, had an international career which included the U.S.A. In 1893–1894 she appeared at La Scala as Fricka in *Die Walküre* and as Anacoana in *Cristoforo Colombo*.

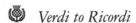 *Verdi to Ricordi*

Genoa, 11 January 1894

Dear Giulio,

As I wrote you yesterday, having no funds in Paris, I must ask you to pay, from my account, in settlement of the enclosed bill, fr.403. These are *Francs,* as you know! This annoys me, and I ask that you have it paid at once, at once, at once, so that those Frenchmen—who tell us so many lovely things (*France will take Piedmont, Austria will take back the Veneto . . . reducing Italy to the great innkeeper of the human race . . . .* as they say!)—may not be able to say that we don't pay our bills promptly! . . Therefore, please, at once, at once. . .

Add. ad.

G. Verdi

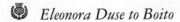 *Eleonora Duse to Boito*

[Dresden, Hôtel Bellevue]
12 January 1894[1]

Blessings to Arrigo — Nothing but blessings. You need not tell me to forgive— I never meant to make any reproach —— never thought of it — never. —I shouted: it is over—I shouted what a wretched and cruel thing it is to live by oneself and for oneself—

Perhaps it had to be this way! [. . .]

Eleonora

NOTE

1. In answer to a missing letter.

 *Ricordi to Verdi*

Milan, Saturday, 13 January 1894

Illustrious Maestro,

The moment I received your letter of yesterday,[1] I sent your Boivin bill to [our office in] Paris with the order to pay it at once. The bill . . . . is all right . . . but are the shirts all right? . . . .

Here we have no wind, but the fiercest cold seasoned by influenza, not really serious, but widespread. By now, 40,000 people seem to have been hit by it. I think La Scala will have to close for some days; besides Mascheroni, 3 singers and 11 members of the orchestra were sick today . . . without counting choristers and dancers!—

I would like to tell you: Come to Milan for a while; here at least there is no wind, and you can go for a walk wearing a good fur coat!— But it is better to wait for the weather to improve, and for the influenza to depart; I hope that will be soon.

It is possible that early next week I may run down there, to hear a few artists at the Carlo Felice; this idea appeals to me, because it would give me the pleasure of greeting you. I am happily anticipating it;[2] meanwhile, I send ahead greeting upon greeting and will bring more in all our names.

Always your devoted and grateful

Giulio Ricordi

NOTES

1. Concerning *Otello*. (*Otello* i, pp. 390–91.)
2. On the following day, January 14, Tornaghi informed Verdi that Giulio had to hear an artist in Bern and planned "to make a trip to Genoa the day after tomorrow." (*Otello* i, p. 392.)

 *Boito to Verdi*

Milan [18 January 1894][1]

[. . .] I am enclosing a little page[2] on which the new entrance of the Fairies in Act III of *Falstaff*[3] is transcribed. [. . .]

NOTES

1. The date is inferred from Verdi's reply, which follows, pertaining, like this letter, mainly to the French *Othello*. (*Otello* i, pp. 392–3.)

1894

2. Missing.

3. Changes made in the French version of the opera, with slight alterations incorporated into the final Italian libretto and score. (See PV p. 351, 2/1 to p. 353, 3/2; Ricordi to Verdi, 19 January; and Verdi to Ricordi, 21 January. See also Hepokoski, pp. 78–80.)

Alice	*(elle débouche avec précaution à gauche avec quelques Fées)*
	Par ici.
Nannetta	*(elle débouche à gauche avec d'autres Fées)*
	Doucement.
Alice	*(elle aperçoit Falstaff et le désigne aux autres)*
	Il est là.
Nannetta	Le bravache
	A grand peur.
Les Fées	Il se cache.
Alice	*(le group entier se porte en avant avec précaution, puis Alice disparait rapidement à gauche)*
	Avancez.
Les Fées	Pas de bruit.
Nannetta	*(elle dispose les Fées à leur places)*
	Glissez-vous pas à pas.
	Commençons.
Les Fées	Ne ris pas.
	(Les petites Fées se disposent en cercle autour de leur Reine. D'autres Fées plus grandes font groupe à gauche)

[Alice	*(she emerges cautiously from the left with some Fairies)*
	This way.
Nannetta	*(she emerges from the left with other Fairies)*
	Quietly.
Alice	*(glimpses Falstaff and points him out to the others)*
	He's there.
Nannetta	The bully
	Is very afraid.
The Fairies	He's hiding.
Alice	*(the whole group comes forward cautiously, then Alice disappears rapidly, at the left)*
	Go forward.
The Fairies	Make no noise.
Nannetta	*(shows the Fairies to their places)*
	Slide there step for step.
	Let's begin.
The Fairies	Let's not laugh.
	(The little Fairies arrange themselves in a circle around their Queen. Other older Fairies form a group at the left.)]

 *Verdi to Boito*

Genoa, 19 January 1894

[. . .] I think those few lines in French will go very well. Now translate them into Italian, without, of course, adding anything, etc., etc. [. . .]

🏵 *Ricordi to Verdi*

Milan, 19 January 1894

Illustrious Maestro,

[. . .] I am sending you the French *Othello* libretto and the galley proofs of the one for *Falstaff*, which is not yet published; this is good, because the new verses can be added to the 3rd act. In fact, I arrived just in time to delay the printing of the French piano-vocal score, and thus we can make the change in the 3rd act.[1]

Now, Maestro, ... forgive me if I ask you a favor . . . even two, while I am at it!—

1. The sooner you can give us the change for the 3rd act, the better, since they can then have the correct edition in Paris at a convenient time.

2. And this is absolutely all!!—
Among the individual numbers, Fenton's Sonnet is requested; but it doesn't have an ending, and while this works very well dramatically, do you think it possible to publish it as a separate piece, and if so, in what way?. . . If it cannot be done, just interrupt my question as Alice does, with a *No, Sir!!* and that is enough.

Oh! . . . . I would like to see you with us today rather than tomorrow; and yet I must tell you to wait a few more days, because the influenza rolls on rather . . . . merrily. On my return [from Bern] I found Ginetta in bed; she is getting better, as is my mother, about whom we were quite worried for a couple of days; fortunately, since yesterday she, too, has been much better. Yesterday I heard that Signora Stolz is also bedridden with influenza!! However, it isn't serious.

Today, after one day of snow and another of rain, we see the sun here and there amid the clouds; so the weather seems to be improving, and with that, general health will return to normal. Then: 1. 2. 3!! departure for Milan, and evviva to our dear, most beloved, most welcome Verdis.

What does not seem to be improving is the financial situation!! . . . Now even the Banca Generale is closed—an enormous loss for commerce and industry!! . . . One could lose one's head, if one still had a head in all this mess.

La Scala reopened Thursday with *Walkiria;* the *Loreley* is still being delayed, because now the protagonist is ill!![2] . . . . . Between the general financial straits and the influenza, our poor theatres!! . .

To confirm what I told you in regard to your semi-annual account; your net credit exceeds 23,000 Lire, which sum is already at your disposal with a check drawn from the Banca Nazionale, to be cashed in Milan.

1894

And now, with a most happy farewell until soon, I remain

Your ever devoted and grateful
Giulio Ricordi

NOTES

1. Boito to Verdi, 18 January.
2. See Ricordi to Verdi, 11 January. Catalani's *Loreley* opened on 24 January.

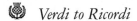 *Verdi to Ricordi*

Genoa, 19 January 1894

[. . .] I don't know where I have put the *Otello* and *Falstaff* librettos in Italian as well as in French. Would you mind sending me *Otello Italian and French, Falstaff Italian and French.* When does La Scala open? And when will I be allowed to come to Milan?—

Addio and greetings to Signora Giuditta and to all of you, living upstairs and downstairs.[1]

Affectionately yours,
G. Verdi

NOTE

1. Presumably the entire family on an upper and lower floor of the house.

Verdi to Ricordi

Genoa, 20 January 1894

Dear Giulio,

In answer to Roger, I said that for *Falstaff* in French half of the *Author's Rights* belong to me, half to the translators, *Boito* and *Solanges*. He sends me this stamped paper to sign.—I said nothing at all about *Falstaff* in Italian, but he includes the rights to it in reference to those of *Otello*.

Now tell me: What are the terms with Boito in Italian, and tell me if I can sign this *traité* which Roger has sent me.—Addio, addio.

Your
G. Verdi

Verdi to Ricordi

Genoa, 21 January 1894

Dear Giulio,

Here are the corrections.¹— On the separate little page you will see the two added bars to the Sonnet.² Do as you please.

On the big page is the addition of those few interjected words for Alice, Meg, Nannetta and Chorus. Thereafter, Alice [and] Meg should disappear, before Nannetta's Song, and go toward the others. So the stage directions must be adjusted.—

In the Minuet I had asked for too much, and it remained cold. If Boito finds half a verse that rhymes with *cortège* to complete the *alexandrine,* everything is fine.

Have fun, then. I still haven't written to Gailhard!³ And you?

Addio, addio.

In haste   G. Verdi

If there are other difficulties, write me ———

NOTES

    1. See Boito to Verdi, 18 January, and Hepokoski, p. 80.

    2. For publication as an individual number (see Ricordi to Verdi, 19 January).

    3. Concerning the French *Othello* at the Paris Opéra.

 Boito to Camille Bellaigue

[In French]   Milan, [22 January] 1894 (Monday)

Thank you, dear friend, thank you for the loving care you have taken with the revision of the French *Falstaff.*¹ Almost all your suggestions will be adopted; I will submit them to Verdi and to Solanges. But you still don't know, since you don't have the translated score before your eyes, how admirably Verdi has been able to *"transpose"* [*Falstaff*'s] Italian nature into French words. Oh, this *Falstaff!* How right you are to love this masterwork. And what a blessing for art when everybody is able to understand it. We will do all we can to reach this goal. The human spirit must be *"méditerranisé,"*² true progress lies only there. [. . .]

NOTES

    1. Boito had sent Bellaigue his and Solanges's translation and had asked for correc-

tions and suggestions. (Nardi, p. 624.) On 12 February Boito writes to Bellaigue: "I am awaiting Verdi in Milan, to submit to him your notes regarding the *Falstaff* translation. Three quarters of your observations have been accepted *con entusiasmo* by Solanges and myself. Thank you" (Scala).

2. Paraphrase of the French sentence "Il faut méditerraniser la musique" in Friedrich Nietzche, *Der Fall Wagner,* vol. ii, p. 907.

Eugenio Tornaghi to Verdi

Milan, 24 January 1894

Illustrious Signor Maestro
Commendatore G. Verdi

Genoa

Giulio has been confined to bed for two days on account of that most annoying influenza. Before he went home, we looked together over Boito's contract for the *Falstaff* libretto. Giulio asks me to let you know that by the terms of this contract Boito is due 10% of the rentals or royalties for performances in Italy and abroad, with the exception of France and Belgium, where he is due the *droits d'auteur* as translator. It seems, then, that for performances with the Italian text in France and Belgium he does not get anything, and that the Agreement proposed by Roger is all right, being identical to the one for *Otello*. Enclosed you will find Roger's letter and the 3 copies of the Agreement.[1]

Giulio has received the proposed changes, and—as soon as he is recovered—he himself will handle the corresponding stage directions together with Boito.

Conveying to you Giulio's best regards, I have the honor to remain, with greatest esteem, your most devoted

Eug. Tornaghi

NOTE

1. Missing.

Eugenio Tornaghi to Verdi

Milan, 29 January 1894

[. . .] Giulio is better, but still not completely over his cold, which greatly troubles him. Today he has written to Gailhard. [. . .]

 *Verdi to Leon Carvalho*

[In French]   Genoa, 11 February 1894

Thank you for your gracious letter.[1] Yesterday I saw Maurel, who repeated what you had already written me in your letter.

It is very, very kind; but all of you forgot a very slight . . . slight detail. You forgot my full eighty years!! At this age one needs tranquillity and rest, and though I feel relatively well, I can no longer stand either the work or the fatigue or the annoyances that are inevitable in the theatre. I know what you will answer me on this subject; but I have known the theatre for a long time (unfortunately) and I know what to expect.—Besides, I can only repeat what I said to Maurel: *If my health, my strength, and my eighty years permit, I shall come to Paris.*

Meanwhile, pay close attention to the role of Alice. It needs first of all, of course, a beautiful, very agile voice; but above all, an actress who has the *devil in her.* Alice's role is not as developed as Falstaff's, but dramatically it is just as important. Alice leads all the intrigues of the comedy. [. . .]

NOTE

1. On 5 February, Carvalho had informed Verdi of the cast for *Falstaff* at the Opéra-Comique. The performers had been chosen in agreement with Maurel and the conductor Jules Danbé (1840–1905) (who also led the premières of *Manon* and *Werther* at the Comique). For the role of Alice, Carvalho suggested the young Louise Grandjean (*Copialettere*, p. 390 n.; see also *Otello* i, p. 396). Louise Grandjean (1870–1934) attended the Paris Conservatory and was engaged at the Opéra-Comique from 1893 until 1902. From 1895 to about 1911 she also appeared at the Opéra. When Grandjean participated in the Paris première of the *Quattro Pezzi Sacri* in 1898, Verdi remembered her as "a good musician and the *bon enfant* at the Opéra-Comique" (in a letter to Boito of 2 April 1898). Her roles included Donna Anna, Aida, Desdemona, Elsa, Brünnhilde, and Isolde. In 1904, she was acclaimed as Venus in *Tannhäuser* at Bayreuth. After the end of her active career, Louise Grandjean became a distinguished professor of voice at the Paris Conservatory.

🌼 *Eleonora Duse to Boito*

[15 February 1894]
At sea—to Cairo—[1]

Arrigo? Is it still possible? Arrigo believes it?
You believe it?
That we are not deceiving ourselves? That we will not deceive ourselves again? That what still remains of this life could be ours? [. . .]

1894

I had wished to die in your care——in a house that was ours—that was far away and in peace——and in the utmost humility— [. . .]

NOTE

1. At the height of her glorious career, "seeking a warm climate and some rest" (Weaver, p. 110).

 Victor Maurel to Verdi

[In French]   Lisbon, 16 February 1894

Dear and illustrious Maestro,

During my brief sojourn in Paris I saw Gailhard. Without telling him that we had talked about the step he has taken, I found out a few things from him that I shall faithfully convey to you.

First of all, your categorical refusal to let *Otello* be given in Italian at the Opéra has disconcerted him exceedingly.[1] It was easy for me to show him the somewhat naive side of his hopes in this respect. To offset the attraction of *Falstaff* at the Opéra-Comique with a new work by Wagner, Massenet, or another composer, I told him, was good old managerial warfare. Wanting to juxtapose Verdi in Italian against Verdi in French, however, could be nothing but an endeavor profitable only to the vanity of the directors of the Opéra. [. . .]

And now let us pass to the Opéra-Comique. I am able to give you an opinion regarding the question of the future interpretation of your *Falstaff*. During my brief sojourn we held two rehearsals with the whole cast.

I listened carefully to Mlle. Grandjean in the role of *Alice*. Here is my exact impression: A pleasant voice, especially in the upper register. A little weak in the low notes. Vocally and musically, she is already quite good and will be excellent when she knows the role by heart. As to her acting, I cannot say anything definite, not having seen her perform in costume. But I have no doubt that she will entirely satisfy you. Mlle. Grandjean has the authority that a good figure bestows upon a woman; her eyes sparkle, her deméanor is serene, she is eager to do well, and she is quite intelligent. What I am saying about her can more or less be applied to the entire cast. The elements for a very fine performance are there, but it is my firm conviction that to achieve it the Maestro will have to attend at least the final rehearsals. The entire production could be far enough along so that you would need only ask for the right nuances, the kind that give life to a work. [. . .]

M. Danbé, the conductor, did not know a single note of *Falstaff*. M. Carvalho has heard only a single performance [in Milan], and under conditions that involved too much commotion to remember details. Thus I will be the only one who can say something useful; but I would greatly prefer not to step out of my role as performer.

M. Carvalho has shared your letter with me. Perhaps I was wrong to read between the lines that you would rather stay away from this new interpretation of your work.—That has made me very sad. During this brief sojourn my conviction remained unshaken, that all Paris is waiting impatiently for the opportunity to render a brilliant homage of sympathy and admiration to the sublime artist, who for so many years has given it such true and lovely artistic enjoyment. Together with many true friends of Italy, I would deplore it if such a beautiful, spontaneous demonstration of justice by the whole capital of France did not directly reach the man who has inspired such proofs of esteem.[2] [. . .]

V. Maurel

NOTES

1. Verdi had insisted on a French translation. (See *Otello* i, p. 395.)

2. Maurel subtly prevails upon Verdi by alluding to his patriotic obligation under present political circumstances. (See Verdi to Giuseppina Negroni Prati, 10 September 1893.)

 Verdi to Camille Bellaigue

[In French]   Milan, 3 March 1894

My dear Monsieur Bellaigue,

I am entirely guilty. Long ago I received your beautiful book *L'année musicale* without telling you a word about it; horrible. . . As an excuse, I could say that lately I have had to shuttle on the railways between Genoa, St. Agata, and Milan, where I am again at present, and from where I shall once more leave in three days. Poor excuse; I repeat: I am entirely guilty.

Your book is very beautiful, and from a genuine expert; your critique is lofty, sincere, and honest. I was particularly surprised by the conference in Geneva.[1]

Apart from the indulgent words on my behalf, for which I thank you, I found confirmation of ideas that have been running through my head for a long time. Everywhere they shout: "the truth . . . the truth . . . ," and perhaps

1894

we are (despite our orchestral and harmonic riches) less concerned with the truth than were artists of other times.

"But music," you say, *"will change again . . . alternating inspirations will cause the two scales of the balance to ascend and descend until . . . ,"* etc. So be it. [. . .]

NOTE

1. Unknown.

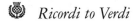 *Ricordi to Verdi*

Milan, 9 March 1894

Illustrious Maestro,

I return the telegram with your kind replies;[1] you will have seen, however, that Count Hochberg's had already been published in the papers. The many telegrams I received confirm the extraordinary success.[2] In Madrid, the press really . . . . . was the press; but the performance,[3] especially the orchestra's, was the *non plus ultra* of ugliness.

I have written to Paris for exact news of the rehearsals so that Boito and I may know how to proceed; and *va sans dire* that *now more than ever* we are convinced that the presence of *Jove triumphant* is necessary!

We are most happy about your good news, but very, very sorry about your departure, which we wish might never have happened![4]— And how about your reception of the Origoni gang!![5] . . . While your kindnesses keep accumulating, we are all left with our mouths hanging open, unable even to say thank you . . . which we do, however, eternally in our hearts. [. . .]

NOTES

1. Missing.
2. In reference to the German *Falstaff* in Berlin on 6 March. Franz Betz (1835–1900), one of the most celebrated Wagnerian baritones of the day, sang the title role in a production that stayed in the repertoire until 1932. On 22 April, following a later performance in Berlin, Ferruccio Busoni drafted these lines—alas never sent—to Verdi: "*Falstaff* provoked such a complete spiritual and emotional upheaval, that I can honestly say it marked the beginning of a new era in my life as an artist." (The entire Italian draft of this letter is translated in Antony Beaumont, *Ferruccio Busoni, Selected Letters*, pp. 53–4.)
3. On 10 February.
4. The Verdis had been in Milan from mid-February until 6 March.
5. Ricordi's little grandchildren.

🏵 *Verdi to Ricordi*

Genoa, 12 March 1894

Dear Giulio,

Received the portrait . . . signed and sent.[1]

Received also your second telegram about the Potbelly in Naples.[2] I hope for the same success *at the sixth performance*, and then I will be content!

And *now to Paris!!* . . you say in the telegram! Alas! Alas! Let it be! But what good would I do there?! More harm than good! And then . . . with almost eighty-one years on my shoulders, undertake a long and tiring journey! It is easy to say that a year ago (by now that's a year younger) I endured the labors of *Falstaff* and the journey to Rome! But I felt the effects of it, and still feel them quite a bit, since my legs don't hold me up as well as before, and now I can walk only slowly and briefly. And just to go to that country where we are so little liked, and where we have so little artistic sympathy for each other! — Moreover, in Paris I don't know anyone anymore and would be as lost as in a desert! Furthermore, it is no longer possible to stay at my old hotel,[3] in which I felt at home (as you all say), and I would have to go to that Grand Hôtel, which I dislike! Lots of woes, you will say! It is true; but woes that poison one's life!—And what need is there to face them when I am convinced that I can't be of any use! Suppose the *troupe,* already completely chosen, were not to my liking, and I didn't believe it capable of performing that opera? I would either have to endure it (a very hard thing for me) or frankly state my opinion, causing bad humor, resentment, and anger all around!

Just let them give *Falstaff* if they wish; but I repeat again that I am convinced that it is better for me, for the opera, and for everyone if it is given without my presence.—

Addio, addio

Your
G. Verdi

NOTES

1. Unknown.
2. Missing.
3. Hôtel de Bade.

1894

🌣 *Verdi to Ricordi*

Monday [Genoa, 12 March 1894]

Dear Giulio,

I received this telegram.[1] I understood it, more or less. Tell me from where it comes, and if this Felix Mottl is the famous conductor.—[2]

You will receive this note before noon tomorrow. Wire me at once to let me know the country and the identity of Mottl —and if it's worth the effort to reply.[3]

G. Verdi

NOTES

1. Missing. Presumably sent in connection with the German *Falstaff* in Berlin on 6 March.

2. Felix Mottl (1856–1911), an eminent Austrian conductor, studied with Anton Bruckner (1824–96). He was an assistant to Richard Wagner at the first Bayreuth Festival in 1876, and conducted there from 1886 to 1902. Mottl edited all of Wagner's vocal scores and composed three operas of his own. He conducted *Parsifal* at Bayreuth in 1886, and, in 1889, *Tristan und Isolde*, which was particularly close to his heart. In addition to his performances at Covent Garden (1898–1900) and the Metropolitan Opera (1903–1904), he was active in Karlsruhe from 1881 to 1904, and from 1903 to 1911 in Munich, where he collapsed and died during his hundredth performance of *Tristan*.

3. Ricordi's answer to this question and a reply to Mottl have not been found.

🌣 *Giuseppina Verdi to G. De Sanctis*

Genoa, 13 March 1894

Briefly, but at once, I answer your letter of 11 March. We knew, actually, Verdi knew, a few hours later about the success of *Falstaff* at the San Carlo in Naples.[1] You will understand that if every labor deserves its reward, a work of art done with so much dedication and inspiration deserves it, too. Now, the best reward for a composer is unanimous, wholehearted applause by a great audience like the Neapolitans, who sensed beautiful things, particularly in the music. Long live *Falstaff* and the Neapolitans, then, who were able to understand and appreciate even those parts of the opera which might have been more successful had they not been lacking in terms of performance, voices, and resources.

[. . .] Thank you for your zeal in giving us the happy news of the great success. But have no illusions about future operas. Verdi has worked enough and has every right to rest! Let others follow his example, not only in regard to his activity, but to his *honest* character in every sense of the word. [. . .]

NOTE

1. On 19 February, presumably under the baton of Arturo Toscanini (see Ricordi to Verdi, 20 September 1893).

 *Verdi to Boito*

Genoa, 14 March 1894

Dear Boito,

Shall I write you? Or shall I not write you? Yes or no? . . . No or yes?

Read if you have time; if not, throw it into the wastebasket, as I have nothing important to tell you.

Tomorrow night Franchetti's opera will be performed.—[1] In Milan I was told such bad things about the libretto that, having read it, I found it not so bad as I had been told. Certainly, the subject is rather naive; the verses are what they are. In spite of everything, good music could be made there, and I wouldn't be surprised if Franchetti, forgoing his puffed-up and heavy style for a moment, has *found* something good. If you go to the theatre, tell me a word about it. You I can trust; and you need not fear that it will turn out as in the case of your Englishman.[2] May God grant that he keep that talent and that tact!

I am well; and I am bored. I do nothing; and I am tired . . . that is, these days I have been working for the three *Potbellies* in Lisbon, Berlin, and Naples! . .[3] Nice things, but also a bit tiresome! Amid these tedious matters, however, there was also a funny note. After the first performance in Berlin I received, as you know, a telegram from the manager of that theatre,[4] and was a bit surprised to see it three hours later, printed in the *Corriere!* Not so bad! But to my great surprise, the very next day I read in the *Corriere* "*Falstaff in Berlin*"*!* What the devil! What's going on! I read, and when I get to the end, I read these words, more or less: "*We are pleased to report a genuine success for Falstaff without the repeat of* 'quand'ero paggio.'"[5] . . Missovulgo[6] ah! Ah! Ah! Ah! Then I burst out laughing for five minutes. . . *Voilà le fin mot!* All of this only to say that he doesn't like that piece! After the first moment of hilarity had passed, however, I wondered . . . *What do these futurists want, these i*[diots]. And why can't something light and brilliant be done in a comic opera? How can that little piece offend the aesthetic sense? Leaving the musical motive aside, it is in the situation. Falstaff, derided for his big belly, says *quando ero paggio ero sottile* [When I was a page I was slim]. . . It is written well for the voice and orchestrated lightly, so that all the words can be heard without being disturbed by the usual (*ill-mannered*) orchestral counterpoints, which interrupt the actual discourse. It is correctly harmonized. . . . What is wrong, then, if it has become popular?!! . . . And this is the way they write critiques! They hardly bother me, since I have finished. And I don't pay attention to them, and never did. But it is bad for the youngsters, who can easily let themselves be dragged into doing something they don't feel like doing. Actually, all the music that is performed nowadays, whether among us or in all other countries, lacks naturalness and isn't sincere. . .

Oh my God, what a long letter! What the devil have I done! Forgive, forgive!

Greetings. Addio, addio.

Affectionately,
G. Verdi

NOTES

1. *Fior d'Alpe* at La Scala, where it received a total of seven performances.

2. Sir Frederick H. Cowen. (See Ricordi to Verdi, 14 December 1893, nn. 1–5.)

3. The first performance of *Falstaff* in Lisbon took place on 27 February 1894, in Berlin (in Italian under Edoardo Mascheroni) on 1 June 1893, in Stuttgart (in German) on 10 September 1893, in Berlin (in German) on 6 March 1894, and in Naples on 19 February 1894.

4. Count Hochberg (see Ricordi to Verdi, 9 March, and Mascheroni to Verdi, 2 June 1893).

5. Audiences everywhere enjoyed repetitions of this jewel in II.ii. but not in Germany, where such interruptions of the action are traditionally not permitted, and applause is seldom expected before the end of an act.

6. See Verdi to Aldo Noseda, 1 April 1890, n. 1.

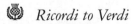 *Ricordi to Verdi*

Milan, 15 March 1894

Illustrious Maestro,

Upon receiving your esteemed letter of the 12th, I wanted to answer you at once; but unfortunately, this was impossible, since on the 13th and 14th I had . . . . two big sessions with the shareholders, one lasting 2 hours, and the other 4 and 1/2—I mean four and a half!

Today I can finally write you—and what else can I tell you . . . other than that your letter really distressed me. [. . .]

How could you possibly think that your presence is useless, since that is exactly what will animate everyone? . . .

About the hotel, rest assured you will feel completely at home; and there will be a little colony of friends to stand guard!! And Boito and I will spare you every possible trouble and fatigue.

I am dumbfounded, however, by what you write regarding the discomfort of the journey!! . . . . But I thought about this, too, and a special car could very well be put at your disposal from Genoa–Turin–Modane–Paris; this way, you would have a most comfortable journey without any inconvenience, and would find yourself in Paris before you knew it. The journey would be more expensive this way, but that would certainly be no problem for you. And if I should also find someone to accompany you, would you like that? . . . .

Concerning your other observations . . . . I wouldn't know what to say; this I know for sure: that your presence in Paris is *everybody's* utmost desire; and that the importance of this first French production of the Potbelly need not be stressed.

I expect to be in Paris with Boito on the 26th; therefore, on the 29th we'll be able to wire you exact details. Thus you could be in Paris on April 1st, always assuming that the opening will be between the 8th and the 12th.— This letter . . . . is rather odd! . . . but being in a tizzy . . . . I can no longer think and write! . . . . Excuse me; answer me with a word of consolation for me and all the others who adore the great Maestro.

Most affectionately Your
Giulio Ricordi

 *Boito to Verdi*

[Milan] 16 March [1894][1]

Dear Maestro,

Last night the audience was divided into three parties: those who were bored and stayed quiet, those who were bored and applauded, those who were bored and hissed. I was bored and stayed quiet. Boredom is an opinion, and it was mine last night.

This *alpine flower* turned out to be rambling nonsense, and to write about it at length isn't worth the price of ink. Franchetti, who navigated well with *Cristoforo Colombo*, drowned in a teacup or, better said, wanted to make a tempest in a teacup and was shipwrecked.

Many become shipwrecked like this because of their mania to *overdo*

1894

and search in their themes for what isn't and cannot be there, *midi à quatorze heures*, as the French say—the French whom *all* of us will go to see in about ten days; *I say all,* that is, you, Signora Peppina, Giulio, and I. It is of the utmost importance that you come along.

I hear (Solanges told me about it; he heard it from someone who was present at the rehearsals), I hear that the preparations for *Falstaff*[2] are proceeding very well from a musical, purely musical, point of view, but that the interpretation of the comedy is totally absent. And it is understandable that it should be so.

That theatre has extremely correct, elegant, and deeply rooted academic traditions which no one dares to violate. For these gentlemen William Shakespeare must produce the effect of a lion turned loose in a shop of Saxe figurines. *Save the china!* This will be the instinctive feeling of those gentlemen; and to save the china, they will be obliged to reduce our lion to impotence.

They will tone down everything, the accents, the inflections, the gestures, the movements, the words, the kisses, the thrashings, the laughter, the fun, the vivacity, the strength, the power, the youthfulness, the folly, the effervescence of the whole opera; and the audience will witness a performance that is very different from what Shakespeare had in mind, from what you have realized, from what all of us want.

Shakespeare is still waiting to be presented to France; he is still waiting for a powerful hand that has the strength and the assurance to interpret him and to reveal who he is.

This hand, Maestro, can only be yours; the mission is sublime and worthy of you. Therefore: *non più parole, che qui sciupiamo la luce del sole.*[3]

The best thing would be for all of us to leave together on the 28th. We'll meet in Turin. Giulio will take care of everything, he will find us a *coupé salon*, and will see to it that during the journey we will sleep as soundly as at home, and that we will eat and drink. We will chat and laugh, and it will be a most delightful excursion. *It is decided.* But time is getting short, and we must reach an agreement in order to wire the hotel.

All the best to Signora Peppina.

Affectionate greetings

from your
Arrigo

Till we all meet again during the journey.

NOTES

1. Postmark: MILANO 16/3/94.

2. At the Opéra-Comique in Paris.

3. Meg in *Falstaff,* I.ii.: "No more words, for here we are wasting the sunlight." (In Shakespeare's *Merry Wives of Windsor,* II.i. 54, Mrs. Ford says, "We burn daylight.")

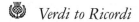 *Verdi to Ricordi*

Genoa, 17 March 1894

Dear Giulio,

You say very well! . . . Everyone says very well! . . . But I, too, say very well when I say that I am almost eighty-one years old, that my strength has diminished daily since I returned from Rome; that I cannot walk as I could a year ago, that I can no longer bear fatigue, noise, etc., etc.

You will spare me the annoyances, you said! . . The intention is good, but you will hardly succeed. However, I take note of your words in case I should feel strong enough to face this journey, which I don't want, because I don't know what consequences it might have, not only in physical but also in artistic terms. I repeat for the hundredth time that my presence at the *Opéra-Comique,* the way matters have now been planned, can be of no use at all, and could even cause much harm. Meanwhile, I know that Delna's voice,[1] splendid as it is, is not low enough for the part of Quickly! What will happen to the quartet, to the 2nd finale, and to so many other low passages throughout? That quartet must be not only musically but also dramatically effective, because it immediately reveals the character of the wives; they are the ones who create the comedy, after all.—I also know that the artist [chosen] for Nannetta[2] is a bit stocky. In Paris, as you know, much attention is paid to the *physique du rôle,* and if she is plump, how will she be able to run, jump, dance, etc., etc.? Perhaps the men will be better, but in this comedy it is the women who ought to be better. I also fear there will be other problems later on.

Despite all of this, it is possible that I might come to Paris entirely against my will. Not, however, without word from you assuring me of the performers' ability; and be sure that they are suited to the roles they must portray.

Today Boito writes me, in a brilliant letter, that we should all go to Paris together on the 26th.[3] No, this is not possible. You told me that you all would go ahead on the 26th; and that, after hearing some rehearsals, you would take the responsibility of wiring me solemnly and prophetically . . .

"Good. *Come to Paris*" or . . . "*Stay in Genoa.*" Tomorrow I will write you about the journey and about lodging. Write me in the meantime.

Affectionately,
G. Verdi

1894

P.S. What a consolation it would be if you found a way to wire me *"Stay in Genoa."* How grateful I would be! Eternally! In this life and the next!

NOTES

1. The French contralto Marie Delna (1875–1932); her voice had been discovered in the kitchen of her father's inn. She made her debut, at seventeen, as Didon in Berlioz' *Les Troyens* at the Opéra-Comique in 1892. Despite Verdi's initial reservations, Quickly became one of her greatest successes, and Verdi is reported to have said that "she is a very great artist [. . .] *If I were twenty years younger, indeed I would write an opera for her!"* (Conati, p. 274.) She participated in the Paris première of Verdi's *Quattro Pezzi Sacri* in 1898, and was the leading contralto of the Opéra from 1899 to 1901. Her long international career took her all over Europe, as well as to the Metropolitan Opera. Delna retired from the stage in 1922 but continued her concert career until 1930. A victim of the stock market crash at that time, she died penniless in a Paris asylum for the poor.

2. Lise Landouzy (1861–1943) made her debut as Rosina in the French version of *Il barbiere di Siviglia* at the Opéra-Comique in 1889. While she enjoyed her greatest success at that theatre, she was a regular guest at the Théâtre de la Monnaie in Brussels, and also appeared in Monte Carlo, Nice, and Aix-les-Bains. After her operatic career ended, Landouzy taught voice in Paris.

3. Boito, however, wrote "on the 28th."

 *Verdi to Maria Waldmann*

Genoa, 18 March 1894

Dear Maria,

Oh, if I had a little time, that is, if I had more time than I do now, I would tell you many, many things that would perhaps end up boring you. But you will understand that my time is a bit limited today and the hours are short; tomorrow will be worse! [. . .]

Don't believe anything they say about my future operas! You know that I am approaching *81!* . . I would be utterly crazy to go through it again. Enough, enough!! . . . [. . .]

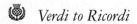 *Verdi to Ricordi*

Genoa, 18 March 1894

Dear Giulio,

I wrote you yesterday that I had more to tell you, etc. . . but since I will probably go to St. Agata on Tuesday,[1] I will pass through Milan, arriving at 12:50 and departing again at 1:30. I couldn't possibly go into town. If you have time, come to the station and we'll talk about everything. Tuesday at 8:00 I will send a telegram to confirm.[2]

Addio, addio.

Affectionately,
G. Verdi

NOTES

1. Verdi decided against this trip, but Ricordi went to see him in Genoa on Thursday, 22 March.

2. Missing.

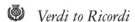 *Verdi to Ricordi*

Genoa, 23 March 1894

Dear Giulio,

Let's recapitulate—We said here:[1]

1. That if you do not find the individuals slated to perform *Falstaff* in Paris satisfactory and, above all, suited to their roles, you and Boito have given me your *word of honor* that you will tell me *"Stay in Genoa."* I have absolute faith in your word of honor.

2. If I come to Paris, I need

a living room;

a room for Peppina;

a room for me;

nearby quarters for the maid.

We shall arrive (we will decide the day) at the Lyons station at about six in the morning. Oh no, what an hour!

You told me that you yourself would make arrangements for the journey. I don't know what these *Wagons Lits* might be like. We want to be by ourselves so we can sleep undisturbed. It makes no difference to me whether the seats are reserved here or in Turin, since I could easily arrange for the journey to Turin with the station master here.— You decide.— But how to assure ourselves of the *compartment you reserved*, and of the day and the hour, if you make the arrangements?. . Tito or Tornaghi, however, might wire me. If you leave on the *27th,* you will arrive on the *28th*, and thus I could get your messages only after two or three rehearsals, that is, at the end of the month. I might be able to leave on the 1st of April, but that is a holiday,[2] so I would postpone my departure until the 2nd. We would be in Paris on the 3rd. If I can rest comfortably during the journey, I could attend the rehearsals the same day, e.g.,

1894

one with the women alone	perhaps these could be done the same
one with the men alone	day from 1 to 3 [and] from 3 to 5.

The next day *all* the singers.
Then onstage with cembalo.
Then with orchestra, if . . . . .

If I have forgotten something, I'll write again.

I haven't finished!

You promised me that you would save me from nuisances! Oh, a thousand thanks, and I trust in your promise! Can I trust you? Don't forget that I am almost 81 years old and nowadays can scarcely endure fatigue! I hold you to your word!

And now tell me: If things at the Opéra-Comique were to go so well that there would be no need for my presence? . . . What a consolation it would be for me if I were to receive word from you saying, *Maestro, stay in Genoa!* What joy! What joy! And how grateful I would be to you.—

Addio for now.

Affectionately,
G. Verdi

P.S. Sauchon wrote me a most eloquent, most beautiful letter! If only half of what he says were true, we would be very content! . . He hardly talks about the performance . . . but about my *Esteemed Person* and about the general desire (so he says) to see me in Paris! Imagine! Yet there is a phrase that doesn't make me too happy: *"Venez . . . apportez à tous le magique appui de vos encouragements!"* . . . So they want nothing else but to hear me tell them . . . *Bravo, bravi, brave, bravoti, bravomi, bravi tutti e felice notte . . . Uhmm!*

NOTES

1. In Genoa, during Ricordi's visit at Palazzo Doria the previous day.
2. Good Friday.

 Ricordi to Verdi

Milan, 23 March 1894

Illustrious Maestro,

In primis et ante omnia [first and foremost], infinite thanks to you and Signora Peppina for your most cordial welcome.[1] I received your letter of yesterday[2] only this morning, and since Boito has left, I cannot give you the information you want. On the other hand, on Sunday, Monday, and Tuesday, there is also Easter vacation at the Opéra-Comique!—Therefore no rehearsals, which will be resumed upon my arrival, that is, next Wednesday. As I told you, I'll leave with Giuditta Tuesday morning in order to be on the battlefield on the appointed day. Hence, on the 29th, 30th, and 31st I shall attend three or four rehearsals with Boito; and be assured, Maestro, that we will wire you the exact details, according to your instructions.

If things go well, I would then ask you to set your departure for the 1st of April, arriving on the 2nd and thus resting the whole day, and to call a rehearsal for the 3rd. As I told you, Tito and I have been busy making your journey most comfortable; and it can be most comfortable, with a bit more money, which will give you no trouble. [. . .] Assuming you change trains in Turin, the six seats would cost about 870 Francs. However, for about 1,000 Francs, that is, 130 or 150 additional Francs, you would have a salon car at your disposal from Genoa to Paris without having to change trains; and this way you would travel as though you were in your home. However, the railway must be notified 2 days in advance. Therefore, if by the 30th I see in Paris that things are going really well, I shall wire Tito to be ready.— Of course, I await your answer giving your approval, as soon as you have received this.

I am constantly receiving enthusiastic news about the rehearsals! I hope . . . . this may not be news generated by unfounded enthusiasm.

I finish with the following news: yesterday I concluded a contract with Cavaliere Pietro Mascagni!! Complete break with his publisher![3] It will be . . . . what it will be . . . or what it is! . . . But, the conditions agreed upon being absolutely fair, I thought it best not to reject *les avances* made to me, since they did not impose upon the House [of Ricordi] a sacrifice that could cause any harm.

It seems that a most violent scene between Sonzogno and Mascagni occurred in Naples, because the former tried to behave like an *emperor* and the latter didn't want to suffer such insolence.

What do you say to that, Maestro? . . .

I await your instructions, hoping that I may be able to tell you, *"Till I see you again"* in a few days in Paris, and here I end.

Greetings to Signora Peppina and to you from your ever most grateful and devoted

Giulio Ricordi

P.S. Of course, I will prepare everything at the hotel, as I know what you like best; and I will be at the *Gare* to receive you.

Boito's address, in case you should need it:

Letters—Grand Hôtel Boul. Capucines.

Telegrams—Grand Hôtel.

1894

NOTES

1. In Genoa on 22 March.
2. Missing.
3. Sonzogno.

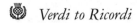 *Verdi to Ricordi*

Saturday, 8 A.M. [Genoa, 24 March 1894]

Dear Giulio,

All things considered, for the journey to Paris, I think the *Sleeping Car* (unpleasant for me as it is) will be better for us
1. because it has a waiter;
2. because it is easy for me to step down;
3. above all, because it shakes less and one feels less of the wheels, etc.

So don't worry about this, since I have been assured that cars going directly to Paris may be boarded here.—

Affectionately,
G. Verdi

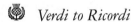 *Verdi to Ricordi*

Genoa, 25 March 1894

Dear Giulio,

As I wired you,[1] I can arrange for my journey here in Genoa.—

[3 illegible words] if you write me to come to Paris, I shall arrive at 6 A.M. on 3 April.

As to the rehearsals, I have already indicated to you what could be done.

I read in a report in the Secolo: *"Although Maestro Verdi's coming here is uncertain, not only the Italian colony but also most Parisian artists are organizing, etc."*

FOR GOD'S SAKE !!!

You have promised to save me from any nuisance, and I am strictly relying on you . . . for the sake of my 81 years!

I've also been sent an issue of *La Tribuna*[2] in which there is an article by *Folchetto*[3] that is really out of place and a blunder! Why does he drag in politics? (This article seems to have been written by an enemy!) If I wanted to get into politics, I would do so in sunlight, in a loud voice, and would never combine it with music! Music is something very different to me; and, furthermore, here only music, music, music is involved! If you see Folchetto before I do, just tell him clearly and frankly that he has taken the wrong course.—Finally, Folchetto ends the article by saying that he hopes to see me in the *"legendary little apartment at the Hôtel de Bade"!* Ahhh!!! I'm glad to hear this, since it means that this *Hôtel* is not in such a state of decay as you yourself had told me! You, who are going to Paris ahead of me, do me the great and enormous favor of giving me complete information; and if it should be habitable at all, reserve me the usual apartment; I believe it is No. 1, right above the staircase on the first floor. Besides, in the Hôtel office they will easily find out that I have stayed there many times, and for months and months.

Furthermore, all the articles in Paris say that I will go to the *première!* Only to the first [performance]?. . No: never, never! I shall go, yes or no, to attend several rehearsals and to state my opinion clearly and frankly: not to *put myself on display* and *give my approval!*

Enough: Happy Easter, bon voyage! I hope . . . I won't say what I hope! . . . Addio, addio.

Affectionately,

G. Verdi

P.S. Maestro's fault![4] I wired yesterday about the contract with Mascagni;[5] if the others [telegrams] are also true concerning Franchetti, etc., etc., etc. *Twice, three times, etc., Maestro's fault.* I am enclosing the *Tribuna* article.

I received the two French *Falstaff* librettos.

NOTES

1. This telegram is missing.

2. Daily political paper founded in Rome in 1893 and, because of its opposition to the fascist regime, compelled to cease publication in 1924. *La Tribuna* contained extensive cultural and literary sections, to which Gabriele D'Annunzio, later a Fascist, contributed under various pen names.

3. Pen name of Jacopo Caponi, critic of the Roman newspaper *Fanfulla*. He translated and enlarged an 1881 biography of Verdi in French, by Arthur Pougain (1834–1921). Writing in Paris, Folchetto says in the clipping, which Verdi enclosed:

> No doubt we will have *Falstaff* in April. The ensemble rehearsals are over, the orchestra rehearsals are just now starting. Maurel,* who arrived last night, pregnant with the intentions of the maestro, is a valuable assistant in the stage direction as well as in the vocal and instrumental performance. It has been announced that Verdi will come to the *première* as he came to that of *Aida,* and that the Italian colony was prepared to welcome him in some way. Now it is asserted that he will not come, as

1894

always for reasons that have something to do with politics.** The Russian-German treaty could change his mind, and perhaps I will see him again in that legendary apartment at the *Hôtel de Bade,* where he likes to stay when he comes to Paris.

Verdi wrote in the margin of the clipping: "*In what can Maurel be useful?" and "**And again with this political mischief!"

4. Verdi refers to himself.

5. This telegram is missing.

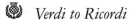 *Verdi to Ricordi*

Genoa, 28 March 1894

Dear Giulio,

I hope you had a safe arrival after a good journey!

If you send me that telegram,[1] send it so that I can receive it during the day on Saturday; otherwise I could not leave Monday morning, since the seats must be reserved at least 24 hours in advance, and I must also get French money. . . . It wouldn't be so bad if I left on Tuesday, after all . . . Perhaps, perhaps [I can give] a bit of pleasure to Maurel, who seems to have said in an *interview* in the *Soir, "What a pleasure if the Maestro didn't come."*

Addio, addio in haste.   Affectionately,

G. Verdi

Greetings to Signora Giuditta for [illegible word] and to Boito!

NOTE

1. Not located.

Verdi to Ricordi

Genoa, 31 March 1894

Dear Giulio,

As I wired you, we shall be in Paris Wednesday morning at 6:45.[1]

If only half of what you tell me about the rehearsal (because of your optimism) is true, . . . I ask myself, *"What am I going to do in Paris?* Put myself on display like the *Ours Martin* [Circus Bear]?" Tell me: is this dignified for an eighty-year-old man? Oh, this is a very hard thing!!

And how is the Divo[2] doing? What does he say? Are we going to have trouble with him, on account of him? . . Addio in haste.

Affectionately,

G. Verdi

NOTES

1. This telegram is missing.
2. Maurel.

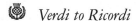 *Verdi to Ricordi*

Genoa, 1 April 1894

Dear Giulio,

I received your letter of the 30th.[1]— May it be, then, as you say! I am sorry, however, that Cajus is weak. In the first finale he is just as important as Ford.

I repeat that we will be in Paris Wednesday at 6:45.

Greetings to all.

Affectionately,
G. Verdi

[. . .]

NOTE

1. Missing.

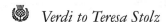 *Verdi to Teresa Stolz*

Paris, 19 April 1894

[. . .] Last night the first *Falstaff*. Good performance onstage. Maurel and Quickly excellent. Marvelous orchestra. Complete effect![1] I don't mention the demonstrations, in spite of the . . . French . . . airs and graces! I conclude by telling you: Good, good, good! But oh dear! How much trouble and fatigue! [. . .]

NOTE

1. The first French performance of *Falstaff,* translated by Boito and Paul Solanges and conducted by Jules Danbé, took place at the Opéra-Comique on 18 April, with Maurel in the title role, Louise Grandjean as Alice, Marie Delna as Quickly, Lise Landouzy as Nannetta, Esther[?] Chevalier as Meg, Gabriel Soulacroix as Ford, and Edmond Clément as Fenton. (See last paragraph of Camille Bellaigue's review in Appendix III.)

The distinguished French baritone Gabriel Soulacroix (1853–1905) studied at the conservatories in Toulouse and Paris. His debut took place in 1878 at the Théâtre de la Monnaie in Brussels. He enjoyed several important successes there, as well as in the French provinces. Between 1881 and 1884, and again in 1891, he sang at Covent Garden. In 1885 he was engaged by the Opéra-Comique, where he appeared, *inter alia,* in Bizet's *Les pêcheurs*

1894

de perles and in the first French production of Puccini's *La Bohème*, in 1898. When the Opéra-Comique caught fire during a performance of *Mignon* in 1887, Soulacroix is said to have saved many lives. He died suddenly in 1905, at the height of his career.

Edmond Clément (1867–1928), who attended the Paris Conservatory and made his debut at the Opéra-Comique in Gounod's *Mireille*, soon became the most brilliant French lyric tenor of his time. He belonged to the company of the Opéra-Comique for thirty-eight years. Clément made his debut at the Metropolitan Opera as Werther in 1909; and he was heard in Boston between 1910 and 1913. He taught voice in Paris, and was still giving recitals as late as 1927.

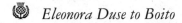 *Eleonora Duse to Boito*

[Paris, 23 April 1894][1]
Hôtel Continental 23 evening arrived at 6
Hotel Continentale No. 201 (3rd floor).

It's almost 7 as I send this.[2] Lenor will wait until 9 this evening if it is *possible* to see Gualdo tonight.[3]

Arrigo will answer her by letter or in person.

Lenor

I'm at the restaurant of the Gare du Nord ——
you can still come for a moment. As tired as I feel, I think I should leave to rest en route ——

Au revoir! — perhaps   E

NOTES

1. On her way from Venice to London (Weaver, pp. 110–1).
2. Presumably by messenger to Boito at the Grand Hôtel, perhaps while he was at a *Falstaff* performance at the Opéra-Comique, or was needed elsewhere during those busy days.
3. See Chronology for 1894, n. 13. To protect themselves, Duse and Boito used the name of their mutual friend, "known as 'gilet bianco' because of his elegant white waistcoats. Now the dapper Gualdo had been stricken by paralysis, and in her distress Lenor wrote Arrigo about the possibility of their taking in their friend." (Weaver, p. 110.)

 *Verdi to Maria Waldmann*

Paris, 24 April 1894[1]
I received your most kind and dear letter,[2] which makes me feel so good! I have no time at my disposal. Tomorrow we return to Genoa.

Thank you, thank you, thank you, my dearest Maria. Peppina sends you her greetings. All the best to the Duke. To you the most cordial handshake.

[G. Verdi]

NOTES

    1. The autograph of this letter, which was published in *Carteggi* ii, p. 266, is missing.
    2. Missing.

 Boito to Camille Bellaigue

[In French]   Paris, [25] April 1894, Wednesday

Dear Friend,
    I just read your article "Apotheosis."[1]
    Knowing how to understand, to love, to express oneself—these are the great joys of the human spirit. You possess them to the highest degree, "Uomo felice." Thank you for the noble pleasure I felt while reading your work.

                                  Your affectionate
                                  [Arrigo Boito]
P.S. The expression "to mediterraneanize music" is not mine. It is Nietzsche's. You know the Bohemian philosopher[2] as well as I, and when I wrote you, I thought you would have recognized the expression.

NOTES

    1. See Appendix III, Bellaigue's review of the first French *Falstaff* at the Paris Opéra-Comique on 18 April.
    2. See Boito to Camille Bellaigue, 22 January, n. 2.

 Verdi to Ricordi

                           Friday [Genoa, 27 April 1894][1]

Dear Giulio,
    Are you all alive or dead?[2]
We are still alive, but could not have taken it any longer.[3]
    At last it's over!
I found a pile of newspapers here and had a look at them. The French are good; better, perhaps, are the German; the Italian ones are half a tone lower. They are subtle, mentioning casually what went well, and emphasizing what went less well. Know-alls!!
    Affectionate greetings to all. Addio.

                                      Your
                                     G. Verdi

1894

NOTES

1. Postmark: GENOVA 27/4/94.

2. Ricordi's following letters show that he and his wife were back in Milan, to where Verdi addressed these lines. (The statement in Abbiati iv, p. 540, and *Carteggio* ii, p. 448, that Ricordi stayed in Paris until early May, is in error. (I must apologize for the same mistake in *Otello* ii, p. 800. H.B.)

3. The Verdis had returned to Genoa on 25 April, after the third performance of *Falstaff* at the Opéra-Comique.

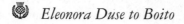 *Ricordi to Verdi*

Milan, 28 April 1894

Illustrious Maestro,

Just as I was about to write to you, I received your very dear note of yesterday giving us the good news we had so much hoped for and for which I just now wanted to ask you.

How much would I have to tell you !! . . . And how much would I like to thank you for all the kindness both of you have shown Giuditta and me.— But you will far better understand my relative silence than all these words.— However, I cannot conceal from you my great satisfaction that, as accomplices in your journey to Paris, Boito and I saw no reason for any regret.

As I had imagined, I am already bogged down here, not only by the hodgepodge of affairs, but also by the troubles involved! . . A hard, very hard life it is to carry on like this for so long.

We found our whole family in good health, which is no small consolation. Let us hope that when the fatigue of the journey is over, Signora Peppina's health will be completely restored.

As for you . . . . . the nuisance of Paris isn't over; there still are autographs and promised dedications! . . . But some other day, when I can give you exact information.

With our most affectionate greetings, while reassuring you of my supreme gratitude,

Your most devoted
Giulio Ricordi

Eleonora Duse to Boito

[London, 30 April 1894]
Savoy Hotel

[. . .] Lenor [. . .] has decided *we should not see each other in London.* It is dangerous at the moment.[1] Arrigo will return *to the well-known house*[2] without *"passing"* through London.—Instead of this, however, there is another plan that is feasible—

Here it is:

Lenor, (if all goes well) will leave London not before 15 or 16 June. On that day Arrigo will come to meet her in Paris.—Could Arrigo . . . —— (will he be able?)——do it? [. . .]

In Paris, *disappearing from the world* for a few days, the two could meet and think about the summer [. . .] .

Eleon

NOTES

1. Duse was still married to Tebaldo Checchi. He was in London, where she was performing at this time. She felt so persecuted that, fearing the Italian staff at the Savoy Hotel, she urged Boito to number his letters and send them only by registered mail. (See Weaver, p. 111.)

2. St. Agata.

 *Ricordi to Verdi*

Milan, 1 May 1894

Illustrious Maestro,

Hoping that you may be completely rested from the many Parisian exertions, I am sending you a bit of work!!— That is, dedications and autographs promised at your departure. Kindly return them all to me, signed and dedicated, so I may then take care of forwarding them.—

I am enclosing an explanatory note for your information.—

I wired you about another complete success of *Falstaff,* in Leipzig.—[1] You will also have news of the enthusiasm in Florence, where another Alice caused surprise; . . . . . she repeated *"Avrò con me dei putti"*[2] 3 times . . . and she is an artist about whom there were many doubts!!—[3]

You will recall that our good friend Sonzogno has taken over the Cannobiana,[4] which he will inaugurate next September.—Now the Dal Verme management would like to have a big season in October–November and to present *Falstaff* with a distinguished cast, of course.—I have not given them any answer, as I first wanted to find out what you think; there are many *pros* and *cons*, positive and negative considerations, and I need not mention them to you, who know them better than I.—Therefore, let me have your frank opinion, and I will be very grateful to you, because I don't want to misjudge; for I might be, subconsciously or not, under the nervous strain of the same old war with Sonzogno.

1894

I hope that your health may always be excellent. Meanwhile, I express my total gratitude with most devoted regards.

Your most devoted
Giulio Ricordi

NOTES

1. Telegram missing.
2. III.i (PV p. 322, 1/2).
3. The otherwise unknown De Marzi. (Abbiati iv, p. 541.)
4. Built in the same year (1778) as La Scala, the Teatro della Cannobiana presented opera and ballet until the 1860s. In 1894 it was demolished and replaced by the Teatro Lirico, which was opened by Edoardo Sonzogno.

 *Verdi to Ricordi*

Genoa, 3 May 1894

Dear Giulio,

No, no, I am not rested at all. Saturday I'll go to St. Agata, and maybe there I will rest . . . but who knows! I heard about Leipzig; and I heard about Florence, and they sent me a nice article in the *Nazione* by *Jarro,*[1] who, I think, was an enemy at one time! Well! He could continue as such, *it wouldn't make any difference.*

I am returning the portraits and frontispieces autographed. . What should I do with that poor music . . . Bertina?[2] I know about the Canobbiana, about Sonzogno, etc., etc. It would be a fight! Why fight? Things are going so well for you, I think, that there is no need to push ahead. My opinion in this case would be to keep quiet and not to give in. *Silence* and *indifference* . . . Oh, indifference is an armor that prevails over all weapons. Besides, it is more dignified.—

Well then, addio. Greet everybody.

Affectionately,
G Verdi

P.S. Wire me as soon as you receive the package with the portraits, etc.—
P.S. Your Mayor and the President of the Exhibition[3] wrote me that I should come on the 6th for the opening of the Exhibition . .
Refuse!!!

NOTES

1. Unknown.
2. Unknown.
3. Esposizioni Riunite di Milano 1894.

Verdi to Ricordi

Milan [St. Agata], 6 May 1894

Dear Giulio,

Arriving here yesterday about 5 o'clock, I found the enclosed letter.[1] A mere bagatelle!! What do you say about it?

I am asking you, who somehow (excuse me) were my secretary during our sojourn in Paris, what to answer . . . after all, this is but the coda of the sojourn in Paris!

Yesterday we passed through Milan, that is, we came through the station, where we stopped only for about 20 minutes.[2]

In haste addio, addio, addio—

Your
G. Verdi

NOTES

1. From the Institute of France, requesting the scores of all the Verdi operas.
2. Between Genoa and St. Agata.

Eleonora Duse to Boito

[London, 8 May 1894]
8 May 8 o'clock

[. . .] The night is over—but Lenor could not sleep.—That so-called work resumed last night seemed to me more than ever the most phenomenal absurdity and shabbiness of my life, and of human life in general. How offensive it is to the soul to mimic life. [. . .]

What misery, Arrigo! [. . .]

What rabble! They make up their eyes, powder their cheeks—throw their hands and mouths wide open—and think they are translating life. [. . .]

Arrigo wonders why Lenor is *so afraid of the world*, and surrounds herself with caution, if she can. The explanation is this—You have fought less than I have to earn your bread. You have lived (yes, perhaps in anxiety—poor Arrigo), but you always had a house. [. . .] I had to *keep working* with such anxiety, and I am a woman. How many sunsets lost, because "you must go to the theatre"; how many days—lost and torn asunder—without learning anything good—and skimming over everything—[. . .]

1894

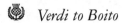 *Verdi to Boito*

[Telegram]   Busseto, 8 May 1894[1]

HAVE BAD COLD AND CANNOT TALK—DELAY YOUR ARRIVAL FEW DAYS—
WILL WIRE

VERDI

NOTE

1. See *Otello* i, pp. 396–8.

 *Ricordi to Verdi*

Milan, 9 May 1894

Illustrious Maestro,

Please excuse my involuntary delay in answering you: As if the usual business weren't enough, the Exhibition has given me a lot of work, which is, fortunately, almost finished by now!— On the whole, the result has been something wonderful, which also deserves to be seen for its originality.

Regarding the letter from the Institute of France, only the collection has to be sent [. . .][1]

NOTE

1. The remainder of this letter is missing.

 *Eleonora Duse to Boito*

[London, 10 May 1894]
From Wednesday to Thursday

[. . .] Teach me! I will teach you!

I felt the hurt you caused me! You will make me repeat the hurt I caused you! [. . .]

We have deceived ourselves so much already. We have also lied, hiding or minimizing *the kind of truths* we were unable to face, that we might be unable to face even today.

Ah! after so many years, what use is life after all?—Look! Even in art (and that is such a small thing in comparison) we did not dare to say everything. Absurd!——— We did not dare, we, one facing the other (in each other's arms), to pick up the pieces from that enormous, phenomenal, absurd plunge into the work of *Shakespeare*.[1] We *kept silent about it,* WE, *afraid* to talk. [. . .]

I am telling the truth when I assert to myself that I would like to *live* again by this love, but to live again, pride and humility are needed on both sides. Truth, truth is needed, the only help! [. . .]

Help me to *protect* our life, not to destroy it! Make me feel *new and alone* on your road——— if you want to walk together with me until the end. Until the end one can and must learn to love.[. . .]

During the days in Paris — I felt the flame, but little lasting joy, and little sweetness. I felt there was still *a world* between us! [. . .]

NOTE

1. Boito's translation of *Antony and Cleopatra,* made for Duse, had been unsuccessful at its première in Milan on 22 November 1888. (See *Otello* ii, p. 799.)

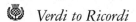 *Verdi to Ricordi*

St. Agata, 10 May 1894

Dear Giulio,

The Institute of France affair is annoying, and, to tell the truth, I had hoped that you would refuse! Anyway, only those operas need be sent which have been tolerated in France: *Ernani, Trovatore, Traviata, Rigoletto, Aida,* the *Messa, Falstaff* . . . that's enough.

Boito wrote me about coming to talk with me—alas!—about this *Othello* at the Opéra.[1] But I had, and still have, a cold and cannot talk, I have no voice! I'll write about it later.

Well then, *Falstaff-Maurel* sick![2] Evviva!

I heard that in the *Falstaff* in Florence De Marzi is singing encores and triple-encores . . . But why not make cabalettas then?

I also saw sauces *"Manon Falstaff,"* fans *"Falstaff Manon"* . . . cookies *"Manon Falstaff"* . . . sweets Giacosa[3] *"Falstaff Manon!"*

What an excellent and providential union this is: *Manon* arm in arm with *Falstaff*.[4]— So if Falstaff, staggering, still makes some headway, he will find in Manon a mighty supporter, who will keep him on his feet and ease his way.[5] Addio, addio and greetings to all.

Affectionately,
G. Verdi

1894

NOTES

1. Presumably Boito wrote this missing letter in Milan after his return from Paris in early May. (See *Otello* i, pp. 396–7.)

2. Postponing the performances of *Falstaff* at the Opéra-Comique.

3. Probably a joking reference to Boito's friend, the sweet-toothed playwright and librettist.

4. Puccini's *Manon Lescaut* was premiered in Turin on 1 February 1893. Next to *Falstaff*, it was the most successful Italian opera of the day. (La Scala presented twenty-two performances of *Falstaff* in 1893 and nineteen of *Manon Lescaut* in 1894.) Harold Rosenthal, discussing the first *Falstaff* production at London's Covent Garden, on 19 May 1894, explains the situation which prompted Verdi's cynical remark:

> Harris [Sir Augustus Harris (1852–96), manager of Covent Garden] had not been particularly enthusiastic about mounting the young composer's [Puccini's] work, and was only persuaded to do so, after much difficulty, by Tito Ricordi and Mancinelli, two of Puccini's greatest friends. The Ricordis were also Verdi's publishers, and while Harris was not told in so many words that he could only produce *Falstaff* if at the same time he took *Manon Lescaut*, it was made plain to him that that was rather the idea in Ricordi's mind. It was suggested that a company of artists for both operas should be imported from Milan; Harris eventually agreed to this but was none too happy about the choice of singers, who were not exactly of the first rank. This did not matter so much with *Falstaff*, which does not cry out for great voices but for a perfect ensemble; *Manon Lescaut*, however, needs first-class Italian voices and a good conductor. Unfortunately, it had neither of these. (*Two Centuries of Opera at Covent Garden*, p. 258.)

Under Covent Garden's second conductor, Armando Seppilli, the Russian Olga Olghina sang Manon; W. Beduschi, Des Grieux; and Antonio Pini-Corsi, Lescaut. This compromise resulted in only two performances of *Manon Lescaut* versus eight of *Falstaff*.

Armando Seppilli (1860–1931) studied composition with Bazzini and Ponchielli at the Milan Conservatory. He accompanied the famous Australian prima donna Nellie Melba (1861–1931) in his own songs.

Olga Olghina (also spelled Olgina and Olghine) (1864?–?), sang leading roles in the premières of *Prince Igor* and *Pique Dame* at St. Petersburg in 1890. She appeared as Manon Lescaut at La Scala in 1894, continuing her career in Warsaw, Helsinki, at the Bolshoi in Moscow, and on other Russian stages into the first years of the twentieth century.

W. Beduschi could not be identified.

5. Verdi had expressed his misgivings about this combination in his letter to Ricordi of 29 March 1893. He also appeared apprehensive about the competition in his letter to Mascheroni of 18 August 1893.

 *Verdi to Boito*

St. Agata, 12 May 1894

Dear Boito,

My voice has returned a bit, but the whole city of Paris still weighs on my stomach and on my legs.

Come here when you want.

Don't forget that the *through train* that stops at Fiorenzuola leaves Milan at 1:30 P.M. and arrives at 3:27.

Till we see each other, greetings to all.

Affectionately,
G. Verdi

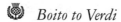 *Boito to Verdi*

Monday, 14 May [1894][1]
Milan

Dear Maestro,

I'll arrive at St. Agata on Thursday and will be at Fiorenzuola on the train you mention. By Thursday I hope you'll be able not only to speak but also to sing, and I hope to be able to sing and talk myself, since for three days I've also had a cold in the head, throat, and chest.

Well then, till we see each other this Thursday.

To be on the safe side, I'll reconfirm my arrival by telegram the day before.

Many good greetings   from your affectionate
Arrigo Boito

NOTE

1. Postmark: MILANO 14/5/94.

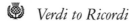 *Verdi to Ricordi*

St. Agata, 14 May 1894

Dear Giulio,

He who gets old inevitably becomes a bore!—

When I was young, it was almost impossible for me to ask my publisher for one of my scores, or for a portrait. Now I must do it either for a *confrère,* or an artist, or for the president of an institute, or for asylums—welfare! That burdens me a lot and causes me grief! If only I could say to you, *"Charge it to my account!"*

Let's get to the point: Please send me the piano-vocal scores of two operas, *Falstaff* and *Otello.* Excuse me and addio, addio. Greetings.

Affectionately,
G. Verdi

1894

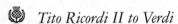 *Ricordi to Verdi*

Milan, 17 May 1894

Illustrious Maestro,

Boito will have brought you my greetings, and I am glad to know he is there, as this means that your cold is gone; it seems, though, that Boito has caught it now.

I received a letter from Tito giving me very good news about the *Falstaff* rehearsals in London; thus he is looking forward to an excellent performance and *mise-en-scène*; it will open the day after tomorrow, Saturday—and I will wire you right away.

Signora Nellie Melba[1] hoped to see you in Milan and present you with the enclosed;[2] unable to have this honor, she asks you to favor her at least with your photograph!!! . . . . In any case, I will send her one, but if you feel like signing one with a simple dedication to her, I would then hand it to Signora Melba.

Boito, who told me that he would return soon, will bring me your news, which we hope will be truly excellent. Meanwhile, affectionate regards from your ever so grateful

Giulio Ricordi

I sent the Institute the operas you indicated to me.

NOTES

1. In May 1894 Melba appeared at La Scala three times each as Lucia and Gilda.
2. Unknown.

Tito Ricordi II to Verdi

[Telegram]   London, 19 May 1894

HAPPY AND PROUD TO ANNOUNCE FALSTAFF TRIUMPH LONDON[1] — PESSINA PERFECT PROTAGONIST — THE OTHER PERFORMERS VERY GOOD[2] — CONDUCTOR MANCINELLI — REGARDS TO SIGNORA PEPPINA

TITO RICORDI

NOTES

1. Harold Rosenthal's account differs:

The regular Covent Garden public was never really enthusiastic about it. *The Times* wrote: "Quite unequivocal was the success of the beautiful work with those whose opinion is of consequence whether in stalls or gallery; but it remains to be seen whether the subscribers and the fashionable world in public will care for an opera which, since it contains no dull moments, allows no opportunities for comfortable conversation during the music." Arturo Pessina "was a far more genial Falstaff than the gloomy cynic presented by M. Maurel, whose make-up and general appearance are exactly imitated" [probably as a result of Verdi's complaint to Mascheroni in his P.S. of 16 August 1893]. Signora Zilli was "a sparkling Alice with a persistent tremolo," Giulia Ravogli "a racy and suggestive" Quickly, Pini-Corsi "a most amusing" Ford (his original part) and Beduschi a "graceful" Fenton. Mancinelli conducted "an admirable performance, though his tempi differ materially from those adopted at the first performance in Milan, which may be supposed to have had the composer's sanction." (*Two Centuries of Opera at Covent Garden*, pp. 258–9. See Verdi to Ricordi, 10 May, n. 5; and G.B. Shaw's review, Appendix IV.)

2. The contralto Giulia Ravogli often appeared with her sister Sofia (1855–1910), a soprano, in Italy and abroad.

 Camille Bellaigue to Verdi

[In French]   Paris, 27 May 1894

Dear and great Maestro,

It is Sunday; it rains, it is stormy; outside it is dark and sad, but inside rosy and merry, since we are playing *Falstaff* in the studio you know.

The day before yesterday we both went to hear your delightful masterwork for the fifth time and never enjoyed it so much. We sat in the corner of the dress circle, from where we divinely heard your divine music. I believe we still did not know *Falstaff,* and we discovered it. What an exquisite, ravishing, intoxicating discovery! During the whole month of May we are living not in the unpleasant spring of this year, but in your score, in the orchestra, the voices, the flowers of your melodies, your harmonies, your sounds. I would like to write again about *Falstaff,* pages upon pages . . . or rather, I do not want to write anything more; I even regret having written. Before beauty we must adore and be silent. Talking about it is almost a sacrilege; true love does not talk. And yet! . . Well, I shall not talk about it anymore; but I will play and play it again without end; and in a few days, I will, we will hear it again. And Maurel will be more repugnant to me than ever.

Recently he massacred the 2nd reprise of *Quand'ero paggio*. I could have thrown my opera glass in his face. At the third reprise I wished him an avenging stroke, but it did not come. And the wretch continued his cursed work. I think the next time he will sing standing on his hands; next year he

1894

will sing on horseback jumping through paper hoops. Not to mention that the entire monologue was cut the other night; no more mournful meditation about the "abject world," no more trills, nothing at all; but the moment the curtain is up, Quickly enters with *Révérance*. That is sad, and the effect of this entrance is immediately destroyed. Did you allow this awful cut? [. . .]

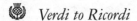 *Verdi to Ricordi*

Milan, 1 June 1894[1]

Dear Giulio,

I received a letter from Paris informing me that Maurel has taken the liberty of making cuts in *Falstaff* here and there!! And what is even worse, he takes out a piece now here, now there on a whim, as if experimenting and to judge which parts are worthy of being tolerated, and which should be forgotten! And then they speak of art. . . of Great Art!! . . *What a joke!!* In this manner, operas become nothing other than exercises to show off the voice, the way of singing or the gesture (affected, of course) of any old artist.

Moreover, I am asked whether I have authorized those cuts! Oh no! Oh no!! I admit, and without regret, that my operas should not be done; but if they are done, I request that it be as I conceived them.

Therefore I turn to you, my publisher, and invoke the contract that exists between us in this regard. Declare, then, in my name to the directors of the Opéra-Comique that *Falstaff* must be performed in its entirety as on the night of the first performance.

Yours as ever,
G. Verdi

NOTE

1. From the end of May until early June Verdi was in Milan to confer about the French *Othello* with Gailhard, Boito, and Ricordi (*Otello* i, p. 400). Although they were in the same city, Verdi chose to protest to Giulio in writing, also in the following note.

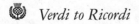 *Verdi to Ricordi*

[Milan] 1 *June* [1894]

Dear Giulio,

Read the enclosed letter.

I think you can translate it into French and send it to your representative in Paris, so that he may contact the directors of the Opéra-Comique to achieve results. I also believe that this declaration will be useful in the future.[1]

G. Verdi

P.S. I couldn't go to the Exhibition today. I'll go tomorrow, if you agree.

NOTE

    1. See similar declarations in Verdi's fight for productions which preserve the integrity and the dignity of art, in *Aida,* pp. 362–7, and *Otello* i, p. 402.

 *Eleonora Duse to Boito*

[London, 7 June 1894]
7 June —

    Here is the itinerary Lenor promised by telegram.[1]— Lenor departs London at 11 in the morning of the 15th. Arrives in Paris at 7 in the evening. Arrigo does not await her at the station, because only people of no importance are met at the station. Lenor (with the maid) checks in at the Hôtel Continental:——alone——it is better. From the station to the Hôtel will take an hour or more. Let's say, then, that Arrigo awaits Lenor at NINE *in the evening*—(no *cards* at the Hôtel) in that square . . . on the way to the rue de la Paix . . . —

    Place Vendôme——

    There is a *Hôtel Bristol at the corner*—I know it—friends of mine stayed there.—So then—Hôtel Bristol—as on that night when you awaited me at the door of the Grand Hôtel.[2] From there we'll go and eat somewhere, and then Lenor herself will tell you her room number, so that you won't have to get it from the porters at the Hôtel. [. . .]

E.

NOTES

    1. Missing, like all others in the remaining Boito-Duse correspondence. (Weaver, pp. 111–4.)
    2. In reference to their brief rendezvous in Paris between 24 and 28 April.

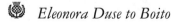 *Eleonora Duse to Boito*

[London, 8 June 1894]
8 June — morning

    [. . .] *Hôtel Bristol* CORNER *of Place Vendôme.*

    The evening of the *fifteenth*—BETWEEN nine and HALF past *nine*—Don't object to waiting for 5 minutes—

1894

No meeting at the station, what an idea! We aren't husband and wife *enough* to *go to the station.* —What an idea! [. . .]

I re-open [the letter]—(I am wrong) to tell you *something* that will make me . . . "highly despised" by you. You'll mock me, that's all, but the other night I went to hear *Falstaff.*

May *God—Arrigo*——forgive me . . . but it seemed such a . . . *melancholy* thing, that *Falstaff.*[1] [. . .]

NOTE

1. This is Duse's only written mention of *Falstaff.*

 Verdi to Camille Bellaigue

[In French]   Busseto-St. Agata, 8 June 1894

My dear Monsieur Bellaigue,

Returned from Milan, where I stayed for eight days to discuss *Othello* matters with Gailhard, Boito, Ricordi, etc. I am a bit late in answering your charming letter of 27 May.

I can imagine your rage at Maurel; it is true, he must always overdo! It is unfortunate, since with his artistic qualities he could avoid these excesses with the approval of the whole world. In spite of this he has much talent, much authority, and is particularly useful in a new piece.[1]

Oh no! oh no! I didn't authorize any cut . . . on the contrary, I am requesting through Ricordi that matters be restored to their former state.

But now, what can I tell you about the splendid words you so kindly said about my *Pancione?*[2] You would almost make me blush if the skin weren't copper-colored at my age.

I'm impatiently awaiting your study of Palestrina and compliment you in advance, sure as I am that it will be very fine.

We, Mme. Verdi and I, remember with great joy the three weeks we spent in Paris, so often in your and your charming Mme. Bellaigue's company.

To both of you, our sincere affection and gratitude.

G. Verdi

P.S. You will see Boito in Paris a few days from now. —

NOTES

1. Unaware of Maurel's incredible behavior, Verdi had wired the directors of the Paris Opéra: "You may engage Maurel for the *Othello* première in October." (*Otello* i, p. 400.) According to Bellaigue's letter of 27 May, Verdi happened to send this telegram the very

same day that Maurel imposed his changes on *Falstaff*. Nevertheless, Maurel was to contribute to the triumph of the first French *Othello* at the Opéra on 12 October.

2. See also Appendix III.

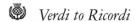 *Verdi to Ricordi*

Busseto, 8 June 1894

Dear Giulio,

Tell me, have you heard anything concerning my protest against Maurel's *coupures* [cuts] in *Falstaff?* [. . .]

Greetings in haste.

Affectionately,
G. Verdi

 *Ricordi to Verdi*

Milan, 9 June 1894

Illustrious Maestro,

Just as I received your esteemed letter, an answer from Paris arrived,[1] which I am transcribing for you:

"Yesterday I went to see M. Carvalho and informed him of Maestro Verdi's letter. He promised me to reprimand M. Maurel, who is wearing him out with his demands. M. Carvalho deeply regrets what is happening, but did not dare to say anything to Maurel, who has been threatening him all the time that he would cancel his contract, talking at every instant about leaving if his whims were not allowed. Maurel went so far as to demand that the *Pique, repic, aspic, etc.,* Chorus[2] be eliminated, on the pretext that it tired him to see people whirling around him. But I obtained a formal promise from M. Carvalho that he would bring an end to the present state of affairs."

I replied that this is all right, observing, however, that I thought it the Maestro's intention that his letter be known also to Maurel. Is this not so? . . . .

This action of M. Maurel's, however, is extremely serious, and I don't understand how Carvalho could let himself be overpowered like that. [. . .]

NOTES

1. In French, apparently sent by Ricordi's Paris representative (see Verdi to Ricordi, 16 June).

2. French translation of the *Pizzica* Chorus in III.ii (PV p. 368, 2/1).

1894

 *Verdi to Ricordi*

St. Agata, 9 June 1894[1]

Dear Giulio,

Excuse me: but all of you haven't acted forcefully enough!

Let us clarify.

1. By contract I have the right [to insist] that my operas be performed as I have written them.

2. The publisher must maintain that right; and if in France, as you said, he has not enough power, I take his place as the author and demand that *Falstaff* be performed as I conceived it. This I formally demand, and I deplore that at the Opéra-Comique performances were given in an outrageous and humiliating way.

It does not concern me if Maurel can be, or wants to be or to remain, overworked.— Why doesn't the management replace him if this is the case? . . But I repeat, this does not concern me. The only thing that concerns me is

That Falstaff be performed in its entirety,

Or that the performances be cancelled.

And this I formally demand of the publisher and owner of the score.

To the friend, then, I will say that he should actively exert himself, since I am not at all disposed to tolerate what I consider an artistic affront.

Your

G. Verdi

P.S. You can proclaim these intentions of mine to everyone; and it would have been better not to have let the abuse occur . . . It will serve in the future.

NOTE

1. If Verdi's date is correct, he would have received Ricordi's letter of 9 June on the same day.

 *Eleonora Duse to Boito*

[London, 11 June 1894]

Morning. 9 o'clock.

[. . .] Never, never, never have I felt so much tenderness for you! I feel *as if I were healing* from the great pain that was gnawing at me for so long,—— not to be *necessary* to you.——God! I suffered for that! Today I no longer feel this way—and it seems to me that I *can*—(I, for a change) *help you.* I want to make life pleasant for you, a steady life —— and remote, and apart . . . [. . .]

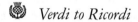 *Ricordi to Verdi*

Milan, 12 June 1894

Illustrious Maestro,

I received your esteemed letter of the 9th, and hasten to tell you that I was about to write you the moment I heard from Paris what Maurel was allowing himself. Only when Boito told me that you would come to Milan, within a day or two,[1] did I wait, to inform you in person. Then came your letter and Carvalho's assurance; this morning, however, I again wired to Paris to find out if everything is now proceeding satisfactorily; I shall let you know if a formal protest to the theatre management would be in order. [. . .]

NOTE

1. The Verdi-Boito correspondence shows no evidence of such a plan.

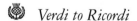 *Verdi to Ricordi*

St. Agata, 13 June 1894

Dear Giulio,

I wrote you recently that you should protest, and in my name . . . but I see that you are hesitating and, oddly enough, are awaiting other telegrams?! For what are you waiting? For the season to end, with Maurel setting a precedent that is damaging to the opera and is an affront to me?!

Addio, addio —
Your
G. Verdi

P.S. For God's sake, don't bother me with the Exhibition.—

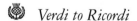 *Verdi to Ricordi*

Busseto St. Agata, 14 June 1894

In case Boito hasn't left yet, I think he should (it is also in his interest), in his name and mine, make the protest to Carvalho. This is no time for *kid gloves.* This precedent must not be tolerated. I am prepared for anything, even to withdraw the score.[1]

Addio, addio.
Your
G. Verdi

1894

NOTE

1. See *Otello* i, p. 402.

 *Ricordi to Verdi*

Milan, 15 June 1894

Illustrious Maestro,

I am confirming to you that yesterday I again wired to protest immediately, in the name of the author and publisher; for your information I enclose a letter from Carvalho[1] and the copy of a letter from Rabourdain,[2] which I just received. I don't know if Boito has left [for Paris];[3] I'll send someone to find out and will give him your message.[4] [. . .]

NOTES

1. Missing.
2. Unknown.
3. He had apparently left in time for his meeting with Duse. (See Duse to Boito, 30 April, and 7 and 8 June.)
4. In Verdi's preceding letter of 14 June.

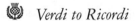 *Verdi to Ricordi*

St. Agata, 16 June 1894

Dear Giulio,

I am not at all of Carvalho's opinion![1]

Let all the praise for the success be Maurel's, but I demand that my property be respected, even to the detriment of my reputation and my material interests in *Falstaff,* as well as in the future *Othello* [in Paris], which concerns us, us alone, and not Carvalho.—But now let things go on just as they are for the few performances that remain—declaring that if they want to do it [*Falstaff*] again, it is going to be different. We have acted too late, and above all I regret that your representative did not express my will to Maurel. If I should be obliged to talk to him personally, it could easily become a serious affair. . . This business was handled too meekly, after all, and might end up hurting *Othello*— [. . .][2]

NOTES

1. See Ricordi to Verdi, 9 June.
2. See *Otello* i, p. 404.

🌼 *Verdi to Giuseppe De Amicis*

St. Agata, 18 June 1894

Dear De Amicis,

Not later than on the morning of 2 July, we will arrive at Montecatini from Milan, where we'll be on Sunday to see the Exhibition. I shall write you the day and the precise hour of our arrival at the spa. [. . .]

We are sorry to hear about the damage caused by the mice! Oh, the damned old houses, and kept in such poor repair; they should all be burned down. [. . .]

🌼 *Verdi to Giuseppe Gallignani*

St. Agata, 20 June 1894[1]

[. . .] Last year, as you may remember, I asked you to use your influence to have my coachman's son accepted at the Conservatory of Parma. You replied that the date for applications was past.

Now I return to the matter. I reiterate the recommendation I made last year, and ask you please to do your best to have my request accepted.

Beg the authorities, implore them on bended knee, in my name. Amen! With a thousand pardons and thanks, I am your

G. Verdi[2]

NOTES

1. In the absence of the original Italian text, this letter is given here, with minor changes, in Edward Downes's translation. (Franz Werfel and Paul Stefan, eds., *Verdi: The Man in His Letters,* p. 426.)

2. In supporting the application of his coachman's son, Verdi may well have remembered his own ill-fated application for admission to the Milan Conservatory in 1832. See Chronology of Verdi, n. 4.

🌼 *Verdi to Giuseppe De Amicis*

Milan, 29 June 1894

Dearest De Amicis,

As I already wrote you, we shall leave here on 1 July and will be in Montecatini Monday morning about 7 o'clock.

We hope to see you there without delay.

1894

Peppina, who, as usual, is not eating, greets you affectionately, and so do I! [. . .]

 *Verdi to Giuseppina Negroni Prati*

St. Agata, 12 August 1894[1]

Dear Signora Peppina,

For some time, even before I went to Montecatini, a thousand things have disturbed me, irritations and troubles of all kinds for myself and others. I don't say this to excuse myself for not having written to you in your sad times![2] No: I have uncommon ideas about this matter. I believe that great sorrows do not call for great words. They need silence, isolation, and, I might say, the torment of thought. Words dissolve, sweeten, and destroy feelings! All formalities suggest something that is little felt, and are a profanation. I do not pretend that I have been a very unfortunate man, but assuming that in my long life I have suffered some great sorrows, I surely drank the bitter cup all alone.

Perhaps I am not right, but I cannot persuade myself that I am wrong.

I thought of you, though, who are so sad; I know and understand how great is the sorrow of this loss. [. . .]

NOTES

1. The date is difficult to decipher and the year might be 1897. Further research may reveal the occasion for this letter and hence the date.
2. Apparently because of the death of a close friend or relative.

 *Verdi to Giuseppe De Amicis*

Busseto St. Agata, 26 August 1894

Dear De Amicis,

Thank you for your kind letter,[1] which I am answering right away, by asking you:

1. If the apartment in the Palazzo Durazzo[2] is large enough for us.
2. If it is true that it is damp, as I have been told.
3. If there is enough light and sun, since it is situated low.
4. How this apartment is heated in the winter, since you know that we need warmth.
5. Be sure to inquire if the bells of the Annunziata [church] will disturb us!

6. Finally, I am very much afraid that the hotel *buses*, city *buses, carriages,* and *carts* may be impossible to tolerate in an apartment situated so low.

Obtain all this information and answer me as soon as possible—but everything in the greatest secrecy.

Peppina thanks and greets you; I, in a hurry, shake your hands.

Affectionately,
G. Verdi

Tell me also what the annual rent for that apartment would be.

NOTES

1. Missing.

2. In view of the problems caused by the owners of Palazzo Doria, Verdi considered renting another apartment in Genoa. (See Verdi to De Amicis, 29 November 1893.) However, he decided to stay at Palazzo Doria, and did so until the end of his life.

🌼 *Verdi to Johann Strauss*

[Paris, 29 September 1894][1]

Falstaff

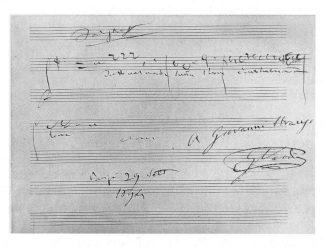

To Giovanni Strauss
G. Verdi

Paris 29 Sept.
1894

NOTE

1. At the time of the fiftieth anniversary of the Waltz King's career, Verdi was in Paris

1894

for the French première of *Othello*, at the Opéra on 12 October. Verdi used to play waltzes by Johann Strauss (1825–99) for others at home, just as he sometimes played "Dormirò sol" from *Don Carlo* when he was alone. Behind the thoughtful courtesy of a famous colleague, as evidenced by this greeting, there was a deep affinity between the two masters, as indicated by Marcel Prawy: "How serene, how laughing, how radiant, how happy was the man, after all, who, violin in hand, made humanity laugh and dance to music grounded in profound, almost frightening melancholy? To what extent did it grow out of his character? Were inner sadness and sorrow its origin?" (*Johann Strauss*, p. 189)

Eleonora Duse to Boito

Ravenna, October 1894

I cannot possibly be in Milan between the 25th and the 30th, as I had thought.

I'm already under way for my next tour, and I'm here—with some poor devils—to hold "rehearsals." I leave here tonight or tomorrow morning—and in three days I must be in Munich. I hardly have time to return to my home[1] to lock the doors, and leave.

I hope to return to Italy in two months, and then I will have to talk to you. I will tell you then, how and why I wanted to destroy every trace of myself, asking you for our letters.[2]

Lenor

MONSIEUR ARRIGO BOITO—GRAND HOTEL—PARIS[3]
DO NOT DESTROY ANYTHING ON YOUR RETURN TO MILAN—FIRST MUST TALK—IF NOTHING INTERFERES I BELIEVE CAN BE MILAN BETWEEN 25TH AND 30TH.

NOTES

1. "I have fixed myself up a little house on the top floor of an old palazzo, in Venice [. . .]," Duse wrote to a friend, in an undated letter, probably in 1894 (Weaver, p. 119).
2. "From triumph to triumph, in a breathless race, without time to look around, to turn back; she must have felt like burning up her very life" (Nardi, p. 607).
3. Telegram from Venice on 14 October, attached to this letter.

Verdi to Ricordi

Paris, Wednesday [17 October 1894]

Dear Giulio,

Welcome home![1]

Falstaff excellent.[2] Most animated staging; the audience has fun and keeps flocking in.

Boito's criticisms are absolutely correct; but in his judgment he forgets that of the audience.

So Falstaff moves too much and doesn't do *quand'ero paggio* well . . . but he repeats it three times.

Delna [Quickly] is good throughout, but tends to exaggerate and might cause *trouble* in the future. She might repeat the narrative three times. Alice [Grandjean] has improved. The quartet is very good and was repeated. Ford sings better than the first one,[3] but has no great voice and some effects are lost. . .

The orchestra is marvelous, even more so than before. All in all *Falstaff*, although a bit exaggerated, hasn't lost a thing as a whole, but has gained in vivacity on the stage, despite a strong tendency toward exaggeration.

Addio, addio

Your

G. Verdi

NOTES

1. While the Verdis enjoyed their last visit to Paris until 22 October, Ricordi had returned to Milan shortly after the opening of *Othello* at the Opéra.

2. *Falstaff* had been revived at the Opéra-Comique on 5 September. Boito had attended a performance and, obviously, expressed his displeasure viva voce to Verdi and Ricordi before leaving Paris. The baritone Lucien Fugère (1848–1935), whom Boito had heard in the summer at Aix-les-Bains, appeared in the title role, replacing Maurel, who sang Iago at the Opéra at that time. Having been denied admission to the Paris Conservatory, and being invited to the Opéra-Comique only in 1877, the young baritone became the favorite artist of that company. A true singing actor, he appeared at the Opéra-Comique in about a hundred operas, including over thirty premières. Massenet dedicated his score of *Don Quichotte* to Fugère, whose distinguished career was among the longest on record, although it involved only a few performances outside of Paris.

3. Unknown replacement for Soulacroix. (See Verdi to Stolz, 19 April, n. 1.)

 Eleonora Duse to Boito

Magdeburg, 22–23 [October] night 94

If Arrigo consents that I talk to him——(*perhaps* it is necessary, *perhaps* I am wrong—) here is my itinerary. After tonight I am free from work. I leave tomorrow for Dresden, where I will stay until the morning of the 25th.[1] The morning of the 25th I'll leave for Berlin, where I will stay until the 28th—or the 29th, and I'll be in Milan (Hotel Cavour) between the 31st and the 3rd.

Perhaps Arrigo will reply to this address: *Berlin—Hotel Continental* if between the 31st and the 3rd I can talk to him————

Eleonora

1894

NOTE

1. Presumably to see her twelve-year-old daughter, Enrichetta, who attended school in that city.

🏵 *Ricordi to Verdi*

Milan, 24 October 1894[1]

Illustrious Maestro,

From Signora Stolz I heard about your excellent journey from Paris to Turin[2]—and I do not doubt that it will have been excellent from Turin to Genoa, where you and Signora Peppina will now be able to rest in tranquillity—and in the excellent health in which I had the pleasure to leave you.[3]

I will not repeat to you, Maestro, the overpowering, yet sweet, emotions I experienced while attending such great events, nor the joy in the highest honors bestowed on our greatest and beloved Maestro. [. . .]

When the mail arrives, Tornaghi opens the pouch of the letters and separates them according to the addresses; those in my name are put on my desk. As I enter my office yesterday morning, I see immediately an envelope in your writing, and open the letter right away. At the same time Tornaghi comes in and says to me: I want to be the first to congratulate you.— I look at him . . . . he looks at me . . . . . we look at each other, then I say:

—But what are you congratulating me for?—

—Come on . . . didn't you see the letter from the Maestro?

—Well, yes—I'm reading it.

—Then take a good look at the envelope—[4]

I look . . . . . . and am flabbergasted!!—I read the letter: there's nothing in it!—[5]

A second letter this morning; another envelope as above, then a *postscript*[6] confirming . . . . .

Is it really true?—What for?—Why? . . . It is easy to guess: I owe this honor to your kindness toward me . . . . . . and so I am not only flabbergasted . . . . but so dumbfounded that I can find no words to express my feelings to you! [. . .]

Summing up, everything was so beautiful that it seems like a dream to me, since almost all the realities of life are dull or sad!—But . . . wherever you are present, everything changes: everything becomes refined by lively colors, and the mind and heart rejoice with respectful admiration. [. . .]

NOTES

1. In answer to Verdi's letters of 21 and 22 October.

2. Teresa Stolz attended *Othello* at the Opéra, then traveled with the Verdis as far as Turin. From there she proceeded to her home in Milan.

3. In Paris, where the Verdis remained until 22 October.

4. On the envelope of his letter of the 21st, Verdi obviously had written "*Cavalier* Giulio Ricordi."

5. Verdi's brief letter of the 21st did not mention that Ricordi and Boito had been named Cavaliers of the French Legion of Honor.

6. The P.S. to Verdi's letter of the 22nd reads: "Greetings to our poet [Boito], your colleague as Cavalier of the Legion of Honor." (See *Otello* i, pp. 418–9.)

 *Verdi to Giuseppe Gallignani*

Genoa, 29 October 1894

The last time I had the pleasure of seeing you at St. Agata, I introduced you to my coachman, Luigi Veroni, whose son hopes to be admitted as a student to your Conservatory. He seems to be most gifted in music, as is stated in his teacher's report.

You had taken such an interest in the matter that I hoped, and am still hoping, for a positive result.

Schools now open on 3 November, and the poor father, Veroni, is all upset, because he has not heard anything. He will present this letter of mine to you, and I hope to hear that his wishes and my hopes are fulfilled. [. . .]

G. Verdi

 Verdi to Giuseppe Gallignani

Genoa, 4 November 1894

Dear Gallignani,

NEMO PROPHETA IN PATRIA . . . . [No one is a prophet in his homeland]

If I had been born in TURKEY, I might have been successful!

Nevertheless, I bow to the Minister's exalted wisdom![1]

How lucky we are!—Governed with such severity, we will become a nation of perfect beings.

Excuse me and addio.

G. Verdi

NOTE

1. To deny the admission of Verdi's coachman's son to the Parma Conservatory (see Verdi to Gallignani, 20 June and 29 October).

1894

🌼 *Verdi to Ricordi*

Genoa, 7 November 1894

Dear Giulio,

What, what?!! *Falstaff* in Berlin[1] a success!!! I didn't expect that![2] I, too, received two long telegrams besides yours.

From *Bock,*[3] together with the entire artistic team, director, etc., etc.

From Count Hochberg in the name of the Emperor!![4] . .

But I think about the telegrams which the artists Pini, Arkel,[5] and others, etc., etc., sent from Madrid; and last night I found an article in the *Epoca Spagnola* that says *"Fiasco."* Whom to believe?

I send you the paper. I send you the two telegrams from Berlin[6] on the condition that you do not publish them.

Moreover, I am sending you: Semi-annual contracts I forgot to give back in Milan.—

The journey was excellent.[7] Farewell to everybody, and be cheerful, which we down here aren't at all. . .

Oh oh oh oh! . . What a surprise and what a joy! Orrigoni has just arrived (saying that Ginetta is here, too) and adding that they will come to have a bite with us at 6. Oh joy   oh joy   oh joy! Addio

Affectionately
G. Verdi

NOTES

1. Reaction to (missing) telegrams concerning a revival of the German *Falstaff* production of 6 March (see Verdi to Boito, 14 March, nn. 3–5).

2. Verdi had considered Mascheroni's Italian *Falstaff* of 1 June 1893 only "a partial success" (Verdi to Ricordi, 2 June 1893), and he doubted the success of the German *Falstaff* of 6 March in Berlin (Verdi to Boito, 14 March).

3. Bote & Bock, prominent music publishing firm in Berlin, founded in 1838.

4. Kaiser Wilhelm II (1859–1941).

5. Teresa Arkel (1861–1929), née Blumenfeld, of German origin, was a dramatic soprano; she studied at the Conservatory of Lemberg [Lvov] in Poland. After her debut in 1884, she sang in Prague, Hamburg, Spain, and Portugal. Specializing in Wagnerian roles, she appeared as Venus in the first Italian *Tannhäuser* at La Scala in 1891. After her retirement from the stage she taught voice in Milan.

6. Missing, like all the other telegrams.

7. From Paris to Genoa between 22 and 23 October.

Verdi to Ricordi

Genoa, 11 November 1894

Dear Giulio,

I'll be in Milan tomorrow, Monday, at 12:50, departing again at once for St. Agata at *1:30.*—If you have something to tell me, come or send [someone] to the station; if you have nothing [to tell me], don't stand on ceremony.——

Tomorrow is the *12th!* A month ago, on the *12th of October,* was the first *Otello* in Paris! Today I received the testimonial from Paris that bears the date *12 October!*

Curious! Very strange, this *12th!!*

It's curious, too, that I have received the foremost decoration from France, the *Cavalier of the Legion of Honor!*

This last one I am again receiving from *France!!* Curious, curious!!!

It's even more curious that the first decoration of *1850* or *1851* was signed
    "Napoleon President of the French Republic"
and this last one
    "Perrier[1] President of the French Republic."
Strange coincidence!!

Addio!

Greetings to all! . .

I am sorry about the illness in your family.

Addio ad.

Affectionately,   G. Verdi

NOTE

1. Jean Casimir-Périer (1847–1907), fifth president (1894–1895) of the French republic.

 Verdi to Unknown Frenchman[1]

[In French]   Genoa, 20 November 1894

Monsieur

What can I say about Gounoud?

When a composer has written operas which have been able to achieve a thousandth performance in a single country, there is nothing left for an individual to add to his glory.

Accept, Monsieur, my respectful compliments.

G. Verdi

1894

NOTE

1. With George Martin's kind permission, this letter and his comments are here given verbatim:

> Verdi, trying hard to be pleasant, marred his effort by misspelling "Gounod." But he did try and succeeded, with a fine Italian hand, in seeming to say something when he really said very little, a social art he practised with difficulty.
>
> His true opinion of Gounod he had written earlier, in 1878 [on 14 October], to his crony Arrivabene, and it probably was the opinion he still held: "Gounod is a great musician, a great talent, who composes chamber and instrumental music in a superior and individual style. But he is not an artist of dramatic fiber. In his hands Goethe's Faust, although turned into a successful opera, has become small. The same is true of Roméo et Juliette and will be true of Polyeucte. In short, he always does the intimate scene well but always weakens the dramatic situations and draws the characters poorly." (*Verdi: His Music, Life and Times*, pp. 552–3.)

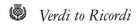 *Verdi to Ricordi*

Genoa, 29 November 1894

Dear Giulio,

Nothing new at all . . . . . doesn't mean nothing.

Peppina has a bad cough! All the teeth I still have are hurting me! And I suffer a lot. Furthermore I'm mostly staying at home, because I do not tolerate well the changes of this season. I eat little and sleep much; I read a lot and am bored *non plus ultra*. Whenever I hear talk of *signatures*, I feel as if I'm getting the shivers!

Ibid. if affairs in Paris, or the Society of Authors, or similar matters are involved, spare me, I beg you. But tell me what it's about.

Orrigoni has given me news of you all. We are glad it was good, and to all of you we wish it always, always will be good.—

Addio ad.

Affectionately,
G. Verdi

 *Boito to Verdi*

2 November [2 December 1894]
Milan

Dear Maestro,

When I think back to Paris, I feel as if endless time had already gone by since those happy days! I had your news from Giulio; while you were passing through Milan[1] we didn't see each other, because you thought I was still at Lake Como, where I spent a week; and I, who had already returned, was not aware of your presence.

I hope your winter visit to us will not take long to come about, and then I will make it up to myself for our encounter gone wrong.

I have finally been to Parma, where I heard good performances of Palestrina: the Mass of Pope Marcellus, and a few madrigals; but as long as I don't hear a completely ideal performance of this music—in which through perfect blending of all parts, this or that most sweetly singing voice emerges lightly, now here, now there—I prefer to hear these sounds in my head and to follow them in the score with my eyes.

I had a truly complete and profound artistic impression of Coreggio[2] this time in Parma. One evening, I was shown the electrically illuminated cupola in the church of San Giovanni. The aisles were immersed in darkness. There were three of us in the church: Mariotti, Corrado Ricci, and I. Suddenly the entire painting on the inside of the cupola lights up, reflected by hundreds of Edison lamps hidden in the ledge, and that sublime masterwork appears as if lit by the sun. A real miracle. Never before had a painting moved me more deeply, not even Velasquez. There I understood the admiration you have for Coreggio. You absolutely must see this cupola in that kind of light. Soon they will also illuminate the even more marvelous one in the cathedral. We all will go there; I would like Camillo to come along, too.

I have seen the charming Massenet, who told me about his visit at Palazzo Doria.[3] *I don't know how Werther* went last night; I didn't go to the performance.

Many kind greetings to Signora Giuseppina and you and to Signor De Amicis. 'Til we see each other soon, I hope.

Your most affectionate
Arrigo Boito

NOTES

1. On 12 November (see Verdi to Ricordi, 11 November).
2. The painter Antonio Allegri da Correggio (1494–1534).
3. Passing through Genoa on his way to rehearsals for the first Italian *Werther,* at the Teatro Lirico in Milan on 1 December, Massenet had paid a visit to Verdi. He tells about this visit (the occasion of which he mistakenly connected with his opera *La Navarraise,* given at La Scala in the season following) in *Mes souvenirs* (Paris, 1912):

> I knew that Verdi was in Genoa and took advantage of passing through that city on the way to Milan, to pay him a visit. Arriving on the second floor of the

1894

ancient Palazzo Doria, where he lived, I could, in a dark corridor, decipher on a card nailed to a door that name radiating so many enthusiastic and glorious memories: VERDI. He himself opened the door. I was quite speechless. His openness, his graciousness, the winning nobility his tall stature* imparted on his whole personality, contributed to our early mutual sympathy. I spent some time in the indescribable charm of his presence, as he talked with the most delightful simplicity, first in his bedroom, and then on the terrace of his room, from which the port of Genoa could be seen, and then the open sea, to the farthest horizon. I had the illusion that he himself was a Doria showing me with pride his victorious fleet. [. . .] About to pick up my suitcase, which I had deposited in a dark corner of the big hallway with high, gilded armchairs in eighteenth-century Italian style, I told him that it contained manuscripts I never part with while traveling. Verdi suddenly grabbed my suitcase, declaring that he did exactly the same, never wanting to part with his work en route. How I wish that my suitcase had contained his music rather than mine! [*Carteggio* ii, p. 459.]

* According to photographs and nearly all the descriptions by his contemporaries, Verdi was not tall.

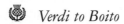 *Verdi to Boito*

Genoa, 3 December 1894

Dear Boito,

Lucky you, who heard a bit of Palestrina. I understand very well that the performance didn't reach your ideal; but in any case, I wish that every city had such solemnities, if only to repair our poor ears, lacerated by an excess of dissonance! The trouble is that all these invented dissonances and orchestral colors are applied senselessly, almost all the time!

And *Coreggio?!?*

A marvelous and seductive painter! So beautiful, simple, and natural that when I see him, I imagine that he never had any teachers! Sometimes grandiose like Michelangelo, except that I love Coreggio's prophets and apostles, while Michelangelo's frighten me! And now a work of charity! — (See earthquake Calabria *Only number*).[1]

Please adjust and rewrite two verses for me

Pietà Signor della miseria mia!   [Have mercy, Lord, on my misery!

Ci salva tu . . . . e ria![2]   You save us . . . . and -ery!]

I have made a [musical] phrase to fit these words, therefore I need these accents; and in the second verse also the accent on the second one. — Even if you don't want the second verse to rhyme, never mind; it's enough for the second verse to be plain. . .

Peppina thanks you and sends you best greetings.

Addio and till we see each other again. Let's hope soon.

Affectionately,

G. Verdi

NOTES

1. Verdi refers to catastrophic news given in a headline in a popular newspaper. To assist the victims of an earthquake that struck Calabria and Sicily on 16 November, 1894, Giuseppe Mantica, a writer and member of parliament, suggested a special issue of the review *Fata Morgana*. As its first contributor, he invited Verdi, who sent him a short composition on 30 November: *Pietà Signor* for a single voice with piano accompaniment. On 3 December, however, the same date as this letter to Boito, Verdi asked Mantica to return the few bars to him, so he might correct and extend them. For this he needed Boito's help. Giuseppe Mantica's brother Francesco, composer and director of the library of the Rome Conservatory, published the article "*Pietà Signor!* Una delle ultime pagine di Giuseppe Verdi" [*Have mercy, Lord!* One of the last pages by Giuseppe Verdi] in the Roman review *Harmonia* of 15 October 1913. In a slightly different version, the Roman review *Rassegna Dorica* published it on 25 March 1941. Both publications contain a facsimile of the short composition—not published by Ricordi—which Verdi dated 6 December 1894 and mailed, along with his calling card, to Giuseppe Mantica. Apparently he had received Boito's correction of 6 December on the same day; otherwise he would have dated the composition 7 December. Presumably the first sketch of *Pietà Signor* is at St. Agata. A photograph of the sketch reveals that the 11th and 13th bars differ from Verdi's autograph in his letter to Boito of 5 December—in which Boito's handwriting is clearly visible—and from the one that appears in the review *Harmonia*.

2. Verdi asks for a word ending with *-ria*, to rhyme with the above *mia*.

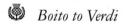

Boito to Verdi

Tuesday [Milan, 4 December 1894][1]

Dear Maestro,

Here it is; see if it fits the musical phrase; the first verse is yours and the second Dante Alighieri's:[2]

> *di me*
> *Pietà, della miseria mia*
> *Agnèl di Dio che le peccata levi.*
>
> [Have mercy on me, on my misery,
> Lamb of God that takes away the sins.]

And all of it together is a paraphrase of the *Agnus Dei*.

Or, if you prefer the effect of the rhyme, here are two other verses:

1894

Pietà di noi, del nostro duol profondo,
O Agnèl di Dio che levi il mal dal mondo.

[Have mercy on us, on our deep sorrow,
O Lamb of God that takes away the evil of the world.]

The paraphrase of this second verse is more complete:
Agnus Dei qui tollis peccata mundi.
The first verse of this second variant would perhaps go better like this:
Pietà di noi, del nostro error *profondo.*
You decide and if it doesn't go well, write me, and I'll try to do better.

Yesterday I happened to receive a piece of red ribbon, sent from Paris; you must have known something about it—actually, I am most suspicious; actually, I firmly believe that the ringleader of the conspiracy was you.[3] Oh Maestro!

In any case, I thank you —
Affectionate greetings

from your
Arrigo Boito

NOTES

1. Postmark: MILANO 4/12/94.
2. *Divina Commedia,* Purgatorio, Canto XVI, verse 18: "l'Agnèl di Dio che le peccata leva" [the Lamb of God that takes away the sins].
3. See Ricordi to Verdi, 24 October, and Verdi to Ricordi, 11 November.

 Verdi to Boito

Genoa, 5 December 1894[1]

Dear Boito,
How beautiful the two verses would be

Pietà di Noi, del nostro error profondo
O agnèl di Dio che levi il mal dal mondo

but the word *Agnèl* sounds bad on the existing notes . . . and I must also stop after the 4th syllable of the second verse.

I transcribe the existing phrase to make myself clearer by inserting the words that would suit me . . . with the understanding that you would arrange them in a better way—

1894

Answer me soon, because they are waiting in Rome.
The culprit is *Ressman*.[2]

NOTES

1. Before Verdi received Boito's letter of the previous day.
2. The Italian ambassador in Paris, Baron Costantino Ressman (1832–99), a native of Trieste, had recommended both Boito and Ricordi as Knights of the Legion of Honor.

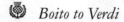 *Boito to Verdi*

[Milan] 6 December [1894][1]

Dear Maestro,

Pietà Signor del nostro error profondo
Tu solo puoi levare il Mal dal mondo.

[Have mercy, Lord, on our profound error,
You alone can take the Evil from the world.]

This way, I think, it might well enough serve the beautiful notes. A few words will have to be repeated, as is already done in the first verse—not too bad on a page that has the character of supplication. Affectionate greetings
Arrigo Boito

NOTE

1. Postmark: MILANO 6/12/94.

Appendix I

How Giuseppe Verdi Writes and Rehearses[1]

Giulio Ricordi

Examination and comparison of one of the first autograph scores, e.g., *I Lombardi* or *Macbeth,* with other more recent ones such as *Aida* or *Otello,* and finally with the autograph score of *Falstaff*, do not reveal any change in Verdi's writing. The same secure hand, the same legibility of the musical score! The pen that has written so many masterpieces commits the notes to the staff with speed and firmness, whether guided by a young hand, or by a hand of almost eighty vital years.

The precision of Giuseppe Verdi's autograph scores is admirable; the composer's ardor when writing causes no confusion or uncertainty; in any new creation, his fervid imagination knows right away how to combine manifold voices with the sounds of the orchestra. We clearly see that the opera pours forth spontaneously all in one entity, yet neatly formed in every line, in every part and detail. Hence the orchestra is not just assisting the voices, it is neither frame nor painting; Verdi does not strain or quibble in search of instrumental effects; they arise naturally with his melodies. Thus we have the perfect fusion of song and instruments, of action on the stage and in the orchestra; thus the complete homogeneity of the various elements uniting to merge into the final product. [. . .]

Verdi's ease in conceiving and writing an opera is absolutely phenomenal. His most creative period occurred between 1849 and 1855, when he wrote *Luisa Miller, Stiffelio, Rigoletto, Trovatore, Traviata,* and *I Vespri Siciliani.* [. . .] The sketches he jots down while composing are very infrequent. For his *Falstaff* he made very few annotations, and on only two pages; with admirable confidence, he then wrote the vocal parts immediately into the orchestra score.

What else?. . . Here are a few absolutely correct dates, perhaps unknown until now: In 1853, for example, Verdi had committed himself to compose two operas, one for Rome, the other for Venice. The writing of the librettos took a long time, and there was not a single note of music until late autumn. Rheumatism in the right arm tortured him; every day he hoped it would subside, but the rheumatism persisted, and still no music!

Precisely on the 1st of November 1852, Verdi began to compose *Il Trovatore.* On the 20th of the same month the opera was not only composed but even completely orchestrated. On the 30th, the score was brought from St. Agata to Cremona and consigned to the publisher Giovanni Ricordi for the engraving of the parts. Verdi had to be in Rome at the beginning of the carnival season 1852–53. Travel by sea was more comfortable; he set out to Genoa for embarkment to Civitavecchia, to proceed from there to Rome. No ship left Genoa, however, until the end of the Christmas holidays. Three days seemed lost in waiting. What to do?—And the contract with Venice? Well, the Maestro uses the time to write the first act of *La Traviata,* leaves for Rome, stages *Il Trovatore* for its première on the 19th of January. A few days later he returns to his tranquil home at St. Agata, and in thirteen days composes the other acts of *La Traviata.* Thus, in only sixteen days, Verdi created this masterwork! [. . .]

The same clarity of conception the Maestro shows in his compositions appears also in the rehearsals. They proceed exactly according to plan, and the opera is ready for performance as arranged long before rehearsals begin. It is not true that Verdi is rough and excessively severe, as is generally believed; the very opposite is the case. With military precision, he comes to the theatre at the established time; he insists, however, for good reason, that all the artists be equally precise, and that no time whatsoever be wasted. As soon as he has arrived at rehearsal and greeted everyone, he begins to work. Verdi is very patient, aware of the vocal and mental limitations of every single artist, and able to achieve the finest results. He requests, above all, clear and exact pronunciation, because the audience must understand and be interested in what the singers wish to express; within a verse he marks a given word that must draw the listeners' attention, and sometimes even the syllable to be emphasized. He does not want a phrase or rhythm to be changed with unnecessary fermatas or rallentandos; he cares for every bar, every note. To achieve elegant diction, he has a certain bar repeated 10, 20, 30 times; and he does the same for exact pronunciation of vowels, which are all too often altered by so-called famous methods of singing.[2]

When the music is known to perfection, Verdi begins to "give color" to the various characters; he points out to each of the singers which character-istic he wants them to present, and what their vocal and physical expression ought to be. All the artists stand around the piano, attentively follow the Maestro's suggestions and try to interpret them, while he, *mezza voce,* indicates the inflections of their particular parts. This is the real point of departure for the so-called *mise-en-scène:* by now more sure of their roles, the performers come to life; the most intelligent ones try some gesture; Verdi observes them attentively, admonishes, encourages, praises, animates them ever more. The piano-vocal scores provided for their study are gradually, almost unknowingly, left on the pianoforte; the artist moves away and mentally begins "to put on," as the Maestro says, the costume of the character involved. Verdi's eyes light up and he no longer takes them off the performer; then two or three singers get together, and Verdi directs their steps, movements, and gestures, making suggestions and corrections. If a move, a gesture does not satisfy him, he himself becomes the character and, declaiming or singing, energetically shows how to interpret the role.

From the rehearsal hall one goes to the stage; the action is outlined and fully developed. The voices are joined by the instruments, and nothing that happens on the stage or in the orchestra escapes Verdi's eyes and ears. The fastidious care he gave to the coaching of the singers, he had already applied to scenery and costumes, which he examines and studies in every detail, requesting alterations until everything is clear and correct. He is the true creator of his opera; he imprints on it his mighty vitality. Thus, in relatively little time, considering the painstaking study of every detail, the new work is ready to face the battle of the first performance.

Last October Verdi was 79 years old; now in his eightieth year he retains his youthful imagination, an indefatigable memory, and downright miraculous strength. His tall and sturdy figure,[3] his fiery and penetrating gaze, his broad and sure gait, awaken respectful admiration in everyone near him.

To illustrate Verdi's activity, it suffices to mention his work during the *Falstaff* rehearsals: from 9 to 10:30 in the morning, revision of the orchestra score, the parts, and the piano-vocal scores; from 12:30 until 4:30 P.M., rehearsal in the theatre. Frequently from 5 to 6 P.M., solo rehearsal with some artist in his drawing room at the Hôtel Milan; from 8:30 to 11:30 P.M. another rehearsal at the theatre![4]

In view of such activity, what else can be said? [. . .]

NOTES

1. Excerpts from an article in *L'Illustrazione Italiana*, p. 23, on the occasion of the *Falstaff* première in Milan on 9 February 1893.
2. See Verdi's letters to Ricordi in November and December 1892.
3. But see Boito to Verdi, 2 December 1894, n. 3.
4. See Giuseppina Verdi to Barberina Strepponi, early February 1893.

Appendix II

Memoirs of Verdi and *Falstaff* in Rome
Eduard Hanslick[1]

This newest opera of the eighty-year-old Verdi makes music history, and its first performance in Rome is a memorable event. [. . .] What an evening in the theatre! A feast of the nation touching every Italian heart! [. . .] At one time I had referred to Verdi and Bellini as the only Italian opera composers appearing inaccessible and untalented for comedy.[2] What an unexpectedly beautiful, significant turn to find the old man, toward the end of his life, breaking away from tragedy and, with the wisdom of blessed age, resting his gaze on the sunny, humorous side of existence!

[. . .] I was deeply moved by the simple cordiality Verdi—here[3] almost unapproachable by any stranger—extended to me, I who have several youthful sins against him on my conscience. Something infinitely mild and noble shines from the modest inner being of this man, who was not made vain by glory, haughty by dignity, or moody by age. His face is deeply wrinkled, his black eyes lie deep, the beard is white; yet his erect posture and sonorous voice keep him from appearing so old. When I mentioned to Verdi the general amazement over the appearance of his *Falstaff*, he replied that to write a comic opera had been his dearest wish throughout his life. "And why didn't you do it?"—"Because nobody cared" [parce que l'on n'en voulait pas]. He added that he had actually written *Falstaff* for his own entertainment. He denied having already begun a *King Lear.* "I'm not twenty years old," he said with a smile more roguish than sad, "but *four times* twenty!"

The luncheon for four was already prepared. The impresario[4] and the conductor Mascheroni appeared. With a witty grin typical only of Italians enjoying a bon mot, Verdi introduced me as "il Bismarck della critica musicale." As a perfect gentleman he also presented my wife with a photograph inscribed to her, and we took our leave most pleasantly impressed.

At night I listened to *Falstaff* with that feverish curiosity which always befalls me when confronting new works of art. Immediately in the first scene I thought of a remark Verdi made during our last conversation. He answered somewhat evasively to the suggestion that he had been influenced by Wagner: "Song and melody," he said, "should always remain the focal point." In *Falstaff* they no longer exist in that absolute sense typical of earlier Verdi operas. Compared with Wagner's second period they still do. Nowhere in *Falstaff* is the voice suppressed or overpowered by the orchestra,[5] nowhere is the memory led by leitmotivs, nowhere is emotion cooled by lofty reflection. On the other hand, the music of *Falstaff* has more the character of a lively conversation and declamation than that of distinctive melody which impresses through its own beauty. The second act of *Ballo in maschera* proves that Verdi knew how to blend the latter kind of music perfectly with the flowing musical expression of comedy. In comparison, Wagnerian influence can be felt in *Falstaff*—albeit only in a broad sense and most liberal interpretation. This is certainly an inestimable method for composers of genius who possess years of experience and technique, but no longer the rich and burgeoning imagination of youth.

The entire structure of the *Falstaff* libretto—and similar modern ones almost as detailed in their wording as legitimate plays—has resulted in a new and different method of composition. Formerly, poetry was defined as "the design to be colored by the composer." This does not apply in any way to the music of earlier operas. Mozart's and Rossini's melodies are greater and entirely different from the mere coloring of a finished design; they are a new and independent entity which, although guided and influenced by the text, creates its own design. It could rather be said that earlier librettos provide the composer only larger or smaller frames with the headings love, rage, happiness. In these frames the composer as musical autocrat created design and color at the same time. The text for Mozart's, Rossini's, and the young Verdi's arias frequently contains only six to eight lines of general content; the composer could do with them as he wished. Compare with this the libretto for *Falstaff*. The monologue "What is honor" is a literal translation from Shakespeare, if I am not mistaken, with yet more detailed additions.[6] There, the composer cannot create anything new and independent; he can only follow word for word to "color" the poet's minutely executed design. The great success of this monologue is actually Shakespeare's and the singer Maurel's; music has little to add, and I cannot say that the effect in the Burgtheater,[7] without music, would be any less. Similar thoughts apply to the jealous Mr. Ford's long soliloquy and to most of the duets, which are dialogues executed in comedy form. Thus, strangely enough, the ancient precept of "design and coloring" belongs only to a far later, namely today's, manner of composition. *Falstaff*'s fast-flowing witty dialogue is initially so formulated that it could be performed even without music. Only a few pieces in *Falstaff* are written for a rounded-out musical form; their melodiousness and clarity are delightful and not lacking in warmth. I was unable to perceive specific power and originality of *melodic* invention except for Fenton's little cantilena "Bocca baciata" recalling the earlier Verdi's sensual charm. The total impression I received is one of a diligently worked-out, delicate, and lively conversational music, which nowhere becomes crude or feeble, transgressing neither by farcical triviality nor by unsuitable pathos. Falstaff has comic power; the other characters do not stand out. The whole thing impresses us as the flowing conversation of an ingenious man of the world, not pretending to dispense new truths or profound thought. A chat rather than powerful musical creation, more esprit than genius. Verdi's *Falstaff* neither bored nor repelled me for a single moment, yet it rarely surprised me with moments of musical beauty.

This sort of theatrical creation by a man in his eighties is unprecedented in music history. In Germany and Italy we have had a few masters who created good sacred music at an advanced age; but no other nation may boast of a composer who at Verdi's age still possessed the dramatic vivacity, the charming whimsy, the secure command displayed in the score of *Falstaff*. Richard Wagner once wrote with regard to Meyerbeer's *Africaine:* at sixty years of age one should stop writing operas—a statement he himself disproved. Six years ago Verdi's *Otello* was greeted as an amazing event. As the even later, and certainly no less colorful, blossom of sixty years' unceasingly prolific talent, *Falstaff* is a small miracle. [. . .] (*Aus meinem Leben,* ii, pp. 282–8.)

NOTES

1. Eduard Hanslick (1825–1904), Richard Wagner's famous adversary, was born in Prague, where he studied music and law. In 1846 he moved to Vienna and soon wrote music reviews. From 1856 until 1895 he taught music history, music appreciation, and aesthetics at the University of Vienna. In 1864 he became music editor of the influential *Neue Freie Presse*. Hanslick's memoirs, *Aus meinem Leben*, are a rare source of information about life, culture, and civilization in nineteenth-century Europe. Hanslick wrote lively sketches of almost every important musician of the age. His friendship with Johannes Brahms, above all, reveals him to be a scholar and musician of good humor and subtle mind, far from the harshly characterized "Veit Hanslich" of Wagner's 1861 prose sketch of *Die Meistersinger von Nürnberg*, who became the pedantic marker Beckmesser in the opera. (See Ernest Newman, *Wagner as Man and Artist,* pp. 26–7.) Hanslick proved to be just as much a gentleman in his encounters with Boito and Verdi. Invited by Giulio

Ricordi to a luncheon with Boito shortly after the *Otello* première in 1887, he replied: "'Impossible. I have written not only severely but unmercifully about his *Mefistofele*, this profanation of Goethe's poem.' [See *Otello* ii, pp. 767–8.] 'He is fully aware of this,' Ricordi remarked, 'nevertheless he looks forward to making your acquaintance; he is a witty, highly educated man.'" "That he indeed had to be," Hanslick wrote in his memoirs, "for meeting me as impartially and cordially as he then did. I listened to his interesting, lively conversation with true delight, and gladly remember the fiery coals his *gentilezza* heaped on my sinful head. Such traits are beautiful and rare and remain unforgettable to me." (*Aus meinem Leben* ii, pp. 300–1.)

2. See Introduction, n. 8.
3. At the Hotel Quirinale in Rome.
4. Presumably Gino Monaldi.
5. See Camille Bellaigue's writings in Appendixes III and V.
6. See Shakespeare, *King Henry IV,* First Part V.i., 130–41.
7. Vienna's leading legitimate theatre.

Appendix III

Review of *Falstaff*[1]

Camille Bellaigue

[. . .] *Falstaff* is a work of life, health, light, and joy. A work of life, of a life
so intense, so natural throughout, that it seems, not imitated, but true; the
life that God gives and not that which has been copied or counterfeited by
man. A work of joy also, despite those people today who think, or pretend
to think, that art is sullen and literature morose; joy is one of the two faces
of the world. Even the most serious and sombre, Shakespeare, Corneille,
Racine, Beethoven, have wished to know and to express that joy. At eighty
years of age, Verdi's tragic genius in his turn has longed for the *gioia bella*
[beautiful joy], as it was called by Mozart,[2] one of those who most loved it.
We wondered how Verdi was going to feel and understand it; now we know.
First, his joy is simple. It has nothing in common with the somewhat
metaphysical joy of a Beethoven, for instance, in the finale of the *Choral
Symphony*. Nor is it joy filled with underlying motives, intentions, and
symbols—the complex, often dense, and heavily Germanic joy of *Die
Meistersinger*. It is the joy of youth, the joy of children, whom we must
resemble to enter the kingdom of wit as well as the kingdom of the soul.
That joy, moreover, is good. Made of gaiety and roguishness, it is also made
of good intentions and good nature. It knows nothing of irony or bitterness.
Laughter in *Falstaff* bursts forth as broadly as in *La Serva Padrona*, but more
indulgently. If, on the other hand, it resounds as clearly as in *Il Barbiere di
Siviglia,* it often sounds with still more finesse and distinction. Compare, in
that respect, the finale of the laundry basket in *Falstaff* and the famous finale
of the *Barber:* the latter, which is admirable, is all of a piece; its beauty
appears abstract and lacking in nuance next to the exquisite delicacy and
princely elegance of Verdi, whose joy is poetic and tender. It lacks neither
the sentiment of nature nor of love. The spirit of the *Barber* is one of dryness

and intrigue; Rossini made Lindoro a gallant and Rosina a coquette. But Verdi, among the bells of his comedy, has mixed a few golden ones, which sometimes, between two bursts of laughter, emit deep notes touching the heart.

As with the libretto of *Otello,* the libretto of *Falstaff* is the work of Arrigo Boito. For a second time, with the same talent, respect, and love, Boito translated Shakespeare for Verdi. I admire that musician-poet, who can be no more than the intermediary between a poet and a musician greater than himself. To be inspired by Shakespeare in order to inspire Verdi truly is not an ordinary task, and to accomplish it in such a manner is no small honor; such modesty, such disinterest is rare; aesthetic honor, as well; few creations of one's own could be as enviable as such a glorious enterprise. Boito has abridged the famous comedy *The Merry Wives of Windsor.* He has simplified the intrigue and has woven together scattered threads of the plot. Boito has filled out Falstaff's character with some qualities borrowed from the character appearing not only in *The Merry Wives* but also in *Henry IV.* So the Italian poem, if it does not include all of Shakespeare's comedy, at least does not include anything that is not by Shakespeare. [. . .]

The plot of *Falstaff* is among the simplest and merriest. As we know, it deals with the attempts of a fat knight on the virtue of Mrs. Alice Ford and Mrs. Meg Page; attempts twice derailed by the honorable and spirited merry wives with the help of their neighbor and friend Dame Quickly and that of Nannetta, Mrs. Ford's daughter. Two rendezvous granted to Sir John both end in his confusion: one, at Mrs. Ford's home, ends in the famous plunge into the Thames; the other, at night in Windsor Park, beneath the legendary Herne's Oak, ends in a mystic fantasy: a masquerade and beatings, which lead to the sinner's confession and the final reconciliation. I forgot—and wrongly—the love affair of Nannetta and young Fenton, which is gracefully blended with the comedy, and which the denouement consecrates in marriage, according to custom. [. . .]

For a long time, action was forbidden to music, and music no longer seemed able to represent action. "Movement does not fit music," repeated those who vie with one another in rendering music dull and paralyzed. They made the art of Haydn, Mozart, and Rossini arthritic. But here is an octogenarian composer telling music, "Get up and walk!"; and it walks, it runs, it is twenty years old. First of all, what a course he has furnished! With Verdi, no feints. He does not grope, he does not spend time preparing: he is off at once with amazing coordination. The double doors open; they fly open in a burst of energy. The introduction, Cajus's quarrel with Falstaff's two henchmen, treated in the style of a classical quartet, takes place with the greatest speed. The principal motif here and there throws off brilliant touches and lights a flame in all corners of the orchestra. It circulates, bounds and rebounds, developing impact, energy, and force. It strikes one instrument, then another; nothing halts it, nothing tires it, and nothing prevails upon it. Apostrophes, replies, and insults fall steadily on it as thick as hailstones. Falstaff, however, impassive, sitting in state, between two bits of repartee, interposes stolid phrases to which the suddenly reduced orchestra abruptly yields. Upon Cajus's exit, he is alone with the two rascals. His character takes shape, body, and soul; all of him is manifested. First the body. *"In this belly,"* he exclaims, *"thunder a thousand voices that proclaim my name."* External voices answer to these "internal voices." Little by little, the orchestra expands its rhythms and timbres; it veritably becomes corpulent; harmonies and sonorities fortify each other. *"Immense Falstaff!"* bellow his comrades; it is no longer just Falstaff; it is all the big-bellied world, the Gargantuas and Sancho Panzas, the power of gross matter, the apotheosis of the flesh, that celebrates, in the manner of a Jordaens painting.[3] From that mass the spirit immediately extricates itself. [. . .] The "Honor Monologue" has psychological depths in which Shakespeare's profound understanding is revealed to whoever knows where to search. In those outbursts of anger and those disdainful silences, now in the plenitude of the orchestra, now in an orchestral void in which a few notes barely sound, Falstaff is whole; he is here with his cynical rages, the insolence of his irony, with his scorn and near disgust for himself and those like him.

The following scene is dazzling for the ear and for the spirit. We remember it, after hearing it, as a fireworks display of melody, harmony, rhythm, and timbre like a musical flowering of the imagination and genius of a twenty-year-old. With nine characters, four women and five men, it is a succession, then a combination, of gossip and chattering unparalleled up to now. The women first show each other the love letters from Falstaff, read them, reread them laughing; and that reading, begun with a pleasing English horn theme, is interrupted; resumed in ever brighter and more colorful keys, the reading concludes with an effusion that Verdi alone could give to the end of a vocal phrase. A male quartet is linked to the female quartet, in a different rhythm and key. Ideas, movements, sonorities, all incessantly renew themselves. Among the various episodes, there are no empty spaces, but, rather, exquisite transitions, musical as much as scenic; the slender and brilliant threads intertwine into a necklace. Delicious, the interlude of the young lovers and their double kiss taken in flight, whose sweetness is prolonged with a farewell that ends in flight. Now the two groups, men and women, unite. The quartet and the quintet, both rapid and both verbal, run together, one encircling the other in harmonious balance. Alone in the midst of this babble, the tenor's voice traces an ideal line in sustained notes around which the other voices swirl. Then the men withdraw, and the women, who always get the last word in this comedy, with laughter and youthful defiance, once more launch an address to the seducer whom they have resolved to admonish.

The two duets—one between Falstaff and Dame Quickly and between Falstaff and Ford—that make up the following scene are very different in style. Dame Quickly comes, representing the two ladies, to entreat Falstaff to visit them. The music here changes pace and language. It is not merely in the rapidity of the rhythms that it searches for and finds high spirits: it is in the intensity of certain notes that are rich in sense and pith; it is in the spicy brevity of certain musical formulas, almost of certain exclamations. But there is always grace and agility; for example, in the amusing *Dalle due alle tre* [From Two to Three O'clock], there are two little triplets; in the two duets, the composer has played with them in the liveliest and most spirited fashion.

We willingly pause at the duet between Falstaff and Ford to praise the musical abundance, truth, and psychological variety, the melodic and instrumental marvels; to point out especially the end, the theme at once elegant and droll with which, on the threshold, the two men exchange courtesies. But we are in a hurry to reach the core of the work, which is truly its head and heart.

The merry wives are completely prepared for their mischievous revenge. There is the screen; there the laundry basket, in which the huge Falstaff will soon be reduced to hiding.

> *Gaie comari di Windsor! È l'ora!*
> *L'ora d'alzar la risata sonora!*

[Merry wives of Windsor! It's time!
Time to raise the loud burst of laughter!]

So the lovable women sing in the original Italian, and all the verve of the comedy sparkles in that song to the glory of laughter, feminine laughter, lovely golden laughter. [. . .]

What a small miracle of music and psychology is the already famous *scherzetto* "When I was page of the Duke of Norfolk!" How formal and shapely such a melody is!! [. . .] And here again is Falstaff with all of his frisky spirit and conceit, but also with the regret—witnessed by two or three low notes from a surreptitious flute—for his trim youth, for the elegance, the breeding and the pedigree of the Shakespearean gentleman that a disorderly and dissipated life has not entirely effaced.

But in the very midst of this scene, in runs Mistress Quickly, announcing the husband: Falstaff only has time to cower behind the screen. Here is the center and the intrigue of the masterpiece, the laundry-basket finale. Everything about it is admirable: the intense vivacity, its dimensions, proportions, and order; yes, perfect order, for there is eurhythmy to the point of giddiness, and yet this whirlwind is harmonious. There are two principal themes in the orchestra at this point, one of *staccato* notes and the other, which is more important, of *legato* notes, turning in a wild spiral, that to some degree recalls the finale of Beethoven's Symphony [No. 4] in B-flat. It is certainly the second theme during which the irrepressible pursuit will unfold.

Here is Ford with his companions, and the hunt begins. The furious theme leads and incites him. He runs forward, passes through the room again and again, leaves and returns, furiously pushing open the doors. He searches the house from cellar to attic; with a leap, he clears the staircase; he knocks over furniture, empties trunks, drawers, dashing forward, searching everywhere for the elusive fat man. The latter, profiting by a lull, hides in the laundry basket, where the merry wives cover him with clothes; at the same time, the young lovers take their place behind the screen, and in the brief ensuing silence, it is charming to hear the young couple sing. But suddenly the mob of pursuers reenters and resumes the search. The theme is also taken up by the full orchestra, and the effect of that brutal, unexpected concussion, which shakes the orchestra with a single blow, is prodigious. Panting, it halts for a second, and a kiss is heard from behind the screen. This time, thinking that they have the guilty pair, Ford and his followers are quiet and consult. Then the most delightful ensemble develops at its ease, scarcely forfeiting any dramatic truth. Falstaff's moans arise from the basket, which is smothering him; in front, to hide this, the women spread their skirts and also show off their voices, agile and velvety as the skirts themselves. And from behind the folded screen, from that asylum in which the two children forget the uproar surrounding them, the exquisite song of their exquisite tenderness takes flight. [. . .] With a feverish hand, Ford finally throws the screen aside: instead of his wife with Falstaff, he finds Nannetta and Fenton. New disappointment, new fury, and, with a new outcry, the hunt begins again. Then the servants, hurriedly summoned by the four women, grab the basket, whose crushing weight is expressed by the orchestra; its weight is tested; it is lifted; it is hoisted to the windowsill, where, to some trills of comic terror in the horns, it is held suspended for a moment. Ford reappears, beside himself; he sees, he understands, and the avenging plunge brings to a close one of the most vivid scenes ever created by music, the art of life *par excellence.*

But the complete life that I mean, that which masterpieces are committed to depict, is not action alone; dreams have their time and place. Shakespeare well knew this, and that is why he was in the end a poet, especially in what Montegut[4] rightly called "the freest of his comedies." Leaving that imbroglio, Montegut asks "if the poet had not anticipated the reader's desire and had suddenly caused a refreshing breeze to circulate by transporting the denouement of the play to Windsor Park, and by crowning it with the romantic legend of Herne the Hunter."[5]

The composer has also anticipated that desire, fulfilled it, and the ardent life of the work becomes calm at the end and is refreshed in the serenity of nature and nocturnal enchantments. This was required for the perfection of our pleasure; it was also required to complete the characters, to add to their graces the final grace of poetry, and to their spirits a little sentiment, a bit of vague tenderness. Obviously light sentiment, which saves the idea of mixed comedy and mystification from banality: Alice's laughter, for example, interrupting the fantastic legend of the Black Hunter so no one will be frightened. Listen to the graceful companions preparing the masquerade, assigning their roles as fairies, *"You will be the Dryade. . . As for you, you will be the Nymph of the Groves. . ."* Their voices are gay and laughing, but beneath the voices, a flute arpeggio is enough to open up the serene perspective of the night, meadows, and forests.

Everyone ends up gaining from that serenity. By moonlight in the royal park, before the haunted oak, the young lover is the first to arrive for the general meeting. Beneath the bluish trees, the gamekeepers' horns sound. After all the day's merriment, here is the sweetness of the night. And the boy, struck by the beauty of the hour, sings for a longer time and more slowly than ever before. If only he could sing the divine sonnet in Italian[6] since it, alas, resists all but musical translation. I do not know a purer melodic line than this, or a melody in which each note exudes more poetry and love. It goes on without repeating itself, following its own exquisite curve; beneath it are grouped echoes the sonnet evokes, softly surrounding it. A timid counter-song answers it. No longer feeling alone, as the Italian sonnet had just said, it trembles with joy on a mysterious chord. Then the notes unite like the lips of those whose desire they sing. *"Bocca baciata non perde ventura!—The mouth that is kissed will come to no harm!"* is the motto and, in a way, the password of love that Nannetta and Fenton had exchanged in their earlier meetings. They exchange it again here, and the orchestra, which had previously been silent to hear them, accompanies them this time and propels them into each other's arms.

At this point the mystic fantasy begins. About the terrified Falstaff a musical fairyland unfolds that the Weber of *Oberon* and the Mendelssohn of *A Midsummer Night's Dream* would have envied. Here everything must be mentioned: Nannetta's call from the distance, where her voice forms delicate and novel chords with the orchestra; the *canzone* itself, on which one could in vain exhaust all the subtleties of the Shakespearean vocabulary; the relaxed cadences, [. . .] and the purposely delayed conclusion, as if the voice could not resign itself to dying away.

Finally comedy reasserts itself. "Apotheosis,"[7] cries Falstaff, derided, beaten, and content; and an astonishing fugue in ten real parts, with solid deep bass and sumptuous Italian sonority, ends the masterpiece in transports of abundant joy.

It is over, and it appears we have still said nothing, have particularly failed to touch the work's foundation and to capture the essence of its music. A complete technical study remains to be done; the pure form must be analyzed: the harmonic treasures, the melodic quality, the rhythmic detail, the instrumental color. A chapter could be written on the psychology of timbres found in *Falstaff*. As for melody, here it is of a particular sort: abundant and brief, like handfuls of sonorous dust. But detail never devours the whole; the Maestro's genius multiplies and does not scatter at all; a sunburst constantly falls on the dust, in which thousands of atoms unite and form a ray of light. Thus the work is at once powerful and delicate, a work of nuances, but also of depth and great meaning. Moreover it is formal and it is healthy. It merely sounds the *réveillé* so long hoped for by the Latin genius. "It is necessary," Boito once said, "to mediterraneanize music."[8] Doubtless not all music, but it is still good that there be a music of the Mediterranean. [. . .] Joy as much as sorrow is the daughter of spirit, and the flame of laughter is equally divine. We have understood it all; all of us have acclaimed the glorious old man who lighted the spark of life. May he deign to accept our modest homage. The great Italian has come among his own, among his former brothers-in-arms, always his brothers-in-art, and his own have fortunately recognized him.

Falstaff has three interpreters of the first rank: first the orchestra, which was marvelous. Then Maurel, who must be praised warmly for the intelligence, verve, and grasp of his role; and also for a talent that would be irreproachable if he always were to refrain from exaggeration and notably from the little horrors—I can find no other word—that the eminent artist permits himself in the second and third encores of the *scherzetto, "When I was page of the Duke of Norfolk."* Delna [Quickly] is as admirably comic today as she was tragic yesterday and will be tomorrow. That young lady is more than a great artist, she is like a masterpiece of nature. A debutante, Miss Grandjean [Alice], is merely a debutante, affected and heavy and endowed with an aggressive voice. Soulacroix [Ford] deserves praise. Landouzy [Nannetta] sang the fairy's song with a very pure voice and style, and Clement did not give us what we expected of him in the delicious role of Fenton.[9]

NOTES

1. Review of the first performance of *Falstaff* in French at the Opéra-Comique, on 18 April 1894. Excerpted from *Revue des deux mondes*, 1 May 1894, pp. 220–8. Translated by John Cullars and Donald Wilson.

2. Probably in reference to Susanna's aria *"Deh vieni, non tardar, o gioia bella . . ."* in the last act of *Le Nozze di Figaro*.

3. Jacob Jordaens (1593–1678), Flemish painter.

4. Émile Montégut (1825–95), distinguished critic of *Revue des deux mondes* and other journals, and translator of Shakespeare.

5. Oddly enough, Bellaigue fails to discuss Act III, Scene 1.

6. In some translated versions he does.

7. See Boito's letter to Bellaigue of 25 April 1894.

8. Ibid.

9. See Verdi's letter to Teresa Stolz of 19 April 1894.

Appendix IV

Falstaff at Covent Garden, 19 May 1894[1]

George Bernard Shaw

Falstaff drew an enormous house on Saturday, and was received with enthusiasm which was quite unforced up to the end of the clothes-basket scene. After that the opera suffered for a while from the play outlasting the freshness of the subject, a fate that invariably overtakes *The Merry Wives of Windsor*, except when the actor who plays Falstaff has an extraordinary power of inventing humorous and varied character traits.

The first scene of the third act was undeniably a little dull. The merry wives cackled wearisomely; Pessina's [Falstaff's] comic stock was exhausted, so that he could do nothing but repeat the business of the earlier scenes; and Mrs. Quickly, who had been charming for the first ten minutes in the novel character of the youthful and charming Signorina Ravogli, gave the final blow to the dramatic interest by not being her detestable old self.

Fortunately, the excitement revived in the forest scene at the end, which is full of life and charm. It ends with a sort of musical practical joke in the shape of a fugue which is everything that a fugue ought not to be, and which, failing more rehearsal than it is worth, has to be execrably sung in order to get the parts picked up. It was listened to with deep reverence, as if Verdi, in his old age, had clasped hands with Sebastian Bach. Always excepting the first scene of the third act, the opera went like wildfire.

Boito's libretto is excellent as far as it is a condensation of Shakespear [*sic*], except that it has not appreciated the great stage effectiveness of Falstaff's description to Ford of his misadventure in the basket, with its climaxes dear to old Shakespearean actors, of "Think of that, Master Brook." His alterations, notably the screen business in the basket scene, make some fun, but they also make the scene in Ford's house quite outrageously impossible. As far as acting is concerned, the weight of the whole opera lies in the scene between Ford and Falstaff at the Garter Inn; and here Pessina played with considerable humor and vigor, though without any particular subtlety.

Pini-Corsi's [Ford's] acting was better than operatic acting generally is; but it hardly satisfied those of us who have seen anything like an adequate impersonation of Ford on an English stage. The women were rather unintelligently and monotonously merry; and on the whole the success was, past all questions, a success of the musical setting, which is immensely vivacious and interesting. The medieval scenery is attractive, especially the garden and the room in Ford's house. The interior of the inn is not sunny enough: modern painting, with its repudiation of the studio light, and its insistence on work in the open air, has made the traditional stage interior look old-fashioned in this respect.

NOTE

1. Eric Bentley, ed., *Shaw on Music*, pp. 185–6. See also Verdi to Ricordi, 10 May 1894; Ricordi to Verdi, 17 May; and telegrams from Tito Ricordi II to Verdi, 19 May 1894.

Appendix V

The Lessons of *Falstaff*[1]

Camille Bellaigue

We wish that the true masterpiece performed again a few months ago at the Opéra would still be there. Already welcomed in Milan, albeit with more respect than admiration, *Falstaff* is hardly conquering his own country. It took him more than a quarter of a century to establish his reign, thanks above all to the unbroken and tireless will of a Toscanini. This summer, having heard *Nerone,* by Boito alone,[2] we recalled Verdi and Boito's *Falstaff.* We reread this score and thought about it again, not without melancholy, in the city and the house where not long ago, at most forty years ago, the two late masters became our friends.[3] We even stayed in the same room we had occupied at that time, near the one where the greater of the two was to breathe his last.[4]

The first lesson of *Falstaff*—we gladly call it the work's foremost virtue—is respect and love for voice and song, that very song which Italy in days of old named, with motherly tenderness, *il bel canto.* At the mere mention of this phrase, pretentious individuals of particular taste will disdainfully hum the *scherzetto,* which immediately became popular: "When I was page to the Duke of Norfolk." But Verdi himself attached little importance to it.[5] He was less impressed with the little piece than was the audience, which he might have reproached for having too much fun hearing and rehearing it. The interpreter, too, usually exaggerates its importance and effect.[6] Out of a chanson, the extremely delicate touch of a mere bit of melody, of vocal music above all, of a witty detail and nothing else, he makes almost an aria, even a bravura piece. A closer look, however, at this chanson, or rather, a closer hearing of it, shows a trait of Falstaff's character. The finesse, the charm of the couplet, and, deep within the orchestra, a few surreptitious notes by the flute reveal the elegance of the fat man, still a gentleman, after all, with the remembrance and regret of bygone youth, which his disorderly life and debauchery could not altogether degrade.

In *Falstaff,* a voice alone or several ones together never cease to sing, especially when they talk or declaim. A single word is melody, as when Quickly greets Sir John on four notes that seem to greet one another: *"Révérence."* The shortest dialogue is always a song, an exchange of sung phrases, no matter how rapid it may be and how quick the replies.

Nowhere has a voice, an Italian voice, been more freely and purely displayed than in young Fenton's amorous sonnet as he awaits the nocturnal rendezvous under the ancient oak tree in Windsor Park, *"Bocca baciata non perde ventura."* Once we have heard these few Italian words, which no translation can render, we can never forget their intoxicating sweetness.

How many passages there are where the voice alone suffices to enchant us! In the midst of the whirlwind in the great finale of the laundry basket, it is again Fenton's youthful, tender voice that rises and soars, at first alone. Soon his young friend's voice joins his own, and the two surge together above the ensemble, which, for a moment, they calm. In the same scene we encounter another melodic halt. To hide Falstaff from the rage of his pursuers and to keep him for their own vengeance, the merry wives have concealed the *"Pancione"* behind themselves. *"Étale la jupe"* [Spread out your skirt], says one of them; *"Étale ta jupe ainsi qu'un rampart"* [Spread out your skirt like a rampart]. Just as we are seeing the protective garments expand, we hear the rhythm broaden in a display of voices.

The voices, always the voices! In the second scene [I.ii], the reading of the same love letter, addressed by Falstaff to two of the four ladies, at first elicits only an overlapping chase of short, lively replies. But these dissolve into unison in a vast and magnificent sonorous flow. The rest of the scene is divided between two groups of female, then of male, voices: a quartet, followed by a quintet, at first apart, then encircling each other. Finally, the extraordinary fugue, ending the opera in a rigorous yet informal manner, is a rare triumph of vocal polyphony on the stage. [. . .]

Verdi's *Falstaff* reminds us all over again of what the role of the orchestra should be in the theatre versus the concert hall, but also of the limits of its power. [. . .] Verdi, dividing voices and instruments in *Otello,* and above all in *Falstaff,* seems to be the only composer since Mozart who has known the most appropriate and equitable choice. With incomparable ease and grace, as if for his own amusement, the eighty-year-old master solved the problem which younger ones today fail not only to solve but even to face. Verdi realized the coexistence of the two elements—too often enemies of the lyric drama or comedy—even better than their balance. The time is gone when an Italian orchestra, even Verdi's, could be treated like a guitar. [. . .] Any operatic masterpiece, even the most famous ones, could be in a melodic, spoken, or symphonic style. But *Falstaff* is all this combined. Open the score to the first page, the first bar. This beginning alone, or this "departure," will give you the most lively impression of a quartet, and a masterful one. The whole introduction (Falstaff's quarrel with his two henchmen) develops in classic instrumental style, just as it began. [. . .] The vast finale of the laundry basket unrolls on a theme, or, rather within a theme, that enfolds it completely in circles of joy, a true "perpetual movement" in which Beethoven might have found the same impulse, the same spirit that launches, also in a spiral, the last *allegro* of his Symphony [No. 4] in B-flat.

This most powerful, yet agile, even delicately suggestive force pours forth all over. For once Nietzsche was right: "The divine walks on light feet."[7] Yet here the orchestra gives all it can. But elsewhere it holds back and grows thinner. It touches lightly, then it suggests. A few bars are all that is needed. [. . .] Not a single character in *Falstaff* ceases to sing as we understand it. Carlyle, I believe, once wrote: "All that touches deeply is song."[8] [. . .]

Falstaff—and this may be its principal merit—is a treasure of musical ideas. In this lyrical comedy there is not a sentiment, not a trait of characterization or gesture, no situation, no movement, hardly a word, which does not immediately create a human being who sings. [. . .]

The history of music, or, rather, of musicians, seems to offer no other example of a similar turn: directly following *Otello, Falstaff.* Not just after *Otello,* but after half a century completely devoted to the expression of tragic passions. From the beginning, and for so long, all that violence! In the end, the very end, so much grace, finesse, and gaiety! In his eighties, the son of a grieving Italy remembered that he was also born in a smiling Italy. Perhaps he did not forget, either, the suffering Beethoven's dedication of his last ode to joy. In a lighter form, it is joy again with which Verdi chose to leave this world, happy to entertain for once, having so often moved. Joy, *gioia bella* as in Mozart, who had known and lavished it so fully,—joy is *Falstaff*'s essence, his very soul. Alas, today's music has hardly any animation. We live with utterly serious, severe, and purposely morose composers. Are they and the rest of us waiting till we are octogenarians to have fun? They had better make haste. Let them read the score of *Falstaff* again. Without imitating that work, they might be inspired to understand and love ideal beauty, so that their enlightened art may grant us at least a few moments of *"l'onesto riso e il dolce giuoco."*[9]

APPENDIX V

NOTES

1. Excerpted from *Revue des deux mondes*, 15 August 1924, pp. 935–43. Translated by John Cullars and Donald Wilson.

2. Arturo Toscanini conducted the first of nine performances of *Nerone* at La Scala in Milan on 1 May 1924.

3. After the *Otello* première at La Scala in February 1887. See *Otello* i, pp. 295, 298.

4. At the Grand Hôtel et de Milan on 27 January 1901.

5. See Verdi to Boito, 14 March 1894.

6. See Bellaigue to Verdi, 27 May 1894, and Appendix III, final paragraph.

7. See Friedrich Nietzsche, *Der Fall Wagner*, vol. 1: "alles Göttliche läuft auf zarten Füssen."

8. Actually, "And deep things are song. It seems somehow the very central essence of us, song; as if all the rest were wrappings and hulls." (Thomas Carlyle, *On Heroes, Hero-Worship, and the Heroic in History* [1841], p. 135.)

9. "The honest laughter and the sweet game." (Dante, *Purgatorio,* Canto XXVIII.)

Chronology of Verdi's Life and Works

1813   Giuseppe Fortunato Francesco Verdi is born on either 9 or 10
        October.[1] He is the only son of the grocer and tavern owner
        Carlo Verdi (1785–1867) and his wife, Luigia, née Uttini
        (1787–1851). His birthplace is Le Roncole near Busseto in
        the Duchy of Parma. Since Parma is under the rule of Napo-
        leon I, the birth certificate is made out in French, in the name
        of Joseph Fortunin François. The child is baptized on 11
        October.

1816   On 20 March Verdi's only sister, Giuseppa Francesca, is born.
        She is mentally retarded and dies on 10 August 1833.

1817   Pietro Baistrocchi, the schoolteacher and organist of Le

Roncole, instructs Verdi in Italian and Latin; presumably he is also the boy's first music teacher.

1820   Verdi substitutes for Baistrocchi as organist at the village church of Le Roncole.

1822   Verdi becomes Baistrocchi's successor as organist and "Maestrino" in Le Roncole.

1823   In the autumn Verdi moves to Busseto, where he lodges for over seven years with the poor illiterate cobbler Pugnatta. In November he enters the school in Busseto and studies under the priest Don Pietro Seletti (1770–1853), who wants him to enter the priesthood.

1825   In the autumn Verdi begins to study music theory and composition with Ferdinando Provesi (1770–1833), the music director at Busseto.[2]

1828   Verdi composes an overture to Rossini's *Il barbiere di Siviglia* and a cantata for baritone and orchestra, after Vittorio Alfieri's (1749–1803) *Saul.*

1829   Beginning in the autumn, and until 1832, Verdi is Provesi's assistant in Busseto and writes church compositions. On 24 October he applies unsuccessfully for the position of organist in nearby Soragna.

1830   On 18 February, after a performance of Verdi's first compositions, Provesi declares that his pupil will soon be "the finest jewel of the fatherland."

1831   On 14 May Verdi moves into the home of his fatherly friend Antonio Barezzi (1787–1867), a well-to-do merchant and music lover in Busseto.[3] Verdi teaches Barezzi's daughter Margherita voice and piano.

1832   Upon application by his father, Verdi is granted a modest scholarship in Busseto. In late May, his father and Provesi accompany him to Milan. In June he applies for admission to the Milan Conservatory but is rejected.[4] In the autumn he gives up his position as assistant in Busseto in order to take private instruction with Vincenzo Lavigna (1766–1836)[5] in Milan. Together with Barezzi's son Giovanni, he lodges at the home of Prof. Giuseppe Seletti, a nephew of Don Pietro in Busseto.

1834   In April Verdi conducts a performance of Haydn's *Creation* in Milan. He directs concerts in Busseto and submits an application to be Provesi's successor.

1835   In July Verdi's studies with Lavigna in Milan come to an end, and he returns to Busseto. On 11 October he applies unsuccessfully for the position of conductor and organist in Monza.

1836   In January Verdi begins the composition of *Rocester,* his first opera. On 20 April he is engaged as Provesi's successor in Busseto. On 4 May he marries Margherita Barezzi (born 4 May 1814). After a brief honeymoon in Milan he conducts and composes in Busseto. On 16 September he completes *Rocester.*

1837   On 26 March a daughter, Virginia, is born. In October *Rocester* is rejected in Parma. On 3 November Verdi offers the opera to La Scala in Milan, but it is refused.

1838   On 11 July a son, Icilio, is born. Virginia dies on 12 August. Between 8 September and 10 October Verdi and his wife, Margherita, are in Milan. He tries again, unsuccessfully, to persuade La Scala to accept *Rocester.* On 28 October he announces that he is resigning as music director in Busseto.

1839   Verdi moves with his wife and son to Milan on 6 February. On 22 October Icilio dies. The première of his opera *Oberto, Conte di San Bonifacio* takes place at La Scala on 17 November. Bartolomeo Merelli,[6] impresario of La Scala, offers Verdi a contract for three more operas.

1840   In early March Verdi begins the composition of a comic opera, *Un giorno di regno.* Margherita is stricken with encephalitis and dies on 18 June. Verdi returns to Busseto on 22 June but is back in Milan in July in order to complete *Un giorno di regno.* On 5 September, with the composer conducting, the opera is a failure at La Scala. Verdi stages *Oberto* at La Scala on 17 October, and in December he leads rehearsals of this work at the Teatro Carlo Felice in Genoa.

1841   The first performance of *Oberto* in Genoa is given on 9 January. Verdi returns to Milan in mid-January. Merelli persuades him to compose *Nabucco,* which he completes in October. On 22 and 23 December Verdi visits the prima donna Giuseppina Strepponi,[7] asking that she intercede with Merelli for the première of the work during the following season.

1842   *Nabucco,* Verdi's first great success, has its première at La Scala on 9 March. Giuseppina Strepponi sings the role of Abigaille; later on she becomes Verdi's mistress and, in 1859, his wife. In June Verdi visits Rossini in Bologna. The rest of the year he spends in Busseto and in Milan.

1843   The première of *I Lombardi alla prima crociata* takes place at La Scala on 11 February. On 20 March Verdi departs for Vienna. On 4 April he conducts the first performance there of *Nabucco* at the Kärntnertor Theatre. On 17 April he attends the first performance of *Nabucco* in Parma, in which Strepponi again appears. Except for a trip to Bologna in late April to see two operas by Donizetti and visit his mother in Busseto, Verdi remains with Strepponi in Parma until the end of May. From 31 May to 10 July he is in Milan. He considers composing a *Re Lear* for Venice. Between 10 July and 1 August he is in Senigallia (Ancona) for the staging of *I Lombardi.* He conducts the work there on 29 July, returning to Milan on 1 August. On 8 October he goes to Bologna for the first performance there of *Nabucco* in the Teatro Comunale. He spends the autumn in Milan. In December he takes part in rehearsals at the Teatro Fenice in Venice for an unsuccessful production of *I Lombardi,* which opens on the 26th.

1844   In early January Verdi is in Verona for rehearsals of *Nabucco* with Strepponi. On 9 March the première of *Ernani* is a great success at the Teatro Fenice in Venice. In mid-March and April Verdi is back in Busseto and Milan. On 11 August he conducts *Ernani* in Bergamo, with Strepponi in the role of Elvira. During mid-August he is in Busseto, where he works on *I due Foscari.* By September he is back in Milan. On 3 October he is in Rome for the staging of *I due Foscari* at the Teatro Argentina; the première on 3 November is well received. In mid-November Verdi returns to Milan. Rehearsals for *I Lombardi* at La Scala are held during December for an opening on the 26th.

1845   The première of *Giovanna d'Arco* at La Scala, on 15 February, is applauded. From the middle to the end of March, Verdi is in Venice to rehearse *I due Foscari* at the Teatro Fenice. On 2 April he returns to Milan, where he breaks with Merelli and La Scala over serious artistic and business differences.[8] Presumably by late May he is again in Venice. On 20 June he leaves Milan for Naples, where, on 12 August, the première of *Alzira* at the Teatro San Carlo is a failure. At the end of the month he returns to Milan and works on *Attila.* On 6 October he purchases the Palazzo Dordoni-Cavalli in Busseto.[9] He spends December in Venice, ill with rheumatism and gastritis.

1846   On 17 March the première of *Attila,* under Verdi's direction, takes place at the Teatro Fenice in Venice. Exhausted and ill, he spends the greater part of the year in Milan. In July he and Andrea Maffei[10] take the cure in Recoaro. In Milan, Varese, and Como he discusses a *Macbeth* libretto with Piave.[11] He settles his parents in the Palazzo Dordoni-Cavalli in Busseto.

1847   On 19 February Verdi and Emanuele Muzio[12] arrive in Florence, where an unusually long series of rehearsals begins for *Macbeth.*[13] With Verdi directing, the première at the Teatro della Pergola on 14 March is cheered. In the spring he works on *I masnadieri* in Milan. In late May he and Muzio leave Milan for London, traveling via the St. Gotthard Pass, Strasbourg, Cologne, Brussels, and Paris. From Paris Muzio goes ahead to London, and Verdi arrives there on 7 June. He meets Giuseppe Mazzini[14] and other Italian exiles. Before Queen Victoria he conducts the première of *I masnadieri* at Her Majesty's Theatre on 22 July. He breaks with the publisher Francesco Lucca.[15] From late July on Verdi stays in Paris with Strepponi. On 26 November the première of *Jérusalem* is given at the Paris Opéra.

1848   Verdi is in Paris during the February Revolution, the abdication of Louis Philippe, and the Proclamation of the Second French Republic. He returns to Milan in early April, after the Cinque Giornate, the five-day revolt there against Austrian rule, which took place from 18 to 22 March. On 25 May he purchases an estate at St. Agata near Busseto and moves his parents there. Traveling through Switzerland, he returns to Paris on 31 May and stays with Strepponi in nearby Passy. On 25 October *Il corsaro* has an unsuccessful première, in Verdi's absence, at the Teatro Grande in Trieste. On 20 December he leaves Paris for Rome.

1849   The première of *La battaglia di Legnano* takes place under Verdi's direction at the Teatro Argentina in Rome on 27 January. Increasingly, Verdi is a symbol for the patriotic movement in Italy; in early February, however, he and Strepponi withdraw to Paris, only to depart on 29 July, partly for political reasons. In early August they arrive at Verdi's Palazzo Cavalli in Busseto. From 2 until 27 October Verdi, accompanied by Antonio Barezzi, is on his way to Naples via Genoa; from there they proceed by sea to Civitavecchia and

then by coach to Rome, where they are put in quarantine
because of the cholera epidemic. In Naples there are violent
arguments with the management of the Teatro San Carlo
concerning *Luisa Miller*. Barezzi must return alone to Busseto
before the opera's delayed première on 8 December. On 13
December Verdi leaves Naples by steamboat for Genoa and
returns from there by coach to Busseto, where he rejoins
Strepponi on 18 December.

1850   At the end of April, Verdi proposes to Piave an opera about
the hunchbacked jester in Hugo's *Le Roi s'amuse*. Among other
projects with Piave and Cammarano,[16] Verdi makes an outline
for a *Re Lear*. In July and August Piave is in Busseto. Between
28 September and 8 October Verdi stages *Macbeth* at the
Teatro Comunale in Bologna. In mid-October he arrives in
Trieste. There, at the Teatro Grande, he stages the première of
Stiffelio on 16 November. In Venice he battles with the
Austrian censors over the text that will develop into *Rigoletto*.
The première of *Gerusalemme,* the Italian version of *Jérusalem,*
takes place at La Scala on 26 December.

1851   Verdi returns to Busseto in early January and separates
himself legally from his parents. On 26 January the censors
approve the revised text of *Rigoletto*. On 19 February Verdi
arrives in Venice; the opera has its première there under his
direction, at the Teatro Fenice on 11 March. On 1 May Verdi
and Strepponi move from the Palazzo Cavalli into the house at
St. Agata, about three kilometers from Busseto. His mother
dies on 28 June; Verdi buries her at Vidalenzo. He then
begins the composition of *Il trovatore,* with reservations about
the libretto. On 10 December he and Strepponi leave St.
Agata for Paris.

1852   Verdi and Strepponi return to St. Agata on 18 March. Work
on *Il trovatore* is interrupted by the death of the librettist,
Cammarano, in Naples on 17 July. Verdi departs for Rome on
20 December. Strepponi accompanies him as far as Livorno,
where he embarks on a ship to Civitavecchia.

1853   The première of *Il trovatore,* under Verdi's direction, is a great
success at the Teatro Apollo in Rome on 19 January. On the
22nd he leaves Rome. From late January to mid-February, in
Busseto or at St. Agata, he works on *La traviata* and is joined
by Piave; from 21 February until early March, in Venice, he

orchestrates the opera. *La traviata* is a fiasco at its première, under Verdi's direction, at the Teatro Fenice on 6 March. He proposes a *Re Lear* to Antonio Somma.[17] On 12 March he returns to St. Agata, and on 15 October he and Strepponi leave for Paris. At the end of the year he begins composing *Les Vêpres Siciliennes.*

1854   In March Verdi is in London to stop unauthorized performances of *Trovatore*. He and Strepponi spend the summer in a rented country house near Paris. Between 1 and 9 October rehearsals of *Les Vêpres Siciliennes* are held at the Opéra. They are interrupted, however, when the prima donna Sofia Cruvelli[18] disappears. On 26 December Verdi conducts *Il trovatore* at the Italian Theatre in Paris.

1855   Under Verdi's direction, the première of *Les Vêpres Siciliennes* takes place at the Paris Opéra on 13 June. He and Strepponi spend August and September at Enghien, near Paris. They return to St. Agata on 23 December.

1856   On 15 March Verdi arrives in Venice, where he stages and conducts *La traviata* at the Teatro San Benedetto with great success. After some trips to Parma and Milan, he works with Piave on a revision of *Stiffelio* at St. Agata in the spring. Thereafter he is in Paris to protect his royalties; he files a suit but loses. From 26 June until 19 July he and Strepponi vacation at the seashore near Venice. On 31 July they leave St. Agata for Paris. At Enghien in September, Verdi works on *Simon Boccanegra* and encounters difficulties with the Venetian censors. For three days Verdi and Strepponi are guests of Napoleon III at Compiègne.

1857   On 12 January the première of *Le Trouvère,* the French version of *Il trovatore,* is given at the Paris Opéra. Verdi and Strepponi leave Paris for St. Agata the next day. The première of *Simon Boccanegra,* under Verdi's direction, is a failure at the Teatro Fenice in Venice on 12 March. In mid-May Verdi leads rehearsals of *Simon Boccanegra* in Reggio Emilia. With Strepponi and Piave he arrives at Rimini in July to stage *Aroldo,* the revised *Stiffelio;* the performance on 16 August is not a success. The Teatro San Carlo in Naples presses him for a *Re Lear*, which continues to occupy him for many years but is never realized. In September and October he works at St. Agata on the libretto to *Gustavo III di Svezia.* In early November this libretto is rejected by the Bourbon censors in Naples. In December Verdi and Antonio Somma change its name to *Una vendetta in domino*.

1858   In early January, in the course of a difficult winter journey with Strepponi from St. Agata to Naples, Verdi orchestrates *Una vendetta in domino* while waiting in Genoa for the ship to Naples. Following their arrival on 14 January, the censors bowdlerize the libretto. Verdi wants to sue, but he is threatened with imprisonment. He and Strepponi leave Naples on 23 April and return to St. Agata on the 29th. From late June until mid-July they take thermal baths at Tabiano, near Parma. In August and September Verdi revises *Una vendetta in domino* under the final title *Un ballo in maschera.* On 23 October he returns with Strepponi—again via Genoa by ship—to Naples for rehearsals of *Simon Boccanegra;* under his direction it is a success at the Teatro San Carlo on 30 November.

1859   In January the words VIVA VERDI (for Vittorio Emanuele Re d'Italia) become the rallying cry of Italians against Austria. After lengthy negotiations *Una vendetta in domino* is approved by the papal censors in Rome as *Un ballo in maschera*. After a stormy sea voyage from Naples between 12 and 13 January, Verdi and Strepponi arrive in Civitavecchia and then in Rome. On 17 February, in Rome's Teatro Apollo, *Ballo* has a successful première under Verdi's direction. On 20 March they return to St. Agata by sea, via Genoa. The Battle of Magenta takes place on 4 June, and Vittorio Emanuele II and Napoleon III arrive in Milan on the 8th. In Busseto on 20 June, Verdi starts a subscription to raise money for "the wounded and the poor families of those who have fallen serving the fatherland." The Battle of Solferino is fought on 24 June; on 11 July the Treaty of Villafranca is signed, and Cavour[19] resigns. Verdi and Giuseppina Strepponi are in Tabiano in July, and on 29 August they are married in a little church at Collonges-sous-Salève, near Geneva, and a few days later they return to St. Agata. On 4 September Verdi is chosen as Deputy from Busseto. Together with delegates from Parma, he is received by King Vittorio Emanuele in Turin on 15 September. On the 17th he visits Cavour on his estate at Leri in Piedmont, and on the 20th he arrives back at St. Agata. In October he provides rifles for the national guard in Busseto.

1860   Between 3 January and 11 March Verdi and Giuseppina are in
Genoa. They enlarge the house and property at St. Agata and
Verdi goes hunting with friends. Sicily and Naples are freed
by Garibaldi, and Italy, with the exception of Venice and
Rome, is unified. Railway travel is initiated in Italy. In July
the Verdis are again in Tabiano; otherwise they spend almost
all their time at St. Agata. They are in Genoa at the beginning of December.

1861   In Turin on 18 January, Cavour persuades Verdi to become a
member of the first Italian Parliament. At its historic opening
on 18 February, as well as in early April, in May, and in June,
Verdi is in Turin as Deputy; otherwise he stays at St. Agata.
Cavour dies on 6 June. From the middle to the end of July, at
St. Agata, Verdi and Piave work on the libretto to *La forza del
destino* for St. Petersburg. Verdi works on the opera until 22
November. On 24 November the Verdis travel with their
little dog, Loulou,[20] from St. Agata to Paris and then St.
Petersburg. In December the illness of the prima donna forces
postponement of the première of *Forza* for one year.

1862   Presumably at the end of January, Verdi is greeted with
ovations in Moscow. In Paris, between late February and 31
March, on the way back from Russia, Verdi meets Boito for
the first time. From 1 until 17 April Verdi is in Turin and St.
Agata. He arrives in London on 20 April, his wife having
preceded him there. The première of Verdi's cantata *L'inno delle
nazioni,* to Boito's words, takes place at Her Majesty's Theatre
in London on 24 May, as part of the International Exhibition.
Between 31 May and 13 June the Verdis return to St. Agata
via Paris and Turin. In late June Verdi is in Turin for parliamentary sessions. In July he and Giuseppina visit her sister,
who is seriously ill in Cremona. Their little dog Loulou dies at
St. Agata.[21] Between early September and the 24th the Verdis
journey from St. Agata via Paris to St Petersburg, where on
10 November the première of *La forza del destino* takes place at
the Imperial Opera. They leave for Paris on 9 December.

1863   From 5 to 11 January the Verdis journey from Paris to Madrid
for rehearsals of *Forza;* the performance there is given at the
Teatro Real, under Verdi's direction, on 21 February. Between
23 February and 14 March the Verdis travel in Andalusia,
arriving in Paris on 17 March for a new production of *Les*

Vêpres Siciliennes at the Opéra on 20 July. Between 21 and 25 July, angered by excessively lax standards at the Opéra, Verdi and his wife return, via Turin, to St. Agata, where he works in his fields. On 30 and 31 July he is again in Turin and on 1 August back at St. Agata.

1864   In late January the Verdis are in Turin for parliamentary sessions. They spend February in Genoa and Turin, March in Turin and St. Agata. In June they are in Genoa, and by July again at St. Agata. After a short sojourn for parliamentary duties in Turin in early October and early November, they return to St. Agata, where Verdi works on a revision of *Macbeth* in French.

1865   On 3 February the revision of *Macbeth* is complete. From 5 February until mid-March the Verdis are in Genoa. Between mid- and late February, the composer visits his ailing father at Vidalenzo, near St. Agata; he goes to Turin in early March. From mid-March until mid-April Verdi alternates between St. Agata and frequent parliamentary sessions in Turin. On 21 April, in Verdi's absence, the French version of *Macbeth* has an unsuccessful première at the Théâtre Lyrique in Paris. In late April Verdi is in Turin for three days; in June he declines to be a candidate for reelection to the Parliament; he resigns his office in September. Between 20 November and 1 December the Verdis journey from St. Agata to Paris for work on *Don Carlos*.

1866   The Verdis return, via Genoa, to St. Agata between 17 and 24 March. On 19 June Italy declares war on Austria. Italy suffers defeat at Custozza on the 24th, and St. Agata is threatened by the war. On 5 July the couple are in Genoa, where they rent an apartment at the Palazzo Sauli. On or about the 20th Verdi completes the instrumentation of the first four acts of *Don Carlos;* between the 22nd and the 24th he and Giuseppina journey from Genoa to Paris. From 19 August to 12 September, at Cauterets, a spa in the French Pyrenees, he composes Act V of *Don Carlos.* In late September he is in Paris to lead the first rehearsals of the work at the Opéra. By early December the instrumentation of the entire opera is completed.

1867   Verdi's father dies in Vidalenzo on 14 January. On 11 March, in the presence of the Emperor and Empress of France, the gala première of *Don Carlos* is not well received. The Verdis leave Paris the next day to supervise the furnishing of their residence in Genoa. Between mid-March and early April Verdi makes several trips to St. Agata for work and the planting of trees in his park. In late May the Verdis adopt the seven-year-old daughter of a cousin of the composer's father. Originally baptized Filomena, she is renamed Maria.[22] The couple spend June in Genoa and St. Agata. On 21 July Antonio Barezzi dies in Verdi's and Giuseppina's arms in Busseto. They are in Genoa and Turin between early and mid-August. Between 18 August and 1 October they visit the International Exhibition in Paris and take the cure at Cauterets. During October they alternate between Genoa and St. Agata. Toward the end of the month they are in Bologna for the final rehearsals of the first Italian performance of *Don Carlo,* which is a triumphant success on the 27th. On 19 November the Verdis travel from St. Agata to Genoa, where they will spend nearly every winter from now on.

1868   From early March to mid-April Verdi is frequently at St. Agata. At the beginning of May he and Giuseppina return there. Verdi's sole meeting with Alessandro Manzoni[23] takes place in Milan on 30 June. In July Verdi alternates between St. Agata and Genoa. Between late August and 15 September the Verdis take the cure at Tabiano; they spend the autumn at St. Agata. On 13 November Rossini dies in Paris. On 13 December Verdi departs for Genoa, where he works with Antonio Ghislanzoni on the revision of *La forza del destino.*

1869   Verdi starts rehearsing *Forza* at La Scala in early January.[24] At the end of the month he and his wife take Maria to a school in Turin. They spend February in Milan. On the 27th the revised *Forza* is enthusiastically applauded at La Scala. The couple return to Genoa the next day. In early April Verdi goes to St. Agata, where Giuseppina joins him at the middle of the month; between late July and the end of August they are again in Genoa. In mid-August Verdi completes a "Libera me" for a *Requiem* in memory of Rossini, which is intended to involve various composers. Verdi severs his long-standing friendship with Angelo Mariani,[25] blaming him for lack of interest in this project, which is not realized. From late August to early September the Verdis are in Tabiano, in the autumn at St. Agata, and from late November on in Genoa.

1870   Verdi and his wife leave for Paris on 26 March; they return to Genoa on 22 April. Negotiations with Cairo lasting several months lead to the composition of *Aida*. Verdi returns to St. Agata on 26 April. Camille Du Locle visits him there in June, and Antonio Ghislanzoni is there from late August to early September; both collaborate with him on the text of *Aida*. On 19 July France declares war on Prussia. From 9 or 10 August until the 13th Verdi is in Genoa. France suffers defeat in the Battle of Sedan on 1 September, and Napoleon III is taken prisoner the next day. The scenery and costumes intended for *Aida* in Cairo are locked up in Paris, which is under German siege. The world première of the opera, planned for Cairo in January 1871, and the European première at La Scala are both in jeopardy.[26] On 13 December the Verdis travel from St. Agata to Genoa. By the end of the year the composition of *Aida* is completed.

1871   On 4 January Verdi declines an offer to succeed Mercadante[27] as director of the Conservatory in Naples. On 18 January the German Reich is proclaimed at Versailles, and on 3 February Rome becomes the capital of Italy. In March Verdi chairs a committee in Florence for the reform of Italian conservatories. He returns to Genoa on the 24th and departs for St. Agata on 23 April. From mid-July to 11 August the Verdis are in Genoa. On 12 August Verdi is in Turin and from 18 or 19 September until the 23rd in Milan to deliver the corrected and expanded score of *Aida* to the intendant of the Cairo Opera, Draneht Bey.[28] The Verdis stay at St. Agata in the autumn and leave for Genoa on 15 November. During this time Verdi makes several trips to Milan to prepare the European première of *Aida* at La Scala. On 20 November, after a performance of *Lohengrin*,[29] the first opera by Wagner to be performed in Italy, Verdi meets Boito by chance in Bologna.[30] In late November and early December, piano rehearsals of *Aida* are held in Verdi's home in Genoa with the cast of La Scala. On 24 December, in Verdi's absence, the première of *Aida* receives ovations in Cairo.

1872   In early January Verdi and his wife arrive in Milan for rehearsals of *Aida,* which triumphs at La Scala on 8 February. The Verdis are in Genoa from 20 February to 31 March, at St. Agata on 1 and 2 April, and arrive in Parma on the 3rd. On

the 20th the first performance of *Aida* in Parma is given at the
Teatro Regio, again with Verdi's staging. The couple return to
St. Agata on the 23rd. In mid-July Verdi is briefly in Genoa,
and at the end of October in Turin and Genoa. In early
November the Verdis arrive for rehearsals of *Aida* in Naples
and spend the entire winter there.

1873   On 30 March *Aida* receives its first performance, with Verdi's
staging, at the Teatro San Carlo in Naples. On 1 April his
string quartet is performed for the first time in his hotel. On
the 10th the Verdis arrive home at St. Agata from Naples.
They spend the first half of May in Parma, Turin, and Genoa,
and return to St. Agata on 16 May. Alessandro Manzoni dies
on 22 May, and Verdi pays a solitary visit to the poet's grave
in Milan on 2 June. On the 25th he and his wife leave St.
Agata for Paris, where he works on the *Requiem* for Manzoni.
They return to St. Agata on 13 September, and from 30
December on they are in Genoa.

1874   On 10 April Verdi completes the *Requiem*. At the end of April
he is at St. Agata, and in early May in Milan for rehearsals of
the *Requiem*. He conducts the work in Milan's Church of San
Marco on the 22nd, at La Scala on the 25th, and, beginning
on June 9, seven times at the Opéra-Comique in Paris. In late
June he journeys to London for negotiations regarding a
performance of the *Requiem;* he returns to Paris on 1 July and
to St. Agata on the 5th. In early September the Verdis move
from the Palazzo Sauli to the Palazzo Doria, near the port of
Genoa. They spend the autumn at St. Agata, and depart for
Genoa on 13 November. In early and mid-December Verdi
goes briefly to St. Agata. On 8 December he is appointed
Senator of the Kingdom.

1875   From 22 to 25 February Verdi is in Milan. In early April he
travels to St. Agata and Milan to rehearse with the soloists of
the *Requiem*. On 14 April the Verdis arrive in Paris; beginning
on the 19th he conducts seven additional performances of the
Requiem at the Opéra-Comique. These are followed by four
performances at London's Albert Hall, beginning 15 May, and
four at the Hofoper in Vienna, beginning 11 June. With the
same singers, Verdi also conducts *Aida* at the Hofoper on 19
and 21 June. Between the 25th and the 28th the Verdis
journey home to St. Agata via Venice. Verdi goes to Milan,

presumably in early July, to correct accounts with the House of
Ricordi. On 15 November he is sworn in as Senator in Rome.

1876   Verdi and Giuseppina are in Genoa from late January until 4
March, then in St. Agata until the 20th. On the 22nd they
arrive in Paris for rehearsals of *Aida* at the Théâtre des
Italiens. There, on 22 April, Verdi conducts the first performance in France of *Aida* in Italian, and, between 30 May and
3 June, three performances of the *Requiem.* The Verdis return
via Turin to St. Agata in mid-June. In mid-August they pick
up their adopted daughter, Maria, following her graduation
from school in Turin. Between 20 August and 1 September
Verdi is alone at St. Agata. From 2 to 3 or 4 September he
visits Giuseppina and Maria in Tabiano and takes them back
to St. Agata. From late October to 9 November he is in
Genoa. On 3 December the couple leave St. Agata for Genoa.

1877   The Verdis are at St. Agata from 3 April to 10 May. Verdi
conducts the *Requiem* in Cologne at the Music Festival of the
Lower Rhine on 21 May. From late May to 19 June the couple
journey home to St. Agata via Holland, Belgium, and Paris.
From early December on they are in Genoa.

1878   Vittorio Emanuele II dies on 9 January; Umberto I becomes
King of Italy; Pope Pius IX dies on 7 February. In early April
the Verdis return to St. Agata. Presumably, they are *en route*
via Milan to Paris between 6 April and the middle of the
month, and in Genoa by the end of the month. In early May
Verdi is briefly at St. Agata; on the 8th he and Giuseppina
return there from Genoa. Maria marries Alberto Carrara
(1853–1925), the son of Verdi's notary in Busseto, on 17
October at St. Agata. In November the Verdis visit the casino
in Monte Carlo and lose money gambling.[31] Toward the end
of the month or in early December they are at the Exhibition
in Paris, thereafter at St. Agata, and by the middle of December in Genoa.

1879   In March Verdi hears a performance of Boito's *Mefistofele* in
Genoa,[32] and Boito pays him a visit. On 20 March he goes
alone to St. Agata for a few days. In mid-April he returns
there with Giuseppina. On 30 May he writes to the French
playwright Adolphe Dennery[33] that he may not be averse to
composing another opera.[34] On 23 June he arrives with his
wife in Milan for rehearsals of the *Requiem.* On the 29th Verdi
conducts the work at a benefit concert at the Teatro Dal

Verme. Boito brings him the outline of his *Otello* libretto. On or about 4 July the Verdis return to St. Agata. On the 14th they are in Genoa and are back at St. Agata by the end of the month. On 18 November Verdi receives Boito's actual libretto to *Otello*. On the 20th he and Giuseppina go to Milan, where Verdi acquires the rights to Boito's *Otello* libretto. By early December the Verdis are back at St. Agata; on the 7th they arrive in Genoa.

1880   On 12 February Verdi and his wife leave for Paris. Between 22 March and 2 April he conducts five performances of *Aida* in French at the Opéra, scoring a magnificent success. On 6 April the Verdis return, via Turin, to Genoa. On the 9th they travel to Milan to attend the first performance of his *Pater noster* and *Ave Maria* at La Scala under Faccio's baton on the 18th. From 19 April to 3 May Verdi alternates between St. Agata and Genoa. From 4 to about 10 May the Verdis visit an exhibition of paintings by Domenico Morelli[35] in Turin. By 11 May they are back at St. Agata. They go to Genoa on 18 November. From 12 to 19 December Verdi is at St. Agata.

1881   On 9 and 10 February and, with his wife, between 24 February and 30 March, Verdi is in Milan for *Simon Boccanegra*. On 24 March the revised version of the opera is given its successful première at La Scala. By the 30th the Verdis are back in Genoa. From 3 to about 14 April, Verdi is at St. Agata. On 2 May he and Giuseppina return from Genoa to St. Agata. From late August to 1 September they visit an exhibition in Milan. Between 11 and 14 November Verdi is in Genoa. On the 22nd he accompanies his wife from St. Agata to Genoa but returns to St. Agata for about a week. In Milan in mid-December he discusses with Boito, Faccio, and Giulio Ricordi improvements in the orchestra of La Scala. On 22 December, after two days at St. Agata, he returns to Genoa.

1882   Verdi is at St. Agata in late April, and from 2 to 18 May in Paris, where he works with Camille Du Locle on a four-act version of *Don Carlos*.[36] At the end of the month he returns, via Turin and Genoa, to St. Agata. From 18 June to early July he and Giuseppina take the cure in Montecatini for the first time. On 10 July they are again at St. Agata, where Verdi works on the revision of *Don Carlos*. They go to Genoa in late November. From mid-December to the 21st Verdi is at St. Agata.

1883   Between late February and early March Verdi spends a few days at St. Agata. In mid-March he completes the revision of *Don Carlos* in Genoa. From early April the Verdis are at St. Agata, and at the end of June in Milan, on the way to Montecatini. On 16 July they return to St. Agata with a stopover in Florence. In early December they are back in Genoa, and after Christmas in Milan for rehearsals of the Italian *Don Carlo.*

1884   On 10 January the four-act version of *Don Carlo* is given its première at La Scala. In mid-January the Verdis are again in Genoa. Verdi returns to St. Agata from 17 to 19 February and again in late April (through 1 or 2 May?). On 6 May he accompanies Giuseppina from Genoa to St. Agata. He is in Milan on or about 21 and 22 May; from 22 to 28 June the Verdis visit Turin to see an exhibition and hear a concert given by Faccio on the 22nd. From 29 June to mid-July they are in Montecatini and in late July in Tabiano. On 23 November Verdi accompanies Giuseppina from St. Agata to Genoa. Between 24 and 29 November he is back at St. Agata, alone. He returns to Genoa on the 30th and, after another brief stay at St. Agata, again on 23 December.

1885   In mid-February and in mid-April Verdi is at St. Agata. On their return from Genoa to St. Agata between late April and 4 May, the Verdis stop for dental care in Milan. They are in Montecatini from early to mid-July. On their return from St. Agata to Genoa between 21 November and 5 December they again see their American dentist in Milan. Andrea Maffei dies unexpectedly in Milan on 27 November. Verdi comforts Clara Maffei and, presumably, also meets Boito. On 21 and 22 December Verdi is at St. Agata.

1886   In late February Verdi spends two days in Milan. On 18 March he departs with Giuseppina and Muzio for Paris. On 11 and 12 April the three travel from Paris to Milan via the Gotthard Tunnel, which opened four years earlier. Between 16 and 29 April they return via Genoa to St. Agata; they arrive in Montecatini on 24 June. On 13 July they hurry from there to Clara Maffei's deathbed in Milan. On the 22nd, presumably, they are back at St. Agata. Verdi is in Milan from 14 until about 16 October. He completes *Otello* on 1 November. Beginning on the 24th, he and his wife spend a few days together in Milan; on 9 December they arrive in Genoa. Between 27 and 30 December he is at St. Agata.

1887   On 1 January Opprandino Arrivabene dies in Rome. On the

4th the Verdis leave Genoa for the rehearsals of *Otello* at La Scala. The première on 5 February is a memorable event. On 2 March the couple return to Genoa; after a brief stay at St. Agata, Verdi is back in Genoa on the 11th. From 30 March to 1 April and also from 3 to 5 May he commutes again between Genoa and St. Agata. On 16 May both Verdis return from Genoa to St. Agata. Between 28 and 29 June they journey via Milan to Montecatini; they return to St. Agata, via Florence, on or about 20 July. Verdi is in Genoa from 9 to 12 August and in Milan from 12 to 14 September. In mid-November he accompanies Giuseppina to Genoa and returns to St. Agata. From the 21st to the 23rd he goes to Genoa via Milan. From the 29th or the 30th, and presumably until 3 December, he is at St. Agata; on 17 December he is in Milan. From the 27th to the 28th he and his wife make the trip from Genoa to Milan and back, in connection with his loan of 200,000 Lire to the House of Ricordi.

1888   In early April the Verdis are in Milan. On or about 5 May they return from Genoa to St. Agata. On 27 June the couple arrive in Montecatini, via Milan. They are back at St. Agata on 11 July to furnish a hospital which Verdi has built and endowed anonymously in nearby Villanova.[37] Tito Ricordi I dies on 7 September. On 5 November the hospital in Villanova opens without any ceremonies. In early December Verdi and Giuseppina are in Milan for his endowment of the Casa di Riposo per Musicisti [House of Rest for Musicians].[38] On 4 December they arrive in Genoa. On the 17th Verdi sees Giulio Ricordi in Milan.

1889   In late February, presumably, Verdi stays for a couple of days in Milan. Between 30 March and about 2 April he makes several round trips between Genoa and St. Agata. On or about 18 April, on their annual journey from Genoa to St. Agata, the Verdis meet Boito in Milan. On their way to Montecatini in late June, Verdi talks about *Falstaff* with him in Milan. Boito gives him an outline of the libretto, which Verdi takes along to Montecatini on 4 July.

[See Chronological Sketches for the remainder of this year through 1894.]

1895   Between 28 January and approximately 7 March the Verdis are in Milan. Concerned with the unexpectedly high costs for the construction of the Casa di Riposo, they meet with the architect, Camillo Boito, and presumably also his brother. While in Genoa, Verdi composes a *Te Deum.* In early May the couple arrive home at St. Agata. In late June they go to Montecatini, passing through Milan, and return to St. Agata on 22 July. In late October Verdi and Giuseppina spend a few days in Milan; in December they are once more in Genoa.

1896   From 16 January to 13 February the Verdis are again in Milan in connection with the Casa di Riposo. From 26 to 28 March Verdi is in Milan, alone. In the spring, Giuseppina Verdi falls ill in Genoa. In late May, Verdi is again in Milan regarding the Casa di Riposo; on 2 June he and his wife are back at St. Agata, and on 11 July they visit the construction site with Arrigo and Camillo Boito and Giulio Ricordi. On the 15th they continue their journey to Montecatini, returning home to St. Agata in early August. From late August to 3 September Verdi makes another trip to Milan for the Casa di Riposo. On 14 October he accompanies Giuseppina on a visit to her sister in Cremona. From late November on the two are again in Genoa.

1897   In early January, in Genoa, Verdi suffers a minor stroke, which is kept secret; he soon recovers. From 22 February to 16 March he and his wife are again in Milan regarding the Casa di Riposo. In early April Verdi makes another trip to Milan. From early May to the 17th, on their way from Genoa to St. Agata, Verdi and Giuseppina are once more in Milan to view the progress of the construction. During the first week of July, on their last trip together to Montecatini, the Verdis stop in Milan; they return home to St. Agata at the end of the month. Verdi works on the *Pezzi sacri,* and in early September he makes a brief trip to Milan and Genoa. Peppina's condition worsens. She dies at St. Agata on 14 November and is buried in the Cimitero Monumentale in Milan on the 16th. The Ricordis and Teresa Stolz come to St. Agata. Boito arrives on Christmas Eve.

1898   On 6 January Verdi, his adopted daughter, Maria Carrara, and Teresa Stolz go to Milan to view the construction of the Casa di Riposo; a further reason for this trip is the printing of the *Pezzi sacri.* Three of them are heard for the first time at the Paris Opéra on 7 April.[39] Verdi is in Genoa between 15 March and 26 April, in Milan from 26 April to late May, and at St.

Agata from late May to early July. In early July he goes to Milan, continuing to Montecatini on the 11th. He returns to St. Agata on 2 August. On about 7 September Verdi goes to Genoa, passing through Milan, and is again in Milan on the 12th; he is back at St. Agata on the 15th. He makes another trip to Milan in late November or early December.

1899   In mid-February Verdi travels from Milan to Genoa. He is again in Milan during mid-May, and by early June back home at St. Agata. In early July Teresa Stolz accompanies him to Montecatini. He returns to St. Agata on or about 3 August. From mid-September to the 24th, passing through Milan, he makes a brief trip from St. Agata to Genoa and back. On 3 December he goes again to Milan, where, on the 16th, he underwrites his endowment for the Casa di Riposo. He spends Christmas in Genoa and observes the New Year with Boito in Milan.

1900   Verdi is in Genoa from 1 March to 5 May; this is his last verifiable stay in that city. From 5 to 22 May he is in Milan, where he dictates his will on the 14th. From 22 May to early July he is at St. Agata; after a few days in Milan, he arrives at Montecatini on 11 or 12 July; he returns to St. Agata in early August. Upon the assassination of King Umberto on 29 July, Verdi makes an unsuccessful attempt to compose a few notes to a prayer written by the Queen. In mid-December he leaves St. Agata for the last time. He celebrates the New Year in Milan with Boito, Teresa Stolz, the Ricordis, and other friends.

1901   Verdi suffers a stroke in his room at the Grand Hotel in Milan on 21 January, and never awakens. He dies at 2:50 A.M. on the morning of 27 January and is buried next to Giuseppina at the Cimitero Monumentale on the 30th. On 26 February both coffins are placed in a crypt in the Casa di Riposo while a choir of nine hundred voices, conducted by Arturo Toscanini, sings the chorus "Va pensiero, sull'ali dorate" from *Nabucco* [Fly, O thought, on wings of gold].

NOTES

1. See Verdi to Clara Maffei, 9 October 1885, n. 1, in *Otello* i, p. 182.
2. In 1799 Provesi had committed a grave crime [. . .]; he stole from the Church of Santa Maria Assunta [at Sissa near Parma], where he was organist. Arrested

and dragged in chains to prison, he languished for nearly two years, untried. Because he was a poet and librettist of no mean skill, Provesi sent all his appeals to the Duke of Parma in verse, but to no avail. No response came to his pleas for clemency. Finally he took another tack, and asked to be tried. Convicted, he was condemned to lifelong exile and to forced domicile in a village in the Apennines. For a man dedicated to music, theatre, and writing, this was rather like being sent to hell, and Provesi soon fled to Busseto, where the police traced him in 1801. In normal circumstances he would have been seized and sent back to Sissa, but in Busseto he enjoyed the patronage of the Cavallis, and thus he was saved. Given an apartment for his wife and child, he was also made director of the Busseto drama academy and music school, and of the organ and orchestra of the Church of San Bartolomeo in Busseto. The importance of the Cavallis can be gauged from the fact that they could oust a rich, church-sponsored organist from his post to make way for a fugitive and ex-convict whose name was never legally cleared in the Duchy of Parma. [Phillips-Matz in Rosen and Porter, eds., *Verdi's "Macbeth,"* pp. 130–1. For the Cavallis, see ibid., pp. 129–36.]

3. Verdi's benefactor and later his father-in-law. On 25 March 1847, Verdi wrote to him from Florence:

> Dear Father-in-law,
>   For a long time I have thought of dedicating an opera to you, who have been for me a father, benefactor and friend. It is a duty I should have fulfilled sooner, and I would have if compelling circumstances had not prevented it.—Now, here is this *Macbeth,* which I love more than my other operas and therefore consider more worthy to present to you. My heart offers it; may yours accept it, and may it be a witness of the lasting remembrance, gratitude, and love borne for you by
> Your most affectionate
G. Verdi

4. Years thereafter, Verdi wrote on an envelope containing this application: "In the year 1832, on 22 June, Application of Giuseppe Verdi to be admitted to the Conservatory of Milan." He added in the third person—"He was rejected." [Fù respinto.] (Autograph at St. Agata.) See Guglielmo Barblan, "Rimpianto per un mancato allievo," *Annuario 1962– 1963 del Conservatorio di Musica Giuseppe Verdi.*

5. Lavigna was a composer and conductor who studied at the Conservatory in Naples. He was engaged as a coach at La Scala in 1809 and, in 1823, as a professor at the Conservatory in Milan. He admired the German classical composers, Mozart in particular, and became the young Verdi's teacher and friend.

6. Merelli studied music with Simon Mayr in his native Bergamo and wrote five librettos for Donizetti, his fellow-student. For thievery in his hometown, Merelli had to give up his studies of law. He managed a theatrical agency in Milan from 1826 to 1830 and various seasons of opera in northern Italy from 1830 to 1835. From 1836 to 1846 and 1861 to 1863 he ruled La Scala, his most coveted goal; he also managed the Kärntnertor Theatre in Vienna from 1836 to 1848. Merelli lived in Vienna again from 1853 to 1855. He was a friend and promoter of Rossini, Bellini, and Donizetti, but his lasting merit was his faith in Verdi's genius, which, after the setback of *Un giorno di regno,* triumphed for the first time with *Nabucco.*

7. See Biographical Sketch.

8. Strepponi's earlier alleged affair with Merelli is said to have contributed to this break. Frank Walker, however, states that "in spite of what Gatti and his innumerable Italian followers have written, it is not true that Giuseppina was Merelli's mistress" (Walker, p. 164).

9. See Walker, p. 195 n., and Phillips-Matz in David Rosen and Andrew Porter, eds., *Verdi's "Macbeth,"* pp. 129–36.

10. Writer and poet (1798–1885) who translated the works of Shakespeare, Milton, Byron, Goethe, Schiller, Heine, and Grillparzer into Italian. Maffei contributed to the libretto of Verdi's *Macbeth*. He was married to Clara Maffei but they separated.

11. Francesco Maria Piave (1810–76) was the librettist of Verdi's *Ernani, I due Foscari, Attila* (with Temistocle Solera), *Macbeth* (with Andrea Maffei), *Il corsaro, Stiffelio, Rigoletto, La traviata, Simon Boccanegra* (first version), *Aroldo,* and *La forza del destino* (first version). When Piave was paralyzed by a stroke, Verdi supported his family and, nine years later, paid for his burial.

12. See Biographical Sketch.

13. Marianna Barbieri-Nini, Verdi's first Lady Macbeth, years later gave a vivid description of those rehearsals. (See Phillips-Matz in Rosen and Porter, eds., *Verdi's "Macbeth,"* pp. 129–36.)

14. Giuseppe Mazzini (1805–72), Republican patriot, apostle of Italian unity, and music enthusiast, wrote a "Philosophy of Music" while exiled in Switzerland in 1835. He asked Verdi to compose a hymn to the text *Suona la tromba* by Goffredo Mameli (1827–49), who lost his life while serving as an adjutant to Garibaldi. In October 1848 Verdi sent Mazzini the requested composition with the words: "May the hymn soon resound amidst the music of the cannons in the plain of Lombardy."

15. Francesco Lucca (1802–72) published Verdi's early works in Milan. He was a trailblazer for Richard Wagner, and a friend of Hans von Bülow.

16. Salvatore Cammarano (1801–52), playwright and librettist, was born into a well-known family of Neapolitan theatrical artists. He wrote, *inter alia,* the texts for Donizetti's *Lucia di Lammermoor* and for Verdi's *Alzira, La battaglia di Legnano,* and *Luisa Miller.* He unexpectedly died in the midst of the creation of *Il trovatore.* The libretto was completed by Leone Emanuele Bardare (1820–?). Cammarano's death may have contributed to Verdi's inability to realize his plan for *Re Lear.*

17. Antonio Somma (1809–65) was a Venetian writer, librettist, journalist, and jurist. He directed the Teatro Grande in Trieste from 1840 to 1847 and wrote the libretto of *Un ballo in maschera* for Verdi.

18. Sofia Cruvelli (1824–1907), a German soprano, was born Johanne Sophie Charlotte Crüwell in Bielefeld, Germany. She was noted for a three-octave range up to high *F.* Some compared her extravagant vocal style to that of Malibran. Verdi thought Cruvelli had Malibran's faults without her virtues. She studied in Paris and Milan, and made her debut in Venice in 1847. She sang at Her Majesty's Theatre in London in 1848 and at the Italian Theatre in Paris in 1854. During Verdi's rehearsals for *Les Vêpres siciliennes* at the Opéra, the prima donna suddenly disappeared without leave.

> Cruvelli reappeared without any explanation and began to sing again. The public surmised, without being corrected, that she had taken an anticipatory honeymoon with a Baron Vigier, whom she later married. The escapade delighted the Parisians and had a good effect at the box office. It also indicated the

lack of discipline at the Opéra. The schedule of rehearsals and performances was thrown off, and the première of the year's most important opera was delayed. Verdi suggested that he and the directors cancel his contract, but they would not. [Martin, *Verdi,* p. 324.]

19. Count Camillo Benso di Cavour (1810–61) was Prime Minister of Sardinia from 1852 to 1859 and from 1860 to 1861. Unlike the Republicans Mazzini and Garibaldi, Cavour wished for a united royal Italy. Under his political guidance Sardinia and France fought Austria in 1859, and Austria lost Lombardy. Disgusted, like Verdi, with the pact Napoleon III made with Franz Josef I, which left the Veneto to Austria, Cavour resigned and retired to his farm at Leri, in Piedmont. Back in office in 1860, Cavour succeeded, with help from Garibaldi and others, in uniting all of Italy, with the exception of Venice and Rome. When Vittorio Emanuele II became King of Italy in 1861, Cavour had achieved the goal of his life, but only a few months before his death.

20. Loulou, a male Maltese spaniel, accompanied the Maestro and his wife on many a journey. His portrait by Filippo Palizzi (1818–99), painted during the Verdis' sojourn in Naples in 1858, still hangs at St. Agata.

21. "A misfortune, a very great one for us, has befallen and deeply upsets us," Verdi wrote to Angelo Mariani from St. Agata on 1 August 1862. "*Loulou,* poor *Loulou,* is dead! The poor little animal! The true friend, the faithful, inseparable companion for almost six years of our life! So affectionate, so handsome! Poor *Loulou!* It's hard to describe Peppina's grief to you, but you can imagine it." (*Carteggi* ii, p. 205.) On Loulou's grave in the park of St. Agata, a stone column bears the often misquoted inscription, "Alla memoria d'un vero amico" [In memory of a true friend].

22. Maria Verdi, often called "Signora Marie," was born on 14 November 1859 and died on 27 June 1936.

23. Alessandro Manzoni (1785–1873), the great Italian poet of the nineteenth century. The novel *I promessi sposi* [The Betrothed], his major work, inspired Goethe and influenced European literature. Verdi revered Manzoni as a saint and dedicated the *Requiem* to him.

24. The first time he set foot in La Scala after his break with Merelli in 1845.

25. Angelo Mariani (1822–73) was among the most celebrated conductors both in Italy and abroad, from Copenhagen to Constantinople. Verdi broke his close friendship with Mariani in 1868, when he felt left in the lurch by the latter's lack of cooperation on a planned Mass for Rossini, which he had begun to compose. Following the break, Mariani dedicated himself to Wagner, and Faccio became Verdi's preferred conductor. (See Biographical Sketch of Teresa Stolz; and Walker, pp. 283–392.)

26. Commissioned by the Viceroy of Egypt, *Aida* could not be performed anywhere before its première in Cairo.

27. Saverio Mercadante (1795–1870) composed some sixty operas and twenty masses, as well as psalms, motets, chamber music, pieces for orchestra, and songs. A pioneer of nineteenth-century Italian music drama, Mercadante inspired Verdi.

28. Draneht Bey, alias Paul Draneht (1815–94), was born Pavlos Pavlidis on Cyprus. During Turkish massacres in 1827, he escaped with his Greek family to Egypt. Mohammed Ali, Egypt's ruler, was so impressed by the teenage refugee that he took him into his service and enabled him to study chemistry, medicine, pharmacy, and even dentistry in Paris. There, Pavlos's professor, the renowned Baron Louis-Jacques Thénard, was so proud of his pupil that he offered him his own name spelled backwards. When Pavlos Pavlidis returned to Egypt, he took up his post with Mohammed Ali as Paul

Draneht; he soon became Draneht Bey and later was elevated to Pasha. A close friend of Ferdinand Lesseps, Draneht Bey was involved in the negotiations for the construction of the Suez Canal. Among numerous other activities, he established the Egyptian railways and was their first superintendent, reformed Egyptian agriculture, and managed the Khedive's opera house in Cairo, which opened in 1869 with *Rigoletto*. In the summer of 1871, Draneht visited Verdi at St. Agata and quarreled with him over the casting of Amneris. (See *Aida,* p. 631–2.)

29. During this performance—conducted by Mariani, whom Verdi did not greet afterwards—he summed up his impressions in a vocal score of *Lohengrin,* which is kept at St. Agata: "Beautiful music, and thoughtful, when it is clear. The action moves as slowly as the text. Result: boredom. Beautiful instrumental effects. Abuse of long notes leading to heaviness. Mediocre performance. Much *verve,* but without poetry and subtlety. In difficult spots, always bad." (For Verdi's detailed comments, see Abbiati iii, pp. 508–11.)

30. The only time, as far as can be established, the two men saw each other between 1862 and 1879. (See Chronology of Boito's Life and Works, 1871.)

31. "You know that I have been in Monte Carlo?" Verdi writes on 19 November to Clara Maffei. "I lost, because I wanted to lose in order to get even sicker of that horrible thing called *gambling*." (Autograph in Braidense; Ascoli, *Quartetto milanese,* p. 370.)

32. On 30 March Verdi writes to Arrivabene: "You talk to me about music, but on my word of honor it seems to me that I have almost forgotten it; the proof of this is that I heard *Mefistofele* a couple of nights ago and understood everything the wrong way. For instance: I had always heard and read that the *Prologue in Heaven* is a perfect whole, something from a genius. . . but when I heard the harmonies of this piece based on dissonances almost all the time, I felt certain I was not in *Heaven* at all."

33. Adolphe Philippe Dennery (also d'Ennery; 1811–99), one of the most popular French dramatists, was author of spectacular shows like *Le tour du monde en 80 jours*, and of librettos, e.g., *Si j'étais roi* (for Adam in 1852) and *Le Cid* (for Massenet in 1885).

34. The autograph of this letter is the property of Signor Giovanni Bergonzi, with whose kind permission it is here translated from the French:

Busseto St. Agata, 30 May 1879

My dear Monsieur D'Ennery,

It is no news to you to hear me repeat that I would be happy to set to music one of your poems, and that I would always consider it an honor to work for the Opéra. But you also know of my hesitations and my fears as to its execution. I repeat to you once again my doubts as to the singers and the *sluggish, tired-out* execution in general: this is to say that the lack of spirit and vigor on the part of the ensembles in my opinion makes a success impossible, unless a remedy is found for it. But this remedy, can the new director [Vaucorbeil] find it? Yet, my dear D'Ennery, allow me to withhold my reply for the time being. It is a serious matter, and one must ponder it seriously. I shall write to you about it later on.

Accept the assurance of my most distinguished sentiments.

G. Verdi

35. Domenico Morelli (?–1901) was a well-known, highly gifted naturalistic painter and one of Verdi's Neapolitan friends. He played a major role by providing Verdi with pictures of characters and locales for some of his operas. (See *Otello* ii, pp. 844–5.)

36. The long and complicated history of Verdi's several versions of this work has been thoroughly researched and edited by Ursula Günther (see Bibliography).

37. See Verdi to Clara Maffei, 16 December, and Muzio to Ricordi, 29 December 1882, in *Otello* i, pp. 136–7, 138.

38. Built by the architect Camillo Boito, Arrigo's brother, the Casa di Riposo was opened on 10 October 1902, Verdi's birthday. In his will, Arrigo Boito left all his future royalties to its endowment.

39. The "trois pièces religieuses"—which Paul Taffanel conducted in Verdi's absence, since the Maestro's physician did not allow him to travel to Paris—were the "Stabat Mater," "Laudi alla Vergine," and "Te Deum." The complete *Quattro pezzi sacri,* including the "Ave Maria," were performed for the first time in Vienna on 13 November 1898.

Chronology of Boito's Life and Works

1842   Born in Padua on 24 February as Enrico Giuseppe Giovanni
        Boito, he is the second son of the portrait miniaturist Silvestro
        Boito (1802–56) and his wife, Giuseppina (née Józefa
        Radolinska), a widowed Polish countess. His brother,
        Camillo, was born in Rome on 30 October 1836, five months
        after the parents' wedding.
1844   The family moves from Padua to Venice.
1851   On 5 September the Venetian musician and writer Luigi Plet[1]
        informs the boys' mother, who is staying in Poland, that her
        husband had deserted his sons. On 24 October Plet writes to
        tell her that nine-year-old Enrichetto shows "more and more

proof that he has a calling in music and composition, since he constantly invents motifs and sonatinas." He writes further that the boy's teacher, Antonio Buzzolla,[2] "asks that I assure you that Enrichetto without a doubt has the talent to become a fine composer." Enrico composes a polka on the tune of "La donna è mobile."[3] Luigi Plet, Giovanni Buzzolla, and Buzzolla's brother Antonio exercise a decisive influence on both Enrico's and Camillo's development.

1853   Abandoned by her husband, the nearly penniless Giuseppina Boito moves to Milan to place Enrico in the Conservatory. Camillo continues his studies in Venice. On 31 October Enrico is enrolled in the Conservatory as a student of piano, violin, and harmony.

1854   On 20 July Enrico's impoverished mother petitions for a scholarship at the Milan Conservatory. It is granted, and the twelve-year-old now studies composition with Alberto Mazzucato,[4] an admirer of Verdi.

1855   At the end of the 1854–55 school year, Lauro Rossi[5] remarks about Enrico's mediocre report: "He has studied with no real energy, and it is to this fact, despite his good intentions, that his meagre progress is to be attributed." He receives praise only for his achievements in French, Italian literature, geography, and mathematics; he is criticized for his deficiency in rhythm. On 31 October Franco Faccio enters the Conservatory and becomes an outstanding student as well as Boito's inseparable friend.

1856   Silvestro Boito dies, allegedly as the result of a brawl.

1858   Boito earns great praise at the Conservatory for a symphony.[6] He spends the summer at the seaside, taking a cure prescribed by his doctor. Almost every year he and his mother move to a different apartment in Milan. Occasional trips with her to Venice provide variety during his school year. On several occasions Camillo visits his mother and brother in Milan. He, too, becomes friends with Faccio, and with Faccio's younger sister Chiarina,[7] who studies voice at the Conservatory.

1859   The liberation of Lombardy from Austrian rule interrupts postal service between Milan and Venice. Camillo is prevented from sending money to his mother and brother. Giuseppina Boito dies on 11 June. On her tombstone the brothers inscribe: "In memory of Giuseppina Boito, cheerful and brave in misfortune. Her two sons—1859." Camillo supports his brother and urges him to make contact with Cesare Cantú,[8] Carlo Tenca,[9] and Filippo Filippi.[10]

1860   On 8 September a patriotic cantata, *Il Quattro Giugno* [The Fourth of June], is performed at the Milan Conservatory in memory of the Battle of Magenta; Boito, for the first time using the name Arrigo, is the author of the text and composer of the first section, while Faccio is the composer of the second part. Both public and press are enthusiastic about the work, even if it is reminiscent of Wagner's "music of the future."

1861   As a joint final examination, on 4 September, Boito and Faccio give their cantata *Le sorelle d'Italia* [The Sisters of Italy], which they dedicate to "Alberto Mazzucato and Stefano Ronchetti-Monteviti,[11] who have, with prudent love and wise counsel, guided us to Art." Boito is responsible for the poetry and for the music of the second section, while Faccio is the composer of the prologue and the first section. Faccio shows the influence of Verdi, while Boito's "germanismo" is seen as disturbing. Detailed reviews treat the youthful work seriously and speak of the musical and dramatic genius of the two friends. A one-year government grant, which they obtain with Camillo's help, enables them to spend some five months in Paris. Tito Ricordi[12] sends them off with a letter of recommendation to Rossini. In late November or early December they arrive in Paris and within a couple of weeks are guests at Rossini's table, and Rossini takes them "under his wings."[13]

1862   Camillo Boito introduces Arrigo and Faccio to prominent artists in Paris. Clara Maffei[14] arranges a meeting with Verdi, and Boito writes the text of *Inno delle Nazioni* [Hymn of the Nations] for him. On 29 March Verdi thanks him with a watch, together with these words: "May it remind you of my name and the value of time."[15] Boito begins work on *Nerone* and *Faust,* which will develop into *Mefistofele.* In early April he leaves Paris to visit his mother's relatives in Poland until autumn. On 19 April he writes to Paolo Reale[16] from Mystki: "At the moment I'm under the magnetic influence of Tacitus and am dreaming of a great opera, which will be christened with a frightful name: *Nero*."[17] In July he sends Faccio his first libretto based on Shakespeare, *Amleto*. On 20 October he is in Vienna on his return to Milan.

1863   In March the comedy *Le madri galanti* [The Gallant Mothers], which he wrote together with Emilio Praga,[18] fails in Turin. In Milan Boito and his brother join the *Scapigliatura,* a belated Italian *Sturm und Drang* movement in revolt against a stereotype establishment. Under Filippi's direction, Boito is a music and theatre critic of *La perseveranza.* After the première of Faccio's *I profughi fiamminghi* [The Flemish Refugees] at La Scala on 11 November, he presents his "Sapphic Ode with Glass in Hand," *all'arte italiana*, which creates a scandal and upsets Verdi.

1864   From January to March Boito and Emilio Praga edit the weekly magazine *Figaro.* Boito translates poems by Heinrich Heine and, in similar style, writes biting, pessimistic, frequently provocative reviews. He also publishes an entire collection of his own poems; one, "Dualismo," earns the praise of Antonio Ghislanzoni. On 29 June he helps found Milan's *Società del Quartetto* (which still exists today); at its first concert quartets of Mozart, Beethoven, and Mendelssohn are played. For the *Giornale della Società del Quartetto,* published by Tito Ricordi and edited by Alberto Mazzucato, Boito writes his well-known article "Mendelssohn in Italia" and other enthusiastic essays on German masters. On 20 December he sends his bizarre poem "Re Orso" [King Bear] "to Giuseppe Verdi, that he may remember me."

1865   At the première of *Amleto* in Genoa on 30 May, Boito's libretto is a greater success than Faccio's controversial music.

1866   On 16 May Victor Hugo writes to Boito: "Bravo, poet, there is a hero in you! You have courage. You have earned Venice. You shall have her. And Rome, as well."[19] Italy fights on the side of Prussia against Austria. Boito, Faccio, and Praga volunteer in Garibaldi's campaign to free the Venetians from Austrian rule. Letters to their sweethearts Vittoria Cima, Eugenia Litta,[20] and Teresa Bellotti[21] tell of their military adventures. Venice is freed, but Istria and the Trentino remain under Austria. Their ideal eludes them; once Boito even turns to drugs.[22]

1867   In March he writes his first novella, *L'alfier nero* [The Black Bishop (in chess)], followed by a second, *Iberia*, and a third, *Il pugno chiuso* [The Closed Fist]. At the same time he is busy with *Il trapezio* [The Trapeze], an unfinished novella set in

China, which was published in 1873–74 in Ghislanzoni's *Rivista minima*, under Boito's anagrammatic pseudonym Tobia Gorrio. In April and May he is in Poland; he returns to Milan in June. There he must bury his brother's only child, three-year-old Casimiro, in the absence of the child's parents. Camillo and his Polish wife separate in the summer. In September the brothers move to another home in Milan. Arrigo orchestrates *Mefistofele*.

1868   The première of *Mefistofele* at La Scala on 5 March is a disaster. After the first rehearsals Mazzucato, the principal conductor at La Scala, had yielded the baton to the composer, who was totally inexperienced. Faccio, concerned, writes from Scandinavia, but the catastrophe cannot be averted. Apart from deficiencies in the performance, the press finds the work too intellectual, too long, and too Wagnerian.[23] Despite discouragement, the young author, once again signing his name Arrigo Boito, protests foolish reform plans of the new Minister of Education, Emilio Broglio, in a candid, stinging "Letter in Four Paragraphs."[24] For the next seven years he will go back to using the pseudonym Tobia Gorrio exclusively.

1869   All that is known about this year is that in November Boito sends the music publisher Francesco Lucca a translation of Wagner's *Rienzi*.

1870   In Ricordi's *Gazzetta musicale,* to which he is a contributor until 1872, Boito (Gorrio) publishes nine articles in a series entitled "La musica in Piazza." In late September he plans a revision of *Mefistofele* in Bologna; by the 30th he is in Venice. From there he sends the first two acts of a libretto, probably *La Gioconda*, to Ponchielli.

1871   In January Boito wants to offer Verdi his text to *Nerone*. Verdi is not opposed to the idea, but he puts off his answer, eventually to decline. Faccio's *Amleto* fails at La Scala on 12 February. Boito spends the summer with friends at Adro,[25] in the province of Brescia, working on the composition of *Ero e Leandro*.[26] On 19 November Boito and Faccio attend a performance of *Lohengrin* in Bologna. Boito meets Verdi at the railway station at 3:00 A.M. the night of the performance; they discuss the discomfort of sleeping on trains.[27] Boito writes enthusiastically to Wagner and publishes his answer in *La perseveranza*.[28] Boito, like Faccio, longs to see Italy united with a Europe where culture is prized in the absence of nationalistic and stylistic prejudice. Their love of Verdi does not preclude honoring Wagner.

1872   On 12 March Lucca publishes Wagner's cantata *Das Liebes-mahl der Apostel,* and Ricordi publishes Joachim Raff's[29] *Zwölf Gesänge für zwei Stimmen,* both of which Boito has translated. At La Scala Faccio conducts *Der Freischütz* in Boito's translation on 19 March. In August Boito takes the cure at the Lido in Venice. Camillo, who continues to support him financially, warns him to be thrifty, since income from translations is not an adequate livelihood.

1873   On 8 August *Un tramonto* [A Sunset], with text by Boito and Praga and music by Faccio's pupil Gaetano Coronaro,[30] is performed at the Milan Conservatory. Boito's Polish aunt Eugenia invites him on a trip to Vienna.

1874   On 24 February Boito successfully petitions the City Council of Milan for the première of Verdi's *Requiem.* His Polish cousin Peter Walewski takes him on a trip to Naples and Sicily. Boito writes *Iram,* a libretto for a never-performed opera by Cesare Dominiceti.[31] He works simultaneously on a revision of *Mefistofele,* on *La Gioconda* for Ponchielli, and on the libretto for *Pier Luigi Farnese* by Costantino Palumbo.[32] Because of a dispute between Palumbo and Edoardo Sonzogno the opera is never performed.

1875   Alfredo Catalani's *La falce* [The Scythe], with libretto by Boito, is presented at the Milan Conservatory on 19 July. The revised *Mefistofele* triumphs in Bologna on 4 October. Faccio writes to Tornaghi from Trieste on 6 October: "I was right to trust the highly effective changes which my friend Boito had made in his extraordinarily distinguished work."[33]

1876   On 15 February Boito writes to Count Agostino Salina:[34] "I am living in the blood and the perfume of Roman decadence at Nero's dizzying court." On 8 April Faccio conducts the first *Gioconda* at La Scala, and the most successful *Mefistofele* in Venice on 13 May. Boito presents the score to Faccio, "his companion in studies, travels, arms, hopes, struggles, defeats, and victories." He completes the libretto to *Semira* for Luigi San Germano[35] in June, but the music is never composed. In the summer Boito goes hiking in the Alps. On 28 August Lucca publishes his translation of *Tristan und Isolde,* followed by the *Wesendonck Lieder*. On 4 November Boito meets Wagner at a performance of *Rienzi* in Bologna. On 26 December *Mefistofele* also achieves success in Turin; Boito raves about Romilda Pantaleoni's performances as Margherita and Elena. She becomes his friend and Faccio's mistress.

1877   Luigi Mancinelli conducts the first *Mefistofele* in Boito's presence in Rome on 4 April. In August Boito is in Ancona for performances of this work, and in September in Trieste, where a further performance of *Mefistofele,* conducted by Faccio, succeeds despite an inadequate cast. At this time a beautiful woman named Fanny[36] enters his life; ill for many years, she will be closely linked with him until her death, in August 1895.

1878   In February Boito is a guest for the first time at Giuseppe Giacosa's country house near Parella, in the province of Aosta.

1879   In early January Boito goes to Turin for the dress rehearsal and first performances of *Ero e Leandro*, composed to his libretto by Giovanni Bottesini. In March he visits Verdi in Genoa, where *Mefistofele* is performed. On 29 June Boito and Giacosa hear Verdi's *Requiem* under the composer's baton at Milan's Teatro Dal Verme. Boito brings Verdi the outline of his *Otello* libretto. He completes the text in Venice and Milan between August and November.

1880   For an exhibition in Turin, which opens in April, Boito is dissatisfied with his setting of "Ode all'Arte" by Giacosa, and it is not published. Together with the French librettist Paul Milliet (1858– ?), he translates *Mefistofele* into French. On 6 July he is in London for the first *Mefistofele* in Italian at Her Majesty's Theatre, and vacations afterwards in Monaco. In September he stays at San Giuseppe in Chiaverano, near Ivrea in Piedmont, and then returns to Milan.

1881   The first *Mefistofele* in Padua on 25 January interrupts Boito's initial collaboration with Verdi on the revision of *Simon Boccanegra*. Faccio conducts this revision at La Scala on 24 March, and *Mefistofele*, under Boito's stage direction, on 25 May. In early July Boito, Faccio, and Giulio Ricordi are guests at St. Agata. Boito stays at Monticello near Monza until August, when he visits the Verdis alone. Presumably during this year he also writes *Basi e bote,* a puppet play in Venetian dialect.[37]

1882   On 18 March *Mefistofele* is given at the Hofoper in Vienna and receives a scathing review from Eduard Hanslick.[38] In August Boito is Vittoria Cima's guest at Villa d'Este, on Lake Como. From 26 to 28 August he is home in Milan, on the way to Arezzo, where Luigi Mancinelli conducts *Mefistofele* and Boito meets the sixteen-year-old Ferruccio Busoni. In September he returns to Villa d'Este. From 26 October on he is once again in Milan.

1883   Boito journeys to Brussels for the first French *Mephistophélès* on 19 January. On the 27th he is in Madrid for the first *Mefistofele* performances in Spain. Retaining vivid memories of the Prado, he vacations at La Spezia and Nervi, visits the Verdis in Genoa on 4 March, and returns to Milan.

1884   In January Boito stays at the Hotel Victoria in Nervi and visits the Verdis in Genoa on the 24th. He travels to Naples on 16 February to attend rehearsals for *Mefistofele*. These are not far enough advanced, so he returns to Nervi by the 23rd and visits the Verdis in Genoa on the 28th. On 3 March he journeys back to Naples for *Mefistofele* at the San Carlo on the 19th. An interviewer's indiscretion threatens to wreck his collaboration with Verdi. In April he visits Faccio and Giacosa in Turin. In Milan, on 15 May, he meets Eleonora Duse for the first time. He arranges for the première of *Le villi*, Puccini's first opera, at Milan's Teatro Dal Verme on 31 May. In the summer he enjoys Alpine tours with Giacosa. Together with Giovanni Verga, they visit Duse at a little spa in the Piedmont. In the autumn Boito is Vittoria Cima's guest at Villa d'Este. From 29 September until 1 October he and Giacosa visit the Verdis at St. Agata.

1885   In January, February, and March Boito is again at the Hotel Victoria in Nervi and a frequent guest of the Verdis in Genoa. On 13 September and 16 October he sees them at St. Agata. In October he also stays at Villa d'Este. On 16 and 17 November he represents Italy at an international conference in Vienna.[39]

1886   In early March Boito visits the Verdis in Genoa. From mid-April into May he stays at Quinto al Mare, a suburb of Genoa. In July he returns to the Villa d'Este. On 14 July, the day of Clara Maffei's funeral, he sees the Verdis in Milan. He spends September at Villa d'Este, working with Giulio Ricordi and

Alfredo Edel[40] on the staging of *Otello*. On 14 October he participates in a production meeting in Milan. Then he and Camille Du Locle[41] begin translating *Otello* into French.

1887   Around the time of the *Otello* première at La Scala on 5 February Boito and Camille Bellaigue become friends, and Boito and Eleonora Duse fall in love.[42] In early March and April Boito continues the *Otello* translation with Du Locle at the Hotel Eden in Nervi. On 23 April, at Nantes, he attends the first *Mephistophélès* in France. He accompanies Rossini's remains from Paris to Florence, arriving on 2 May; Rossini is entombed in the church of Santa Croce the following day.[43] Boito visits St. Agata in June, accompanies Duse on a tour through Sicily and Calabria, meets her in other cities, and in mid-August begins translating *Antony and Cleopatra* for her in a farmhouse they share near Bergamo. By the end of September he is once again with Giacosa at St. Agata. In early and late October he stays at Villa d'Este. Meanwhile he is summoned to Rome concerning reforms of Italian conservatories. Asked to preside over the International Music Exhibition of 1888 in Bologna, he goes to that city in early November. Later that month and in December he sees Duse in Turin; Boito considers marriage and the adoption of her child. In December he returns to the Hotel Eden in Nervi.

1888   Until 24 March he works on *Nerone* in Nervi, with intermittent visits to the Verdis in Genoa and, in late January, to Duse in Rome. In early April he meets her in Turin, and the Verdis in Milan. In early May he travels to Bologna for the opening of the International Music Exhibition. Presumably, he attends there the first Italian *Tristan und Isolde,* in his translation, on 2 June. From mid-June until late August he stays at San Giuseppe, near Ivrea in Piedmont. Duse joins him there in early July. On 17 September he meets her in Pisa, is then at Villa d'Este, sees her briefly in Milan on 3 October, and returns alone to San Giuseppe. Giovanni Mariotti offers him the direction of the Conservatory in Parma, but Boito declines. In long letters he gives advice and encouragement to Duse during the rehearsals for *Antony and Cleopatra* in his translation for her. He stays away from the première on 22 November in Milan[44] and remains anonymous as translator. In December he returns to Milan.

1889   In January Boito is again at San Giuseppe and with Duse in Naples; on the way to that city, he probably sees the Verdis in Genoa. In February he is in San Remo, in Genoa, and back in Milan. On 18 and 28 April he writes to Duse about his inspiring meetings with Verdi in Milan at that time.

[See Chronological Sketches for the remainder of this year through 1894.]

1895   During the spring, together with Giacosa, Giulio Ricordi, and Ulrico Hoepli,[45] Boito makes improvements in the protection of authors' rights. In early June, with Camille Bellaigue and his wife, Boito visits the Verdis at St. Agata. His ailing secret friend Fanny dies in August. In mid-October he participates in the transfer of a Polish relic to a delegation from Poland.[46] On or about 20 October he sees the Verdis at St. Agata. He spends Christmas with them in Genoa.

1896   In mid-February and mid-April Boito visits the Verdis in Genoa. From late August to mid-September he is at Cuasso al Monte on Lake Lugano, where Duse visits him. From the end of October until 5 November he stays at St. Agata. He spends New Year's Eve in Milan.

1897   From late May to early June, and again in mid-October, Boito is at St. Agata, and in August at Aix-les-Bains. On 10 November, in Paris, he and Paul Taffanel[47] agree to perform Verdi's *Pezzi sacri*[48] at the Opéra in April 1898. Giuseppina Verdi dies at St. Agata on 14 November. Boito hurries to Milan for her funeral. He stays with Verdi at St. Agata from Christmas Eve until New Year's Day.

1898   Velleda Ferretti, a thirty-five-year-old woman in Milan, who is separated from her husband, begins to play a major role in Boito's life. He has known her since she was a child, having met her in the salon of Countess Maffei and more frequently in later years at St. Agata and the Palazzo Doria. He sees Verdi in Milan between 6 January and 15 March, and visits him, on his way to Paris, in Genoa on 27 and 28 March. He attends the rehearsals of the *Pezzi sacri;* and Paul Taffanel conducts the première at the Opéra on 7 April. On 28 May Boito hears these works conducted by Arturo Toscanini in Turin. Camillo Boito's wife, Madonnina, dies on 24 June. Arrigo stays with his brother from mid-August until early September. From the middle to the end of October he is

Verdi's guest at St. Agata. On 24 November he sees Duse "for the last time" at the Hotel Hassler in Rome.[49] The farewell—the result of separations caused by Duse's touring and her affair with D'Annunzio, as well as Boito's own attachments to the late Fanny and to Velleda Ferretti—means "more than death" to both of them.[50]

1899   Boito is Verdi's steady companion in Milan until the Maestro's departure for Genoa toward the middle of February. In March he stays at the Pension Anglais in Nervi. In early April he spends Easter with Verdi in Genoa. In August he vacations at Lavarone near Trent. From late October until early November he is again at St. Agata.

1900   On 1 March Boito awaits Verdi in Genoa and in mid-April spends Easter with him. In August he writes to Camille Bellaigue from Castione della Presolana in the Province of Bergamo, about Verdi's excellent health. Together with other friends, Boito celebrates Christmas and the New Year with the Maestro at the Grand Hotel in Milan.

1901   On the nights of 26 and 27 January, Boito and Giacosa are at Verdi's deathbed.[51] In May the publisher Emilio Treves[52] releases Boito's text to *Nerone;* Giulio Ricordi announces the première of the work at La Scala for the following year, with Tamagno in the title role. "What music is called for by a poem such as this!" Bellaigue writes to his friend on 7 July.[53] Critics, however, accuse Boito of ignorance and falsifications of historical facts.

1902   At Sirmione on Lake Garda, Boito writes to Bellaigue on 5 January: "With my own hands I have created the instrument of my torment. My dear friend, what work this is! And how few notes there are today that are truly worthy of going into the score!"[54] He cancels the première planned by Ricordi.

1903   In late May Boito suffers his first attack of angina pectoris, which will later prove fatal. Velleda Ferretti falls ill. In July Boito and her brother take her to Dr. Paul Dubois[55] in Bern. Two months later she is completely recovered. Boito hears lectures by Dubois at Bern University and the two become friends. Back in Italy, he sees the Bellaigues in late September.

1904   In the spring Boito meets the Bellaigues in Rome. He leaves his studio in Milan and works on *Nerone* at increasingly rare intervals. On 24 October he awaits another visit by Bellaigue in Milan.

1905   Among countless letters concerning musical, literary, and general intellectual interests, Boito writes to Tito Ricordi II on 10 December, warmly recommending the young composer Riccardo Zandonai.[56]

1906   On 3 September Boito is in the Apennines when Giacosa dies at Colleretto Parella in Piedmont. At the funeral Giacosa's daughter informs Boito of one of her father's last thoughts: "Tell Boito that his friendship was one of the purest joys of my life, and also my pride."

1907   For most of the year, evidently, Boito is in Milan.

1908   Boito's friend François Coppée[57] dies in Paris on 17 May. On 9 June Boito presumably sees Bellaigue in Milan. In late June he is at Lake Garda, in early July back in Milan. In November he meets the Bellaigues in Rome. During this time Boito is also friendly with Paul Bourget.[58]

1909   On New Year's Day Boito writes to Bellaigue from Messina. At Easter he is in Sirmione on Lake Garda. The composer Giuseppe Martucci, a friend of both Boito and Toscanini, dies in Naples on 1 June. In the same month Boito awaits a visit by Bellaigue in Milan.

1910   The landscape painter Carlo Mancini,[59] one of Boito's oldest friends, dies on 12 March; Boito honors him with a fine obituary. To Bellaigue he complains in a letter of 15 June: "This tyrant of mine [Nerone] keeps pressing me to himself, to my torment."[60] His dream of a *St. Matthew Passion* under Toscanini's direction does not materialize; on 23 November, he writes to Giuseppe Depanis:[61]

> Yesterday, at a board meeting of the Società del Quartetto, the beautiful dream of the *St. Matthew Passion* once again blazed forth.
>
> For this fervent wish we had in mind the exhibition in Turin, and the possibility of a joint fraternal effort between Turin and Milan [. . .].
>
> The *St. Matthew Passion* is the *Divine Comedy* of music. It requires above all the guiding spirit of a great and profound artist, one who knows it from every angle, who understands it, worships it, and who knows how to give it the right meaning and interpretation. For this one needs Toscanini. He is in New York and will later be in Rome, and won't have the time to study that tremendous text. Even Toscanini needs many months to master it.

> And then, beginning with the execution of the figured
> bass of the organ, material and technical difficulties appear
> everywhere.
>
> Where does one find the hundred and eighty beautifully
> rehearsed voices that are needed to form the three choruses?
> Where does one find the soloists worthy of this tragedy? The
> risk of betraying the miraculous work with a mediocre per-
> formance makes me shudder. No, dearest friend, it was an
> illusion![. . .][62]

All the same, as evidenced in a letter to Bellaigue on 30 March 1911, Boito occupies himself for months with this project.

1911   On 7 March the poet Fogazzaro dies; Boito attends his funeral. In Vicenza, Boito, with Renato Simoni,[63] walks through the streets of Palladio, sharing Bellaigue's enthusiasm for the architect. In late April Boito is an influential supporter of the movement to establish a Museum of La Scala. On 25 July he confides to Bellaigue: "I am writing the final notes of the long work [*Nerone*], not without sadness." [64]

1912   Boito is appointed chairman of a committee to establish a Scala Museum, and becomes president of the Società del Quartetto. In early March Velleda Ferretti's brother, Adolfo, commits suicide; her eighteen-year-old daughter becomes incurably ill; and Boito comes to the aid of his friend. On 17 March he is named Senator of the Kingdom. Giulio Ricordi dies on 6 June, without seeing his wish for the completion of *Nerone* fulfilled. Arturo Toscanini and Antonio Smareglia[65] remain faithful to Boito in their belief in this work.

1913   In mid-April Boito travels by automobile through the Apennines to Siena. He is in Busseto on 10 October for the centenary of Verdi's birth, and dictates the text of a memorial tablet to be attached to the house of Antonio Barezzi. In late November he is impressed by the great Verdi festivals taking place in Rome.

1914   With Luigi Mancinelli, Boito attends the first performance of *Parsifal* in Italy, conducted by Tullio Serafin[66] at La Scala on 9 January. On 28 June Camillo dies, and Arrigo writes to Bellaigue on 7 July: "From now on I believe I am no longer the man I was; the burden of age is heavier because of the blows of fate rather than because of the years."[67]

1915   On 20 May Boito casts his vote in the Senate for Italy's entry into the war. In Venice he sees once more Tiepolo's great fresco in the dome of the Church of the Scalzi. Four months later he learns that this work of art has been destroyed by an aerial bomb. On 30 August he travels to Rome. On his return there, in late November, he visits Duse for the first time since they parted in 1898. He returns to Milan on 2 December, but sees Duse again in Rome several times before Christmas.[68]

1916   Duse sees Boito in Milan in the summer and visits him once again at his home in September. His health is declining; his concentration and creative powers diminish.

1917   In May Boito visits the front. In the summer he and Duse briefly meet for the last time, at the home of Antonietta Pisa Rizzi[69] in Milan. In the autumn Boito's shock at Italy's defeat at Caporetto aggravates his angina pectoris. Duse is worried and arrives in Milan on Christmas Eve, but does not want Boito to learn of her presence.

1918   Aware that she is near, Boito sends Duse, via Velleda Ferretti, a gold fragment from a mosaic in San Marco, as a remembrance of Venice. Duse leaves Milan on 17 January. In the spring Boito is brought to the nursing home of Dr. Bertazzoli in the Via Filangeri.[70] On 19 May he writes to Duse for the last time: "I'll probably spend July in a little house at Villa d'Este that Donna Vittoria has kindly put at my disposal."[71] There, according to Carlo Gatti, it is his intention to finish *Nerone* "within two months, working two hours each day." He dies in the nursing home on the morning of 10 June. His body is cremated and his ashes are brought to the Cimitero Monumentale in Milan.

NOTES

1. Cantor of the San Marco Chapel in Venice (*Carteggi* iv, p. 114). See also Nardi, pp. 35–9.

2. Antonio Buzzolla (1815–71) was a composer and conductor. In 1831, he played in the orchestra of the Teatro La Fenice in Venice as flutist and later as violinist. His first opera, *Il ferramondo,* was successfully performed in Venice, at the Teatro San Benedetto, in 1836. He then studied at the Conservatory in Naples under Mercadante and Donizetti until 1839. Two of his other operas were less acclaimed in Venice in 1841 and 1842, but his many compositions for voice and piano in the Venetian dialect have never lost their appeal.

In 1843 Antonio Buzzolla conducted in Berlin and then toured Poland and Russia. In 1847 he was conductor of the Italian Theatre in Paris. Back in Venice, he participated in the uprising of 1848. The Teatro La Fenice produced two more of his operas in that year and in 1850. In 1855 he was appointed *maestro di cappella* at San Marco. As a composer of distinguished church music, he was invited to contribute to the *Requiem* for Rossini, which Verdi planned in 1869 (Nardi, pp. 36–9).

3. Not traced (see Nardi, p. 36).

4. Alberto Mazzucato (1813–77) was appointed to the faculty in 1839, and was director of the Conservatory from 1872 until his death. He headed the orchestra of La Scala from 1858 to 1868. He was also an editor of Ricordi's *Gazzetta musicale* and the author of several books on music theory and appreciation. Among other writings of importance, he translated Berlioz's *Great Treatise of Instrumentation and Orchestration* into Italian. For the intended *Requiem* for Rossini he contributed a *Libera me,* parts of which Verdi incorporated into his *Requiem* for Manzoni.

5. Lauro Rossi (1812–85) was a versatile composer, an impresario in Mexico from 1835 to 1843, director of the Conservatory in Milan from 1850 to 1871, and director of the Conservatory in Naples from 1871 to 1878.

6. Not traced.

7. See Boito to Verdi, 16 March 1890, n. 2.

8. Cesare Cantù (1804–95) was a very active writer, historian, and pedagogue. Among countless other publications, he was the author of a historical novel, *Margherita Pusterla,* and the editor of the 35-volume *Storia Universale.*

9. Carlo Tenca (1816–83) was a writer, a politician, the founder and editor of various periodicals, an unyielding opponent of the Hapsburg rule in Italy, and Clara Maffei's lifelong partner.

10. Filippo Filippi (1830–87), Italy's most influential music critic, was respected and feared throughout Europe. After his graduation in law at Padua in 1853, with little, if any, formal education in music, he became the music editor of a journal in Venice. Thereupon, Tito Ricordi invited him to write for *La gazzetta musicale* in Milan. In 1859 Filippi was appointed music and art critic of *La perseveranza,* a prominent Milan newspaper, in whose pages he courageously and passionately propounded his often controversial ideas until his death. During frequent trips abroad, which he described in his book *Musica e musicisti,* he attended the premières of *Don Carlos* in Paris and *Aida* in Cairo. As a special correspondent he covered Tsar Alexander's coronation in Moscow in 1881 and was sent to London, Madrid, Constantinople, Weimar, and Bayreuth for the inauguration of the Festival House in 1876. Filippi's judgments of Wagner's as well as Verdi's works varied between enthusiasm and rejection. Along with his quest for journalistic sensationalism, Filippi annoyed Verdi with his repeated allusions to Wagner's influence on his operas. (See *Aida* and *Otello.*)

11. Stefano Ronchetti-Monteviti (1814–82), a composer, was from 1859 professor at the Conservatory in Milan.

12. See The Life of Giulio Ricordi, n. 1, above.

13. Weinstock, *Rossini,* p. 135.

14. See Introduction, n. 7.

15. Autograph at Istituto di Studi Verdiani.

16. Banker in Milan and President of the *Società Milanese degli Artisti.*

17. De Rensis, p. 250.

18. Emilio Praga (1839–75)—poet, painter, playwright, and librettist—was father of Marco Praga (1862–1929). Between 1857 and 1859, Emilio traveled throughout Europe

and in Paris discovered Baudelaire's *Fleurs du mal*. This book had a decisive influence on the remainder of his short life. In 1862 he married and also published his first volume of poetry. His father's death, in 1864, forced him to support his family. In 1865 he became a teacher of Italian literature at the Milan Conservatory, but he fell victim to drink, causing his wife and son to leave him. Boito and other friends could not prevent his untimely death.

19. Nardi, p. 207.

20. Eugenia Litta (1837–?) was described by Balzac in a letter to her mother as an enchanting child. She was splendidly instructed in music and literature, and was married at the age of eighteen to Count Giulio Litta Visconti Arese. She maintained a fashionable salon in Milan and was considered one of the most beautiful women in Europe. Arrigo Boito and Emilio Praga were simultaneously enamored of her.

21. An intimate friend of Vittoria Cima.

22. On 17 October 1908 Boito wrote to Camille Bellaigue: "When I was young and an admirer of Baudelaire, I let my nerves succumb to the joys of hashish; the lesson lasted a week and the fun a few days. Once, my brother found me unconscious on my bed, and after that I didn't indulge again." (Autograph at La Scala.)

23. On 21 April, a few weeks after this fiasco, Rossini wrote to Tito Ricordi: "Give my regards to Boito, whose beautiful talent I infinitely esteem. He sent me his libretto to *Mefistofele*, from which I perceive that he wants too soon to be an innovator. Don't think that I am fighting against the innovators! I only wish that one may not do in one day what can only be achieved in many years." (*Lettere di G. Rossini*, p. 322.)

24. Published in the Milan newspaper *Il Pungolo* on 21 May 1868. (Nardi, *Scritti*, pp. 1285–92.) Verdi, too, condemned the plan of the Minister and Rossini's public endorsement. (See *Carteggi* ii, pp. 28, 348; iii, pp. 48, 53–4, 58–9, 64; iv, p. 174.) In protest, Verdi sent back the medal of the Commendatore of the Crown of Italy, which had recently been bestowed on him.

25. He was invited by the widowed Countess Ermelina Dandolo and her son, Enrico II. (See Boito to Verdi, 25 March 1890, n. 7.)

26. Originally planned as a two-act lyric tragedy. Boito incorporated some of its music into his revision of *Mefistofele*.

27. Nardi, p. 335.

28. Ibid., p. 336. The autograph of this letter, in the archive of La Scala in Milan, differs from its published form in Wagner's *Sämtliche Schriften und Dichtungen*, vol. 9, pp. 287–91. Actually, Wagner sent this four-page letter from Lucerne on 7 November 1871 "al Signor Boito, suo vero amico!" He addresses him as "Dear Friend," and signs himself "with cordial greetings Your Richard Wagner." (See Introduction, n. 15.)

29. Swiss composer and conductor (1822–82), a friend of Hans von Bülow, and from 1877 to 1882 director of Dr. Hoch's Conservatory in Frankfurt am Main.

30. See Ricordi to Verdi, 11 February 1890, n. 2.

31. Dominiceti (1821–88) was stranded while conducting on tour in Bolivia, and there amassed a fortune working in a tin mine for eighteen years. He composed, *inter alia*, a series of operas and was, from 1881 until his death, a highly respected professor of composition at the Conservatory in Milan.

32. Palumbo (1843–1928) was an esteemed pianist and composer from Naples, where, in 1873, he was named professor at the Conservatory.

33. Autograph at House of Ricordi.

34. Count Agostino Salina (1830–1906), a music enthusiast, was for over thirty years a member of the board of directors of the Teatro Comunale in Bologna and also president of the *Società del quartetto* there. Salina's support was primarily responsible for the première of Boito's revised *Mefistofele*.

35. San Germano (1846–1904) composed four operas, of which one succeeded, and two—including *Semira* to Boito's libretto—were never completed.

36. We are not authorized to mention the full name of this lady. We know that she was two years older than Boito, married to a commoner, and a very beautiful friend of Donna Vittoria Cima. This relationship was to last quite a few years, even past 1884, the year in which Eleonora Duse entered Boito's life. Perhaps Fanny was, at first, a woman who brought him peace; when her health gradually failed, Boito remained close to her and comforted her until he closed her eyes in August 1895. [Nardi, p. 424. See Boito to Verdi, 9 August 1892, n. 2.]

37. The music historian Carlo Gatti (1876–1965) reported on 30 June 1918 in the *Illustrazione italiana:* "Boito confided to his friends that at one time he had set to music a comedy he had written in Venetian dialect." Raffaello De Rensis (1880–1970), Gatti's colleague, declared that Boito had extracted from *Basi e bote* only a little serenade, which does not appear in the libretto. The composer and pianist Riccardo Pick-Mangiagalli (1882–1949), from 1936 until 1949 director of the Milan Conservatory, succeeded in obtaining and composing Boito's text. His opera was performed at Rome's Teatro Argentina in 1927 and at La Scala in 1932.

38. See Appendix II, n. 1.

39. See *Otello* ii, p. 770.

40. Italian painter and costume designer of Alsatian origin (1856–1912). He began as an illustrator for the House of Ricordi; after 1875 he designed costumes for *Simon Boccanegra, Mefistofele, Don Carlo, Otello,* and other operas at La Scala. His designs for popular non-operatic extravaganzas brought him fame in Paris, London, and New York. (See *Otello* ii, p. 827.)

41. A librettist and opera producer (1832–1903) representing the avant-garde in the French operatic life of his day. He completed the text of Verdi's original French *Don Carlos* for its première at the Paris Opéra on 11 March 1867. This period marked the beginning of his close friendship with Verdi. Early in 1868 Du Locle accompanied the eminent Egyptologist Auguste Mariette (1821–81) on a journey through Egypt. This association culminated in the creation of Verdi's *Aida*.

During the Franco-Prussian War the Verdis were deeply concerned about the fate of the Du Locle family in Paris. When Du Locle experienced financial setbacks, he borrowed from Verdi; his failure to repay the Maestro punctually put their friendship to a severe test. Years later, Charles Nuitter arranged their collaboration on the four-act version of *Don Carlos,* which led to a reconciliation.

Du Locle made French translations of *Aida* (with Nuitter) and, with Verdi's assistance, *La forza del destino* and *Simon Boccanegra.* On his own he translated the first two acts of *Otello,* and he also wrote a drama, *André Chénier.*

Du Locle managed the Opéra-Comique, with Adophe de Leuven (1800–84) from 1870 until 1874, when he became sole director. As such he promoted contemporary composers—among them Bizet, whose *Carmen* he commissioned and produced on 3 March 1875. A few weeks later, Verdi conducted seven performances of the *Requiem* on the same stage. Economic difficulties—aggravated by the initial fiasco of *Carmen*—and a heart condition forced Du Locle to resign as director of the Opéra-Comique on 5 March 1876, just one year after the ill-fated *Carmen* première. Only forty-four years old at the time, Du Locle had lost not only his illusions but also the enthusiasm, vision, and energy that had fathered *Aida* and *Carmen*.

42. A year later, on 20 February 1888, Boito wrote to Eleonora Duse: "Un anno abbiamo vissuto nel sogno! un anno esatto, nè un'ora più, nè un'ora meno." [For a year we have lived in a dream! Exactly one year, neither an hour longer, nor an hour less.] (Nardi, p. 528.)

43. Weinstock, *Rossini*, pp. 373–4.

44. The outcome was not good. Duse, of course, was applauded; but in general the public was cold, and the adaptation was condemned. [. . .] Boito had allowed himself many liberties. There were not only sizable cuts, but also transpositions of lines, rearrangements. Since Boito's English was scant (if it existed at all), he based his work on the French translation of François-Victor Hugo, son of the poet, whose versions of Shakespeare have been described as "bourgeois" and "unpoetic." [Weaver, p. 760.]

45. Born in Switzerland as Ulrich Hoepli (1847–1935), he became an apprentice in a Zurich bookstore at the age of fourteen. Years in Leipzig, Breslau, Vienna, and Trieste added to his knowledge of making and selling books. In 1870 he founded a publishing house in Milan and produced, for the first time in Italy, over 6,000 volumes dealing with the arts and sciences. In 1911 he established a foundation for needy students in Zurich; and in 1930 he funded a large planetarium in Milan.

46. The heart of the Polish national hero Tadeusz Kosciuszko (1746–1817) was a relic in a chapel of the villa Negroni Prati at Vezia, a suburb of Lugano in the Swiss canton of Ticino. Kosciuszko, who had died in Switzerland, had willed the physical remains of his heart to the young daughter of his hosts, who became the Countess Emilia Morosini (a close friend of Verdi's in Milan and the mother of Giuseppina Negroni). Boito accompanied the Polish delegation to Rapperswil on Lake Zurich, where the relic was then kept in exile at a Polish museum until being brought to the cathedral in Warsaw in 1927. It was discovered in the ruins of the cathedral after World War II and was finally laid to rest in the chapel of Warsaw's royal palace.

Boito had written to Verdi from Milan on 9 October: "I will leave for Vezia on the 14th; on the 15th I will travel with the heart of Kosciuszko, and by the 17th I will be back in Milan." Verdi referred to the solemn occasion in a letter to Giuseppina Negroni Prati on 12 October: "Boito has also written me about the well-known relic in your possession, and about the ceremony that is to take place. I might not have had the heroic courage to deprive myself of this property, but I praise and admire you."

47. A flutist and conductor (1844–1908), considered the founder of the present French method of flute pedagogy. At the Paris Opéra, he conducted the first *Othello* in October 1894, and the first performances of three of Verdi's *Quattro pezzi sacri* in April 1898.

48. As part of a series arranged by the Société des Concerts at the Conservatory, the program containing three of the *Pezzi Sacri*—without the "Ave Maria"—was presented, contrary to normal practice, at the Opéra. (See Chronology of Verdi's Life and Works, n. 39.)

49. Weaver, p. 209.

50. Ibid.

51. Giuseppe Giacosa left a precise account of Verdi's last hours (*Rassegna dorica*, 25 February 1941).

52. In 1861, in Milan, Emilio Treves (1834–1916) founded a publishing house under

his name; it continues to be prominent in Italy. From 1871, his brother Giuseppe (1838–1904) was administrator of the firm and assisted Emilio in his fight for authors' rights.

53. Autograph at La Scala.

54. Ibid.

55. Swiss professor of neuropathology (1848–1918) at the University of Bern and author of several books, *inter alia,* on the influence of the mind on the body. Boito became immersed in Dubois's lectures at Bern, and from then on Dubois and his entire family spent nearly every holiday with Boito at Lake Garda.

56. Riccardo Zandonai (1883–1944) was a pupil of Pietro Mascagni and composed several operas, of which only *Francesca da Rimini* (1914) is still in the Italian repertory. Influenced by Richard Strauss, he also wrote symphonic poems, as well as choral works and music for films.

57. Coppée (1842–1908) was a poet, librarian, and archivist of the Théâtre Français. He was a member of the French Academy after 1884.

58. Bourget (1852–1935), author of novels, essays, critical reviews, travel books, and poetry, was a member of the French Academy. He traveled in the United Kingdom and the United States. As a Christian moralist he saw man's salvation in Christianity. His writings impressed the young Thomas Mann (1875–1955).

59. The son of a wealthy Milan family, Carlo Mancini (1829–1910) studied at the Brera Academy and could afford worldwide travel. Even in his seventies, Mancini traveled in Egypt, India, and Burma, returning with some 350 sketches which are now at the Galleria d'Arte Moderna in Milan. Considered one of the finest Italian landscape painters of the late nineteenth century, he brought to his romantic landscapes a knowledge of geology and botany. He was also a musician.

60. Autograph at La Scala.

61. Giuseppe Depanis (1853–1942) was a writer, critic, impresario, and passionate Wagnerian in Turin. In December 1876 Boito wrote to Giulio Ricordi from that city: "Depanis is a rare and intelligent model of an impresario who is a gentleman and an artist."

62. De Rensis, pp. 130–1.

63. Renato Simoni (1875–1952) was an influential journalist, dramatist, librettist, and, from 1914 until 1952, theatre critic for the *Corriere della sera.* He suggested the composition of *Turandot* to Puccini and wrote for motion pictures as early as 1916. He directed films and plays beginning in 1936, and in 1948, he did so together with Giorgio Strehler in Verona. He bequeathed to the Museo Teatrale alla Scala his vast library of over 40,000 volumes, collections of periodicals, pictures, statues, costumes, masks, and autographs. Boito gave him, *inter alia*, François-Victor Hugo's French translations of *Othello, Henry the Fourth,* and *The Merry Wives of Windsor*, in which he had made his notes for the librettos of *Otello* and *Falstaff*.

64. Autograph at La Scala.

65. Antonio Smareglia (1854–1929), a native of Trieste, became a music enthusiast as a student at the Technical College in Vienna. He studied composition under Faccio and Coronaro at the Milan Conservatory, and wrote—under Wagner's influence—ten operas, which were also successful in Austria and Germany. Johannes Brahms and Hans Richter gave their support to Smareglia in Vienna, as did Boito and Toscanini in Milan. His opera *Bianca di Cervia* enjoyed ten performances at La Scala in 1882. Smareglia lost his eyesight in 1900, but was able—thanks to an outstanding memory—to dictate the complete score of his opera *Oceana* (which was premiered at La Scala in 1903, under Toscanini's

direction) and to be active as a professor at the Conservatory in Trieste from 1921 until his death.

66. Tullio Serafin (1878–1968) began at the age of eleven to study composition at the Milan Conservatory. He played violin and viola in the orchestra of La Scala and assisted Toscanini. Following his debut as a conductor in 1903 with *Aida* in Ferrara he ranked among the most renowned of his generation.

67. Autograph at La Scala.

68. Weaver, pp. 300–1.

69. Antonietta Rizzi, a close friend of Eleonora Duse, was born into a highly cultured family in Milan. She was married to Giulio Pisa, a banker and patron of the arts.

70. Dora Setti, *Eleonora Duse ad Antonietta Pisa*, p. 124.

71. Ibid.

The Life of Giulio Ricordi

Giulio Ricordi was born in Milan on 19 December 1840 and died there on 6 June 1912. He was Tito Ricordi's eldest son[1] and became the official director of the music publishing firm in 1888, shortly before his father's death. Giulio had, however, already been de facto director since 1868. Gifted as a writer, musician, painter, and businessman, he began, at the age of twenty-two, to do distinguished work in his father's firm. From 1866 until 1902 he edited *La gazzetta musicale di Milano*, a prominent monthly journal that, in the sixty years of its existence, published the most important news concerning musical life and events throughout the world. He founded two reviews—*Musica e musicisti*, in 1902, and *Ars et labor*, in 1906, that reflect his idea of linking all the arts. Under the pseudonym J. Burgmein, he composed piano and chamber music, symphonic works, songs, ballets, and operettas, which were performed during his lifetime. On 29 January 1862 he married Giuditta Brivio (1838–1916); they had four children. His appointment to the City Council of Milan from 1885 to 1889 increased his prestige and influence on musical and cultural matters in the Lombard capital.

Apart from his special ties with Verdi, this outstanding publisher combined a sure sense for both art and business. Ricordi worked on behalf of nearly all the important Italian composers, librettists, and conductors of his day. As Verdi's publisher and producer at La Scala and other opera houses, "Signor Giulio" wrote *Disposizioni sceniche* [Production Books] for *Aida*, *Simon Boccanegra*, and *Otello;*[2] they not only reflect Verdi's own intentions for the staging of his works but also provide evidence of Giulio's active role in production. His vast achievements are all the more astonishing in light of the fact that he was very frequently ill.

"Immaculately dressed in a formal, rather severe style, a black tie neatly tied round a high stiff collar, the short beard carefully trimmed, the corners of his moustache slightly turned up, and invariably with a slightly quizzical, ironic expression on his countenance, Giulio suggested a diplomat rather than a hardboiled publisher."[3]

His biographer Giuseppe Adami[4] sees Giulio

> at La Scala while an opera in his property is being rehearsed. [. . .] On such days Ricordi has no time to eat or sleep. His life is on the stage. As the publisher, he guards his own rights, bawling and raging all over the place; as the artist, he takes care of the staging; as the critic, he instructs, counsels, and leads the singers; as the painter, he designs a costume or a set. [. . .] Whoever encounters Giulio Ricordi in the street on the eve of an artistic feast of this kind does not recognize him. He walks faster, does not see anybody, has grown taller and slimmer. [. . .] His habitual irony is gone, giving place to an almost morbid nervousness. [. . .] But after a complete and rousing success, our Giulio should once more be seen as the enthusiastic artist, clapping his hands, embracing the composer and the conductor, and even—may Signora Ricordi not hear us—the female singers, especially if they are pretty. [. . .]

After the première of *Otello* in 1887, Ricordi took the young Puccini under his wing and protected him when the shareholders of the House of Ricordi threatened to drop the fledgling composer after the failure of an earlier opera, *Edgar*, at La Scala in 1889. In his stubborn fight for Puccini, Giulio showed the same power of conviction, perseverance, diplomacy, and persuasion that had enabled him to win so many arguments with Verdi and on Verdi's behalf. The paternal tone of his letters to Puccini, however, reveals an entirely different attitude from the filial one in the letters to his "illustrious Maestro." Ricordi's firm belief in his protégé, on the other hand, made him even resort to such questionable tactics as talking Franchetti[5] out of his own *Tosca* libretto, in favor of the publisher's preferred composer.

Significantly, "Ars et Labor" is the motto of the House of Ricordi. Its well-known trademark, three connected rings, suggests three generations of Ricordis—Giovanni, Tito, and Giulio—responsible for the worldwide fame of their firm. These three rings, however, might also be seen as a symbol of the publisher's collaboration with his composers and librettists, the triumvirate of Giuseppe Verdi, Giulio Ricordi, and Arrigo Boito, which brought about two of the greatest miracles in the history of opera, *Otello* and *Falstaff*.[6]

NOTES

1. Tito Ricordi (born in Milan 29 October 1811, died there 7 September 1888) enlarged the famous publishing firm founded by his father, Giovanni (1785–1853), the son of a glazier.

Giovanni Ricordi had been a violinist, prompter, and music copyist at the Carcano and Lentasio theatres in Milan. In 1807, at Breitkopf & Härtel in Leipzig, he studied the latest methods of engraving on copper. Upon his return to Milan with a printing press, he founded his own publishing house on 16 January 1808. In 1814, he was engaged as copyist and prompter at La Scala; in 1815, Simon Mayr introduced him to the young Donizetti, whose publisher he became. Francesco Lucca worked as a music engraver in Ricordi's shop and later became his major competitor. Unlike his colleagues, Giovanni Ricordi soon enjoyed a reputation of high esteem for his authors and the protection of their rights. Being associated with La Scala's impresario, Bartolomeo Merelli, Ricordi published the works of many contemporary composers. His correspondence with Verdi, beginning in 1844, attests to their friendship and collaboration. (See Roosevelt, pp. 134–40.)

Tito Ricordi inherited a solidly established, flourishing business—and also his father's friendly relationship with Verdi. An excellent pianist, Tito was personally acquainted with Schumann, Liszt, Meyerbeer, and other contemporary musicians. In 1842 he founded *La gazzetta musicale di Milano.*

He fought successfully for the rights of composers, and in 1864 was one of the founders of the Quartet Society in Milan. He expanded the buildings that housed his establishment and, as an outstanding lithographer, introduced important technical innovations into his printing facility. Under his leadership the House of Ricordi acquired several other Italian music publishing firms and opened branches in various cities in Italy, in Paris, and in London. Three months before his death, after years of bitter opposition, Tito Ricordi succeeded in annexing the publishing house of Francesco Lucca to his own.

By maintaining continuous contact with the management of La Scala and other Italian opera houses, Tito showed an interest in all phases of the production of operas published by his firm. Despite occasional business differences, he remained on intimate terms with Giuseppe Verdi throughout his life. Upon learning of Tito's death, the Maestro could not hold back his tears.

2. See *Otello* ii, Documents I and II.

3. Mosco Carner, *Puccini*, pp. 52–3.

4. Adami, *Giulio Ricordi e i suoi musicisti*, pp. 165–6.

5. The composer Alberto Franchetti (1860–1942) was also published by Ricordi. (See Ricordi to Verdi, 3 December 1890, n. 1, and 30 September 1892; also Verdi to Ricordi, 9 October 1892, n. 4.)

6. See also Introduction, pp. xxxii–xxxiv.

Biographical Sketches

CAMILLE BELLAIGUE was born in Paris on 24 May 1858 and died there on 4 October 1930. Bellaigue, Hanslick, and Filippi were among the most enlightened music critics in nineteenth-century Europe. All three were trained in both law and music. Camille Bellaigue won first prize in piano performance at the Paris Conservatory in 1878. In 1884 his first music critique was published in the *Correspondent*. From 1885 until his death, he wrote chiefly for the *Revue des deux mondes*. Bellaigue's numerous articles are found in *L'Année musicale* (1886–91), *Un siècle de musique française* (1887), *Psychologie musicale* (1894), *Portraits et silhouettes de musiciens* (1896), *Études musicales et nouvelles silhouettes de musiciens* (1898), *Impressions musicales et littéraires* (1900), *Mozart* (1906), *Mendelssohn* (1907), *Les Epoques de la musique* (1909), *Verdi* (1912), *Notes brèves* (1911, 1914), *Propos de musique et de guerre* (1917), *Souvenirs de musique et de musiciens* (1921), and *Paroles et musique* (1925).

Upon reading the young critic's review of the *Otello* première in Milan, Arrigo Boito responded with enthusiasm and expressed heartfelt wishes for Camille Bellaigue, who was to become a very close friend. His wishes were so completely fulfilled that fourteen years later Boito could write to Bellaigue, "You are the most fortunate man I know."[1]

A most harmonious human being, Camille Bellaigue was closely akin to another dear friend of Boito, Giuseppe Giacosa, and also to Paul Dubois— all three of them well-adjusted family men. Bellaigue's *joie de vivre* was mirrored in the warmth and refinement of his home in Paris, where he and his wife, Gabrielle, his "madonna," would spend evenings reading and playing music. Vacations were spent with their children and many books in the Pyrenees, in Italy, or in Switzerland. And at St. Agata, the Bellaigues were welcomed by the Verdis with open arms.

Like Boito, Bellaigue was interested in all areas of art. He often sought Boito's advice on a variety of publications and rejoiced in his praise as, for example, when Boito wrote to him on 1 March 1899.

> I have read your article "Mazzini–Wagner"[2] and I applaud you as always and with all my heart. This time, you consider your subject from an even higher point of view than is usual for you, enabling you at first glance to make this comparison, which is odd, or at least unexpected, and yet so valid, and which lends your beautiful work so much charm.[3]

Above all else, Boito was Bellaigue's spiritual guide in the realms of Dante, Shakespeare, and Bach. The following lines, written on 27 September 1904, cemented their natural affinity:

> My dear Camille,
> "Toi—moi" *all right.* That's invigorating for a friendship. Using first names has other advantages, too: it seems to rejuvenate the partners (which does me much good). It cherishes truth, and makes discussion easier by eliminating the possibility of anger resulting from the most heated differences of opinion. One fine day you will say to me: "You're [tu] an ass!," and this will have no consequences at all, while "Sir, you [Vous] are an ass!" . . . after this, a duel must be fought. Let's use first names, then, dear Camille; it will prolong our lives.[4]

At this time, too, Boito played for his friend the final scene of *Nerone.* Six years after Boito's death, Bellaigue attended the première of this work in Milan and wrote, perhaps not without understandable prejudice: "No one understood the relationship of word and note, of language and music, better than Boito, the poet and musician."[5]

NOTES

1. In a letter written, in French, in May 1901 (De Rensis, p. 332).

2. According to a police report in Dresden, Richard Wagner was a spiritual ally of the Italian patriot Giuseppe Mazzini. Wagner's intimate relationship with Malvida von Meysenburg, the "friend and confident of the dreaded conspirator G. M. . . . used as an agent by Mazzini" (*Carteggi* iv, p. 55), was to prove, for the authorities, his contamination by the Italian socialist. This "dreaded conspirator" was, however, more philosopher than politician, and an erudite Wagnerian. In 1835, exiled in Switzerland, Mazzini wrote his *Filosofia della musica,* which appeared in the Italian review *L'italiano* in Paris in 1836 and as a book in Milan in 1897. Boito refers to Camille Bellaigue's review of this book in the *Revue des deux mondes* of 15 February 1899 (pp. 918–34), in which his friend discusses "les idées musicales d'un revolutionnaire italien" involving a somewhat utopian synthesis of German and Italian music. (See Chronology of Verdi's Life and Works, 1847.)

3. French autograph at La Scala; dated 1899 by De Rensis, p. 324.

4. French autograph at La Scala; De Rensis, pp. 338–9.

5. From Bellaigue's review of the première of *Nerone* at La Scala on 1 May 1924 (*Revue des deux mondes,* 1 July 1924, pp. 217–26).

CAMILLO BOITO was born in Rome on 30 October 1836 and died in Milan on 28 June 1914. He was six years older than his brother, Arrigo. At the time of his birth, his father, Silvestro, was painting a number of miniature portraits of Pope Gregory XVI, who was a fellow native of Belluno. Later Silvestro Boito sojourned with his wife and Camillo in Naples and Florence, and with his wife's relatives in Poland; finally, in about 1840, the family took up residence in Padua. In 1848, Camillo, not yet twelve years old, joined his father in the Venetian uprising against the Austrian garrison. Evidently because of marital difficulties, his mother left shortly thereafter for her native Poland, leaving the children in the care of their father. When he disappeared from Venice without a trace, friends there took care of the boys until their mother's return. Camillo watched over his younger brother for the rest of his life. At the age of fourteen Camillo entered the Academy of Fine Arts in Venice; he also studied singing. In 1856, shortly after completing his studies, he was appointed to the chair in architecture at the Academy, enabling him to support his mother and brother. On a fellowship he visited Florence and Rome. He fled Venice in 1859 because of threats of arrest by the Austrian occupation and took refuge in Milan, where he was soon named professor of architecture at the Brera Academy of Fine Arts, a position he held for forty-eight years.

On several visits to his relatives, Camillo became acquainted with cities in Poland and Germany, and he married a Polish cousin. Their unhappy marriage was dissolved in 1867, following the death of their three-year-old son, Casimiro, whom Arrigo, in the parents' absence, buried in Milan. Camillo remarried after twenty years, on 12 October 1887; his bride was the young Marchesa Madonnina Malaspina, whom Piero Nardi describes as

> a creature worthy of the house into which she had entered. She herself had a poetic vein [. . .] and she left behind works of verse and prose that are essentially comparable to her husband's. [. . .] When she felt her death approaching, she pretended to be unaware of it and spoke with a smile of the future so as not to cause her husband and her brother-in-law any distress.[1]

Madonnina died on 24 June 1898.

Camillo Boito was one of the most important figures in Italian architecture and art history during the second half of the nineteenth century. Like his brother, he possessed a truly aristocratic culture and had a thorough grounding in the humanities. He was a clear, deeply probing thinker and pedagogue, and in articles, stories, and lengthy volumes he treated a wide variety of subjects. His *Gite di un artista* (Milan: Hoepli, 1884) tells of Bavaria and Crakow, among other places. His chief works on art history are *Il duomo di Milano* (Milan, 1889); *Ornamenti di tutti gli stili*, a comprehensive textbook of architectural styles; *Architettura del Medio Evo in Italia,* 2 vols. (Milan: Hoepli, 1880); and the journal *Arte italiana decorativa ed industriale,* which he founded and published himself. *Questioni pratiche di Belle Arti* (Milan: Hoepli, 1893) is a collection of previously published essays that cover artistic competitions, methods of instruction in architecture, and, most important, the restoration of monuments, an area in which he set guidelines that are still followed today.

"Architecture must maintain a firm hold upon the past, in order to be a monument to an era and to a people," he writes in the introduction to *Architettura del Medio Evo in Italia.* In so saying, he applies Verdi's observation "Torniamo all'antico; sarà un progresso" [Let us return to the past; it will be progress][2] to the realm of architecture. Camillo Boito laid the theoretical and practical foundations—far removed from the principles of historical rationalism of the prominent French architect and art historian Eugène Viollet-le-Duc (1814–79)—of the criteria that are still applied today to the restoration and reevaluation of architectural monuments. Boito knew that works of art do not adhere entirely to a single style, but change and grow. Yet contemporary Italian writers on art, he states,

> advise us to adhere to the Moorish style for our theatres, the Gothic style for our churches, the Greek for the entrances to our city residences, the Roman for our commercial buildings, the communal style of the Middle Ages for our public buildings, the English Tudor style (or else the Italian or French Renaissance style) for our homes, and so on and on; for each sort of building they advocate a different style. There are those who want to see our cemeteries in the Egyptian style, while others take pleasure in calling for the forms and concepts of the Chinese and the Turks. A poet rightly said: "Toujours l'honnête homme ouvrit—La fenêtre des vieux âges—Pour aérer son esprit." [The gentleman opens always—The window of ancient times—To refresh his spirit.] We are so nakedly exposed that a courtesan, as Shakespeare says, would catch a cold.

Camillo Boito's literary achievements were scarcely less distinguished than his architectural ones— even if Arrigo considered them of less lasting value and prohibited the filming of one of his brother's stories.[3] All the same, Luchino Visconti made a film in 1954 based on Camillo Boito's best-known story, *Senso,* which deals with a Venetian noblewoman and her lover, an Austrian lieutenant who is executed before her eyes. In his stories, favorite themes are the passions of women and conflicts brought about by the Scapigliatura. *Storielle vane,* his first volume of stories, appeared in 1876, followed by *Senso—Nuove storielle vane* in 1882; both books were published in Milan by the firm Fratelli Treves. A complete edition of both volumes was released in Florence in 1970 by the publisher Valecchi.

"Physically weary but of sound mind, I bequeath to my beloved brother all of what little I possess," reads Camillo Boito's will. "Then I shall wait, in a niche of the crematorium, until Arrigo, after he has fulfilled his obligation to art, and at as late a moment as possible, is reunited with me."[4] Camillo died on 28 June 1914 in the house he shared with his brother, Via Principe Amedeo No. 1, in Milan.

Camillo Boito's most important buildings are the funeral chapel of the Ponti family in Gallarate (situated 41 kilometers from Milan on the Milan-Domodossola railway), built in 1867; the hospital and cemetery in Gallarate, 1872; the Palazzo delle Debite in Padua, 1877; the Museum of Padua, 1878; the grand staircase of the Palazzo Franchetti in Venice, undated; and the Casa di Riposo per Musicisti in Milan, which was opened on 10 October 1902. With this, his last building, which had been commissioned by Verdi, Camillo Boito also erected for himself and his brother a most fitting monument.

NOTES

1. Nardi, p. 618.
2. See Boito to Verdi, 4 October 1887, n. 3.
3. Nardi, p. 728.
4. Ibid., p. 699.

ELEONORA DUSE was born at Vigevano, in Lombardy, on 3 October 1858, and died in Pittsburgh on 21 April 1924. This renowned Italian actress played a major role in Boito's life. The child of traveling players, she was born and died in hotel rooms. At the age of four she was beaten and forced onto the stage to entertain the public. As a fifteen-year-old she played Shakespeare's Juliet in the arena at Verona. Her rise was slow and arduous and full of reverses. Duse's first triumph came in Naples in 1879, with Emile Zola's *Thérèse Raquin.* She had an unhappy affair with the fashionable Neapolitan journalist Martino Cafiero[1] and bore a child who died soon after birth. She then played in Turin to half-empty houses and was on the verge of giving up the stage when the appearance of Sarah Bernhardt,[2] her later rival, gave her new confidence. In September 1881, she married Tebaldo Checchi,[3] a colleague of mediocre talent, and in January 1882 their daughter, Enrichetta,[4] was born. Duse had a brief liaison with the actor Flavio Andò,[5] who had been her Turiddu in the Turin première of Giovanni Verga's *Cavalleria rusticana* in 1884; as a result she separated from Tebaldo Checchi during a South American tour in 1885.

Eleonora Duse's encounter with Arrigo Boito in May 1884, her second meeting with him in February 1887, and their passionate love affair all held a profound meaning for her, one that continued beyond his death. "He awakened in her a conscious awareness of transcendental values," the actress Eva Le Gallienne writes in her biography of Duse.[6]

> Arrigo Boito was not only an artist, but a scholar, and not only a scholar, but a man of high ideals and deep spiritual fervor. He was seventeen years older than Duse, and became her guide, her mentor, her "Saint." She not only loved him, she revered him. [. . .] He was gentle and unselfish, modest and discreet. Unlike D'Annunzio, he loved her more for what he could give her than for what she could give him. From him she gained her knowledge of poetry and music, of great literature and philosophy. [. . .] She seldom spoke of Boito—her feelings for him were too deep. But years later she confided [. . .] that she had loved him more than any other human being; she felt he had preserved and developed in her that innate integrity of character and spirit, which, without his sustaining goodness, she might so easily have lost. Though life separated them and she went on to other, lesser, loves—their friendship endured until his death in 1918.

Duse immersed herself in Shakespeare with Boito, and he translated *Antony and Cleopatra* for her, but, with characteristic modesty and discretion, he avoided the première in Milan on 22 November 1888. When she played Cleopatra in St. Petersburg in March 1891, Anton Chekhov maintained that he understood every word she spoke, although he knew no Italian.[7] And the celebrated Austrian actor Josef Kainz, who was performing in Russia at the same time, "shouted, cheered, waved his hat, as people do when a monarch passes by."[8]

In Lisbon ladies laid their capes under her feet. In Turin students unharnessed the horses of her coach so that they might bear their idol to her hotel on their shoulders. Admirers in St. Petersburg threw roses in her path, New Yorkers called her "The Passing Star," in Washington she was invited to the White House, and Queen Victoria received her at Windsor Castle. By the mid-1890s, however, Luigi Pirandello[9] felt that she suddenly had lost enthusiasm for nearly all her former roles.

Gabriele D'Annunzio, whom Duse met in 1894, effected this change; he became her lover and, inspired by her, wrote his first play, *La città morta.* For years she gave herself to D'Annunzio and his works, even supporting him financially; but "the indignation and humiliation she suffered through his all-consuming egotism and heartlessness left her wounded and dismayed."[10] Exhausted by the strain of a tour through Germany, England, and France in 1904, she begged him in vain to postpone the première of *La figlia di Iorio,* a lavish production she had financed largely through major loans. Instead, D'Annunzio entrusted the principal role to Irma Gramatica,[11] while openly enjoying adventures with other women. Duse broke with him, but the separation was long and painful. Abandoned and bankrupt, she was on the brink of suicide, when, in March 1904, the Berlin banker Robert von Mendelssohn—a remote descendant of the composer—assumed her debts.

Duse continued to perform all over Europe and South America. At the height of her fame, after a performance of Ibsen's *Lady from the Sea* in Berlin on 25 January 1909, she unexpectedly retired from the stage for fourteen restless years. "Born, it seems, to *imitate* life, without possessing it," as she wrote to her daughter in 1918,[12] Duse read and traveled, establishing no roots and finding no peace, yet forming many friendships in all walks of life—with Isadora Duncan[13] and Rainer Maria Rilke,[14] with peasants and soldiers. During the war she went to the front to comfort the wounded, but with death all around her, she had no use for the theatre.

> She was tormented by a desire to serve, and frustrated by the knowledge that there was so little she could do, so little she could give. She felt compelled to abandon her solitude and join in relief work in the hospitals, with the Red Cross, and at the front. She detested ostentation and made every effort to remain anonymous; she undertook the most humble and menial of tasks.[15]

Meanwhile, she became fascinated and seriously involved with the cinema, which she perceived as a medium of art and poetry. In September 1915 D. W. Griffith[16] invited her to appear in his silent films, but, unable to meet with him beforehand, she declined. *Cenere,*[17] produced in Italy the following year, remains the only visual record of her art.

Arrigo Boito, her "Santo," now in his seventies, came to see her in Rome in 1915, and, over the course of the next two years, she had three more nostalgic reunions with him in Milan. In 1919, Duse, a grandmother by now, spent seven weeks with her daughter's English family in Cambridge. Her savings were consumed by the war, and Germany's inflation reduced her deposits in the Mendelssohn Bank in Berlin. Needing money as well as spiritual solace, though suffering from emphysema and asthma, she decided to return to the stage. In June 1923, after an absence of seventeen years from the London stage, her six performances there drew capacity audiences. On 29 October she opened a New York season with *The Lady from the Sea* in a gala performance at the Metropolitan Opera House. Ten additional performances in five weeks took place at the Century Theater, followed by a triumphant but exhausting tour across the United States. Between lengthy railway journeys, Duse needed oxygen tanks in every hotel and dressing room, but she also enjoyed the company of old and new friends. Her engagements took her as far as Chicago, Detroit, New Orleans, Havana, Los Angeles,[18] and San Francisco. On 5 April 1924, in Pittsburgh, appearing in Marco Praga's play *La porta chiusa* [The closed door], she spoke her last words onstage: "Sola, sola" [Alone, alone]. In a freezing rain, while waiting before a locked door of the theatre, she caught an inflammation of the lungs and died in her hotel on 21 April. She rests in the little cemetery of Asolo in the Veneto, where she felt at home.

NOTES

1. Martino Cafiero (1841–84) was a writer, journalist, and founder of two newspapers in Naples, where his indiscretion almost destroyed Verdi and Boito's collaboration on *Otello*. (See *Otello* i, pp. 156–9).

2. Sarah Bernhardt (1844–1923), one of the most extraordinary personalities in theatre history, was born in Paris as the illegitimate daughter of a law student and a notorious Dutch courtesan. She wanted to become a nun, but the Duke of Morny, half-brother of Napoleon III and one of her mother's lovers, arranged her admission to the school of acting at the Paris Conservatory, where, however, she did not distinguish herself. Thanks to the Duke's intervention, she was accepted, on probation, by the Comédie-Française; but she was dismissed in 1863 on disciplinary grounds. Eventually, in 1868, she was successful at the Théâtre Odéon; the following year she triumphed there in a play by François Coppée.

During the Franco-Prussian War of 1870–71, Bernhardt established a military hospital at the Theatre Odéon. Thereafter she appeared in French classical dramas and works by Victor Hugo, who spoke of her "golden voice" and was deeply moved by her portrayal of Doña Sol in his *Hernani*. In 1879, overcoming violent stage fright, Bernhardt conquered London audiences for the first time. In 1880, with her own company, she toured all over the world, performing exclusively in her native French, as Duse appeared only in her native Italian. Racine's *Phèdre*, Marguérite Gautier in *La Dame aux Camélias* by Dumas fils, and the title role of Eugène Scribe's *Adrienne Lecouvreur* were among Bernhardt's most celebrated roles. Victorien Sardou directed her in flamboyant style in *Fédora, Tosca,* and other plays of his own.

While on a South American tour in 1905, Bernhardt injured her right knee while jumping off the parapet in *La Tosca;* ten years later her leg had to be amputated. Nevertheless, she visited soldiers at the front in 1916. Sacha Guitry, Maurice Rostand, and Louis Verneui wrote plays for her in which she could act while seated. A Hollywood film, *La Voyante*, was made at her home in Paris, where she died in 1923.

3. Tebaldo Checchi (1844–1918) was employed by the Argentine Foreign Ministry in Buenos Aires after his separation from Duse in 1885.

4. In 1908, when Enrichetta married Edward Bullough, a young teacher in Cambridge, her mother's fervent hope came true: to see her settled in England rather than anywhere else. "Throw away that stupid married name of your mother," she urged her daughter, "and that stupid *Duse as well.*" (Weaver, p. 284.)

5. Flavio Andò (1851–1915) performed with Duse for the first time in Naples in 1879, and continued to play leading roles with her after their short-lived affair. She respected him as an elegant, versatile actor and skilled director, but was reported to have called him "handsome, though stupid."

6. The American actress Eva Le Gallienne (1899–1991), in *The Mystic in the Theatre: Eleonora Duse,* pp. 164–5.

7. Anton Pavlovitch Chekhov (1860–1904), dramatist and short-story writer, in a letter to his sister on 16 March 1891.

8. Josef Kainz (1858–1910), in Weaver, p. 88.

9. Luigi Pirandello (1867–1936), dramatist and novelist.

10. Le Gallienne, p. 170.

11. Both Irma Gramatica (1873–1962) and her sister Emma (1876–1965) appeared on the stage until the end of their lives.

12. Weaver, p. 329.

13. Isadora Duncan (1878–1927), American dancer.

14. The Austrian poet (1875–1926) worshiped Duse from afar. With her in mind he had rewritten his youthful play *The White Princess,* dedicating it to her in 1904. During the summer of 1912, he met her for three weeks in Venice, and Duse asked him for a translation of the play, but by then he had lost interest in it.

15. Le Gallienne, pp. 177–8.

16. David Ward Griffith (1875–1948), American film pioneer.

17. After a novel of the same name by Grazia Deledda (1875–1936), a Sardinian writer influenced by Giovanni Verga. Deledda was awarded a Nobel Prize in 1926.

18. In *The Los Angeles Times* of 20 February 1924, Charles Chaplin (1889–1977) wrote:

> She is obviously and frankly a very old woman; yet there is something about her that suggests a pitiful child. I suppose this is the simplicity of her art. [. . .] Behind the child is a great heart that is fed upon experience. [. . .] Of course, the sum of these is the perfect artist: the simple, direct child soul; the experienced craftsman in technique; the heart that has been taught the lesson of human sympathy, and the incisive analytical brain of the psychologist. [. . .] So great is her dramatic power, so tremendous is her knowledge of dramatic technique, that [. . .] I confess it drew tears from me. [. . .] It was the finest thing I have seen on the stage.

FRANCO FACCIO was born in Verona on 8 March 1840 and died in Monza on 21 July 1891. He was the son of a modest hotelier. He received a strict Catholic upbringing and was supposed to enter the priesthood, but he went on to become a composer and an important conductor. He and Arrigo Boito were fellow students at the Milan Conservatory in 1855. United by common ideals and artistic aspirations, they became the closest of friends, remaining so until Faccio's horrible death from syphilitic dementia.

From 1861 to 1862, after completing their studies, Faccio and Boito visited Paris together and met, among others, Rossini, Verdi, Berlioz, and Gounod. After returning to Milan, Faccio achieved fame with his opera *I profughi fiamminghi,* which had its première at La Scala on 11 November 1863. His *Amleto,* to a libretto by Boito, failed in its first appearance in Genoa on 30 May 1865.[1] Nonetheless, in 1870 Verdi hailed Faccio as "one of our finest" young musicians.

A brief military episode in the summer of 1866, when Italy joined forces with Prussia in a war against Austria, interrupted Faccio's and Boito's artistic activities. For a few weeks they took part in Garibaldi's campaign, about which Faccio kept a lively and sometimes amusing diary.[2]

In 1867 Faccio conducted *Il trovatore, Ernani, Rigoletto, Un ballo in maschera,* and other Italian operas in Berlin, where he also became acquainted with *Lohengrin* and *Tannhäuser.* Thereafter, he was active in Scandinavia. In 1868 he was appointed professor at the Milan Conservatory. In 1869 he became a conductor at La Scala and, shortly thereafter, its artistic director. After *Amleto* failed there on 9 February 1871, as it had in Genoa in 1865, he withdrew the work from the repertory and gave up composing.

In 1872 he conducted the European première of *Aida,* in 1881 the revised versions of *Simon Boccanegra* and *Mefistofele,* and in 1884 the revised version of *Don Carlo*—all at La Scala. In addition to Puccini's early operas and the French repertory, Faccio introduced Weber's *Der Freischütz* to La Scala in Boito's translation, with recitatives he had composed himself. Faccio also introduced symphonic concerts to La Scala, his programs including many classical and romantic works by German composers; he especially revered the music dramas of Richard Wagner, shedding tears over *Parsifal.* Writing to a friend between the première of *Otello* and the revival of *Lohengrin* at La Scala, he declared: "A year ago you witnessed the glorious triumph of Italian art on this great stage. This time let us hope that you can be present at the triumph of German art. The one need not exclude the other."[3]

After successful performances of the revised version of Boito's *Mefistofele* in Venice in 1876, in Trieste in 1877, in Verona and Brescia in 1878, and in Barcelona in 1880, Faccio helped the work achieve its breakthrough at La Scala on 5 May 1881. In March 1886, with the first Italian production of Bizet's *Les pêcheurs de perles* at La Scala, he celebrated his thousandth appearance as an operatic and symphonic conductor.

In 1887, in conjunction with the world première of *Otello* at La Scala, he led the work in Rome and in other Italian cities; the first performances of *Otello* in London took place in July 1889. After that, he traveled with Giulio Ricordi, Puccini, and the stage designer Alfred Hohenstein to Bayreuth in connection with the preparations for the first Italian *Meistersinger* at La Scala. This performance, on 26 December 1889, at last signaled Wagner's triumph in Italy. It was also Faccio's final success: incurably ill, he could only lead two more performances of *Die Meistersinger,* and in a revival of *Simon Boccanegra* on 15 January 1890 he appeared on the podium for the last time.[4]

Mattia Battistini,[5] Telramund in *Lohengrin* conducted by Faccio in 1888, spoke of him as "energetic and severe, but not a tyrant. Extremely precise, but not to the point of pedantry. He had absolute control over the orchestra, the artists, and the audience."[6] Giuseppe Depanis said that "the orchestra, the chorus, the artists were under the spell of the little man, who with a sweep of his baton [. . .], unchained and calmed the tempest of polyphony, the audience responding without restraint. This mysterious rapport between the stage, the orchestra, and the audience, a true magnetic current, was Faccio's most outstanding merit."[7]

As the successor to Angelo Mariani and the predecessor of Arturo Toscanini, "the little Italian devil," as the Viennese called Faccio, had such an enormous international reputation that G. B. Shaw placed him on the same level as Hans Richter, Felix Mottl, and Hermann Levi.[8]

NOTES

1. On 31 July 1863 Verdi wrote to Clara Maffei: "Faccio ought to place his hand on his heart and write as he feels, without worrying about anything else; he should have the *boldness* to try new ways, and the *courage* to defy opposition." (*Carteggi* iv, p. 83.) After the première of *Amleto,* Verdi, again writing to Clara Maffei, summarized the general impression: "If Faccio really has talent, then I believe he has to stay away from professors at the conservatory, writers on aesthetics, and critics, and neither study nor listen to any music for ten years." (Nardi, p. 183.)

2. Massimiliano Vajro quotes from this diary in his biography of Boito, *Saggio di bibliografia boitiana,* pp. 103–9.

3. Giuseppe Depanis, *I concerti popolari,* p. 74.

4. See Ricordi to Verdi, 11 and 23 February 1890; also Budden, *The Operas of Verdi* iii, p. 427.

5. Mattia Battistini (1856–1928) was called "the King of Baritones" in his time. Massenet rewrote *Werther* for his exceptional vocal range. Wagner admired his Wolfram in an Italian *Tannhäuser* at Rome's Teatro Argentina in 1881. Battistini sang well into his seventies, appearing in over eighty operas. He never ventured to the United States; an early voyage to South America made him fearful of transatlantic travel. He refused to sing *Falstaff,* since his slim figure would have had to be disguised for the "man-mountain."

6. De Rensis, *Faccio e Verdi,* p. 209.

7. Ibid.

8. Quoted in *Enciclopedia dello Spettacolo* (Rome: Casa Editrice Le Maschere, 1957), iv, p. 1774.

GIUSEPPE GIACOSA was born at Colleretto Parella, in Piedmont, on 21 October 1847, and died there on 3 September 1906. He was an unusually prolific playwright and librettist. The son of an attorney, he took a law degree and practiced for a time in his father's office in Turin, but after his first theatrical successes he decided to devote the rest of his life to the stage. Next to Franco Faccio and Camille Bellaigue, he was to become Arrigo Boito's closest friend.

Giacosa married in 1877. In 1885 he taught history and literature at the Academy of Fine Arts in Turin, but withdrew often to the town of Ivrea, near his birthplace, for periods of intense work. Brief journeys to southern Italy, Sicily, France, and Germany opened the world to him, but he preferred the rather bourgeois family life on his native soil.[1]

In 1888 he moved to Milan, where simultaneously he became director and lecturer at the Academy of Dramatic Arts and professor of dramatic literature at the Conservatory. After only one year he left the Academy, and in 1892 he resigned from the Conservatory as well.

In the autumn of 1891 he accompanied Sarah Bernhardt on a tour of North America with a five-act play, *La Dame de Challant,* which he had written for her in French. In *Impressioni d'America* (Milan, 1899) he gives a lively account of this journey, which took him as far as the Midwest and Toronto. He also wrote about the history and the people of his Piedmont homeland; and, a passionate alpinist, he described his wanderings over the mountains of Val d'Aosta. His work is extraordinarily wide-ranging and includes stories and an imposing series of verse dramas. A close friend of Giovanni Verga and Emile Zola, he turned toward naturalism at the beginning of the 1880s and became, next to Verga, the most important representative of verismo on the Italian stage.

In 1883, the year before her first encounter with Arrigo Boito, Eleonora Duse appeared in Florence and Rome in two premières of works by Giacosa. In the autumn of 1891 she played in the first performance in Turin of *La Signora di Challant,* his Italian version of *La Dame de Challant.*

Giacosa's brooding drama *Tristi amori,* which had been inspired by Boito, was a failure at its première in Rome in 1887 because of its stark realism. Some months later, however, Eleonora Duse brought the work to triumphant success in Turin. Today it is considered his finest work, next to *Come le foglie.*

Come le foglie has been compared to Chekhov's *Cherry Orchard,* while *Il più forte,* Giacosa's last work (1904), is reminiscent of G. B. Shaw's *Mrs. Warren's Profession.* Outside Italy, Giacosa is possibly best known today for his librettos for Puccini's *La boheme* (1896), *Tosca* (1899), and *Madama Butterfly* (1903; in collaboration with Luigi Illica[2]). During his lifetime, however, Giacosa was appreciated as a playwright in Germany and Austria: in January 1892 he attended the first performance in German of *Tristi amori* in Frankfurt am Main, and in the autumn of 1895 he gave a lecture in Dresden on "Il cosmopolitismo e il teatro." On 9 October of the same year, the Burgtheater in Vienna gave the first performance of Arthur Schnitzler's[3] *Liebelei* on a double bill with Giacosa's *Diritti dell'anima,* and toward the end of November 1900 Giacosa traveled to Berlin for a German version of *Come le foglie.*

Countess Elena Albertini Carandini[4] cherished her childhood memory of riding in a cab in Milan and stopping at a confectioner's shop in the company of her beloved grandfather, Pin, as he was called by everyone who knew and loved this kind and happy man.

In the last years of his life, Giacosa often took the waters at Carlsbad. In Milan in 1906, as he lay dying of heart failure, D'Annunzio is said to have remarked to Marco Praga, "A voice is gone from the city—the voice that had power to express the grief of all mankind as the old king of melody was reunited with the mysteries of his beginnings."[5] D'Annunzio was referring to a eulogy that Giacosa had delivered at a tribute to Giuseppe Verdi at La Scala on 1 February 1901.

Giacosa died on 3 September 1906 in the little mountain village of his birth. He was buried in the tiny cemetery of Colleretto Parella on a brilliant autumn day; among the mourners was Arrigo Boito, who had been his friend for more than thirty years.

NOTES

1. Eleonora Duse, his complete opposite, called Giacosa *"bourgeois to the roots of his hair"* (Weaver, p. 125).

2. A journalist and librettist in Milan, Luigi Illica (1857–1919) also wrote a number of other librettos, including *Andrea Chénier* and *Siberia* for Umberto Giordano.

3. Viennese physician and poet (1882–1931).

4. See Introduction, n. 11.

5. Nardi, *Vita e tempo di Giuseppe Giacosa,* p. 879.

EDOARDO MASCHERONI was born in Milan on 4 September 1852 and died at Ghirla, near Varese, on 4 March 1941. He was twenty-one years old when he conducted *Macbeth* and *Un ballo in maschera* in Brescia. Five years later he led the first Italian performance of *Fidelio* in Rome. By 1888 Verdi had overcome his initial reservations about Mascheroni, who soon became his devoted young "Farfarello."[1]

"You cannot believe what an impression the music made on Mascheroni. He jumped from his chair and burst out into continuous exclamations of enthusiasm," Ricordi wrote to Puccini on 5 November 1892, after having played the first two acts of *Falstaff* for the young conductor.[2] After Faccio's premature death, Verdi and Boito recommended Mascheroni to La Scala, where he conducted *Otello* on 15 February 1892 and the première of *Falstaff* on 9 February 1893. In addition to the premières of many new works, including Catalani's *La Wally* (1892), he conducted the first performances at La Scala of *Tannhäuser, Der Fliegende Holländer,* and *Die Walküre.*

The première of *Falstaff* and the ensuing tour in 1893 were the crowning achievements of Mascheroni's career. He left La Scala after only four seasons, thereafter conducting in Germany, Spain, Portugal, and Buenos Aires. In Rome, with *La Gioconda,* he inaugurated the new Teatro Adriano in 1898; he returned there for the theatre's twenty-fifth anniversary with *Norma, La Traviata, Lohengrin, Andrea Chénier,* and *Otello* in 1923. Arguments with Mascagni, whose *Iris* he was to première at Rome's Teatro Costanzi in 1898, led to his withdrawal, and judging from a letter Puccini sent to Ricordi, he did not endear himself to Puccini either. After conducting in minor Italian theatres, his youthful enthusiasm burnt out, and perpetually in the shadow of Toscanini, Mascheroni retired to his villa near Varese in about 1925. The very qualities of faithful and scrupulous adherence to the wishes of the composer, which endeared him to Verdi, were not appreciated by the venerable maestro's successors.

A successful composer of chamber music, Mascheroni was praised by D'Annunzio for his magnificent *Requiem Mass.*[3] In addition to a second *Requiem* commissioned by the King of Italy, Mascheroni composed songs, pieces for orchestra, and two less fortunate operas, *Lorenza* and *Perugina.*

NOTES

1. See Chronological Sketch 1893, n. 6.
2. Marek, p. 157.
3. In the Roman paper *La Tribuna*, 20 February 1888.

VICTOR MAUREL was born in Marseilles on 17 June 1848 and died in New York on 22 October 1923. An artist of splendid vocal abilities and extraordinary skill as an actor, he studied singing in his native city and made his debut there in 1867. Not wishing to remain in the shadow of the famous bass-baritone Jean-Baptiste Faure (1830–1914) of the Paris Opéra, he decided in 1869 to make his career in Italy. On 19 March 1870, in the première of *Il Guarany* by the Brazilian composer Antonio Carlos Gomes, Maurel made his first appearance at La Scala. Between 1873 and 1879 he appeared in each spring and summer season at Covent Garden, and in 1873–74 he made his debut in the United States and in Russia. He shone as Mozart's Don Giovanni and Figaro, and as Wagner's Wolfram and Telramund; in Gounod's *Faust* he alternately sang Mephistopheles and Valentin. Among his memorable characterizations of Verdi roles were Amonasro in the first performance of the French *Aida* at the Paris Opéra (1880), Simon Boccanegra in the revised version (1881), and in the première performances at La Scala as Iago (1887) and Falstaff (1893).

In 1892, at the Teatro Dal Verme in Milan, Maurel sang the first Tonio in Leoncavallo's *Pagliacci*; in 1894 he was the first Iago at the Metropolitan Opera in New York. He returned to New York for the seasons of 1895–6 and 1898–9, while in the years 1894, 1896, and 1897, and from 1900 to 1903, he appeared at the Opéra and the Opéra-Comique in Paris. He sang in Monte Carlo in 1897, at Covent Garden in the 1904–5 season, and in 1905 also at the Teatro San Carlo in Naples. Thanks to his early study of painting, this man of many talents even made a name for himself as a scenic designer for Gounod's *Mireille* at the Metropolitan Opera in 1919. He ended his career as a voice teacher in Paris and New York, where, from 1909 until his death in 1923, he was beset by serious financial hardship.

Among various publications, Maurel wrote an especially informative book, *Dix ans de carrière—1887–1897*. Besides a detailed description of the first production of *Otello* at La Scala, including his own ideas and an analysis of the roles in the work, this 423-page volume contains photographs of the author, a discourse on voice instruction, reminiscences of Verdi in an essay on *Falstaff,* and letters from America, in which Maurel gives an account of industry and economy in the United States, of the American character, and of the arts. Subsequent chapters deal with vocal technique and the singing profession, with the art of opera in general, with emotion in the theatre, with instruction at the Paris Conservatory, and with producing *Don Giovanni*—again including keen analyses of the roles in that work.

For all his obvious intelligence and culture, Maurel had one major liability: he was a capricious star, and he stretched Verdi's patience to the breaking point. Verdi's correspondence with Giulio Ricordi paints a picture of Maurel as a boundlessly ambitious, vain, arrogant, and willful artist, who, along with his wife, was aggressive to the point of tactlessness, daring even on occasion to disregard the author's intentions. In particular, Verdi was enraged by the star's astonishing liberties with the score of *Falstaff* at the Opéra-Comique.

Despite these irritating contradictions, we would do well to listen to the judgment of Maurel's great colleague Lilli Lehmann,[1] who translated his *Dix ans de carrière* into German. On 3 April 1899, she wrote him a letter, from Boston, in French, that reads like a farewell:

> You have given me so much that the gratitude of my entire life will not be enough to thank you; the feeling that you have brought happiness to a woman at a certain moment, the most critical one in her spiritual life, will give you some small satisfaction and will convince you that your kindness to me was not squandered, that it will remain buried in my heart forever. [. . .] My love and friendship for you were no earthly flame, I assure you. [. . .] The ideal of a fine man of enormous powers, with a clear and penetrating intelligence, of rare goodness, an artist of the highest rank, who knows much and understands all, who forgives every error and after such a long and great career is a diligent worker—is it any wonder that I hold him in such high esteem, that I love him with all my heart?[2]

NOTES

1. In her autobiography, *Mein Weg* (Leipzig, 1913), pp. 217–8, the German soprano speaks of Maurel with similar enthusiasm; she also wrote an inspired foreword to her German translation of *Dix ans de carrière*.

2. Theodore Front of Los Angeles, California, kindly placed the autograph of this letter at my disposal.

EMANUELE MUZIO was born at Zibello, in the Province of Parma, on 24 August 1821 and died in Paris on 27 November 1890. He was a cobbler's son and, like Verdi, came from a village near Busseto. In April 1844, on Antonio Barezzi's recommendation, he became Verdi's only pupil, his assistant, and devoted friend. In 1847 he accompanied Verdi to Florence and London for the premières of *Macbeth* and *I masnadieri*. Muzio's total love and reverence for his Maestro are reflected in the unsophisticated reports of these travels he sent to Barezzi—genuine testimonials to Verdi's life and work in those feverishly busy "galley years."

Muzio taught and composed in Milan after that city's abortive uprising in 1848. In 1850 he conducted the inaugural performance at the Italian Theatre in Brussels, where his opera *Giovanna la pazza* was successfully premiered the following year. His second opera, *Claudia,* was given in Milan in 1853 and 1855. In 1858 he became a conductor of the Royal Opera Orchestra in London. There followed extensive concert and opera tours of North America during the time of the Civil War; an unhappy marriage, later dissolved, to a young American singer; and the death of his only son soon after birth.

In 1869 Muzio conducted *Rigoletto* at the dedication of the Khedive's opera house in Cairo, and he led a concert at Ismailia for the opening of the Suez Canal. During the season of 1873–4 he led the first performances of *Aida* in New York and in several other American cities. In 1876 Muzio resigned as artistic director of the Italian Theatre in Paris, a post he had assumed in 1870. He remained in Paris as a voice teacher, and Adelina Patti, whose first New York performances he had conducted in 1859–60, was one of his students. In 1875 Verdi asked him to participate in the preparations for performances of the *Requiem* in Paris, London, and Vienna; and at the music festival in Cologne, in 1877, Muzio once again assisted the Maestro with rehearsals of this work.

For all his gifts, Muzio lacked self-confidence. But Verdi looked after him like an older brother and also asked Clara Maffei to be helpful to him. "He has dreams which will never be realized. He has an excellent heart, but not enough of a head to know the world and himself," Verdi wrote her from Paris on 3 October 1848,[1] and again, from Busseto on 21 June 1851, "You know how capable and how good he is, and that he has a big heart; he is a little rough and a bit of a bear, almost like me, but I repeat, with an excellent heart."[2]

Shortly before his death, in a Paris hospital, without a friend beside him, Muzio wrote one last letter to his Maestro.[3] He stipulated in his will that all the letters he had received from Verdi should be destroyed, in order to prevent their commercial exploitation.

NOTES

1. Autograph in Collezione Enrico Olmo, Chiari; Ascoli, *Quartetto milanese,* p. 92.
2. Autograph, ibid., p. 98.
3. See Muzio to Verdi, 22 October 1890.

GIUSEPPE PIROLI was born in Busseto on 16 February 1815 and died in Rome on 14 November 1890. He was a childhood friend of Verdi. He was raised in poverty but became a distinguished lawyer and politician. In 1848 he was nominated secretary of the regency of Parma and in that position represented Parma's subsequent provisional government. He taught penal law at the University of Parma and was persecuted by Carlo III, a Bourbon ruler imposed on Parma by the Congress of Vienna. In 1859 Piroli was elected deputy of the Assembly of Parma. In this capacity he proposed the decree that united the province of Parma with the Kingdom of Italy. Like Verdi, Piroli belonged to Cavour's liberal party, which opposed the clerical and radical socialist parties. In 1866 he joined the Council of State in Rome and was nominated vice president of the Chamber. In 1884 he became a senator.

Mourning the death of his lifelong friend and legal adviser, Verdi described Giuseppe Piroli, in his letter of 6 December 1890 to Maria Waldmann, as "a learned, frank, sincere man, of a rectitude not to be equalled. A friend, constant and unchanging for sixty years."

TERESA STOLZ was born at Elbekosteletz, Bohemia, on 5 June 1834 and died in Milan on 23 August 1902. She had eight brothers and sisters, five of whom became professional musicians; overcoming initial setbacks, she became the most famous member of the family. After her studies at the Conservatory in Prague from 1849 to 1851, and later with renowned Italian coaches, she appeared in Bohemian and probably German theatres, as well as in Tiflis, Odessa, and Constantinople. Her rise to fame, however, began in 1864, when she sang Leonora in *Il trovatore* at Spoleto and a number of other roles, including Gilda, Lady Macbeth, and Amelia, in Bologna, Palermo, Florence, and Cesena. Under contract to La Scala in 1865, she won particular acclaim in *Giovanna d'Arco* and *Lucrezia Borgia.* Thereupon Verdi chose her for the first performance of the Italian *Don Carlo* at Bologna in 1867; her triumphal interpretation of the role of Elisabetta established her overnight as the greatest Verdi soprano of the late nineteenth century. This brilliant reputation was confirmed by her appearances in *La forza del destino, Aida,* and the *Requiem.* Teresa Stolz's vocal power and technique, her wide vocal range, and her noble, sensitive phrasing inspired Verdi to add "O patria mia" to the Nile scene of *Aida.*[1]

As a witness to a performance of Verdi's *Requiem* in Paris in the spring of 1875, Blanche Roosevelt[2] reported to *The Chicago Times* that

> Madame Stoltz's [*sic*] voice is a pure soprano, with immense compass and of the most beautiful quality one ever listened to, from the lowest note to the highest. Her phrasing is the most superb I ever heard, and her intonation something faultless. She takes a tone and sustains it until it seems that her respiration is quite exhausted, and then she has only commenced to hold it. The tones are as fine and clearly cut as a diamond, and sweet as a silver bell; but the power she gives a high C is something amazing. She is said to be the greatest singer in the world; and I presume it is true, as I cannot possibly imagine any one greater than she. [. . .][3]

Teresa Stolz's broken engagement to Verdi's one-time friend, the conductor Angelo Mariani, and her subsequent relations with Verdi have occasioned much gossip and speculation. Even Frank Walker's thoroughly probing research gives no definite answer as to the true nature of her connection to the Maestro and his wife, whose company she often shared.[4] After Giuseppina Verdi's death in 1897, she remained Verdi's most faithful companion until he died. She survived him by less than two years.

NOTES

1. See Verdi to Ricordi, 12 August 1871 (*Aida*, p. 202).

2. Blanche Roosevelt (1853–98) was the daughter of J. R. Tucker, a U.S. senator from Wisconsin, but she took the name of her mother, who was supposedly related to Theodore Roosevelt. (*Otello* ii, p. 854.)

3. See Roosevelt, pp. 73–4.

4. See Walker, pp. 393–446; and Wechsberg, *Verdi,* pp. 139–62. Phillips-Matz provides ample information in her biography of Verdi, and George Martin sums up the question on pp. 588–90 of his biography.

GIUSEPPINA STREPPONI VERDI was born in Lodi, in Lombardy, on 6 September 1815 and died at St. Agata on 14 November 1897. After the early death of Margherita Barezzi, she became Verdi's companion and, later, his second wife. Her father, Feliciano Strepponi (1767–1832), a well-known composer, gave her instruction in voice and piano. From 1830 to 1834 she studied at the Milan Conservatory, and went on to become one of the most outstanding sopranos of her time. She achieved her greatest successes in operas such as *L'elisir d'amore, Lucia di Lammermoor,* and *La sonnambula,* and Donizetti wrote the title role of his opera *Adelia* for her; but dramatic roles such as Norma damaged her voice.

While Verdi lost his first wife and their children, Strepponi was also beset with tragedy: after her father's death she was forced to support her entire family and two children she had had out of wedlock. Her life appeared ruined. Her star was falling just as Verdi's was beginning to rise with his *Nabucco,* in which she sang the part of Abigaille in the première, in 1842. However, the role was far too dramatic for her. Later, in performances of *I Lombardi* and *Ernani,* she further overtaxed her vocal resources, and in 1846 she retired from the stage to teach voice in Paris.

At this time, Verdi wrote her a letter that, in accordance with the terms of her will, would one day be buried with her. In Busseto, Verdi and his "whore" became the objects of small-town gossip, which perturbed even

Antonio Barezzi, his benefactor and former father-in-law. In response, Verdi wrote him from Paris on 21 January 1852:

> In my house there lives a lady—free, independent, and as much devoted to solitude as I, with the resources to protect her from misfortune of any kind. Neither she nor I need answer to anyone for our actions; but on the other hand, who knows what our relationship is? How do we occupy ourselves, what ties do we have, what rights do I have over her and she over me? Who knows whether she is my wife or not? And in case she is, who knows for what particular motives, with what intentions we avoid publicizing it? Who knows whether this is good or bad? Why might it not be a good thing? And if it were a bad thing, who has the right to hurl a curse at us?[1]

Seven years later, on 29 August 1859, the couple were married in a church ceremony at Collonges-sous-Saleve, then an Italian village in Savoy across the border from Geneva. Ten years later, on 8 March 1869, Giuseppina Verdi wrote to Giulio Ricordi, "Is it true, Giulio, that *in Verdi's case the man is greater than the artist?* For many years now, I have had the privilege of living close to him, and there are moments when I don't know which is greater—my love, or the awe I feel before him, before his heart and his character."[2]

With notable literary interests and linguistic gifts, Giuseppina Verdi often assisted her husband with his correspondence, particularly in French. She shared and encouraged his friendships, accompanied him in nearly all his travels, and, by means of a secret visit to Clara Maffei, she even brought about a meeting with Alessandro Manzoni. A letter she wrote to Verdi on 21 April 1880[3] contains a prophetic remark: "If you bring about an *opéra comique*, you cannot climb any higher. So try to adjust yourself to live as long as Methusalah (966 years), if only to please the one you love." How well she knew what was on his mind!

Despite many periods of depression—such as that caused by her husband's infatuation with Teresa Stolz—which are reflected in her diaries, Giuseppina Verdi was a partner of rare influence and importance. Modestly, she once said about herself:

> I haven't studied, I don't have a flair for any art, for science or literature; but I love the arts and literature, and I sense many things by intuition . . . When I know that the house is clean, that Verdi isn't missing any of his buttons, and the dinner doesn't turn out too badly, I pick up a good book and put to it a thousand questions about things of which I know nothing.[4]

Edmondo De Amicis,[5] a cousin of Giuseppe De Amicis, gives a lively description of this extraordinary woman, who sang in the première of *Nabucco* and witnessed the triumph of *Falstaff*:

The position of Verdi's wife, in some respects resembling that of a prince consort to a queen, was not easy. But Signora Giuseppina was so well qualified—by nature as well as by acquired traits—that in this difficult relationship she never, I believe, allowed even the slightest discord to arise. Her justifiable pride never descended to vanity, never rose to haughtiness; and only an observer without insight could have labeled as idolatry the quite obvious reverence in which her great love for her husband manifested itself. Her constant thought seemed to be to bring serenity and a smile to that face, over which the sovereign passion of his art laid a veil of austerity and almost of sadness, which would not be raised by any breeze of human praise. In this, nature helped her, for it had endowed her with a very fine sense of humor, rare among women, and the ability to apply it with grace and admirable effectiveness, without ever lapsing into slander or ridicule. She could say, wittily: "Who knows what Victor Hugo would give to be able to attend his own funeral!" But she did not say this without first having stated that she admired the poet to the point of being frightened by him. [. . .]

In her face, the features of earlier beauty remained almost unchanged, even towards her seventieth year; the persistent blonde of her graying hair and rosy complexion lent her, at first sight, a youthful appearance; her clear eyes, however, had a naturally severe expression, which was in contrast to the cheerfulness of her spirit. [. . .] She spoke with great simplicity, rather slowly—not through impediment, but out of caution, almost putting her words and sentences, which were few and always to the point, through a sieve; she was never sententious, even when discussing her own art; every judgment she expressed was in the form of a doubt; the charm of her conversation was never deprived of that common sense which had made her such a useful adviser to the Maestro when there was still no other bond between them than that of art. [. . .]

Whoever has not read her letters has not known her well; in them, she displayed, even better than in her conversation, every quality of mind and spirit. Her mastery of epistolary form seemed in her to be a gift of nature as the beauty of her voice had been; and exercising this ability was among her most enjoyable occupations. Her letters reveal a perfect harmony of handwriting, style, wit, and sentiment—in all of these there was the same grace. She could write a fine page about nothing at all, by playing with words, by turning a particular thought round and round, so to speak, and toying with it with the agility of a humorous writer experienced in all the subtleties of the art. Even affection was frequently expressed in the form of a joke, but in a very delicate way, like a smile in an eye moist with emotion. They were harmonious, brilliant letters, in which one discerned many gentle fragrances, as in a bouquet, and never even a trace of affectation or pedantry, never a sentence that betrayed the intention or the consciousness of writing well. In having such a masterful letter writer for a wife, who often saved him the trouble of taking up his pen, without offending the correspondents (who from a literary point of view gained thereby)—in this, too, Verdi was fortunate. [. . .] The Signora's letters were doubly precious when the Maestro added a few lines of his own at the bottom of the last page, in that bold, irregular handwriting of his, which seemed to come from the hand of a giant for whom the pen is too small an implement. The contrast between the two hands gave a faithful image of their different natures, and almost made comprehensible the gentleness which the writer of the letter bestowed upon the life of the writer of the postscript. In fact, she bestowed so much of it upon his life that if she had died fifteen years earlier, I believe Verdi's creations would have ended with *Aida*.[6]

NOTES

1. *Copialettere,* p. 128.
2. *Carteggi* ii, p. 14.
3. *Carteggi* iv, pp. 274–5.
4. Abbiati iv, p. 431.
5. Edmondo De Amicis (1846–1908) was a writer, an officer in the Italian-Austrian War of 1866, and an active socialist. His *Sketches of a Soldier's Life* (1868) ranked, next to his novels, among the most popular stories in Italy. Of similar interest are his descriptions of travels he undertook, after 1870, to Spain, the Netherlands, London, Moscow, Paris, and Constantinople. His portrait of Giuseppina Strepponi Verdi appears in *Nuovi ritratti letterari ed artistici*, pp. 225–30.
6. For the most reliable account of Giuseppina Strepponi's life with Verdi, based on letters and documents, see Walker, pp. 164, 282 and 393–446; and Phillips-Matz, whose view of Strepponi is a more realistic and negative one. See also her article "A Time of Stress" in *Opera News*, 5 January 1991.

MARIA WALDMANN was born in Vienna in 1844 and died in Ferrara on 6 November 1920. She dedicated herself to the Italian mezzo-soprano repertoire. She was heard with Teresa Stolz in September 1869 in a production of *Don Carlo* in Trieste. Thereafter she sang in Moscow and at La Scala, where, during the 1871–2 season, she appeared in both *La forza del destino* and the European première of *Aida*.

Despite Verdi's initial reluctance to engage Waldmann for that première, she became his favorite Amneris, enjoying his and his wife's affectionate friendship. Usually with Teresa Stolz as Aida, and frequently under Verdi's direction, Maria Waldmann also appeared as Amneris in Parma, Padua, Naples, Cairo, Vienna, Paris, and other cities. Verdi then chose her for the mezzo-soprano part in the *Requiem,* which she sang under his baton in its first performance in 1874 in Milan, in 1875 at the Opéra-Comique in Paris, at the Albert Hall in London, at the Hofoper in Vienna, and, once again, at Milan's Teatro Dal Verme in 1879.

Blanche Roosevelt, who heard her sing the *Requiem* with Teresa Stolz under Verdi's baton in Paris in 1875, reported:

> Madame Maria Waldmann, if possible, has a grander voice for a contralto than Madame Stoltz [*sic*] has for a soprano. It certainly is rare to hear such quality of tone in any female voice. Many times one would think it the tenor, and only when one would look at her and see some slight quiver of the otherwise motionless form, could he realize that it was a woman singing. [. . .] She is a very lovely person, with golden hair and sweet oval face. She was also dressed in white, with great elegance and taste; but the dress didn't amount to anything—it was the singing. [. . .]¹

Apart from her extraordinary vocal merits, Maria Waldmann's attractions for Verdi were her personality and artistic temperament, qualities similar to those he had found in her compatriots of the Austro-Hungarian Empire— Teresa Stolz, Antonietta Fricci, Anna D'Angeri, and Gabrielle Krauss.

When Blanche Roosevelt met Maria Waldmann in Paris in 1875, she remarked to Verdi, who concurred, that "she seems sweeter off the stage than even on. How modest she is, and so young! [. . .] She said that she never would have her picture taken, and that she detested publicity of any sort."² Verdi regretted, yet sympathetically understood, Maria Waldmann's decision to end her career at the age of thirty-four, when she became the Countess, and later the Duchess, Galeazzo Massari of Ferrara.³

NOTES

1. Roosevelt, p. 74.
2. Ibid., pp. 80–1.
3. See Verdi to Maria Waldmann, 10 July 1876 (*Aida,* p. 403), and her correspondence with both the Verdis in *Carteggi* i, ii, and iv, a revealing and enchanting documentation.

Select Bibliography

Arrigo Boito

OPERAS

Mefistofele. Prima rappresentazione Milano, 5 Marzo 1868, rinnovato Bologna 4 Ottobre 1875: Partitura d'Orchestra. Milan: G. Ricordi & C., 1919. 467 pp. Plate no. 115310.

————. Rappresentata al teatro communitativo di Bologna il 4 Ottobre 1875. Canto e pianoforte riduzione di M. Saladino. Milan: R. Stabilimento Ricordi, 1875. 271 pp. Plate no. 44720.

————. *Disposizione scenica per l'opera Mefistofele di Arrigo Boito* [revision]. Milan: G. Ricordi, n.d. Plate no. 45401.

Nerone: Tragedia in quattro atti. Libretto. Milan: Fratelli Treves, 1901.

————. Opera completa per canto e pianoforte. Riduzione di Ferruccio Calusio. Milan: G. Ricordi, 1924. 415 pp. Plate no. 119599.

————. Partitura d'Orchestra. Milan: G. Ricordi & C., 1925. 586 pp. Plate no. 119751. Miniature score.

LIBRETTOS FOR GIUSEPPE VERDI

Inno delle nazioni. In Piero Nardi, ed., *Arrigo Boito: Tutti gli scritti.* Verona: A. Mondadori, 1942. 1363–4.

Simon Boccanegra [Revision]: *Melodramma in un prologo e tre atti* di F. M. Piave [and Arrigo Boito], Musica di Giuseppe Verdi. Milan: G. Ricordi, 1881.

Otello: Dramma lirico in 4 atti. Versi di Arrigo Boito. Musica di Giuseppe Verdi. Milan: Edizioni Ricordi, 1886–7.

————. Libretto di Arrigo Boito. Musica di Giuseppe Verdi (1813–1901). Milan: G. Ricordi & C. S.p.A., 1978.

Falstaff: Commedia lirica in tre atti. Libretto di Arrigo Boito. Musica di Giuseppe Verdi (1813–1901). Milan: G. Ricordi & C. S.p.A., 1978.

Giuseppe Verdi

ORCHESTRA SCORES

Falstaff. Milan: G. Ricordi & C. [c. 1893]. 472 pp. Plate no. 96180.

Falstaff. Commedia lirica in tre atti. Milan: G. Ricordi & C. [c. 1912]. 464 pp. Plate no. 113953. Miniature score. Reprints: New York: Broude Bros.; New York: International Music Co.; New York: E. F. Kalmus (folio and miniature score).

Falstaff. Milan: G. Ricordi & C. [1951]. 394 folios, 788 pp. Facsimile of the Autograph. 10 dedication copies printed for individuals; 500 numbered copies sold.

Falstaff. Commedia lirica in tre atti. Milan: G. Ricordi e C. [c. 1954]. 464 pp. Plate no. P.R. 154. "Nuova edizione riveduta e corretta." Miniature score.

See also Chusid, Martin, *A Catalog of Verdi's Operas*.

EARLY PIANO-VOCAL SCORES OF **FALSTAFF**

Falstaff. Commedia lirica in tre atti. Milan: R. Stabilimento Tito di Gio. Ricordi e Francesco Lucca di G. Ricordi & C. [c. 1893]. 461 pp. Plate no. 96000. Numerous reprints to date.

Falstaff. Lyrical Comedy in three acts. Milan and London: G. Ricordi & Co., 1893. 471 pp. Plate no. 96342. Italian-English. English translation by W. Beatty Kingston. Numerous reprints to date.

Falstaff. Lyrische Komödie in drei Akten. Milan and Leipzig: G. Ricordi & C. [c. 1893]. 411 pp. Plate no. R. & C. 96370. German translation by Max Kalbeck.

Editions and Letters

Arrivabene, Count Opprandino. *Verdi intimo: Carteggio di Giuseppe Verdi con il Conte Opprandino Arrivabene (1861–1886)*, ed. Annibale Alberti. Milan: A. Mondadori, 1931.

Boito, Arrigo. *Lettere di Arrigo Boito*, ed. Raffaello De Rensis. Rome: Società Editrice di "Novissima," 1932.

———. *Arrigo Boito: Tutti gli scritti*, ed. Piero Nardi. Verona: A. Mondadori, 1942.

———. *Carteggio Verdi-Boito*, eds. Mario Medici and Marcello Conati in collaboration with Marisa Casati. 2 vols. Parma: Istituto di Studi Verdiani, 1978.

———. *Eleonora Duse–Arrigo Boito: Lettere d'amore*, ed. Raul Radice. Milan: Il Saggiatore, 1979.

———. *Verdi–Boito Briefwechsel*, ed. and trans. Hans Busch. Berlin: Henschelverlag, 1986; Frankfurt am Main: S. Fischer Verlag, 1986.

——— *The Verdi-Boito Correspondence*, eds. Marcello Conati and Mario Medici, trans. William Weaver. Chicago: The University of Chicago Press, 1994.

Du Locle, Camille. "Der Briefwechsel Verdi–Nuitter–Du Locle zur Revision des 'Don Carlos,'" Part I, ed. Ursula Günther. *Analecta musicologica: Studien zur italienisch-deutschen Musikgeschichte* IX/14 (1974): 414–44.

———. "Der Briefwechsel Verdi–Nuitter–Du Locle zur Revision des 'Don Carlos,'" Part II, ed. Gabriella Carrara Verdi and Ursula Günther. *Analecta musicologica: Studien zur italienisch-deutschen Musikgeschichte* X/15 (1975): 334–401.

Faccio, Franco. *Franco Faccio e Verdi: Carteggi e documenti inediti,* ed. Raffaello De Rensis. Milan: Fratelli Treves, 1934.

Florimo, Francesco. "Verdi and Francesco Florimo: Some Unpublished Letters," ed. and trans. Frank Walker. *Music and Letters* 26/4 (1945): 201–8.

Gomes, Antonio Carlos. *Carteggi italiani raccolti e commentati da Gaspare Nello Vetro.* Milan: Nuove Edizioni, 1977.

Hiller, Ferdinand. *Aus Ferdinand Hillers Briefwechsel,* ed. Reinhold Sietz. 7 vols. Cologne: Arno Volk, 1958–70.

Meyerbeer, Giacomo. *Briefwechsel und Tagebücher,* ed. Heinz Becker. 3 vols. Berlin: Verlag Walter de Gruyter & Co., 1960.

Nuitter, Charles-Louis-Etienne. See Du Locle, Camille.

Petrarca, Francesco. *Lettere di Francesco Petrarca. Delle cose familiari: libri ventiquattro. Lettere varie: libro unico,* ed. Giuseppe Fracassetti. 5 vols. Florence: Le Monnier, 1863–67.

Ricordi, Giulio. *Giuseppe Verdi–Giulio Ricordi: Corrispondenza e immagini 1881–1890,* Catalogo della mostra a cura di Franca Cella e Pierluigi Petrobelli. Milan: Edizioni del Teatro alla Scala, 1981.

Rossini, Gioacchino. "Le lettere di Rossini a Verdi," ed. Gabriella Carrara Verdi. *Biblioteca* 70/3 (1973): 9–16.

———. *Lettere di G. Rossini,* ed. G. and F. Mazzatinti and G. Manis. Sala Bolognese: Arnaldo Forni Editore, 1975.

Verdi, Giuseppe. *I copialettere di Giuseppe Verdi,* ed. Gaetano Cesari and Alessandro Luzio. Milan: Comune di Milano, 1913.

———. *Giuseppe Verdi Briefe,* ed. Franz Werfel, trans. Paul Stefan. Berlin: Paul Zsolnay, 1926.

———. *Verdi: Lettere inedite,* ed. Giuseppe Morazzoni. Milan: La Scala e il Museo Teatrale e Libreria Editrice Milanese, 1929.

———. *Carteggi Verdiani,* ed. Alessandro Luzio. Vols. i and ii: Rome: Reale Accademia d'Italia, 1935; vols. iii and iv: Rome: Accademia Nazionale dei Lincei, 1947.

———. "Four Unpublished Letters from Verdi," ed. and trans. Frank Walker. *Music and Letters* 29/1 (1948): 44–7.

———. *Letters of Giuseppe Verdi,* ed. and trans. Charles Osborne. New York: Holt, Rinehart and Winston, 1971.

———. *Verdi's Aida: The History of an Opera in Letters and Documents,* ed. and trans. Hans Busch. Minneapolis: University of Minnesota Press, 1978.

———. *Verdi Briefe,* ed. and trans. Hans Busch. Frankfurt am Main: Fischer Taschenbuch Verlag, 1979.

————. *Giuseppe Verdi: Autobiografia dalle lettere,* ed. Aldo Oberdorfer. New ed. rev. by Marcello Conati. Milan: Rizzoli, 1981.

————. *Verdi's Otello and Simon Boccanegra (revised version) in Letters and Documents,* ed. and trans. Hans Busch. 2 vols. Oxford: Clarendon Press, 1988.

————. *Carteggio Verdi–Ricordi 1880–1881,* ed. Pierluigi Petrobelli, Marisa Di Gregorio Casati, and Carlo Matteo Mossa. Parma: Istituto di Studi Verdiani, 1988.

————. *Carteggio Verdi–Ricordi 1882–1885,* ed. Franca Cella, Madina Ricordi, and Marisa Di Gregorio Casati. Parma: Istituto Nazionale di Studi Verdiani, 1994.

————. *Nuovi inediti verdiani: Carteggio di Giuseppe e Giuseppina Verdi con Giuseppe De Amicis (Genova, 1861–1901),* ed. Leonello Sartoris. Genoa: Editrice Lo Sprint s.r.l., n.d.

Zoppi, Umberto. *Angelo Mariani, Giuseppe Verdi e Teresa Stolz in un carteggio inedito.* Milan: Garzanti, 1947.

Secondary Works

Abbiati, Franco. *Giuseppe Verdi.* 4 vols. Milan: G. Ricordi, 1959.

Abert, Anna Amalie. "Verdi." In *Die Musik in Geschichte und Gegenwart,* vol. 13. Kassel: Bärenreiter Verlag, 1966. 1426–57.

Adami, Giuseppe. *Giulio Ricordi e i suoi musicisti.* Milan: Fratelli Treves, 1933.

Apel, Willi. *Harvard Dictionary of Music.* 2d ed. Cambridge: Harvard University Press, 1969.

Ardoin, John. "Three Facsimiles." *Opera Quarterly* III/4 (Winter 1985–86): 38–47.

Ascoli, Arturo di, ed. *Quartetto milanese ottocentesco.* Rome: Archivi Edizioni, 1974.

Ashbrook, William. "Arrigo Boito." In Stanley Sadie, ed., *The New Grove Dictionary of Music and Musicians.* London: Macmillan Publishers, 1980. Vol. II, pp. 863–7.

————. *Donizetti and His Operas.* Cambridge: Cambridge University Press, 1982.

Auden, W. H. "A Genius and a Gentleman." Review of *Letters of Giuseppe Verdi,* ed. by Charles Osborn. *The New York Review of Books* 18/4 (1972): 17–18.

Aycock, Roy E. "Shakespeare, Boito and Verdi." *The Musical Quarterly* 58/4 (1972): 588–604.

Bacchelli, Riccardo. "Verdi e Shakespeare." *Rassegna musicale* 21/3 (1951): 201–3.

Barbiera, Raffaello. *Il salotto della Contessa Maffei e la società milanese.* Milan: Fratelli Treves, 1896.

Barblan, Guglielmo, "L'opera di Giuseppe Verdi e il dramma romantico." *Rivista musicale italiana* 45 (1941): 93–107.

————. "Rimpianti per un mancato allievo." In *Annuario 1962–63 del Conservatorio di Musica Giuseppe Verdi.* Milan, 1963. 171–85.

————. "Spunti rivelatori nella genesi del *Falstaff.*" In *Atti del I° Congresso Internazionale di Studi Verdiani.* Parma: Istituto di Studi Verdiani, 1969. 16–21.

————. *Toscanini e la Scala,* ed. Eugenio Gara. Milan: Edizioni della Scala, 1972.

————. "Il sentimento dell'onore nella drammaturgia verdiana." In *Atti del III° Congresso Internazionale di Studi Verdiani.* Parma: Istituto di Studi Verdiani, 1974. 2–13.

————. "Un prezioso spartito del *Falstaff.*" Milan: Edizioni della Scala, n.d.

Bauman, Thomas. "The Young Lovers in *Falstaff.*" *19th Century Music* IX/1 (Summer 1985): 62–9.

Beaumont, Antony, trans. and ed. *Ferruccio Busoni, Selected Letters.* New York: Columbia University Press, 1987.

Bekker, Paul. *The Changing Opera,* trans. Arthur Mendel. New York: W.W. Norton, 1935.

Belforti, Adolfo. *Emanuele Muzio: L'unico allievo di Giuseppe Verdi.* Fabriano: Stabilimento Tipografico Gentile, 1895.

Bellaigue, Camille. *Verdi.* Paris: H. Laurens, 1912; 1927.

————. "Arrigo Boito—Lettres et Souvenirs." *Revue des deux mondes* 46/6 (15 August 1918): 900–15.

————. "Nerone." *Revue des deux mondes* 22/7 (1 July 1924): 217–26.

Bentley, Eric, ed. *Shaw on Music.* New York: Doubleday & Company, 1955.

Bie, Oskar. *Die Oper.* Berlin: S. Fischer, 1913; 1923.

————. "Verdi und Wagner." *Die neue Rundschau* 24/1 (1913): 644–55.

Blom, Eric. "Verdi as Musician." *Music and Letters* 12/4 (1931): 329– 44.

Bonavia, Ferruccio. *Verdi.* London: Oxford University Press, 1930.

Bragaglia, Leonardo. *Verdi e i suoi interpreti (1839–1978).* Rome: Bulzoni Editore, 1979.

Bria, Giovanni. "Die *Gran Scena del Sonnambulismo* in Giuseppe Verdi's *Macbeth.*" Zurich: Lizentiatsarbeit der Philosophischen Fakultät der Universität Zurich, 1988.

Britten, Benjamin. In "Verdi—A Symposium." *Opera* 2/3 (February 1951): 113–5.

Brusa, Filippo. "Il *Nerone* di Arrigo Boito: La musica." *Rivista musicale italiana* 31 (1924): 392–443.

Budden, Julian. *The Operas of Verdi.* 3 vols. London: Cassell; New York: Oxford University Press, 1973–81.

————. *Verdi.* Master Musicians Series. London and Melbourne: J. M. Dent & Sons, 1985.

————. "Falstaff: Verdi e Shakespeare." Parma: Teatro Regio, 1986.

Bülow, Hans von. *Briefe und Schriften,* ed. Marie von Bülow. 8 vols. Leipzig: Breitkopf & Härtel, 1896–1908.

Bülow, Marie von. *Hans von Bülow in Leben und Wort.* Stuttgart: J. Engelhorns Nachf., 1925.

Busch, Fritz. *Der Dirigent,* eds. Grete Busch and Thomas Mayer. Frankfurt am Main: Fischer Taschenbuch Verlag, 1990.

Busch, Hans. "(Signed) G. Verdi." *Opera News* 36/19 (1972): 8–11.

————. "Verdi as His Own Interpreter." *Your Musical Cue* 1/2 (1973): 4–10.

————. "Destined to Meet." *Opera Quarterly* 5/2,3 (Summer–Autumn 1987): 4–23.

SELECT BIBLIOGRAPHY

Busoni, Ferruccio. *Scritti e pensieri sulla musica,* eds. Luigi Dallapiccola and Guido M. Gatti. Milan: G. Ricordi, 1954.

Büthe, Otfried, and Almut Lück-Bochat, eds. and trans. *Giuseppe Verdi Briefe zu seinem Schaffen.* Frankfurt am Main: G. Ricordi, 1963.

Cafasi, Francesco. *Giuseppe Verdi, fattore di Sant'Agata.* Busseto: Cassa di Risparmio, n.d.

Cambiasi, Pompeo, ed. *La Scala: Note storiche e statistiche, 1778–1906.* Milan: G. Ricordi, 1906.

Caponi, Jacopo. See Folchetto (pseudonym).

Carlyle, Thomas. *On Heroes, Hero-worship, and the Heroic in History.* London: James Fraser, 1841.

Carner, Mosco. *Puccini: A Critical Biography.* 3d rev. ed. New York: Holmes & Meier, 1992.

Cassi, Paolo. "Gerolamo Magnani e il suo carteggio con Verdi." In *Vecchie cronache di Fidenza.* Milan: Stabilimento Tipografico Gazzetta dello Sport, 1941. 129–35.

Cazzulani, Elena. *Giuseppina Strepponi.* Lodi: Edizioni Lodigraf, 1990.

Cella, Franca, and Pierluigi Petrobelli, eds. *Giuseppe Verdi–Giulio Ricordi: Corrispondenze e immagini 1881–1890.* Milan: Teatro alla Scala, 1982.

Celletti, Rodolfo. *Le grandi voci.* 3 vols. Rome: Istituto per la Collaborazione Culturale, 1964.

———. "La vocalità di Falstaff." Parma: Grafiche Step Editrice, n.d.

Celli, Teodoro. *"Falstaff."* Teatro alla Scala Stagione 1980/81 [Program], 86–91.

Cenzato, Giovanni. *Itinerari verdiani.* Milan: Ceschina, 1955.

Cesari, Gaetano. *"Nerone* di Boito al Teatro alla Scala." *Musica d'oggi* 6/4–5 (1924): 109–24.

Checchi, Eugenio. *Giuseppe Verdi: Il genio e le opere.* 3d ed. Florence: G. Barbera, 1926.

Chop, Max. *Giuseppe Verdi.* 3d ed. Leipzig: Reclam, 1938.

Chotzinoff, Samuel. *Toscanini: An Intimate Portrait.* New York: Alfred A. Knopf, 1956.

Chusid, Martin, ed. *A Catalog of Verdi's Operas.* Hackensack, NJ: Joseph Boonin, 1974.

———, and William Weaver, eds. *The Verdi Companion.* New York: W. W. Norton, 1979.

Ciampelli, Giulio Mario. *Le opere verdiane al Teatro alla Scala (1839–1929).* Milan: La Scala e il Museo Teatrale e Libreria Editrice Milanese, 1929.

Conati, Marcello, ed. *Interviste e incontri con Verdi.* Milan: Edizioni Il Formichiere, 1980.

———. *Encounters with Verdi,* trans. Richard Stokes. London: Victor Gollancz; Ithaca, NY: Cornell University Press, 1984.

Cone, John Frederick. *Adelina Patti: Queen of Hearts.* Portland: Amadeus Press, 1993.

Confalonieri, Giulio. *A Hundred Years of Concerts at "La Società del Quartetto" of Milan.* Milan: La Società del Quartetto, 1964.

Conrad, Peter. "Operatic Shakespeare." In *Romantic Opera and Literary Form.* Berkeley: University of California Press, 1977. 43–69.

Costantini, Teodoro, ed. *Sei lettere inedite di Giuseppe Verdi a Giovanni Bottesini.* Trieste: C. Schmidl, 1908.

Covington, Richard. "The Aria Never Ends in the Opera That's Casa Verdi." [La Casa di Riposo.] *Smithsonian* 26/9 (December 1995): 93–8.

Craft, Robert. "The Giant of Busseto." *The New York Review of Books* 22/4 (1975): 3–4.

Croce, Benedetto. *La letteratura della Nuova Italia, saggi critici.* Vol. I. 2d ed. Bari: Giuseppe Laterza e Figli, 1921. 257–74.

Dallapiccola, Luigi. "Reflections on three Verdi operas." *19th Century Music* 7/1 (Summer 1983): 55–62.

De Amicis, Edmondo. *Nuovi ritratti letterari ed artistici.* Milan: Fratelli Treves, 1908–9; 1920.

Dean, Winton. *Essays on Opera.* Oxford: Clarendon Press, 1990.

De Angelis, Alberto, ed. "G. Verdi e il Senatore G. Piroli: Un epistolario inedito." *Musica d'oggi* 18/3 (1940): 59–63.

De Filippis, Felice. *Il Teatro di San Carlo.* Naples: Città di Napoli, 1951.

———. "Verdi e gli amici di Napoli." *Bollettino quadrimestrale dell'Istituto di Studi Verdiani* 1/3 (1960): 1365–72.

Degrada, Francesco. *Il palazzo incantato: Studi sulla tradizione del melodramma dal Barocco al Romanticismo.* Vol. II. Fiesole: Discanto Edizioni, 1979.

Della Corte, Andrea. "Verdi e Boito inediti nei ricordi di Edoardo Mascheroni." *Musica d'oggi* 7/7 (1925): 214–43.

———. *Giuseppe Verdi.* Turin: Edizioni Arione, [1939].

———. *Le sei piu belle opere di Giuseppe Verdi.* Milan: Treccani, 1957.

———. *Toscanini visto da un critico.* Turin: ILTE, 1958.

Depanis, Giuseppe. *I concerti popolari ed il Teatro Regio di Torino: Quindici anni di vita musicale: Appunti-Ricordi.* 2 vols. Turin: S.T.E.N., 1915.

De Rensis, Raffaello. *L'Amleto' di Arrigo Boito.* Ancona, 1927.

———. *Arrigo Boito: Aneddoti e bizzarrie poetiche musicali.* Rome: Fratelli Palombi, 1942.

———. *Arrigo Boito: Capitoli biografici.* Florence: G. C. Sansoni, 1942.

———, ed. *Critiche e cronache musicali di Arrigo Boito (1862–1870).* Milan: Fratelli Treves, 1931.

———, ed. *Franco Faccio e Verdi: Carteggi e documenti inediti.* Milan: Fratelli Treves, 1934.

Destranges, Etienne. *L'Evolution musicale chez Verdi. Aida—Othello—Falstaff.* Paris: Fischbacher, 1895.

———. *Consonnances et dissonances: Etudes musicales.* Paris: Fischbacher, 1906.

Duault, Alain. *Verdi, la musique et le drama.* Paris: Gallimard, 1906.

Duncan, Isadora. *My Life.* New York: Boni & Liveright, 1927.

Dupré, Giovanni. *Pensieri sull'arte e ricordi autobiografici.* Florence: Successori Le Monnier, 1880.

Einstein, Alfred. *Greatness in Music.* New York: Oxford University Press, 1941.

―――. *Music in the Romantic Era.* New York: W. W. Norton, 1947.

Enciclopedia della Spettacolo. 9 vols. Rome: Le Maschere, 1954–62.

Escudier, Léon. *Mes souvenirs.* Paris: E. Dentu, 1863.

Fellner, Rudolph. *Opera Themes and Plots.* New York: Simon and Schuster, 1958.

Ferrari, Paolo Emilio. *Spettacoli drammatico–musicali e coreografici in Parma dall'anno 1628 all'anno 1883.* Parma: L. Battei, 1884.

Fétis, François Joseph. *Histoire générale de la musique.* Paris: Librairie de Firmin Didot Frères, 1869.

Filippi, Filippo. *Musica e musicisti: Critiche, biografie ed escursioni.* Milan: Libreria Editrice G. Brigola, 1876.

Fioretto, Giovanni, ed. *Le poesie di Giuseppe Giusti.* Verona: H. F. Münster, Carlo Kayser Successore, 1877.

Fleming, Shirley. "A Noisy Bantling in Old New York." *High Fidelity* 13/10 (1963): 82–9.

Foerster Lovedat, Lilian. "A Plan of Action." *Opera News* 27/6 (1962): 9–13.

Folchetto, ed. and trans. *A. Pougin: Giuseppe Verdi-Vita aneddotica con note ed aggiunte di Folchetto.* Milan: Ricordi, 1881.

Fortis, Leone. "Il vecchio maestro." *Gazzetta Musicale di Milano* XLV/49 (7 December 1890): 773–5.

Friedlaender, Maryla. "How *Aida* Was Written." *Opera News* 6/18 (1942): 20–5.

―――. "*Aida* and the Cult of Isis." *Opera News* 11/10 (1946): 10–2.

―――. "*Aida's* Milan Premiere." *Opera News* 17/12 (1953): 27–8.

Fusero, Clemente. *Eleonora Duse.* Milan: dall'Oglio, 1971.

Gál, Hans. "A Deleted Episode in Verdi's *Falstaff.*" *The Music Review* 2 (1941): 266–72.

―――. *Drei Meister—Drei Welten: Brahms—Wagner—Verdi.* Frankfurt am Main: S. Fischer, 1975.

―――, ed. *The Musician's World: Great Composers in Their Letters.* New York: Arco Publishing, 1966.

Gara, Eugenio, ed. *Carteggi Pucciniani.* Milan: G. Ricordi & C., 1958.

Garibaldi, Luigi Agostino, ed. *Giuseppe Verdi nelle lettere di Emanuele Muzio ad Antonio Barezzi.* Milan: Fratelli Treves, 1931.

Gatti, Carlo. *Verdi.* 2 vols. Milan: Alpes, 1931. Milan: A. Mondadori, 2d ed., 1951; 3d ed., 1953; new rev. ed., 1981.

―――. *Verdi nelle immagini.* Milan: Garzanti, 1941.

Genest, Émile. *L'Opéra-Comique; connu et inconnu.* Paris: Fischbacher, 1925.

Gerhartz, Leo Karl. *Versuch über Falstaff: Zu autobiographischen Aspekten von Verdis letzter Oper.* Goldschmidt Festschrift. Dortmund, 1986.

Gerigk, Herbert. *Giuseppe Verdi.* Potsdam: Athenaion, 1932.

Ghislanzoni, Antonio. *Gli artisti di teatro.* 2d ed. Milan: Ultra, 1944.

Giani, R. "Il *Nerone* di Arrigo Boito. La concenzione e il poema." *Rivista musicale italiana* 31 (1924): 235–392.

Gibelli, Vincenzo. *Anton Chechov: Poeta della vita russa.* Milan: Giuffre Editore, 1970.

Girardi, Michele. "French Sources of *Falstaff* and Some Aspects of Its Musical Dramaturgy," trans. William Ashbrook. *Opera Quarterly* 11/3 (1995): 45–63.

———. *"Dal labbro il canto estesiato vola . . .* Sir John Falstaff da Shakespeare a Boito sino a Verdi." Parma: Grafiche Step Editrice, n.d.

Godefroy, Vincent. *The Dramatic Genius of Verdi.* 2 vols. London: V. Gollancz, 1975; New York: St. Martin's Press, 1978.

Gossett, Philip. Review of *Letters of Giuseppe Verdi,* edited by Charles Osborne. *The Musical Quarterly* 59/4 (1973): 633–9.

———. "Verdi, Ghislanzoni, and *Aida*: The Uses of Convention." *Critical Inquiry* 1 (1974): 291–334.

Gourret, Jean. *Dictionnaire des chanteurs de l'Opéra de Paris.* Paris: Éditions Albatros, 1982.

Gräwe, Karl Dietrich. "Shakespeares dramatische Charaktere und Verdis Operngestalten. Über das Verhältnis von Dramentext und Opernlibretto." In *Atti del I° Congresso Internazionale di Studi Verdiani.* Parma: Istituto di Studi Verdiani, 1969. Pp. 120–5.

Gray, Cecil. "Verdi and Shakespeare." *Opera* 2/3 (February 1951): 118–23.

Grout, Donald Jay. *A Short History of Opera.* New York: Columbia University Press, 1954.

Guglielmi, Edoardo. "Itinerario di *Falstaff.*" Parma: Teatro Regio, 1986.

Gui, Vittorio. "Arrigo Boito." In *Enciclopedia della Musica,* vol. I. Milan: Ricordi, 1963. Pp. 283–4.

Günther, Ursula. "Zur Entstehung von Verdis *Aida.*" *Studi Musicali* II/1 (1973): 15–71.

———. "Documents inconnus concernant les relations de Verdi avec l'Opéra de Paris." In *Atti del III° Congresso Internazionale di Studi Verdiani.* Parma: Istituto di Studi Verdiani, 1974. Pp. 564–83.

Hanslick, Eduard. *Die moderne Oper: Kritiken und Studien.* Berlin: A. Hofmann, 1875.

———. *Die moderne Oper.* Vol. III: *Aus dem Opernleben der Gegenwart.* Berlin: Allgemeiner Verein für Deutsche Litteratur, 1884.

———. *Suite: Aufsätze über Musik und Musiker.* Vienna and Teschen: K. Prochaska, 1885.

———. *Die moderne Oper.* Vol. IV: *Musikalisches Skizzenbuch.* Berlin: Allgemeiner Verein für Deutsche Litteratur, 1888.

———. *Aus meinem Leben.* 2 vols. Berlin: Allgemeiner Verein für Deutsche Litteratur, 1894, 1911.

———. *Die moderne Oper.* Vol. IX: *Aus neuer und neuester Zeit.* Berlin: Allgemeiner Verein für Deutsche Litteratur, 1900.

———. *Music Criticisms, 1846–99,* ed. and trans. Henry Pleasants. Baltimore: Penguin Books, 1963.

Hawks, Francis L. *The Monuments of Egypt.* New York: George S. Putnam, 1850.

Helbling, Hanno. *Arrigo Boito.* Munich and Mainz: Piper-Schott, 1995.

Henriot, Patrice. "*Aida* ou la subjectivité ensevelie." *L'Avant-Scène Opéra* 4 (1976): 4–8.

Hepokoski, James A. "Verdi, Giuseppina Pasqua, and the Composition of *Falstaff.*" *19th Century Music* 3/3 (March 1980): 239–50.

———. *Giuseppe Verdi: Otello.* Cambridge: Cambridge University Press, 1987.

———. *Giuseppe Verdi: Falstaff.* Cambridge: Cambridge University Press, 1993.

———. "Overriding the Autograph Score: The Problem of Textual Authority in Verdi's *Falstaff.*" *Verdi Newsletter* 22 (1995): 27.

Heuberger, Richard. *Erinnerungen an Johannes Brahms.* Tutzing: Hans Schneider, 1971.

Holl, Karl. *Verdi.* Berlin: Karl Siegismund, 1939.

Hopkinson, Cecil. *A Bibliography of the Works of Giuseppe Verdi.* 2 vols. New York: Broude Brothers, 1973; 1978.

Hughes, Spike. *The Toscanini Legacy.* London: Putnam, 1959.

———. "An Afternoon at St. Agata." *Opera News* 32/9 (1967): 8–13.

———. *Famous Verdi Operas.* Philadelphia: Chilton, 1968.

———, and Barbara McFadyean. *Nights at the Opera.* London: Pilot Press, 1948.

Humbert, Jean. "*Aida* entre l'égyptologie et l'égyptomanie." *L'Avant-Scène Opéra* 4 (1976): 9–14.

Hume, Paul. *Verdi: The Man and His Music.* New York: E. P. Dutton, 1977; London: Hutchinson, 1978.

Humphreys, Dena. "Verdi's Peak of Progress." *Opera News* 12/8 (1948): 11–5.

Huret, Jules. "Une répétition de *Falstaff.*" *Le Figaro* (Paris), 5 April 1894.

Hussey, Dyneley. *Verdi.* London: J. M. Dent, 1940.

Irvine, Demar. *Massenet: A Chronicle of His Life and Times.* Portland: Amadeus Press, 1993.

Istel, Edgar. "Verdi und Shakespeare." *Jahrbuch der Deutschen Shakespeare Gesellschaft* III (1917): 69–124.

———. "A Genetic Study of the *Aida* Libretto," trans. Otto Kinkeldey. *The Musical Quarterly* 3/1 (1917): 34–52.

Kerman, Joseph. *Opera as Drama.* 2d ed. New York: Vintage Books, 1959.

———. *Contemplating Music: Challenges to Musicology.* Cambridge: Harvard University Press, 1985.

Kerner, Leighton. "Verdi's Green-eyed Monster: Jealousy Themes in *Otello* and *Falstaff.*" *Opera News* 60/10 (1996): 12–4.

Kimbell, David R. *Verdi in the Age of Italian Romanticism.* Cambridge: Cambridge University Press, 1981.

Klein, Herman. *The Reign of Patti.* New York: Century, 1920.

Klein, John W. "Verdi's Attitude to His Contemporaries." *The Music Review* 10/4 (1949): 264–76.

Kolodin, Irving. *The Metropolitan Opera 1883–1966: A Candid History.* New York: Alfred A. Knopf, 1966.

Kovacs, Janos. "Zum Spätstil Verdis." In *Atti del I° Congresso Internazionale di Studi Verdiani.* Parma: Istituto di Studi Verdiani, 1972. 132–44.

Kozma, Tibor. "Heroes of Wood and Brass: The Trombone in *Aida.*" *Opera News* 16/18 (1952): 264–76.

Krehbiel, Henry E. *Chapters of Opera.* New York: Henry Holt, 1908.

———. *A Book of Operas.* New York: Macmillan, 1909.

Kühner, Hans. *Giuseppe Verdi in Selbstzeugnissen und Bilddokumenten.* Reinbeck bei Hamburg: Rowohlt, 1961.

———. "Verdi e la Germania." In *Atti del I° Congresso Internazionale di Studi Verdiani.* Parma: Istituto di Studi Verdiani, 1969. 364–6.

Landon, H. C. Robbins. *Das kleine Verdibuch.* Salzburg: Residenz Verlag, 1976; 2d ed., Hamburg: Rowohlt, 1982.

Le Gallienne, Eva. *The Mystic in the Theatre: Eleonora Duse.* New York: Farrar, Straus & Giroux, 1966.

Lehmann, Lilli. *Mein Weg.* Leipzig: S. Hirzel, 1913.

Lessona, Michele. *Volere e Potere.* Florence: G. Barbera, 1882.

———. *Dalla Traviata al'Otello.* Rome: Istituto Grafico Tiberino, 1941.

Levi, Primo. *Verdi.* Rome: Stab. Tip. della *Tribuna,* 1901.

———. *Domenico Morelli nella vita e nell'arte.* Rome and Turin: Casa Editrice Nazionale Roux e Viarengo, 1906.

Lippmann, Friedrich, ed. *Colloquium Verdi—Wagner Rom 1969.* In Analecta musicologica 11. Cologne and Vienna: Böhlau, 1972.

Lipsius, Marie (pseud. La Mara). *Musikerbriefe aus fünf Jahrhunderten.* 2 vols. Leipzig: Breitkopf & Härtel [1886].

Loewenberg, Alfred, ed. *Annals of Opera 1597–1940.* Totowa, NJ: Rowman and Littlefield, 1978.

Lombroso, Cesare. "Il fenomeno psicologico di Verdi." *Gazzetta Musicale di Milano* XLVIII/10 (5 March 1893): 159–60.

Lualdi, Adriano. "Arrigo Boito—Un' Anima." *Rivista musicale italiana* 25 (1918): 524–49.

Lunari, Luigi. "Falstaff: genesi di un personaggio." Program of Teatro alla Scala 1980–81. 130–1.

Luzio, Alessandro. *Garibaldi—Cavour—Verdi.* Turin: Fratelli Bocca, 1924.

Mackenzie, Alexander C. *A Musician's Narrative.* London: Cassell & Co., 1927.

Macnutt, Richard. "The Ricordi Firm." In Stanley Sadie, ed., *The New Grove Dictionary of Music and Musicians.* London: Macmillan Publishers, 1980. Vol. XV, pp. 851–5.

Mancinelli, Luisa. *Giuseppe Verdi: Ricordi personali.* Genoa: Narcisi, 1936.

Mann, Golo. "Der Brief in der Weltliteratur." In *Deutsche Akademie für Sprache und Dichtung.* Darmstadt Jahrbuch 1975. Heidelberg: Lambert Schneider, 1976. Pp. 77–99.

Marchesi, Gustavo. *Giuseppe Verdi.* Turin: Utet, 1970.

———. *Giuseppe Verdi e il Conservatorio di Parma (1836–1901).* Parma: Tipolito la Ducale, 1976.

———. *Verdi.* Milan: Fabbri Editori, 1979.

———. *Arturo Toscanini.* Turin: Utet, 1993.

———— and Mario Pasi. *Verdi: La Vita, I Viaggi*. Parma: Ugo Guanda Editore, 1993.

Marek, George R. *Puccini*. New York: Simon and Schuster, 1951.

————. "*Falstaff*—Boito's Alchemy." *Opera Quarterly* I/2 (Summer 1983): 69–72.

Mariette, Edouard. *Mariette Pacha: lettres et souvenirs personnels*. Paris: H. Jouve, 1904.

Marlowe, Roger. "Verdi and Shakespeare." *The Music Review* 20 (1959): 228–32.

Martin, George. *Verdi: His Music, Life and Times*. New York: Dodd, Mead, 1963.

————. *The Red Shirt and the Cross of Savoy: The Story of Italy's Risorgimento, 1748–1871*. New York: Dodd, Mead, 1969.

————. *Aspects of Verdi*. New York: Dodd, Mead, 1988.

Martinelli, Aldo. *Verdi: Raggi e penombre*. Genoa: Studio Editoriale Genovese, 1926.

Massenet, Jules. *Mes Souvenirs, 1848–1912*. Paris: Pierre Lafitte, 1912.

Matz, Charles. "Blanche Roosevelt." *Opera News* 27/20 (1963): 26–8.

Maurel, Victor. "À propos de *Falstaff*." In *Dix ans de carrière 1887–1897*. Paris: Imprimerie Paul Dupont, 1897; New York: Arno Press, 1977.

Mazzini, Giuseppe. *Filosofia della musica*. Florence: Cuaraldi, 1897, 1977.

Merkling, Frank. "Verdi's musical Egypt." *Opera News* 14/19 (1950): 12–5, 26–8.

Meyers Handbuch über die Literatur. Mannheim: Bibliographisches Institut, 1964.

Micheli, Giuseppe. "Sei lettere di Verdi a G. Mariotti." *Aurea Parma* 1–2 (1941): 35–46.

Mila, Massimo. *Il melodramma di Verdi*. Bari: G. Laterza e Figli, 1933, 1961.

————. "Verdi e Hanslick." *Rassegna musicale* 21/3 (1951): 212–24.

————. *Giuseppe Verdi*. Bari: G. Laterza e Figli, 1958.

————. *L'arte di Verdi*. Turin: Einaudi, 1980.

Minardi, Gian Paolo. "Sir John sul palcoscenico di Sant'Agata." Parma: Grafiche Step Editrice, n.d.

Mingardi, Corrado. "Composizioni giovanili di Giuseppe Verdi in quattro programmi inediti della Filarmonica Bussetana del 1838." *Biblioteca* 70/1 (1970): 39–44.

————. "Verdi e Berlioz." *Biblioteca* 70/1 (1970): 45–9.

————. "Una nuova terribile lettera di Verdi contro i bussetani." *Biblioteca* 70/2 (1971): 27–30.

————. "Con Verdi in Casa Barezzi." Busseto: Amici di Verdi, 1985.

————. *Verdi e il suo ospedale, 1888–1988*. Piacenza: Comune di Villanova sull'Arda, 1988.

————. "Con Verdi nella sua terra." Busseto: Amici di Verdi, 1989.

————. "Il Maestro in villa." *Po* 4 (1995).

Modugno, Maurizio. "Il cammino discografico di Sir John Falstaff, cavaliere." Parma: Grafiche Step Editrice, n.d.

————. "Il Falstaff nei giudizi della stampa dell'epoca." Parma: Teatro Regio, 1986.

Monaldi, Gino. *Verdi e Wagner*. Rome: Civelli, 1887.

————. *Verdi, 1839–1898.* Turin: Fratelli Bocca, 1899, 1926.

————. *Cantanti celebri del secolo XIX.* Rome: Nuova Antologia, 1907.

————. *Le prime rappresentazioni celebri.* Milan: Fratelli Treves, 1910.

————. *Il Maestro della Rivoluzione italiana.* Milan: Società Editrice Italiana, 1913.

————. *Le opere di Giuseppe Verdi al Teatro alla Scala.* Milan: G. Ricordi, 1914.

————. *I miei ricordi musicali.* Rome: Ausonia, 1921.

————. *Verdi aneddotico.* L'Aquila: Casa Editrice Vecchioni, 1926.

Montefiore, Tommaso. "Roma a Verdi." *La Tribuna* (Rome), 17 April 1893.

————. "Ancora del *Falstaff*." *La Tribuna* (Rome), 19 April 1893.

Moravia, Alberto. "The Anachronism of Verdi," trans. William Weaver. *High Fidelity* 13/10 (1963): 79–81.

Morenz, Siegfried. *Die Begegnung Europas mit Ägypten.* Zurich: Artemis, 1969.

Munger, Edmund. "*Aidas* of the Past." *Opera News* 12/18 (1948): 30–1.

Munisteri, Peter P. "Antonio Ghislanzoni, Poet of *Aida*." *Opera News* 5/22 (1941): 25–6.

Nardi, Piero. *Vita di Arrigo Boito.* Verona: A. Mondadori, 1942.

————. *Vita e tempo di Giuseppe Giacosa.* Milan: A. Mondadori, 1949.

Newman, Ernest. *Wagner as Man and Artist.* New York: Vintage Books, 1924.

————. *More Opera Nights.* London: Putnam, 1954.

————. *Seventeen Famous Operas.* New York: Alfred A. Knopf, 1955.

————. *Great Operas.* 2 vols. New York: Vintage Books, 1958.

Nicolaisen, Jay. *Italian Opera in Transition, 1871–1893.* Ann Arbor: University of Michigan Press, 1981.

Nietzsche, Friedrich. *Der Fall Wagner.* Vol. II: *Friedrich Nietzsche Werke,* ed. Karl Schlechta. Munich: Carl Hanser Verlag, 1965.

Noseda, Aldo (Il Misovulgo). "La nuova opera di Verdi." *Il Corriere della sera* (Milan), 27 November 1890.

Noske, Frits. "Ritual Scenes in Verdi's Operas." *Music and Literature* 54/4 (1973): 415–39.

————. *The Signifier and the Signified: Studies in the Operas of Mozart and Verdi.* The Hague: Martinus Nijhoff, 1977.

Nugent, Marian. "First American *Aida*." *Opera News* 11/10 (1946): 24, 32.

Orsini, Luigi. *Giuseppe Verdi.* Turin: Società Editrice Internazionale, 1949.

Osborne, Charles. *The Complete Operas of Verdi.* New York: Alfred A. Knopf, 1970.

Pagano, Luigi. "Arrigo Boito: L'artista." *Rivista musicale italiana* 31 (1924): 199–234.

Parker, Roger. "One Priest, One Candle, One Cross: Some Thoughts on Verdi and Religion." *Opera Quarterly* 12/1 (1995): 27–34.

Phillips-Matz, Mary Jane. "First Ladies of the Verdi Premieres." *Opera News* 18/15 (5 January 1954): 10–1, 30–1.

————. "Peppina Redeemed." *Opera News* 19/8 (1954): 4–6, 26.

————. "Great Opera Houses: Cairo." *Opera News* 27/6 (1962): 26–9.

————. "The Truth about *Traviata*." *Opera News* 28/9 (11 January 1964): 24–5.

————. "Verdi's Gardener." *Opera News* 29/19 (20 March 1965): 28.

————. "The Verdi Family of S. Agata and Roncole: Legend and Truth." In *Atti del III° Congresso Internazionale di Studi Verdiani.* Parma: Istituto di Studi Verdiani, 1969. Pp. 216–21.

————. "New Verdi Documents." *Verdi Newsletter* 4 (1978).

————. "Chatelaine to the End: New Light on Giuseppina Strepponi." *Opera News* 43/12 (27 January 1979): 16–8.

————. "Generations: A Work in Progress [on the Uttinis]." *Opera News* 52/10 (30 January 1988): 26–9.

————. "Public Sinners." *Opera News* 53/5 (November 1988): 24–6.

————. "A Time of Stress." *Opera News* 55/8 (5 January 1991): 10–13, 44.

————. *Verdi: A Biography.* Oxford and New York: Oxford University Press, 1993.

————. "Verdi's Heir [Puccini]." *Opera News* 60/12 (2 March 1996): 12–5, 23.

Piamonte, Guido, ed. "*Falstaff* alla Scala dal 1893 al 1967." Program of Teatro alla Scala, 1980–81. Pp. 100–1.

Pinagli, Palmiro. *Romanticismo di Verdi.* Florence: Vallecchi, 1967.

Pinzauti, Leonardo. "*Aida* e *Lohengrin.*" In *Atti del III° Congresso Internazionale di Studi Verdiani.* Parma: Istituto di Studi Verdiani, 1974. Pp. 401–7.

Pizzetti, Ildebrando. *Musicisti contemporanei.* Milan: Fratelli Treves, 1914.

————. "Pizzetti commemora Boito." *Musica d'oggi* 6/4–5 (1924): 127–8.

Pizzi, Italo, ed. *Ricordi verdiani inediti, con undici lettere di Giuseppe Verdi.* Turin: Roux e Viarengo, 1901.

Pleasants, Henry. *The Great Singers.* New York: Simon and Schuster, 1966.

————, ed. and trans. *Music Criticisms 1846–99.* New York: Penguin Books, 1950.

Pompeati, Arturo. *Arrigo Boito, poeta e musicista.* Florence: Battistelli, 1919.

Porter, Andrew, "Only Verdi." *The New Yorker*, June 21, 1976, 98–103.

————. *Music of Three Seasons: 1974–1977.* New York: Farrar, Straus & Giroux, 1978.

————. "Giuseppe Verdi." In Stanley Sadie, ed., *The New Grove Dictionary of Music and Musicians.* London: Macmillan Publishers, 1980. Vol. XIX, pp. 635–45.

————. "A Miracle of an Opera." *San Francisco Opera Magazine* (*Falstaff* issue, 1989).

Pougin, Arthur. *Verdi: Histoire anecdotique de sa vie et ses oeuvres.* Paris: Calman Levy, 1886.

————. *Verdi: An Anecdotic History of his Life and Works,* trans. James E. Matthews. New York: Scribner & Welford, 1887.

Prawy, Marcel. *The Vienna Opera.* New York: Praeger, 1970.

————. *Johann Strauss: Weltgeschichte im Walzertakt.* Vienna: Verlag Fritz Molden, 1975.

Prod'homme, Jacques-Gabriel, ed. "Unpublished Letters from Verdi to Du Locle (1866–1876)," trans. Theodore Baker. *The Musical Quarterly* 7/4 (1921): 73–103.

————. "Lettres inédites de G. Verdi à Léon Escudier." *Rivista musicale italiana* 35 (1928): 1–28, 171–97, 519–52.

————. "Lettres inédites de G. Verdi à Camille Du Locle (1868–1874)." *La Revue Musicale* 10 (1929): 97–112; 11 (1930): 26–36.

Rachleff, Owen. "Israel and Egypt." *Opera News* 27/6 (1962): 24–5.

Reich, Willi. "Unbekannte Verdi Dokumente." *Melos* 18 (1951): 48–51.

Resasco, Ferdinando. "Verdi a Genova: ricordi, aneddoti ed episodi." Genoa: Pagano [?], 1901.

Reyer, Ernest. *Notes de musique.* Paris: G. Charpentier, 1975.

Ricci, Corrado. *Giuseppe Verdi e l'Italia musicale all'estero.* Bologna: Reale Accademia Filarmonica, 1889.

————. *Arrigo Boito.* Milan: Fratelli Treves, 1919.

Ricordi, Giulio. "Un'opera nuova di Giuseppe Verdi." *La Gazzetta musicale di Milano* XLV/48 (30 November 1890): 757.

Rinaldi, Mario. *Verdi e Shakespeare.* Rome: De Sanctis, 1934.

————. *"Aida" di Giuseppe Verdi.* Florence: Monsalvato, 1943.

————. *Verdi critico: i suoi giudizi, la sua estetica.* Rome: Ergo, 1951.

Rod, Edouard. "Le Néron de M. Boito." *Revue des deux mondes* 61/15 (1 July 1901): 219–28.

Roncaglia, Gino. *L'ascensione creatrice di Giuseppe Verdi.* Florence: G. C. Sansoni, 1940.

————. *Verdi regista.* Modena: Società Tipografica—Editrice Modenense, 1956.

————. *Galleria verdiana: Studi e figure.* Milan: Curci, 1959.

Roosevelt, Blanche. *Verdi, Milan and "Othello."* London: Ward & Downey, 1887.

Rosen, David. "The Staging of Verdi's Operas: An Introduction to the Ricordi *Disposizioni sceniche.*" In *International Musicological Society Report of the Twelfth Congress, Berkeley, 1977.* Kassel: Bärenreiter, 1981. Pp. 444–53.

————, and Andrew Porter, eds. *Verdi's "Macbeth": A Sourcebook.* New York and London: W. W. Norton, 1984.

Rosenthal, Harold. *Two Centuries of Opera at Covent Garden.* London: Putnam, 1958.

————, ed. *The Mapleson Memoirs: The Career of an Operatic Impresario, 1858–1888.* London: Putnam, 1966.

————, and John Warrack, eds. *The Concise Oxford Dictionary of Opera.* Oxford: Oxford University Press, 1964, 1973, 1979, 1980.

Rosselli, John. *Music and Musicians in Nineteenth Century Italy.* Portland: Amadeus Press, 1991.

Sacchi, Filippo. *Toscanini: Un secolo di musica.* Milan: Longanesi, 1960.

Sachs, Harvey. *Toscanini.* London: Weidenfeld and Nicolson, 1978.

Sams, Eric. "Eduard Hanslick." In Stanley Sadie, ed., *The New Grove Dictionary of Music and Musicians.* London: Macmillan Publishers, 1980. Vol. VIII, pp. 151–3.

Sartori, Claudio. *Casa Ricordi, 1808–1958: Profili storici.* Milan: G. Ricordi, 1958.

————. "La Strepponi e Verdi a Parigi nella morsa quarantottesca." *Nuova rivista musicale italiana* 8/2 (1974): 239–53.

Scarsi, Giovanna. *Rapporto Poesia–Musica in Arrigo Boito.* Rome: Editrice Delia [1973].

Scheit, Gerhard. *Dramaturgie der Geschlechter.* Frankfurt am Main: Fischer Taschen-buch, 1995.

Schlegel, August Wilhelm. *Vorlesungen über dramatische Kunst und Literatur.* 3 vols., Heidelberg: Mohr und Zimmer, 1809–1811. 2 vols., Bonn: K. Schröder, 1923.

Schlitzer, Franco. *Inediti verdiani nell'archivio dell'Accademia Chigiana.* Siena: Ticci, 1953.

Schmidl, Carlo. *Dizionario universale dei musicisti.* 2 vols. Milan: Sonzogno, 1887, 1926–28; supplement, 1938.

Schonberg, Harold C. *The Lives of the Great Composers.* New York: W. W. Norton, 1970.

———. "Always Strictly Business." Review of *Letters of Giuseppe Verdi,* edited by Charles Osborne. *The New York Times Book Review,* 12 March 1972, 6–7, 12.

Schuh, Willi, ed. *Hugo von Hofmannsthal—Richard Strauss: "Der Rosenkavalier" Fassungen—Filmszenarium—Briefe.* Frankfurt am Main: S. Fischer, 1971.

———. *Richard Strauss: Jugend und frühe Meisterjahre—Lebenschronik 1864–1898.* Zurich: Atlantis Verlag, 1976.

Seltsam, William H., ed. *Metropolitan Opera Annals: A Chronicle of Artists and Performances, 1883–1947.* New York: H. W. Wilson, 1947.

Severgnini, Silvestro. "Immagini di Verdi da *Otello* a *Falstaff.*" Program of Teatro alla Scala, 1980–81, pp. 106–9.

Shakespeare, William. *King Henry IV, Parts 1 and 2,* ed. A. R. Humphreys. London: Methuen, 1930.

———. *King Henry V,* ed. John H. Walter. London: Methuen, 1967.

———. *The Merry Wives of Windsor,* ed. H. J. Oliver. London: Methuen, 1985.

Shaw, George Bernard. *London Music in 1888–89 as Heard by Corno di Bassetto (Later Known as Bernard Shaw).* New York: Vienna House, 1973.

———. *Music in London 1890–94.* 3 vols. New York: Vienna House, 1973.

Sheean, Vincent. *Orpheus at Eighty.* New York: Random House, 1958.

Sietz, Reinhold, ed. *Aus Ferdinand Hillers Briefwechsel.* 7 vols. Cologne: Arno Volk, 1958–70.

Signorelli (Resnevic), Olga. *Eleonora Duse.* Rome: G. Casini, 1955.

Singher, Martial. *An Interpretive Guide to Operatic Arias: A Handbook for Singers, Coaches, Teachers, and Students.* (Translations of the texts of the arias by Eta and Martial Singher.) Philadelphia: The Pennsylvania State University Press, 1983.

Spotts, Frederic. *The Bayreuth Festival.* New Haven: Yale University Press, 1994.

Stedman, Jane W. "*Aida's* Ethiopia." *Opera News* 13/6 (1949): 11–3.

———. "Slaves of Love and Duty." *Opera News* 21/5 (1957): 10–3.

Stefani, Giuseppe. *Verdi e Trieste.* Trieste: Comune di Trieste, 1951.

Stendhal, M. de. *Rome, Naples and Florence by Stendhal,* ed. and trans. Richard N. Coe. London: John Calder, 1959.

———. *Life of Rossini,* ed. and trans. Richard N. Coe. Rev. ed. London: Calder and Boyars; New York: Orion Press, 1970.

Stevenson, Florence. "Ancient Places III: Journey to Memphis." *Opera News* 40/17 (1976): 13–5.

Strauss, Franz and Alice, and Willi Schuh, eds. *A Working Friendship: The Correspondence between Richard Strauss and Hugo von Hofmannsthal*, trans. Hans Hammelmann and Ewald Osers. New York: Random House, 1961.

Stuckenschmidt, Hans Heinz. *Ferruccio Busoni*. Zurich: Atlantis Verlag, 1967.

Tassoni, Giuseppina Allegri. "Una gloria della scenografia parmense." *Aurea Parma* 32/1 (1948): 3–13.

Tebaldini, Giovanni. "Ricordi verdian." *Rassegna Dorica* XI/1, 3–6 (January and March–June 1940).

Tintori, Giampiero, ed. *Duecento anni di Teatro alla Scala. Cronologia opere—balletti—concerti 1778–1977.* Milan: Grafica Gutenberg Editrice, 1979.

Toscanini, Arturo. "La sinfonia dell'*Aida*." Interview, *Il Teatro Illustrato* (1913).

Toye, Francis. *Verdi, His Life and Works.* London: W. Heinemann, 1931; New York: Alfred A. Knopf, 1934, 1946.

———. "Verdi over Fifty Years." *Opera* 2/3 (February 1951): 105–10.

Vajro, Massimiliano. *Saggio di bibliografia boitiana.* Pozzuoli, 1950.

———. *Boito.* Brescia: La Scuola, 1955.

Vaughan Williams, Ralph. In "Verdi—A Symposium." *Opera* 2/3 (February 1951): 111–2.

Vetro, Gaspare Nello. *L'allievo di Verdi Emanuele Muzio.* Parma: Edizioni Zaea, 1993.

Vivanti, Annie. "Verdi's *Falstaff*: A Visit to the Composer." *Daily Graphic* (London), 14 January 1893.

———. "Giosuè Carducci." *Nuova Antologia* (Rome), 1 August 1906.

Wagner, Richard. *Sämtliche Schriften und Dichtungen.* 12 vols. Leipzig: Breitkopf & Härtel, C. F. W. Siegel, R. Linnemann, 1911.

Walker, Frank. "Verdi and Francesco Florimo: Some Unpublished Letters." *Music and Letters* 26/4 (1945): 201–8.

———. "Vincenzo Gemito and His Bust of Verdi." *Music and Letters* 30/1 (1949): 44–5.

———. "Verdi and Vienna." *Musical Times* 92/1303 (September 1951): 403–5; 92/1304 (October 1951): 451–3.

———. "Mercadante and Verdi." *Music and Letters* 33/4 and 34, 1 (1952–53): 311–21, 338.

———. *The Man Verdi.* London: J. M. Dent & Sons, 1962; University of Chicago Press, 1982.

Wallner-Basté, Franz, ed. and trans. *Verdi aus der Nähe: Ein Lebensbild in Dokumenten.* Zurich: Manesse Verlag, 1979.

Waltershausen, Hermann W. von. "Shakespeares Einfluss auf die Musik." In *Jahrbuch der Deutschen Shakespeare-Gesellschaft* 64 (1928): 13–42.

Weaver, William. "Of Poets and Poetasters: Verdi and His Librettists—from Solera to Boito." *High Fidelity* 13/10 (1963): 109–13, 171.

———. *The Golden Century of Italian Opera from Rossini to Puccini.* London: Thames & Hudson, 1980.

———. "Verdi, Shakespeare, and the Italian Audience." *English National Opera Guide* 7. London: John Calder; New York: Riverrun Press, 1981. Pp. 23–6.

————. *Duse: A Biography.* London: Thames & Hudson; New York: Harcourt Brace Jovanovich, 1984.

———— "Italy on His Mind." *Opera News* 58/10 (1994): 20 3.

————. "In Other Words: A Translator's Journal." *New York Times Book Review,* 19 November 1995.

————, trans. *Seven Verdi Librettos.* New York and London: W. W. Norton, 1977.

————, ed. and trans. *Verdi: A Documentary Study.* London: Thames & Hudson, 1977.

————, and Simonetta Puccini, eds. *The Puccini Companion.* New York and London: W. W. Norton, 1994.

See also Chusid, Martin.

Wechsberg, Joseph. *Verdi.* New York: G. P. Putnam's Sons, 1974.

Weingartner, Felix. "Verdi, der Begründer der modernen Spieloper." *Signale für die musikalische Welt* LXXI/41 (8 October 1913): 1451–4.

Weinstock, Herbert. *Rossini.* New York: Alfred A. Knopf, 1968.

Weiss, Piero, ed. *Letters of Composers through Six Centuries.* Philadelphia: Chilton, 1967.

Weisstein, Ulrich, ed. *The Essence of Opera.* New York: Free Press, 1964.

Werfel, Franz, and Paul Stefan, eds. *Verdi: The Man in His Letters,* trans. Edward Downes. New York: L. B. Fischer, 1942; 2d ed., New York: Vienna House, 1970.

Werner, Klaus-Günter. *Spiele der Kunst: Kompositorisches Verfahren in der Oper* Falstaff *von Giuseppe Verdi.* Frankfurt am Main: Lang, 1987.

Williams, Stephen. *Verdi's Last Operas.* London: Hinrichsen, 1950.

Wolff, Stephane. *L'Opéra au Palais Garnier (1875–1962): Les oeuvres, les interprètes.* Paris: Deposé au journal *L'Entr'acte* [1962].

Ybarra, Thomas Russel. *Verdi: Miracle Man of Opera.* New York: Harcourt Brace, 1955.

Zervudachi, Despina Draneht. *Twilight Memories.* Lausanne: Georges Jaccard, 1939.

Index

Hans Busch (1914–1996) was Opera Theatre stage director and professor emeritus at the Indiana University School of Music. Professor Busch directed at the Metropolitan Opera and at many other leading opera houses in the United States, Europe, and South America. He was author of similar documentary studies focusing on *Aida, Otello,* and the revised *Simon Boccanegra,* as well as two volumes of Verdi correspondence published in German.